People and Computers XIV - Usability or Else!

Springer

London
Berlin
Heidelberg
New York
Barcelona
Hong Kong
Milan
Paris
Singapore
Tokyo

Sharon McDonald, Yvonne Waern
and Gilbert Cockton (Eds)

People and Computers XIV
– Usability or Else!

Proceedings of HCI 2000

 Springer

Sharon McDonald, BA (Hons), MSc, PhD, CPsychol
School of Computing, Engineering and Technology, University of Sunderland, Sunderland SR6 0YN

Yvonne Waern, PhD
Department of Communication Studies, University of Linköping, Linköping, Sweden SE 581 83

Gilbert Cockton, MA (Cantab), PGCE, PhD, FRSA
School of Computing, Engineering and Technology, University of Sunderland, Sunderland SR6 0YN

ISBN 1-85233-318-9 Springer-Verlag London Berlin Heidelberg

British Library Cataloguing in Publication Data
A catalog record for this book is available from the British Library.

Typesetting: by *Winder.*
Printed and bound at the Athenæum Press Ltd., Gateshead, Tyne and Wear
34/3830-543210 Printed on acid-free paper SPIN 10766894

Contents

Usability and System Evaluation 309

Preface: HCI 2000 — Usability or Else!

... or else we meet at the next year's HCI conferences of course! Still, it is heartening as the People and Computers conference series edges past unlucky XIII that usability is a cornerstone of the emerging digital economy and the information society. When Wall Street and European finance centres demand due diligence checks on dotcom usability (with financial service consultancy rates to match), we know that someone somewhere is now taking HCI really seriously. Maybe this really will be the decade when HCI comes of age. Fingers crossed!

Next year's British HCI Conference will be in France, joint with the Francophone IHM conference (http://www.shu.ac.uk/hci2001). This marks a major step towards a regular truly European HCI Conference. For many years, the British HCI Conference series has filled this role, and we have moved towards more international conference committees in preparation for truly European HCI Conferences. For the second HCI conference in succession, a papers and proceedings co-chair comes from outside the UK. With typically British caution towards the 'continent' we have written this preface in two parts from opposite sides of the North and Baltic Seas. With due British manners, we let Yvonne Waern start with her Scandinavian view of HCI 2000.

Yvonne's Bit

It is a particular favour to serve in a conference committee, and particularly to serve as a papers and proceedings co-chair. It is like following a child from conception to birth. First, we have the proud father, who conceived the conference as "Usability, or Else!" Who would that be if not a young, energetic man, i.e. Gilbert Cockton? He has been a leader in all our efforts, particularly when Sharon McDonald, who serves as the real mother of the conference, broke her arm in an accident. Imagine all the pain that she went through, as well as everybody around who were concerned about her as well as about the conference baby.

One of our ideas had been to make this one of the first HCI conferences that was concerned with e-business. Plenaries apart, there were few e-business papers proposed. Isn't e-business relevant to HCI researchers?

What did we get instead? Well, something old, something new, something borrowed and something blue! To the 'old' and ever valuable belong papers on formal modelling (see Process, Methodology and Design Methods). We should never forget that this is an issue that may have to be resolved repeatedly, as new challenges arrive for HCI. The 'new' papers include ideas about home terminals (see The Context of Interaction: People, Places and Actions) — home electronics and 'invisible' computers will certainly be issues for HCI in the future! The 'borrowed' are — well every living research community has to relate to its own work as well as to others. The borrowing is a part of research growth and we see it everywhere (see Process, Methodology and Design Methods)! The 'blue' shocks the traditionally minded – maybe the challenging title of "Are user studies harmful?" is a sign from the Nordic cold blue sky, where one's sight may be clearer than in more Southerly places?

We are proud to say that the quality of the papers is, as always, extremely high. This is due primarily to the papers, of course, but also to our most competent committee of reviewers. The reviews alone would fill up a book and that would be interesting reading! We hope that all paper proposers benefit from their reviews. This is a learning process for everyone who submits and reviews — maybe we should consider having our HCI students reading not only the papers but also their reviews! To compare the final papers with the paper submissions would be a challenge.

The only thing I regret is that we could not create an even more international proceedings. There are papers from around the world (Japan, New Zealand, USA, Brazil, Finland and the Netherlands) and only two papers sessions at the conference contain only UK papers, but overall most authors are from the UK. Volume 2 of the proceedings extends this with contributions from South Africa, Italy, Denmark, and Sweden. With HCI 2001 joint with IHM 2001 in France, we hope that future HCI conferences can extend their international balance as well as reach.

Now, with the date of publication/birth soon due, we all feel filled with happiness as well as apprehension. Will everything be alright? Will the proceedings be received as we hope? How will audiences and readers react to our selection of accepted papers? Time will tell — in the meantime I can only say that everybody has done her and his best!

Yvonne Waern
Linköping University, Sweden
A papers and proceedings chair and a fly on the back of the working ox
of Sharon and Gilbert.

Oxtail Soup as Desert

Yvonne's kind yet somewhat unjustified comment (she did work hard, don't let her deceive you!) left Sharon and I with the dilemma of which of us was the front and which the back of the Ox. The British artist Damien Hirst could cut us both down the middle from skull to loin, but we'd rather avoid ending up in London's Tate Art Gallery as "General and Technical Chairs Divided". Still, our financial worth as underpaid academics would clearly multiply considerably if we sacrificed ourselves to the services of contemporary art!

As with many British HCI Group conference proceedings, we have not imported the artificial constraints imposed by three paper conference sessions into the proceedings' structure. The proceedings begin with invited papers from two of plenary speakers who miraculously found time to prepare papers within the demands of their busy working lives. We are grateful to all our distinguished plenary speakers, but extra thanks are due to Jerry and Jim for their extended efforts on behalf of HCI 2000. Summaries of the other plenary presentations can be found in Volume 2 of the proceedings (available from the British HCI Group, http://www.bcs-hci.org.uk/).

The remainder of the proceedings groups papers under the three broad HCI headings of Context, Design and Evaluation, reflecting the key activities underlying the design of interactive systems that demonstrably fit their context of use. Such systems need to be designed using the best interactive technologies to fit known contexts of use and then evaluated to demonstrate this fit. As we accepted 11 papers on design, we have separated general papers on design methods and process from specific design innovations. The remaining papers divide almost equally between studies of the context of use and the evaluation of interactive systems.

As with previous British HCI Group conferences, we see a continuing diversification of HCI methods and application areas, demonstrating yet again that HCI as a field continues to expand both in terms of its own knowledge and methods and in terms of the application domains in which these are applied. At the same time, previous HCI 'knowledge' is not ignored, but is returned to with a critical eye to ensure that developments in HCI are built on the strongest possible foundations.

So there you are, for Yvonne it was a question of marriage and childbirth, for Sharon and I it is one of food and expensive contemporary art — demonstrating no doubt a Scandinavian focus on people versus a Northern English focus on stomachs and wallets. Until next year when IHM-HCI in Lille will hopefully deliver promising Gallic romance, gourmet French food and expensive merchandise in equal measure, we'll do our best for European integration at Sunderland by letting Yvonne pay the bill for taking the conference committee people out to dinner.

Sharon McDonald
Gilbert Cockton
School of Computing, Engineering and Technology, University of Sunderland, UK
The other papers and proceedings chairs, forever undecided on their Ox-endedness.

The Conference Committee

Conference Chair	Gilbert Cockton, *University of Sunderland*
Technical Programme	Sharon McDonald, *University of Sunderland*
Papers and Proceedings	Sharon McDonald, *University of Sunderland*
	Yvonne Waern, *Linköping University*
	Gilbert Cockton, *University of Sunderland*
Short Papers and Posters	Susan Turner, *Napier University, Edinburgh*
	Phil Turner, *Napier University, Edinburgh*
Organisational Overviews	Lynne Hall, *University of Northumbria at Newcastle*
Panels	Andrew Monk, *University of York*
Tutorials Co-Chairs	Darryn Lavery, *Microsoft, USA*
	Fintan Culwin, *South Bank University, London*
Doctoral Consortium	John Dowell, *University College London*
Industry Day	Mary Jones, *BT Labs*
	Peter Windsor, *Usability Ltd*
Social Programme	Linda White, *University of Sunderland*
	Mary Holmes, *University of Sunderland*
Proceedings	Russel Winder, *King's College London*
Publicity	Nina Reeves, *Cheltenham and Gloucester College*
Treasurer	Bob Steele, *Sheffield Hallam University*
British HCI Group Liaison	Chris Roast, *Sheffield Hallam University*
European Liaison	Phillipe Palanque, *Université de Toulouse, France*
Asia-Pacific Liaison	Jackie Moyes, *Hiser Group, Australia*
Americas Liaison	David Caulton, *Microsoft, USA*
Conference Management	Digital Media Network, *University of Sunderland*
Exhibition	Richard Wilson, *Industrial Liaison and Careers Consultant, West Sussex, UK*
Website	Lynn Devaney, *Digital Media Network, UoS*
Publisher Liaison	Russel Winder, *King's College London*

The Reviewers

Ghassan Al-Qaimari, *Royal Melbourne Institute of Technology, Australia*
Jackie Archibald, *University of Sunderland, UK*
Sandrine Balbo, *CSIRO-MIS, Australia*
Ian Benest, *University of York, UK*
Nigel Bevan, *Serco Usability Services, UK*
Ann Blandford, *Middlesex University, UK*
Chris Bowerman, *University of Sunderland, UK*
Stephen Brewster, *University of Glasgow, UK*
Carol Britton, *University of Hertfordshire, UK*
Jean-Marie Burkhardt, *Université Paris V Rene Descartes, France*
Samantha Campion , *Independent Human Factors Consultant, UK*
Chaomei Chen, *Brunel University, UK*
Dave Clarke, *Visualize Software Ltd, UK*
Martin Colbert, *University of Kingston, UK*
Karin Coninx, *Limburgs Universitair Centrum, Belgium*
Iain Connell, *University of York, UK*
Mary Czerwinski, *Microsoft Research, USA*
David Darvill, *BC Research Inc, Canada*
Andrew Dearden, *Sheffield Hallam University, UK*
Mark Dunlop, *Risoe National Laboratory, Denmark*
Emmanuel Dubois, *University of Grenoble, France*
Daphne Economou, *Manchester Metropolitan University, UK*
Alistair Edwards, *University of York, UK*
David England, *Liverpool John Moores University, UK*
Sue Fenley, *King's College London, UK*
Alan Ferris, *AIT plc, UK*
Claude Ghaoui, *Liverpool John Moores University, UK*
Simon Grant, *Information Strategists, UK*
Phil Gray, *University of Glasgow, UK*
Ashok Gupta, *University College London, UK*
David Hawdale, *Serco Usability Services, UK*
E.G. Henderson, *Cranfield University, UK*
Hans-Jürgen Hoffmann, *Darmstadt University of Technology, Germany*
Kasper Hornbæk, *University of Copenhagen, Denmark*
Ismail Ismail, *University College London, UK*
Phillip Jeffrey, *GMD FIT, Germany*
Chris Johnson, *University of Glasgow, UK*
Lorraine Johnston, *Swinburne University of Technology, Australia*
Matt Jones, *Middlesex University, UK*
Alistair Kilgour, *Real Axis Consulting, UK*
Robert Macredie, *Brunel University, UK*
Panos Markopoulos, *Technical University of Eindhoven, The Netherlands*
Jon May, *University of Sheffield, UK*
Andrew Monk, *University of York, UK*
Michelle Montgomery Masters, *University of Glasgow, UK*
Sonali Morar, *Brunel University, UK*
Ian Newman, *Loughborough University, UK*
Julian Newman, *Glasgow Caledonian University, UK*

Laurence Nigay, *University of Grenoble, France*
Kenton O'Hara, *The Appliance Studio, UK*
Eva Olsson, *Uppsala University, Sweden*
Eamonn O'Neill, *University of Bath, UK*
Robert Pedlow, *Telstra Research Laboratories, Australia*
Annelise Mark Pejtersen, *Risoe National Laboratory, Denmark*
Rakhi Rajani, *Brunel University, UK*
Nina Reeves, *Cheltenham, Gloucester College of HE, UK*
Dimitrios Rigas, *University of Bradford, UK*
Chris Roast, *Sheffield Hallam University, UK*
Tony Rose, *Canon Research Centre, UK*
Angela Sasse, *University College London, UK*
John Seton, *BT Advanced Communications Research, UK*
Brian Shackel, *Loughborough University, UK*
Robert Steele, *Sheffield Hallam University, UK*
Mark Treglown, *University of Nottingham, UK*
Leon Watts, *UMIST, UK*
Maggie Williams, *PC Magazine, UK*

Plenaries

Usability and Profits in the Digital Economy

Gerald (Jerry) L Lohse

University of Pennsylvania, Sansom Place West, Room 106, 3650 Chestnut Street, Philadelphia, PA 19104–6107, USA

Tel: *+1 215 573 7345, +1 484 431 7698*

Fax: *+1 215 573 8817*

EMail: *lohse@wharton.upenn.edu*

URL: *http://ecom.wharton.upenn.edu/,*
     http://opim.wharton.upenn.edu/~lohse/

With a third of the of the world's $60 trillion economy going online by 2010, usability issues become critical to corporate survival. To increase their value in this new business landscape, e-commerce HCI professionals must expand their understanding of marketing issues driving the digital economy. Areas that have been the exclusive domain of marketers such as branding, customer service, store shopping behaviour, consumer loyalty, pricing strategies, product displays, privacy, and trust now require a detailed understanding of human–computer interaction to maximise the quality of the customer experience. Firms should be investing in a total customer experience strategy that includes usability issues. Small changes in the interface can impact the quality of the customer experience and the profitability of companies. Thus, the ability of HCI professionals to contribute to the profitability of firms in the digital economy is enormous. This paper explores five years of research documenting how HCI issues impact profitability online.

Keywords: branding, privacy, loyalty, pricing, consumer behaviour.

1 Introduction

E-commerce is transforming every aspect of business, sending companies scrambling to cope with the new market realities of doing business online. By

2010, one-third of the world's $60 trillion economy will be conducted online (Lohse, 2000). The USA Department of Commerce projects that by 2006, half of USA workers will be information technology workers or in a field that uses information technology heavily. The shift to a digital economy will have severe implications for companies that cannot adapt. In the United States, half of the current Fortune 2000 will not survive the decade.

With a third of the economy online, issues of how people interact with the technology become mission critical to corporate survival. Human–computer interaction (HCI) is important not because the masses are experiencing computers for the first time, but because the user interface has a direct and quantifiable impact on profits. New corporate titles such as 'Director of Making Stuff Easy' and 'VP of Ease of Use' demonstrate that HCI issues matter to senior management.

E-commerce HCI professionals must expand their understanding of marketing issues driving the digital economy to increase their value in this new business landscape. Marketing issues are deeply intertwined with user interface design issues because the issues subsume their real-world counterparts. For example, bricks and mortar customer service is replaced with online product descriptions, search functions, gift shopping services, and information pages. Cashier checkout is the online shopping cart and the order form. Shopping experience and atmosphere are now evoked by the consistency of the interface, the quality of the interface, and expressiveness of the graphics. Now more the ever, the promise of electronic commerce and online shopping will depend to a great extent upon the interface, how people interact with the computer and usability.

Jakob Nielsen (1993) defines the five components of usability as learnability, efficiency, memorability, errors, and satisfaction. From an engineering perspective, these five parts create an objective and measurable basis for quantifying and evaluating 'usability'. For Internet interfaces, search features, navigation, and minimising data entry errors are clearly at the core of usability. But the quality of the online customer experience depends on much more than these 'pure' usability components defined by Nielsen. Areas that have been the exclusive domain of marketers such as branding, customer service, store shopping behaviour, consumer loyalty, pricing strategies, product displays, privacy, and trust now require a detailed understanding of human–computer interaction to maximise the quality of the customer experience.

Usability is a necessary but not sufficient condition for a high quality customer experience. If a consumer can't figure out how to return an online purchase, then provide a toll free phone number for customer support with a real person. Designers can create the best interface possible to provide online customer support, but inadequate staffing that delays a timely response to inquiries will ruin the quality of the customer experience. Thus, the quality of the customer experience is a strategic issue. Simply handing it off to the technology team, or graphic designers, or a 'usability expert', does not give the holistic, strategic treatment that customer experience requires. It requires a corporate wide effort. The quality of the customer experience drives the success or failure of a site. Firms should be investing in a total customer experience strategy that includes tactical graphic design and usability issues. Small changes in the interface can impact the quality of the customer experience and the profitability of companies. Thus, the ability of HCI professionals to contribute to the profitability of firms in the digital economy is enormous. This paper explores these opportunities and challenges facing the HCI e-commerce community.

2 The Four 'Ps' of Marketing: Price, Product, Promotion, and Place

Marketing begins with a discussion of the four 'Ps': price, product, promotion and place (distribution and logistics). The fundamental rule of marketing is that firms never compete on price unless they truly are the price leader based on manufacturing efficiencies or scale. Rarely are there two price leaders in any market. While consumers may applaud a death spiral price war, shareholders cringe. Online retailers fear increased price sensitivity and comparison shopping, resulting in razor thin profit margins. Compared to other media, electronic shopping lowers physical or monetary search costs for product information (Alba et al., 1997; Bakos, 1997). Most economic models of search (Bakos, 1997) expect that increased search would lead to lower prices, as consumers explore a larger number of vendors, reducing both the average price paid and the dispersion of prices (Smith et al., to appear). Both Bailey (1998) and Brynjolfsson & Smith (1999) find that online prices for identical books differed on average by 33% for books and 25% for CD's.

Since most firms never want to compete on price, how do companies design sites to differentiate their products from those of the competition? A study by Lynch & Ariely (1998) designed the user interface of an online wine store to vary the search cost for price vs. quality information, and for comparing across two competing electronic wine stores. At these sites, consumers spent their own money purchasing wines from the two merchants who sold some overlapping and some unique wines. Results showed that making price information more accessible does not necessarily have ruinous effects on price sensitivity. In fact, price sensitivity decreased with the usability of quality information. Making store comparisons easy increased price sensitivity for overlapping wines but not for unique wines.

Lohse & Johnson (1998) also found that presentation of product information on the screen strongly influences price sensitivity. In a study examining the effect of rearranging product information on choice behaviour, subjects chose a lower price product in the price format and a higher price product in the quality format. Coefficients from the multinomial logistic regression model found that price was weighted higher in the price format than in the quality format whereas subjects weighted quality higher in the quality format than in the price format.

Johnson et al. (1999) found that wallpaper, a seemingly inconsequential design element, can influence choice of low or high priced products. Dollars embedded in green wallpaper primed thoughts about money, increasing the importance of price. In the purchase of a car, a flame-like background primed for safety and increased the importance of safety. This subliminal priming effect was repeatedly found in multiple studies using multiple primes and product classes.

These three examples illustrate that retailers can design the user interface to offset the price sensitivity of consumers. Web sites that make it hard for consumers to find information about the quality of products, increase the price sensitivity of consumers. Interfaces that uniquely differentiate products to show the value added will translate into increased revenues. The design must highlight the value proposition to the consumer: better service, faster delivery, more product variety, and higher quality products.

On the Internet, brand differentiation includes the use of dialog and interaction. Email, chat, focus groups, and early feedback on products and services, engage the customer proactively. The longer you are able to keep a potential customer on the web site, the more likely they will buy. For example, 60% of book purchases are unplanned impulse buys. Selling coffee inside a bookstore provides marketers an opportunity to let product displays, floor design, and promotions sell the books. Online communities allow members to talk to other members. Member generated content increases repeat visits to a Web site. Other atmospheric elements and changing content help keep customers coming back again and again.

Broadband will create an opportunity to create user irresistible web sites according to Peter Max, a popular USA artist. But current penetration in the USA is 500,000 households with DSL and 1.5 million with cable modem. It may be 10 years before there is even 50% broadband penetration in the USA. So unless your target audience has broadband, don't design graphics laden sites as if people had broadband. Hoque & Lohse (1999) found that display ads were more effective in traditional paper yellow pages than in the new electronic media. Online ads with extensive graphics have long download times that preclude the effectiveness of the graphics. This suggests a business opportunity to market value-added design services that create more effective electronic yellow pages advertisements within the current design constraints of the Web.

Jakob Nielson is right! No amount of 'graphic glitz' will keep someone coming back to shop on a Web site. An online seller of fashion clothing and accessories, boo.com, learned this lesson the hard way about the density of graphics on the site. As one critique pointed out:

> "The much-hyped e-tailer boo.com finally shut its doors this week. No surprise there. Back in November — at the time Boo was most slathered with press hype — we stated here: 'With a slow and difficult customer experience, boo.com is headed for failure.'" (http://www.goodexperience.com/archives/1199.html#111199)

Companies must manage customer expectations about the delivery of products ordered online. Both eToys and Toys-R-Us experienced fulfilment problems during the 1999 Christmas season. Customers sent e-mail inquiries to check the status of their orders but due to the sheer volume of requests it took up to nine days to answer those inquiries. Undaunted by the slow response to their email inquiries, customers phoned in droves to check the status of their orders. Again, neither store had sufficient phone support staff in place to respond to the volume of inquiries. This example illustrates the importance of the quality of customer service in being responsive to the customer. HCI designers can increase overall satisfaction with the experience by sending email to let the customer know where the product is, when the package will arrive, how it will be shipping and whether shipping and handling charges are included in the price. Designers can create an optimal interface for customer interaction but if there isn't sufficient staffing the overall quality of the customer experience suffers. Clearly, we are still a long way from clicking on an item and having it appear on your doorstep each and every time.

3 Online Consumer Buying and Spending Behaviour

Started in November of 1997, the Wharton Virtual Test Market (WVTM) is an ongoing survey of Internet users concentrating on electronic commerce. In the first survey, Bellman et al. (1999) found that time starvation and leading a 'wired' lifestyle were the most significant factors associated with online buying and spending. People leading a more 'wired' lifestyle use email to keep in touch with family and friends. Buyers have been on the Internet for years as compared to months for non-buyers. And, finally, online buyers use the Internet regularly at work and believe it has improved their productivity.

So what does this mean for HCI? A time-starved consumer does not want a printer that says the toner cartridge is low. This reinforces the existing buying pattern of shopping physical stores to find and buy a replacement cartridge. It is more likely that a time-starved consumer will never want to run out of toner. Another design might have the printer logon to the Internet, pop-up an order entry screen to order a replacement toner cartridge and time it so that it arrives before the old one is completely out. Time starved consumers with a wired lifestyle want a value proposition that saves them time in their busy life: real time, not just mouse clicks! Companies that recognise how to service wired, time-starved customers will become more profitable in the digital economy.

People who buy online do not necessarily become repeat buyers. Lohse et al. (to appear) found that 15% of people who tried online shopping in 1997 did not buy again in 1998. While half of these dropouts became online buyers again in 1999, it is much harder to convince a dropout to come back to online buying than it is to make an online buyer dropout. People who have had a bad experience — usually some form of delivery problem, billing error, or a stock-out not mentioned on the Web site — can take years to convince to try online shopping again. Other surveys have found similar lists of complaints — for example Andersen Consulting (2000) and Boston Consulting Group (2000) — and agree that an online buyer's first trial of a company's Web site is critical. The quality of the initial customer experience is important for converting visitors and first-time buyers into repeat customers.

The most important change in consumer behaviour is a slow down in the rate of per person online spending. While total online spending per person is increasing for the majority of online shoppers (80%), the rate of increase is slowing. The Internet adoption rate will inevitably slow down. The people who rapidly adopted the Internet in its first years were the most affluent and educated in the population, and those most familiar with computer technology. In the United States, the Internet population has started looking more and more like the general population. Companies will have to plan their Web site design for an audience that is less time starved, less Web savvy, less educated, earning less, less tolerant of new technology, more price sensitive, and more likely to be female. The increasing frustration with new technology increases the need for a simple and easy to use design.

Bellman et al. (1999) forecast that total business-to-consumer (B2C) sales will be $97.4 billion in 2004. Currently, online sales to consumers are only 0.6% of total retail sales in the USA, which at the end of 1999 were close to $3 trillion. The online B2C market is only a fraction of the online business-to-business (B2B) market, and looks likely to remain so in the future. Our findings reinforce others, for example Reuters (2000) and Weber (2000), who warn investors to downgrade expectations that Web retailing will grow to rival other forms of shopping. Internet shopping will be just another way of shopping, and online shopping will only be a minor part of an online shopper's total retail spending.

While online sales may not be as important a threat to traditional retail as the hype of the last few years suggested, time spent online has grown exponentially over the last three years, and after three years online. The more years a person has been online, the more comfortable they become with the security and privacy hazards of using the Internet, although concern about privacy and security remain high. Part of this comfort comes from knowing more about how to keep their information secure. More experienced Internet users check whether sites use secure encryption before revealing personal information, and know significantly more about 'cookie' technology. Online retailers can increase sales and the number of repeat buyers by educating online consumers about the security of online transactions.

4 Privacy

Every time a consumer goes online, their click stream data are recorded in Web server log files, which can be analysed to generate profiles of their online habits and preferences for electronic marketing. However, differences in regulation between countries may prevent the use of these data. To understand global policy implications regarding privacy and security, Bellman et al. (2000) surveyed 2,901 people globally. Worldwide, Bellman et al. (2000) consistently found a high level of concern about online privacy and security. Specifically, people don't like their data being shared or sold to other companies. Consumers agree that Web sites are collecting too much information. Companies are more likely to get data if they ask for a limited set of items rather than ask for everything. Consumers from the USA were the only ones in our sample to disagree that governments should regulate data collection practices. However, even people in the USA. slightly agree that government legislation is needed to safeguard sensitive personal medical and financial data. The greater concern about online privacy and security in countries outside the USA is largely due to a lack of knowledge about technological safeguards, such as secure socket layer (SLL), the posting of privacy policies and TRUSTe, clickstream data and log files. Finally, fears about privacy and security of online transactions are significant predictors of whether a person will buy online. Specifically, trusting businesses to provide sufficient protection of personal data is critical.

The best way to obtain people's trust is to not share their data or sell it to other companies, and keep their data safely out of the reach of hackers. Only when consumers trust online companies with their data will those companies be able to make the most of the possibilities offered by database marketing. Seals of approval, brand, fulfilment, and site design communicate trust to consumers (Hoffman et al., 1999). Seals of approval include symbols, like VeriSign, TRUSTe, SLL lock or key, and Visa, assure the visitor that security has been established. Brand signals information about trust related to delivery promises and the visitor's possible previous experience. An electronic mail confirmation reduces fears associated with privacy and security as well as increases the level of trust with the company. A professionally designed site with good navigation and design attributes connotes quality and professionalism that are part of a brand's image. Trust also is indicated by how orders will be processed, by information on how to seek recourse if there are problems, as well as by information about back orders for out-of-stock items.

5 Quantifying the Effect of Interface Design Features On Sales

Given the resources needed to launch a retail store on the Internet or change an existing online storefront design, it is important to allocate product development resources to interface features that actually improve store traffic and sales. In order to quantify tradeoffs among different interface redesign alternatives, Lohse & Spiller (1998; 2000) examined the relationship between interface design features and traffic and sales data. In August 1996, monthly store traffic, dollar sales and a set of 36 interface features were measured for a sample of 28 online retail stores. Monthly store sales averaged nearly $64,000 and traffic averaged 54,893 unique visits per month. Annual 1996 sales at this cybermall exceeded $22 million.

Using a stepwise regression approach, Lohse & Spiller (1998; 2000) identified the set of interface design features that had the largest influence on Internet store traffic and monthly sales. The variables in the traffic regression model explains 88% of all variance in the store traffic data; the sales regression model explains 76% of the variance in dollar sales data. For the monthly sales data, product list navigation features that reduce the time to purchase products online account for 61% of the variance in monthly sales. Other factors explaining the variance in monthly sales included: number of hyperlinks into the store (10%), hours of promotion (4%) and customer service feedback (1%).

Information search costs are a major determinant of both store traffic and sales. But the new media is not frictionless. Some information search tasks take longer online; others are shorter. Because of the cost involved with launching an online catalogue or information service, it is important to allocate product development resources to design features that increase the effectiveness of the media.

Diligence in browsing a store is not a virtue Internet retail marketers should expect from their customers. Navigation features that make it easier for customers to find products are essential for a successful online retail store. After all, if customers can't find what they want, they can't buy the product. The regression suggests that improving navigation of product lists, product search, and increasing the use of hyperlinks within a store are the primary areas of opportunity. Product list navigation explained 61% of the variance in monthly sales. Additional product list information such as price, a thumbnail image, and a longer descriptive product name had the largest impact on sales. Lohse & Spiller speculated that this facilitates purchase decision making at the point consumers initially view the product.

Hyperlinks are like an additional store entrance that increases traffic into the store. The number of links into a store explained 10% of the variance on monthly sales. Hyperlinks aid the discovery of new and useful information and allow the user to obtain more detail as needed. The links should be as context specific as possible. The sale of a Walkman CD player should have a link to buy batteries. A shirt can be linked to pants and a matching sweater. Such links reduce the effort of browsing by directing customers to related items. In a survey of 130 apparel stores for women, Spiller & Lohse (1997) found that 95% of the stores did not have hyperlinks among related products. Because hyperlinks provide an opportunity to up-sell and cross-sell, online retailers should not waste opportunities to link to related products.

It is difficult for designers to anticipate a user's navigation path. Since everyone will not come in the front door, every web page must have consistent navigation links (site map, index, etc.) to move around on the site. Complex URLs that use a foreign naming convention make them nearly impossible to use as site navigation aids. Clearly communicate the structure of the site on the home page (master index) and link to the master index from every page on the site.

Larger stores attract more traffic. However, this traffic does not necessarily translate into higher sales. One reason for this outcome is that consumers may not find the products they are looking for in larger stores. Improved search functions or other shopping modes should overcome this low conversion to sales.

The checkout process is more complicated than necessary (Jarvenpaa & Todd, 1997). If the checkout process is too long, customers balk and sales are lost. According to Kadison et al. (1998), 67% of online shopping carts are abandoned. Also, consumers enter a lot of repetitive information such as name, address, and credit card information. Ideally, this could be entered once and allow the customer to checkout once even though purchases are from multiple stores. Hoque & Lohse (1999) view the one-click-to-purchase approach of amazon.com and 1–800–Flowers (http://www.1800flowers.com/) as recognition that every additional mouse click reduces the possibility of a purchase.

At a real department store, it is easy to undo a purchase during checkout. Just tell the clerk that you have changed your mind and only want the pants but not the shirt. On the Internet, the undo button for one store emptied the entire shopping cart leaving the customer to start over (Spiller & Lohse, 1997). Inconsistent menus do not allow customers to review the contents of the shopping cart from any page in the store. Some order forms do not provide customers with important information such as does the price include shipping and handling, when will the order be shipped or whether an item is out-of-stock. Finally, a real sales clerk provides service at checkout, asking, for example, if you found everything that you were looking for. There is no analogue online, suggesting an opportunity to develop such a feature in the future.

Despite the advances in online retail stores since 1996, recent studies summarised by Nielsen in 1998 found similar navigation problems (http://www.useit.com/alertbox/981018.html). For example, even when starting on the correct home page, users only found information they were searching for 42% of the time, 62% of shoppers gave up looking for the item they wanted to buy online, 40% of first time purchasers fail to make a repeat purchase because of a negative experience, and 50% of sales are lost because people can't find products on the web site. A 1999 report by Mark Hurst (http://www.goodreports.com/) also found similar problems with web site navigation. In user tests, 39% of shoppers failed in their buying attempts because the site was too difficult to navigate and 56% of search attempts failed.

6 Do Consumers Comparison Shop Before They Buy?

Adamic & Huberman (1999) found that the top 1% of sites on the Web capture 50% of all visits to the Web. This is consistent with the idea that consumers are limiting their search to just a few of the most popular sites. Johnson et al. (2000b) look at number of stores consumer browse and shop using data collected by Media Metrix. The panel data includes every URL visited from a random sample of 10,000 households in the USA over a two-year period. Johnson et al. (2000b) focused on three categories: compact disks, books, and travel services.

Two patterns are striking in the data: first, the current level of search is low, initially ranging from 1.1 stores for books to 1.8 for travel. In fact, 70% of the CD shoppers, 70% of the book shoppers, and 36% of the travel shoppers were observed as being loyal to just one site throughout the duration of our data. It is hard to comparison shop if consumers only go to one store. Secondly, while more active shoppers visit more sites, there is no evidence that experience increases the number of sites visited. One might expect the greatest amount of search for travel services, both because prices can change over time and because this is a more expensive purchase. However, findings demonstrate that experience leads to a slight decrease in the number of visited sites.

Contrary to a widely held belief, online consumers don't comparison shop before they buy, despite apparently limitless shopping opportunities a mouse-click away. There was no empirical evidence to support Nielsen & Norman (2000) claim that comparison-shopping is a major reason consumers shop online. The study underscores that brand identification is more important than ever. People flock to those sites and products that they know, have used and liked. Thus, design strategies that create a sticky web site are critical.

7 Cognitive Lock-in Makes a Web Site Sticky

Electronic commerce and marketing on the Internet is thought to reduce search costs and decrease brand loyalty. "The competition is only a click away" is a common phrase in the popular press. Johnson et al. (2000a) describe a cognitive lock-in mechanism for building loyalty to a Web site. Consider a first visit to a new supermarket. Some learning takes place regarding the aisle location of some favourite product classes, the shelf location of some favourite brands, and a preferred shopping pattern through the store (Kahn & McAlister, 1997). This knowledge of the layout of a physical store, which increases with subsequent visits, makes the store more attractive, relative to the competition. Johnson et al. (2000a) argue that the same process happens with virtual stores. A similar argument has been commonly made about learning software, such as word processors. The experience with one system raises the cost of switching to another, and has been used to explain the slow conversion from WordPerfect to Word, for example.

Johnson et al. (2000a) used panel data from Media Metrix from July 1997 to June 1998. The number of individuals in the panel averaged 19,466 per month, roughly two per household. The URL of each Web page viewed by individual members of the household, the date and time at which it was accessed, and the number of seconds for which the Web page was the active document on an individual's computer screen, are captured. Johnson et al. (2000a) selected books, music, and travel because these categories register the highest numbers for repeat visits and repeat purchasing among online merchants.

To study consumer shopping behaviour, Johnson et al. (2000a) tested whether the power law of practice applies to visits to Web sites, and helps explain why some sites are 'stickier' than others. Not surprisingly, people become more efficient browsing a Web site the more they visit that site. Over time, visitors are more likely to buy from the Web site they find the easiest to use. Although they may have to pay a price penalty for not shopping around, online customers can be locked-in to their favourite Web sites because of the cognitive switching costs. Cognitive lock-in goes a long way toward explaining why very little comparison-shopping is observed in the Media Metrix data set, with most panelists being loyal to just one store in any of the books, music, and travel categories (Johnson et al., 2000b).

The major implication of the power law of practice is that one of a Web site's strongest assets is a simple navigation design that can be learned rapidly. The layout of a site is one of the primary drivers of its repeat traffic. Managers of Web sites with rapid learning rates should not change the navigation design. Altering the navigation design of a site reduces the cognitive lock-in effect. If your customers have to learn your site design all over again, they might learn someone else's instead. Of course, customers come back on repeat visits to find new content, and the more varied the content the more they will be encouraged to return. So content should be refreshed often. Furthermore, users must be able to transfer learning from pages they have visited to pages they have not seen before. Managers with locked-in customers can increase the expected life-time value of these customers by adding new opportunities for them to buy from the site, as, for example, online bookstores amazon.com and barnesandnoble.com did when they added music, videos, and other products to their lists of items for sale. Cognitive lock-in not only involves site navigation but also includes customisation, personalisation, recommendations, and easy checkout.

8   Minimise Data Entry Errors

Everything about business-to-consumer (B2C) issues raised in this paper applies to business-to-business (B2B) web sites as well. However, the implications are much larger! Cisco claims to have the most advanced e-commerce site in the world (Lohse,

2000). Cisco sells Internet network equipment. In 1996, Cisco noticed 25% of their orders contained errors. They developed an online equipment-ordering system that verified the order as it was placed to ensure compatibility of all the components. As the Internet grew, Cisco's volume of business has grown dramatically. In the last five months of 1996, Cisco did $100 million worth of business. In 1997 their online sales amounted to $1 billion; in 1998, $4 billion; and in 1999, $11 billion (60% of their orders) were placed online. This represented an annual saving to them of $367 million, net of the capital investment in the system. In addition, 90% of all of their software updates are communicated automatically online, while 70% of their technical support and service is handled online. General Electric's maintenance, repair, and operations costs increased 16% between 1982 and 1992, while prices declined. GE also noted that 25% of its invoices (1.25 million) contained errors and had to be reworked because the purchase order, receipt and invoice did not match. GE's Lighting piloted an online procurement system that not only helped eliminate those errors but also decreased labour costs, identified more suppliers, and procured goods faster. Streamlining MRO purchases in all 12 business units will save GE over $500 million annually. These examples from Cisco and GE illustrate how designing systems to minimise order entry errors impacts profitability.

9 Summary

Quality of the customer experience is critical! A business must anticipate the needs of its customer or they will go elsewhere. The quality of the customer experience includes usability. However, usability doesn't measure consumer loyalty or satisfaction with timeliness of order delivery or tell a company whether its web site has helped reduced costs or bring in new business. Knowing when and what customers are buying allows a firm to determine the physical flow of products and better manage fulfilment. Making sure the pages load quickly during periods of peak demand is essential to delivering a quality customer experience. Hits, page views and average session length are not the metrics for measuring the quality of the customer experience. A drop in conversion rates (visitors to buyers), average order size, or repeat purchases indicate a problem with the site.

Usability will lead to profits in the digital economy. It is very clear that the very survival of firms will depend to a large extent on the quality of the user interface. But usability, *per se*, is not sufficient by itself to insure profitability. The HCI community must go beyond usability to influence the design of features historically left to the exclusive domain of marketers such as branding, customer service, store shopping behaviour, consumer loyalty, pricing strategies, product displays, privacy, and trust. Only a combined understanding of human–computer interaction and these underlying marketing issues will lead to designs that maximise the quality of the customer experience and therefore profitability of online retailers.

References

Adamic, L. A. & Huberman, B. A. (1999), The Nature of Markets on the World Wide Web, Technical Report, Xerox Palo Alto Research Center. http://www.parc.xerox.com/ist1/groups/iea/www/novelty.html.

Alba, J., Lynch, J., Weitz, B., Janiszewski, C., Lutz, R., Sawyer, A. & Wood, S. (1997), "Interactive Home Shopping: Incentives for Consumers, Retailers, and Manufacturers to Participate in Electronic Marketplaces", *Journal of Marketing* **61**(3), 38–53.

Andersen Consulting (2000), "9 Out of 10 Online Holiday Shoppers Experienced Problems", http://www.andersen.com/news/newsarchive/1.00/newsarchive_011000. html. Press Release, 2000.01.10.

Bailey, J. (1998), Electronic Commerce: Prices and Consumer Issues for Three Products: Books, Compact Discs, and Software, Technical Report 98(4), Organisation for Economic Cooperation and Development (OECD).

Bakos, J. Y. (1997), "Reducing Buyer Search Costs: Implications for Electronic Marketplaces", *Management Science* **43**(12), 1676–92.

Bellman, S., Johnson, E. J., Kobrin, S. & Lohse, G. L. (2000), An International Survey of Concerns about Internet Security and Privacy, Working Paper Wharton Forum on Electronic Commerce.

Bellman, S., Lohse, G. L. & Johnson, E. J. (1999), "Predictors of Online Buying: Findings from the Wharton Virtual Test Market", *Communications of the ACM* **42**(12), 32–8.

Boston Consulting Group (2000), "Winning the Online Consumer: Insights into Online Consumer Behavior", www.bcg.com/consumer_promise/form.asp.

Brynjolfsson, E. & Smith, M. D. (1999), Frictionless Commerce: A Comparison of Internet and Conventional Retailers, Working Paper, MIT.

Hoffman, D. L., Novak, T. P. & Peralta, M. (1999), "Building Consumer Trust Online", *Communications of the ACM* **42**(4), 80–5.

Hoque, A. Y. & Lohse, G. L. (1999), "Designing Interfaces for Electronic Commerce: Predicting How Information Search Costs Influence Consumer Choice", *Journal of Marketing Research* **36**(3), 387–94.

Jarvenpaa, S. L. & Todd, P. A. (1997), "Consumer Reactions to Electronic Shopping on the World Wide Web", *International Journal of Electronic Commerce* **1**(2), 59–88.

Johnson, E. J., Bellman, S. & Lohse, G. L. (2000a), What Makes a Web Site "Sticky?" The Power Law of Practice and Cognitive Lock-in, Working Paper Wharton Forum on Electronic Commerce.

Johnson, E. J., Lohse, G. L. & Mandel, N. (1999), Computer-based Choice Environments: Four Approaches to Designing Marketplaces of the Artificial, Working Paper Wharton Forum on Electronic Commerce.

Johnson, E., Moe, W., Fader, P., Bellman, S. & Lohse, J. (2000b), "Modeling the Depth and Dynamics of Online Search Behavior", Paper presented at the 2000 INFORMS Marketing Science Conference. The Anderson School, UCLA.

Kadison, M. L., Weisman, D. E., Modahl, M., Liew, K. C. & Levin, K. (1998), "The Look to Buy Imperative", *Forrester Report* **1**(1). http://www.forrester.com/ER/research/report/0,1338,2603,FF.html.

Kahn, B. E. & McAlister, L. (1997), *Grocery Revolution: The New Focus on the Consumer*, Addison–Wesley.

Lohse, G. L. (2000), "State of the Web", *Wharton Real Estate Review* **4**(1), 19–24.

Lohse, G. L. & Johnson, E. J. (1998), "What You See Is What You Choose: The Effect of Rearranging Product Information on Consumer Choice", Presentation at Informs Marketing Science Conference: Marketing Science and Technology, Insead, France, July 10–13.

Lohse, G. L. & Spiller, P. (1998), "Electronic Shopping: The Effect of Customer Interfaces on Traffic and Sales", *Communications of the ACM* **41**(7), 81–7.

Lohse, G. L. & Spiller, P. (2000), "Internet Retail Store Design: How the User Interface Influences Traffic and Sales", *Journal of Computer Mediated Communications* **5**(2).

Lohse, G. L., Bellman, S. & Johnson, E. J. (to appear), "Consumer Buying Behavior on the Internet: Findings from Panel Data", *Journal of Interactive Marketing* .

Lynch, J. & Ariely, D. (1998), Interactive Home Shopping: Effects of Search Cost for Price and Quality Information on Consumer Price Sensitivity, Satisfaction with Merchandise Selected, and Retention, Working Paper, Duke University.

Nielsen, J. (1993), *Usability Engineering*, Academic Press.

Nielsen, J. & Norman, D. A. (2000), "Web site usability", Information Week, http://www.informationweek.com/773/web.htm.

Reuters (2000), "E-Tailers Make Alterations", News Wire Article. March 2, Reuters Ltd, Palo Alto, http://www.wired.com/news/print/0,1294,34708,00.html.

Smith, M. D., Bailey, J. & Brynjolfsson, E. (to appear), Understanding Digital Markets, *in* E. Brynjolfsson & B. Kahin (eds.), *Understanding the Digital Economy*, MIT Press.

Spiller, P. & Lohse, G. L. (1997), "A Classification of Internet Retail Catalogs", *International Journal of Electronic Commerce* **2**(2), 29–56.

Weber, J. (2000), "The Last Mile", The Industry Standard, March 27, http://www.thestandard.com/article/display/0,1151,13277,00.html.

Asynchronous Negotiated Access

James Hollan & Scott Stornetta

Distributed Cognition and HCI Laboratory, Department of Cognitive Science, University of California, San Diego, La Jolla, California 92093, USA

EMail: *{hollan, stornetta}@cogsci.ucsd.edu*
URL: *http://hci.ucsd.edu/*

Scheduling access to people and selectively sharing the state of one's activities are essential elements of collaborating with others. These processes are fundamental to arranging face-to-face meetings and coordinating access to shared information. Examples include scheduling meetings, contacting others in real time (by phone or instant messaging), and checking on the changing status of a jointly-authored document. In this paper, we first discuss challenging social and technical problems associated with scheduling and sharing activities and then describe a novel computational technique designed to help mediate access to people and their work products. We argue that providing effective negotiated-access will be an issue of growing significance as computational and wireless technologies make us increasingly and perhaps overly accessible.

Keywords: collaboration, coordination, managing interruptions, mediating access, scheduling.

1 Introduction

Consider the everyday task of scheduling a meeting. If those involved are in close proximity, the most common approach is for the person initiating the meeting to speak directly with the other people they want to meet with to compare calendars, share the state of relevant activities and commitments, discuss options, and ultimately decide on a mutually agreeable meeting time.

When the parties are not in close proximity, a similar process of negotiation often takes place over the phone. In both cases, the parties participate in real time.

Scheduling by phone is complicated because it is often difficult for parties to reach one another. What frequently results is a game of phone tag. One party tries to reach another, is unable to, and leaves voice-mail indicating an interest in finding a time to meet. The other party returns the call, more often than not fails to reach the original caller, and leaves voice-mail in response. The process routinely entails multiple iterations, with the participants leaving suggested times to meet, confirming previously mentioned times, or proposing new times. The negotiation is inefficient and frequently tedious. The process is further complicated as the number of meeting participants increases.

People commonly remove themselves from scheduling negotiations by having a secretary participate on their behalf. A principal virtue of this is the secretary is available by telephone throughout the day, so the back and forth problem of phone tag ends as soon as people initially contacted call back. The secretary has access to their employer's calendar as well as knowledge of other constraints and is able to negotiate a time for the appointment.

A process similar to this phone-tag negotiation is now often carried out via electronic mail. A person proposes a meeting in email, perhaps suggesting potential times for the to-be-scheduled meeting, and the process proceeds through email acceptance or counterproposal until a time acceptable to all involved is negotiated. Though this process may be less frustrating than phone tag, it can still stretch out over an extended period before agreement is reached. It is also possible that by the time one of the participants responds another participant's schedule may have changed due to the lack of timely response to a suggested potential time or to a conflicting obligation arising. It is the nature of asynchronous interactions that a proposed time may no longer be valid by the time all parties respond and commit to it.

2   Negotiated Access: A Proposal

In this paper, we propose a negotiated-access mechanism that alleviates a number of problems associated with arranging access to people and coordinating information sharing. It is implemented via a lock-and-key technique that supports asynchronous interaction and provides flexible boundaries between less urgent and more urgent access. In addition, it allows control over timing of access and permits tailoring of access level to specific individuals or groups. We first describe our negotiated-access proposal in the context of arranging meetings and then show that it is a general approach to a wide spectrum of problems.

2.1   Scheduling: Problems with Calendar-sharing Approaches

Let's continue with the meeting scheduling example and look at a calendar-sharing approach. In this model, all parties keep appointment calendars in electronic form using compatible software. Someone wanting to schedule a meeting can view other people's calendars, see the times they are available, choose an appropriate time, and notify everyone involved of the meeting time, without the other parties ever needing to be involved in the negotiation.

Although calendar-sharing software has enjoyed modest acceptance, it has not been made to work well in practice. First, such systems require all parties to maintain their calendars in electronic form and to continually ensure that they are up to date. The payoffs for these added burdens are often not equitably distributed. There are large costs associated with keeping schedules updated, and payoffs frequently may not be worth the effort for many of those involved. Grudin (1987) discusses this in terms of who does the work and who gets the benefit. He notes that such systems often fail because while requiring everyone involved to keep their calendar online and current, often only managers derive benefit. Second, because such schemes allow people to view and modify the calendars of others, calendar sharing is limited to close associates who feel comfortable allowing such access. While it is not an uncommon practice for people working within the same organisation to use calendar-sharing systems, they fail to meet the needs of those who:

1. do not use the same software;

2. are in separate organisations without needed connections;

3. do not find the reward-to-effort tradeoff suitably beneficial; or

4. do not feel comfortable sharing their calendars.

Knowing a person's schedule provides valuable information about their activities and raises complex confidentiality and security issues. In some calendar-sharing software, this is addressed in part by masking out the details of appointments. When someone else is viewing the calendar, only times available are presented but this is still information not everyone wants to share. If there is even one person an individual does not feel comfortable sharing his or her schedule with, then there is incentive not to participate in calendar sharing. Without universal acceptance of the sharing scheme, the whole process can become fragile and break down. In a significant number of situations, for the reasons listed above, it is simply not practical to use calendar-sharing software to schedule a meeting.

2.2 Scheduling: Negotiated-access Approach

To help describe our proposed negotiated-access approach, consider scheduling a simple two-person meeting. For example, imagine Irving wants to schedule a meeting with a business associate Roberta. He begins by composing an email message to her. It might be something like:

```
Roberta,

I've been thinking more about your proposal and would
like to discuss it.  I'm in and out of the office a
lot this week, so the best thing to try is probably
scheduling a time that both of us are available.
You can choose a time for us to talk simply by clicking
on the link at the bottom of the page.  That link gives
you a one-time access to my calendar, and will allow you
to pick a time for us to talk.  Look forward to talking
with you, and hope things are going well.  - Irving
```

After completing his email, Irving specifies restrictions on possible times for the meeting and on when scheduling can take place. For example, he might restrict the meeting to times he is free in the next two weeks and indicate that Roberta will only have one-time access to schedule. A program could then be run to insert a specially constructed URL at the bottom of the page. The completed email message might look like:

```
From: Irving@equi-pose.com
To: Roberta@hci.ucsd.edu

Roberta,

I've been thinking more about your proposal and would
like to discuss it.  I'm in and out of the office a
lot this week, so the best thing to try is probably
scheduling a time that both of us are available.
You can choose a time for us to talk simply by clicking
on the link at the bottom of the page.  That link gives
you a one-time access to my calendar, and will allow you
to pick a time for us to talk.  Look forward to talking
with you, and hope things are going well.  - Irving

http://www.equi-pose.com/cgi-bin/Irving/?token=roberta-1
```

After Roberta receives the email and decides she wants to schedule the meeting, she simply clicks on the URL.* Roberta will then see a Web page displaying Irving's calendar with only the times he is available to meet with her. This Web page is generated by a program that is run in response to Roberta's click. It checks the token to ensure it is the unique token that was used to specify the meeting Irving requested and if verified allows Roberta one-time access to the calendar to choose an appointment time within the constraints Irving imposed. Once Roberta selects a time, the token *roberta-1* is deactivated. If Roberta or anyone else attempts to use the URL at a later time, they will not be allowed access to Irving's calendar. Cryptographic processes can be used to make the token secure and infeasible to guess. We discuss this and other variations later. Finally, Irving is automatically notified, by email or other means, that Roberta has confirmed their meeting.

2.3   Scheduling: *Negotiated-access Advantages*

Notice how this process removes problems associated with approaches mentioned earlier. Irving did not send a proposed set of meeting times explicitly in his email. Instead he sent a token that provides a mechanism to access a filtered view of his calendar. If in the interim between when he sent the message and Roberta responded his calendar changes, the filtered view Roberta will see can still be current. Irving and the automated negotiation process retain control over possible times until the other party responds. However, also notice that Roberta benefits from this process by being presented choices that are current at the time of access and the effort required of her is minimal. The effort to specify the filter and generate the associated token is done by Irving, the person wanting to schedule the meeting.

Advantages of the proposed process are further illustrated in the following situation. Suppose an employer needs to meet with eight job candidates applying for a position opening. He has a block of four hours during which he can conduct interviews, and he would like to meet for 30 minutes with each candidate. In a

---

*Note that there are two parts to the URL: a path to a cgi-bin program for accessing Irving's calendar and a parameter that is the token used to generate the filtered view and schedule the meeting.

conventional system the employer might propose specific times in email messages to the candidates. However, the times proposed to a given candidate may not work for that person, whereas he or she could be available at a time proposed for a different candidate. If one candidate could swap times with another, then potentially everyone's scheduling needs could be satisfied. Unfortunately, working through this might take several rounds of email.

Our proposed token-based mechanism offers significant improvements for negotiating access. For example, the employer could send out eight emails, each with a separate token, but with each token giving access to the same four hour block. After the first candidate who accesses the calendar chooses a time, that time slot is marked as used. The next candidate to access the calendar sees only the seven remaining choices, and so on for the other candidates. This example is a special case of scheduling a general multi-person meeting. What we want to highlight is the unique flexibility provided by asynchronous negotiated access to a filtered and dynamically updated database of state information. Arranging any multi-person meeting may benefit from application of the process disclosed here.

While the negotiated-access mechanism does not eliminate all possible problems (e.g. one of the candidates might have a particularly constrained schedule with demands that cannot be met), it can still simplify the negotiation process and minimise its duration. It should be clear that the underlying mechanism could be modified so that respondents can indicate subsets of the possible times that fit their schedules, or even indicate priorities for those times. Then as each person accesses the schedule via their token the schedule is in an updated state based on all previous interactions. While the mechanism could be varied to support posting individual time constraints when the scheduling negotiation is to find a mutually agreeable time, this introduces additional complexities. Here we want to emphasise the advantages of the basic method we propose:

1. The time involved in scheduling negotiation is minimised for all involved.

2. Each person negotiates their constraints within the context of the current state of the evolving schedule and in many cases doesn't need to be further involved.

3. Unlike calendar sharing approaches, special software is required only of the person initiating scheduling.

4. The added work required to specify a filter falls only to the meeting initiator.

2.4 Instant Messaging: Similar Problems

The same fundamental scheduling problems exemplified above in arranging meetings are also confronted in a variety of other situations. Consider instant messaging for example. The recent growth in instant messaging (IM) systems, as well as wireless access, presages a world where one is continuously available for interaction. In such a setting, there will be a growing need to restrict and negotiate access.

Instant messaging and similar chat facilities evolved from the *talk* command on early Unix systems. Talk was used for synchronous short text-based interactions, while email was used for longer messages sent asynchronously. This mechanism was adequate so long as:

1. the number of users on the system remained small;

2. users were likely to be acquainted with each other (which was typically the case, by virtue of working in the same small group); and

3. they were only logged on the system a relatively small fraction of their day.

Over time, this basic mechanism was expanded to handle collections of computers connected via multiple networks and resulted in a very large number of aggregate users. As a consequence, condition (1) no longer held. If all current users were notified each time a new user logged on, this would create almost constant interruptions. In addition, as networks grew larger, most users were no longer associates, in either a social or work-related sense. Thus, condition (2) no longer held. Users don't want information about their presence or absence on the system to be broadcast to other users they don't even know. These circumstances led to the creation of *buddy lists*, collections of people with whom one wishes to have instant messaging communication. Thus, today when a user logs onto the system, only those people who have the user on their buddy list are notified.

Instant messaging has now expanded beyond text to include voice. A real-time audio channel can be opened and remains continuously on, analogous to a text-based IM window remaining on the screen. While this is advantageous when both parties desire increased access to each other, the audio version of IM can be even more invasive than a text version, and leads to the need to further regulate access in situations where parties want to insulate themselves, at least temporarily, from access. In addition, the growth of wireless connectivity and other *always-on* systems creates a situation in which users can be logged on nearly continuously. In such circumstances, condition (3) no longer holds. As a result, additional means will increasingly be needed to regulate one's availability for instant messaging and similar forms of access.

2.5 Instant Messaging: Negotiated-access Approach

Many problems people confront in instant messaging derive from the absence of a negotiation mechanism being available at the time one individual wants to access another. While professors might want to provide students in their classes with instant messaging access, they likely also want to be online at times without that access being granted. The same mechanism described above to aid meeting scheduling can also be employed to provide negotiated-access for instant messaging. In this case, each individual or group can be provided with a token similar to the one used in the scheduling example. The token is used to negotiate access in the same lock-and-key method[†] described earlier. Just as in the case of meeting scheduling, the identity of the token is checked and the associated filter determines whether access to the

---

[†]A Web-based server technology, similar to the calendar example, can be employed to act as a negotiation intermediary. The negotiation could result, for example, in selectively and temporarily altering buddy-list members.

person they seek is made available. Since access can be tailored to the token, at the same instant people could be available for IM to one set of individuals (perhaps those with whom they are working to meet an approaching project deadline) and not to others. Notice that negotiations can take into account any information available in the database at the time of attempted access. This is particularly advantageous because it gives all parties fine-grained control over access.

2.6 Pagers, Cell Phones, and Wireless Email: Inner and Outer Circles of Access

In addition to instant messaging, pagers and cell phones further increase our accessibility and the need to regulate access. In fact, some people use access to their pager and cell phone numbers to distinguish between an *outer circle* of acquaintances and a more intimate *inner circle* of friends. They do this by simply giving the outer circle only their office phone number, and giving the inner circle their pager or cell phone number. A difficulty arises when there is a need, perhaps involving an urgent matter, for someone from the outer group to reach them via their pager or cell phone. To facilitate this, one is motivated to reveal one's cell phone or pager number. The side effect of this is that the inner circle expands, as it's not possible to ask the person to forget the number. It's also socially awkward to say: now that we've taken care of this issue, please don't ever call me on my cell phone again. Again, people can make use of secretaries to negotiate this form of access. The secretary determines which calls merit urgent contact and can connect a call without disclosing the cell phone number. Automated personal assistants (see for example, http://www.wildfire.com/) attempt to simulate this same process. Nevertheless, it still often leads to the need to query the person to see if they desire to take the call, which can be disruptive and time-consuming.

Allowing one more person access to the inner circle is at least a nuisance. As this process is repeated for multiple exceptional circumstances, the advantages of having the inner circle can seriously degrade. These outer/inner distinctions are present in the two previous examples as well, namely:

MEDIUM	OUTER CIRCLE	INNER CIRCLE
Telephone	Work Number, Phone Book Listing	Cell or Pager Number
IM	Public Directory	Buddy List
Meetings	No Calendar access	Calendar

The emergence of wireless email services is also starting to lead to a two-tier system of email accounts in which those in the outer circle are given one's main email address and those in the inner circle are given one's mobile email address. Below we discuss how our proposed negotiated-access process can be applied to these new examples but to assist exposition we first discuss a generalisation of the process.

3 Generalisation of Negotiated Access

As we enter a world of increased connectivity via the Internet and wireless, the associated technologies (e.g. pagers, cell phones, and wireless email) intensify the need for a practical method to negotiate access. Key issues include:

- maintaining, and hopefully increasing, individual control over the management of interruptions;

- supporting controlled access to personal information such as one's calendar and to shared information and work products to aid collaboration;

- creating a common integrated process for access negotiations;

- sharing the effort required for negotiation in appropriate and effective ways between the parties involved; and

- minimising the need for participants to devote time unnecessarily to the negotiation process itself.

It is desirable that the method avoid the problems mentioned earlier: proposed times for scheduled events being out-of-date, losing control over sensitive information, requiring parties to use identical software, and creating burdensome overhead for all involved in the negotiation process. In addition, an effective solution should permit access to the privileges of an inner circle on a limited basis and provide a socially acceptable way for access to be withdrawn after the temporary need has passed.

Rather than providing specific instantiations of our negotiated-access proposal to handle pager, cell phone, and wireless email access, here we describe a generalisation applicable to these and other areas. It allows people to efficiently negotiate access to others, to personal state information, and to shared work materials, while minimising the need for synchronous interaction during negotiation. To implement the process requires:

1. a database of state information and filters;

2. a unique token generator;

3. a checker of tokens;

4. a process of applying a filter to authorise access and possibly generate a customised view of selected database information; and

5. a communication mechanism.

In the general case, a person sends a token to others he or she wishes to access. The originator maintains control over the period when a token and associated filter is valid as well as the process of negotiation. The receivers of tokens or their agents can, during the period the tokens are valid, use them to participate in a negotiated interaction with an agent of the originator. An agent can be a person or a computational process. The sender's agent uses the token and potentially additional information to select a filter from a database in order to dynamically configure and execute the negotiated interaction. This process can selectively reveal information to the token receivers, allow them to modify selected portions of the sender's database of state information, or result in running a program to interface with other applications.

The filter and token combination provide the lock-and-key access mechanism alluded to earlier. They are created at the time one initiates a new instance of negotiated access. In the case of scheduling, this involves specifying the meeting constraints, duration the token is valid, and parameters used to configure the calendar view parties will be given and access privileges they will have. In the cases of instant messaging, pager, cell phone, or wireless email access, the token enables potential access. Access is determined by the associated filter and state information in the database. For example, a cell phone call from one's spouse might always be able to reach one but during an important meeting others might not have cell phone access. The database can contain information about an individual's location, schedule, state of work materials, status of various projects, desire to currently limit access, and a range of other information. While this information can be entered manually, there is the promise that portions of it can be included and updated without conscious effort, as the byproduct of other activities. For example, location information could, at times, be automatically updated when GPS chips start to be incorporated in cell phones, cars, and other devices.

Our generalisation of the negotiated-access mechanism can also provide limited duration access to privileges of an inner circle. Upon the need for such access, a specific filter customised to the particular circumstances can be created. Of course, it could also result from modifying a previously configured filter. Negotiated access[‡] can then be exercised via the associated token at the convenience of the parties to whom one extends such privileges. The token might permit paging, placing a cell phone call, creating an IM connection, sending wireless email, or any combination of access. The token and execution of the associated filter determines whether access is granted. Suppose, for example, it results in a cell phone connection. After the call concludes, the token might be deactivated as an automatic result of the filter. Note that the state of one's inner versus outer circle then reverts to what it was prior to the event. Notice also that the same mechanism can be used to further refine inner-outer distinctions to create multiple categories. This enables individuals to be temporarily recategorised so as to move them either inwardly to grant them additional access or outwardly to further restrict access. At any time access may be denied due to state information present in the database. For example, a called party may be in a location in which all filters automatically disable cell phone access.

The generalised negotiated-access process can be modified to permit additional discretion to all parties, to make it more convenient, to use multiple communication channels, and to increase the security of the process. While we don't elaborate these modifications here, we do want to emphasise token security. The only requirement for a token is that it be unique. It can be generated using cryptographic techniques. If the intended recipient of a token has a known digital signature, then one could require both the token and a digital-signature test of identity to gain access. In fact, with a known digital signature, one can dispense with the token altogether, simply using the digital signature as the token.

[‡]This can take a variety of forms. The token could be passed via a Web connection, as described in the previous examples, or over a wireless network. The token could be a phone number to be called with extra digits to be keyed in once a connection to a server application is established. The token could even be constructed to be appropriate to be used in a verbal interchange with a person's secretary.

4 Summary

Currently we are at the beginnings of widespread wireless connectivity and ubiquitous computing. The Web is merging with a variety of technologies: cell phones, laptop computers, hand held organisers, information appliances, and GPS and other sensors. The capability for access anytime and anywhere is here. The increasing frequency of cell phone calls at inappropriate times testifies that people no longer can easily control access. Devices can determine where they are located and can make a range of information available to users as well as make users available to others or their devices.

We have proposed a general technique that promises to assist in mediating access. It capitalises on advantages afforded by computation(Hollan & Stornetta, 1992). We first described the negotiation technique in the context of problems involved in scheduling meetings and then showed that similar issues, which at first may seem unrelated but in fact have much in common, arise in other contexts. One such activity, gaining immediate access, is currently of growing importance because of expanding connectivity via wireless technology.

Cell phones and related technologies make it possible to be constantly available for synchronous interaction. At times, this can be advantageous but the associated costs and benefits result in a complex tradeoff space for designers as well as users. The negotiated-access mechanism we describe can influence these tradeoffs as well as assist in arranging access to people and coordinating information sharing. It is implemented via a token-based lock-and-key technique that supports asynchronous interaction and provides flexible boundaries between less urgent and more urgent access. In addition, it allows control over timing of access, permits tailoring of access level for specific individuals or groups, and provides limited duration access to privileges of an inner circle without expanding and degrading the value of maintaining an inner circle and without offending those granted only temporary access. The implementation we sketch for meeting scheduling, instant messaging, and access via pagers, cell phones, and wireless email, does not require all parties to share the same software, allows late-binding of details to better support negotiation during changing circumstances, and minimises overhead in the negotiation process. While many issues need to be further elaborated, not the least of which is the results from our prototype implementations, what we propose is a novel and promising approach to an increasingly significant problem.

References

Grudin, J. (1987), Social Evaluation of the User Interface: Who Does the Work and Who Gets the Benefit?, *in* H.-J. Bullinger & B. Shackel (eds.), *Proceedings of INTERACT '87 — Second IFIP Conference on Human–Computer Interaction*, Elsevier Science, pp.805–11.

Hollan, J. & Stornetta, S. (1992), Beyond Being There, *in* P. Bauersfeld, J. Bennett & G. Lynch (eds.), *Proceedings of CHI'92: Human Factors in Computing Systems*, ACM Press, pp.119–25.

The Context of Interaction:
People, Places and Actions

Requirements are in the Eyes of the Beholders

Phil Turner

HCI Research Group, School of Computing, Napier University, Edinburgh EH14 IDJ, UK

EMail: *p.turner@dcs.napier.ac.uk*

It will be demonstrated that the perceived attributes or characteristics of information artefacts can act as constraints on the ways in which people use and interact with them. This is particularly true when the information artefacts behave as boundary objects within organisations. Yet despite the different uses to which these information artefacts are put the user interfaces to them are typically uniform. The proposed approach brings together insights from activity theory, affordances and personal construct theory, and adopts repertory grids as its principle means of investigation. Finally, the consequences of this approach to design of local user interfaces to information artefacts is considered.

Keywords: requirements, information artefacts, boundary objects, repertory grids, affordances, activity theory.

1 Introduction

The prevailing attitude of the major software vendors to the design of user interfaces to their products appears, steadfastly, to be *one size fits all*. Despite the recognition that users vary in terms of their IT expertise; for example Carroll & Mack (1985) among many others, vary among themselves; for example Dillon & Watson (1996) and between cultures; for example Hoft (1996), little has been done to tailor user interfaces for individuals beyond simple customisation. This problem has been exacerbated by the relatively recent discovery that people work together in groups (*sic*) and these groups differ from one to another in terms of their makeup and working practices and work content.

Consider the functioning of an information-centric office. In such an organisation there will perhaps be a number of information systems. (Hereafter the more precise term *information artefact* will instead be adopted, an information artefact being "any artefact whose purpose is to allow information to be stored, retrieved, and possibly transformed" (Green & Benyon, 1996).) Thus an information artefact such as a central database may be used by different groups of individuals within the organisation many of whom will have different needs and perceptions of this information artefact. And it is these differing perceptions which are of interest here. These heterogeneous perceptions arise from an individual's work or frame of reference, as Bucciarelli observes:

> "... consider this page in front of you. [...] A naïve empiricist would sense its weight and estimate its size; another reader might note its colour or texture; a chemist on the design team would describe its resistance to discoloration, its acidity, and its photosensitivity. A mechanical engineer would be concerned with its tear or its tensile strength, its stiffness, and its thermal conductivity. An electrical engineer would speak of its ability to conduct or hold a static charge. All of these attributes of the object, the same artefact, are understood within different frames of reference, and they might all contend in a design process ..." (Bucciarelli, 1994, p.71)

Similar observations have been made of so-called boundary objects (Star, 1989). A boundary object is a shared object of working, such as a document or file, or more generally an information artefact, which exists at the boundaries or intersections of different work-groups and may be regarded as a vehicle for communication about work. Individuals in different work-groups necessarily perceive these objects in different ways according to their individual and group needs. A successful boundary object allows individuals in different work-groups to interpret the same material in different ways according to their individual and group needs. Mark (1997) has reported the use of 'conventions', the means by which the different perspectives and work-groups can achieve a shared understanding or common method for handling information artefacts, and by implication a shared understanding of their characteristics. She notes that the conventions must be articulated, be consistent among users, and sufficiently flexible to be able to adapt to contingencies. Mambrey & Robinson (1997), in work paralleling Mark's (both studies related to the German POLITeam project) focused on the role and behaviour of boundary objects in the flow of work between government offices in Bonn and Berlin. They found that artefacts such as documents and folders become inscribed with a history or log reflecting changing, and not necessarily predictable, properties — going from, for example, 'incoming email' to 'request to' or 'private work in progress' to 'public information'. By contrast, a failure of boundary objects to support crucial characteristics is illustrated in Star & Ruhleder's (1994) account of a large scale system for sharing research information between groups of nematode researchers. Here it is observed that judgements of trust and reliability "require knowledge of the community that is not captured in any formal system."

Having established that people perceive and work with information artefacts in different ways, a resultant challenge for user interface designers is how to create individual or small group tailored local user interfaces (LUI) based upon these perceptions. Rather than adopting a task analytic approach (Benyon, 1992) or the use of contextual analysis, for example Beyer & Holtzblatt (1998), or any of the many variations on participatory design, for example, or an ethnographic enquiry, for example Hughes et al. (1994), or a cognitive work analysis (Vicente, 1999), a theoretical and practical framework is proposed (and subsequently demonstrated) which establishes perception as a possible basis for user interface design.

1.1 Perception as Action

Gibson and Wartofsky are among a number of researchers who have linked perception to action. Gibson (1986) has emphasised the biological aspects of this in terms of animals exploiting their ecological niches, later coining the term 'affordance' to embody this idea. This concept of affordances is both attractive and elusive. An affordance is described as the reciprocal relationship between an animal and its environment: an affordance is a resource or support that the environment offers an animal; the animal in turn must possess the capabilities to perceive it and to use it. Thus an affordance is "a specific combination of the properties of (a thing's) substance and its surfaces taken with reference to an animal". Affordances are said to exist independently of the animal or individual evolved. While the HCI research community has to some extent embraced the idea of affordances; for example Anderson (1993), Gaver (1991), Gaver (1995), Norman (1988)) affordances remain paradoxically easy to identify but difficult to design in to an artefact.

Expanding on Gibson's ecological/biological approach, Wartofsky has focussed on the learned aspects of perception. Writing from a cultural-historical perspective (typified by activity theory) Wartofsky treats perception as an historical process having been culturally acquired and one which continues to expand with additional individual or group experience. His argument begins, like Gibson's, with the recognition that perception is a functional aspect of the interactions between animals and their environments. He observes that there is a reciprocal relationship between the animal and its environment: while the perceived world of the animal can be treated as a map or an image of the animals activities, the senses of animals themselves are shaped by the purposive interactions which the species has with the environment, or as he puts it, "Rather, the very forms of perceptual activity are now shaped to, and also help to shape an environment created by conscious human activity itself. This environment is the world made by *praxis* — nature transformed into artefact, and now embodying human intentions and needs in an objective way." An excellent example of this may be found in Goodwin & Goodwin's (1998) study of operational staff at an airport. The study demonstrates how perceptions of information artefacts (flight information displays, documentation linking flights, destinations and aircraft, the position of the aircraft themselves on the stand ...) and their perceived properties or characteristics are shaped by the histories of both the personnel involved and the artefacts themselves. The Goodwins further observe that such perceptions are always grounded in particular organisations, tasks and mediating artefacts.

Thus the perceived (or identified) characteristics of artefacts, computer based or otherwise, have consequences for the ways in which the artefacts are used. Next, an elicitation technique for these percepts is described.

1.2   Perception in Action

Repertory grids were devised by Kelly (1955) as a means of identifying the elements of an individual's (social) life. Underlying repertory grids is Personal Construct Theory * which takes as a central premise that humans are constantly developing and testing hypothesis about their social reality, thus conceptualising people as 'scientists'. Interestingly as Shaw & Gaines (1992) have pointed out there are surprising synergies between personal construct theory and the above remarks about affordances. Kelly's use of the term 'construct' is closer in meaning to percept than it is to concept, as percept carries with it 'the idea of its being a personal act'. (Kelly (1955, p.70), quoted in Shaw & Gaines (1992)).

While the initial uses of repertory grids were in the exploration of such things as attitudes and neuroses, they have also been used in knowledge elicitation; for example Shaw & Gaines (1987), Shaw & Gaines (1992), to some extent in information system and HCI design; for example Dillon & McKnight (1990), McCarthy & O'Connor (1999) and in understanding job design; for example Hassard (1987). At its simplest (and there are a number of variations on the detail) the analyst seeks to elicit a set of *elements* and *constructs* from an individual. These elements, which may take a variety of forms, are in some sense the major components of the domain of interest. In the case study to be described later in the paper, the elements consist of the information artefacts (e.g. paper forms; procedures; information systems and so forth) in the system to be described. The elements are then used to elicit a further set of dimensions or constructs by which the elements can be distinguished. Thus a grid can be constructed consisting of x elements and y constructs which affords subsequent analysis.

2   The Student Enrolment Process

This section illustrates this approach using data from a live case study where the brief was the design of an automated workflow system to support the undergraduate student enrolment process. Enrolment is a well established set of procedures which nonetheless change every year, for example, last academic year has seen the introduction of a tuition fee. The enrolment process is deeply arcane in its custom and practice which are lost in the mists of bureaucracy and apocryphal history. However it is largely centred round a single form (the enrolment form) which is generated, checked by students, validated by staff, used to collect data from several different sources, and finally divided so that its parts are distributed to different destinations.

2.1   Student Enrolment

At the beginning of each academic year, a pre-printed paper enrolment form is generated for each student by the faculty, bearing as much information about the student's personal details and choice of course as is available. When students arrive to enrol, the appropriate academic course leader checks the academic-related information (evidence of qualifications, choice of options ...) adding any details

---

*Numerous detailed accounts of Personal Construct Theory and repertory grids are available elsewhere; for example Kelly (1955), Fransella & Bannister (1977).

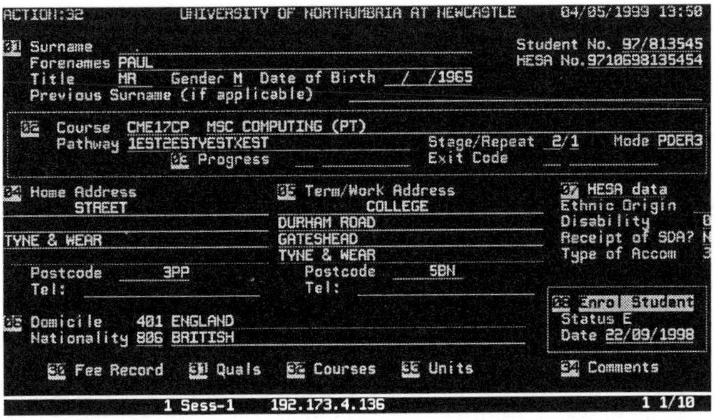

Figure 1: The SAS (with a student's details obscured).

which may be missing and signs the form to authorise enrolment. Some academics also use this as an opportunity for informal counselling. Next, administrative staff not only check (and add, as necessary) personal details, but check that evidence of some reliable means of paying the fees is provided. Details are entered by administrators into the student administrative system — the SAS. In some cases, not all the data required by the SAS is immediately available, so either provisional data is entered or fields are left blank, which will subsequently generate an error report. The student is requested to bring the missing material as soon as possible and it is entered when available. This is an informal work-around, not part of the official process. Once past the administrative staff, students move on to finance and out of the scope of this study. From the student's point of view, enrolment is not only their official entry to the university, but the all-important tear-off part of the form provides evidence that will allow them to join the library and the students' union, log on to computer systems and pay a reduced rate of local tax. The activity of enrolling students is realised in practice by a number of its component actions. Each action has a goal, for example, to collect fees, to check the student's qualifications and so forth which are achieved by one or more individuals using one or more information artefacts. Administrative goals include getting data quickly into the system while academics, in contrast, *inter alia* are concerned with estimates of teaching numbers.

2.2 The SAS

The existing SAS system is hosted on a mainframe and is accessed via a telnet session from a PC. The SAS has a character based user interface and supports a number of sub-systems designed to administer student admissions, a marks recording system and a student record system. The student admissions system has no less than 10 different screens which are used to input data (witness the 1/10 at the bottom of Figure 1).

3   Mapping Perceptions of Individual Work

Individuals were drawn from two different communities for this investigation. The first and larger group were drawn from the departmental office, which is typical of those to be found in a large university. The departmental staff are information workers dealing with not only the student enrolment tasks just described, but the administration of student records, staff and student queries and so forth. The staff are organised hierarchically with a senior administrator *J*, her deputy and four administrators and two secretarial support staff. Interest was not so much what they did (i.e. the content and context of their work) but what information artefacts were used in the enrolment process and how they differentiated among them.

The other group of stakeholders were drawn from the academic staff and were very typical of lecturers with little or no involvement in the enrolment process itself but who are, of course, direct users of the enrolment information.

3.1   *Procedure*

The method adopted involved using repertory grid to elicit perceptions about the range of information artefacts and their perceived characteristics (following the technique described in Fransella & Bannister (1977). All of the departmental administrative staff and a number of the academic staff were asked individually:

- To identify the information artefacts (elements) which are used in enrolment and so forth. We aimed at the recommended minimum of eight to ten elements from each participant. Each elicited element was then written on a separate piece of card.

- Then using the triad approach, we asked each participant in turn to identify at least eight characteristics by which the elements differed. The triad approach involves taking three elements at random (in practice this was done using three cards chosen at random) and asking the participant, "In what way or ways do any two of these elements resemble each other and which is different?" A typical answer may be something like, "these two are important and this one is less important", creating the bipolar construct of 'important — less important'.

- The participants then were presented with all *x* information artefacts and for each perceived characteristic asked to rank the element on a five-point scale. Thus if an information artefact was rated as 'very important' it might attract a weighting of 1, while a less important element would be rated 4 or 5. Table 1 is an illustration of this, elements represented by capital letters.

The resulting data were then analysed using the University of Calgary's WebGrid II software[†].

3.2   *Results*

Of the output from the analysis software, two aspects will be considered in some detail. The first is a multi-dimensional map of the perceived world of the individual in this context. The constructs act as an organising framework, while the information

---

[†]Webgrid II may be found at http://gigi.cpsc.ucalgary.ca/WebGrid/WebGrid.html

	1	2	3	4	5	
Important	A	C	E	D	B	Less important
		F				
		G				

Table 1: A sample repertory grid.

---

artefacts are found in clusters in this *n*-dimensional space. The second is a set of dendrographs graphically representing the correlations between the elements (information artefacts in this instance) and the correlations between the constructs.

In all 11 repertory grids were elicited, eight from the administrative staff and three from the academic staff. The former proved too varied and of interested; the latter proved to remarkably uniform (and dull) and were very close in character to the results from the more junior administrative staff. Give this, only the data from the administrative staff will be examined in detail.

3.3 Maps of Individual Percepts

Figures 2–4 are multi-dimensional maps representing the percepts of *J*, *C* and *D* respectively. Clearly *J*'s world is richer and more diverse than the others, again reflecting the make-up of her job and her knowledge and experience. Inspection alone of these figures reveals that the elements (identified by an 'X' and an appended label) are distributed widely across the constructs (which are represented by axes) in *J*'s map while they are grouped in two main areas, ignoring a singleton, in *C*'s map; again *D*'s world lies between the two in terms of complexity.

The use of repertory grids in mapping the administrators' work has thus demonstrated that perceived characteristics are a meaningful concept; that the range of information artefacts and their perceived characteristics vary dramatically with an individual's job and range of responsibilities (probably as a function of the amount of discretion involved) or as a function of their different work histories in cultural-historical terms. (For the sake of completeness it should be noted that the academics' perception of the enrolment process were primarily centred on their need to have some understanding of likely student numbers for time tabling purposes.)

3.4 Perceived Characteristics

Figures 5–7 are dendrograms for three of the administrative staff. To the top of each figure are the elicited constructs with a scale to the right (100–50) which is a measure of this correlation. Interestingly many of these perceived characteristics are highly correlated. Highly correlated constructs may indicate that the different perceived characteristics are effectively synonyms and may be consolidated (it should be noted that the repertory grids method allows for iteration to further clarify highly correlated constructs but this was not pursued in this case). Examining the figures in turn. Figure 5 is a detail from the analysis of *J*'s elicited perceived characteristics. *J*, as already noted, is a highly skilled and knowledgeable departmental manager with more than a decade of experience in the job. Her perceived characteristics are greater in number than her colleagues and include what might be judged to

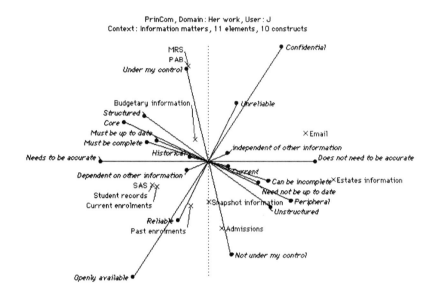

Figure 2: J's map.

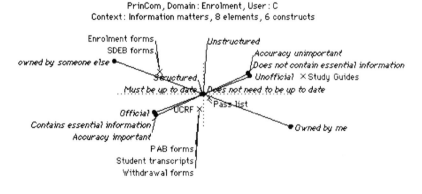

Figure 3: C's map.

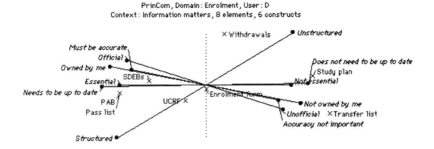

Figure 4: D's map.

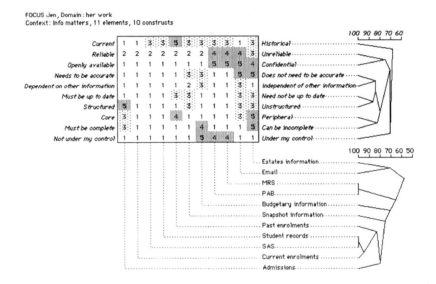

Figure 5: J's dendrogram.

be more sophisticated range of constructs such as dependent — independent on other information; current-historical; as well as construct which appear in the other two figures such as reliable-unreliable; up to date — not up to date and so forth.

Figure 6 provides an interesting contrast to the last figure as it is the equivalent detail for *C*. This member of staff holds a junior position in the office and perhaps not unsurprisingly there are fewer perceived characteristics and information artefacts in her world. It is fair to say that *C*'s range of duties are much more limited than *J*'s and the degree of discretion limited. The working world of this individual appears to verge on the monochromatic. There are relatively few information artefacts identified and these are perceived as being effectively identical (see the grouping

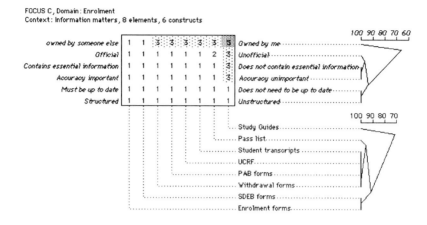

Figure 6: C's dendrogram.

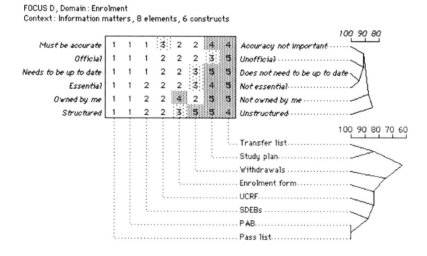

Figure 7: D's dendrogram.

of PAB, UCRF, Withdrawal list and Transfer list — these refer a set of administrative forms and procedures). The same is true of the constructs.

Finally, Figure 7 is a detail from administrator *D*'s elicited information artefacts and constructs. *D* is an experienced member of staff in charge of the administration of an entire cohort of students and the figure is an illustration of the middle ground she occupies between *J* and *C*. *D* who is one of *J*'s key administrators has significant more experience and responsibilities than the junior members of staff. While *D*'s world is populated with the same set of constructs and elements as *C*, her perception of their relationship is more complex as witnessed by the lower levels of correlation among them.

4   A Local User Interface for Local People

If this is to be anything more than a mere academic curiosity, these data must be translatable into design recommendations reflecting the individuals' perceptions of their working world. What is immediately obvious is that *J* requires access to more information artefacts than the others and needs to exercise a greater degree of flexibility in the way in which she works with them. *C*, and to a lesser extent *D*, has a simpler view of her world; forms must be complete, are important, must be accurate, official and up to date; *J*'s world has, in contrast, many shades of grey. At a trivial level this appears to amount to a simple reflection of job description. However in considering the impact of perceived characteristics on the design of information artefacts, Robertson & Robertson's (1999)) definition of functional requirements as 'things the product must do' and non-functional requirements as 'properties the product must have' is useful. Thus the above perceptions of the information artefacts used in enrolment are effectively **contextualised non-functional requirements** on, in this instance, a redesigned local SAS.

4.1   Redesigning the SAS

The current student enrolment system, as already described, is mediated by the enrolment form which has to be completed at enrolment and then keyed into the student administrative system (SAS) via a character-based green screen. The SAS requires that all fields of the student records must be completed (the administrative staff privately admitting that dummy data is entered to 'keep the system happy').

The proposed redesign of the system required the creation of a local database to hold student details (and to deal with the boundary object problem — more of which later), uploading the relevant data to the existing SAS only when it is complete. This would also provide academics with the opportunity to obtain rough figures of students registered on particular courses, etc., without recourse to the complexities of the SAS, a requirement which had been identified in the wider analysis work. This redesign also afforded an opportunity to demonstrate the usefulness of the contextualised non-functional requirements.

As already noted, many of the perceived characteristics of the information artefacts used in enrolment are highly correlated and in this instance, several can be consolidated in an overall 'confirmed — provisional' dimension. The next section explains how this was incorporated in the re-design.

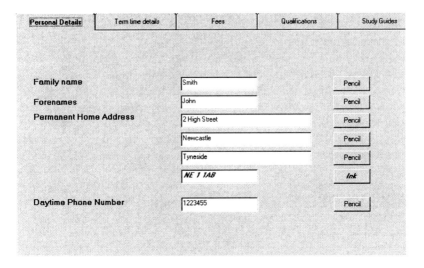

Figure 8: A detail from the revised SAS.

4.2   The Pencil and Ink Metaphor

It is common practice (certainly within the United Kingdom) to use a pencil to complete fields on paper forms when the required information is provisional or uncertain and to subsequently ink over the pencil to confirm the information. And it is this pencil and ink metaphor which was adopted based on *J*'s data. *C*'s data, and to a lesser extent, *D*'s data are consistent with the current SAS and its use (in effect they work as data entry clerks). However *J*, being the manager of the office, and being responsible for the enrolment process, and being the point of contact within the office for other departments and work groups, necessarily needs greater flexibility to deal with the dynamically changing enrolment data.

The prototype consisted of a Visual Basic user interface to an underlying MS Access database. While the interface itself proved very simple to create, articulating the metaphor proved to be problematical. Figure 8 is a detail from the prototype user interface. As can be seen, fields which are confirmed are shown in normal font ('ink'), those which are still provisional in bold italics ('pencil'). Each field has an accompanying button which permits its contents to be toggled to the other state.

4.3   Evaluation of the Redesign

J found the idea intuitive, appealing and well suited to her needs, but was emphatic that the pencil/ink feature should only be available to her and her senior staff (i.e. her deputy and one other). More junior members of the team were thought likely to be confused by the scope for discretion and would not have sufficient experience to make the judgement required, a position which is entirely consistent with the data from the repertory grids. The potential for obtaining rough local student statistics was less well received. *J* explained that to be meaningful, local data must be integrated with that originating from multiple sources elsewhere in the university.

While academics might consider the local information to be sufficiently accurate for their purposes of, for example, ordering approximately the right number of handouts, this was not the case for the administrative function with its object of keeping precise records of student numbers. Finally, *J* stressed that Faculty and Finance offices would not be able to work with provisional enrolment data. Thus it can be seen that while the pencil and ink metaphor was well received and expected to be of value for the senior administrative staff, it was judged to be effectively useless outside the narrow boundary of the departmental office.

5 Discussion

5.1 *Perceived Characteristics are Real*

The use of repertory grids has demonstrated the practicality of eliciting the perceived characteristics of information artefacts and how different perceptions of, and requirements on, the same set of information artefacts can vary even within the same stakeholder group. However there is a need for some consolidation of these perceptions to be usable as a source of contextualised non-functional requirements. This consolidation can be achieved by 'eye' as was done here, in the case of the confirmed — provisional dimension, or by statistical re-analysis of the entire set of repertory grids for the relevant local group of stakeholders.

5.2 *Preserving Invariant Information to Resolve Contextual Boundary Problems*

Green & Benyon's use of a data-centric model of information artefacts — ERMIA — which is an augmented entity-relationship modelling technique provides an interesting backdrop to the work reported here. The purpose of an ERMIA analysis is to reveal the invariant properties of information artefacts. Essentially ERMIA seeks to answer the question, "When the 'same' information is made available in two different representations what is it that remains the same?" (Green & Benyon, 1996, p.810). That which remains the 'same' being described as the conceptual structure of the information artefact.

To conclude, it seems that the underlying conceptual structure needs to be understood in order to construct information artefacts which are usable **across** boundaries and the perceived characteristics of the information artefacts **within** boundaries to construct contextualised user interfaces. So, to the non-functional requirements of information artefacts which are most frequently defined in terms of usability (e.g. learnability, memorability and so forth) or cognitive dimensions (Green, 1989) their perceived characteristics are now added.

Acknowledgements

Thanks to the academic and administrative staff from the School of Computing and Mathematics, University of Northumbria at Newcastle, for their generous cooperation. The support of EPSRC Grant GR/M12148 is also gratefully acknowledged.

References

Anderson, B. (1993), Metaphor, Affordances and Interface Design, Poster presentation at HCI'93.

Benyon, D. (1992), "Task Analysis and Systems Design — The Discipline of Data", *Interacting with Computers* **4**(2), 246–59.

Beyer, H. & Holtzblatt, K. (1998), *Contextual Design: Defining Customer-centered Systems*, Morgan-Kaufmann.

Bucciarelli, L. L. (1994), *Designing Engineers*, MIT Press.

Carroll, J. M. & Mack, R. L. (1985), "Metaphor, Computing Systems, and Active Learning", *International Journal of Man–Machine Studies* **22**(1), 39–57.

Dillon, A. & McKnight, C. (1990), "Towards a Classification of Text Types: A Repertory Grid Approach", *International Journal of Man–Machine Studies* **33**(6), 623–36.

Dillon, A. & Watson, C. (1996), "User Analysis in HCI — The Historical Lessons from Individual Differences Research", *International Journal of Human–Computer Interaction* **45**(6), 619–63.

Fransella, F. & Bannister, D. (1977), *A Manual for Repertory Grid Technique*, Academic Press.

Gaver, W. (1991), Technological Affordances, *in* S. P. Robertson, G. M. Olson & J. S. Olson (eds.), *Proceedings of CHI'91: Human Factors in Computing Systems (Reaching through Technology)*, ACM Press, pp.79–84.

Gaver, W. (1995), Oh What a Tangled Web We Weave: Metaphor and Mapping in Graphical Interfaces, *in* I. Katz, R. Mack & L. Marks (eds.), *Companion Proceedings of CHI'95: Human Factors in Computing Systems (CHI'95 Conference Companion)*, ACM Press.

Gibson, J. J. (1986), *The Ecological Approach To Visual Perception*, Lawrence Erlbaum Associates.

Goodwin, C. & Goodwin, M. H. (1998), Seeing as a Situated Activity: Formulating Planes, *in* Y. Engestrom & D. Middleton (eds.), *Cognition and Communication at Work*, Cambridge University Press, pp.61–95.

Green, T. R. G. (1989), Cognitive Dimensions of Notations, *in* A. Sutcliffe & L. Macaulay (eds.), *People and Computers V (Proceedings of HCI'89)*, Cambridge University Press, pp.443–460.

Green, T. R. G. & Benyon, D. R. (1996), "The Skull Beneath the Skin; Entity-relationship Modelling of Information Artefacts", *International Journal of Human–Computer Interaction* **44**(6), 801–28.

Hassard, J. (1987), "FOCUS As a Phenomenological Technique for Job Analysis: Its Use in Multiple Paradigm Research", *International Journal of Man–Machine Studies* **27**(6), 251–80.

Hoft, N. L. (1996), Developing a Cultural Model, *in* E. M. del Galdo & J. Neilsen (eds.), *International User Interfaces*, John Wiley & Sons.

Hughes, J., King, V., Rodden, T. & Anderson, H. (1994), Moving Out of the Control Room: Ethnography in Systems Design, *in* R. Furuta & C. Neuwirth (eds.), *Proceedings of CSCW'94: ACM Conference on Computer Supported Cooperative Work*, ACM Press, pp.429–39.

Kelly, G. A. (1955), *The Psychology of Personal Constructs*, Norton.

Mambrey, P. & Robinson, M. (1997), Understanding the Role of Documents in the Hierarchical Flow of Work, *in* S. C. Hayne & W. Prinz (eds.), *Proceedings of ACM Group'97*, ACM Press, pp.119–127.

Mark, G. (1997), Merging Multiple Perspectives in Groupware Use: Intra- and Inter-group Conventions, *in* S. C. Hayne & W. Prinz (eds.), *Proceedings of ACM Group'97*, ACM Press, pp.19–28.

McCarthy, J. C. & O'Connor, B. (1999), "The Context of Information Use in a Hospital as Simultaneous Similarity–Difference Relations", *Cognition, Technology and Work* **1**(1), 25–36.

Norman, D. A. (1988), *The Psychology of Everyday Things*, Basic Books.

Robertson, S. & Robertson, J. (1999), *Mastering the Requirements Process*, Addison–Wesley.

Shaw, M. L. G. & Gaines, B. (1987), "KITTEN: Knowledge Elicitation and Transfer Tool for Experts and Novices", *International Journal of Man–Machine Studies* **27**, 251–80.

Shaw, M. L. G. & Gaines, B. (1992), "Kelly's "Geometry of Psychological Space" and its Significance for Cognitive Modelling", *The New Psychologist* pp.23–31.

Star, S. L. (1989), The Structure of Ill-structured Solutions: Boundary Objects and Heterogeneous Distributed Problem Solving, *in* L. Grasser & M. Huhns (eds.), *Distributed Artificial Intelligence*, Pitman, pp.37–54.

Star, S. L. & Ruhleder, K. (1994), Steps Towards an Ecology of Infrastructure: Complex Problems in Design and Access for Large-scale Collaborative Systems, *in* R. Furuta & C. Neuwirth (eds.), *Proceedings of CSCW'94: ACM Conference on Computer Supported Cooperative Work*, ACM Press, pp.253–64.

Vicente, K. J. (1999), *Cognitive Work Analysis: Towards Safe, Productive, and Healthy Computer-based Work*, Lawrence Erlbaum Associates.

On Change and Tasks

Peter J Wild & Robert D Macredie

Centre for Living Information Systems Thinking, Department of Information Systems and Computing, Brunel University, Uxbridge, Middlesex UB8 3PH, UK

Tel: *+44 1895 274 000 ext 3684/2328*

Fax: *+44 1895 251 686*

EMail: *{Peter.Wild,Robert.Macredie}@brunel.ac.uk*

URL: *http://www.brunel.ac.uk/research/clist*

This paper observes that task analysis, despite its prominence in many HCI approaches, embodies a limited perspective on change sources and manifestations. The paper starts with a critique of the change management perspective of TA methods and illustrates the argument with two examples — Interacting Cognitive Subsystems, and Task Knowledge Structures. Following this, we examine some broader change sources, manifestations and their implications. The paper continues by presenting an overview of work in its formative phase that broadens the change perspective of the Task Knowledge Structures approach. The paper concludes with an overview of some open issues in change management.

Keywords: change, task analysis, context, task knowledge structures, interacting cognitive subsystems.

1 Introduction

Monk (1997, p.111) observes that task fit is "the most important attribute of a usable system". Over the history of Human–Computer Interaction (HCI) there has been continual stress on the importance of tasks as the focus of effective interactive systems design; for example (Carroll & Rosson, 1992; Gould & Lewis, 1985; Johnson et al., 1988; Johnson et al., 1995). HCI has developed methods for the analysis of tasks in order that interactive systems have greater task fit than reliance on luck or intuition alone. Task analysis (TA) methods break down into generative and evaluative methods. The former are concerned with the generation of requirements and interactive system designs and try to ensure that an interactive system reflects a task's structure. Evaluative methods use psychological theory to evaluate the effectiveness of interactive systems, attempting to evaluate the cognitive implications of particular task structures. We have seen an evolution of generative methods to cover more of the context of use of interactive systems; and of evaluative methods to account for a level of cognitive complexity greater than just simply skilled task performance. Despite this evolution, the TA community appears to have a limited view of change in the environments of interactive systems and little consideration has been made for wider sources and manifestations of change.

One example of change is the European Single Currency (Euro). The consequences for interactive systems are wide and varied[*]. They range from the seemingly simple addition of new key bindings for the Euro symbol, through to redevelopment and enhancement to deal with an altered form of currency exchange. Even Britain, who was not in the scheme at its launch, has been heavily affected due to its important role in foreign exchange markets. Consequently, many people have worked to ensure their organisations were able to perform tasks under the new system. In the long term, the Euro may affect the way that money is exchanged both inside the European Community and between the community and the rest of the world. In this example, interactive systems and the tasks they support have been affected, not by technical changes but political and economic ones. Furthermore, the changes needed are both revolutionary and evolutionary rather than the type amenable to a one-shot application development process. As such, we can see that wider changes in interactive systems contexts can affects tasks, altering the task requirements and the level of task fit of interactive systems and by implication their usability.

There are implications of this lack of deeper consideration of change for TA methods. Can we, for example, argue that generative TA methods allow us to examine the context of tasks when change, as a major part of contemporary organisational life is ignored? In turn, can our evaluative TA methods cope with usability evaluations that involve more than simple comparison of different interactive system designs and ignore deeper issues of learning and alteration of task structures[†]?

Within this paper our concern is with change and the implications for task analysis. We start with a critique of change management practices in TA, offering examples of how the criticisms apply to two contemporary TA methods, Interacting Cognitive Subsystems and Task Knowledge Structures. The paper continues with an examination of sources and manifestations of change and some of their implications for tasks. The next section presents a proposal for ameliorating the limited change perspective in one particular TA method, that is, Task Knowledge Structures (Johnson et al., 1988; Johnson et al., 1995).

---

[*]Between the original submission and the paper being revised we have seen: the introduction of share dealing in the UK in Euros; severe doubts about the viability of the Euro as a strong international currency; and the admission of Greece to the scheme.

[†]In fairness this limited view of change appears to exist in methods claiming greater contextual awareness, for example Beyer & Holtzblatt (2000), and in other design disciplines Alexander (1975).

1.1 Task Analysis and Change: A Critique

We make two criticisms of the change management approach predominant in TA methods. The first is that TA methods are biased towards managing the implications of technological change. The second that TA methods approach to change management embodies a limited view of interactive systems and their role though time in organisations.

TA methods have mostly been concerned with the implications of technological change. This is understandable; new interaction devices and styles have developed and have had to be examined to understand their impact upon usability. In understanding the implications of technological change, Carroll & Rosson (1992), for example, suggest that we adapt our tasks to new interactive systems and in turn, the altered interactive systems inspire new tasks. However, even with this heavy emphasis on technological change, Barnard & May (1993) point out that TA methods have been overtaken by change; gaining deep insights into command line interaction by the time Graphical User Interfaces had become dominant. The Euro example presented earlier shows how wider types of change affect interactive systems and their context and this suggests that TA has a limited consideration of the context of use of many interactive systems.

A key issue here is that changes in a task's context may affect the structure of the task and will have usability implications. For example, for any task that has some form of payment or billing sub-task the Euro brings a number of options. We could ignore the Euro; after all, here in the middle of nowhere only local people use our shop. We try and accommodate the Euro in our transactions; after all, whilst Britain is not a member state many of our airports carry passengers from all over Europe. We could agree to accept payment in Euros assuming the exchange rate is favourable. Then we need to decide whether to leave the decision about suitable rates of exchange up to individual staff members. Decisions about what to do would have to take into account volume of sales, number of suppliers, type of product, or the political view of users and managers. Even such a seemingly small issue such as a new currency has many implications for task structure.

The second criticism that can be made about change management in TA methods is that they are oriented to single projects, that is, the development of a single interactive system with a final sign off point. Even projects concerned with upgrading a user interface to an existing application have adopted the view that the interactive system is finished and that it is enough to enhance its use interface so that it is more usable; for example (Johnson et al., 1995; Wesson et al., 1997). Despite the presence of design iteration; for example Gould & Lewis (1985), interactive systems can still be seen as embodying fixed points where all stakeholders agree what the requirements are and how they should be implemented (Paul, 1993). This is evidenced in the notion of attribute specification; for example (Wixon & Wilson, 1997), or the notion of a 'Generalised Task Model' (Johnson et al., 1988). Whilst usability attributes can be reconsidered, Dillon (2000, p.120) notes that it is only occasionally that "the operational targets for user performance are revised". Similarly, the TA literature has no reports of a generalised task model being revised once the implementation of an interactive system is complete, suggesting that they are considered complete and generic enough to account for all instantiations of a task. TA methods support Gould & Lewis's (1985) call for early focus on tasks, but seem to abandon users after an interactive system is delivered. However, studies of interactive systems development; for example Fitzgerald (1990) and Fitzgerald et al. (1999) show that many resources are used in evolving interactive systems and that 60% to 80% of post-delivery changes are due to alterations to requirements. Furthermore, it is not simply the case than increased or more effective analysis will prevent changes to requirements, as anecdotal evidence suggests that a period as small as six months can alter requirements significantly (Fowler, 1998).

There are clearly situations when a new interactive system is apt. These situations can be viewed as HCI's equivalent of changing which side of the road vehicles travel on. In these situations, TA methods offer rich techniques for the generation, design and evaluation of interactive systems. However, TA methods adopt only one approach to change management, the single project. This limited view on change may be a further barrier to the acceptance of TA methods because much interactive systems development is grouped under maintenance. This is a particular concern when we consider Software Engineering's interest in change (Brooks, 1995) and issues covered by TA and HCI such as: user interface design; consistency and task support (Collins, 1994); task scenarios (Graham, 1996); and modelling of user's goals (Antón & Potts, 1998). We welcome software engineering's concern with these issues, but there is no guarantee that they are driven by the same concern with usability as HCI.

1.2   Change and Task Analysis: Two Cases

Within this section we examine two contemporary approaches to TA with respect to varying change source and manifestations. The first method is Interacting Cognitive Subsystems (ICS) (Barnard & May, 1999), which derives an evaluative method from a sophisticated unified theory of cognition; the second is Task Knowledge Structures (TKS) (Johnson et al., 1988; Johnson et al., 1995) a generative theory of tasks that comprises of an information gathering method Knowledge Analysis of Tasks (KAT) and a task representation. Despite the great strengths and maturity of these approaches the process of applying TKS and ICS in design assumes that the interactive system being developed will be static and not be subjected to pressures for change.

1.2.1   Interacting Cognitive Subsystems

The ICS framework presents a unified theory of cognition that builds on several facets of cognition to enable reasoning about the consequences of cognitive tasks, including HCI tasks. When applied to HCI contexts via a method known as Cognitive Task Analysis (CTA), ICS has an explicit consideration of long term changes in cognitive activities, that of the progression from novice via intermediate to expert. This approach to change management is limited and we can observe two issues. Firstly, it is often the case that users reach a plateau in their knowledge about an interactive system. At this stage, little else is learnt about the functionality of an interactive system (Rosson, 1983), or a limited set of features accounts for the bulk of usage of an interactive system; for example (Draper, 1984). Hence, the fidelity of the novice-expert progression of ICS approach can be questioned. Secondly, the ICS approach as used in HCI assumes that the interactive system stays the same across time. This is explicitly represented in the novice-intermediate-expert (NIE) representation format. However, with issues such as environment change, tailoring, and the task-artefact cycle we suggest that this path is too idealised. If an interactive system changes, what are the implications for the ICS approach? We cannot assume that all changes will be a natural progression for a user. Yet in fairness to the ICS approach it has been applied to language comprehension, cinematography and unipolar-depression, none of which exhibits the novice-intermediate-expert progression used in the cognitive task modelling approach. Owing to the richness of ICS (Barnard & May, 1999) this is an issue of process and 'suitable' use of ICS constructs may allow these non-inherent constraints to be tackled.

1.2.2 Task Knowledge Structures

The TKS development process involves the development of several extant task models which are subjected to 'generification' processes that produce a generic task model (GTM). This GTM is 'designed' to produce a designed task model and is used to generate candidate interactive system designs. Concerning TKS change management, we have three criticisms. The first is that whilst the process allows for considerable iteration in the design phase, the overall approach to change management is reminiscent of Lewin's (1958) unfreeze–change–freeze change management model. Iteration is only carried out in the design phase; once an interactive system is agreed upon, it is frozen. No case is made for task centred design in post delivery alterations.

Our second criticism surrounds the realism of the notion of a generic task model (GTM). This notion is that if the analyst samples across a wide enough spectrum of task supporting artefacts (e.g. for document preparation: pen and paper; typewriter; typesetting; and word processor) we gain a generic model of the task. We do not deny that abstraction should be encouraged and TKS use of generification and focus on centrality and representativeness is powerful. Our objection to this notion is that it can be used to counter our arguments about change. Because a GTM supposedly covers the structure of all possible instantiations of a task, it therefore guards against changes in the environment of an interactive system. We can counter this with several points. Firstly, TKS embodies a limited view of change and its management that there is no way of verifying this use of the GTM notion. Secondly, it ignores the innovative and transformational nature of design (Carroll & Rosson, 1986) and the impact this has on the ways of performing tasks.

Our final criticism is that with shorter development cycles and resource pressures, developers — the people who are predominately meant to analyse tasks — may not have the opportunity to generalise across different task supporting artefacts. In most contexts, we would be safer to assume that most designers will not be attempting a generic model of the task. After all, it is these sorts of time and resource pressures that provide a motivation to Monk's (1997) TA approach, which has less abstraction from the original task context.

Yet, the paradox of the current TKS process is that TKS themselves are not assumed static. They are altered through phenomena such as memory degradation, exploration and the development of expertise. Yet the process of applying TKS embodies a limited view on change. In Section 4 we return to the issue of TKS and how we think these process constraints can be overcome. In the next section we take a look at different changes sources, manifestations and reactions and some of their implications for tasks.

2   Change Sources, Manifestations and Reactions

We argue that there is a need for a deeper appreciation of other sources and manifestations of change other than those associated with technology and one-off development of interactive systems. Within this section we present the contextualisation of change that underlies our work. Within our contextualisation there are change sources; different manifestations of change; and reactions to change.

2.1   Sources of Change

Weinrich & Koontz (1993) regard organisations as having five change sources in their environment. In turn Kanellis et al. (1996) view an organisation as having three major sources of change in their internal environment.

2.1.1   Organisational Environment Change Sources

Technological change sources are concerned with the knowledge we have about ways of carrying out our tasks. Each new wave of technology puts pressure upon the previous 'solutions' that served before it. For example the vacuum tube industry has been relegated to manufacturing products for sound amplification equipment rather than for an essential component of computers. In some cases, new technology replaces old artefacts; for example, word processors have replaced typewriters. This does not imply that the task an artefact supports becomes obsolete; as Carroll & Rosson (1992) have noted, tasks tend to evolve with each new wave of technology.

Economic change sources cover issues such as suppliers, prices, customers, and the general economic environment. Economic influences are likely to affect a task domain in a top-down fashion; that is, the goals and intentions that organisations have with respect to a task domain will alter. Different solutions to problems and the resultant tasks may be favoured depending on shifts in the economic environment. Other tasks may no longer be needed or be reduced in their frequency. For example, if the Euro becomes a success, currency exchange between member countries will no longer apply, and its centrality to travel in Europe will change.

Social change sources cover issues such as the attitudes, beliefs, customs, desires and expectations of people. Changes in the social environment can have a great impact on organisations and the task performed, that is, social changes can pre-empt technology. An example would be the change in attitude towards personal credit; over the last twenty years it has become increasingly common to use credit facilities. This has led to the proliferation of a range of supporting technologies for credit transactions and has affected traditional debit accounts through the introduction of debit cards.

Political-legal change sources cover issues such as the set of laws, regulations, government agencies and their actions that affect organisations. The policies of government can affect organisations, either through constraint, such as laws and anti-monopoly legislation, or freedom, through free trade agreements.

Ethical sources condition the accepted organisational practice and conduct. They provide an often-neglected aspect of an interactive system's context. Recent years have seen greater awareness of 'green' issues and ethical investment. Whilst not always having an immediate impact upon interactive systems functionality, changes in ethics will affect organisations and at some stage they are likely to have to change work practices. In particular this may have implications for the types of changes that are accepted in a task domain (e.g. deforestation) and the overall state of a task domain after changes have been made (e.g. pollution).

2.1.2   Change Sources within an Organisation

Organisational Structure is concerned with the overall allocation of formal responsibilities between departments and the staff within them. Organisational structure is also concerned with the links and coordination between roles. One prevalent trend during the 1990s was the move away from strictly structured hierarchies to smaller, more flexible cross departmental teams; for example Hammer & Champy (1993). This puts greater pressure on interactive systems to be more flexible in their operation and to either embody fewer assumptions about the reporting structure in an organisation, or to be configurable to different structures.

Culture can be viewed as a combination of the ideologies, beliefs and set of values present in an organisation. Kast & Rosenzweig (1985) note that organisational culture may be broken down into: goals and values; the psycho-social system; and the managerial role. The first of these is concerned with what goals an organisation holds and how these are affected and mediated by values. Some of these can be scoped towards the domain, however the values within an organisation are harder to articulate in terms of the domain. The psycho-social system is concerned with the interaction between an individual's feelings and the social environment of the organisation. Typically this would cover issues such as motivation and morale. The managerial role is concerned with the mediation between the role of managers both as progenitors and recipients of change.

Politics pervade organisations because they bring together people with often diverse backgrounds and views on how goals should be achieved. Political factors are important, understanding the wider political implications of change management is necessary. For example, usability problems were given as a reason for rejection of an interactive system by the users in Markus's (1983) case study; there were wider political factors at play in the acceptance and use of IT artefacts, and these were concerned with the distribution of power that was implied by the new IT artefact.

2.2   Manifestations of Change

Our next concern is the manifestation that a change can have. Between them Kanellis et al. (1996) and Vicente & Rasmussen (1992) suggest five dimensions for describing change manifestations. From these dimensions it is possible to build permutations such as 'sudden temporary undesired' to describe a particular manifestation. Table 1 illustrates the five dimensions using examples from motoring. These dimensions are not put forward as absolute, but as a provisional approach for the description of

Dimension	Example of each extreme
Gradual —	Phasing out of leaded petrol
Sudden	The side of road driven on
Temporary —	Road works
Permanent	New road
Desired —	Reduction in pollution
Undesired	Traffic jams
Familiar —	Home street
Unfamiliar	New town being visited
Expected —	Rush hour
Unexpected	Accident

Table 1: Characterising change manifestations.

change. We acknowledge that these dimensions may only describe the view of single stakeholder groups, and that multiple assessments of the a change manifestation may need to be made. For example, the CATWOE analysis of Soft Systems Methodology (Checkland & Scholes, 1990) could be used to scope how aspects of a change manifestation apply.

2.3   *Reaction to Change*

Our next consideration is what happens when changes manifest themselves. Kanellis et al. (1996) suggested four generic reactions to change:

- Insulation from the change. For example, the organisation could adapt an interactive system to take security measures against unwanted system entry.

- Resistance to the change. A particular stakeholder group may resist the introduction of a new interactive system, or an organisation may form alliances with others against a common competitor.

- Acceptance of the change. Within an interactive system context, this can involve phenomena such as stakeholder innovation, adaptive maintenance, tailoring or the traditional approach of introducing new technology.

- Ignore the change. The change may not be deemed relevant to a particular stakeholder group.

3   Moving Task Analysis Forward?

In Section 1.2.2, we offered several criticisms of the change management process within the TKS approach. We tempered our criticisms by noting that the change management approach is a process issue rather than an inherent feature of TKS. Elsewhere we noted (Macredie & Wild, 2000) that generative TA methods could help the evolution of an existing interactive system by identifying: what functionality needs to be added; what task knowledge is likely to be transferred; what training is needed; and produce models that avoid biases of particular stakeholders. Hence, efforts have been made to use TKS in the process of dealing with post-delivery changes to interactive systems. This opens the TKS approach to scenarios where interactive systems are changing in an incremental manner, and where changes in task requirements may be due to wider change sources and manifestations than technology and one shot development alone. The main contribution here is in using a TA method in a new context and the resulting experiences and recommendations gained from this. Thus, in much the same way that the TKS process has evolved to integrate participatory design concerns; for example Keep & Johnson (1997), this use of TKS allows for a process with greater consideration of concerns about change into a task-centred approach.

We use TKS because: it is a mature approach to task centred design; it has been used in many domains in cooperation with many other approaches; and it has a rich model of the task. However, we stress that this research is still in its formative stages. TKS has been used informally and retrospectively; currently pilot studies are being undertaken in order to gain deeper insights about the role of TA in general and TKS specifically in dealing with wider sources and manifestations of change.

We also acknowledge that alternative ways of purposefully evolving interactive systems are available, such as object orientation and evolutionary development. However, unlike other approaches, the constructs of TA allow the systematic focus on tasks as a key issue in usability (Macredie & Wild, 2000). This is in contrast to the architectural benefits of object orientation or the managerial benefits of evolutionary development[‡].

3.1   Flexibility Analysis of Tasks

Fitzgerald (1990) offered empirical evidence that 70% of enhancements to interactive systems are due to predictable organisational changes. Furthermore, these changes could be identified by stakeholders within organisations but were not communicated to users and developers. He suggested that the result of meetings with stakeholders about areas of possible change should be input into interactive system development; and the implications examined to ensure that the changes are easily applicable. As it stands, flexibility analysis is little more than an exhortation to consider change in conjunction with stakeholders; there is no explicit focus on tasks and or of how usability is affected by changes to existing interactive systems.

We use 'change meetings' with prominent stakeholders to discuss how envisaged task models can be made to be more flexible. Our concern here is with opening an envisaged task model to wider views about its purpose in the organisation and how different sources, manifestations and reactions to change such as those discussed in Section 2 will affect tasks. The richness of the TKS representation allows many micro and macro task issues to be discussed. The general format for the workshops is akin to Fagin inspections. The process is concerned with criticising the task model's fitness for purpose, that is given pressures for the evolution of an interactive system:

[‡]See Macredie & Wild (2000) for further arguments about flexibility analysis, tailoring and object orientation.

- what needs to be done;

- do we have an existing interactive system to deal with it; and

- what are the usability implications of these options.

At this formative stage of research heuristics for consideration of TKS elements are available and these currently focus upon: Roles; Goals; Task Objects; Centrality and Representativeness; and Task Exceptions:

Roles: We can examine roles to consider whether a role faces overload, under-load, fragmentation, and whether too many roles are assigned to a user or interactive system.

Task Goals: Changes in task goals tend to reflect higher level shifts in an organisation. In contrast, changes to subgoals tend to reflect alterations to an interactive system.

Task Objects: As a result of change are we altering or monitoring more objects in a task domain? Are we dealing with virtual objects rather than physical ones (or vice versa)? Are there new attributes to consider or has the representativeness of an object or attribute changed? For example, if the price of gold rises, then silver may become a more representative metal for jewellery.

Centrality and Representativeness: Are the key elements of a task changed? Are the most frequent tasks altered? For example, one recent trend has been the shift to electronic payment methods. This is likely to have had an impact upon the representativeness of cash for payment, yet it is unlikely that payment will alter in its centrality to transactions. However, the payment sequence may be altered to account for new fraud checks. In contrast, pre-payment systems such as those being introduced in petrol stations and supermarkets are likely to impact upon the centrality of taking payment in consumer purchasing tasks.

Task Exceptions: These are another source of information about the evolution of tasks and the altered requirements of an interactive system. Task exceptions are discussed in more detail in Section 3.3.

3.2 Alternative Domain Model

TKS views a domain from the perspective of the user and represents it as objects with attributes and the allowable actions on objects. With regards to change this leaves us with the ability to make assertions that object attributes can be, or have, changed. For a richer consideration of domains in relations to tasks and change we use the Abstraction Hierarchy (Rasmussen et al., 1994). The Abstraction Hierarchy represents a task domain as a five-layer hierarchy ranging from the physical location of objects through to the goals/intentions held towards the domain. We are interested in the AH because it allows broad distinctions between different types of task domain. For example some such as process control, are largely causal in nature whilst others are more abstract in nature, such as interactive timetables or library databases. This allows discussion of how changes are likely to affect a domain.

However, one potential weakness of the Risø Abstraction Hierarchy approach is that it relies solely on the use of unstructured interviews to gain knowledge about a domain (Rasmussen et al., 1994). TKS in contrast has a rich set of knowledge elicitation methods including interviews, questionnaires, concurrent and retrospective protocols, observation, card sorting, repertory grids, rating scales, frequency counts, and analysts performing the task. These can be used to create both a traditional TKS task representation and a representation using the theoretical equipment of the Abstraction Hierarchy. By bringing these two together, we gain:

- Richer knowledge elicitation practice for the development of an abstraction hierarchy.

- Data about the centrality and representativeness of elements of the abstraction hierarchy.

In using the AH to represent the domain, we have come to concur with Monk (1997) that goals should be expressed as states in a domain, rather than the traditional process orientated expressions such as 'boil water in kettle'. This has two advantages:

- it enables analysts and users to more easily recognise generic states, objects and actions. It avoids description of goal achievement with current technology and helps focus on the purposive reason behind the current task execution; and

- expressing goals as states allows the more effective expression of commonality between different tasks.

Thus, the goal expression 'have hot water' has commonality with the making of hot drinks and the washing of items, but not with 'have fed donkey'; and will enable the identification of task sub-components that may transfer across to existing interactive systems. This could allow users to use an alternative interactive system to support an evolved task rather than the alteration of an interactive system. For example, rather than adding charting facilities to an interactive system we may facilitate using and importing charts from another application.

3.3 Task Exceptions

In some task domains an increase in the occurrence of task exceptions can be an indication that an interactive system is undertaking more of the routine work in a domain and that a user's task is becoming centred around supervision and problem solving. In other task domains exceptions mean that things are going wrong that are beyond the control of the user. For example, within a petrol station the primary task exceptions are dealing with aspects of the domain that have ceased to function as required. Currently, legal and contractual considerations prevent the cashier from intervening to repair equipment such as the jet or car wash. Equipment failure of this nature can lead to considerable frustration to staff and customers and in turn leads to more task exceptions such as: refund; redirection to alternative facilities; attempting to keep a good customer through incentives.

However, hand in hand with TKS's notion of a generic task model is a tendency to take a normative view of task models. In applying TKS to interactive systems evolution, we have found a need to analyse and describe Task Exception (Monk, 1997; Saastamoinen, 1995). The rich knowledge elicitation of Knowledge Analysis of Tasks allows us an effective way of doing this. As well as the rich task representation of TKS we add extra indicators to elaborate motivations and conditions of task exceptions. For example within a petrol station, the exception task, 'have fire', is *sudden* in onset, *unwanted* and actions are oriented towards *insulation* from the change.

3.4   Deeper Understanding of Changes to Task Structures

For deeper considerations of changes to task structure, we move away from the TKS approach and turn to the Interacting Cognitive Subsystems (Barnard & May, 1999). Previously, ICS has also been used in the examination of the usability implications of different task structures and offers a rich framework in which to ground analysis. Space precludes a more detailed overview, but two issues have motivated our use of ICS. How does a user deal with changes in an interactive system and how do they unlearn past task knowledge? In dealing with the first issue, our analyses focus on the subsystem for dealing with the knowledge of existing tasks structures (the propositional subsystem) and how alterations to tasks and interactive systems are resolved through interaction with other subsystems. With the second consideration our analyses are concerned with the level of automation of goal formation and task execution and how insights from ICS can be used to motivate alterations to interactive systems that facilitate usability in evolving interactive systems.

4   Conclusions

Within this paper, our concern has been the implications of change and we have offered two main contributions. The first is to open a debate about the change management approach predominant in TA methods. With TA playing such an important role in the endeavour of HCI, it is important that TA methods are able to cope with change as a major part of the contemporary interactive system context. The key issue is that alterations in task structure are very likely to have implications for usability, and richer analysis and more iteration prior to delivery of an interactive system will not prevent the task context from changing. Arguing that the limitations of contemporary TA methods are an issue of process and perspective, we have suggested that certain additions to the methods may enable them to be used in contexts where wider sources and manifestations of change are present.

Two elements of our work — change workshops and the contextualisation of change — can be used in conjunction with other approaches such as usability engineering (Wixon & Wilson, 1997) contextual and scenario based design (Beyer & Holtzblatt, 2000; Carroll, 1995).

However, change remains a challenge for HCI as a whole; partly because it is an area that has been neglected and partly because for scientific endeavours as a whole it is a difficult area (Casti, 1991). We noted in Section 3.1 that Fitzgerald's (1990) case study suggested that 70% of the changes an interactive system faced could be seen coming, retrospectively at least, by people in the organisation. The issue of predictability remains an open one in science, particularly in open systems such as organisational interactive systems. In the intermediate period we can assume that knowing something about the knowledge people have about the tasks they perform can allow us to make qualitative predictions about how work will be affected by changes in task context.

Acknowledgements

The authors acknowledge the valuable comments made by the three anonymous reviewers. Members of CLIST are acknowledged for their ongoing commentary, in particular Prof Ray Paul, Dr Mark Lycett and Dr Lynne Baldwin.

References

Alexander, C. (1975), *The Oregon Experiment*, Oxford University Press.

Antón, A. & Potts, C. (1998), The Use of Goals to Surface Requirement for Evolving Systems, *in* K. Torii (ed.), *Proceedings of the the 20th International Conference on Software Engineering (ICSE'98)*, IEEE Computer Society Press, pp.157–66.

Barnard, P. J. & May, J. (1993), Cognitive Modelling for User Requirements, *in* P. F. Byerley & P. J. B. J. May (eds.), *Computers, Communication and Usability: Design Issues, Research and Methods for Integrated Services*, Elsevier Science, pp.101–145.

Barnard, P. J. & May, J. (1999), "Representing Cognitive Activity in Complex Tasks", *Human–Computer Interaction* **14**(1/2), 93–158.

Beyer, H. R. & Holtzblatt, K. (2000), "Contextual Design: Using Customer Work Models to Drive System Design". Tutorial notes for a tutorial session at CHI'2000.

Brooks, F. P. (1995), *The Mythical Man-Month*, second edition, Addison–Wesley.

Carroll, J. M. & Rosson, M. B. (1986), Usability Specifications as a Tool in Iterative Development, *in* H. R. Hartson (ed.), *Advances in Human–Computer Interaction*, Ablex, pp.1–28.

Carroll, J. M. & Rosson, M. B. (1992), "Getting Around the Task–Artefact Framework: How to Make Claims and Design by Scenario", *ACM Transactions on Office Information Systems* **10**(2), 181–212.

Carroll, J. M. (ed.) (1995), *Scenario-Based Design: Envisioning Work and Technology in System Development*, John Wiley & Sons.

Casti, J. L. (1991), *Searching for Certainty: What Science Can Know about the Future*, Scribners.

Checkland, P. B. & Scholes, J. (1990), *Soft Systems Methodology in Action*, John Wiley & Sons.

Collins, D. (1994), *Designing Object-oriented User Interfaces*, Benjamin/Cummings (Addison–Wesley).

Dillon, A. (2000), Group Dynamics Meet Cognition: Combining Socio-Technical Concepts & Usability Engineering in the Design of Information Systems, *in* D. Coakes, D. Willis & R. Lloyd-Jones (eds.), *The New SocioTec*, Springer-Verlag, pp.119–25.

Draper, S. W. (1984), The Nature of Expertise in Unix, *in* B. Shackel (ed.), *Proceedings of INTERACT '84 — First IFIP Conference on Human–Computer Interaction*, Vol. 2, Elsevier Science, pp.182–186.

Fitzgerald, G. (1990), "Achieving Flexible Information Systems: the Case for Improved Analysis", *Journal of Information Systems* **5**(1), 5–11.

Fitzgerald, G., Philippidis, A. & Probert, S. (1999), "Information Systems Development, Maintenance, and Enhancement: Findings from a UK Study", *International Journal of Information Management* **19**(4), 319–28.

Fowler, M. (1998), *Keeping It Soft. Distributed Computing.*, 101 Communications.

Gould, J. D. & Lewis, C. H. (1985), "Designing for Usability — Key Principles and What Designers Think", *Communications of the ACM* **28**(3), 300–311.

Graham, I. (1996), "Task Scripts, Use Case and Scenarios in Object Oriented Analysis", *Object Oriented Systems* **3**(3), 123–42.

Hammer, M. & Champy, J. (1993), *Reengineering The Corporation*, Brealey Publishing.

Johnson, P., Johnson, H. & Wilson, S. (1995), Rapid Prototyping of User Interfaces Driven by Task Models, *in* J. M. Carroll (ed.), *Scenario-based Design*, John Wiley & Sons, pp.209–46.

Johnson, P., Johnson, H., Waddington, R. & Shouls, A. (1988), Task-related Knowledge Structures: Analysis, Modelling and Application, *in* D. M. Jones & R. Winder (eds.), *People and Computers IV (Proceedings of HCI'88)*, Cambridge University Press, pp.35–62.

Kanellis, P., Paul, R. J. & Crick, A. (1996), An Archetype for Researching Information Systems Flexibility, *in* S. Wrycza & J. Zupancic (eds.), *The Fifth International Conference on Information Systems Development*, Gdansk University Press, pp.147–61.

Kast, F. E. & Rosenzweig, J. E. (1985), *Organisation and Management*, McGraw-Hill.

Keep, J. & Johnson, H. (1997), "Generating Requirements in a Courier Despatch Management System", *ACM SIGCHI Bulletin* **29**(1), 51–3.

Lewin, K. (1958), Group Decision and Social Change, *in* E. E. Maccoby, E. Newcombe & R. Harley (eds.), *Readings in Social Psychology*, Holt, Rhinehart and Winston, pp.459–73.

Macredie, R. D. & Wild, P. J. (2000), "An Evaluation of the Potential of Task Analysis in the Evolution of Interactive Work Systems", *Cognition Technology & Work* **2**(1), 7–15.

Markus, M. L. (1983), "Power, Politics and MIS Implementation", *Communications of the ACM* **26**(2), 430–45.

Monk, A. F. (1997), Lightweight Techniques to Encourage Innovative User Interface Design, *in* L. Wood & R. Zeeno (eds.), *User Interface Design*, CRC Publishing, pp.109–29.

Paul, R. J. (1993), "Why Users Cannot Get What They Want", *ACM SIGOIS Bulletin* **14**(2), 8–12.

Rasmussen, J., Pejtersen, A. M. & Goodstein, L. P. (1994), *Cognitive Systems Engineering*, John Wiley & Sons.

Rosson, M. B. (1983), Patterns of Experience in Text Editing, *in* A. Janda (ed.), *Proceedings of CHI'83: Human Factors in Computing Systems*, ACM Press, pp.171–5.

Saastamoinen, H. (1995), "Case Study on Exceptions", *Information Technology and People* **8**(4), 48–78.

Vicente, K. J. & Rasmussen, J. (1992), "Ecological Interface Design: Theoretical Foundations", *IEEE Transactions in Systems, Man and Cybernetics* **22**(4), 589–605.

Weinrich, H. & Koontz, H. (1993), *Management: A Global Perspective*, McGraw-Hill.

Wesson, J., de Kock, G. & Warren, P. (1997), Designing for Usability: A Case Study, *in* S. Howard, J. Hammond & G. K. Lindgaard (eds.), *Human–Computer Interaction — INTERACT '97: Proceedings of the Sixth IFIP Conference on Human–Computer Interaction*, Chapman & Hall, pp.31–8.

Wixon, D. & Wilson, C. (1997), The Usability Engineering Framework for Product Design & Evaluation, *in* M. Helander, T. K. Landauer & P. Prabhu (eds.), *Handbook of Human–Computer Interaction*, second edition, North-Holland, pp.653–88.

How Effective Are User Studies?

Sari Kujala & Martti Mäntylä

Laboratory of Information Processing Science, Helsinki University of Technology, PO Box 5400, FIN-02015 HUT, Finland

Tel: *+358 9 451 3250*

Fax: *+358 9 451 3293*

EMail: *sari.kujala@hut.fi*

URL: *http://www.hut.fi/˜skujala/*

Not much empirical evidence has been presented to evaluate the usefulness of user studies or the optimal amount of resources to allocate to them. This study is an initial step towards understanding the costs and benefits of user studies in the early stages of product development. In a case study, a psychologist, rather than a designer, performed a user study and developed design propositions. The results were compared with a baseline design process with usability tests. The results show that the user study was useful although the investment of 46 person hours was modest. The design propositions based on the user study results made the product more usable and desirable for the users.

Keywords: user-centred design, user study methods, user involvement, consumer products, mobile users.

1 Introduction

The importance of an early focus on users and tasks was recognised early in the Human–Computer Interaction field (Gould & Lewis, 1985), and this principle can be claimed to be the essential part of incorporating the user point of view into design work. Usability and utility cannot be seen in isolation from users, their needs, goals, characteristics, skills, knowledge, behaviour, and contexts.

How then should the early focus be implemented in product development? The literature suggests that customer-developer mutual understanding and user participation are important factors in the successful development of systems. For example, Keil & Carmel (1995) found that more successful software development projects employed more direct links to users and customers.

However, in the longitudinal field study of Heinbokel et al. (1996) projects with high user participation showed lower overall success, fewer innovations, and a lower degree of flexibility. Their results also suggest that high user participation and even user orientation correlates negatively with team effectiveness and quality of team interaction. Heinbokel et al. (1996) explain that user participation disturbs the process of software development. The participation projects had to deal with several problems related to developer-user relations that were not present in projects without user participation. Users, for example, got new ideas and demanded changes in a late stage of development.

An approach to overcoming the negative effects of user participation is to gain direct user contacts by designer-controlled user studies. Designers control user studies as they decide when and how to contact users. Users, for example, can be observed at work or they can be interviewed in order to gather user needs. The focus is more on user behaviour than on their opinions. Many user study techniques and user-centred processes have been produced and reported on (Bauersfeld & Halgren, 1996; Beyer & Holtzblatt, 1996; Beyer & Holtzblatt, 1998; Hackos & Redish, 1998; McGraw & Harbison, 1997; Simonsen & Kensing, 1997; Viller & Sommerville, 1999; Wixon & Ramey, 1996; Wood, 1997).

Not much empirical evidence is available to support the idea that user studies are beneficial in the early stages of product development. In real-life, design projects are often characterised by scarce personnel, tight schedules, and uncertainty. While case studies and experiences are useful, we also need empirical evidence to estimate what is an efficient investment to gain reasonable results from user studies — that is, how to *optimise* user studies.

An often-referred to cost-benefit analysis that supports early user involvement is the case of Digital Equipment Corporation (Wixon & Jones, 1996). A baseline new product designed with little involvement by human factors professionals experienced disappointingly low initial sales. The second version of the product was developed with extensive involvement by usability professionals. Wixon & Jones (1996) claimed that their methods had a great effect on the product's commercial success, and indeed sales exceeded predictions by 30% to 60%. These results are certainly very promising, but they are inconclusive. As a variety of usability techniques were used in the Digital Equipment Corporation case study, no specific grounds or mechanisms for the improvement could be shown. In addition, many other companies have designed successful products without any special usability involvement.

This study is an initial step towards understanding the costs and benefits of user studies in the early stages of product development. We try to evaluate the utility of the user studies in a case study. A psychologist, rather than a designer, performed a user study and made design propositions with the help of the results. The utility of the results was compared with a baseline process, which included usability tests.

2 User Study Framework

Our user study framework is aimed at design tasks in which the users cannot be specified in advance, long lasting observations of users are difficult or impossible to arrange, and the time frames available are short. We found the framework useful for the design of a personal digital assistant (PDA) application and the present case study has a similar product type.

The user study framework is a combination of a contextual type semi-structured interview technique, and a modified version of the think aloud method. By combining different techniques, the user study framework makes it possible to gather efficiently different kinds of information: detailed non-verbal information (skills, selection rules and values), domain specific knowledge (goals, tasks, and sequences), and an overall picture of user world. In this way, the techniques included in the user study framework support each other in a complementary way.

2.1 Technique 1: Semi-Structured Interview

First, semi-structured interviewing is used to get a general overview of usage and users. The technique is influenced by the earlier work of Bauersfeld & Halgren (1996), Beyer & Holtzblatt (1996; 1998), and Wood (1997). The interviews are carried out in the natural settings of potential users using their own task-related language. The idea is to gain deeper understanding and help the user to remember details by seeing and perhaps trying the tools and artefacts being discussed. The users are encouraged to show artefacts and give demonstrations. The user study framework provides suggested topics for the interviews to ensure the necessary information will be gained about users and their use contexts.

Topics include:

Background information:
> The typical questions are about age, profession, technical orientation, previous computer experience, work experience, and educational level.

User's goals and preferences:
> Examples of such questions:
> What is the meaning of the product for you?
> What is the most important goal in your work?

User's knowledge, skills, and experiences:
> For example:
> How do you solve the problem you mentioned?

Current processes:
> For example:
> Could you describe your usual tasks?

The context of using a tool:
> Examples of such questions:
> Where do you use your product?
> Which kinds of tools do you carry with you?

The pros and cons of the current tools and processes:
> Examples of such questions:
> What is the meaning of this procedure?
> Why do you find this useful?

The specific problems and requirements of the user:
> Examples of such questions:
> What is most troublesome in this task?
> Which kinds of important things are you unable to do?

2.2 *Technique 2: Think Aloud Method*

The think aloud method is used to obtain more detailed information about how users use their present tools and what beliefs, theories, skills, etc., delineate the use. In the modified version of the think aloud method the user is asked to tell how he/she uses a tool or an artefact by thinking aloud during the imagined use. The user has the tool in hand, imagines his/her typical use situations, and tells how he/she would use the tool in these situations. For example, a user is asked to describe how he uses his calendar during a day or to show how he performs a task with his device. The idea is to gather more detailed information about ways of use, values, skills, and selection rules, in this way. The interviewer asks clarifying questions when needed.

2.3 *Analysing and Documenting*

The results of the user study are described in written documents under predefined headings and a collection of specified diagrams. Headings were background information, goals, tasks, tools, use descriptions in thinking-aloud sessions, needs at work, and other needs. The task hierarchy diagram is a concrete interpretation of the results in order to support design work, particularly dialogue design. Use situations, the places of use, procedures, probable user roles, tasks and sub-tasks are described from the point of view of using the future system.

3 Case Study

The user study was conducted for a large Finnish company. The study was focused on a set of functions of a portable communications device aimed at supporting mobile users. The set of functions and their interface were already designed in the baseline design process, and now the functions were redesigned independently and without knowledge of the earlier design. A hypothesis of the user study was that the existing product could be improved by matching the functions and their labels more closely with the needs and the expectations of the users.

3.1 *Users*

Six users were interviewed in their work places. The user group was selected together with the designers. The users were expected to need the specific functions of the product because of their type of work. The six users who participated in the study had different occupations, which nevertheless shared similar characteristics in regard to their product usage as they all had mobile jobs. Four of them were users of a previous model and the remaining two owned the model with the functions concerned.

3.2 User Study Procedure

The user study framework was used as earlier described. The interviewer first asked some general questions and then she asked questions from each prescribed topic. Every time a user mentioned a problem or a device function, the modified think aloud method was used. The user was asked to show, with his or her own product, how he or she deals with the problem or carries out a task.

One psychologist performed the user study and developed design propositions. While conducting the studies, the psychologist also videotaped its progress, and made notes. The psychologist analysed and documented the interviews. The notes made during the interviews were the main source of the results, but the videotapes were checked to complete the notes. The psychologist used the results to synthesise a new set of functions and their labels, intended to support users.

3.3 Validation of the User Study Results

The results of the user study were validated by three comparisons with the baseline process, in which the original functions had been developed. The comparative design process was typical for this company. The process was very iterative and rapid prototyping was used. The user target segment was defined by product marketing, but it was not based on market research or a user study. The user interface team included a marketing representative, but the only direct link to users was through usability tests. The prototypes were usability tested three times in different phases of the design and the users participated in the usability tests totalled 33. Only the prototype tested latest included the functions under consideration entirely, because the requirements changed during the design process. Eight users participated in this usability test. More details on the process and the product are not available for confidentiality reasons.

Three different comparisons with the baseline design process were used.

3.3.1 Comparison 1

Figure 1 describes the first comparison made with the baseline process. Three designers who had participated in the baseline design process were interviewed to find out what kind of information they had applied when they created the original functions during this process, and what kinds of needs they expected users to have. Additional baseline knowledge was found by studying documentation of the design work.

The designers' existing information was then compared with the information gathered with the user study in order to determine what new information had been generated. The rationale of this analysis is that to be useful the user study should produce new information. Designers can use the new information as a basis of their decision making.

3.3.2 Comparison 2

Comparison 2 is illustrated in Figure 2. The results of the two latest usability tests performed and reported during the baseline design process were compared with the user study results. The idea was to find out whether it is possible to get similar or better information than that gained from usability tests earlier in the design process by the user study. If so, we judge user studies to be cost-effective by guiding design

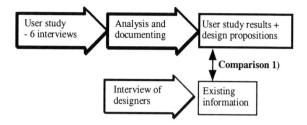

Figure 1: The illustration of the comparison 1.

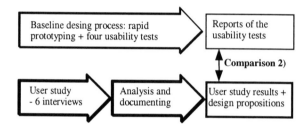

Figure 2: The illustration of the comparison 2.

work towards a promising direction earlier in the process and reducing the number of iterations needed to converge with a good result.

3.3.3   Comparison 3

Finally, the usability of the concrete design propositions created in the case study process was compared with the usability of the baseline functions. Comparison 3 is illustrated in Figure 3. To be judged truly useful, the user study method must ultimately produce more usable and desirable products. A comparative usability test was performed with eight users. While the actual functionality of the product could not be changed on this occasion, we tested whether the improved new functions and specifically their labels would make any difference in use.

The users were divided into two groups on the basis of their previous knowledge of the original functions studied. Group 1 included four experienced users who had used the product including the original functions for about six months. They were first interviewed to find out how they understood and used the functions. In the actual test, the four users were asked to perform tasks demonstrating how they used the original device functions expected to be problematic on the basis of user studies.

Group 2 consisted of four users of an older model. They were asked to do the

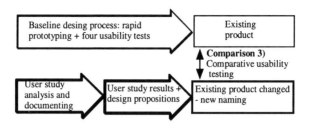

Figure 3: The illustration of the comparison 3.

same tasks as group 1 using the newer model and the improved functions. The aim was to test whether the improvements that were identified on the basis of the user study results would help using the product. After testing, the users were interviewed about their opinions and expectations towards the two versions of the functions. In particular, they were asked to select one alternative for their own use.

4   Results

The results of the user study included general descriptions of users, their typical patterns of use, frequencies of functions they used, their wishes and needs, and one summarised sequence diagram depicting the optimal overall usage. Some usability problems of their present product were also identified. Eight new functions were created to meet the user requirements. Three out of the eight functions were already available in the original model in some form, but one of these baseline functions seemed not to work in an optimal way from the users' point of view. The new design proposition included partly different functionality and partly different labels for the functions.

The designers found the most useful information gained by the user studies to be the identified use ways. The user study revealed the contexts in which the users actually used the devices and how the users used their devices in those specific contexts. This user group utilised their devices rather narrowly and it became clear that their main motivation was simply to use the one main function. They were not ready to invest time or effort in becoming familiar with the many additional functions available in their products.

4.1   Costs

Table 1 represents the total time, 46 hours, spent on the user study. These hours include 10 hours spent on reporting and creating the design propositions. The user visits included interviews and travelling time, but not the nine hours users spent on interviews. The interviewees and the users that participated in the usability tests received small presents. The prescribed interview topics made the preparation of the interview questions fairly straightforward and this preparation took only two hours.

The phase of the study	Hours
Preparing the interview questions	2
Making the user visits (6)	15
Documenting the results for each user	19
Study report	10
Total	46

Table 1: Estimate of the total number of person hours spent on the user study.

The baseline product was designed within the large company, and the design team could not offer any estimation of the time spent on design. Thus, the benefits of the user study were estimated by comparing them with other characteristics of the baseline design process. A rough estimation of the resources allocated to the usability tests can be derived from the fact that 33 users participated in them.

4.2 Benefits

The benefits of the user study were estimated by comparing them with the characteristics of the baseline design process as it was described in the case study overview.

4.2.1 Comparison 1

Three designers who had participated in the baseline design process were interviewed to find out what kind of knowledge they had applied when they created the original functions during the baseline design process. The interview showed that the designers incorrectly expected the users to have similar pattern of use to the one they used themselves.

Many of the users' needs and wishes were already recognised, but designers had found it difficult to distinguish the essential ones. The designers found the results of the user study to be useful for understanding the priorities of the users, their use contexts, and their specific ways of use.

4.2.2 Comparison 2

The analysis of the usability test results of the baseline process showed clearly that the user study results predicted most of the problems that had surfaced in the usability tests and the overall reactions of the users. In particular, all conceptual problems could be predicted by user studies.

Even though the baseline functions did offer solutions to real user problems, their structure and names did not match the natural use situations. Therefore, users had difficulties in conceptually understanding the functions.

4.2.3 Comparison 3

The usability of the concrete design propositions created in the case study process was compared with the usability of the baseline functions. The comparative usability test supported the usefulness of the user studies. Six users out of eight selected the new functions with new names for their use, and also the other two preferred some

Product	User group	Number of users	Problems	Mean time spent (min)
Existing	Experienced	4	9	9.51
Changed	Novices	4	8	8.18

Table 2: Results of the comparative usability test.

of the new names. In particular, the users thought that the new names matched their use better than the baseline ones.

Table 2 summarises the results of the comparative usability test. Altogether, the four experienced users of the baseline product spent slightly more time performing the tasks than the four novices using the new names. Two experienced users had already learned to use the functions, but two other experienced users had as many problems (nine) as the novices (eight) did together.

The novices had more difficulties with some specific user interface features than the experienced users (five vs. two problems), but they had fewer problems in completing the task and understanding it conceptually. This finding supports the idea that by simply renaming the functions according to user study findings they can be made easier to associate with intended and useful usage.

Our heterogeneous users diverged in some of their opinions. Not all users needed the more advanced functions, while some of them found them very important. The owners of the newer model seemed to be slightly more advanced than the owners of the older model in this respect. In the user study most of the users had older models; in retrospect it might have been useful to interview users more similar to users with the newer model (for example, people who use competitive products). Still, the general findings were very similar for both groups.

5   Conclusion

Our results show that the user study was useful although the investment was modest. All three comparisons made with the baseline design process and its results suggest that the benefits of the user study outweigh the costs.

First, the user study can provide more information for the designers. The designers' model of the user behaviour was slightly different from the model that emerged from user studies. The designers' model was based mainly on their experiences within their company and their own behaviour or that of their colleagues. The baseline design process included usability tests, but the tests did not seem to offer usable information about user behaviour.

Moreover, the user study results can help to prioritise the user needs. The case showed that an early user study can transform design to become a more informed activity. However, there is a gap between the user study results and the design ideas: the results have to be interpreted and different solutions have to be synthesised and selected.

The case study showed that users are different. Iterative design process is still needed to test the solutions and to identify and eliminate those specific ideas that are not fit for general use. Some of these marginal ideas are complementary, but it is important to distinguish the ideas that are disturbing to some users in order to exclude them or to use them for segmenting the product into several models intended for different groups of users.

Second, the user study results can predict and avoid future usability problems. By comparing the user study results with those achieved by two baseline usability tests it became clear that the user study could have offered important information earlier in the design process. Of course the comparison was made afterwards and the success of the prediction would have depended on the interpretation of the results.

While the gap between user study results and implementation makes usability tests necessary, we believe that user study results make the system more focus on its real use and the right conceptual structure is found early in the design process. In particular, user studies improve later usability tests by making them more focused towards real use contexts and tasks. Usability tests based on incorrect concepts and tasks do not give very useful results.

Finally, the results of the user study helped the inexperienced psychologist to design a better product than the one developed in the design team of the large company with the help of usability tests. The design propositions based on the results made the product more usable and most of the users selected the new versions even if they had used the baseline model. The users liked most of the ideas based on the user study, but some ideas were ambiguous. Some users used different methods and they expected to have a slightly different interface.

All in all, our results suggest that it would be profitable to do more user studies in the early stages of design. Furthermore, the results imply that our user study framework indeed provides an attractive way to start a design.

We also think it is likely that the user study could help decision making and shorten development time, but it is difficult to show explicitly on the basis of this case study. Further work should validate different user study methods in real development contexts and show their effects on development processes and teamwork.

Further, the question arises whether designers are able to do effective user studies themselves and should be studied. Interviewing requires social skills, and the costs of the interviewing training needed are unclear.

Acknowledgements

This research has been supported by the Academy of Finland through the project 'Smart Products in an Information Society', and Technology Development Centre (TEKES). The authors wish to acknowledge the helpful comments provided by Marjo Kauppinen and Anu Mäkelä. A draft for this paper has been presented as a short paper in CHI'2000 conference.

References

Bauersfeld, K. & Halgren, S. (1996), "You've got three days!" Case Studies in Field Techniques for the Time-challenged, *in* Wixon & Ramey (1996), pp.177–95.

Beyer, H. & Holtzblatt, K. (1996), "Contextual Techniques", *Interactions* 3(1), 44–50.

Beyer, H. & Holtzblatt, K. (1998), *Contextual Design: Defining Customer-centered Systems*, Morgan-Kaufmann.

Gould, J. D. & Lewis, C. H. (1985), "Designing for Usability — Key Principles and What Designers Think", *Communications of the ACM* **28**(3), 300–311.

Hackos, J. T. & Redish, J. C. (1998), *User and Task Analysis for Interface Design*, John Wiley & Sons.

Heinbokel, T., Sonnentag, S., Frese, M., Stolte, W. & Brodbeck, F. C. (1996), "Don't Underestimate the Problems of User Centredness in Software Development Projects — There Are Many!", *Behaviour & Information Technology* **15**(4), 226–36.

Keil, M. & Carmel, E. (1995), "Customer–Developer Links in Software Development", *Communications of the ACM* **38**(5), 33–44.

McGraw, K. L. & Harbison, K. (1997), *User-centered Requirements: The Scenario-based Engineering Process*, Lawrence Erlbaum Associates.

Simonsen, J. & Kensing, F. (1997), "Using Ethnography in Contextual Design", *Communications of the ACM* **40**(7), 82–8.

Viller, S. & Sommerville, I. (1999), Social analysis in the Requirements Engineering Process: From Ethnography to Method, *in* F. M. Titsworth (ed.), *Proceedings of International Symposium on Requirements Engineering RE'99"*, IEEE Computer Society Press, pp.6–13.

Wixon, D. & Jones, S. (1996), Usability for Fun and Profit: A Case Study of the Design of DEC Rally Version 2, *in* M. Rudisill, L. C., P. B. Polson & T. D. McKay (eds.), *Human–Computer Interface Design: Success Stories, Emerging Methods, and Real-world Context*, Morgan-Kaufmann, pp.3–35.

Wixon, D. & Ramey, J. (eds.) (1996), *Field Methods Casebook for Software Design*, John Wiley & Sons.

Wood, L. E. (1997), "Semi-structured Interviewing for User-centered Design", *Interactions* **4**(2), 48–61.

Function Allocation for Computer Aided Learning in a Complex Organisation

Chris Johnson & Bryan Mathers

Department of Computing Science, University of Glasgow, Glasgow G12 8QQ, UK

Tel: *+44 141 330 6053*
Fax: *+44 141 330 4913*
EMail: *johnson@dcs.gla.ac.uk*
URL: *http://www.dcs.gla.ac.uk/~johnson*

Laurillard's conversational model of educational practice supports the introduction of Computer Aided Learning (CAL) techniques into complex organisations. A particular strength of this approach is that it guides the allocation of tasks between human instructors and automated assessment tools. Previous applications of Laurillard's approach have focussed on teaching practices within Schools and Colleges. In contrast, we extend the use of her model to analyse the allocation of training activities within a regional fire service. This, in turn, guides the development of CAL resources that are intended to support, rather than replace, the tasks currently performed by Training Officers.

Keywords: computer aided learning, function allocation.

1 Introduction

Function allocation is a neglected and critically important aspect of Computer Aided Learning (CAL). The division of responsibilities between human trainers and computer applications can determine the successful acquisition of both technical knowledge and practical skills (Laurillard & Taylor, 1994). For example, human mediation is important if CAL systems do not keep pace with the rate of change in an organisation. This applies to curriculum changes in a school syllabus. It also applies to commercial organisations whose working practices are revised after

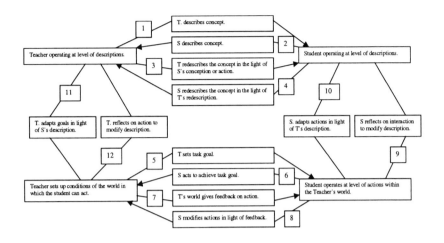

Figure 1: Laurillard's Conversational Model for Effective Education.

the introduction of new equipment or in response to regulation (Cohen et al., 1995). Most commercial training materials are out of date "as soon as they are published". In consequence, tutors and trainers must make their students aware of the inadequacies of CAL resources. Human intervention is important because the introduction of CAL technology has a profound and often unpredictable impact upon learning practices within organisations (Hewitt & Tscheligi, 1995).

1.1   Models of Function Allocation in CAL

The previous section has argued that the development of education resources is better supported if designers explicitly considered the allocation of educational functions between a teacher and their computer systems. Unfortunately, few techniques can be recruited to support this task. Most existing methods focus upon the support that particular media or narrative techniques provide for student learning styles. Laurillard's (1993) Conversational Framework provides one approach that can be used to support function allocation in CAL. Her model describes twelve steps that are necessary to support the effective transfer of knowledge and skills between a student and their teacher. These different stages are illustrated in Figure 1.

Figure 1 illustrates how both students and teachers contribute to the learning process. The right-hand components of the diagram represent the iterative process by which students modify their view of the concepts that they are being taught. The left-hand components of Laurillard's model describe the iterative process that informs the teacher's interaction with the student. Most of the tutor's tasks in Laurillard's model can be performed by either a human instructor or by an appropriate CAL tool. For example, Stage 5 involves the tutor in establishing task objectives for the student. This could take the form of an essay title set by the teacher. Alternatively, it might be implemented as a computer generated construction task embedded within a virtual reality simulation. This paper, therefore, sets out to determine whether Laurillard's model can help designers to identify appropriate allocations of training tasks within a complex and dynamic organisation (Montgomery, 1997). There is considerable evidence that such domain characteristics help to determine appropriate function allocations between human trainers and CAL applications (Plowman, 1996). However, most of this evidence focuses on educational practices in Universities or in schools. This paper, therefore, looks beyond these conventional settings to examine the impact of function allocation within the training mechanisms of one of Scotland's regional Fire Brigades.

2   The Fire Brigade Case Study

This paper focuses on the introduction of CAL techniques to support the training of fire fighters. In order to understand the reasons why CAL was needed, it is important to understand the existing training regime. The Fire Brigade is divided into a number of watches. Each watch will, typically, rotate between day and night shifts. If the watch is on day shift then the Officer in Charge selects a practical training task from a manual held in each station. These tasks are intended to provide the fire fighters with the practical skills that are necessary to perform their duties. For instance, they can involve drills that are intended to build up the fire fighters' skills through simulation. For instance, Figure 2 shows a fire fighter using Lukas cutting equipment to practice rescue skills during a simulated road traffic accident. The practical drills are supported by further 'free' sessions that are used to correct any problems, catch up on missed sessions or train with special equipment. If a watch is on night shift and practical training is no longer possible then a technical training activity will be selected. These, typically, involve lectures that last three-quarters of an hour and are delivered by a Training Officer. Between five and ten minutes are then spent in question and answer sessions. Each technical session covers one of seventy-three subjects that form part of a two-year cycle. Fifteen of these topics are considered to be of special importance and are, therefore, repeated annually. Completion of these various tasks is recorded on the individual's training card. However, training activities are interrupted if the watch is called to an incident.

2.1   The Impact of Function Allocation on Training

Senior officers viewed CAL as a cost-effective means of raising standards in both practical and technical training. There was a concern, however, that automated systems should be targeted to provide the greatest support in areas where existing training techniques were perceived to be weakest. A questionnaire was, therefore, issued to two fire stations within the brigade. A total of twenty-seven returns were received.

Attitudes towards computer instruction packages and human tutors are partially determined by the amount of experience that an individual has in their occupation (Lave & Wenger, 1991). This has important consequences for the introduction of CAL into organisations such as the Fire Brigade. In particular, highly experienced individuals will, typically, react more positively to human trainers who are perceived to have shared some of their experiences. Conversely, experienced individuals are

Figure 2: Fire fighter using Lukas Cutters during a practical exercise.

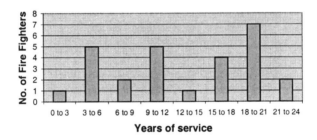

Figure 3: Histogram showing experience within the Fire Brigade.

more likely to distrust CAL tools whose programmers may be viewed with skepticism and distrust. Figure 3 presents the range of experience within the two stations that were studied. As can be seen, only one fire fighter had less than three years experience. The majority had served in the brigade for more than twelve years. Such findings emphasise the importance of function allocation. There is a danger that experienced fire fighters may become alienated if training tasks are simply transferred from human instructors to CAL systems. Designers must, therefore, carefully consider the way in which such systems are to be integrated into the existing training practices of human tutors.

The questionnaire went on to assess the fire fighters' attitudes towards existing training methods. At the start of the project, they did not have access to any CAL systems. Training consisted of lectures and videos as well as drill-based instruction. It was also recognised that many fire fighters viewed 'real' incidents as an important means of acquiring new knowledge and reinforcing key skills. Figure 4 presents the fire fighters' assessment of their training mechanisms in terms of 'ease of learning'.

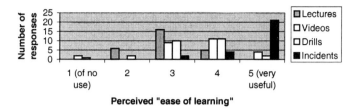

Figure 4: Histogram showing perceived 'ease of learning' in the Fire Brigade.

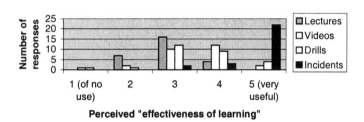

Figure 5: Histogram of perceived 'effectiveness of learning' in the Fire Brigade.

From the histogram, it is apparent that the fire fighters believed 'real' incidents to be the easiest means of learning about their occupation. This finding has important health and safety implications. Incidents should reinforce training gained by other means. They are clearly not a satisfactory delivery mechanism for basic instruction.

The fire fighters identified lectures and video presentations as their least popular training methods. This is interesting for two reasons. Firstly, lecture based training is the primary mechanism by which human tutors deliver technical material to the fire fighters. Secondly, video presentations are perhaps the closest approximations to CAL tools that many of the fire fighters have experienced. The results of Figure 4 indicate that neither resource is being effectively deployed. Figure 5 presents the fire fighters' response to the perceived effectiveness of different training methods. As can be seen, there is a strong correlation between these results and the responses shown in Figure 4. Lectures and videos are perceived as being relatively ineffective training mechanisms in comparison to incident based training.

Figures 4 & 5 provide few insights into those features that reduce the effectiveness of lecture based training. Similarly, they do not identify those attributes that increase the perceived effectiveness of 'real' incidents. These, more detailed, perceptions were addressed by two further questions. Fire fighters were encouraged to write down their feelings about the best and worst aspects of fire training. Table 1 presents a summary of their responses.

Topic	Frequency
Practical work	7
New experiences	7
Specific parts of training	5
Teamwork	3
Nothing	2

a. What do you enjoy most about fire training?

Topic	Frequency
Repetitiveness	18
Ladder drills	3
Too in-depth	2
Nothing	2

b. What do you hate most about fire training?

Table 1: Categorisation of responses to open questions about training methods.

Table 1a re-iterates the importance of practical training. It reveals that activist learning styles characterise many people who are attracted by, or are recruited into, the Fire Brigade. For example, the importance of new experiences suggests that any revised function allocation between human and computer-based training should continue to provide a varied menu of training experiences. Similarly, if more training functions are to be implemented within CAL systems then there is a clear concern that this should not jeopardise the benefits of team-based learning that seem to be a significant strength of existing practices. Table 1b provides evidence of further requirements for any revised function allocation. The fire fighters' antipathy towards repetitive exercises reinforces the importance of new experiences in Table 1a. The fire fighter's irritation with detailed training exercises is an interesting finding. It, perhaps, suggests a need to continually situate exercises within 'realistic' scenarios. However, the limited scope of the survey provides insufficient evidence to reach firm conclusions about this.

The initial analysis indicated that there was scope for improving training practices within the Fire Brigade. Senior staff in this organisation viewed CAL as a primary means of achieving such improvements. There was an implicit view that the re-allocation of training activities between computer-based training systems and human instructors would alleviate some of the problems that were revealed by our survey. The questionnaire also suggested that any re-allocation of training functions towards CAL tools must exploit the positive features of incident-based learning and avoid the problems of lecture-based training. Unfortunately, the questionnaire did not provide detailed evidence about the exact ways in which function allocation might be used to achieve these objectives. Nor did it identify ways in which the intervention of human instructors and CAL systems might be integrated to support the technical training and practical expertise of the fire fighters.

3   Analysing Function Allocation in Complex Organisations

This section describes two practical problems that must be addressed if Laurillard's conversational framework is to guide the allocation of training tasks between CAL systems and human instructors.

3.1 Existing Function Allocation in the Technical Cycle

Laurillard's model was primarily intended to promote a conversational view of education in which tutors and students maximise their shared view of any topic. Montgomery (1997) has, however, shown that her framework can also be used as a practical design tool. Activity-implementation charts provide check-lists that analysts can use to note whether each of Laurillard's stages is supported by either human tutors, CAL systems or some other mode of learning. Montgomery focussed on University education. In contrast, Table 2 shows how activity-implementation charts can also be used to analyse technical training within the Fire Brigade. A blank in the Teaching Mode column indicates that a learning activity is not supported by the current allocation of educational tasks. Table 2 shows that many of Laurillard's learning activities are not explicitly supported. In particular, the use of traditional lecturing techniques leaves little room for the task-based activities in Laurillard's conversational model. If Montgomery is to be believed then this indicates an important opportunity for increasing the intervention of either human tutors or CAL applications. Such opportunities illustrate a basic point about function allocation; it is only possible to derive an appropriate allocation of responsibilities between automated and manual systems if designers can identify necessary functionality in the first place.

An important insight from our application of Montgomery's techniques was that problems still exist even if training activities already support a particular stage in Laurillard's model. For example, Table 2 indicates that fire fighters have an opportunity to describe key concepts in either written or spoken form; each technical lecture is followed by an open session of questions and answers. This is a key component in Stage 2 of the conversational framework. However, initial observations revealed that some fire fighters failed to ask any questions after technical training sessions. This is an important problem. Laurillard's dialogue depends upon the tutor being able to gauge their students' understanding through the questions that they ask. It also relies upon students testing whether or not they have correctly understood the key concepts that are being taught. Low levels of student participation in conventional lectures short-circuit the dialogue that Lauillard views as being essential to effective education.

3.2 Existing Function Allocation in the Practical Cycle

Table 3 extends our application of activity-implementation charts to analyse the practical training that is provided by the Fire Brigade. This shows that the stages of Laurillard's model are better supported for practical training than they are for technical training. This imbalance perhaps results from the perceived importance of practical skills within the organisation. However, it also confirms the senior officers' view that function re-allocation, through the increased use of CAL techniques, offers the greatest benefit to technical training activities.

Our analysis identified a number of concerns about the use of Laurillard's model to assess function allocation. In particular, Montgomery's approach focuses upon the role of human tutors and CAL applications within controlled environments, such as Universities or Schools. It does not consider the ways in which 'real' events can be

Activity	Function allocation	Example
1. The learner listens to a teacher's exposition.	Human	Officer in charge gives a lecture. Fire fighter reads lecture notes/watches training video.
2. The learner describes the conception as they understand it, in the form of an essay or verbally.	Human	Fire fighter asks question at end of lecture
3. The teacher re-describes the conception to the learner based upon activity 2 and provides feedback.	Human	Officer in charge explains answer to question.
4. The learner attempts activity 2 again.	Human	Fire fighter confirms their understanding of Officer in Charge's response.
5. The teacher sets a goal for the learner to complete.		
6. The learner attempts the goal set in activity 5.		
7. The teacher provides feedback regarding the learner's attempt at the task described in activity 6.		
8. The learner modifies their actions in the light of feedback provided by the teacher.		
9. The learner reflects on the interaction in order to modify their grasp of the concepts.	Human	Call-out provokes reflection on technical training.
10. The learner modifies their actions in the light of reasoning at the 'public' level of descriptions.	Human	Fire fighter alters behaviour in practical exercise on basis of technical material.
11. The teacher modifies the task set to address some need revealed by the learner's descriptions or actions.		
12. The teacher examines the learner's actions and modifies their description of the original conception.		

Table 2: Activity–Implementation Chart for technical training in the Fire Brigade.

used to reinforce practical skills and technical knowledge. This is important because Section 2 demonstrated that fire fighters perceive incidents to be the most efficient and effective means of training. The importance of these learning opportunities is also recognised by the Fire Brigade. Experience gained during real incidents is logged in the training records of individual fire fighters. Future work might address this limitation of Laurillard's model by introducing additional rows into activity-implementation charts. There must be some mechanism by which tutors can refine their drills in the light of student performance not only in simulations but also in real-world incidents, e.g. Table 4.

There is a strong reliance upon human support for the acquisition of practical skills by fire fighters. Question and answer dialogues again provide their instructors

Activity	Function allocation	Example
1. The learner listens to a teacher's exposition.	Human	Instructor demonstrates drill. Fire fighters watch video demonstration.
2. The learner describes the conception as they understand it, in the form of an essay or verbally.	Human	Fire fighters ask questions for clarification
3. The teacher re-describes the conception to the learner based upon activity 2 and provides feedback.	Human	Questions answered by instructor
4. The learner attempts activity 2 again.	Human	Fire fighters reformulate question.
5. The teacher sets a goal for the learner to complete.	Human	Drill specified by instructor from manual.
6. The learner attempts the goal set in activity 5.	Human	Fire fighters perform drill.
7. The teacher provides feedback regarding the learner's attempt at the task described in activity 6.	Human	Instructors comment during drill and perform formal debriefing.
8. The learner modifies their actions in the light of feedback provided by the teacher.	Human	Fire fighters repeat drill if time allows.
9. The learner reflects on the interaction in order to modify their grasp of the concepts.	Human	Turn taking in drills may allow time for reflection as others perform task.
10. The learner modifies their actions in the light of reasoning at the 'public' level of descriptions.	Human	Fire fighter uses drill during call-out.
11. The teacher modifies the task set to address some need revealed by the learner's descriptions or actions.	Human	Instructor alters complexity of drill by adding/removing tasks, time pressures etc.
12. The teacher examines the learner's actions and modifies their description of the original conception.	Human	Completion of individual record cards.

Table 3: Activity–Implementation Chart for practical training in the Fire Brigade.

10. The teacher examines the learner's actions in real incidents and revises their training regime accordingly		

Table 4: Extension to Activity–Implementation Charts for practical training.

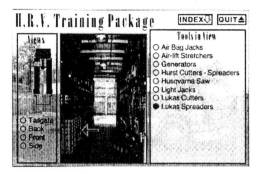

Figure 6: The heavy rescue vehicle training package.

with the primary means of assessing whether or not they have acquired the skills that are being demonstrated. This has important implications for revised function allocations. Video clips and desktopVR techniques can provide fire fighters with useful guidance about the performance of practical tasks. However, the introduction of these CAL resources must not jeopardise the feedback that is necessary if tutors are to be sure that fire fighters can perform the tasks that are demonstrated to them. Similarly, the introduction of CAL resources should not jeopardise the feedback that is necessary if fire fighters are to gauge whether or not they have successfully acquired the necessary practical skills.

4   Using Function Allocation to Guide the Application of CAL

This section applies the previous analysis to target the use of CAL within a complex, organisation.

4.1   Using CAL to Increase Learner Participation in Technical Presentations

Our initial survey suggested that the lecture-based presentation of technical material provided limited opportunities for fire fighters to interact with their instructors. This analysis was supported by the relatively weak support for Stages 2 and 4 of Laurillard's model that was identified in Table 2. Many fire fighters did not play an active role in the question and answer sessions that were intended to reinforce technical material. A number of authors have argued that CAL tools can be used to address such concerns (Cohen et al., 1995). Fire fighters are likely to be less reticent in exploring problem areas with the assistance of a computer-based tool than they are in asking questions in front of their colleagues. CAL tools can also reduce the problems that arise when training sessions are interrupted by a call-out. Fire fighters can work through a package at their own speed and resume their interaction when other duties permit.

These claims were tested by the development of a CAL tool that provided an introduction to the equipment carried on a Heavy Rescue Vehicle (HRV). A central concern was to avoid the criticisms of lecture-based presentations that were revealed

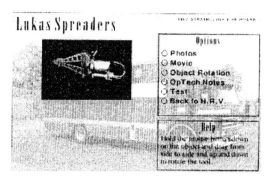

Figure 7: Multimedia Resources in the heavy rescue vehicle training package.

by the initial survey. The main design aim was, therefore, to maximise interaction with the subject material. The principle technical means of achieving this was through the application of desktopVR. In particular, the photo-realistic facilities of QuicktimeVR were used to construct a three-dimensional representation of the storage area inside the HRV. This approach provides high levels of support for activist learning styles; fire fighters can use their keyboard and mouse to move inside the vehicle itself (Johnson, 1998). Equipment can be located either through exploration using the desktopVR view, shown in the middle panel of Figure 6, or by selecting an item from the list on the right. The HRV package was intended to move some of the technical teaching duties away from the Training Officers and onto a CAL application. It was, therefore, necessary to provide more detailed information about each item of equipment on the vehicle. For example, fire fighters could have accessed the text from a conventional lecture through hypertext links in the QuicktimeVR model. This would have ignored many of the benefits from reallocating training activities to CAL systems. Alternatively, Figure 7 shows the different multimedia resources that were provided for the HRV package. Detailed textual material was presented in the form of technical notes. Images of the equipment 'in action' were presented through video clips. Our initial survey indicated that such diversity was extremely important from the users' perspective. Fire fighters accessed the multimedia resources by selecting from an option list that was provided for each item of equipment. This enabled fire fighters to choose the information resource that best met their needs. They were not constrained by the pre-determined ordering of material in a lecture.

Two further features of the HRV package emerged as a direct result of our work into function allocation. The first of these concerned the presentation of particular items of equipment. Our need to improve upon the passive nature of traditional lectures persuaded us to support three-dimensional interaction with these objects. The aim was to increase the fire fighters interaction with the material in a CAL tool in a manner that is difficult, or impossible, to achieve given the constraints upon human instructors in conventional lectures. The intention was to enable fire

Figure 8: Object rotations in the heavy rescue vehicle training package.

fighters to directly manipulate the equipment so that they could observe significant details, such as power connections. Figure 8 shows the results of this approach for Lucas cutters. QuicktimeVR techniques were again used to enable fire fighters to manipulate three-dimensional views of the HRV equipment using a conventional keyboard and mouse.

The second contribution of function allocation was in the integration of video material into the HRV package. It has already been noted that both human instructors and video presentations were perceived as being less effective than direct involvement in incidents. In developing a CAL system to replace some aspects of human instruction, it was important to learn as much as possible from criticisms of the existing approaches. Video was, therefore, used to illustrate the practical application of rescue equipment within simulated rescues. This approach is shown in Figure 6.

The HRV package was intended to reduce the reticence that some fire fighters exhibited during question and answer sessions. This was identified as a significant problem because Laurillard's model stresses that learners must be provided with the opportunity to verify that they have correctly understood key concepts. CAL helps to address such concerns because fire fighters can use an automated system to check their understanding in their own time. They can also consult a CAL application without exposing any possible confusion to their colleagues or to a Training Officer.

4.2   Using CAL to Structure Student Interaction in Technical Presentations

Montgomery's (1997) Activity-Implementation charts can also be used to assess the impact of changes to an existing task allocation. For example, the HRV package supported Stage 1 of Laurillard's model. It addressed the fire fighters' criticisms of conventional lectures by enabling them to interact more directly with technical training material. One side effect of this was to weaken support for Stages 3 and 12. The introduction of a computer based system actually reduced the opportunity for the trainer to modify their material in response to the changing needs of their students and of the Fire Brigade. The HRV package was designed as a self-contained product and could not easily be updated by Training Officers. This is a significant weakness. If fire fighters reported usability problems or identified further informational needs then Training Officers were forced to provide ad hoc support through additional lectures or printed documentation. This reduced the benefits to be gained from allocating training tasks to a CAL tool.

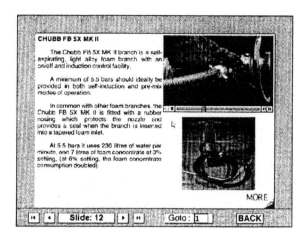

Figure 9: The self-instruction slide package.

A second package was, therefore, developed to provide Fire Brigade personnel with means of extending and maintaining their CAL resources. This approach is supported by Laurillard's conversational view of education because human instructors can tailor the presentation of material to support their students needs. Training Officers, rather than external designers, can direct the allocation of CAL tools to those areas that they consider to offer the best rewards. Unfortunately, this approach also creates a new set of design problems. The HRV package was tailored to support particular training activities. In contrast, the new user interface was to provide fire fighters with access to the wide range of material that Training Officers wanted to present. This included information about safe lifting procedures as well as details about the effective use of breathing apparatus and good operating practices for rescue equipment. A slide metaphor was chosen and Training Officers were provided with a tool to link-in text and multimedia resources. The result can be thought of as a highly simplified version of Microsoft's PowerPoint interface. Figure 9 illustrates the results of using this tool to generate a training package about foam delivery systems.

The Slide Package again shows that Laurillard's model can be used to identify weaknesses and omissions in the existing division of labour between human instructors and computer-based training packages. The HRV package did not enable Training Officers to tailor the presentation of material in response to changing user needs. The Slide Package overcame these objections by enabling officers to create their own CAL resources. It is important to emphasise, however, that the use of such educational models does not replace iterative design techniques. For example, the decision to use a slide metaphor owes more to Lydia Plowman's (1996) study of narrative in multimedia than it does to Laurillard's conversational model of educational tasks. The Slide Package enabled fire fighters to browse material in any order that they chose. However, there was also a tuition mode in which they could follow a pre-determined order that had been specified by the instructor. Slide 1 and then slide 2 and then slide 3. Such linear and causal sequences were not supported within the HRV package. The problems that unstructured exploration can create for the users of CAL systems emerged through user testing, mentioned in Section 5, rather than through the analytical use of function allocation techniques.

4.3   *Using CAL to Support Common Understanding in Technical Training*

In retrospect, the HRV and Slide Packages failed to address many of the fundamental concerns raised by Laurillard's model. The HRV package supported the presentation of material, embodied in Stage 1 of the model. The Slide Package enabled Training Officers to update CAL material in Stages 3 and 12. They did not, however, provide any support for Stages 4–8 in Table 3. These stages focus on the use of tasks and exercises to provide students with feedback about their understanding of key concepts. These stages also provide the tutor with feedback about the need to improve their delivery techniques. A third package was, therefore, developed to address the failings of previous applications. An important concern was to deliver a flexible and extensible assessment system that could be tailored by Fire Brigade staff in the same way that the slide package could be extended. We were also concerned to support a diverse range of comprehension tools to avoid the fire fighters' antipathy towards repetitive training exercises.

Further analysis also revealed that certain questions should be classified as 'need to know'. From the fire fighters' perspective, it was important that they could identify these questions as being critical to their understanding of the topic. From the instructors' perspective, these questions helped to assess both the fire fighters' grasp of the central topics but also the performance of their instructional systems in indicating the degree of importance associated with particular topics. This issue is especially important where training functions are being re-allocated away from human instructors towards CAL systems. Training Officers use a myriad of rhetorical techniques to emphasise the importance of key topics during a lecture: repetition, prosodic stress, visual movements and expressions. Many of these cues are entirely lost when training tasks are transferred to CAL systems. Figure 10 presents a self-assessment exercise that was developed to accompany the foam tutorial in Figure 9. This screen implements a photographic multiple-choice question. Fire fighters are provided with feedback after each selection and are encouraged to provide further input if they make an incorrect selection. In this case, the question has not been marked as 'need to know'. If this were the case then the screen would indicate the significance of the question.

Self-assessment techniques, such as that shown in Figure 10, provide fire fighters with a mechanism by which they can gain feedback about their understanding of key topics. Our analysis of Stages 7 and 12 in Laurillard's model also indicates that it is important for Training Officers to get feedback about the effectiveness of their training techniques. For this reason, the Comprehension Package provided logging facilities. Tutors can track the performance of individual fire fighters as well as groups of students. It is important to emphasise, however, that this system was intended to aid individual comprehension rather than provide a

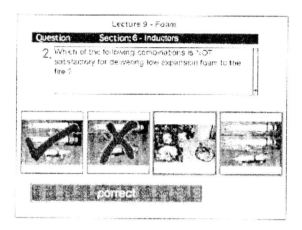

Figure 10: A photographic multiple choice question.

means of assessment. Our intention was to raise the level of understanding within the group rather than to achieve a normal distribution of marks around the mean. Even so, the development of this tool raised important social questions about the use of logging techniques. Any analysis of this topic must consider not only the fire fighters' attitudes but also the attitudes of their Trades Union representatives.

Stage 11 of Laurillard's model centres on the way in which a teacher modifies a task to address some need revealed by the learner's previous descriptions or actions. Such modifications can be automated through the application of user models to adapt questions in response to students' interaction. However, this approach could not easily have been adopted in this project. Firstly, the user model would have had to cover the vast range of technical and practical subjects that the Training Officers supported through the Slide Package. Second, it was difficult to envisage a user model that could be developed and maintained by the Training Officers as they observed successful or unsuccessful adaptations by the user model. The application of user models was, therefore, rejected in favour of simplifying the mechanisms by which questions were generated. Figure 11 illustrates the Training Officer's interface that was used to develop the questions that the Comprehension Package presented to the fire fighters.

5 Assessing the Effectiveness of Revised Function Allocations

Designers must have some means of assessing the utility of particular function allocations. A number of different perspectives must be taken into account. For instance, any reduction in the tutor's load may be supported by Training Officers but rejected by the fire fighters. Further problems arise because changes in function allocation can have longitudinal effects that are difficult to predict and to measure. The validation of such effects is a research area in its own right. We decided to

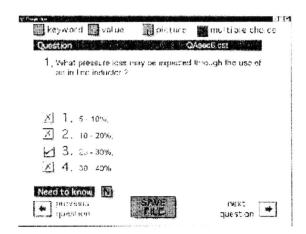

Figure 11: Question generation in the comprehension package.

focus on whether the Comprehension Tool helped to reinforce the fire fighters' understanding of particular topics. A matched subject design was adopted; each fire fighter was paired with another officer of equivalent rank. Each member of the pair was then randomly assigned to one of two groups. Both groups were given access to the foam resources that had been developed using the Slide Package. One group was then given the Comprehension Tool. They were encouraged to use it to identify areas that they might not have understood from their use of the foam tool. The second group was given a pencil and paper test without any feedback about the accuracy of their responses. One week later both groups were re-tested using the Comprehension Tool. It was hypothesised that the group that had access to the self-assessment tool would achieve significantly higher scores than the group that had performed the pencil and paper test. This hypothesis would support the claim that fire fighters could use the Comprehension Tool to improve their grasp of the core material after using the Slide Package, as suggested by Stages 6 and 8 in Laurillard's model. A weakness in this experimental design is that learning effects might improve the results of the group that already had some experience with the Comprehension Tool. These effects were minimised by ensuring that both groups were confident in the use of the tool before the second test.

A T-test failed to show any significant differences in the re-test scores between those who had access to the Comprehension Tool and those who sat the pencil and paper test (see Tables 5 & 6). A number of reasons explain this finding. Firstly, the Comprehension Tool was used for the re-test. As mentioned before, this application was intended to reinforce key concepts rather than to achieve a normal distribution of marks. Secondly, there were some minor problems in applying ranking techniques to the two watches. The evaluation was forced to match the station officer in the second group with a sub-officer in the first group. Thirdly, problems arose from the context

Rank	Number	Comprehension Tool Paper test?	Score 1	Score 2
Sub officer	1	Paper	72	76
Leading fire fighter	2	Comprehension tool	60	56
Leading fire fighter	3	Comprehension tool	80	68
Fire fighter	4	Paper	36	44
Fire fighter	5	Paper	88	84
Fire fighter	6	Comprehension tool	64	52
Fire fighter	7	Paper	40	40
Fire fighter	8	Comprehension tool	52	32

Table 5: Results for the first group of fire fighters.

Rank	Number	Comprehension Tool Paper test?	Score 1	Score 2 * post fire
Station officer	1	Comprehension tool	96	88*
Leading fire fighter	2	Paper	80	60*
Leading fire fighter	3	Paper	92	80
Fire fighter	4	Comprehension tool	68	48
Fire fighter	5	Comprehension tool	64	68
Fire fighter	6	Paper	52	40*
Fire fighter	7	Comprehension tool	84	64
Fire fighter	8	Paper	60	60

Table 6: Results for the second group of fire fighters.

in which the evaluation was conducted. In the middle of the second session, one of the watches was called out to attend a fire. The results for the second group are, therefore, split between those who were tested one week after initial exposure to the foam package and those who were tested one week after that. These minor concerns hide a deeper sense of unease about the evaluation of function allocation in complex organisations. The Slide Package and Comprehension Tool enabled the Fire Brigade to develop and maintain their own CAL resources. Training Officers, therefore, determined the extent to which automated tools supported their training activities. They controlled the detailed allocation of training duties between human instructors and CAL systems. Unfortunately, we could provide them with little guidance about how to assess the impact that such allocations would have upon the knowledge, skills and 'real world' performance of fire fighters.

6 Conclusions and Further Work

Laurillard's model is principally an analytical tool. It can be used to determine whether human instructors and CAL tools support key stages in knowledge acquisition and skill development. It provides limited support for the constructive design of new tools. This argument has been illustrated by the implementation of CAL systems that were intended to support the existing training allocation within the Fire Brigade. Our work focused on the technical training areas that were demonstrated to have the poorest coverage of the stages in Laurillard's model. The initial attempts produced an interactive training tool for a Heavy Rescue Vehicle. This was intended to avoid the pitfalls of conventional lectures by increasing user participation and interaction with the technical material. The principle means of achieving this was through the application of desktopVR techniques. The decision to exploit these techniques was based on feedback from the Fire Brigade rather than the insights gained from theoretical models of function allocation. However, Laurillard's approach did provide a valuable means of assessing the application of this new CAL tool. Her model emphasises the importance of changing educational resources in response to the tutor's observation of student performance. The HRV tool was developed as a stand-alone application. It could not be easily modified by Training Officers.

A second CAL application was developed to avoid the limitations of the HRV package. This tool was specifically developed to provide Fire Brigade instructors with means of tailoring the presentation of training resources. A slide-show metaphor was adopted. This provided a generic interface to a range of multimedia resources that could be linked in by the instructor. Again, Laurillard's model was used as a means of critically evaluating the new task allocation that was created by the introduction of this tool. A particular weakness was that although the CAL resources improved the exposition of technical material, they did little to help fire fighters determine whether or not they had correctly understood this material. This weakness corresponded to at least two stages of Laurillard's model that were not covered after the introduction of the Slide Package. We, therefore, developed a Comprehension Tool that could be used by fire fighters as a self-assessment package.

We were anxious to establish that the application of Laurillard's model resulted in a better function allocation than had existed before the introduction of our new CAL systems. This raised a host of methodological and practical problems. The methodological problems centred around the identification of a suitable evaluation technique that might demonstrate the utility of a function allocation. This is a research area in its own right. The value of any division of tasks is likely to be a highly subjective concept. In our case study, the fire fighters had a different perspective from the Training Officers. The Training Officers had a different perspective from the Senior Officers and so on (Lave & Wenger, 1991). In anticipation of the results of on-going research in this area, we decided to use a more focused empirical approach. This failed to identify any significant differences between groups that had access to our Comprehension Tool and those that did not. The results of this validation exercise were almost certainly affected by the practical problems of conducting such tests within complex organisations. Subjects could not be exactly ranked as the method required nor could we prevent offices from being called away to attend a fire during one of our evaluation sessions.

This paper has presented the practical experiences of using function allocation techniques within a complex organisation. It has demonstrated that Laurillard's model can be extended from University education to the more practical training problems of a Fire Brigade. Above all, however, we have identified the pressing need for appropriate evaluation techniques that might be used to assess the utility of changes in training allocations. During the later stages of this project, we became aware of the complex criteria that were being applied to assess the success or failure of our systems. Some people were interested in the financial benefits that might be derived from allocating training duties to CAL tools. Others saw this as an opportunity to provide fire fighters with more varied material and, in particular, to support activitist learning styles. Some individuals wanted to ensure that the Fire Brigade investigated 'leading edge' technology. They were less worried about establishing the 'effectiveness' of that technology. Finally, there was a concern that the introduction of new technology might distance fire fighters from the experience that human instructors could impart from their own first-hand experiences.

Acknowledgements

Alan Thompson helped with the design and implementation of some of the systems described in this report. Thanks are due to the members of Glasgow Interactive Systems Group (GIST) who provided valuable advice and encouragement with this research.

References

Cohen, A., Candland, K. & Lee, E. (1995), The Effect of a Teacher-designed Assessment Tool on an Instructor's Cognitive Activity, *in* K. Nordby, P. H. Helmersen, D. J. Gilmore & S. A. Arnessen (eds.), *Human–Computer Interaction — INTERACT '95: Proceedings of the Fifth IFIP Conference on Human–Computer Interaction*, Chapman & Hall, pp.405–9.

Hewitt, T. & Tscheligi, M. (1995), Advanced Interaction in University Based Education, *in* K. Nordby, P. H. Helmersen, D. J. Gilmore & S. A. Arnessen (eds.), *Human–Computer Interaction — INTERACT '95: Proceedings of the Fifth IFIP Conference on Human–Computer Interaction*, Chapman & Hall, pp.423–30.

Johnson, C. W. (1998), On the Problems of Validating DesktopVR, *in* H. Johnson, L. Nigay & C. Roast (eds.), *People and Computers XIII (Proceedings of HCI'98)*, Springer-Verlag, pp.327–38.

Laurillard, D. (1993), *Rethinking University Teaching: A Framework for the Effective Use of Educational Technology*, Routledge.

Laurillard, D. & Taylor, J. (1994), "Designing the Stepping Stones: An Evaluation of Interactive Media in the Classroom", *Journal of Education Television* **20**(3), 169–84.

Lave, J. & Wenger, E. (1991), *Situated Learning: Legitimate Peripheral Participation*, Cambridge University Press.

Montgomery, M. (1997), Developing a Laurillardian Design Method for CAL, *in Proceedings of Ed-Media '97*, Association for the Advancement of Computing in Education.

Plowman, L. (1996), "Making Sense of Interactive Multimedia", *British Journal of Educational Technology* **27**(2), 92–105.

Connections, Locations and Shared Workspaces: What Should the User Understand about Network Services for Online Collaboration?

Merja Ranta-aho, Maria Köykkä & Raila Ollikainen

Human Factors in Telecommunications, Communications Laboratory, Helsinki University of Technology, PO Box 2300, FIN-02015 HUT, Finland

Tel: *+358 9 451 2355*
EMail: *merja.ranta-aho@hut.fi*
URL: *http://www.comlab.hut.fi/hft/*

Users of networked services may benefit from a simple but correct understanding of the underlying network technology in the service. Many technical concepts like network connections are present already in the task model held by the user. Attempts to hide them in the user interface of computer applications using network services in the name of simplifying usage may in fact cause confusion. This paper presents an analysis of some concepts needed in networked multimedia services that, we find, should be communicated to the user correctly in the user interface.

Keywords: mental models, network services, usability, learning, user interface design.

1 Introduction

During the 90s, working with the computer has become also working in a computer network. Services for online collaboration have grown more complex, from audio-only or text-based real-time or non-real time communication to real time collaboration with audio and video connections and collaborative manipulation of digital objects. Examples of these services are collaborative virtual environments, often in the WWW, and desktop multimedia conferencing.

Research on the usage of these systems has concentrated on topics such as comparison of the quality of interaction mediated by the system to face-to-face collaboration, group and communication dynamics, and the effect of various media and the quality of the media on collaboration (Fussell & Benimoff, 1995; Olson & Olson, 1997; Kies et al., 1997). This paper will discuss another viewpoint: how much of the underlying network operations of the system should the user understand to be able to work with the system efficiently and without fatal errors?

2 Constructing Mental Models of Computer Systems

A characteristic of the human mind seems to be that it constructs models of the external world to aid activity, learning and problem solving. The concept of mental models has been utilised especially in the context of human–computer interaction. A definition by Carroll & Olson (1988) views a mental model (of a computer system) as "a rich and elaborate structure, reflecting the user's understanding of what the system contains, how it works and why it works that way". The mental model can be mentally 'run', and its behaviour observed.

Mental models are not fixed representations, but they evolve and eventually change as the user interacts with the system and learns more about it. Norman (1983) states that mental models generally are incomplete and unstable and that different models get confused with each other. Lack of detail is not necessarily a problem, actual incorrectness (in respect to the actual system) of the user model can, instead, be hard to correct. It is easier to add new details to an existing model than it is to change established views of something (Argyris, 1991). Norman (1983) points out that people are reluctant to use mental effort to revise mental models, if this can be avoided by additional, simple physical effort. In addition, prior knowledge and beliefs will affect later perception of the system and interpretation of events, see for example Rumelhart & Norman (1978), and also in line with constructivist learning theories.

The computer system user's mental model includes both models of the computer system and of the task domain (Neale & Carroll, 1997). The user is required to maintain a model of both domains and to construct a mapping between them (Payne et al., 1991; Payne, 1992). To assist the user in doing this, traditional user interface guidelines (Nielsen, 1993) and the conceptual design approach (Norman, 1986) suggest that the user interface concepts should map to user task concepts rather than to those of the underlying system. This leads to hiding from the user technical details that are not necessary for the user to know.

The practice of hiding the system level from the user does not always work. It may be easier to introduce new technical concepts at the user interface level than to try to hide them totally, as the result might be contradicting other user interface guidelines like user control or consistency, see for example Nielsen (1993; Shneiderman, 1998), and even in good attempts to hide technical concepts, there probably is some part of the user interface, typically some 'advanced' features, where these new technical concepts must be encountered. For the user, revising a user model at a later stage of learning is more difficult than constructing it correctly from the beginning, as was stated earlier. As users seem to build a naïve explanation of the system architecture level anyway (Ranta-aho, 1997) — so it might be best to support the user model formation on the system architecture level correctly from the beginning.

There are several problems in having a faulty representation of a technical system. The full potential, e.g. the advanced functions of the system may stay unused. Even worse, user errors may occur that the user is not aware of or is unable to correct. User models different from the actual system architecture cause problems e.g. for some World Wide Web users, who are unaware of information security risks — and are also resistant to correct information about the WWW (Ranta-aho, 1997).

Not all system level concepts are difficult, and many of them can be explained very easily in a simple level of detail. In network services, some of the technical concepts may actually be, of course in a very general level, part of the user's mental model of the task she is engaged with.

3 Network Services for Online Collaboration: Connecting Locations Through Shared Workspaces?

The user's view of the task is an important starting point in designing interactive systems, as conceptual design supporters such as Norman (1986) and Clark & Sasse (1997) conclude. For collaboration online, a reference for the user task might be same-place, real time collaboration (Fussell & Benimoff, 1995). In online collaboration, evidently, some kind of a service is used to make a network connection to some other location, to the other participants, in user interfaces of multimedia conferencing services often metaphorically represented as 'placing a call' or 'joining a meeting'. To replace the physical common workspace, online services for collaboration create what Fussell & Benimoff (1995) call a 'shared work space'.

Network connections, locations connected to and the shared workspaces for collaboration are not technical details irrelevant to the user, but rather, an essential part of the user's mental model for the task. They are this only on a simple level, but the actual system is more complex. Multimedia network applications have different kind of complex connection options:

- A connection to a service provider may be needed before actual application connections can be made (e.g. the connection to the Internet service provider before the browser can operate).

- Several connections can be made simultaneously by the computer.

- One connection may have several components: e.g. separate connections for different media in a videoconference call.

- The bandwidth of the connection may be selectable.

- Various technical parameters of the connection may be selectable, that affect the perceived quality of the connection.

Implicit in the concept of network connection is that there are different locations connected with each other. On the user task level, the simple concept of location is 'the place where I am' or 'the place where the partner is located'. Locations may refer not only to physical locations of other persons, but locations of information. When working with a computer, the personal computer is a simple example of an information location. In networked computers and services, different locations are connected by network connections and some may be separated by access control; the terms 'connector' and 'separator' are used by Dieberger & Frank (1998).

The shared workspace in a network application, like a shared whiteboard, 3D environment, chat board, aims to reproduce the workspace or visualising tools used in actual, same-place collaboration (Fussell & Benimoff, 1995). For being able to collaborate efficiently, users need information of the actual nature of the shared workspace and other locations they interact with:

- What do others see? Can any user customise her own view?

- What is the location of a file or the shared workspace — does one have access to something located on someone else's computer, or is there truly some shared space that both can access and retrieve independently of each other?

- Who else other than the collaborators is able to access the shared workspace?

- Are the available functions of the workspace equal for both, or does one user control what the others can do?

The described concepts: connections, locations and shared workspaces, should be presented in the user interface of network services clearly. Failing to do this, usability problems arise that lead to user errors and inefficient work practices. This was demonstrated in usability tests of three different applications, two multimedia conferencing systems and one 3D virtual environment for communication, which will be described in the next section.

4   Usability Problems of Network Services for Collaboration

4.1   *Methods*

For an analysis of the concepts that the user needs to understand in network services for collaboration, usability tests of three different online services for collaboration were conducted. The purpose of the tests was not to evaluate the quality of these specific applications, and the results should not be taken as any indication of their quality. Details of the tests are presented in Table 1.

Test users were recruited from outside the companies involved. For the Arena World tests, the participants did not know each other in advance. For the two multimedia conferencing applications, recruiting pairs that knew each other in advance created a more natural situation. During the tests, users were located in different rooms, and an experimenter was present for each test user. The users

Application	Test users	Functions used in test tasks
Arena World 1.0 WWW 3D multi-user virtual world with avatars, one-to-one and group audio chat and general and restricted-participants text chat and text messages; access to video and audio clips and 2D information content; a pilot application, used with Netscape Navigator and Real Player	N=12; 15–44, half of them with prior experience of 3D computer games and/ or 3D virtual worlds Criteria: use computer daily or almost daily	• Combination of a general text chat, private person-to-person text messages and private chat groups • Person-to-person audio chat • Logging in and exiting
FVC Picturetel Live and Live Share plus Point-to-point multimedia conferencing application with application sharing, shared whiteboard, text chat and file transfer; commercially available	N=12; 20–45 Criteria: at least basic computer skills with Microsoft Windows knowledge	• Audio-video conferencing and joint editing with the whiteboard and application sharing • Parameter setting for connection
Microsoft Netmeeting 2.11 Conferencing application with audio conferencing, text chat, file transfer, shared whiteboard and application sharing; commercially available	N=8; 20–25 Criteria: at least basic computer skills with Microsoft Windows knowledge	• Collaboration and negotiation tasks with application sharing and audio discussion

Table 1: Usability test details for the tests conducted.

were given realistic collaborative tasks to do with other test users. Arena World as a multi-user application was tested with three simultaneous users, the multimedia conferencing applications with a pair of users.

Sasse (1996) suggests, that for analysing what kind of models the user holds of a system, both performance results and verbal accounts of user beliefs should be collected. In the tests, the performance of the users was videotaped using either a video camera recording the screen and all discussion, or a combination of a screen capturer and video camera (for audio mainly) mixed together. The users were interviewed both during and after the test tasks, among other issues also about their beliefs about how the system was functioning, especially in situations, where the result of interaction with the system was not as intended. Another, rich source for user verbalisations was their discussion with the other test user(s).

4.2 Analysis of User Problems: What Did the Users Not Understand?

Many of the usability problems encountered by the test users did not involve expressed misunderstandings about the functioning of the system either on the application or system level. Examples of these problems were not recognising an icon, difficulties of locating items by visual search from the screen or from the right-mouse-button menu, complaints about too long action sequences and lack of needed functionality. Solving the problems did not require explanations of the functioning of the system. They were left out from this analysis.

In total, 9 of the usability problems found in the three applications could be attributed to a false understanding of the underlying system and the functionality it provides, based on user explanations of the situations and their expressed beliefs about the operation of the system. Two of the problems occurred in two different applications, others in only one. These problems are analysed here further.

4.2.1   Problems With Understanding Connections

In Arena World, there were several places, where the user could start viewing a movie or listening to the radio. If this was done, the user could not join audio chat before terminating the movie or radio program, because there could only be one audio component received at a time. This was not understood, but users failed to start audio chatting and thought that the function just did not work. This was due to the insufficient understanding of the connection with the virtual world: that it consisted of several components, of which only one at a time could be audio.

Although starting to use Arena World involved giving a user name and password, there was no exit button in the application, but the users had to use the browser's back button to exit. No user found the correct way of exiting the application without lots of searching and guidance by the experimenter. This problem could be related to unclear methods for terminating the connection: if one logs on, she expects to log off, also.

In Picturetel, when making a call, an audio-video connection was established, but the connection for the shared whiteboard had to be made separately. Some of the user couples did not notice that their whiteboards were not in call with each other. They both had opened locally the whiteboard and thought that they are using that in collaboration.

In Picturetel, setting various technical parameters of the connection including audio coding, video coding and speed of data transfer was also tested. These parameters influenced each other, as most of them affected the transmission capacity needed for one component (audio, video or data) of the connection. Only from a deep inspection of the manual could it be found, that the connection actually had components, and that they influence each other. Most users had difficulties in understanding how they should set the parameters for optimal performance.

4.2.2   Problems with Understanding Locations and Shared Workspaces

In Arena World, one shared workspace was the text chat. There was a general text chat visible to all users, and a private chat for each user, where the user could invite others to join. Every user had one single chat output area and one chat input area. The user could select by pressing buttons below the chat output area, which chat room she wanted to be in. Only the discussion of that chat room was displayed in the chat output area. All of the users had difficulties in establishing a text chat discussion otherwise than in the general chat. The users found the way to invite others to their own private chat rooms. Accepting an invitation automatically moved the invited user to the room she was invited to, but the inviters did not move themselves there. This was due to the false understanding of the characteristics of the chat output area and poor feedback on the current participants in each chat room — a wrong understanding of what was really shared with other participants.

In both multimedia conferencing applications' application sharing, the application runs on the owner's computer, and the remote user can see the application window and use the commands of the application and thus, for a small part, control the other user's computer. The users have to take turns in using the cursor. The save command naturally saves the file on the owner's computer, and the only way for the remote user to get the file is by file transfer. The applications also had a shared whiteboard, where both users could work simultaneously and save their common work independently. With these two functionalities, the users had several difficulties:

Users had difficulties on saving their files after an application-sharing task. Owners of the application successfully saved files on their hard disk but the remote users expected themselves to be saving the file on their own hard disk with the save command. Also, almost nobody understood clearly the data security risks in application sharing: if the other person is allowed to edit files on the other's computer, she may also be doing some harm. This problem could be described as failing to understand the location and also technical functioning of the shared workspace.

The users who had an application-sharing task before a Whiteboard task had expected Whiteboard to work like application sharing and they started taking turns in drawing. The other way round, a similar phenomenon occurred, but it was very soon clear for the users, that there was only one cursor and that they had to start taking turns. Here the first experience clearly influenced the way the users understood the second, quite similar functionality — the differences between the shared workspaces provided by the whiteboard and application sharing were not pointed out clearly.

Picturetel users did not understand what detaching in application sharing means. The detach function can be used when a shared application has been opened and the remote user wants to do some work on other areas of the desktop than on the shared application. The users did not understand that they have to detach in order to do something else in their desktop when a shared application was opened.

In NetMeeting, in application sharing, the owner of the application had difficulties in understanding whether the remote user is able to see the same than she after sharing the application. The owner thought that after sharing the application the remote user is able to see everything the owner sees for example the actual conferencing application window.

5 Conclusions

The usability tests revealed nine usability problems that could be attributed to false understanding of the functioning of the application. To be able to use the application correctly, the users needed to understand partly the system architecture level functioning of the application; relying solely on the user interface level information was not sufficient. Especially the exact nature, possibilities and restrictions of the shared workspace were in all cases difficult to understand.

In Section 3 it was suggested, that connections, locations and shared workspaces are part of the task model the user of a collaborative network application has. This means, before all, that the user expects to meet these concepts and is aware that they exist. When asked, all users were able to give some kind of an explanation of how the application worked. The models they gave included the concepts of locations, connections and shared workspaces. This could mean, that the concepts are not difficult for the user to understand — the challenge is to present them in a simple but correct way in the user interface.

The challenge in the design of user interfaces for network services for online collaboration is not to hide network aspects of the system. It is also not to make the user *aware* of the network, as the user already knows it exists. Instead, as long as little consistency exists between applications, the user expectations of how things work will vary a lot. The main difficulty is to identify the network aspects that should be presented for the user, and to design the presentation in a clear and consistent manner.

References

Argyris, C. (1991), "Teaching Smart People How To Learn", *Harvard Business Review* **69**(3), 99–109.

Carroll, J. M. & Olson, G. M. (1988), Mental Models in Human–Computer Interaction, *in* M. Helander (ed.), *Handbook of Human–Computer Interaction*, North-Holland, pp.45–66.

Clark, L. & Sasse, M. A. (1997), Conceptual Design Reconsidered — The Case of the Internet Session Directory Tool, *in* H. Thimbleby, B. O'Conaill & P. Thomas (eds.), *People and Computers XII (Proceedings of HCI'97)*, Springer-Verlag, pp.12–5.

Dieberger, A. & Frank, A. U. (1998), "A City Metaphor to Support Navigation in Complex Information Spaces", *Journal of Visual Languages and Computing* **9**(6), 587–622.

Fussell, S. R. & Benimoff, N. (1995), "Social and Cognitive Processes in Interpersonal Communication: Implications for Advanced Telecommunications Technologies", *Human Factors* **37**(2), 228–50.

Kies, J. K., Williges, R. C. & Williges, B. H. (1997), Desktop Video Conferencing: A Systems Approach, *in* M. Helander, T. K. Landauer & P. Prabhu (eds.), *Handbook of Human–Computer Interaction*, second edition, North-Holland, pp.979–1002.

Neale, D. C. & Carroll, J. M. (1997), The Role of Metaphor in User Interface Design, *in* M. Helander, T. K. Landauer & P. Prabhu (eds.), *Handbook of Human–Computer Interaction*, second edition, North-Holland, pp.441–62.

Nielsen, J. (1993), *Usability Engineering*, Academic Press.

Norman, D. A. (1983), Some Observations on Mental Models, *in* D. Gentner & A. L. Stevens (eds.), *Mental Models*, Lawrence Erlbaum Associates, pp.7–14.

Norman, D. A. (1986), Cognitive Engineering, *in* D. A. Norman & S. W. Draper (eds.), *User Centered System Design: New Perspectives on Human–Computer Interaction*, Lawrence Erlbaum Associates, pp.31–62.

Olson, G. M. & Olson, J. (1997), Research on Computer Supported Co-Operative Work, *in* M. Helander, T. K. Landauer & P. Prabhu (eds.), *Handbook of Human–Computer Interaction*, second edition, North-Holland, pp.1433–56.

Payne, S. J. (1992), On Mental Models and Cognitive Artefacts, *in* Y. Rogers, A. Rutherford & P. Bibby (eds.), *Models in Mind: Theory, Perspective and Applications*, Academic Press, pp.103–18.

Payne, S. J., Squibb, H. & Howes, A. (1991), "The Nature of Device Models: The Yoked State Space Hypothesis and some Experiments with Text Editors", *Human–Computer Interaction* **5**, 415–44.

Ranta-aho, M. (1997), The WWW Surfing Metaphor — Harmful for the Novice User, *in* K. Nordby (ed.), *Proceedings of the 16th International Symposium of Human Factors in Telecommunications '97*, Loeren Grafisk A/S, pp.443–50.

Rumelhart, D. E. & Norman, D. A. (1978), Accretion, Tuning, and Restructuring: Three Modes of Learning, *in* J. W. Cotton & R. L. Klatsky (eds.), *Semantic Factors in Cognition*, Lawrence Erlbaum Associates.

Sasse, M. A. (1996), Eliciting and Describing User's Models of Computer Systems, PhD thesis, School of Computer Science, The University of Birmingham.

Shneiderman, B. (1998), *Designing the User Interface: Strategies for Effective Human–Computer Interaction*, third edition, Addison–Wesley.

Informing the Design of an Online Financial Advice System

Elizabeth Longmate, Paula Lynch[†]& Chris Baber

Educational Technology Research Group, School of Electronic and Electrical Engineering, University of Birmingham, Edgbaston, Birmingham B15 2TT, UK

Tel: *+44 121 414 4795*
EMail: *e.longmate@bham.ac.uk*

Electronic delivery of financial products is a convenient method of providing consumers with information on, and access to, goods and services. This paper considers the specific area of online financial advice and how, through the application of stakeholder requirements and design recommendations criteria, a 'personalised' approach can be developed. This paper identifies the requirements of two groups of stakeholder (potential end-users and financial advisers) to inform the design of an online advice system. Interviews with financial advisers identified the interaction process with clients. This was supported by a series of discussion groups involving potential users to identify and understand user experiences and attitudes towards advisers, the Internet and online advice. The data gathered formed the basis of a set requirements used to develop a concept interface to an online financial advice system.

Keywords: online advice, discussion groups, requirements gathering, scenarios.

1 Introduction

There has been a proliferation of Web sites offering the visitor personalised advice on a myriad of topics from finance to health to hairdressing and cookery; see for example the following Web sites[*]:

[†]NCR Knowledge Lab
[*]All URLs quoted in this paper were known to refer to valid Web pages on 2000.05.09.

Interactive Investor: http://www.iii.co.uk/
Ask Alice: http://www.columbia.edu/cu/healthwise/alice.html
Betty Crocker: http://www.bettycrocker.com/
Vidal Sassoon: http://www.vsassoon.com/consultation/

This study looks at the potential of an online financial advice system that it capable of dispensing comprehensive, intelligent advice (i.e. a recommendation regarding a decision or course of action) via the World Wide Web. The aims of the study are to understand the key stakeholder requirements, and to develop design recommendations and concepts for such a system. This paper will begin by outlining the trends that are reshaping consumer requirements for online financial advice, as well as exploring traditional face-to-face methods.

1.1   E-commerce and the Move to Online Advice

A key area in the rapid growth of e-commerce is in the financial and insurance services sector. The move to develop online financial advice is inspired by two key factors. 27% of British adults, for example, now use the Internet at least once a month (see http://www.nielsenmedia.com/interactive/). There is also an increasing use of the Internet as a tool for browsing and comparing the prices of goods and services (reported on the same Nielsen Media Web pages). Browsing is already common for computer software and hardware products, but it is on the increase for banking and financial services, investments and insurance sectors (GVU, 1998). A recently commissioned Mori poll (see http://www.mori.com/) showed that 3.1m people now use the Net to manage their personal finances. This represents nearly a third of the people currently estimated to be online in Britain. The driving force behind the move to online advice is the changing patterns of financial management. Social and economic changes have also altered the way people value their time and money. With people spending longer hours than ever before working, they place a higher premium on their leisure time. As such they are likely to be receptive to the notion of time saving products and services. The drive for change comes from increased consumer sophistication and increased competition between financial service providers. Consumers are more demanding in the services and products they expect from their financial provider. In addition, the reduced level of job security and the expectation of no or little state pension provision in the future have led to increased concern over personal financial planning. E-commerce, therefore, is an attractive proposition as it offers both convenience and the ability to customise products and services on a large scale, (Kalakota & Frei, 1998).

There are currently several different sources of financial information and advice available online. The Motley Fool UK Web site (http://www.fool.co.uk/) for example, offers general advice and discussion about financial issues. The Wells Fargo Web site (http://www.wellsfargo.com/) has a series of financial planners allowing customers to calculate mortgage repayments and pension provision projection. Personal money management software such as Quicken (see http://software.quicken.com.au/products/personal.htm) or Microsoft Money (see http://www.microsoft.com/money/) also claim to incorporate an 'adviser'. This warns users if they are approaching a budget limit or minimum balance.

There are a number of interactive online financial advice services. The Interactive Investor Web site (http://www.iii.co.uk/) is an online financial information provider giving up to date news on products and developments within the industry. In addition, once registered on their site, the user can email a query to a panel of independent financial advisers. A reply is issued within 24 hours containing general advice with a request for more detailed personal information in order to make a more appropriate recommendation. The Royal Bank of Canada Web site (http://www.royalbank.com/retirement/quizzes/irpq/irpq.html) tries to make the interaction with the customer a little more personalised by inviting them to fill in an investor risk profile quiz. This includes multiple choice statements such as "If the market experienced a sudden downturn my first reaction would be to ...". The output is an investor profile aimed to help the customer pinpoint the type of investment suitable for them. However, Internet users want *personalised* advice. They are more likely to request personalised content on financial and business news compared with news, shopping and health (see the Nua Internet surveys at http://www.nua.ie/surveys/index.cgi?f=vs&art_id=905355505&rel=true).

1.2   Establishing Current Trends in Financial Management

Financial advice encompasses a wide range of services and information, from skimming through a leaflet in the bank to having a comprehensive financial review with a financial adviser. The adviser experience is also multi-faceted. A meeting will differ depending on the issues discussed, who called the meeting and its location. Traditionally, the advice process is carried out in a face-to-face situation either at the adviser's office, bank branch or at the client's home. Advisers are either independent in which case they are free to recommend and give advice on any product or they are tied to a particular company and can only sell and promote their products. It is important to try and establish the ways in which people currently manage and think about their financial affairs and to understand where the adviser fits into that scheme.

In terms of attitudes towards and usage of financial advisers at the moment, a survey carried out by Loughborough University for NCR Knowledge Lab (see http://www.knowledgelab.ncr.com/) provides some interesting findings, (Howcroft et al., 1999). The key findings from this work were that consumers rely upon financial advisers when selecting more complex financial products where the consumer's knowledge is relatively low and their uncertainty high, i.e. investment products, credit based products (mortgages and personal loans) and insurance. Respondents generally acted upon the advice when it concerned credit based products rather than investment or current account products. The importance of being able to see the adviser was dependent on the type of product. Whilst motor or house insurance were typically bought over the telephone, purchasing life assurance tends to be carried out during a face-to-face interaction. The perceived significance of independent financial advisers was high with respondents suggesting they would consider using their services in the future. The survey also highlighted the importance of a personal recommendation when choosing a financial adviser, and the development of a good relationship.

1.3   Aims and Objectives

The aim of this study is to produce a set of design guidelines based on requirements gathered from the two stakeholder groups: 1. financial advisers; and 2. potential users. A design concept for an online financial system based on these guidelines will indicate an understanding of:

- The knowledge and information required by financial advisers to make recommendations and give advice. Also the way they interact with the client in order to reach decisions.

- The requirements of the user, and how the user views and understands the current interaction process.

- User reaction and opinion to the concept of online or computer based financial advice.

2   Documenting and Describing the Financial Advice Process

This part of the work focused on two qualitative sessions. Firstly, interviews with financial advisers and secondly, a series of discussion groups with consumers.

2.1   Method for Interviews With Financial Advisers

Due to the limited access available to financial advisers, a data accumulation approach was taken to documenting the financial advice process. Five financial advisers were interviewed with the aim of generating a normative description of the financial advice process. To this end, the first adviser was interviewed using a semi-structured interviewing technique. This is an adapted form of the critical decision method, (CDM). This asks questions, or probes, around a specifically recalled incident, (Klein et al., 1989). The probes related to the adviser's goals, options and to analogous situations, for example, 'did the situation remind you of a similar set of circumstances?' The description of the process was drawn up in a flowchart and was then shown to the second adviser for modification. This iterative development process continued with the remaining advisers

2.1.1   Participants

Five financial advisers were interviewed. One was independent, one was currently a financial advice trainer and the other three were tied advisers. Of the tied advisers, two had more than three years experience and one was newly qualified.

2.1.2   Procedure

The participants were given a brief introduction to the nature of the discussion and assured that their comments would only be presented as general points. The advisers were told that the aim of the interview was to help the development of a flowchart, which described the advice process. They were then introduced to the CDM methodology. The CDM comprised of two main sections:

- Advisers were asked to recall an incident in which they gave financial advice. By focusing on a particular event, the aim is to elicit thoughtful information rather than encouraging them to reveal the textbook or standard approach to making a decision and a recommendation. The adviser's recollection was not limited by any intervention except for any minor points of clarification. This process creates a context for understanding for the interviewer and assists recall on the part of the interviewees, (Klein et al., 1989).

• Having recalled the incident and presented the information, a variety of probes were used to elicit factors involved in making decisions and giving advice. Initial pilot studies led to the revision of the probes to ensure that the final set were appropriate and not misunderstood. All the sessions were taped and transcribed.

2.1.3 Analysis and Results

The flowchart (Figure 1) produced provides a normative description of the financial advice process. The tasks outlined in bold indicate that the customer is present during this stage. The flowchart represents the collective opinion of all the financial advisers. It also highlights the importance of enabling the client to think about motivations and priorities. These are referred to as the 'soft facts'. Discussion is an important part of the process and both soft and hard, financial, facts have to be elicited in a careful order.

The interviews were transcribed and analysed using content analysis. Four key themes emerged from the interviews, giving examples by 'painting pictures', 'moving the goal posts', extracting information and trust.

Painting pictures: The advisers used a wide range of techniques in order to elicit the information necessary to make decisions, offer advice and give appropriate recommendations. In addition to gathering the hard facts and figures about a client's financial circumstances through a 'fact find' questionnaire they established 'soft facts', relating to attitudes, concerns and real motivations. The data allowed the adviser to identify the key needs of the customer and assists the customer in recognising these needs as well.

> " In terms of how do you find out more information it is purely in terms of questioning not about facts and figures but asking them what interests them. We try to show the customer how in the event of x happening how their personal lifestyle would be affected and how it is possible for that still to be protected going forward." (Male, experienced adviser)

Soft issues are sometimes difficult to establish. Advisers found that presenting 'what if' scenarios and painting pictures was helpful if the client was having difficulty understanding a concept. Scenarios served two purposes. Firstly, creating an almost disturbing image in order to get the client thinking about relevant areas of financial planning; and secondly, by painting positive pictures in order to motivate and move the customer towards the selling point. There also appears to be *example* story telling as found in advertising in which a client identifies with the description of another client's circumstances. Direct questioning still seems to be a major part of the process and one that cannot be avoided if all the facts are to emerge.

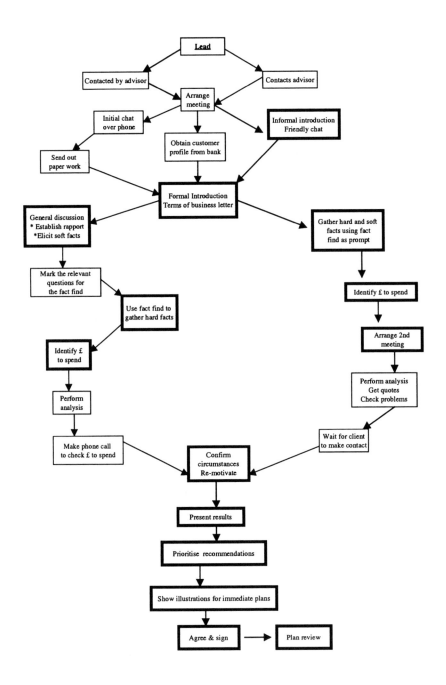

Figure 1: Flowchart describing the financial advice process.

Moving the goal posts: All the advisers acknowledged that the clients' goals changed and shifted during the course of the meetings. This was usually because the client approaches the meeting with just one need or goal in mind and has not considered the 'knock on effects' of their goal. The advisers will start with the client's most important goal, but then illustrate its dependency on many other factors. Advisers also suggested that clients are often unsure of an appropriate focus or set of priorities in their situation.

Extracting information: The advisers identified that a key skill is knowing how to elicit all the relevant information from the client. Whilst the advisers could not think of many times when clients had purposely not told them the full facts, there were occasions when it did not seem obvious to disclose certain information. The advisers reiterated the point that it was difficult to make recommendations when all the relevant underlying attitudes and aspirations had not been disclosed. Advisers often had to adapt their behaviour or change their language in response to customer's body language or needs.

Trust: A key factor in establishing the desired, long-term relationship was to develop a rapport with the clients. Many of the advisers spoke of having informal discussions with the clients and maintaining a chatty atmosphere. The advisers suggested that the tone of the interaction was very important. Whilst it was appropriate to be as relaxed as possible about financial matters with some clients, others may require a more businesslike approach to the subject. Most of the advisers found that with the relaxed atmosphere comes trust. Although some clients liked to see full and detailed explanations of the recommendations, many trusted the adviser and agreed with their recommendations immediately.

Overall, several important themes emerged from these interviews. Firstly, the adviser does not follow a rigid procedure but takes his, or her, cue from the natural flow of the conversation and explores topics and directions taken by the client. This is shown in the flowchart, Figure 1. Secondly, that "soft facts sell the products". Eliciting the client's attitudes and preferences is vital if appropriate advice is to be given. Targeting these attitudes and concerns also motivates the client to take the advice and think about the 'bigger picture'.

2.2 Method for Eliciting Consumer Opinion

Discussion groups are a way of capturing a wide, representative sample of opinion. Focus groups are discussion-based interviews, which thrive on the group dynamics. An issue raised by one participant may stimulate ideas from others, (Jordan, 1998). The aim of running the groups was threefold:

- To understand the process in which consumers get or would like to get financial advice.

- To get a better understanding of the issues associated with using the Internet for obtaining advice and then more specifically financial information.

- To identify the key consumer issues associated with the design of future online financial advice systems. The discussion groups also provided an opportunity to present the participants with different scenarios of obtaining financial advice. Usage scenarios can be used to help express more clearly functionality and to concretise user requirements, (Mack, 1995; Carroll, 1995).

2.2.1   Participants

The participants (21 Male, 24 Female) were recruited through an agency according to several screening criteria. All participants were in paid employment, were in socio-economic groups B or C1 and used the Internet at least once a fortnight. A $2 \times 2 \times 2$ design structure was used. Two age conditions, 25–35 and 45–55, gender and two experience conditions, those who had seen an adviser in the last 12 months and those who had not. An extra group containing people who had never seen an adviser group was also included. A total of ten groups (1 pilot and 9 test groups) were run as single sex groups with 3–6 members per group. All discussions were video taped and then transcribed.

2.2.2   Procedure

The following key areas were discussed:

- Sources of financial advice and information.

- Experience and attitude towards financial advisers.

- Reasons for not visiting a financial adviser.

- Ideal financial advice.

- Experience and attitude towards the Internet.

- Online advice.

2.2.3   Scenarios

The moderator showed the group three scenarios, presented as storyboards, describing different ways of obtaining financial advice:

Face to face: This described the traditional face-to-face meeting with an adviser.

Emailing a query: This scenario showed a person emailing a query to a panel of financial experts.

Future online financial advice system: This scenario outlined the idea of an online adviser.

The moderator described each scenario in turn. Participants were asked to describe what was good and bad about the three different ways of getting financial advice and to discuss what features would be important in an online financial advice system.

2.2.4 Results

The sessions were analysed using content analysis. Some general points and themes emerged from the discussions as well as opinions and ideas relating to the three scenarios.

The discussions revealed a great deal about participants attitudes and experiences towards their finances.

In general, finance was regarded as a dull but necessary topic. The participants thought the process of gaining financial advice should be made less stressful. Whilst some people kept a close eye on their finances, others turned their attention to the issue when the need arose. The need can be related to a specific milestone such as turning thirty or to a change in circumstances, i.e. divorce:

> "You tend to look at things when they directly affect you" (Female, 25–35, has not seen adviser)

Sources of financial advice and information: All the groups made use of a variety of information sources regarding their finances. Newspapers, the television and radio were mentioned. Some people relied upon their friends and family for advice whilst others had built up a close relationship with their accountant in preference to a financial adviser.

Experience and attitude towards financial advisers: All the groups had a generally negative perception of financial advisers and gaining financial advice. The process was confusing, long-winded and pressurised. Actual experiences with financial advisers seemed to be polarised. A *good* experience would be relaxed, informative and would leave customers feeling positive about resolving their finances. A *bad* experience in which things were rushed and pressurised left the customer feeling confused and angry.

Reasons for not visiting a financial adviser: Several reasons were highlighted. One of the main ones was lack of money and the assumption that an adviser would only want to see people who had a large sum of money. The younger groups in particular thought that the wide choice of services, products and providers available meant that given enough time it was possible to sort things out on their own. Finally, some people who had not visited an adviser were discouraged by the technicalities of the process and were concerned about being able to find a trustworthy adviser.

The ideal financial advice: The following factors were mentioned:

- Provides all information — the good and the bad points.
- Trustworthy.
- Quick and flexible.
- No pressure or time limits.
- Tailored to your needs in terms of aims and language.

The Internet: The Internet was regarded with enthusiasm. The speed, convenience and the ability to make comparisons were mentioned as favourable features. The older groups were perhaps more enthusiastic towards the Internet but at the same time felt a little worried about the technology. There were mixed concerns over disclosure of personal information and credit card details. Positive experiences helped allay some of the fears over credit card fraud and not having to give name and address made disclosure more acceptable:

> "I think it's sort of toe in the water job. Try it once and get something, see how successful that is and then build your confidence." (Male, 45–55, not seen an adviser)

Online advice: The Internet was thought to be a very good source of information, the group however were not sure that it was possible to obtain specific advice online, i.e. advice tailored to specific needs and requests. Whether or not people were comfortable with the concept of online financial advice depended to some degree on the type of product and the amount of money involved.

2.2.5 Attitudes Towards the Scenarios

The *face-to-face scenario* (see Section 2.2.3 for details) was still thought to offer several positive features. The opportunity for detailed discussion was highlighted, and participants felt it was more appropriate when large amounts of money were concerned. However, this scenario offers the user little control of timing and location of the advice sessions.

The *emailing a query to an expert scenario* was convenient and could be used at the user's own pace but the male groups in particular thought that the three to four day wait for a response was not acceptable.

A *future online financial system* was thought to be a possibility by the groups. Consumers would want such a system to provide an immediate response, be convenient and to help them prepare before visiting a real adviser. The males, predominantly expressed fears over disclosure of personal details online and the groups were concerned that the system would not be able to describe all the possible issues surrounding their finances.

3 Discussion

Most commerce in the real world depends on relationships between people (see http://www.communities.com/company/papers/commerce_n_society/commerce_society.html). One aim of this study was to examine social issues in the financial adviser experience and how these would compare with an online system. Several important factors emerged from the discussion groups and are discussed below.

3.1 Trust

Trust develops over time and is often the result of one or more positive and reinforcing experiences. An absence of pressure was mentioned as a key factor in the development of trust as was having a transparent system, i.e. one that pointed out both the good and the bad points. Trust is also enhanced when a tailored service is provided rather than a general service based on preconceptions.

As an online financial system would be dealing with personal and private information, the issue of trust in terms of security and privacy is likely to play a key role in the acceptance of any such system. A study by Cranor et al. (1999) examined the nature of the concerns regarding privacy on the Internet. Using an online survey revealed that Internet users are more likely to provide information when they are not identified. Given a scenario concerning a banking Web site, over a half of respondents said they would provide information about their income, investments and investment goals in order to receive customised investment advice. Whilst just over a third said they would also supply their name and address to receive an investment guide booklet by mail. The survey found three other criteria which, in common with the GVU (1998) survey, emerged as highly important factors in terms of deciding whether or not to disclose. These were:

- Whether information is used in an identifiable way.

- The kind of information collected.

- The purpose for which the information is collected.

3.2   *Disclosure*

Although participants expected to have to disclose personal details they did not always find it an easy task. There was a gender split in terms of attitudes towards disclosing online. This finding matches a study by Weisband & Kiesler (1996). These researchers showed that computer administration of questionnaires led to an increase in self-disclosure in comparison with face-to-face interviews. They also found that females disclose more than males, (Weisband & Kiesler, 1996; Foubert & Sholley, 1996). Interestingly the Weisband & Kiesler (1996) study noted that the size of the effect had decreased in recent years as a result of increased public knowledge of computers and improvements in graphical user interfaces (GUIs). Computer interfaces are now capable of having the 'look and feel' of a paper questionnaire or form. These changes may have increased respondents' sense of the computer interaction as an evaluation or test situation and consequently reduced their self-disclosure.

A study by UIE (see http://www.uie.com/) found that people tended to want to purchase products and services following a familiar set of conventions when buying online, as when in a traditional sales situation. The order in which personal information is disclosed is important. In a physical shop, the sales script allows the shopper to browse, examine and check prices without disclosing personal information. It is only after the customer has decided to buy an item do they have to reveal personal information in the form of name and credit card details. When the sales script is violated and the Web site demands personal details before allowing access to the information, customers often feel uncomfortable and are driven away from the site.

3.3   *Control*

Participants wanted to feel more in control of the financial advice process. They saw the use of the Internet as a means of achieving this control. A few people saw it as an opportunity to remove the 'real' adviser altogether whereas for others, in particular the women, it meant having more control over their knowledge and feeling better prepared for meetings with 'real' financial advisers:

> " I think also my worry was from the first time was, will he laugh at me? At the small amount I'm talking about?" (Female, 45–55, has seen an adviser)

3.4   Independent vs. Branded

People wanted to receive independent advice. They liked the idea of having a wide range of products to choose from and disliked the idea of a tied adviser. However, this was offset against the need for any Web site offering online advice to be run by a well-known name. Branding is very important in terms of trust and disclosure.

3.5   Real Contact

The option to contact a real adviser was seen as a useful addition to the online system. Very few of the participants thought that such a system could or would be used in isolation. Its use would compliment the face-to-face process. A computer-based system would lack social context information such as tone of voice, eye contact, nods or smiles, (Kiesler et al., 1984; Sproull & Kiesler, 1991). Being able to establish contact and therefore trust with a real adviser was another important factor.

3.6   Convenience

Participants thought the Internet would be more convenient in terms of choosing when and where to receive financial advice and information could be studied and digested carefully, rather than having everything crammed into a short period of time. (Some of the participants could only manage to see an adviser during their lunch hour).

3.7   Interrelated Themes

The themes are highly interrelated. Real contact, disclosure and brand, for example, have an affect on trust. The variables within the groups (gender, good or bad experience, sophistication and confidence) also have an effect upon the themes. Gender has an effect upon disclosure, whereas the level of confidence and sophistication as regards financial issues affects control.

3.8   Design Recommendations and Concepts

The design recommendations are made on the basis of stakeholder requirements. The design should:

- Allow the collection of hard and soft facts.

- Allow the user to explore possibilities and to try out different scenarios.

- Should provide explanations and recommendations with 'why'.

- Should not violate the sales script by forcing the user to give too much personal at the beginning of the process.

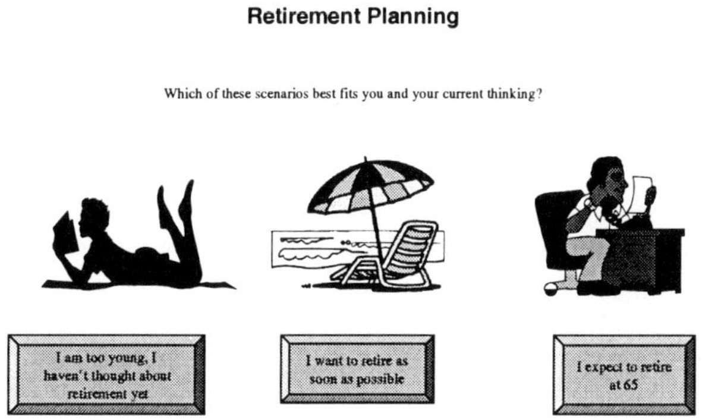

Retirement Planning

Which of these scenarios best fits you and your current thinking?

I am too young, I haven't thought about retirement yet

I want to retire as soon as possible

I expect to retire at 65

Figure 2: Visual concept illustrating the design recommendations.

- Be easy to use and employ clear and simple language.

The design recommendations were then translated into a visual concept (see Figure 2). This idea represents the requirements of the stakeholders and illustrates how an implementation of these requirements might appear.

The concept makes use of scenario inclusion (Carroll, 1995). It attempts to communicate complex issues to users through the uses of scenarios and narratives. This approach has been shown to be effective in facilitating communication about system features between stakeholders (Cooper et al., 1999). The design concept might include a combination of direct questioning, scenarios, examples and self-recognition. The user, for example, might consider a variety of 'what if' scenarios, exploring possibilities and identifying and associating with different examples of the clients presented on the computer. Users could alter the scenarios to match their own details and in this way, both the hard and soft facts could be collected.

4 Conclusion

Currently those interested in using the Internet to sort out their finances are more likely to access intermediary Web sites offering information and comparative quotes for financial services companies rather than buying financial services direct from a provider such as the banks (Emmett, 1999). Taking this approach to sorting out one's financial affairs is however far from easy; it involves a lot of Web browsing and the inputting of duplicate information. Any future online financial advice system needs to be intelligent and comprehensive. Importantly, an online financial system will be intended to complement but not substitute, face-to-face communication between customers and financial advisers.

The design of the interface will have a great effect upon the tone, appeal and the usability of the system. The discussion groups revealed the desire for personalisation in financial advice but also the differences between people's personal tastes and attitudes. This view was also expressed during the user evaluations. Some users thought that a light-hearted tone of the system would not appeal to those who wanted to take the whole process very seriously. The issue of customising the interface in order to reflect user tastes is an issue, which requires further attention. Future work might also focus on engaging the thoughts and requirements of the third stakeholder group, i.e. the financial institutions. This is in terms of incorporating requirements for regulatory bodies, choices and independent advice.

In terms of whether a system like this would be accepted and used, most people thought they would be happy and willing to try an online financial adviser. There appear to be a number of potential uses for the system. As an addition to current resources it would also lead to more productive meetings with the financial adviser. The system may help prepare users for what to expect from an adviser meeting, and perhaps alleviate the problem of not feeling eligible. It may be used by those lacking the free time to see an adviser or as a way of gaining extra knowledge or getting a clear life stage overview. The design will also affect the important factor of the system's trustworthiness. Although trust is affected by personal variables such as level of sophistication and confidence, factors such as the amount of real contact available and branding also play a role.

This project has taken a scenario-based approach to the implementation of stakeholder requirements, rather than concentrating on more traditional aspects of HCI and interface design. In this way, the requirements of the advisers and the potential users of an online financial system have been implemented through a scenario based design concept instead of the more typical online form. The acceptability of the concept may also have implications for the design of other Web-based systems dealing with the disclosure of personal information.

Acknowledgements

This work forms part of an MSc sponsored project. I am grateful to everyone at NCR Knowledge Lab for the advice and assistance I received during the project, and to Alex Gibb for his useful comments on earlier drafts.

References

Carroll, J. M. (1995), Introduction: The Scenario Perspective on System Development, *in* J. M. Carroll (ed.), *Scenario-Based Design: Envisioning Work and Technology in System Development*, John Wiley & Sons, pp.1–17.

Cooper, L., Williams, D. & Baber, C. (1999), A User Centred Deployment Methodology, *in* D. Harris (ed.), *Engineering Psychology and Cognitive Ergonomics*, Ashgate, pp.313–27.

Cranor, L. F., Reagle, J. & Ackerman, M. S. (1999), Beyond concern: Understanding Net Users' Attitudes About Online Privacy, Technical Report, AT & T Labs-research. http://www.research.att.com/library/trs/TRs/99/99.4/99.4/, last accessed 2000.05.31.

Emmett, S. (1999), "Interface. Banking on an Online Service.", *The Times*. 1999.08.11.

Foubert, J. D. & Sholley, B. K. (1996), "Effects of Gender, Gender Role and Individualised Trust on Self-Disclosure", *Journal of Social Behaviour and Personality* **11**(5), 277–88.

GVU (1998), GVU's 10th WWW User Survey, Technical Report, Georgia Tech Graphics, Visualization & Usability Center. http://www.gvu.gatech.edu/user_surveys/, last accessed 2000.05.31.

Howcroft, B., Hewer, P., Hamilton, R. & Beckett, A. (1999), Consumer Behaviour and the Corporate Strategies of Financial Institutions, Technical Report, Loughborough University Banking Centre.

Jordan, P. W. (1998), *An Introduction to Usability*, Taylor & Francis.

Kalakota, R. & Frei, F. (1998), Frontiers of Online Financial Services, *in* M. J. Cronin (ed.), *Banking and Finance on the Internet*, John Wiley & Sons, pp.19–75.

Kiesler, S., Siegel, J. & McGuire, T. (1984), "Social Psychological Aspects of Computer-mediated Communication", *The American Psychologist* **39**(10), 1123–34.

Klein, G. A., Calderwood, R. & Macgregor, D. (1989), "Critical Decision Method for Eliciting Knowledge", *IEEE Transactions in Systems, Man and Cybernetics* **19**(3), 462–72.

Mack, R. L. (1995), Discussion: Scenarios as Engines of Design, *in* J. M. Carroll (ed.), *Scenario-Based Design: Envisioning Work and Technology in System Development*, John Wiley & Sons, pp.361–86.

Sproull, L. & Kiesler, S. (1991), *Connections: New ways of Working in the Networked Organisation*, MIT Press.

Weisband, S. & Kiesler, S. (1996), Self-disclosure on Computer Forms: Meta-analysis and Implications, *in* M. Tauber, V. Bellotti, R. Jeffries, J. D. Mackinlay & J. Nielsen (eds.), *Companion Proceedings of CHI'96: Human Factors in Computing Systems (CHI'96 Conference Companion)*, ACM Press, pp.3–10.

Introducing Internet Terminals to the Home: Interaction Between Social, Physical, and Technological Spaces

Wai On Lee

Microsoft Corporation, One Microsoft Way, Redmond, WA 98052–6399, USA

EMail: *waionl@microsoft.com*

A field study was carried to examine the effects of introducing Internet terminals to the home. The results showed that the acceptance of an Internet terminal such as the WebTV set-top box is dependent on existing technologies, the availability and use of spaces in the home, the social structure and dynamics within the home, and the nature of information and communication needs within the home and with the community outside. The results are interpreted using Venkatesh & Mazumdar's framework in which the home is conceptualised as three interrelated spaces: social, technological, and physical. Analysis of the findings showed how the new technology changes the dynamics and the relationships in and between these spaces and how the home in turn reconstructs itself as part of the process of appropriation. I conclude by drawing out design implications for Internet terminals in the context of the home.

Keywords: internet terminals, field study, home, co-usage.

1 Introduction

With the advent of set-top boxes that provide Internet access via the television, the convergence of television and computer is increasingly becoming a reality (Mountford, 1992; Markoff, 1994; Rose, 1996). These devices effectively turn the television into low cost 'Internet terminals' that allow users to browse the World Wide Web and send/receive electronic mail from the comfort of their living room.

To understand the effects of these devices and the factors that influence their success, a number of ethnographic and in-home field studies have been carried out over the past three years. In this paper, I report on one of these studies. The purpose of the study was to examine the effect of these devices in the initial stages of uptake in the home.

Research of the home and home technologies provides valuable clues about possible effects of this type of technology and the factors that might influence its use. For example, studies of the use of the home PC revealed that teenagers often lead the rest of the family in the use of the Internet and that there was a need for providing more help for adults to get started with the use of the Internet on home PCs (Kraut et al., 1996).

Although Internet terminals essentially provide a subset of the functionality of the home PC, a number of important differences make further research on their impact on the home necessary. First, in contrast to the PC, the stripped down functionality and the specificity of Internet terminals may make them easier to get started and used. Second, the incorporation of these devices into the centre of a home raises interesting questions concerning how such devices might transform home activity and how they could be integrated into the lives of people in different home environments. Research of the home has emphasised the importance of the life-stage of the family, people's daily routines, and home spaces in determining the types of activities they are involved in as well as the coordination and management of activities in the home (O'Brien & Rodden, 1997; Venkatesh & Mazumdar, 1999).

In this field study, participants were given such a device (the WebTV Internet Terminal 1.0) and followed their first four weeks of usage. I was particularly interested in its effects on people in different home settings (e.g. different life-stages, family size) as well as people with different exposure to technology, particularly computer technology. The goals of this study were therefore to try and qualitatively understand how this type of technology could be integrated into the homes of people in different home settings and to understand what the results have to say about the design of the this type of technology.

2 Method

Ten homes with different profiles within 30 mile radius of Redmond, Washington, were recruited for the study. Each home was visited four times over a period of 6 weeks at the beginning of 1997:

Visit 1. The purpose of this visit was to establish participants' entertainment, information, and communication needs and habits. Ten homes were chosen from sixteen based on how closely they fitted our participant profile (e.g. whether they truly had no PC experience, whether they had children that might be able to use such a device) and their information and communication needs (e.g. did they have any interests or hobbies that might be supported by the Web?). However, since the emphasis of the study was towards providing a detailed qualitative understanding of the home rather than to make quantitative comparisons between groups, the selection of the participating homes was one that was biased towards variety rather than towards balanced contrasting groups. The homes chosen were six homes without any PC experience (two homes with singles living alone, two with families, and two with retired couples) and four homes with a home PC and Internet connection (one home with a single, one home with a young couple, and two with families with children). All the families were two parent families with 2–3 children between 6–14 years of age.

Visit 2. The chosen homes were notified and visited 2–3 weeks after the initial visit. In this visit, the data collection procedure was explained and the set up process videotaped. Participants were asked to install the device so that they could use their VCR to record their usage in the first week.

Visit 3. Participants were visited again after they had one week of experience with the device. The focus of this phase was to examine their initial learning experience.

Visit 4. After three more weeks of usage, participants were visited again to examine their experience with the device and the state of their knowledge of the device. After the visit, the device was offered to them for $100 (about 1/3 of the original price at the time). Those who decided to purchase the device were given the device for free.

The following data collection methods were used:

- In-depth semi-structured interviews in all 4 visits.

- Naturalistic observations in all 4 visits.

- Diaries from visit 2 onwards.

- Video recording on visits 1 and 2.

- VCR recording between visit 2 and visits 3.

- Questionnaires.

3 Findings

The results will be presented in order roughly matching the order of the visits. I first examine the installation of the device, users' learning, and usage of it before examining the effects of the use of the device on existing home technologies. Next, the results are examined using a theoretical framework for understanding technology integration within the home. Finally, I conclude by examining the implications of the results for the design of Internet terminals and their acceptance in the home.

3.1 Installation and Initial Learning

3.1.1 Existing Configuration of Home Technologies

The make up of the home and its existing technologies posed numerous problems for the installation of the device. I found that most TV cabinets and stands were already cluttered with electronic devices such as VCRs, game console, stereo equipment, and cable boxes. As a result, many participants had difficulty finding a suitable location for the WebTV device. The range of possible locations for the box was further restricted by the short video and audio cables provided. The positioning of the device away from the TV screen also caused subsequent problems since users typically pointed their input devices to the TV screen rather than to the receiver in the WebTV device.

3.1.2 The Home Environment

Since most homes did not have telephone sockets near TVs, there was a need to connect long telephone cords across doorways and rooms. In one home, the participant had to connect 3 cords (a total of 100 feet) before it was long enough to reach the telephone socket.

In some homes the telephone cord was left dangerously strewed across doorways. Having realised the danger of leaving a telephone cord on the floor (particularly with two young children around), the father of one home rewired the cord overhead to the ceiling fan before taping it to the frame of a light socket and down to the telephone socket (and thus posing potential dangers). Many of the homes only connected the device when they needed to use it and disconnected it when they finished.

3.1.3 Understanding Consumer Electronics

Only four out of ten homes were able to successfully install WebTV without assistance within the one-hour limit (these were one PC family, two non-PC families, and one non-PC single). The most common problem was that participants did not realise they had to switch their TV or VCR to an 'external input mode', and if they did realise this, had difficulty figuring out *how* to do it.

3.1.4 Learning from One Another and Learning in Isolation

In non-single homes, one member of the household would typically show others things that he/she had learned or found. In these homes, learning by watching others was also common. For example, the mother of a non-PC family reported that she would look over the father's shoulder when he was using the system to pick up anything that she hadn't discovered.

Participants thought the device was easy to learn and reported few problems in using the system. After a few minutes of exploration participants were able to use the remote control to move the yellow rectangular focus around the screen and enter into various links (see Figure 1). However, detailed interviews showed that some critical features in WebTV were not discovered and used (e.g. Call-waiting option, Send, Save). In homes where there was primarily a single user, the inability to discover some of the critical features was particularly noticeable. For example, one retiree had not been able to discover the use of Save (favourites) after four weeks of usage. Video recordings and subsequent interviews indicated that he had followed the procedure for saving a sample favourite without reading the text on the screen. As a result, this participant thought Favourites were something that the system provided.

4 WebTV Usage

The aggregate of usage from the ten sites over the four weeks as abstracted from their diaries is shown in Figure 2.

Figure 1: WebTV home page.

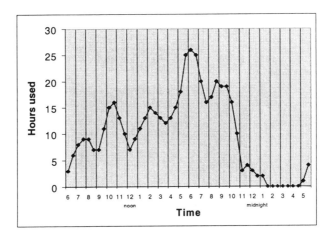

Figure 2: Aggregated usage in the first four weeks.

The most popular time for using WebTV was between 5.30 PM and 7 PM. The usage tapered off as the evening progressed so that by ten o'clock few users used it. The surprisingly high usage of WebTV in the late morning and early afternoon were probably due to the temporal patterns of the retirees and homemakers in this study. For example, the mother of a PC family would only start using the system after breakfast, when all the children had gone to school.

4.1 Web Usage

Participants in this study accessed a wide variety of Web sites due to the differences in their life-stage and interests. The most regular Web activities for the participants were: searching for information on personal or immediate interests (e.g. cancer, pop singer, travel, soccer); a couple browsed the Web looking for contractors to build their vacation home; the father of a PC family checking on stock prices; children browsing games and general children Web sites; parents reading news from on-line newspapers; browsing the Spotlight link of the day; a parent and a child browsing Web sites of countries and places for educational purposes.

Much of the access to these sites was via the 'Explore' feature (a Web page with links to a variety of interesting Web sites). The system's daily Web site suggestion 'Spotlight' on the Home page was also well liked by a number of the participants. In particular, one retiree checked it out daily and enjoyed reading the content a great deal. However, participants also complained that they didn't know where to find useful, interesting, or entertaining Web sites.

There were a number of reports of people within a household Web browsing together. For example, the parents of a non-PC family would guide one of their children through a Web site about Egypt or Ireland to teach them about that country. However, there were also reports of conflicts because of the need for individual use of the device. For example, the daughter and son of one non-PC family (ages 9 and 6, respectively) would argue as to who gets to use WebTV first. Families with teenage children also reported that Web browsing tended to be done in isolation because of the different interests of the family members (see examples).

4.2   Email Usage

Participants who were able to find people with whom they could regularly correspond with were able to incorporate the use of WebTV email into their lives. For example, one retiree emailed his golfing buddies to arrange to play golf; the mother of the PC family emailed friends back in the East Coast to maintain their relationship; one retiree emailed his son and granddaughters in Alaska.

In line with other studies of Internet usage of home PCs, for example Kraut et al. (1996), there was more email usage than Web browsing. Interviews of participants' routines and analysis of their diaries suggest that email was used on a regular basis and was engendering the development of routines in using the device.

Not all the participants were able to establish a regular email correspondence network during the study. For example, although one of the non-PC single had emailed a number companies and people (including some old friends), they did not continue to correspond on a regularly basis. As a result, the usage of the device decreased dramatically after the first week for this participant.

In addition, a number of participants have complained about the lack of privacy regarding their email usage because of the public nature of using the WebTV device. On the other hand, participants in other homes had reported enjoying using the system with other people. For example, the retirees would write letters to friends and families together.

5   Co-usage and Conflicts of Usage

Throughout the study, a number of participants pointed out that the facility for side-by-side co-usage was an important positive aspect of the device and that they highly treasured the instances where they were able to share their Internet experience with other people in the home. In this study, I found the following types of co-usage:

Show and tell. A person showing other(s) what he or she had found.

Turn taking. A group of people taking turns exploring a Web site. In the case of email, one person would write one part and another person would write another in a way that resembles the sharing of telephone conversations, see for example Frohlich et al. (1997).

Guide. A person helping other(s) through a Web site by helping them to resolve difficulties in it and suggesting possible actions to take within the site. In the case of email, guiding occurs when a person helps other(s) in the phrasing and spelling.

Surrogate. A person controls the input device by carrying out the actions for another person.

Joint. A group of people jointly deciding how to navigate within a Web site. In the case of email, two people or more might be jointly composing the mail, negotiating, and contributing to the content.

Unsurprisingly, the use of an Internet terminal in the heart of the home also created conflicts amongst its users. In this study, I found conflicts in:

Control. Two or more people compete for who gets to use the input devices to navigate the Web.

Content. Two or more people disagree on where they should navigate to in the Web.

Usage privacy. A person needing the quietness and solitude in using the system.

Visual privacy. A person may be concerned that what is displayed on the screen can be seen by others.

5.1 Home Life-stage and Users' Needs

An important factor that influenced the extent to which individual or co-usage was the life-stage of the family or members of the home. In the homes I visited, I found:

- Families at a stage where the children were acquiring independence and exploring outside the family unit, the time to use the Internet terminal alone was important because of their different interests.

- Families at a stage where children still involved the parents in many of their information gathering and communication activities, the Internet terminal facilitated the guiding environment they needed. This is not to say that conflicts did not occur for these participants, but their interests and home activities (partly as a result of the life-stage the family) were such that these instances were infrequent and easily resolved.

- For a couple in the beginning of their relationship and a couple of grandparents, the device facilitated the co-usage and added to their enjoyment of browsing the Web and doing email.

In the context of Web browsing, I saw a couple in the early stages of their relationship finding that going to the Web to look for their dream vacation home particularly rewarding. Elsewhere, a parent guiding a six year old through a Web site describing another part of the world by explaining the meaning of the text and pictures.

In the context of email, for families at the stage where children need help with their writing a parent would typically guide them. Parents would also suggest that they 'write together' (e.g. let's write a letter to grandma). The quality of their writing was in part supported by the guidance of parents. Such increase in children's capabilities due to support is well known in developmental research (Vygotsky, 1978). However, what is revealed here is that installation of the Internet terminal in this environment naturally lends itself to this type of activity.

6   The Bottom Line: Purchasing the WebTV Device

Eight out of ten homes were willing to pay the $100 to keep the WebTV device after four weeks of usage. Although this was a high percentage of acceptances, we should bear in mind that these ten sites have been pre-selected as sites that have the potential for 'needing' such a device in the first place.

The two homes that did not purchase the system were a PC family and a Non-PC single. For the PC family, they rationalised that they have a PC already and the fact that the WebTV was more limited than the PC in terms of functionality (at the time the limitations include: the lack of video playback, inability to download files, etc.). Similarly, the non-PC single commented that the limited nature of Web browsing on WebTV and the fact that he would like to buy a PC in the future to be the reasons for his decision. Interestingly, this was the same participant who was unable to establish a regular email corresponding network.

For the homes that decided to purchase the system, email was reported to be the primary reason for purchasing the system for non-PC participants. These participants felt that although the Web was interesting and useful, it was not 'indispensable'. In contrast, many participants felt that email had become entrenched in their lives that they could not do without it. In a subsequent email a few days after the study, one retiree wrote:

> "My decision to keep the Web system is based on the fact that I really like the system & all that it offers. It would probably be worth it simply because of the E-Mail capabilities. We love exchanging letters with our Grand-children & other family & friends. Plus the fact that this system is already in place. Also all the Web Sites that we can obtain information from. [...] To lose it now would probably put us into withdrawals of some kind."

For PC owners, the decision was primarily socially motivated rather than utilitarian. Although one PC family also cited that the device was easy to use for the entire family, the main reasons had little to do with system's features *per se* but on the consequence of having these features on the TV in the living room and being able to use the system with other household members. For example, the female of

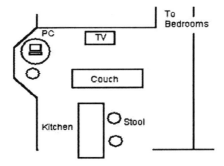

Figure 3: Partial floor plan of family A's home (WebTV device was on top of the TV).

the couple cited the fact that WebTV allowed them to use the system together as a major motivation factor in wanting to purchase the system.

7 Two Examples

To illustrate the interaction between different factors and the rich detail involved in the process of appropriation that ultimately leads to the acceptance or rejection of the WebTV device, I will briefly describe two of the homes studied. The two homes are comparable in terms of their make-up and provide interesting contrasts in their experience with the WebTV device.

7.0.1 Family A (Rejected the Device)

This family was a PC family with three children, ages 14, 12 and 10 who went to the same local school. The WebTV device was installed on the TV in the family room. This TV was rather small (about 15 inches) and old (about 10 years old) and consequently the display quality that resulted from the WebTV system was not ideal. Although there was another TV in the home, it was located in the parents' bedroom and was not used for watching TV by the parents except before bed and was generally perceived to be off-limits by the children. The effect of this was that when one person was using the WebTV, others could not watch TV and visa-versa.

The main activity area of the house can be conceptually divided into: PC usage, TV viewing, cooking, and eating (see Figure 3). Although the PC and TV were physically close together, they were conceptually separated. The activities that went on and the participating household members in these areas were also very different. PC usage tended to be private, where individuals of the family played games, did homework, surfed the Web, and emailed. In contrast, TV area was public, where they watched TV, read, relaxed, and played.

Although initially excited about the use of the WebTV device, after a week of usage, the mother of this family complained about the lack of privacy and difficulty in 'concentrating' because her children would be 'running about' around her. She also complained that the children would get in front of the TV when she was using the device. Further probing revealed that in this family, the TV/couch area was centre of activity for the children. The area between the TV and the couch was used as a general play area, typically when they weren't watching TV. As a result, the use of WebTV effectively took this area away from them and since there wasn't an equivalent area in the house, the children naturally played in the same areas or hung around their mother when she used the device.

This conflict of usage was not local to parent-children but was also present between the children. Although the children had used the WebTV device a number of times, it was mostly by themselves or with their own friends rather than with each other, and never with a parent; e.g. the 12 year old daughter had emailed her school friends a number of times gossiping about people at school but quickly stopped because the youngest would be reading what she was writing and reading. In this family, the children were at an age that they were acquiring independence and had their own interests that intensified the need for individual usage of the WebTV.

The mother of this family commented that after a few days of trying, she had resorted to using the WebTV device when the children had gone to school. However, this too did not last long because her email was still coming through to her PC. She remarked that most of their friends had "not been able to deal with two email addresses" and had continued to send email to their PC. As a result she continued to do email on the PC.

When the time came for deciding whether they wanted to keep the device for a nominal fee, they unanimously declined the offer with little hesitation.

7.0.2   Family B (Accepted the Device)

This family was a non-PC family with two children (ages 9 and 6) who were home schooled. This family had one TV, a relatively new (3 years old) and big TV (35″) in a room near the back of the house, away from the dining area (which was the main activity area of the house).

After a week of WebTV usage, the father had rearranged their TV area by moving an end-table in front of a comfy chair to create a 'mini workstation' to place all the remote controls required to use the WebTV device, to rest the keyboard whilst typing, and to place notes they needed for using the device.

Although initially skeptical about the usefulness of the device, particularly because they were thinking about getting a PC, the parents commented a number of times on how much they liked the product. In particular, they commented on the benefits of email and being able to guide their children in using the Web for educational purposes.

Even though they had never had an email account for the home (the father had just started to use email at work and the rest of the family had never used email prior to the study) they were able to establish a network of email correspondents relatively quickly; e.g. the father used the Web to search for this brother's email address in the East Coast and quite quickly started corresponding with him regularly. Most of the family's email correspondences were with friends and family members that the entire family knew.

It should be noted that the life-stage of the family was such that the children were dependent on a parent when using the device; e.g. the youngest needed help in typing and composing email. In addition, the family liked to do things together

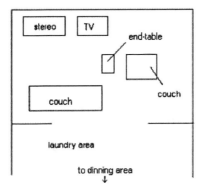

Figure 4: Partial floor plan of family B's home.

(in particular, the parents, a parent and a child). The public nature of the WebTV therefore lends itself to co-usage in this family; e.g. the parents co-wrote emails to friends in another part of the state. Typically, the father would type and the mother would add to the content, help to compose, pointing out spelling mistakes, and better phrasing. A parent would also guide a child surfing the Web as well as in composing emails. Conflicts still occurred in this family, e.g. the two children would sometimes quarrel as to who gets on the WebTV first. However, as part of the process of appropriation in this family, it was easily resolved by the establishment of rules (e.g. taking turns), and more importantly, the fact that one of the parent could be with the other child in the main activity area of the house (the dining area), away from the TV room where the WebTV was being used (see Figure 4).

The family enthusiastically took up the offer of purchasing the device even though they were on a modest income and were thinking of purchasing a PC.

7.1 The interaction Between Social, Physical, and Technological Spaces

The examples illustrated some of the factors that were influential in the introduction, use, and ultimately the acceptance of a new technology in the home. To try and understand these findings in a more systematic fashion, it is important to distinguish the social, physical, and technological spaces of the home and their reciprocal relationships with the new technology. Venkatesh & Mazumdar's (1999) theoretical conceptualisation of technologies in the home is a useful starting point for framing some of the issues pertinent in the findings. The framework conceptualises the home in terms of three interacting spaces:

Social: refers to the home social structure, home activities, life-stage of the family, social dynamics between and among family members.

Physical: refers to the spatial organisation of the home in terms of the physical divisions, whether conceptual or concrete, within the home.

Technological: refers to the configurations of home technologies, the use of these
  technologies.

As illustrated above, the social space of family A was such that family members
were old enough and had different interests that required individual use of the device.
This conflicted with the public nature of the device as embedded in the physical
and technological spaces of the home. The readily available PC in its relatively
private setting therefore provided a better alternative given the needs of this family.
The introduction of the device in an area that was normally perceived and used for
interaction with other members of the family caused conflict and competition for that
space, particularly because an alternative physical space for interaction didn't exist
in the home.

In contrast, the social space of family B was such that the public nature of the
device lends itself to co-usage activities that the family members desired. What was
a cause of conflict in the previous family was an important benefit in this family at
this stage of their lives. In addition, the family actively modified the physical space
and the technological space to accommodate for change to support the additional
activities of information seeking and external communication in a space that was
normally used for leisure and entertainment. In this process of appropriation, what
was an 'overloaded' space in the previous family became a 'multi-purpose' space or
a space that was more dedicated to the use of the WebTV device.

The ability to establish a email network as a result of relationships outside
the home was also found to be a major influence on the continue usage of the
device (e.g. the inability of a non-PC single to establish a email correspondence
network who subsequently rejected the device). Moreover, the nature of the social
relationships outside the home and their interaction with the social space within
the home also influenced *how* the device was required to be used. As shown in
family B, corresponding with family or friends that all the family knew and cared
about allowed the WebTV to serve the co-usage needs of this family well. In contrast,
as appropriated within family A, the daughter of the family who wanted to have
private email conversations with her school friends found the public nature of the
device and the prying eyes of her younger sister to be problematic. The extent of
the need for individual or co-usage was therefore determined not only by the internal
social, physical, and technological space, but also by the world in which these spaces
are embedded, in particular, the types of social relationships, the community and
social groups the household members belonged to, and how they interact with the
social space within the home.

8   Design Implications

Given the above analysis, I will briefly consider some of the near term implications
on how the design of Internet terminals can take advantage of this understanding:

Technological Space: To overcome the problems created as a result of embedding
  a new technology into existing technological space, future designs need deal
  with enabling the remote control receiver to be closer to the TV screen as well

as providing longer connection cables so that the device can be connected without major overhaul to the existing consumer electronics configuration.

There is also a need for supporting users' conceptual understanding of technologies as a result of the introduction of the Internet terminal. In this regard, alternative technologies that by-pass the need for such understanding might also be beneficial; e.g. Internet ready TVs and transmission via TV cable rather than telephone might mitigate some of the usability problems caused by the existing technological configuration and users' (lack of) understanding of them.

Finally, features that enable the smooth transfer from existing technology to new technology such as automated transfer of email from old email account to the new account, or the automated updating of email directory of the users' contacts would allow the new technology to be used without putting the burden of updating email addresses on email users.

Physical Space: As shown in the examples, the availability of physical spaces for displaced social activity is important to the uptake of an Internet terminal within the home. Users need to be guided in the deployment of this type of device to ensure that conflicts are minimised; e.g. providing suggestions in documentation for the most appropriate setting for the device given the particular needs of the home. Obviously, creating new physical spaces is difficult for most homes to do, manufacturers of such device therefore need to come to terms with the fact that this type of device may not be suited for all homes. Alternative types of Internet terminals, such as an Internet terminal with a dedicated monitor, portable Internet terminals, etc., may be more suitable for some home environments (e.g. an Internet terminal with a dedicated monitor may be more suitable for large families with frequent individual usage needs but only has one TV that is situated in an open-access area).

Social Space: In contrast to most work environments, where there may be official or non-official experts to ask for help, learning within some home environments can be a lonely activity. Setting up communities of WebTV users (which is now being constructed), in particular, WebTV users who might know one another may facilitate the learning of the system over time.

Designs of Internet terminals of this type also need to capture the opportunities for co-usage rather than designing them out. In the context of parent-child co-usage, rather than provide tools to help children writing on their own (e.g. by suggesting construction, content ideas, spelling and grammar checking, etc.), it may be more valuable to focus on creating opportunities for and support the process of co-usage, co-learning, and guided learning between a parent and a child; e.g. suggesting topics and concepts that might be too difficult to understand by the child, noting and storing spelling mistakes, grammar usage, that can be used as opportunities for teaching by the parents. In the past, this kind of design direction may have been avoided because of the private nature of the PC and the focus on work/productivity, but may now be worth exploring given the opportunities provided by new technologies of this type.

Finally, future designs need to keep in mind the larger social space in which the home is part of and that for many users the maintenance of relationships via email in the home may be the primary reason for using this type of device. Internet terminals for the home should therefore be designed for this purpose; e.g. providing a record of when a user last wrote to a person, when it was time to write again, who else they might need to write to as a result of writing to this person, etc. These kinds of personal information flow management are typically emphasised in studies of work, for example Winograd & Flores (1986), but may be just as important (if not more so) in the management and maintenance of relationships in life.

Acknowledgements

I would like to thank Nancy Bell and Alladi Venkatesh for discussions on the theoretical conceptualisation of the home. Thanks also to Cynthia Duval and Geoff Corso for their comments on an earlier version of the paper.

References

Frohlich, D. M., Chilton, K. & Drew, P. (1997), Remote Homeplace Communication: What is It Like and How Might We Support It, *in* H. Thimbleby, B. O'Conaill & P. Thomas (eds.), *People and Computers XII (Proceedings of HCI'97)*, Springer-Verlag, pp.133–53.

Kraut, R., Scherlis, W., Mukhopadhyay, T., Manning, J. & Kiesler, S. (1996), "The HomeNet Field Trial of Residential Internet Services", *Communications of the ACM* **39**(12), 55–65.

Markoff, J. (1994), "I Wonder What's on the PC Tonight", *The New York Times* **3**, 1. May 8th.

Mountford, S. J. (1992), When TVs are Computers are TVs, *in* P. Bauersfeld, J. Bennett & G. Lynch (eds.), *Proceedings of CHI'92: Human Factors in Computing Systems*, ACM Press, pp.227–30.

O'Brien, J. & Rodden, T. (1997), Interactive Systems in Domestic Environments, *in* G. C. van der Veer, A. Henderson & S. Coles (eds.), *Proceedings of the Symposium on Designing Interactive Systems: Processes, Practices, Methods and Techniques (DIS'97)*, ACM Press, pp.247–59.

Rose, F. (1996), "The End of TV as We Know It", *Fortune* p.58. December 23.

Venkatesh, A. & Mazumdar, S. (1999), New Information Technologies in the Home: A Study of Users, Impacts, and Design Strategies, *in Proceedings of EDRA conference*, pp.101–6.

Vygotsky, L. S. (1978), *Mind In Society. The Development of Higher Psychological Processes*, Harvard University Press.

Winograd, T. & Flores, F. (1986), *Understanding Computers and Cognition: A New Foundation for Design*, Addison–Wesley.

Process, Methodology and Design Methods

User Involvement in the Design of Human–Computer Interactions: Some Similarities and Differences between Design Approaches

Mathilde Bekker & John Long[†]

IPO, Center for User-System Interaction, PO Box 513, 5613 MB Eindhoven, The Netherlands

Tel: *+31 40 247 5239*
Fax: *+31 40 243 1930*
EMail: *{M.M.Bekker, J.B.Long}@tue.nl*

[†] *Ergonomics & HCI Unit, University College London, 26 Bedford Way, London WC1H OAP, UK*

EMail: *J.Long@ucl.ac.uk*

This paper reviews user involvement in the design of human–computer interactions, as advocated by a selection of different approaches to design. The selection comprises: User-Centred Design; Participatory Design; Socio-Technical Design; Soft Systems Methodology; and Joint Application Design. The review reveals a preliminary identification of non-configurable and configurable 'attributes' of user involvement in design, and their associated 'values', which characterise the similarities and differences between the design approaches. The attributes and values are intended in the longer term to support designers to compare and contrast various design approaches and to make more informed choices about the configuration of user involvement in design practice. Requirements for future research into the better understanding and configuring of user involvement are proposed.

Keywords: user-centred design, user involvement, participatory design, socio-technical design, soft systems methodology, joint application design.

1 Introduction

In Human–Computer Interaction (HCI) research, designing with the user in mind has become a generally agreed principle. However, a survey of usability specialists showed little consensus concerning the term 'User-Centred Design' (UCD) (Karat et al., 1996; Karat, 1997). In general, specialists agree that users should be involved in the design process to ensure the development of usable systems. However, UCD is understood to encompass a wide variety of different design activities. In addition, different interpretations of the term UCD result from the wide range of design approaches which include some form of user involvement.

Design approaches differ in the rationale they propose for user involvement and how such involvement should be implemented. A main difference between approaches is the role envisaged for the user in the design process. For example, design approaches differ in whether they support design for, with, or by the users (Eason, 1995). 'Design for users' does not require the users themselves to be involved. Instead, they are 'represented' by the designers or usability specialists, who use theories and findings about human behaviour to inform design. In some cases, users may be consulted as only one of a set of possible information sources. 'Design with users' requires users, through a representative role, to have some indirect input to the design process. 'Design by users' requires the users themselves to be directly involved in the design process. These important differences indicate the non-unitary nature of UCD.

There are, however, some risks related to the lack of clarity as to what design approaches advocate. First, designers may choose an approach without understanding the underlying ideas. As a consequence, the approach might be used incorrectly, leading to undesired outcomes. Second, practitioners, may, whether knowingly or not, claim that they have used a particular design approach, when in fact they have failed to do so. As a consequence, others may be misled about the design process and so its strengths and weaknesses. In an effort to provide more clarity about similarities and differences between design approaches, this paper presents a review of a selection of design approaches that advocate user involvement.

Other papers have discussed similarities and differences between user involved design approaches. However, these papers have generally considered at most two approaches. For example, (Carmel et al., 1993) compared Joint Application Design (JAD) and Participatory Design (PD). PD has been compared to UCD (Carroll, 1996) in an introduction to a special issue of the journal 'Human–Computer Interaction' on PD.

This paper reviews user involvement in design, as advocated by a selection of different approaches to the design of human–computer interactions. The paper is concerned with the similarities and differences between design approaches (i.e. the underlying assumptions associated with a proposed combination of design methods and techniques), rather than with the individual design methods and techniques that might comprise a design approach. The aim of the paper is a preliminary identification of non-configurable and configurable 'attributes' of user involvement in design, and their associated 'values', which characterise the similarities and differences between these approaches. Non-configurable attributes are attributes that are descriptive of design approaches, but are fixed and so cannot be changed by the designer for a specific design project. Configurable attributes are also descriptive but can be realised by different values and can be changed by the designer for a specific design project. In the longer term, the identification and description of these attributes and values is intended to support designers:

- to understand better the similarities and differences between design approaches; and

- to make more informed choices about the configuration of user involvement in design practice.

The paper reviews the different rationales for involving users in design. Then, the non-configurable and configurable attributes, identified in five different design approaches, are presented and summarised in table form. Subsequently, the most salient similarities and differences between the design approaches are discussed and an example is given of how user involvement might be configured for a hypothetical design context, by use of the configurable attributes and values. Finally, the ideas presented in the paper and recommendations for future work are discussed.

2 Rationale for User Involvement

As mentioned in the introduction, a number of different rationales have been proposed for user-involvement in the design of user-computer interactions. Design approaches originated in different countries, having different cultures and often with different underlying assumptions about why users should be involved in design. Overviews of the rationales for user participation have been presented elsewhere; for example (Greenbaum, 1993; Muller et al., 1997; Bjerkness & Bratteteig, 1995). These overviews identify the following different rationales for user involvement in design:

- Political or ethical rationale. User involvement is justified, because users should have a right to influence decisions affecting their work practice.

- Pragmatic rationale (efficiency, effectiveness, and quality). User involvement is justified, because it leads to more usable systems, and so to people working more efficiently and effectively.

- Commitment and 'buy-in' rationale. User involvement in design is justified, because it leads to greater commitment to the final design. Users are able to develop realistic expectations for the design and so reduce their resistance to change.

- Theoretical or philosophical rationale. User involvement in design is justified, because designers can never understand the users' work well enough (Ehn,

1988). For users to be able to contribute to design, they need to practise 'involved acting' (for example, trying out design ideas themselves), and not just 'detached reflection' (for example, only reading about and reflecting on design ideas) (Ehn, 1988).

Thus, there is a wide range of rationales for user involvement in design.

3   Design Approaches Advocating User Involvement

In this section, five design approaches are reviewed. Over the years, many design approaches have been developed, in different research areas. This paper presents only a selection of such approaches. The selection, however, includes approaches developed in different traditions and different cultures. This paper trades off depth for breadth of coverage. The aim is not to detail the different design approaches *per se*, but rather to identify salient aspects of each approach, as they concern the similarities and differences between design approaches and the configuration of user involvement by designers.

The selection of these approaches reflects influences from different cultures (for example, those from North America, Scandinavia and the UK) and different research areas (for example, systems thinking, design group dynamics and design philosophy). The two major HCI design approaches are User-Centred Design (UCD) and Participatory Design (PD). Socio-technical Design (STD) is distinguished by its ethical approach to the design of (social) systems. Soft Systems Methodology (SSM) has its foundation in systems thinking. Last, Joint Application Design (JAD) is an approach that has been developed in industry to improve the efficiency of design processes. It should be noted that neither JAD nor SSM were developed specifically to involve users in design, but primarily to improve the design problem-solving process in general. Many of the terms to describe design approaches are used in different ways in the literature, for example, some so-called UCD approaches, on further examination, appear more like a socio-technical design approach. These differences in interpretation hinder designers' understanding of the differences between these approaches and so the configuration of user involvement in design.

Based on a review of the literature, these design approaches are described in terms of attributes and their values, which reflect the similarities and differences between the approaches. The attributes are divided into two types: non-configurable and configurable. Non-configurable attributes (NCA) cannot be changed by designers, for example, 'when' the approach was developed, its values being the decades '1960s', '1970s', etc. Non-configurable attributes, although not changeable, are nevertheless considered to support understanding by designers of the configuration of user involvement in design by identifying the similarities and differences between design approaches. Configurable attributes (CA) can be changed by designers, for example, 'user representation', its values being 'direct' and 'indirect'. Configurable attributes are considered to support the making of more informed choices by designers about the configuration of user involvement in design, as well as better understanding.

A preliminary identification of attributes of user involvement, characterising the differences between the approaches, is based generally on the roles that users

Attributes	UCD	PD	STD	SSM	JAD
	Values				
Time	Late 1970s	Late 1960 — early 1970s	Early 1970s	1970s	Late 1970s
Location	USA	Scandinavia	UK	UK	USA
Rationale	Pragmatic	Political, Philosophical	Political, Commitment and buy-in	Pragmatic, (Political)	Pragmatic
Background / theory	Human information processing, Subjective experience of user, Social context of computing	Labour relations, Group learning	Socio-technical systems theory	Systems thinking	Group dynamics, Software engineering
Themes	Knowledge of the user, Iterative design, Evaluation with simulations, etc.	Democracy of the workplace, Empowerment, Conflict resolution	Social impact, Balance of social and technical constraints	Ill-defined problems, Different world views	Teamwork, Accelerated design, Completeness

Table 1: Design approaches: Non-configurable attributes and values.

and designers play in the design process; and how and when the users are involved in that process. Each of the approaches is discussed in terms of these preliminary attributes. The attributes of user involvement, together with some examples of the values they might take, are highlighted in bold, on first mention only. A list of attributes and values, discussed in Sections 3.1 to 3.5, appears in the Section 4. 'Similarities And Differences'. Table 1 shows the non-configurable and Table 2 the configurable attributes and values for the design approaches.

3.1   User-Centred Design

UCD was developed in the late 1970s (**NCA: time: 1970s, 1960s**) in the USA (**NCA: location: USA, UK, Scandinavia**). The development coincided with the change of computer users from mainly experts, such as engineers and programmers, to less expert users, such as managers and teachers (Grudin, 1990). This development required an approach to design with a better understanding of the range of end-users. As a generic term, UCD requires the representation of users' interests in design to ensure the development of efficient and usable systems. In some versions of UCD, no direct user involvement is required, users' interests being indirectly represented by usability experts or by theories and models of user behaviour (**CA: user interest representation: direct; indirect**). In general, UCD includes design approaches that combine UCD principles and UCD techniques (Karat, 1997). Gould & Lewis

Attributes	UCD	PD	STD	SSM	JAD
	Values				
User interest representation	Indirect	Direct	Direct	Indirect, Direct	Direct
User role	Design for, Design with	Design by	Design with	Design for, Design with	Design with
Developer role	Expert or facilitator	Emancipator	Facilitator	Expert, Facilitator	Facilitator
User involvement timing	Mostly early and late	Throughout	Throughout	Mostly early (not clearly stated)	Mostly early
User representation	Representative set	All prospective users	All prospective users	Representative set	Some users, Representative set
User design influence	Product	Process and product	Process and product	Product	Product
Stakeholder education	Emphasis on developer education	Mutual education of stakeholders	Mutual education of stakeholders	Emphasis on developer education	Emphasis on developer education
Stakeholder agreement	Cooperation	Cooperation / conflict†	Cooperation	Cooperation	Cooperation
User involvement process	Specifiable	Unspecifiable, Partly specifiable‡	Specifiable	Specifiable	Specifiable
Design problem scope	Task fit	Task, Social and Political fit	Task and Social fit	Task, Social and Political fit	Task fit
User control	Weak	Strong	Strong	Weak	Weak
User design problem (assumed to be)	Ill-defined, Well-defined	Ill-defined	Ill-defined	Ill-defined	-Unclear-
User involvement structure	Present	Present	Present	Unspecified	Present
User information source	One of many (minor)	Main source (major)	Main source (major)	One of many (minor)	One of many (minor)

†some versions assume cooperation between employers and employees, other versions assume inherent conflict between employers and employees.

‡some versions assume that methods, and user involvement cannot be specified; other versions assume that partial specification is possible.

Table 2: Design approaches: Configurable attributes and values.

(1985) propose the following design principles: early focus on users and tasks; empirical measurement; and iterative design. The principles aim to incorporate human factors knowledge into the design process and the techniques aim to involve the users efficiently into the design process. UCD is based on theories about human information processing, subjective experiences of users, and the social context of computing (Draper & Norman, 1986, p.3). The users' role varies from passive (users are consulted as sources of information by the design team) to more active user participation (some user representatives are part of the design team) (**CA: user role: active; passive; none**). The developer's role is often that of an expert that represents the users' interests (Eason, 1995) (**CA: developer role: emancipator; facilitator; expert**). According to a survey of design practice, users are most often involved early and late in the design process, and less frequently in the design activities themselves (Wilson et al., 1996) (**CA: user involvement timing: throughout; early; late**).

3.2 Participatory Design

In Scandinavian countries, user participation in design was initiated in the 1960s by concern for the relationship between work and democratic values (**NCA: themes: democracy of the workplace; iterative design**) (Bjerkness & Bratteteig, 1995, p.75). Projects, involving politically motivated user participation (**NCA: rationale: political; social; philosophical; pragmatic**), were carried out in the 1970s prompted by the Scandinavian Trade Unions. The system developer played an 'emancipator' role (Bjerkness & Bratteteig, 1995, p.85). PD emphasises active user involvement, throughout the design process, to ensure all prospective users (**CA: user representation: all; representative set; some; none**) influence both the design process and the product (**CA: user design influence: process; product**). In this way, user de-skilling, resulting from the introduction of new technology was to be avoided. An important aspect of PD is the opportunity it provides for the mutual education of various stakeholders (for example, users and developers teaching one another about their work) (**CA: stakeholder education: users; developers**). A number of design approaches were developed along these lines, differing mainly in the assumptions as to whether employers and employees are in inherent conflict or are able to reach some form of agreement, termed, respectively, 'Collective Resource' approach and 'Cooperative Design' approach (**CA: stakeholder agreement: cooperation; conflict**) (Bjerkness & Bratteteig, 1995). In the present paper, these approaches are considered under the general term Participatory Design.

Some proponents of PD oppose a method-oriented approach altogether. They argue that a method, described as a series of linear or sequential steps, cannot guarantee a solution to a design problem. However, others argue that such a methodological description can be used as a basic structure for a more complex process that may be less easily understood (Muller et al., 1997, p.260–1) (**CA: user involvement process: specifiable; partly specifiable; unspecifiable**). More recently, some PD methods have been developed that cover the complete development life cycle, for example, MUST*(Kensing & Blomberg, 1998) and Cooperative Experimental System Development (CSED) (Grønbæk et al., 1997).

3.3 Socio-Technical Design

STD was developed in the UK as a reaction to the failures of introducing new technologies into society. Studies of introducing new technology into a social system, without considering the consequences for that system, identified problems indicating deficiencies of 'technological determinism' (Eason, 1988; 1997). As a consequence, socio-technical systems theory was developed to support the joint optimisation of the social and the technical sub-systems (Emery & Trist, 1969).

STD aims to combine technological and social considerations to ensure that the systems being developed fit into the social context (**CA: design problem scope: social-fit; task-fit; political-fit**). Examples of STD methods that have been developed include ETHICS (Effective Technical and Human Implementation of Computer-based Systems) (Mumford, 1993), and the set of design techniques developed by researchers working at HUSAT Research Centre in the UK (Eason, 1988). The users' role in STD varies from passive to active involvement. The developer's role is often that of a facilitator (Mumford, 1993). STD emphasises the ethical aspects of introducing technology into society. It supports users' control over changes in their workplace, through which it aims to improve the chances of the final system being accepted (**CA: user control: strong; weak**).

3.4 Soft Systems Methodology

SSM was developed in the 1970s in the UK. It builds on ideas of 'systems thinking' developed earlier in the 1950s and 1960s. 'Hard' systems engineering was advanced to support the development of well-specified systems to achieve their objectives. The shortcomings of systems engineering lay in its assumption that the need for a particular system had already been specified (Checkland & Scholes, 1993, p.16). However, often the major problem is to determine that need. Many design problems are ill-defined and may not be readily specifiable. Because of the assumption that problems are well-defined, the 'hard' systems engineering approach may fail, when the problem turns out to be not readily specifiable or even unspecifiable. SSM offers an organised set of principles, which support the process of 'managing' (in the broad sense) real-world problem situations and determining through which changes such situations may be modified in an acceptable and desirable manner (Checkland & Scholes, 1993, p.5).

SSM is a development methodology which extends systems thinking to incorporate ill-defined design problems (**CA: user design problem: well-defined; ill-defined**). It uses models to compare descriptions of real-life situations and, on a meta-level, it assesses how well the development methodology has been used to learn about how to apply SSM. It has been applied to a wide range of application domains, as described in 'Soft Systems Methodology in Action' (Checkland & Scholes, 1993). Checkland & Scholes, also discuss how SSM has evolved through the lessons learned from its use in a number of case studies. The role that users play

---

*MUST is a Danish acronym for theories of, and methods for, design activities.

in this process is unclear. As reflected in their descriptions of case studies, users' roles vary from passive to representative. The developer often plays an expert or facilitator role.

3.5   Joint Application Design (JAD)

JAD[†] was developed by IBM in the late 1970s to facilitate group design sessions. It aimed to develop shorter design cycles and to improve communication between the people involved. It is a structured approach, based on organised and facilitated meetings. It has been taken up by other companies, because it offers a structured approach for involving users in design (**CA: user involvement structure: present; absent**). The underlying ideas are based on theories about group dynamics. An independent facilitator is responsible for organising the meetings, planning the agenda and facilitating the contributions of the participants (for example, designers, users, managers, etc.). The user constitutes one possible information source for the design approach and, as such, often has a consultative or representative role (**CA: user information source: major; minor**). Users are mainly involved in the earlier phases of the design process, that is, initiation, analysis and design (Wood & Silver, 1989, p.19).

The characterisation of the different design approaches in terms of the NCAs and the CAs and their values has now been completed. The next section considers the similarities and differences between design approaches, as reflected by the attributes and values.

4   Similarities and Differences

The backgrounds of five design approaches that advocate user involvement have been described in Sections 3.1 to 3.5. Non-configurable attributes and values appear in Table 1, and configurable attributes and values in Table 2.

Obviously, different rationales for involving users in design have different consequences for the development of design approaches and for the configuration of user involvement in design. This section discusses some of the similarities and differences between the selected design approaches and in particular those reflected in the attributes of user involvement.

Who is involved in the design process differs between the approaches. In some approaches, with a political rationale for involving users in design, such as PD and STD, much care is taken to ensure the involvement of all people whose life may be influenced by the new system or product (**CA: user representation**). Other approaches, such as SSM and JAD are less explicit about how to select and involve an appropriate set of users.

The different approaches also differ in how they involve users in the design process. Some, such as UCD, are not necessarily participatory, while others such as PD put much emphasis on active and direct user involvement (**CA: user role; CA: user interest representation**). Most approaches propose a compromise involvement, in which the users have a representative role. That is, they have a say

---

[†]Generic names for JAD include: Joint Application Design, Joint Application Development, Joint Application Requirements (Carmel et al., 1993).

in some matters, but do not control the design process (**CA: user control, CA: user design influence**). The pragmatically oriented approaches, such as UCD, JAD and SSM, put more emphasis on the design process that is to be followed, than on the specific role that users should play. Furthermore, the approaches differ in when they propose to involve users (**CA: user involvement timing**). PD and STD propose active user involvement throughout the design process, whereas JAD involves users early on in the design process.

5   Example of Configuring User Involvement in Design

To illustrate the potential application of the descriptions of the design approaches in Tables 1 & 2, a hypothetical example is given of how non-configurable and configurable attributes might support better understanding and more informed choices by designers. Suppose a designer has to decide on the configuration of user involvement in an organisation strongly committed to the pragmatics of the market place, but with some, albeit limited, sensitivity to the social context of the workplace. The fact that the UCD approach is more compatible with this design situation, in terms of its attributes and values (**NCA: rationale; pragmatic, and: background theory; human information processing**), than, for example, the PD approach (**NCA: background theory; labour relations, and themes; democracy of the workplace**) can be understood from the descriptions in Table 1. Again, supposing the designer, cited earlier, has to decide on user involvement in the following design situation. During a two-week project, a design team, consisting of a software engineer and an industrial designer are to redesign a logging system for customer queries, used by the help-desk of a computer support group. The main aim of the redesign is to improve the completion of the form for the customer's initial query. The designer decides on the following values for the configurable attributes, based on the time constraints and the main aim of the redesign. The user is asked for some direct input (**CA: user interest representation**), early and late in the redesign process (**CA: user involvement timing**), because the designer wants to ensure a good task-fit. The design team designs for, and with, the user (**CA: user role**), mostly taking an expert and facilitator role (**CA: designer role**), because the designer wants input and feedback from the user. The user has medium control over the design (**CA: user control**), because the designer wants the user to have some influence, but wants final design decisions to be taken by the design team. The user is one of the sources of information (**CA: user information source**), because the designer integrates the users' input with other knowledge, such as design principles.

These decisions, configuring user involvement in design, are expressed in a plan for the design project. The team plans to observe and interview some of the users about their use of the query form. Based on these findings, and the application of some design principles, the design team plans to make an initial design proposal. They plan to adjust the proposal, using feedback on these ideas from some of the users, and to implement the changes. Although hypothetical, this example, illustrates how the attributes and values might inform the configuration of user involvement in the design process.

6   Discussion and Future Work

There are some limitations to the review of design approaches described in this paper.

First, there are methods that combine ideas from various design approaches, and which therefore do not neatly fit into one category. Some design approaches have adopted ideas from other design approaches, as they evolved over time. For example, some PD methods have incorporated some aspects of the more pragmatic rationale underlying UCD (Carroll, 1996), which is a form of configuring a design approach according to design contexts.

Second, because the review identifies attributes of design approaches, it supports a comparison of approaches only at this level. After deciding which design approach(es) to apply, more explicit choices on the level of design techniques need to be made. Other reviews are available to support designers in making decisions at this lower level. For example, the user-requirements framework handbook (Maguire, 1997) presents a review of the advantages and disadvantages of a selection of design techniques.

The review of the design approaches in this paper covers an initial set of attributes, and related values, of user involvement in design. This list illustrates some important differences between the design approaches discussed in this paper. However, it is only a preliminary list of attributes and additional research and development would be required to realise the potential of the approach. First, the list of attributes and values needs to be expanded. The different design approaches would need to be systematically and exhaustively examined to ensure that all the important attributes and values had been identified. Second, the attributes and values, as reported here, cannot be claimed to be coherent. Some attributes are very closely related, and so difficult to distinguish. For example, the value 'design by' **(CA: user role)** is closely related to strong user influence **(CA: user control)**. Third, designers need to use the attributes and values, to configure user involvement in design, to test whether the attributes and values are fit for the purpose for which they are intended, that is, support for design.

7   Conclusions

The paper identifies attributes of design approaches. It is important to understand the underlying similarities and differences between design approaches in order to configure a design approach suitable for design practice. The paper offers a review of a set of design approaches to support designers:

- to better understand the similarities and differences between design approaches; and

- to configure user involvement in design.

The review identifies similarities and differences between the selected design approaches, and thus allows designers to compare and contrast these approaches, so supporting understanding. The review shows that different rationales of approaches lead to different implementations of user involvement (for example, how and when users are involved). The politically oriented approaches put emphasis on giving users an active role in a major part of the design process, whereas the more pragmatically oriented approaches put more emphasis on applying an effective and possibly structured design process, where the users sometimes play a more limited role.

Acknowledgements

The authors wish to thank Floris van Nes and Matthias Rauterberg for their useful comments on an earlier version of this paper.

References

Bjerkness, G. & Bratteteig, T. (1995), "A Discussion of Scandinavian Research on System Development", *Scandinavian Journal of Information Systems* **7**(1), 73–98.

Carmel, E., Whitaker, R. D. & George, J. F. (1993), "PD and Joint Application Design: A Transatlantic Comparison", *Communications of the ACM* **36**(4), 40–8.

Carroll, J. M. (1996), "Encountering Others: Reciprocal Openings in Participatory Design and User-centred Design", *Human–Computer Interaction* **11**(3), 285–90.

Checkland, P. B. & Scholes, J. (1993), *Soft Systems Methodology in Action*, second edition, John Wiley & Sons.

Draper, S. W. & Norman, D. A. (1986), Introduction, *in* D. A. Norman & S. W. Draper (eds.), *User Centered System Design: New Perspectives on Human–Computer Interaction*, Lawrence Erlbaum Associates.

Eason, K. (1988), *Information Technology and Organisational Change*, Taylor & Francis.

Eason, K. D. (1995), "User-centred Design: For Users or by Users?", *Ergonomics* **38**(8), 1667–73.

Eason, K. D. (1997), Understanding the Organisational Ramifications of Implementing Information Technology Systems, *in* M. Helander, T. K. Landauer & P. Prabhu (eds.), *Handbook of Human–Computer Interaction*, second edition, North-Holland, pp.1475–95.

Ehn, P. (1988), *Work Oriented Design of Computer Artefacts*, Gummessons.

Emery, F. E. & Trist, E. L. (1969), Socio-technical Systems, *in* F. E. Emery (ed.), *Systems Thinking*, Penguin, pp.281–96.

Gould, J. D. & Lewis, C. H. (1985), "Designing for Usability — Key Principles and What Designers Think", *Communications of the ACM* **28**(3), 300–311.

Greenbaum, J. (1993), "PD: A Personal Statement", *Communications of the ACM* **36**(4), 47.

Grønbæk, K., Kyng, M. & Mogensen, P. (1997), Toward a Cooperative Experimental System Development Approach, *in* M. Kyng & L. Mathiassen (eds.), *Computers and Design in Context*, MIT Press, pp.201–338.

Grudin, J. (1990), The Computer Reaches Out: The Historical Continuity of Interface Design, *in* J. C. Chew & J. Whiteside (eds.), *Proceedings of CHI'90: Human Factors in Computing Systems*, ACM Press, p.261.

Karat, J. (1997), "Evolving the Scope of User-centred Design", *Communications of the ACM* **40**(7), 33–8.

Karat, J., Atwood, M. E., Dray, S. M. & Ratzer, M. (1996), User Centered Design: Quality or Quackery?, *in* G. van der Veer & B. Nardi (eds.), *Proceedings of CHI'96: Human Factors in Computing Systems*, ACM Press, pp.161–2.

Kensing, F. & Blomberg, J. (1998), "Participatory Design: Issues and Concerns", *Computer Supported Cooperative Work* **7**(3/4), 167–85.

Maguire, M. (1997), RESPECT User Requirements Framework Handbook, WP5 Deliverable D5.1, Technical Report, HUSAT Research Institute.

Muller, M. J., Haslwanter, J. H. & Dayton, T. (1997), Participatory Practices in the Software Lifecycle, *in* M. Helander, T. K. Landauer & P. Prabhu (eds.), *Handbook of Human–Computer Interaction*, second edition, North-Holland, pp.255–97.

Mumford, E. (1993), The Participation of Users in Systems Design: An Account of the Origin, Evolution and Use of the ETHICS Method, *in* D. Schuler & A. Namioka (eds.), *Participatory Design: Principles and Practices*, Lawrence Erlbaum Associates, pp.257–70.

Wilson, S., Bekker, M. M., Johnson, H. & Johnson, P. (1996), Costs and Benefits of User Involvement in Design: Practitioners' Views, *in* A. Sasse, R. J. Cunningham & R. Winder (eds.), *People and Computers XI (Proceedings of HCI'96)*, Springer-Verlag, pp.221–40.

Wood, J. & Silver, D. (1989), *Joint Application Design. How to Design Quality Systems in 40% Less Time*, John Wiley & Sons.

Concurrent Usability Engineering

Pekka Ketola

Nokia Mobile Phones, PO Box 83, 33721 Tampere, Finland

EMail: *pekka.ketola@nokia.com*

Usability engineering lifecycle models have problems matching with concurrent product development practices. In this paper we describe what problems there are between usability engineering lifecycle and concurrent product development process and describe an example how this problem is handled at Nokia Mobile Phones.

Current descriptions for usability engineering lifecycle describe how the work is done during one engineering lifecycle or in a product development project from the very beginning of design to the product launch and to the collection of field feedback. However, in mature development organisations usability engineering is continuous and often parallel work from one product to another and the engineering practice should take this continuity into account. In addition to this, product development is naturally divided to three different phases that set different requirements for the engineering work. These phases are concept work, actual product development and evaluation of the product on the market.

Keywords: usability engineering, human-centred design, lifecycle, product development, concurrent engineering, software engineering, project management.

1 Introduction

In organisations that have continuous product lines yielding new versions of products one after the other, the usability engineering (UE) should be streamlined with the parallel product development and with the flow of new products. Normally it is not possible to follow any existing usability engineering lifecycle from the beginning to the end with all product projects — it is simply too resource consuming and many organisations are not mature to support usability engineering well enough (Earthy, 1998).

At Nokia Mobile Phones (NMP) the product development is based on Concurrent Engineering Process (CEP) (Heikkinen, 1997). CEP is a systematic engineering approach to the integrated, concurrent design of products and their related process (Heikkinen, 1997, p.10). It helps to manage all parallel product design activities, from the design of single software (SW) feature to the ramp-up of factories. From the product design point of view concurrent engineering process starts from a given product concept and ends at the launch of a product. The alternate and fundamentally different approach for CEP is sequential development, where R&D, design, manufacturing and support are more linear than parallel activities.

The concept is often designed by a different process and by different resources than the actual product. Very often, right after the product is launched, the human resources that designed the product start with new design projects. This kind of work practice doesn't fit well to usability engineering lifecycle thinking because of human and organisational reasons.

In this paper we propose ideas for usability work target setting in the framework of usability engineering lifecycle. Systematic approach helps to focus usability work in a way that takes the company's product development into consideration as an entity. Target setting is divided according to the major phases of product development: concept work, development and verification.

This kind of focusing is useful in organisations where:

- The product development is continuous.

- Future products are directly based on the earlier versions, like updates of SW based applications for example in PC's, or new improved versions of existing appliances, like mobile phones.

- New technologies are often introduced and embedded to products.

Target setting also gives better opportunities to plan the usability engineering and human resources for a specific project.

2 Usability Engineering Lifecycles

The common usability engineering lifecycle is generally accepted and slightly varying versions of it are presented in literature. The following table (Table 1) shows the main points in three versions (Nielsen, 1993; Mayhew, 1999; ISO, 1999) of usability engineering lifecycle activities as they are originally presented.

Table 1 shows that each usability engineering lifecycle model can be basically divided into two similar development stages. It also shows that each lifecycle model ends by collecting feedback from the real use of the system. These stages are:

Phase 1: Concept Major actions: Study the potential users of the product, create initial design ideas with usability goals.

Phase 2: Product development Major actions: Design the product, iterate the design through testing.

Nielsen (1993)	Mayhew (1999)	ISO (1999)
Know the user	Requirement analysis (User profile, task analysis, platform capabilities/constraints, general design principles, usability goals)	The active involvement of users, a clear understanding of user and task requirements
Competitive analysis		An appropriate allocation of function between users and technology
Setting usability goals		The iteration of design solutions. Multi-disciplinary design
Parallel design		Use existing knowledge to develop design solutions.
		Understand and specify the context of use. Specify the user and organisational requirements
Participatory design	Design/Testing/Development (Work re-engineering, CM design, CM mockups, iterative evaluation, screen design standards, prototyping, iterative evaluation, detailed UI design, iterative evaluation)	Use existing knowledge to develop design proposals. Make the design solution more concrete using simulations
Coordinate design of total interface		Present the design solution to users and allow them to perform tasks
Apply guidelines and heuristic analysis		Alter the design in response to the user feedback and iterate this process until objectives are met
Prototyping		Manage the iteration of design solutions
Empirical testing		Provide design feedback
Iterative design		Assess whether objectives have been achieved
Collect feedback from field use	Installation (user feedback)	Field validation
		Long-term monitoring

Table 1: Usability engineering activities.

Phase 3: Evaluation Major actions: Get feedback and validate the design before and after product launch.

2.1 Disconnected Lifecycles

Unfortunately, each usability engineering lifecycle model is formally missing the link to the previous or parallel work, for example to earlier usability evaluation of a similar input technology, and the link to usability engineering that is made before or in parallel to the current lifecycle, for example to another design project in the same company. In other words, although feedback is collected from the field, it is not taken into account when new lifecycle starts.

Because this kind of information input is not included in usability engineering lifecycle models there is a risk that the needed information is not used though it may be available. In this situation the effectiveness of usability engineering is very much dependent on the experience and activity of individual designers or on the maturity of the organisation.

At NMP the product development is done in multiple sites, even in different continents (USA, Europe, Asia). The problem of disconnected lifecycles is seen clearly in projects that continue the work that has been done in an earlier project in a different continent and that has ended for example one year before the new project started. The physical and temporal distances of projects create discontinuity in information flow. Another challenge is the constant lack of resources and fast development tempo which means that after the product launch it is difficult to concentrate or have resources on collecting field feedback, especially through long term monitoring, while new projects are already waiting for you.

Disconnected lifecycles are not so problematic when an existing product is improved by iterative design and with long lasting product concept.

2.2 Cooperative Design and Usability Engineering

It is very typical that the design of SW interface and the overall mechanics and hardware of the product are designed by separate organisational groups or even by different companies. For example when a WindowsCE (see WindowsCE Home Page http://www.microsoft.com/windowsce/) application is designed that should run on all WindowsCE compatible platforms the hardware interface may have features that are not optimal with the SW user interface, like sizes and positions of command buttons.

Usability engineering lifecycle models do not give very much support for this kind of parallel or disconnected design of SW and mechanics. Nielsen (1993), Mayhew (1999) and ISO (1999) define the design of total interface and iterative prototyping in product development phase (Phase 2) but the purpose of these actions is primarily the verification of a SW interface.

When a new product, like a mobile phone, is designed then hardware (HW), mechanics and UI are typically designed in parallel. Product hardware and mechanics are design areas where the final design often freezes earlier than software UI design. If usability evaluations of the whole user interface (mechanics and UI) are done too late in the project then mechanical design can't be changed anymore and possible usability problems have to be solved in the design of software UI. For example, if the bad 'touch' of a keypad produces input errors then the input sensitivity must be corrected with software changes. A better solution in this case, instead of iterative design, would be to separate the usability evaluation of mechanics and the evaluation of UI design.

3   Concept Work

A concept describes what the system can do, what it could look like and what features there should be in it. Depending on the application area it can be, for example, an idea for industrial design or an idea about user interaction and interface.

As an example of product UI concepts, Figure 1 shows two UI concepts for Nokia mobile phones. The first concept (on the left) is based on two softkeys and *roller* (middle button). The second concept with less command buttons is based on one softkey and *Navi Key* (leftmost button).

Figure 1: Two mobile phone UI concepts.

Product development is the realisation of concept work, except if the new product is for example an updated version to a previous one. Thus, concept work is not always needed in order to create a new product, or concept work has been done much before the actual product development.

Concept work is creative by its nature. In this phase the concept development team tries to find ways to improve an existing design or to create a new one by designing a newt concept. Methods like contextual design (Beyer & Holtzblatt, 1998) or human-centred design (ISO, 1999) are typically used in this phase. Concept work is not part of concurrent engineering process but it precedes it.

The first part (Phase 1) of traditional, for example Nielsen (1993), usability engineering lifecycle is a powerful tool during concept work. In concept work the work should concentrate on two organisational issues that are not well-defined in lifecycle models. *Learning from the past* and from reference products is needed in order to avoid the mistakes already done and even to create fresh and innovative design ideas. Surprisingly, the same design mistakes are often reproduced, for example because the development team either doesn't have capability to identify the problems or it is not linked to earlier or parallel design work, doesn't know about existing problems in other products or because there is some company-based reason to maintain the existing design.

The other focus in this phase is *designing for the future* (Nielsen, 1993, p.71). Very often the product under development won't be the last one. There will be new versions of the same product or there will be new products that are different but contain same interaction elements. Also, sometimes the same concept work is used as a platform for several products. This means that documentation of usability efforts should be made in the way that does not only help the current project but that is valuable also in the future, and for different product development teams.

Concept phase in the product development is thus an activity that should focus on lessons-learned issues as input data and also as output data in addition to the actual design and usability engineering work. In the concept phase it is important to create documents that can be utilised by the primary product project and also by other development projects. One way to verify that correct information is collected and documented is to define documentation requirements for this phase. Requirements help also the usability person(s) to focus on valid tasks.

A product concept doesn't define the details for UI design, for example the sizes of UI objects and items in menus. On the other hand a good and well-documented concept can give good guidelines to support design and decision making in the actual design phase.

4   Product Development

In the product development phase, which can be handled as a separate entity from the concept work, a project defines and implements the actual product. User interface and interaction is designed, software and hardware implemented and other needed actions are done, such as marketing activities and building the product lines in the factory to produce products. Depending on the organisation and development process this phase contains activities that are linear or, very often, parallel.

In the product development phase the focus of the usability work is clearly product oriented. All user interface design and usability work is made in order to get the product to the market in time and with the desired quality including usability. Compared to the concept phase this phase is very different. Typically, concept work has given the fundamental design ideas and perhaps defined and verified the basic interaction principles and addressed latent and overt user needs. In a concept the data is described by rough descriptions or prototypes. During product development these ideas must be refined and implemented in a user-friendly way and verified in the given time-frame and budget.

Usability engineering in this phase should focus on effectively and actively verifying the actual implementation by iterative usability testing. However, the amount of iterative design is often limited by project timetable, budget and available resources.

In product design phase the usability work should focus on issues that can be considered as *usability risks*. Risks can be for example new unexplored communication technologies, input tools that haven't been used in earlier products or interaction sequences that are different from earlier implementations. Usability risk areas should be followed and evaluated with more attention than *safe* areas.

When a usability risk comes true it can lead to the failure of the whole product. There are several examples in history of products that have failed because a concept or a technology has been implemented in an unusable way, for example:

- Apple's Newton (Earthy, 1998, p.110) failed because of poor utility.

- First implementations of predictive input mechanism (T9) in mobile phones failed because of input *errors*.

- First digital cameras failed because of poor user *satisfaction*.

- Web browser in Nokia 9000 had problems with *learnability* due to inconsistencies (Hjelmeroos et al., 1999).

- Many Web sites fail because of poor *efficiency* (Nielsen, 1998).

All these examples have new and innovative design solutions and hence usability risks.

The focus of the usability work is on the product and the documentation should primarily support the design of this specific product. This far the traditional usability engineering lifecycle definitions can be used as described in Phase 2 (Table 1).

5 Evaluation

In some phase of design there comes the point when no longer work can be done in order to improve a product because it must hit the marketplace or when no more changes are allowed because the design must be frozen. This point is typically few weeks before the manufacturing starts depending on the amount of system testing that is needed.

When this deadline is reached it is time to start the field evaluation of the product and to continue iterative design in order to make the following products better. After product launch it is easier to arrange field studies and competitor evaluations in public because confidentiality issues are no longer restricting the work. Especially in high-technology areas, like in the mobile phone industry, the competition and secrecy restrict sometimes efficiently beta testing and large-scale field testing before product launch.

In the evaluation phase the usability efforts should focus on producing data for forthcoming products and for new versions of the same product because there is no way to improve the user interaction and UI design in the present product. From a usability engineering point of view it would be useful to think of field verification as the starting point of concept or product design instead of end point i.e. field verification of product 1 would be the start of design for product 2.

From the organisational point of view it is valuable to keep the usability resources that were allocated in the project in their positions a little longer in order to do the usability evaluations because they are the best persons to evaluate and build the overall picture of the work done and to get the needed data from real users (Bærentsen & Vredenburg, 1999, p.74).

6 Case: Usability Engineering Lifecycle in Mobile Phone Development

Nokia is the world's leading mobile phone supplier and a leading supplier of mobile and fixed telecom networks including related customer services. Nokia also supplies solutions and products for fixed and wireless data communication, as well as multimedia terminals and computer displays (Nokia, 1999). Nokia Mobile Phones has a long history in user interface design and usability engineering (Kiljander, 1999). It is not more than 16 years since the very first mobile phones (Figure 2) with small displays were developed (Pulkkinen, 1997, p.109).

Since then the sizes of devices have collapsed, functionality in terminals and network services has increased and functionality from other appliances, like personal computers, has been adapted and integrated to mobile phones. This development together with mass markets has created enormous needs for ease of use and simplicity in product design (Figure 3).

The UI design and usability work that is being done in Europe, Asia and USA is based on human-centred design. The following example describes a situation where

Figure 2: Mobira Talkman (5 kg, 1984).

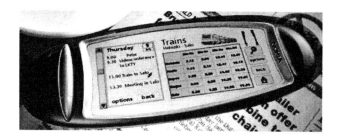

Figure 3: A future terminal vision (˜100g).

it is reasonable to think about usability engineering lifecycle not as a continuous project but as three focused entities.

6.1   Organisation

People that are directly related to usability work at NMP are divided into four functions: concept designers, product designers, feature designers and marketing. The functions may be located physically and sometimes temporally in different places. For example a concept that is designed in Europe can be implemented in Asia after two years.

Concept designers create new product concepts and bring usability-tested concepts to product designers. *Product designers* start their work with a given concept in order to design a complete product by following the concurrent engineering process. *Feature designers* design and specify how each feature, like answering an incoming call, should function across different platforms and product categories. Field feedback is gathered primarily by *marketing activities*, like customer contacts and surveys. Some of the feedback is gathered via concept designers (for example in competitor/reference product evaluations). Also in many cases the product project organisation is maintained for product update activities and in these cases projects sometimes gather, document and use the usability information by themselves.

6.2   Product Development and Usability Engineering

The product development practices at NMP are not optimal for applying UE lifecycle as a continuous process as proposed in literature. The arguments against using and reasons why UE lifecycles fail are:

- Product development from concept work to field feedback is not a continuous process, but rather three independent and connected processes.

- Product development is always linked to many other product and technology development projects.

- Field feedback from a working prototype is difficult to implement into the product because the design is typically frozen before any feedback can be collected.

- Beta-testing is not possible (as with software products).

- New and unexplored UI technologies are constantly introduced to products. The problem with these is that it is difficult to involve and teach the users a technology that has perhaps never earlier existed in order to do participatory design.

Instead, we have developed a way to focus usability engineering according to organisational functions. This has given us many advantages:

- Usability experts and designers can use their time effectively and they can focus on manageable design and interaction entities.

- Results and information about UE activities are effectively documented and spread within the organisation.

- Different groups can concentrate on their competence areas. For example, a concept designer can concentrate (design and evaluate) on larger problems and interaction principles in a concept, while a feature designer can finalise and evaluate the details of the concept using his experience and knowledge from other products.

Figure 4 shows a realistic example of the focused and parallel design of products. After the concept X has been designed, the concept designers start to specify the details of each feature. At some point a project X is started to make a product of the concept with the brand new feature Y, for example predictive text input. Later another project is started to make another version (X.2) of the same product. And finally, a new project is started to design a new product (Z) with different concept but with the same feature (Y).

Simultaneously there are three projects implementing the same feature (Y). The challenges for usability engineering is to verify that usability information is efficiently transferred between projects, that field feedback is collected early enough for X.2 and Z and that no overlapping work is done.

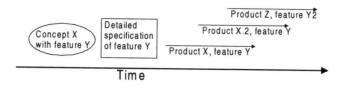

Figure 4: Focused and parallel design.

6.3   *Concurrent Product Development and Usability Engineering*

Development of the final product in NMP product projects has been based on concurrent engineering process since early 1990's (Pulkkinen, 1997, p.141). Concurrent engineering process ensures that both software and hardware quality of the product will be satisfactory. Currently there is no coherent process definition covering how usability engineering should be handled during the development process.

The development of new mobile phones and other personal devices is very much centred around ergonomic hardware and mechanics. Because usability engineering lifecycle definitions are primarily targeted at software developers they don't give much support for this part of product development or to integration of hardware and software from a usability point of view.

Concurrent engineering can be applied in many ways because it is basically a collection of methods, tools and work practices (Heikkinen, 1997, p.10). NMP has applied concurrent engineering process by defining milestones (E0–E5) for product development. The first milestone (E0) is reached when it has been verified that the product can really be implemented and the last milestone (E5) is reached when the design is completed and factories have made the first devices to be delivered to users. Thus, design and decision making proceeds with large intervals of concurrent working by all life-cycle perspectives.

Concurrent engineering process based product development gives an *opportunity for usability engineering*. It is possible to plan usability engineering resources and activities according to product timetables, milestones and product definitions. Concurrent engineering process also enables coordination and timing of usability activities between different projects. This is very economic and efficient especially when there are limited usability resources in the organisation.

7   Conclusions

In this paper we have described some usability engineering issues that we have observed and learned in the context of concurrent product development at Nokia. It is a description of problem areas that are a consequence of the marriage of dynamic product development process and static usability engineering process. These problem areas have very practical consequences.

It is not always reasonable to apply a complete usability engineering lifecycle in companies that have an intensive and continuous product development flow. Limited human resources and the discontinuity between different product development phases cause problems. In other words, usability engineering methodologies that are meant for sequential product development are not optimal for concurrent product development. Problem areas with usability engineering lifecycle models are:

- Documentation requirements or guidelines are not defined. If usability information and knowledge needs to be transferred and maintained there must be standard and general documentation practices.

- Usability evaluation of mechanical design and software design should be handled as separate but parallel issues until it is possible to test integrated design (prototypes).

- There is no separation of risk and safe areas in usability engineering. Risk areas can be foreseen and those issues should get more emphasis than safe issues.

- It is difficult to apply traditional usability engineering when the product contains features from which there are no previous knowledge and nobody really understands the nature of the feature. Examples of this in the context of mobile phones are: introduction of predictive text input, Bluetooth communication (see The Official Bluetooth Website http://www.bluetooth.com/) and GPRS (Nokia, 2000) connection technology.

- Field evaluation is almost impossible to do early enough in order to improve the evaluated product. The connection of field-feedback activities and product development is one of the main problems in usability engineering. Thus, a lot of UI design validation (usability testing) effort should be put to early design phases.

- Parallel projects are not taken into account. The principles for synchronisation of usability engineering activities between projects should be defined.

Good usability documentation practices in the company are critical for successful usability engineering in the long run. Without well-documented usability information it is not possible to build knowledge from everyday work and from findings that are obtained from usability evaluations.

Concept work, design, implementation and evaluation form a development sequence that is continuous within a product and between products and it clearly has a different focus or purpose during different development phases.

Continuity means that if the usability engineering lifecycle is correctly applied the organisation can build usability-related knowledge from the past and current experiences, and use it efficiently for future products. Understanding the need to focus the overall usability work helps the organisation to use usability resources effectively and intelligently.

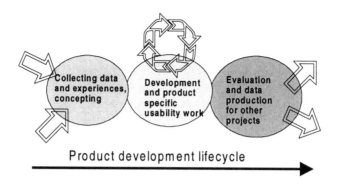

Figure 5: Usability work flow.

Following figure (Figure 5) shows the main product development phases (circles) and usability work foci (arrows) in one product development cycle. The arrows also describe the flow of usability related information during the product development.

The first phase consists of creating and collecting the initial design data (input) to produce a product. The second phase is the actual development of the product. During this phase the project focuses on creating and using the data in order to create the specific product. In the last phase all data is used as output in order to be used by other products or by forthcoming versions of the same product. For example, usability evaluations about keyboards are used to make a better keyboard for the next product.

Usability engineering lifecycle, human-centred design or any other given design methodology, as such, doesn't ensure that the usability work in an organisation is done in an optimal way or that the products will be usable. By defining the work foci the organisation is capable of understanding better what usability related actions in the product design process needs to be done, why they must be done and when certain things must be done.

Existing concurrent engineering process models do not include usability related activities, except as general requirements for quality. When any organisation applies concurrent engineering process in product development it doesn't get support from the process definition to apply usability engineering. On the other hand, by combining concurrent engineering process and usability engineering models intelligently it is possible to create a powerful method in order to manage usability engineering during product development.

There are several indications that in many organisations other development processes, for example the Waterfall process (Royce, 1970), are being replaced by some type of concurrent engineering process (Heikkinen, 1997, p.20). This means that there is a growing need to develop concurrent process models that include usability engineering. The future research will describe and evaluate a usability extension to concurrent engineering process. The extension defines what, when and how usability-engineering activities should be handled when product design is based on concurrent engineering development process.

References

Bærentsen, K. B. & Vredenburg, K. (1999), "A Contribution To The Design Process", *Communications of the ACM* **42**(5), 73–7.

Beyer, H. & Holtzblatt, K. (1998), *Contextual Design: Defining Customer-centered Systems*, Morgan-Kaufmann.

Earthy, J. (1998), Usability Maturity Model, Technical Report, Information Engineering Usability Support Centres.

Heikkinen, M. (1997), A Concurrent Engineering Process for Embedded Systems Development, Technical Report, VTT Offsetpaino Espoo Finland.

Hjelmeroos, H., Ketola, P. & Räihä, K. J. (1999), Coping with Consistency under Multiple Design Constraints: The Case of the Nokia 9000 WWW Browser, *in* S. Brewter & M. Dunlop (eds.), *Proceedings of the 2nd Workshop on Human–Computer Interaction with Mobile Devices*, pp.51–6. http://www.dcs.gla.ac.uk/mobile99/.

ISO (1999), "ISO 13407 International Standard. Human-centred Design Processes for Interactive Systems". International Organization for Standardization, Genève, Switzerland.

Kiljander, H. (1999), User Interface Prototyping Methods in Designing Mobile Handsets, *in* A. Sasse & C. Johnson (eds.), *Human–Computer Interaction — INTERACT '99: Proceedings of the Seventh IFIP Conference on Human–Computer Interaction*, Vol. 1, IOS Press, pp.118–25.

Mayhew, D. J. (1999), *The Usability Engineering Lifecycle*, Morgan-Kaufmann.

Nielsen, J. (1993), *Usability Engineering*, Academic Press.

Nielsen, J. (1998), "Failure of Corporate Websites". http://www.useit.com/alertbox/981018.html, last accessed 2000.06.10.

Nokia (1999), "Nokia In Brief". http://www.nokia.com/inbrief/units/index.html, last accessed 2000.06.10.

Nokia (2000), "A Phone Call — But Not As We Know It". http://www.nokia.com/networks/17/gprs/applications.html, last accessed 2000.06.10.

Pulkkinen, M. (1997), The Breakthrough of Nokia Mobile Phones, Technical Report, Acta Universitatis Oecenomicae Helsingiensis.

Royce, W. (1970), Managing the Development of Large Software Systems, *in Proceedings of IEEE WESCON*. Reprinted as Royce (1987).

Royce, W. (1987), Managing the Development of Large Software Systems, *in Proceedings of the 9th International Conference on Software Engineering (ICSE'87)*, ACM Press, pp.328–39. Reprint of Royce (1970).

Usability Capability Models — Review and Analysis

Timo Jokela

University of Oulu, Department of Information Processing Science, PO Box 3000, 90014 University of Oulu, Finland (Also at Nokia Mobile Phones, Oulu, Finland)

Tel: *+358 40 547124*
Fax: *+ 358 8 553 1890*
EMail: *timo.jokela@oulu.fi*
URL: *http://www.tol.oulu.fi/english.html*

Usability capability models are used for assessing the ability of development organisations to develop usable products. We have identified quality criteria for usability capability models and analysed the strengths and weaknesses of the existing models. The analysis reveals that there are differences both in the quality of the structure of the models and in the extent that they cover phenomena related to user-centred design. Our conclusion is that process assessment approach forms a good basis for a usability capability model. However, the existing models should be extended with new organisation and business related processes. In addition, also non-process perspectives as skills, resources, technology, and culture in user-centred design should be covered.

Keywords: usability capability, usability capability model, user-centred design, process assessment, generic capability model.

1 Introduction

Usability is defined as one of six main software quality attributes in the standard ISO (2000). It is defined as follows:

> "The capability of the software product to be understood, learned, used and attractive to the user, when used under specified conditions."

Figure 1: Effective user-centred design leads to usable products.

Another definition of usability is that one in the standard ISO (1998a) where usability is defined in a broader sense:

> "The extent to which a product can be used by specified users to achieve specified goals with effectiveness, efficiency and satisfaction in a specified context of use."

We use this definition in the context of this paper.

How to design usability? The prevailing paradigm is user-centred design (UCD) which is:

> "an approach to interactive system development that focuses specifically on making systems usable"

as defined in ISO (1999). Effective user-centred design leads to usable products, Figure 1.

In practice, the position of user-centred design in the development organisations is problematic. When we examine software intensive systems and products that are in the market, we can observe that many of those represent poor level of usability. This seems to be true also with many companies that have had dedicated resources for user-centred design for years. Some of the products that a company brings to the market may represent good usability, while some other products of the company may fail in usability either partially or even seriously. The problematic position user-centred design has been a topic of many presentations and panels in conferences and seminars. For example, there was a tutorial (Bloomer & Wolf, 1999), a panel (Rosenbaum, 1999) and an interview of Don Norman and Janice Rohn (Anderson, 2000) at CHI'99. In addition, the author shares these experiences, having acted as a usability practitioner in a large development organisation.

We define *usability capability* as follows, Figure 2: *The characteristic of a development organisation that determines its ability to consistently develop products with high and competitive level of usability*[*].

In development organisations with high level of usability capability, user-centred design is effective and efficient which leads to usable products. Low usability capability level means either non-existent or ineffective user-centred design which results to poor usability of products.

---

[*]Refer the definition of *capability* in Trillium (1994): "The ability of a development organisation to consistently deliver a product or an enhancement to an existing product that meets customer expectations, with minimal defects, for the lowest life-cycle cost, and in the shortest time."

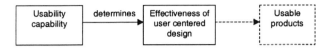

Figure 2: Usability capability determines the ability of a development organisation to perform effective user-centred design and thereby to develop usable products.

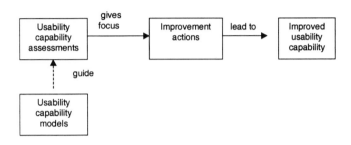

Figure 3: Usability capability assessments guide improvement actions of usability capability.

How do we improve the usability capability of development organisations? The first step in an improvement process is to understand the current status: What are the strengths and weaknesses in user-centred design in the organisation? In the world of software development, *process assessment models* have been introduced as a basic method for analysing the current organisational status. By performing process assessments in software development organisations, one can identify the strengths and weaknesses of in the practices of software development, and use this information to focus organisational improvement actions.

Analogously, *usability capability models* have been introduced for assessing the status of usability capability in the world of user-centred design. Through usability capability assessments, one can identify the strengths and weaknesses in user-centred design in a development organisations, and get guidance for improvement actions to raise the level of usability capability, as illustrated in Figure 3.

In the software development world, assessments are a widely established practice. In the world of user-centred design, however, assessments are still an activity that is performed rather seldom.

The objective of this paper is to review and analyse the existing usability capability models. Our background for the analysis is in our experience (Kuutti et al., 1998) in performing usability capability assessments using the INUSE Processes model (Earthy, 1998b). We have found the assessments very useful. We, however, also found some weaknesses in the model: it did not recover all those problems that the practitioners had encountered (Jokela & Abrahamsson, 2000). These experiences inspired us to examine the other existing models, too. This paper reports those findings.

In the following section, we will give an overview of the existing usability capability models. Then we identify quality criteria for the analysis, and analyse the existing models trying to understand the strengths and problems of each model. In the final section, we draw conclusions and propose paths for further work with the models.

2   Overview on the Existing Usability Capability Models

In this section, we briefly describe six existing usability capability models. Although they are identified by different terms (not 'usability capability model'), they all address the same theme: they try to define those characteristics of development organisations that are relevant for effective user-centred design. We use the term 'usability capability model' to cover all of these models.

We examine the following usability capability models, listed in chronological order:

- Stages of Acceptance of User-centred Design, by Ehrlich & Rohn (1994).

- Trillium, by Trillium (1994).

- Usability Leadership Assessment, by IBM (Flanaghan, 1995).

- Humanware Process Assessment, by Philips (Gupta, 1998).

- Usability Maturity Model: Processes, by the INUSE project (Earthy, 1998b).

- Usability Maturity Model: Human-centredness Scale, by the INUSE project (Earthy, 1998a).

Three of these usability capability models — Trillium, Philips, and INUSE Usability Maturity Model: Processes, *INUSE Processes* — have their origin in the Capability Maturity Model (CMM) (Paulk et al., 1993), Bootstrap (Kuvaja et al., 1994), and the international standard ISO (1998b). The rest of the models have a different approach to process assessment — we call them *generic capability models*. The most important background to these models is probably the quality model of (Crosby, 1978).

The reader should have some knowledge about the process assessment and quality models to understand thoroughly the usability capability models. In the context of this paper, however, it is not feasible to explain these models in detail.

2.1   *Ehrlich & Rohn*

The work by Ehrlich & Rohn cannot be regarded as a 'model' — it presents four 'stages of acceptance of user-centred design' only with brief descriptions (10 to 20 lines of text per each stage). It is included here since it is one of the early efforts to define usability capability and it is presented in a well-known book (Bias & Mayhew, 1994). The four different stages for usability capability — skepticism, curiosity, acceptance, and partnership — are briefly described in Table 1.

Stage	Description
Skepticism	Organisations that have never been involved with UCD. It is unclear what benefits it will bring. If a UCD expert is involved at all, he or she is brought late in the development cycle with no real influence.
Curiosity	Open-minded about the benefits of UCD, but needs to be educated about UCD. A UCD person may influence some overt characteristics of the product.
Acceptance	UCD people are part of the team from the beginning. Their role and expertise are appreciated as an important part of product development.
Partnership	The team is seamless entity. Products that are not only more usable but also more useful. The UCD people are likely to be driving some or all of the project.

Table 1: Ehrlich & Rohn define four stages of acceptance of user-centred design.

2.2 Trillium

Trillium is a process assessment model for development of telecommunication products, developed by Bell Canada. It is a large model covering widely different processes of product development. It also includes a number of usability practices. Trillium is well documented and of public domain, and can be downloaded from the Web. Its origin is in the CMM.

At the top level of the model, Trillium defines eight *capability areas* of product development, each of which are composed of *roadmaps*. One capability area is *Customer Support* where *Usability Engineer* is one roadmap, containing a number of *usability practices*. In addition, the roadmaps *User Documentation* and *User Training* include some more usability practices.

Trillium defines five levels of capability: from Level 1 (lowest one, *unstructured*) to Level 5 (highest one, *fully integrated*). Different usability engineering practices are categorised at different levels of capability, as illustrated in Table 2. The categorisation means that the practices at Level 2 are regarded as the most important ones while the practices at Level 4 are relevant only after the practices of at Levels 2 and 3 are carried out.

2.3 IBM: Usability Management Maturity

The IBM model is quite broad; it covers organisational, skills and process aspects. There is only limited documentation available about the IBM model, without any references to other models. The only documentation publicly available is the one delivered at the CHI'95 in a special interest group session.

The IBM model defines nine *attributes* of *usability management maturity* that fall into three different categories, as illustrated in Table 3.

All these attributes are evaluated through benchmark statements. Examples of *benchmark statements* are (attribute 1):

Level of capability	Examples of usability practices
Level 2: repeatable	• existing competing products are assessed
	• customer/user locations are visited by designers before initiation of design
	• users are involved in the design process
Level 3: defined	• comparative analysis of competing products is performed at appropriate points in the product life-cycle
	• users are visited to determine how the system is used
	• measurable levels are specified for important usability goals
	• prototyping is used to help develop all user interfaces
	• user documentation is developed formally
	• the training material is verified and validated formally
Level 4: managed	• evolution of user needs and abilities is projected
	• the rationale for the user interface design is explicitly documented
Level 5: fully integrated	(no usability practices at this level)

Table 2: Usability practices are categorised at different levels of capability in Trillium.

- Organisation accepts the value of user-centred tools and technology.

- Management sets a positive tone about usability and considers usability, as well as schedule and cost, to be important.

- The organisation understands the value of measurements of and users' productivity and satisfaction.

- The organisation values HCI skills in the development team.

The capability is assessed separately for each attribute with scale $1\ldots5$ (1 = low, 5 = high).

2.4 Philips: Humanware Process Assessment

Another process assessment model is one developed by Philips called 'Humanware Process Assessment'. There is a tutorial available about the approach.

The model uses the terminology of CMM. It identifies ten key process areas. Four of these are engineering processes:

1. *Understanding Use.* Design teams develop a shared understanding of how the product is expected to be used in practice, based on information from user studies.

Category	Attributes
Organisation	1. Organisation Awareness: Awareness at all organisational levels of the importance of usability in product development)
	2. Organisation Activities: Activities at all organisational levels to insure a prominent focus on usability
	3. Improvement Actions: Management's actions to improve the current focus on usability
Skills	4. HCI Skills and Impact: HCI skills and impact of the staff responsible for usability
	5. HCI Resources: Resources available for usability work
Process	6. Early and Continual User Focus: Ensuring an early and continual focus on the user during software development
	7. Integrated Design: All elements of the external design are developed in parallel by multi-disciplinary teams
	8. Early and Continual User Test: Conducting early and continual user testing throughout the development process
	9. Iterative Design: Ability to modify product design based on feedback from usability activities.

Table 3: The IBM model comprises of nine attributes that fall into three categories.

2. *Creation and Simulation.*   Mock-ups and prototypes are produced and evaluated.

3. *Humanware Evaluation.*   Design solutions are evaluated against usability criteria to ensure that these are met.

4. *Humanware Quality Assurance.* Before market release, products are evaluated with end users or the customer.

The first three processes form an iterative cycle. The outcome of the processes is two documents: User-centred User Requirements and User Interaction Specification.

In addition, the model defines the following, market and management oriented key process areas:

5. *Humanware in Market Intelligence.* End user and customer information is gathered to guide decisions on future products.

6. *Humanware in Market Feedback.* End-user and customer feedback relating to products in use is gathered to identify strengths and weaknesses of current designs.

7. *Humanware Responsibility.* A coordinator drives the policy on Humanware throughout an organisation; Humanware quality is managed for each product

development programme; a team of individuals is responsible for carrying out Humanware activities.

8. *Humanware Project Management.* The Humanware activities are resourced and scheduled in a dedicated Humanware project plan.

9. *Humanware Communications.* Communications are promoted to ensure that the Humanware policy in the organisation is implemented effectively.

10. *Integration of Humanware into the PCP.* Existing procedures are extended to include Humanware activities to ensure they are carried out as an integral part of the Product Creation Process.

2.5 INUSE Usability Maturity Model (UMM): Processes

The INUSE project developed a well-documented process assessment model that is based on the format of the software process assessment model defined in ISO 15504. The model contains seven processes:

- Ensure HCD content in system strategy.
- Plan the human-centred design process.
- Specify the user and organisational requirements.
- Understand and specify the context of use.
- Produce design solutions.
- Evaluate design against requirements.
- Facilitate the human-system implementation.

The processes HCD.2–HCD.6 are derived from ISO 13407. Each process is defined with *a purpose statement*. In addition, there are identified a set of *base practices* for each process. Assessments are typically carried out through analysing the extent and quality to which the base practices are implemented.

As an example, the purpose of the process HCD.4 is "to identify, clarify and record the characteristics of the stakeholders, their tasks and the organisational and physical environment in which the system will operate". The related base practices are:

- Identify and document user's tasks.
- Identify and document significant user attributes.
- Identify and document organisational environment.
- Identify and document technical environment.
- Identify and document physical environment.

Each of the processes is assessed independently, using the scale of capability that is defined in ISO 15504. The levels of capability are illustrated in Table 4.

The INUSE Processes model is the basis of the technical report TR ISO 18529, which will appear in the near future.

Level of capability	Description
Level 0: Incomplete	Organisation is not able to carry out the process.
Level 1: Performed	The process achieves its purpose. Individuals carry out processes.
Level 2: Managed	The quality, time and resource requirements for the process are known and controlled.
Level 3: Established	The process is carried out in a manner specified by the organisation and the resources are defined.
Level 4: Predictable	The performance of the process is within predicted resource and quality limits.
Level 5: Optimising	The organisation can reliably tailor the process to particular requirements.

Table 4: There are six levels of capability in the INUSE Processes model.

2.6 INUSE Usability Maturity Model (UMM): Human-centredness Scale

The INUSE Usability Maturity Model: Human-centredness Scale, *INUSE HCS*, is based on the IBM model, Sherwood-Jones' Total System Maturity model (Sherwood-Jones, 1995), ISO 13407, and on quality stages of Crosby (1978). The INUSE HCS model has one dimension that is "intended for use in the assessment of the human-centredness of an organisation or department". It defines five increasing levels of maturity of human-centred processes, from *unrecognised* to *institutionalised*.

The model defines a set of management practices that an organisation needs carry out to achieve each level. As in Trillium, different usability engineering practices are categorised at different levels of capability, as illustrated in Table 5.

3 Quality Criteria

What kind of characteristics should a good usability capability model have? Our criteria arise from two different perspectives. The first one is related to the *structure* of the models: What is the quality of the model from the viewpoint of structure? The other perspective is the *coverage* of the model: To what extent a model covers real world phenomena that are relevant to usability capability?

3.1 Structure of the Models

We have identified the following characteristics that are relevant to the quality of the structure the capability model:

Basis. A solid basis increases the strength of a model. Such a solid basis is for example a proven and recognised meta-model that the usability capability model is built on.

The extent of documentation. There should be adequate documentation about the model. We can examine the models only based on the available documentation.

Level of capability	Examples of management practices
Level A: Recognised	• Problem recognition. Management and staff are aware that there is a need to improve aspects of the systems under development concerned with their use.
Level B: Considered	• Quality in use training. • Human-centred methods training.
Level C: Implemented	• Active involvement of users. • Provide appropriate human-centred methods. • Maintain quality in use techniques. • Develop appropriate skills.
Level D: Integrated	• Integrate HF processes with quality system. • Manage iteration of design solutions.
Level E: Institutionalised	• Systematic improvement of quality in use. • Acceptance of human-centred skills.

Table 5: Organisation needs to carry out management practices to achieve capability levels.

Unambiguity. A good model should be easy to understand and the constructs and relationships should be defined and described unambiguously and consistently. A model should be such that the assessors need not do interpretations about the statements of the models.

Flexibility. A good model should be such that it can be flexibly used in different situations and organisations. The model should reveal the different bottlenecks of user-centred design and it should be possible to examine organisations that are different in size and tradition in user-centred design. A model should not contain statements that may cause disagreements within professional community.

It certainly is possible to identify more criteria than the ones above. However, we have found these criteria as relevant ones — probably partly because we have found that shortcomings in these areas are problematic in the models that we studied.

3.2   Coverage of Real World Phenomena

It is important that the model covers widely the relevant issues that might have impact on the usability capability. In the following, we identify the most essential elements of a development organisation that usability capability models should cover. More detailed discussion can be found in (Jokela & Abrahamsson, 2000).

3.2.1   Performance of User Centred Design at Project Level.

A good model should recover the following aspects from development projects:

- The extent to which the development process incorporates the activities and follow the principles of user-centred design.

- The extent to which there are user-centred design skills available in the project.

- The extent to which user-centred design activities are carried out with appropriate procedures, methods, tools and technology.

- The extent to which the results from user-centred activities are used so that they have an impact in the design of the product.

- The extent to which the development team is committed to user-centred design.

At a poor capability level there are no user-centred activities carried out in a project. Alternatively, if there are some, they are carried out in an inappropriate and inefficient way. In an ideal scenario user-centred design has a significant role, the development team understands and appreciates the role of user-centred design experts, efficient methods are used, project staff respect user-centred design work, and results are used in the design. A capability model should be able to make a distinction in performance between different projects.

3.2.2   Usability in Business Strategy

As discussed earlier, it is typical that the impact of user-centred design may vary from project to project. A capability model should recover the extent to which user-centred design is implemented in the all product development projects, throughout the organisation.

Our understanding is that user-centred design can achieve the position as an organisation wide routine only if usability and user-centred design are a part of business strategy. Project development managers see user-centred design typically as a new risk — meaning more cost and activities. Hakiel's (1999) conclusion is that in order to make user-centred design routine, there should be demand to it from the product owners.

At a poor level of capability, the business management does not recognise need for a human-centred process and does not understand the business benefit of producing usable products. At high level of capability, the management has recognised the benefits of usability to the business, follows the competitive situation in usability in the market, and does actions to ensure the competitive level of usability of the products that the enterprise develops.

3.2.3   Keeping the Resources for User-centred Design at A Competitive Level.

An organisation needs to act in order to keep its user-centred design resources at a competitive level in the future. In an organisation of high level usability capability, the senior management is concerned about the ability of the organisation to meet the competition in usability, and performs appropriate actions to keep the ability for user-centred design at a competitive level.

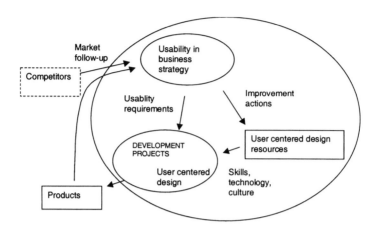

Figure 4: Elements of usability capability are performance of user-centred design in development projects, usability in business strategy and user-centred design resources.

A capability model should be able to make a distinction between different organisations: those, which do actively actions to keep their ability and resources in user-centred design at a competitive level, and those, which do not.

3.2.4   Summary: Elements of Usability Capability

Elements of usability capability are performance of user-centred design in development projects, usability in business strategy and user-centred design resources, Figure 4. A good usability capability model should cover all these different perspectives.

4   Analysis of the Models

In this section, we present the main findings of our analysis of the usability capability models one by one[†]. We analyse the models from the perspectives of structure and coverage, as discussed above. In the end of the section, we summarise the result in the Table 6.

4.1   *Trillium*

Structure: Trillium is based on CMM but has many differences compared with it. There is thorough documentation about the model, which is in the public domain. The practices are well defined, easy to understand, with clear guides for interpretation, etc.

Trillium classifies usability practices at different levels of capability. A relevant question is that is the classification the right one? For example, someone may disagree that the practice "existing competing products are

---

[†]We exclude Ehrlich & Rohn (1994) because of its very limited documentation.

assessed" is at Level 2 while the practice "users are visited to determine how the system is used" is at Level 3. In other words, the model claims that the previous practice is more important than the latter one. There are certainly almost as many opinions on the classifications as there are usability experts.

Coverage: The Trillium model covers a large number of usability practices, and thus has a rather wide coverage. At a high level of capability, e.g. at Level 4, the model requires that there needs to be performed many user-centred design practices throughout the organisation. However, the model does not address issues like the skills, culture and influence of usability experts.

The practices of Trillium cover solely engineering aspects — i.e. related to the implementation of the user-centred design activities. The model does not identify any business management activities that would motivate projects to apply user-centred design practices. It also lacks a specific process for the development of user-centred design resources.

Summary: Trillium is well documented but inflexible. It covers well engineering practices but does not include management practices nor addresses issues like culture or skills.

4.2   The IBM Model

Structure: The internal structure of the model is weak — due to the limited documentation. There is no reference model; there are no definitions for terms — even if the names of the attributes are quite easy to understand. Also the rating of attributes require a lot of interpretation, too. It is not possible to do assessments without making strong interpretations about the model. For example, there is a benchmark statement "The organisation demonstrates an understanding of HCI principles". Does this cover all organisations? If it does, how to interpret when the understanding is high in some parts of the organisation while very low in some other parts of organisation?

On the other hand, the model is very flexible in the sense that all of its nine attributes can be evaluated separately.

Coverage: The model is covering, including organisational, process and skills aspects. Business management actions are mostly missing, as in all of these models.

Summary: The model is covering but the documentation is too limited and ambiguous.

4.3   Philips

Structure: The model refers to CMM but states that it is "not a maturity model". There is not much documentation about the Philips model available. It contains short definitions for ten 'Humanware' processes.

Coverage: A significant feature of the Philips model is that it includes six engineering processes (key process areas). There are processes that address on ensuring the influence of user-centred design resources in projects, and on usability at the business strategy level. There is no dedicated process for continuous development of user-centred design resources.

Summary: The strong point is that the model includes widely also other but engineering processes. The available documentation is very limited.

4.4   INUSE Processes

Structure: The INUSE Processes model is probably the most advanced model. It is well documented, based on the format defined in ISO 15504. However, the statements related to the process HCD.1 (Ensure HCD content in system strategy) and HCD.7 (Introduce and operate the system) that are not at the same level of maturity as in the engineering processes.

For example, the purpose statement of the HCD.1 is rather abstract ("The purpose of the process *Ensure HCD content in systems strategy* is to establish and maintain a focus on stakeholder and user issues in each part of the organisation which deal with system markets, concept, development and support"). In addition, some of the base practices of the engineering processes are somewhat ambiguous (e.g. " Set and agree the required functions and performance of the system in terms of the total experience of the relevant stakeholders and/or the user organisation with the system".)

Coverage: Four processes (HCD.3–6) that are taken from ISO 13407 describe well the engineering activities of user-centred design that should take place in product development projects. The main shortcoming is in the inadequate covering of activities related other but engineering processes. In larger organisational context, the model is missing similar types of processes that are missing from the Trillium but are to some extent in the Philips model (development of user-centred resources, and senior management activities that would motivate the projects to apply user-centred design practices). In addition, non-process issues (skills, culture, and technology) are missing.

Summary: Has a strong basis, well established assessment criteria and practices. Easy to expand to cover more processes. Business related processes and non-process aspects missing.

4.5   The INUSE Usability Maturity Model: Human-centredness Scale

Structure: The model is well documented. However, there are some limitations in the structure. One limitation is that it has only one dimension ('human-centredness'). While this might work in a smaller organisation, applying the model to a bigger organisation may be problematic. In addition, one dimension makes the model inflexible.

Another problem is in how the management practices are allocated at different levels. Like in the Trillium model, "what to put at each level" is arguable. There are management practices at different levels that do not depend on each other. For example, in management practices of the attribute 'HF Technology' at Level C may exist to large extent (e.g. "provide appropriate human-centred methods") while the training issues addressed at Level B may be at rather low level.

Coverage: The INUSE HCS is based on several other models, and thereby covers a wide spectrum of different perspectives: engineering, management, cultural and improvement. This is the strong point of the model.

Summary: A good reference model that covers widely the different aspects of usability capability. The strongest limitation is its one-dimensional structure, which makes it difficult to use the wide coverage of the model in a flexible way.

4.6 Summary

We have examined usability capability models from the perspectives of structure (basis, documentation, unambiguity, flexibility) and coverage of usability capability (user-centred design implementation, usability in business strategy, improvement actions). The results are summarised in Table 6.

Our analysis indicates that there are different strengths and weaknesses in the different models. The process assessment models (Trillium, Philips, and INUSE Processes) have a solid structure that is derived from the software process assessment models. Especially the INUSE Processes model has a strong basis; it is based on a standard ISO 15504. However, the process assessment models do not cover all essential aspects. First, process assessment inherently excludes aspects such as skills, technology, and culture in user-centred design. These are critical elements to examine especially in organisations with short tradition in user-centred design. Second, these models do not include all the relevant processes — especially those that management should do related to user-centred design, and those that address on the improvement of the ability of user-centred resources of the organisation. The Philips model is the most advanced from this perspective.

We find the lack of non-process aspects as a clear shortcoming in the process models. One fundamental element of usability capability — if not the most important one — is the user-centred skills that are in the organisation. However, the process models do not address this (until perhaps at the high levels of capability). This is why we do not give full scores to the process models in 'user-centred implementation'.

The generic capability models — the IBM model and INUSE Human-centredness Scale — address also some of those issues that process models do not cover. However, they have some clear weaknesses. The available documentation about the IBM is inadequate which makes the internal structure of the model weak. It is not possible to do assessments without making strong interpretations about the model. The INUSE HCS has also a wide coverage — one of its sources is the IBM model. The model is also well documented, but the one-dimensional approach restricts its flexible application: it prioritises practices in an order that many may disagree with.

Model	Type	Structure				Coverage of usability capability			
		Reference model	Documentation	Unambiguity	Flexibility	UCD Implementation	Usability in business strategy	Improvement actions	
Trillium	process	×[1]	× × ×	× ×	×	× ×	×	×	large set of practices but arguable prioritisation
IBM	generic	-	× ×	×	× × ×	× ×	×	× ×	wide coverage and flexible but ambiguous
Philips	process	×[2]	×	×	× × × ×	× ×	× ×	×	larger set of processes that in INUSE Processes but limited documentation
INUSE Processes	process	× × ×[3]	× × ×	× ×	× × × ×	× ×	×	×	strong basis and structure, main weaknesses in coverage
INUSE HCD	generic	×[4]	× × ×	× ×		× ×	× ×	× ×	wide coverage but arguable priorities

1. Refers to CMM but has many differences compared with it.
2. Refers to CMM but has very little documentation.
3. The format is compliant with ISO 15504. Processes are based on ISO 13407.
4. Similar type of levels as Crosby (1978) defines.

Table 6: Different usability capability models have different strengths and weaknesses. (Scale: × — low, × × × — high)

5 Conclusions and Further Work

Usability capability models are used for analysing the ability of development organisations to develop usable products. We have identified quality criteria for usability capability models and analysed the strengths and weaknesses of the existing models. The analysis reveals that there are differences both in the quality of the structure of the models and in the extent that they cover phenomena related to user-centred design.

The analysis was mainly based on our experiences as acting as practitioners and in carrying out assessments. We have experimented the INUSE Processes model in practice three times now. Apart from that, our analysis was done 'on paper': we examined the other models using the available documentation. Thereby our analysis is somewhat biased: we know the INUSE model much better than the other models. On the other hand, only the Trillium model has documentation, the quality of which is comparable with the documentation of the INUSE models.

Although also the INUSE Processes model has some weaknesses, we find it as the best choice. It has a solid basis on two recognised standards: ISO 15504 and ISO 13407. The model is also the basis of the forthcoming technical report TR ISO 18529. The structure makes it easy to improve and expand the model. However, more work is required to identify and define other but engineering type of processes; especially those related to business management activities, human factors involvement, and resource and competence improvement activities. Also some engineering processes need refinements; for example some base practices should be defined more unambiguously. The model should also be expanded with a non-process dimension that covers issues as skills, technology, and culture.

One challenge for the future work is in how to define new processes. It is technically easy to define a new process and add it to the capability model. It is much more challenging to define a process (purpose statement, base practices) that is useful, unambiguous, consistent and easy to use. Another topic for further research is to learn more about the practical use of the models: What are the most useful ways to apply models in different organisations and situations, and to what extent do the models truly help in improving the usability capability of development organisations? Also models and assessment practices of non-process aspects should be developed.

Although we have identified some shortcomings in the existing models, we want to emphasise the usefulness the models. Our experience is that assessments give a very good starting point for improvement actions in user-centred design. With further research, we hope to make the models work even better. We plan to carry out research in the KESSU project together with Helsinki University of Technology, Buscom, CCC, Nokia Mobile Phones, Nokia Networks and Teamware Group. Work in this area is done also in CHS project HFICMM that is carried out in UK by DERA CHS, Lloyd's Register and Process Contracting Ltd.

References

Anderson, R. (2000), "Organisational Limits to HCI. Conversations with Don Norman and Janice Rohn", *Interactions* **7**(3), 36–60.

Bias, R. G. & Mayhew, D. J. (eds.) (1994), *Cost-Justifying Usability*, Academic Press.

Bloomer, S. & Wolf, S. (1999), Successful Strategies for Selling Usability into Organizations, *in* M. W. Altom & M. G. Williams (eds.), *Companion Proceedings of CHI'99: Human Factors in Computing Systems(CHI'99 Conference Companion)*, ACM Press, pp.114–5.

Crosby, P. B. (1978), *Quality is Free: The Art of Making Quality Certain*, McGraw-Hill.

Earthy, J. (1998a), Usability Maturity Model: Human Centredness Scale, Technical Report, Lloyd's Register of Shipping. INUSE Project, http://www.lboro.ac.uk/research/husat/eusc/.

Earthy, J. (1998b), Usability Maturity Model: Processes, Technical Report, Lloyd's Register of Shipping. INUSE Project, http://www.lboro.ac.uk/research/husat/eusc/.

Ehrlich, K. & Rohn, J. (1994), Cost Justification of Usability Engineering: A Vendor's Perspective, *in* Bias & Mayhew (1994), pp.76–8.

Flanaghan, G. A. (1995), Usability Leadership Maturity Model (Self-assessment Version), *in* I. Katz, R. Mack, L. Marks, M. B. Rosson & J. Nielsen (eds.), *Proceedings of CHI'95: Human Factors in Computing Systems*, ACM Press.

Gupta, A. (1998), Humanware Process Improvement: The Philips Approach to Institutionalizing the Principles of User-centred Design, Tutorial at HCI'98.

Hakiel, S. (1999), Sufficient and Necessary Conditions for Routine Deployment of User-centred Design, *in Proceedings of the IEE Colloquium 010: Making User-centred Design Work in Software Development*, IEE.

ISO (1998a), "ISO 9241-11 International Standard. Ergonomic Requirements for Office Work with Visual Display Terminals (VDTs). Part 11: Guidance for Specifying and Measuring Usability". International Organization for Standardization, Genève, Switzerland.

ISO (1998b), "ISO/DIS 15504 Draft International Standard. Software Process Assessment". International Organization for Standardization, Genève, Switzerland.

ISO (1999), "ISO 13407 International Standard. Human-centred Design Processes for Interactive Systems". International Organization for Standardization, Genève, Switzerland.

ISO (2000), "ISO 9126 International Standard. Information Technology — Software Product Evaluation — Quality Characteristics and Guidelines for their Use". International Organization for Standardization, Genève, Switzerland.

Jokela, T. & Abrahamsson, P. (2000), Modelling Usability Capability — Introducing the Dimensions, *in* F. Bomarius & M. Oivo (eds.), *Proceedings of Profes 2000*, Vol. 1840 of *Lecture Notes in Computer Science*, Springer-Verlag, pp.73–87.

Kuutti, K., Jokela, T., Nieminen, M. & Jokela, P. (1998), Assessing Human-centred Design Processes in Product Development by Using the INUSE Maturity Model, *in* S. Nishida & K. Inoue (eds.), *Proceedings of the 7th IFAC/IFIP/IFORS/IEA Symposium on Analysis, Design and Evaluation of Man–Machine Systems (MMS'98)*, IFAC, pp.89–94.

Kuvaja, P., Similä, J. et al.(1994), *Software Process Assessment and Improvement — The BOOTSTRAP Approach*, Blackwell.

Paulk, M. C., Weber, C., Carcia, S., Chrissis, M. & Busch, M. (1993), The Capability Maturity Model for Software Version 1.1, Technical Report SEI-93-TR-024, Software Engineering Institute.

Rosenbaum, S. (1999), What Makes Strategic Usability Fail? Lessons Learned from the Field, *in* M. W. Altom & M. G. Williams (eds.), *Companion Proceedings of CHI'99: Human Factors in Computing Systems(CHI'99 Conference Companion)*, ACM Press, pp.93–4.

Sherwood-Jones, B. (1995), Total Systems Maturity, Technical Report, BAeSEMA Glasgow, UK.

Trillium (1994), Model for Telecom Product Development & Support Process Capability, Technical Report, Bell Canada.

Hardening Soft Systems Conceptual Modelling

Dan Diaper

School of Design, Engineering & Computing, Bournemouth University, Talbot Campus, Fern Barrow, Poole, Dorset BH12 5BB, UK

EMail: *ddiaper@bournemouth.ac.uk*

There are many ways in which Soft Systems Methodology (SSM) is soft to advantage. While 'bubble and arrow' diagrams are a popular style of depicting SSM conceptual models, SSM explicitly accommodates alternative systems modelling approaches, without affecting its other desirable soft properties. Two, harder notations and methods to the 'bubble and arrow' style of conceptual modelling are proposed. First, if a similar graphical notation to it is to be used, then SSM conceptual analysts should profit from adopting the more rigorous notation and methods of software engineering's Data Flow Diagram (DFD) analyses. Second, the formal method Simplified Set Theory for Systems Modelling (SST4SM) has been designed so that it requires little mathematical knowledge to understand and use. The SST4SM algebraic expressions in tabular systems models are claimed to be easy to construct and reason with, even by the mathematically challenged. The use of the SST4SM method is claimed to lead to systems models that are better in many ways from those likely to arise from the 'bubble and arrow' type approaches. Furthermore, the size of an SST4SM system model, which can be grown iteratively, is not as limited as graphically based conceptual models.

Keywords: soft systems methodology, formal methods, software engineering, structured methods, systems analysis, systems models, conceptual models, set theory, Venn diagrams, simplified set theory for systems modelling (SST4SM), data flow diagrams (DFDs).

1 Introduction

Formal methods are hard. They are hard in several ways. First, there are the hard-soft distinctions most often associated with Checkland's Soft Systems Methodology — SSM (Checkland, 1972; 1978; 1981; Checkland & Wilson, 1980; Patching, 1990). SSM is methodologically soft in that it is not precisely described, relying on the skills and 'common sense' (Patching) of the systems analyst, and it is highly flexible in the iterative application of its seven main stages. SSM is also soft in that it deals with soft problems, which tend to involve system elements, most commonly people, whose behaviour is unpredictable. Critically, soft methods applied to soft problems are intended to elucidate a better understanding of problems. In contrast, hard methods, which include the formal ones, are well defined and prescriptive in their usual application to hard problems. Hard problems are ones directed towards a particular, predetermined class of solution. This paper argues for using harder notations and methods on soft problems.

Second, there is the hard-easy distinction. Clearly formal methods are hard in this second sense for many people who work in areas such as Human–Computer Interaction (HCI) and who do not have a strong mathematical background. Of course, SSM is also hard in this sense for people who are relatively unfamiliar with the rich, multiple perspectives approach of social scientists.

Formal methods might seem anathema to SSM and, of course, vice versa. This paper will argue otherwise. There are two aspects of the approach described in this paper that allows a desirable integration. First, the formal method will substitute for only one of the representations used by SSM, the conceptual model, so that the other soft methodology and soft problem aspects of SSM are undisturbed. This is explicitly allowed for in SSM and is represented in Figure 1 as '4b Other systems thinking'. This is a similar extension to the Multimedia approach; for example to SSM's rich pictures (Avison et al., 1992; Avison & Taylor, 1997) and Brown's (1992) use of grounded theory to improve SSM's 'rigour' (Kreher, 1993).

Second, the formal method to be used, Simplified Set Theory for System Modelling (SST4SM), has been especially developed as an easy formal method that can be used by the mathematically challenged. That the integration is desirable is due to the intended function of SST4SM, which is to provide a means to aid analysts reason about complex systems. By definition, systems are complex in that they involve the emergence of properties caused by the interaction of elements of different types.

The paper will briefly introduce SSM and suggest how its conceptual modelling approach can be made more rigorous. SST4SM is introduced and it is illustrated how SST4SM can substitute for an SSM conceptual model in a text book example.

2 Soft Systems Methodology

SSM's primary usage has been for the analysis of soft problems concerning 'human activity systems'. Figure 1 redrawn from Patching (1990) illustrates SSM's main stages in which the bubbles represent analysis processes which have associated with them one or more representations. It is critical to stress that when used, there is considerable iteration between the SSM stages. Indeed, every bubble in this graphical model of the methodology could be considered to be connected to every other bubble.

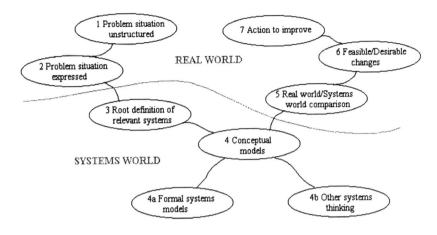

Figure 1: Stages in the Soft Systems Methodology; after (Patching, 1990).

Checkland's use of the term 'Formal systems model' in stage 4a is unfortunate as his is not a formal model in the mathematical sense, but a structured one as used in software engineering to describe methods such as Structured Systems Analysis and Design Method — SSADM (Downs et al., 1988; Ashworth & Goodland, 1990; Eva, 1994). Such structured methods involve the definition of a notation, often a diagrammatic one, and rules and heuristics about how to construct and use it. Data Flow Diagrams (DFDs), Entity Relation Diagrams (ERDs), Entity Life Histories (ELHs) and State Transition Diagrams (STDs) are typical examples of such structured notations used in software engineering. They have the important property that, while it is always possible to produce alternative, valid models using these notations, they possess a graphical syntax such that it is possible to produce models which are incorrect in the same sense that a putative sentence in English can be grammatically incorrect. This is not the case with SSM's 'bubble and arrow' conceptual model notation and this is an example of SSM being methodologically soft.

While formal models share the above syntactical quality with the structured ones, they accrue additional properties due to their mathematical nature. If only formal methods were easy, then their advantages as hard methods could be more readily exploited. First, for example, the precision and hence 'clarity' (Harrison & Thimbleby, 1990) they provide facilitates talking about the model, even to oneself. Second, formal methods support mathematical proof. While proof is not, at least currently, a major aspect of the SST4SM method, one type of proof automatically provided by SST4SM is that of the logical completeness of the SST4SM systems model. Also, the method's filtering techniques are dependent on the formal properties of the SST4SM representation. Third, formal models can support analysts reasoning about complex systems and SST4SM has been especially designed for this purpose. As a hard method it forces analysts to consider their systems model in some detail and specifically directs them to consider particular combinations of aspects that are generally not considered in other systems modelling methods. Furthermore, analysts' effort is focused on understanding the systems model and using it as a tool to reason with, and not on its formality. Fourth, non-graphical formal notations, like SST4SM's, are capable of modelling systems that have many sub-systems. There is an upper limit on graphical representations with respect to their size, after which they become difficult for people to deal with holistically.

Apart from the overall, multiple perspective, soft systems approach of SSM, its critical stages, that make it distinctive from other approaches, are its central ones, and the two distinctive, associated graphical representations are 'rich pictures' and 'conceptual models'. Both these graphical representations have their own, very different, notation.

2.1 SSM Conceptual Models

A conceptual model in SSM is primarily, first developed from a prose description, the 'root definition', which uses the 'CATWOE' acronym (Clients, Actors, Transformation, Worldview, Owner and Environment) to describe a perspective (W) of a system; a major, positive soft aspect of SSM is that it encourages the development of a number of such perspectives.

A conceptual model describes how a system transforms its environment. Arguably, conceptual models are the most important representation used in SSM because they explicitly relate the systems and real world models. Thus, they are one of the main ways used in SSM to reason about the nature of the soft problems being addressed. Graphically, a typical SSM conceptual model shows the system boundary, its inputs and outputs and within the system, sub-systems and their relationships, represented by arrows.

One example root definition (Patching, 1990, p.148), relating to a British County Council's provision of care to its less-able residents, and showing the use of the CATWOE acronym, is:

> "A system owned by the Director (O) of the Social Services Department, operated by professional and administrative staff of a Department (A), to manage given resources effectively and efficiently (T) to deliver caring services to clients of the Department (C), within the constraints of the County Policy for the provision of care in the County (E)."

Figure 2a is re-drawn from Patching's conceptual model which was developed from this root definition. The style of this SSM diagram is a common one. The criticisms below of Figure 2a as a conceptual model of a system are based on the view that there is a distinction between: (i) the many admirable aspects of the soft systems approach to soft problems of SSM; and (ii) notational and methodological softness, in the pejorative sense of sloppy modelling.

Floating Arrows: It is fairly common in SSM conceptual models for inputs and outputs to the system to not be directed to particular sub-systems. 'Service management needs' is an example of this and a reasonable question for analysts to ask is "Which sub-systems deal with this input from the systems' environment?" There are a number of possible answers to such a question, for example:

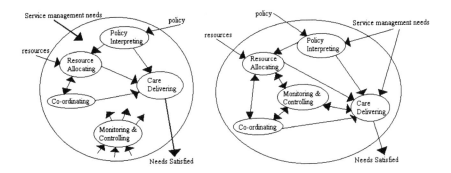

Figure 2: Example SSM conceptual models. 2a. Copied from (Patching, 1990). 2b. One possible conceptual model consistent with 2a.

- all the sub-systems have this input;

- all except, for example, the 'Monitoring & Controlling' sub-system; or

- there are other parts of the system not shown that deal with this input.

There are similar problems with the 'Monitoring & Controlling' sub-system which are exacerbated by having three floating inputs and outputs, e.g. 'Are there really three, or does this merely indicate 'many'?' Such questions are important because other people, such as colleagues and clients, may see and try and use these models during a SSM exercise.

The point is that if the analyst has considered such issues, then they should be represented in the conceptual model; if they have not been considered, then they should have been because any change to a high level model is likely to cause large changes, or create new, lower level models. Indeed, there is a plausible argument that the higher the level of model, the more precisely, and accurately, it needs specifying.

Arrow Semantics: Unlike DFDs, for example, SSM conceptual models do not usually label the arrows, nor have a dictionary associated with them which might define their properties. While it is conventional for the main inputs and outputs that are transformed by the system to be shown using thicker lines, the meaning of all the lines, simplistically, what flows along the arrows, are unlikely to be identical. In contrast, in a DFD only one sort of thing, which can be formally defined, data, flows between its system entities.

Furthermore, in this example, 'Resources' are an input to the system and it could be argued, depending on the precise definition of things, including arrows, which will themselves depend on subtle differences of systems perspective (W), that it is 'Resources', rather than the 'Service management needs' that are really the input that is transformed by the system. Alternatively, it can be argued that the transformations achieved by a system are the transformations of all its environmental inputs to all its outputs. NB Forcing analysts to define things, including the relationships between things, is an example of how a representational notation can encourage analysts to reason about the system they are modelling. In SSM terms, such reasoning based on defining things can lead to both different conceptual models of the same systems perspective (W) and to different or new systems perspectives.

Arrow Direction Arrows can be either uni- or bi-directional in a SSM conceptual model and it is difficult in Figure 2a to immediately apprehend why one arrow is bi-directional and the others are not. More importantly, excepting this one instance, the sub-systems only communicate with one another in one direction. This has consequences such as 'Policy Interpreting' and 'Care Delivering' being isolated from the other sub-systems, except via the ambiguously floating, 'Monitoring and Controlling' sub-system. It would be more plausible to make most of, if not all, these arrows bi-directional as, for example, most, if not all, acts of communication, can be considered as two-way. A method that encourages analysts to consider, for example, what the 'Policy Interpreting' sub-system knows about the state and processes of 'Resource Allocating' should lead to a better model.

The above criticisms do not suggest that the Figure 2a conceptual model is wrong, but that it is too methodologically soft to encourage and support analysts' reasoning about the system and its components. Figure 2b shows a possible alternative conceptual model to Figure 2a using the SSM notation for such models. Figure 2b is only one of a number of possible models that would differ depending on how the analyst constructing the model solves problems such as "Which sub-system considers 'Service management needs'?", which in Figure 2b, it has been decided, are the 'Policy Interpreting' and 'Care Delivering' sub-systems. Alternatives to 2b might depend, for example, on how the 'Coordinating' sub-system is defined with respect to what is transmitted via the 'Monitoring & Controlling' sub-system. This, for example, would affect whether arrows are uni- or bi-directional.

Overall, the problem with SSM's conceptual models is that they are too soft to support adequately reasoning about the system they purport to represent. Unlike highly structured models such as DFDs, which have a well specified graphical syntax and which demand that the semantics of all entities are defined, the softness of SSM's conceptual models fails to encourage analysts to ask questions about the system being modelled. This criticism is not to do with the level of detail, but with what is described at a particular level of detail. Indeed, there is not a lot of difference in how analysts using DFDs work and how SSM analysts work when constructing conceptual models, even though they are applied to hard and soft problems respectively, and that DFDs concentrate on only a single, data, perspective and that the system of interest is exclusively a software system. Diaper et al. (1998), for example, describe how a data flow analyst works thus:

> "... the software engineer is attempting to understand the world and represent some simplified abstraction of it that is useful for the purpose ... Such tasks are appropriate for people and exploit the power of the

human mind as an information processing device capable of dealing with complex, multivariate problems.

... Most advocates of DFDs accept that it (the construction method) is a heuristic-based process requiring a lot of skill and experience to achieve success. ... "

For SSM analysts who wish to continue to use the SSM conceptual model style of notation, then it is proposed that they would benefit from using the DFD notation and construction heuristics. Apart from, trivially, changing the definition of the system boundary, all that is required to implement this proposal is that data, as defined for DFDs, is much more broadly defined for SSM. For example, SSM arrows would represent the flow of something between system processes (sub-systems) and to terminators (entities outside the system boundary). The 'something' that flows could be physical, informational, financial, social power, data, etc. Whatever it is, however, it should be defined, even if only by some text. Furthermore, the DFD decomposition process is strictly hierarchical, because it enforces a data flow integrity rule (Pressman, 1987) and, of course, SSM's definition of sub-processes as being hierarchical (e.g. Patching) is thus identical to that used by levels of DFDs. The advantage of this proposal for SSM analysts is that the discipline required to construct good and correct DFDs can be used in the same way to encourage reasoning about the SSM conceptual model, even though the latter is being applied to a soft problem. In addition, there are plenty of Computer Assisted Software Engineering (CASE) tools that support DFD construction and these could be used by SSM analysts without change to the software.

Underneath the above proposal is the assumption that constructing and reasoning about conceptual models is not easy. It must be harder to build an adequate systems model compared to a model that uses a formally defined, single perspective, such as data as used in DFDs. While Patching suggests that constructing initial conceptual models is not difficult, any disagreement with him is not to do with people's abilities to generate one or more conceptual models, but about the quality of these models and the completeness, at various levels, of the sets of models generated. If analysts modelling with DFDs profit from using a hard notation and method, and given that constructing good systems models is more difficult than constructing DFDs, then SSM analysts are also likely to benefit from using a DFD-like approach because it will encourage them to ask more questions of the model they are building. One way to characterise the methodological softness of SSM's conceptual modelling approach is that it allows systems analysts to be too easily satisfied with the systems models that are constructed.

The proposal to use a DFD-like approach need not change SSM analysts' current practices, except that it offers the opportunity to extend them. This proposal is thus similar to that of Brown (1993) who made "one very modest proposal in an attempt to open up a new option for SSM practitioners, to stimulate debate and generate learning". Furthermore, there is nothing to prevent analysts using a DFD-like notation for SSM conceptual models for modelling only some sub-systems.

The next section will introduce an alternative modelling notation and method to that based on SSM's notation.

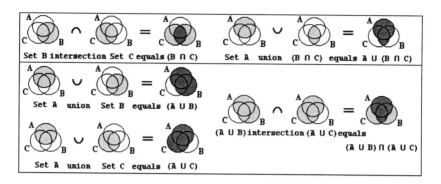

Figure 3: An example of how Venn diagrams can be used for logical proof.

---

3 Simplified Set Theory for System Modelling

SST4SM as a formal method is general, and its use as an alternative for SSM conceptual modelling is but one example of how SST4SM can be applied. The primary design goal for the development of the formal SST4SM notation was that the SST4SM algebraic expressions must be able to be generated automatically in a manner that requires no mathematical competence. SST4SM has two components: (i) a notation; and (ii) a method of generation and use. The generation method can be done manually by an analyst for modelling systems with a small number of system elements (sets) and the software for initial model generation with larger systems involves a simple program of a couple of hundred lines of code.

The SST4SM formal notation is so simple that, if sensible set names are used, then substituting, for example, 'the interaction of' for ∩ (intersection) and 'and' for ∪ (union) produces meaningful English-like sentences logically identical to the algebraic expressions. This is a deliberate design feature of SST4SM's notation, copied from the original work on Task Analysis for Knowledge Descriptions — TAKD (Diaper, 1989; Diaper & Johnson, 1989). It is assumed that for most people learning a notation is not a problem, whereas actually doing mathematics is hard, or even, very hard.

3.1 Set Theory

The justification for basing SST4SM on set theory is simply that all modern mathematics is based on it (Ross & Wright, 1988). SST4SM is intended as a basis, and first step, towards a simplified first order predicate calculus that can be used by the mathematically challenged.

One attraction of working with set theory is that for small numbers of sets there is a formal proof method that is graphical, Venn diagrams. It is therefore possible, for example, to prove the identity of apparently dissimilar set theoretic expressions without recourse to manipulating algebraic equations. Figure 3 illustrates the Venn diagram method of proof for the distributive law of set algebra:

$$A \cup (B \cap C) = (A \cup B) \cap (A \cup C)$$

In Figure 3, in the top left, the sets B and C are shown in light grey and their resulting intersection $(B \cap C)$ is in dark grey. In the top right the set A and $(B \cap C)$ are in light grey and their resulting union, $A \cup (B \cap C)$, is in dark grey. Similarly in Figure 3's lower left hand panel, the resulting unions of the sets A and B, and A and C, are shown first in dark grey and their intersection, $(A \cup B) \cap (A \cup C)$, on the far lower right of the figure, results in the identical four areas being shaded in dark grey as in the final result in the upper right hand panel. Thus, since the dark grey areas that represent $A \cup (B \cap C)$ and $(A \cup B) \cap (A \cup C)$ are the same, then these two set theory expression are proved to be logically identical.

SST4SM represents a solution to two problems with set theory that makes it difficult. First, the Venn diagram method, for proof and for reasoning about what is being modelled, is strictly limited to very small numbers of intersecting sets (5 regularly shaped sets if all can intersect with each other). This is too small for most useful systems modelling applications. Except with small numbers of sets, or when there are few set intersections, set theory algebra must be applied to the algebraic expressions.

Second, the concept of sub-sets, particularly when they intersect, leads to a large number of possible arrangements of sets, each of which has a different algebraic expression. For example, with just three sets there are 14 different arrangements of the sets and, if one cares about how each of the three sets is related to each other, as is almost inevitably so in systems modelling applications, there are 50 possible logical expressions to describe every possible arrangement of three sets.

3.1.1 SST4SM and Set Theory

There are five ways in which SST4SM differs from traditional set theory and it is these that warrant its title of 'Simplified'. First, SST4SM abandons the sub-set concept entirely and instead represents all set relationships by the single pattern in which all sets can intersect with all other sets. Second, the basic components of an SST4SM expression are set intersections rather than sets as in set theory. Thus while 'A' in an expression stands for the set A in set theory, it stands for that part of set A that does not intersect with any other set in SST4SM. Third, SST4SM allows set intersections to be directional. Interaction direction information may be represented as a set intersection element. Fourth, SST4SM expressions are never algebraically reduced to simpler expressions. This makes them easy to understand but at the expense of mathematical elegance. They can relatively easily be read as English-like sentences. Fifth, the SST4SM expressions that form a logically complete SST4SM systems model can be generated automatically without a knowledge of set theory algebra.

3.2 The SST4SM Notation

The complete notation of SST4SM, in set theory terms, is as follows:

U	Universal set	Every set that is included in the model
=	Equals	$A = B$ The elements in sets A and B are the same
∪	Union	$A \cup B$ Everything in set A and set B
∩	Intersection	$A \cap B$ Things common to sets A and B
****	Complement	$A \backslash B$ Everything in set A that is not in set B
∈	Is an element of	$x \in A$ x is a member of the set A
∅	Empty set	$A = \emptyset$ The set A contains nothing

The following is often used in SST4SM for convenience:

∗ The union of all set intersections not specified to the left of this operator

For example, with two sets, A and B, the full SST4SM expression of $\{A\}\backslash\ast$ is: $\{A\}\backslash\{(A \cap B) \cap (B)\}$. In these SST4SM expressions the 'A' and 'B', when alone, are set intersections and in set theory terms are their complement, i.e. 'A' $= A\backslash B$ and 'B' $= B\backslash A$.

Unlike traditional set theory, an SST4SM expression delineates compound set intersections of interest by simply combining (union) the relevant, individual set intersections. Each SST4SM expression is basically a list of every possible set intersection, joined within the expression by the union operator (∪). Each expression is in two parts. On the left are all the set intersections that are members of the set of interest. On the right are those that are not of interest, and indicated with the complement operator (\). The next section illustrates the use of the SST4SM notation to describe a SSM based conceptual model.

3.3   An Example SSM Model to SST4SM Model Conversion

The purpose of this section is to demonstrate that a SST4SM systems model can be used to represent a SSM conceptual model. The aim is thus to show that, although the representational formats are different, the SSM and SST4SM models are logically identical. The example is contrived so that formal proof is possible via Venn Diagrams.

Figures 2a & b are examples of SSM conceptual models. Their validity, i.e. how well they model the real world, is irrelevant for the purpose of demonstrating the conversion of a SSM conceptual model into a formal one, expressed using SST4SM, i.e. it is sufficient that they are typical SSM conceptual models that an analyst might produce.

Ignoring the floating 'Monitoring & Controlling' and 'Service Management Needs' for a moment, then Figure 4a represents the identical model, using a Venn diagram of four sets, each represented by a circle, to that in Figure 2a. Each set corresponds to one of the four SSM conceptual model sub-systems connected by arrows. Set intersections in Figure 4a correspond to the arrows in Figure 2a. The arrows within the intersections in Figure 4a are set elements and indicate the direction of interaction between sets.

Unlike the SSM models of Figure 2, it is possible to represent the Venn diagram of Figure 4a as set theory algebraic expressions. For example, the relationship between 'Policy Implementing' and 'Resource Allocating' is:

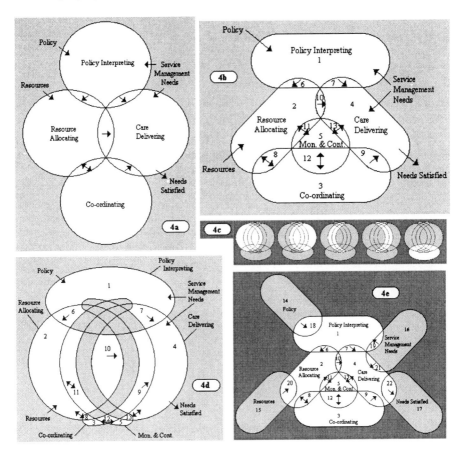

Figure 4: Venn diagram based systems models of Figure 2. 4a. A four set systems model. 4b. A five set systems model. 4c. The sets of the fruit bowl Venn diagram in which all sets intersect. 4d. A five set, fruit bowl Venn diagram logically equal to 4b. 4e. A nine set systems model.

$$\text{Area} = \{\text{PolicyInterpreting} \cap \text{ResourceAllocating}\}$$
$$\{\text{"Pol.Int.} \rightarrow \text{Res.All."}\} \in \{\text{PolicyInterpreting} \cap \text{ResourceAllocating}\}$$

NB Elements of set intersections ($\in$) are represented in text in this paper and placed in quotations.

'Service Management Needs' inputs to the system have been added to two of the four sets in Figure 4a, consistent with the explicit decision on this represented in Figure 2b. It is not possible to easily add a fifth set to represent 'Monitoring & Controlling'. Indeed, using circles it is only possible for Figure 4a to represent the SSM conceptual model using four sets because of the relatively small number of intersections between the sets. 'Monitoring & Controlling' can be added to create a five set Venn diagram, Figure 4b, that is logically identical to the SSM conceptual model in Figure 2b, by using regular, but none circular shapes.

Like Figure 4a, it is only possible to draw Figure 4b because of the small number of set intersections. It takes considerable graphical skill to produce such legal Venn diagrams and the graphical solution can be very different for even very small changes to the SSM conceptual model. SST4SM deals with the most complex possible relationship between sets, where every set intersects with every other set in every possible combination. In the case of a five set model, such a Venn diagram would have 31 different areas within it ($2^n - 1$, where n is the No. of sets). Figure 4c represents the 'Fruit Bowl' Venn diagram that uses regular shapes to represent five sets that all intersect, including intersecting with no other sets. Reading from left to right in Figure 4c, the fruit bowl consists of two circular sets, two banana shaped sets, and the oval dish shaped set they rest upon.

Figure 4d is the SST4SM model, expressed as a fruit bowl Venn diagram, that is logically identical to that in Figure 4b, and therefore, of course, also identical to the Figure 2b SSM conceptual model. NB Empty sets ($\emptyset$) are shown in grey in Figure 4d. Model identity can be proved by checking that each of the numbered areas in Figures 4b & d represent the identical intersection of sets. For example, area 6, which was described above using set theory, can be written in the SST4SM notation thus:

Area$_6$ = {Policy Interpreting $\cap$ Resource Allocating}\$*$

{"Pol.Int. $\leftarrow$ Res.All."} $\in$ {Policy Interpreting $\cap$ Resource Allocating}\$*$

The use of the $*$ notation is stylistically important here as it represents the other 29 areas of the Venn diagram. While the difference between the set theory and SST4SM expressions appears trivial, it is less so when more complicated parts of the model need to be referred to. For example, if an analyst wished to consider a sub-system model that examined 'Resource Allocating' but ignored 'Policy Interpreting', then the set theory expression for this sub-system can be reduced to:

Sub$-$system = Research Allocating\Policy Interpreting

The set 'Research Allocating' corresponds to the following numbered areas in Figure 4b: 2,6,8,10,11. The set 'Policy Interpreting' corresponds to areas 1,6,7. The complement operator (\) functions as a negative and since area 6 is common to both sets then the area of interest is specified by the set theory expression as corresponding to areas: 2,8,10,11.

The same numbered areas on Figure 4d are represented by the logically identical, but unreduced, SST4SM expression:

Sub$-$system   =   {{Res.All.} $\cup$ {Res.All. $\cap$ Coord.} $\cup$ {Res.All. $\cap$ CareDel.} $\cup$
                          {Res.All. $\cap$ Mon.&Con.}}\$*$

The sequence of each of the parts of the expression separated by the union operator ($\cup$) corresponds to the following numbered areas in Figure 4d: 2,8,10,11.

This is identical to that described by the reduced set theoretic expression. SST4SM expressions are not limited to intersecting pairs and the notational approach encourages systems analysts to consider complex interactions between many sub-systems.

SST4SM is not a graphical system modelling method. It represents a systems model in a tabular format. With larger numbers of sets, there is no Venn diagram arrangement possible that meets the criterion of all the sets intersecting in all possible ways. A full SST4SM analysis of Figure 2b requires 9 sets, the five sub-system ones and the four that are outside, but interact with, the system: 'Policy', 'Resources', 'Service Management Needs' and 'Needs Satisfied'. The very small number of set intersections does allow a Venn diagram to be drawn using these 9 sets, and this is shown in Figure 4e. The complete SST4SM systems model in Table 1 can be checked against the corresponding numbered areas in Figure 4e.

The SST4SM systems model represented in Table 1 is organised according to the five identified sub-systems and each consists of an ordered list of all relevant sub-system components. NB Where repetition occurs in the table, this is indicated in italics. Apart from the directional elements of the intersecting sets, a few example elements as members of the single set expressions are included. These would have arisen during the use of the SST4SM method, which is described in the next section. To save space, only the SST4SM algebraic expressions are given in Table 1. These can be read as English like sentences using substitution. For example:

$$\text{"System External"} \in \text{Policy} \backslash * \qquad (1)$$

$$\{\text{Policy} \cap \text{Policy Interpreting}\} \backslash * \qquad (2)$$

$$\text{"} \rightarrow \text{"} \in \{\text{Policy} \cap \text{Policy Interpreting}\} \backslash * \qquad (3)$$

The interaction of Equation 1 "System External" 'Policy', and Equation 2 'Policy' and 'Policy Interpreting', Equation 3 "from" 'Policy' and "to" 'Policy Interpreting'.

It is feasible to automate such an English-like natural language output. On the other hand, the re-writing of SST4SM algebraic expressions in a naturalistic style might be a valuable activity for analysts to do manually as another way to encourage them to think carefully about their systems model.

The SST4SM systems model example in Table 1 demonstrates that a SSM conceptual model involving 9 system elements can be modelled using SST4SM. While it looks cumbersome compared to the graphical elegance of both Figure 4e and Figure 2b, to which the SST4SM tabular systems model is logically identical, the point is that Figure 4e can only be drawn because of the very small number of intersections involved. The equivalent of Figure 4e for most system models with 9 sets that analysts might wish to construct cannot be drawn as Venn diagrams. In effect, what SST4SM allows the analyst to do is to convert a structured, SSM conceptual model into a formal, SST4SM algebraic one. Obviously the reverse conversion can also be done. SST4SM allows such model conversion without requiring the analyst to carry out any algebraic manipulation. Furthermore, the SST4SM method is not as limited as 'bubble and arrow' graphical representations with respect to the number of system elements it is able to comfortably model.

	Element Examples	Area No.
Policy Sub-system		
Policy Interpreting \ *	"Matching policy and needs ..." ∈ Policy Interpreting	1
{Policy ∩ Policy Interpreting} \ *	"→" ∈ {Policy ∩ Policy Interpreting} \ *	18
{Policy Interpreting ∩ Service Management Needs} \ *	"←" ∈ {Policy ∩ Service Management Needs} \ *	19
{Policy Interpreting ∩ Resource Allocating} \ *	"→" ∈ {Policy Interpreting ∩ Resource Allocating} \ *	6
{Policy Interpreting ∩ Care Delivering} \ *	"→" ∈ {Policy Interpreting ∩ Care Delivering} \ *	7
Resource Allocating Sub-system		
Resource Allocating \ *	"finance, procedures ..." ∈ Resource Allocating	2
{Resources ∩ Resource Allocating} \ *	"→" ∈ {Resources ∩ Resource Allocating} \ *	20
*{Policy Interpreting ∩ Resource Allocating} \ **	*"→" ∈ {Policy Interpreting ∩ Resource Allocating} \ **	6
{Care Delivering ∩ Resource Allocating} \ *	"←" ∈ {Care Delivering ∩ Resource Allocating} \ *	10
{Resource Allocating ∩ Coordinating} \ *	"↔" ∈ {Resource Allocating ∩} \ *	8
{Resource Allocating ∩ Monitoring & Controlling} \ *	"↔" ∈ {Resource Allocating ∩} \ *	11
Coordinating Sub-system		
Coordinating \ *	"account, records, meetings ..." ∈ Coordinating	3
*{Resource Allocating ∩ Coordinating} \ **	*"↔" ∈ {Resource Allocating ∩ Coordinating} \ **	8
{Care Delivering ∩ Coordinating} \ *	"←" ∈ {Care Delivering ∩ Coordinating} \ *	9
{Coordinating ∩ Monitoring & Controlling} \ *	"↔" ∈ {Coordinating ∩ Monitoring & Controlling} \ *	12

Table 1: SST4SM systems model table. NB Repeated expressions are shown using italic.

Care Delivering Sub-system

Care Delivering*	"Meals on Wheels delivery staff ..." ∈ Care Delivering	4
{Service Management Needs ∩ Care Delivering}*	"→" ∈ {Service Management Needs ∩ Care Delivering}*	21
{Policy Interpreting ∩ Care Delivering}*	"→" ∈ {Policy Interpreting ∩ Care Delivering}*	7
{Care Delivering ∩ Resource Allocating}*	"←" ∈ {Care Delivering ∩ Resource Allocating}*	10
{Care Delivering ∩ Coordinating}*	"←" ∈ {Care Delivering ∩ Coordinating}*	9
{Care Delivering ∩ Monutoring & Controlling}*	"↔" ∈ {Care Delivering ∩ Monitoring & Controlling}*	13
{Care Delivering ∩ Needs Satisfying}*	"→" ∈ {Care Delivering ∩ Needs Satisfying}*	22

Monitoring & Controlling Sub-system

Monitoring & Controlling*	"administer, compare..." ∈ Monitoring & Controlling	5
{Care Delivering ∩ Monitoring & Controlling}*	"↔" ∈ {Care Delivering ∩ Monitoring & Controlling}*	13
{Resource Allocating ∩ Monitoring & Controlling}*	"↔" ∈ {Resource Allocating ∩ Monitoring & Controlling}*	11
{Coordinating ∩ Monitoring & Controlling}*	"↔" ∈ {Coordinating ∩ Monitoring & Controlling}*	12

External to the System

Policy*	"Matching policy and needs ..." ∈ Policy	14
Resources*	"money, personnel, buildings ..." ∈ Resources	15
Service Management Needs*	"elderly, at risk ..." ∈ Service Management Needs	16
Needs Satisfied*	"hot meals, monitor elderly ..." ∈ Needs Satisfied	17

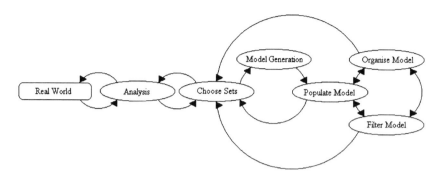

Figure 5: The SST4SM Method.

3.4   Systems Modelling with SST4SM

Unlike the previous section, this section is concerned with the validity of conceptual systems models, i.e. with the quality with which they model, and even predict, the real world. While the previous section demonstrated that SST4SM can represent an existing SSM systems model, this section claims that if the SST4SM method is used to model a system, then it will produce a better systems model, better specified and more accurate, than using what is at least one popular SSM approach.

Just as it was argued in Section 2.1, that improving the rigour (hardness) of methodological notations and methods helps analysts construct and reason about systems, so the primary argument for using SST4SM as an alternative for SSM conceptual modelling is that it provides a high level of analyst support. Its use is probably particularly appropriate for systems models with, at least, tens of system elements (sets), where graphical notations tend to fail because, for example, they loose their 'at a glance', holistic simplicity.

3.4.1   The SST4SM Method

The SST4SM method is designed to be used iteratively so as to support, as easily as possible, creation and reasoning by systems analysts. Figure 5 shows the method as a systems model based on a DFD-like notation. What flows between the method's stages in Figure 5 are various versions of the systems model. Input and output to SST4SM is via the 'Analysis' process which in the context of this paper is the rest of SSM, except the conceptual modelling stage which SST4SM is replacing. An example, alternative approach to the 'Analysis' process and its relationship to the 'Real World' is provided by Dowell & Long's framework of the general HCI design problem (Long, 1986; 1997; Dowell & Long, 1989; Long & Dowell, 1989).

In SST4SM, analysts choose sets such that each set represents a systems element, equivalent to a sub-system in a SSM conceptual model. A logically complete SST4SM model is automatically generated following set selection. This initial model has every set intersecting with every other set. Intersections represent interactions between two or more systems elements (sets). The complete list of SST4SM expressions for more than a few sets is very large. For example, with 10 sets there are initially 1023 expressions (2^n-1) in the initial SST4SM systems model.

The remaining three SST4SM techniques, 'Populate Model', 'Filter Model', and 'Organise Model' are used to reduce the initially large SST4SM model to a structured, very much smaller, meaningful one. These three stages are briefly described below.

The analyst associates with each set intersection, elements which represent meaningful real world examples. It is these elements which *populate* the SST4SM model. Elements can be expressed in any way the analyst chooses, including natural language. What an analyst is doing is simulating aspects of the real world, which is one common way in which analysts work (Diaper et al., 1998). SST4SM's *filtering* process basically involves an analyst identifying set intersections that are meaningless, i.e. no meaningful real world examples can be imagined to populate the set. Starting by populating the two set intersections means that as soon as a meaningless set intersection is identified then it, and all the expressions with greater numbers of intersection that contain it, can be removed from the model. Identifying even a small number of such meaningless set intersections generally results in the removal of most (e.g. up to about 90%) of the initial SST4SM systems model table. There is also an equivalent, bottom-up, filtering technique. It is usually convenient for the analyst to *organise* the filtered table of SST4SM model expressions in a format different from SST4SM's default ordering. A common effect of all these techniques is to cause the systems analyst to change or increase the number of sets in the systems model.

The analyst cycles around the various stages of SST4SM and the output is the model that is sent to the 'Analysis' process. The SST4SM method encourages the analyst to reason about the systems model they are constructing by providing a structured way of applying quite simple heuristics in a flexible way. The output SST4SM model is a formal, logical model of the system expressed, albeit clumsily, in set theory. It can have associated with it quite naturalistic English descriptions of the sets, and the set elements, the real world instances, can be displayed. The model has been created, however, without the analyst having to apply any set algebra.

For example, the SST4SM expressions, based on a Table 1 SST4SM systems model, that represents the three sub-system interactions by which 'Service Management Needs' influences 'Needs Satisfied', and ignoring the 'Monitoring & Controlling' sub-system, are:

$$\text{Sub–system\_1} \quad = \quad \{\{\text{Ser.Man.Needs} \cap \text{CareDel.}\} \cup \text{CareDel.} \cup$$
$$\{\text{CareDel.} \cap \text{NeedsSat.}\}\} \backslash *$$

Figures 4d & e Areas: 21, 4, 22.

$$\text{Sub–system\_2} \quad = \quad \{\{\text{Pol.Int.} \cap \text{Ser.Man.Needs}\} \cup \text{Pol.Int.} \cup$$
$$\{\text{Pol.Int.} \cap \text{CareDel.}\} \cup \text{CareDel.} \cup$$
$$\{\text{CareDel.} \cap \text{NeedsSat.}\}\} \backslash *$$

Figures 4d & e Areas: 19, 1, 7, 4, 22.

$$\text{Sub}-\text{system\_3} \;=\; \{\{\text{Pol.Int.} \cap \text{Ser.Man.Needs}\} \cup \text{Pol.Int.} \cup$$
$$\{\text{Pol.Int.} \cap \text{Res.All.}\} \cup \text{Res.All.} \cup$$
$$\{\text{Res.All.} \cap \text{Coord.}\} \cup \text{Coord.} \cup$$
$$\{\text{CareDel.} \cap \text{Coord.}\} \cup \text{CareDel.} \cup$$
$$\{\text{CareDel.} \cap \text{NeedsSat.}\}\} \backslash *$$

Figures 4d & e Areas: 19, 1, 6, 2, 8, 3, 9, 4, 22.

The above SST4SM equations basically describe, in the conventional 'bubble and arrows' SSM conceptual model style of Figure 2, three routes within the systems model. Their parts can be checked against the numbered areas in Figures 4d & e. The equations can be used to reason about the system, even when no graphical representation is available, for example, by identifying unique, common and shared systems elements, i.e. combinations of set intersections.

In a proposed process re-engineering exercise (Stages 6 and 7, Figure 1), for example, where the brief requires not changing the 'Care Delivering' and 'Controlling and Monitoring' parts of the system, the following SST4SM equations would be some of those generated:

$$\text{Sub}-\text{system\_1\_Re}-\text{Eng.} \;=\; \emptyset$$

$$\text{Sub}-\text{system\_2\_Re}-\text{Eng.} \;=\; \{\{\text{Pol.Int.} \cap \text{Ser.Man.Needs}\} \cup \text{Pol.Int.}\} \backslash *$$

$$\text{Sub}-\text{system\_3\_Re}-\text{Eng.} \;=\; \{\{\text{Pol.Int.} \cap \text{Ser.Man.Needs}\} \cup \text{Pol.Int.} \cup$$
$$\{\text{Pol.Int.} \cap \text{Res.All.}\} \cup \text{Res.All.} \cup$$
$$\{\text{Res.All.} \cup \text{Coord.}\} \cup \text{Coord.}\} \backslash *$$

$$\text{Sub}-\text{system\_3\_Re}-\text{Eng.} \;=\; \{\{\text{Sub}-\text{system\_2\_Re}-\text{Eng.}\} \cup$$
$$\{\text{Pol.Int.} \cap \text{Res.All.}\} \cup \text{Res.All.} \cup$$
$$\{\text{Res.All.} \cap \text{Coord.}\} \cup \text{Coord.}\} \backslash *$$

The first equation indicates that Sub-system_1 is not a candidate for re-engineering. The second and third show that both other sub-systems have things that might be re-engineered. The fourth equation, which arises by simple substitution, and is a way of representing sub-sets, shows those parts of Sub-system_3 that can be changed without effecting Sub-system_2. Considerable numbers of SST4SM equations such as the above can be easily generated by adding, subtracting, combining and substituting, common and different parts of SST4SM expressions that represent sub-systems of interest. Analysts' effort is then focused on understanding such expressions, not on generating them, which could be automated in a CASE tool, i.e. it doesn't require intelligence, and can be done manually without any recourse to doing, hard, mathematics. Converting SST4SM algebraic expressions into English-like sentences is one technique that helps analysts understand their SST4SM systems model and it encourages them to think up examples with which they can populate and filter the sub-systems of interest.

The downside of SST4SM is that it produces a tabular systems model rather than a graphical one, although sub-systems of up to 5 sets can use the fruit bowl model. On the plus side, and particularly because the SST4SM method is designed to allow analysts to grow the systems model iteratively, an SST4SM systems model can meaningfully model very large systems and, with little effort on the part of analysts, the method can present manageably sized alternative views of a system and its sub-systems.

4 Summary, Discussion, Conclusions and Future Research

SSM's '4b Other systems thinking' (Figure 1) explicitly recognises that alternative ways of representing conceptual models can be used within the rest of SSM. This paper proposes two ways of improving what is still currently an example of a favoured SSM conceptual modelling style. First, it is suggested that 'bubble and arrow' graphical SSM conceptual models, in the style of Figure 2a, would profit from adopting a more DFD-like notation and method of model construction and use. Adopting this proposal would not change SSM's approach to dealing with soft problems.

Second, that using the SST4SM notation and method can provide alternative, better systems models to graphically based conceptual models. SST4SM accrues many advantages by creating a formal systems model, while, unlike other formal methods, its methods require no algebraic manipulation. It is claimed that SST4SM is able to model more complex systems than those that can be comfortably accommodated using graphical representations. The SST4SM method forces analysts to consider detailed examples of the meaning of parts of the systems model and so actively encourages a critical appreciation of what is being modelled. The SST4SM method also actively encourages analysts to consider alternative sub-systems in much more complex ways than the graphical ones. Given that conceptual models are a major way that SSM explores a system of interest as a soft problem, then the quality of such models must be of critical importance. Furthermore, that an SST4SM systems model can be converted into a bubble and arrow style diagram even allows the possibility of SSM analysts working with SST4SM and then showing their results to the less expert as a graphical model.

The SST4SM notation and method does require learning and practice. SST4SM is methodologically firm; it is as hard as possible, without excluding exploiting the intelligence and skills of analysts, which is a methodologically soft approach. Given that the SST4SM notation and method replaces the necessity for analysts to undertake any set algebra, then it does not appear to be much harder than other things taught on many undergraduate computing and information systems degree programmes.

Notwithstanding the difference between dealing with hard and soft problems, it obviously must be more difficult to model systems, in the SSM sense of systems, than it is to build single perspective models such as software engineering's DFDs, STDs, etc. Systems model analysts therefore need as much support as they can get from the notations and methods they use so that they can concentrate their efforts on understanding the systems model and the real world it purports to represent. SST4SM is easy in that it does not require any great knowledge of mathematics, and its formal, algebraic output table can be readily translated into English-like sentences. Systems, by definition, are complicated, so it is inconceivable that one could develop an adequate approach to systems modelling that is, for example, easy, quick, cheap, accurate and predictive. SST4SM has not been designed to be analyst effort free, but has been designed so as to focus the analyst's attention on a systems model in a variety of different ways.

SST4SM has been developed using a number of systems examples and a paper describing these, and the SST4SM notation and method more completely than was possible in this paper, is in preparation. SST4SM has also been compared to various tree and tabular models of systems (Diaper, 2000). It is particularly easy to describe organisational structures, people's roles, object and information flows, etc. using SST4SM. Additional techniques have been developed that allow SST4SM to be used as a task analysis method, currently called Simplified Set Theory Task Analysis (SSTTA). Work is in progress on 'bridging the gulf' between anthropocentric requirement specifications and computer-centric design ones (Diaper, 1990; 2000) using SSTTA to model both the software system and the general system using the same formal method (Zhu et al., 1999; Diaper & Zhu, 1999). Apart from extending SST4SM's range of application, by increasing the number of different systems models, for different purposes, developed using it, future research will investigate extending SST4SM to a simplified, first order predicate calculus while still retaining its ability to be understood and used by the mathematically challenged.

References

Ashworth, C. & Goodland, M. (1990), *SSADM: A Practical Approach*, McGraw-Hill.

Avison, D. E. & Taylor, V. (1997), "Information Systems Development Methodologies: A Classification According to Problem Situation", *Journal of Information Technology* **12**(1), 73–81.

Avison, D. E., Golder, P. A. & Shah, H. U. (1992), "Towards an SSM Toolkit: Rich Picture Diagramming", *European Journal of Information Systems* **1**(6), 397–407.

Brown, A. D. (1992), "Grounding Soft Systems Research", *European Journal of Information Systems* **1**(6), 387–95.

Brown, A. D. (1993), "Soft Systems Methodology: A Case for User-dependent Methodology — A Reply", *European Journal of Information Systems* **2**(4), 309–11.

Checkland, P. (1972), "Towards a Systems-Based Methodology for Real-world Problem Solving", *Journal of Systems Engineering* **2**(1), 9–38.

Checkland, P. (1978), "The Origins and Nature of 'Hard' Systems Thinking Applied Systems Analysis", *Journal of Applied Systems Analysis* **5**(1), 99–100.

Checkland, P. & Wilson, B. (1980), "Primary Task and Issue-based Root Definitions in System Studies Applied Systems Analysis", *Journal of Applied Systems Analysis* **7**(1), 51–4.

Checkland, P. B. (1981), *Systems Thinking, Systems Practice*, John Wiley & Sons.

Diaper, D. (1989), Task Analysis for Knowledge Description (TAKD), *in* D. Diaper (ed.), *Task Analysis for Human–Computer Interaction*, Ellis Horwood, pp.108–159.

Diaper, D. (1990), Simulation: A Stepping Stone between Requirements and Design Simulation and the User Interface, *in* A. Life, C. Narborough-Hall & W. Hamilton (eds.), *Simulation and the User Interface*, Taylor & Francis, pp.59–72.

Diaper, D. (2000), The Model Matters: Constructing and Reasoning with Structural Models, To be submitted.

Diaper, D. & Johnson, P. (1989), Task Analysis for Knowledge Descriptions: Theory and Application in Training, *in* J. Long & A. Whitefield (eds.), *Cognitive Ergonomics and Human–Computer Interaction*, Cambridge University Press, pp.191–224.

Diaper, D. & Zhu, H. (1999), Systems And Task Analysis Method Integration, Research proposal to the ESRC/EPSRC.

Diaper, D., McKearney, S. & Hurne, J. (1998), "Human–Computer Interaction and Software Engineering: Integrating Task and Data Flow Analyses using the Pentanalysis Technique", *Ergonomics* **41**(11), 1553–82.

Dowell, J. & Long, J. (1989), "Towards a Conception for an Engineering Discipline of Human Factors", *Ergonomics* **32**(11), 1513–35.

Downs, E., Clare, P. & Coe, I. (1988), *Structured Systems Analysis and Design Method: Application and Context*, Prentice–Hall.

Eva, M. (1994), *SSADM Version 4: A User's Guide*, McGraw-Hill.

Harrison, M. D. & Thimbleby, H. W. (eds.) (1990), *Formal Methods in Human–Computer Interaction*, Cambridge Series on Human–Computer Interaction, Cambridge University Press.

Kreher, H. (1993), "Critique of Two Contributions to Soft Systems Methodology", *European Journal of Information Systems* **2**(4), 304–8.

Long, J. (1997), Research and the Design of Human–Computer Interactions or 'What Happened to Validation', *in* H. Thimbleby, B. O'Conaill & P. Thomas (eds.), *People and Computers XII (Proceedings of HCI'97)*, Springer-Verlag, pp.223–43.

Long, J. & Dowell, J. (1989), Conceptions of the Discipline of HCI: Craft, Applied Science and Engineering, *in* A. Sutcliffe & L. Macaulay (eds.), *People and Computers V (Proceedings of HCI'89)*, Cambridge University Press, pp.9–34.

Long, J. B. (1986), People and Computers: Designing for Usability, *in* M. D. Harrison & A. Monk (eds.), *People and Computers: Designing for Usability (Proceedings of HCI'86)*, Cambridge University Press, pp.3–23.

Patching, D. (1990), *Practical Soft Systems Analysis*, Pitman.

Pressman, R. S. (1987), *Software Engineering: A Practitioner's Approach*, second edition, McGraw-Hill.

Ross, K. A. & Wright, C. R. B. (1988), *Discrete Mathematics*, second edition, Prentice–Hall.

Zhu, H., Jin, L. & Diaper, D. (1999), Testing Software Requirements with Task Analysis, *in*
     *11th. International Conference on Software Engineering and Knowledge Engineering
     (SEKE'99)*, Knowledge Systems Institute, pp.239–45.

A Model for Extensible Web-based Information Intensive Task Oriented Systems

Cecilia Cunha, Clarisse de Souza, Violeta Quental[†] & Daniel Schwabe

Informatics Department, [†] Languages Department, PUC-Rio, R. Marquês de São Vicente 225 – Gávea, Prédio RDC – sala 500, Rio de Janeiro – RJ – 22453-900, Brasil

Tel: *+55 21 529 9462*

Fax: *+55 21 511 5645*

EMail: {*ceciliak,clarisse,schwabe*}*@inf.puc-rio.br,*
   violetaq@let.puc-rio.br

We propose an interface-driven approach to eXtensible Web-based Information-intensive Task-oriented Systems (X-WITS). This paper describes representation dimensions and a unifying language which is the basis for the construction of extensions and generation of texts, such as descriptions or narratives of interaction flows between end-users and X-WITS. X-WITS general architecture is presented, as well as an extension scenario which enlightens the proposal's main characteristics. The proposal is discussed in view of its theoretical underpinnings: Semiotic Engineering and End-User Programming.

Keywords: end-user programming, Web-based systems development and maintenance, augmented transition networks (ATN), workflow systems, semiotic engineering.

1 Introduction

Our work is motivated by the fact that it is nearly impossible for a single piece of software to provide solutions for every specific problem a particular user may have in a given domain of activity (Myers, 1992). Although this is widely known and accepted by software designers and developers, it is nevertheless true that extensible applications (i.e. applications that users can themselves reprogram and change) are difficult to design, develop, and use.

Our own work in Semiotic Engineering (de Souza, 1993; 1999; Barbosa & de Souza, 2000) has explored some aspects of human meaning assignment processes that highlights the nature of the difficulties posed by extensible applications. These difficulties stem from the fact that human interpretation of signs (e.g. user interface signs appearing on computer screens) yields an indefinitely long chain of associations among other signs.

An example of this process in action, technically called 'semiosis' (Peirce, 1931; Eco, 1984), occurs when users take a text editor, such as MS Word, and use it for preparing slide presentations or for designing data capture forms. These related usages not only attest to the wide spectrum of applicability (Fischer, 1998) of this software, but give evidence of an indeterminate semiosic path evolving from text editing: an association with slide preparation and drawing, with form-filling, and other possible connections not mentioned here.

Thus, the applicability of software is the result of semiosis as performed by users, designers, or both communities. They all generate potential requests for maintenance or for new software releases (or products). Popular applications may end-up with unwieldy loads of maintenance and/or redesign requests.

End-User Programming (EUP) is part of the solution to take some of the maintenance burden away from software designers. It can also be a more satisfying alternative to end-users themselves, who can build desired features. Semiotically, EUP environments can be regarded as an indirect form of meaning negotiation between end-users and application designers. By developing extensions, end-users are metaphorically writing a message back to the designers about how they receive and evaluate the application and about how it could be enhanced to meet an unpredicted need.

With this scenario in mind, we are developing an EUP environment for Qualitas, a Web-based Workflow System, currently running in its beta release for a community of about twenty users engaged in teamwork. Supporting EUP in this environment requires enriched representations for activities, tasks, roles, interaction and information structures.

In this context, there is another fundamental aspect to consider: the usability of such representations as perceived by end-users. We will discuss one usability dimension by placing pragmatic issues related to the range of operations an end-user can perform and the mechanisms by which this is achieved. More specifically, we will describe a representation language that integrates parts of the application's domain model (such as tasks and roles) and the interaction model (such as interfaces and documentation). This language is a kind of *lingua franca* for designers, developers and empowered end-users (i.e. a language they can all use for their own purposes). From it, lower-level implementation code or schemata can be derived, as well as natural language texts which can explain and/or describe aspects of the application's model. The representation language also plays the role of a common linguistic reference for translations to and from other interface languages such as the ones we may build for a complete and fully usable EUP environment.

An extension scenario will be described next. Since our main intent is to explore X-WITS extension capabilities, this scenario does not focus on its Information Intensive aspect. It is important to notice that the hypertext navigation and the natural language generation mechanisms support this aspect and are powerful features of this system, especially when the task to be accomplished involves decision making.

2 Extension Scenario in Qualitas

Qualitas is an application for assisting users (technicians) in providing services to customers. As part of the service provision workflow a technician has to draft a service proposal. The technician communicates with the customer and registers information about the service request/proposal.

Let us suppose a technician wants to develop an application extension enabling customers to post their requests directly into the system*.

Basically, an extension is the result of a manipulation of a copy of the current workflow, which is depicted as a flow of user-interactions called Interface Network. Figure 1 shows a schematic view of an extension (or a new workflow) creation, after the user has copied the first three interfaces and their corresponding processing.

Each box, except for 'Make Proposal', represents an interface[†] that appears to end-users as they interact with the application. The interface title, as it appears to end-users during interaction, is shown in the upper part of a box. The lower part displays the roles of employees that can interact with the interface. Clicking on a box triggers the interface layout. Horizontal arrows indicate system processing (called actions). Vertical and diagonal arrows indicate hypertext navigation.

Note that the user did not copy the connection between the interfaces: 'Fill Out Service Type' and 'Customer Detailed Information'. This navigational anchor was eliminated because the customer will be entering the service data now. Anchors can also be created if desired.

The user looks at the new workflow and realises that only Technicians can interact with the interfaces (lower part of the boxes). She wants to allow customers to use them, so she refers to the interface property called Role. But 'Customer' is not a possible value, so at this point the extension task has to be shared with the application developer.

X-WITS does not provide the power of a general programming language to end-users. The idea is to induce them to keep consistency with the original design or designer's message, in semiotic terms. Although there is no guarantee that consistency will be kept, end-users are guided to adapt the message, without replacing it or introducing negations of it. Consequently, some restrictions are imposed on the set of possible extensions. Structurally new objects, relationships or behaviour cannot be created from scratch. Extensions are an adaptation or a different combination of existing solutions. Users may, as explained later, create new objects structurally equal or similar to existing ones or change the processing between two interfaces, always based on the existing representation.

---

*For the sake of definiteness during the presentation of this scenario, we will assume that the customer is male and the technician is female.

[†]An HTML form or a hypertext Web page. Multimedia and hypermedia interfaces are not yet included.

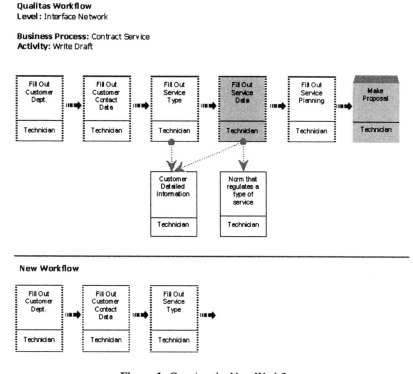

Figure 1: Creating the New Workflow.

The creation of the new role 'Customer' is prevented because it implies new relationships, attributes, and behaviours for this object. It would be transformed from a passive object, about which information is stored, into an active one, which can change information about other objects, thus distorting the original design. In future work we plan to investigate the use of metaphoric mechanisms (Barbosa, 1999; Barbosa & de Souza, 2000), in which the role 'Customer' could be extended in view of the role 'Technician'.

In a collaborative programming situation (Nardi, 1993), both the user and developers decide that she should continue extending Qualitas, using 'Technician' as a temporary role. In the meantime, designers will create the role 'Customer'.

The next interface to be copied ('Fill Out Service Data') captures details about services (see Figure 2). However some information should not be provided by a customer (e.g. the material the technician would hand out). Also, there are navigational links that are useless to customers, such as the one to 'Customer Detailed Information', represented by the underlined content $current_customer(name)$. The user will then adapt this interface. The radio buttons represent the set of possible changes that can be made to the corresponding highlighted fields and the interface.

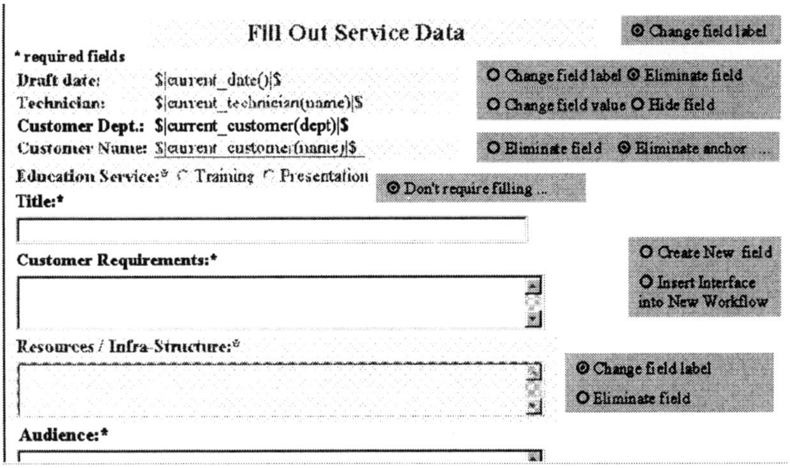

Figure 2: Adapting an Interface.

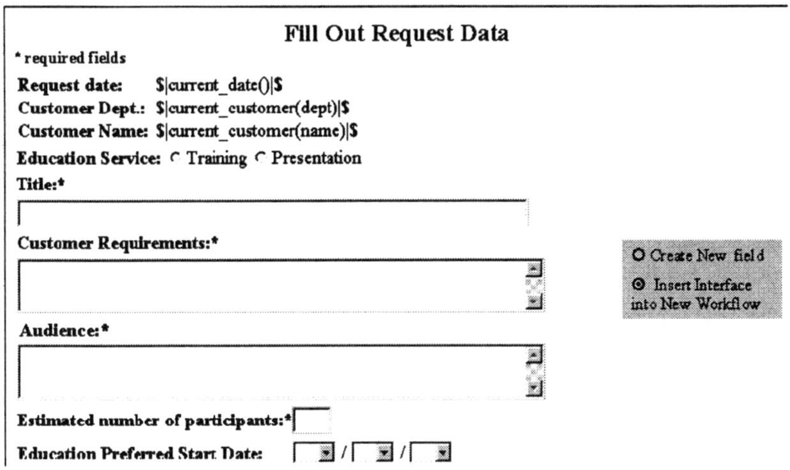

Figure 3: Adapted Interface.

In the adapted interface (Figure 3), the title was changed to 'Fill Out Request Data', which semantically means the creation of a new object 'Request', similar to a Draft object. The navigational anchor to customer information was eliminated — the $current_customer(name)$ field is not underlined. In the new Interface Network, the navigational arrows would not appear anymore. The fields 'Technician' and 'Resources/Infrastructure' were also eliminated, so this information will not be available during the processing of this interface. Input data for field 'Education Service' is not required (no * symbol).

Now the action (arrow) that processes the interface 'Fill Out Service Data' will be copied. However, it will not work as is because of the eliminated fields. The extension environment describes the problems encountered and proposes solutions such as:

This action may only be executed if the following rule is satisfied: "There is a technician responsible for the service."

The information 'technician' is not available for this action. Possible solutions are:

1. *To not check the rule.*

2. *To make this information available by assigning it a fixed value.*

3. *To make this information available by adding it to the previous interface.*

Information expected to be saved into the database is not available. Please inform how to proceed in each case. Resources/Infrastructure:

1. *Don't save this information into the database.*

2. ...

The user solves these problems and moves on. She skips the interface 'Fill Out Service Planning'. Then she wants to turn the Request into a Proposal, connecting the new workflow with the rest of Qualitas' original workflow (box 'Make Proposal' in Figure 1).

She goes back to the action just adapted and tries to add this step. However the system warns that to become a proposal, a request should have a responsible technician. Thus, she decides to create a new interface which assigns a technician to a request.

She determines that only Coordinators are entitled to allocate technicians to requests. Notice that users can make extensions whose parts are targeted at other users, with roles different from their own. As future work we plan to describe mechanisms that guide users to do this in a collaborative way.

After composing the interface, she creates its processing mainly by indicating that each information available should be saved in the database and that the request should become a proposal (change of object state).

The user decides the extension is ready to be tested. Tests are handled in an environment separated from Qualitas itself in order to protect the original system. When the user finishes testing, she can make the extension available at the application interface. Mechanisms which could help the end-user connecting an extension to the current interface are planned for, although, they are out of the scope of this paper.

During execution, problems not anticipated by users might happen, such as a power failure or exceptions occurring during action execution. This is a subject which deserves special attention and we plan to discuss it in future work.

3   X-WITS Architecture and Representation Language

3.1   *General Architecture*

The general architecture proposed for eXtensible Web-based Information-intensive Task-oriented Systems (X-WITS) is composed of two models: The Domain Model and The Interface Model.

The Domain Model is composed of a Task Definition Representation and an Information Representation.

Qualitas' Task Definition Representation is actually the representation of the workflow system. It is a top-down representation (WMC, 1999) where, at the top level, there is a set of business processes. At the next lower level, each business process is represented as a network of activities. In order to support the extension environment, one more level of detail is added to the representation. Each activity is represented as a network of interfaces. Each interface is a representation of the actual system Web page. The Interface Network is the abstract representation upon which end-users build extensions, as shown in Figure 1. It is processed by the representation language that will be described in Section 3.2.

The Information Representation presents the domain information as information units related to each other. Each information unit has different perspectives, such as:

- The interface perspective, which is used when adapting or creating an interface during extension.

- The natural language (NL) perspective, which holds information such as a noun's gender and is used when generating text for summaries or system messages.

Our model allows the generation of workflow summaries and explanations which contain navigational anchors. Summaries can be generated based on the internal representation language that is presented in the next section. The NL generation and the navigational perspectives support the information intensive facet of X-WITS. They provide contextualised information to end-users, which is especially important for decision-making tasks.

Together, the Domain and the Interface models enable interface adaptation or the creation of new ones during extension. Briefly, in the Interface Model, an interface is defined as a composition of the commonly known input fields and output fields in addition to trigger fields. Trigger fields fire the processing of an interface and/or the display of another interface. Each field type has a corresponding set of widgets that can be selected during extension.

We will now present a representation language which integrates the elements of the different models and ultimately specifies the interpreter of the extension environment. The representation language can also be used to generate explanations or descriptions about the system's underlying model and functioning.

3.2   *The Representation Language*

The representation language is formalised as an Augmented Transition Network (ATN), (Woods, 1970) which is an Interface Network processor. The use of grammars as formalisms to represent and process flexible workflows has been previously presented (Glance et al., 1996). However, we propose an explicit representation of the connection between workflows and their corresponding interfaces, thus enabling the interface-driven approach to application extension. In Semiotic Engineering terms, the ATN represents not only the designer's message about the task oriented domain but also the relationship between this message and the decisions about how it should be conveyed to end-users. This explicitness enables end-users to provoke changes at the domain level (e.g. the workflow structure) by manipulating interfaces. Ultimately, the interface-driven approach to EUP allows users to take advantage of their knowledge about the user-interface to construct extensions, thus maximising the usability of the extension environment.

Each state of the ATN represents an abstraction of an interface in the Interface Network. The various arc types are the actual representations of the structures, actions and sequences of interaction that put the interface network into effect. When moving from one state to the next, actions are executed and interactions take place. ATN registers serve as (global) variables which hold information to be shared among different states or interfaces. In general, registers are instances of elements of the Domain and Interface models.

We will now show how the Interface Network can be represented and processed by the ATN. The first example represents the interaction in which the technician informs the customer's department. An ATN state is an abstraction for the interaction to follow (which is specified in the arc sets exiting that state). The integration between the Domain and the Interface Model permeates all productions.

```
"Fill Out Customer Department"
cat(Data_Entry,
     test(security),
     (
     action(setr 'Interface'
            getdb [table: 'Customer' ;field:'CustDept']),
     action(setr 'Webpage01'
            quote generate-htmlform ['Interface']),
     action(setr 'CustDept' form_input),
     action(setr[Customer],
            buildq[CUSTOMER_OO.Dept,getr[CustDept]]),
     )
     terminate(to "Fill Out Customer Contact", post_test)  )
```

'Fill in Customer Department' is the initial state. It has one arc associated to it (CAT). TST arcs for error-handling are omitted for brevity. The ACT arc is traversed if a security test is performed successfully. It tests whether user has access to this interface network path. For that, information from the Task Definition Representation (roles allowed to interact with an interface) and from the Information Representation (current user's role) are used in conjunction.

A successful traversal triggers 4 actions: getting information about the different Customer Departments, by using the database perspective of the Information Model; generating an HTML form for the retrieved items, according to the Interface Model, and assigning it to an indexed Web page under construction; reading input from the form and loading it into a register variable ('CustDept'); and finally building a new Customer information unit and assigning the value of 'CustDept' to its department attribute. This creates an instance of Customer in the Domain Model. Termination of traversal is achieved with an indication of the destination state ('Fill in the Customer Contact') and a test of the pre-conditions it requires.

The state 'Fill Out Customer Contact Data' has subsidiary networks, such as the interaction for 'Filling Out the Customer's Name', described below:

```
"Fill Out Customer Name"
cat(Data_Entry,
     test(Validate_Input),
     (
     action(setr 'Interface'
             getdb[table: 'Customer'; field: 'CustContName']),
     action(setr 'Webpage02' generate-htmlform[Interface]),
     action(setr 'Webpage02'
             generate-htmltext[CUSTOMER_OO.Dept])
     action(setr[CustContName], form_input),
     action(setr[Customer],
             buildq[CUSTOMER_OO.Name, getr[CustContName]]),
     )
     terminate(to "Fill Out Customer Address", post_test)  )
```

This state builds the first part of the HTML form. Its header is generated by the third action and shows the department informed in the previous state, demonstrating how registers hold information and make it available among different interfaces. Registers keep contextual information which is useful for hypertext navigation (Schwabe et al., 1996). The information intensive aspect of X-WITS relies on this, especially in cases where a hypertext navigation and consequent NL text generation are the main resources for providing background information that influence a decision-making process.

Specification of the interaction for 'Filling Out Service Type':

```
"Fill Out Service Type"
cat(Data_Entry,
     test(Validate_Input),
     (
     action(setr 'Interface
             getdb[table:interface; field:ServType]),
     action(setr 'Webpage03 generate_htmlform[Interface]),
     action(setr 'Webpage03
             gen_navigational_anchor[Interface, Customer_OO]),
     action(setr[ServType],form_input),
     action(setr[Service],
             buildq[SERVICE_OO.Type, getr[ServType]]),
     )
     terminate(to "Fill Out Service Data", post_test)  )
```

This step builds the HTML form used to inform service type. The third action uses the navigational perspective of the Customer information and creates an anchor to detailed information about this customer, which has been specified in a previous interface. This navigational anchor allows the delivery of customer detailed information, thus supporting the information intensive aspect of X-WITS.

The ATN, as an interpreter, is responsible for validating new workflows. So, our EUP solution can be viewed as the activity of writing new texts within this grammar. As an ATN, it allows for an infinite number of new texts, a characteristic that presents some level of flexibility to extension development.

ATNs' generative power allows the automatic generation of system documentation and extension environment interfaces, among other resources. The ATN is a base language, upon which translations to different languages can be made, such as pseudo-NL or graphical language. This aspect enhances the productivity of maintenance tasks. For instance, an end-user developed extension, that does not require intervention of designers, may have at least one automatically generated documentation, which could still be refined later on. By regularly providing documentation, the reuse of extensions among users and designers is promoted.

4   Discussion

4.1   Semiotics and Semiotic Engineering

Studies in Semiotics and Computational Semiotics present assorted contributions to our work. They provide a motivating scenario by helping us to understand and reinforce the need for development of extensible applications (see Introduction).

Our development is based on the Semiotic Engineering (de Souza, 1993) approach, in which a software application is a message that is sent from its designer to intended end-users.

We have taken this perspective on the design of the X-WITS model. In Qualitas, we have formally described the group model as part of our message to the end-users (Prates, 1998). In this paper we would like to focus on the usage of the Interpretive Abstraction Principle and the Semiotic Continuum Principle (de Souza, 1999). These principles describe the relationships that must hold between the different languages that take part in an extensible application. In X-WITS, they were applied for the translation of the ATN into more abstract languages — the ones users deal with. Thus, the different languages are likely to maintain co-referentiality (Draper, 1986). This allows end-users to recognise the common patterns and meanings among the different languages they deal with, and consequently maximises usability and communicability (Prates et al., 2000).

The application of these principles in the construction of X-WITS also represents a contribution to the development of research in Semiotic Engineering. Future implementation and tests will allow us to achieve more concrete conclusions on how these principles can be used to enhance the usability, applicability, and communicability of extensible software.

The content of a designer's message is his/her understanding of the domain tasks and of how these tasks should be performed by end-users. This approach distinguishes our work from Freeflow (Dourish et al., 1996), in which the user can choose between different strategies to achieve a certain goal (forward or backward chaining). While in Freeflow an end-user chooses among these strategies at runtime, in our proposal s/he is presented with the strategies that the designer found suitable, but if they are not satisfactory, the user can build his/her own strategy in the extension environment. This distinction favours different approaches to user-interface design. Our work favours a pre-defined step-by-step approach to problem solving and a user-interface design that guides end-users, such as wizards. On the other hand, the proposal of Dourish et al. (1996) implies a 'do-it-yourself' approach to problem solving and a more Object Oriented interface in which the end-user decides the next step.

As mentioned, an EUP language (EUPL) enables end-users to manipulate the designer's original message in order to create their own messages. Thus, extensions can be viewed as an indirect communications or meaning negotiations between end-users and designer. To enable this indirect communication, two main features are crucial: a shared and relatively stable space of (primitive) meanings and a language to articulate the meanings. Primitive meanings are references from which new meanings are introduced. In our proposal, the primitive meanings are established in the original designer's message and represented in the ATN specification.

As a natural consequence, primitive meanings should not be replaced during extensions and new meanings should be created when in opposition to existent ones (Eco, 1976). Although these considerations lead to restrictions on the set of possible extensions, they guarantee indirect communication between the designer and end-users (extension development) will remain possible along time. Not only will the original designer's meanings remain stable and available to be used in conjunction with new meanings, but for every new meaning it should be possible to establish a relation, or track the original or primitive meaning, thus facilitating the interpretation of these new meanings. In future work we will discuss that this is also indispensable for extensions that are targeted at other end-users, since their common ground of understanding is also the original designer's message. We also plan to observe if and how the insertion of new meanings may change the context, and consequent path of interpretation of the original meanings.

4.2   End-User Programming

End-User Programming techniques can be categorised as (Cypher, 1993):

- Parameter Configuration: the user is presented with a set of parameters, of which values may be changed and, as effect, the application will change.

- Macro Recording: the user records a set of steps carried through at the interface under a label and, later on, uses this label to execute the sequence of steps associated with it.

- Programming by Demonstration: similar to Macro Recording; distinguished by the fact that this technique tries to overcome the problem of literal interpretation of steps. For example, where a step of saving a file called 'Paper.txt' is recorded in Macro Recording literally, in Programming by Demonstration this step could be recorded as '*.txt', where * would stand for the name of the current file. In Macro Recording, a repetitive task would be saved as a sequence of the same task many times. In Programming by Demonstration, a loop command would be generated.

- Programming Languages: the extensible application offers a programming language to the end-user.

The Parameter Configuration and the Programming by Demonstration techniques present limitations when analysed from a semiotic perspective. In Parameter Configuration, the designer tries to anticipate the extensions users will want to do (in order to provide the set of parameters and their values), which is very hard or even impossible to achieve given the definition of the semiosis concept and its unlimited characteristic. The Programming by Demonstration falls into the same problem, since the designer tries to anticipate the generalisation the user is looking for.

The Programming by Demonstration and the Macro Recording techniques present as an advantage, the fact that end-users can extend the application through the User-Interface Language (UIL), benefiting of this knowledge to develop extensions. Although, the Macro Recording technique presents the problem of literally recording each step, thus limiting the reuse of the macro in different situations or contexts.

Providing a Programming Language to end-users overcomes the problems previously mentioned but raises others since users should not be expected to know how to program. So how could they be enabled to manipulate variables, conditions and iterations, in sum, to use a programming language? Advances are taking place. Scripting languages can be a solution, in which end-users program by using parts of the domain jargon (Nardi, 1993). DiGiano (1996) proposes a gentle introduction to the end-user programming language, mainly by showing its connections with the UIL at the UIL itself.

Ideally end-users should be provided with the power of a programming language and they should also be able to reuse the knowledge they acquired at the UIL. DiGiano (1996) proposes the exposure of the EUPL in connection with the UIL at the UIL. Our proposal goes the other way around and exposes the the user interface at the extension environment. Consequently, the meanings conveyed through the UIL, in addition to the ones conveyed in the extension environment, the designer message, are the programming building blocks provided to end-users.

In Oval (Malone et al., 1995) these building blocks are namely Objects, Views, Agents and Links. It provides end-users a radically tailorable tool that can be used to construct a large range of applications for cooperative work. The tool reaches its goal in the sense that various kinds of applications can be constructed, especially due to the generality of the primitive building blocks. They are the common and stable ground of meanings shared by the end-users and rest in a very abstract, domain independent level. The authors then argue that some tailoring features (such as the definition of new object types), or maybe the creation of new and complete applications, may be done by experienced end-users (e.g. power users or programmers). They conclude that Oval provides a wide spectrum of tailoring options and that many users would only make changes to applications developed by others.

This is the focus in our proposal: end-users should be able to extend an application by resorting on the domain jargon they already know, usually not as generic as the building blocks proposed by Oval (Nardi, 1993). Our ATN (and all the languages derived from it) expresses the common set of meanings that are shared by designers and the community of end-users and that are used throughout the application. Moreover, mechanisms that impose restrictions on the set of possible extensions, in order to try to preserve these meanings along time, are proposed.

A contribution of our proposal to EUP remains on the common representation language from which all the other application languages can be derived. This enables the content of the designer message about the domain to be shared among the different languages in a consistent manner. Another contribution is the user interface driven approach to application extension, where interfaces are the main building blocks that end-users manipulate to achieve extensions.

5   Conclusion

X-WITS helps the delivery of flexible Web-based workflow applications. Flexibility by selection (Heinl et al., 1999) offers multiple alternative execution paths to the end-users and can be provided by the application designer. But, as stated by the authors, "flexibility by selection is limited by the requirement that it has to be anticipated and has to be included (directly or indirectly) into the workflow type specification". The semiosis concept points to the requirement to handle unpredicted situations or user needs. So, the proposed extension environment provides some level of "flexibility by adaption", in which an unforeseen execution path can be incorporated. Workflow adaptations may take place on one or more specific running workflow instances or deliver a new workflow path that does not affect the running instances. In our proposal, only variants of the current workflow are generated — the end-user extensions coexist with the designer's workflow and are not new workflow versions that replace the current one. It is important to emphasise that the possible adaptations are restricted, so that they are potentially consistent with the original designer's message. One of our challenges is discovering how far it is possible to augment flexibility and preserve the designer's message at the same time. As a result we should be able to continue our work on defining general criteria and guidelines that may help developers of EUP environments evaluate and enhance their own work (de Souza, 1999; de Souza & Barbosa, 1996).

The strength of this proposal relies on the described representation language — the ATN. It represents the designer's message and serves as a common ground that is used for the indirect communications mentioned: from the designer to end-users (e.g. in the UIL), from the end-users back to the designer (when developing extensions) and from one end-user to another (when developing extensions targeted at other users). It may also support direct communications, for instance when designers and end-users develop extensions or maintain the system in conjunction. We have discussed why this common ground should be preserved throughout application usage and this is reflected at the described example.

It is possible to derive different languages from the ATN. By deriving many languages from the ATN, always following the principles proposed by (de Souza, 1999), the chances of successfully getting the designer's message across is increased and thus application usability, communicability and applicability are potentialised.

In future work we plan the further specification of the proposed models and representation language as well as the implementation and validation of this proposal. Then we should be able to evaluate the costs involved in the development of X-WITS. Literature points that the development of flexible systems is costly (Nardi, 1993). This may not be different with X-WITS, since it requires representations that will be made explicit to end-users, so that they can be manipulated. The trade-off remains on the fact flexible systems should reduce maintenance costs and increase user satisfaction.

We also foresee a set of different directions that can be pursued. The discussion about exception handling and EUP in groupware systems should be further explored, as well as the evaluation of how analogical mechanisms (e.g. metaphors) could be used during extension, as proposed by (Barbosa, 1999; Barbosa & de Souza, 2000). It should also be interesting to see how the automatic generation of pseudo-NL documentation and help system, enhanced with navigational mechanisms, will work for the extensions developed by the end-users.

6 Acknowledgements

We would like to thank Raquel Prates, João Luiz Elias Campos, Anna Hester and our sponsors CNPq, TeCGraf and Petrobras.

References

Barbosa, S. D. J. (1999), Programação Via Interface, PhD thesis, PUC-Rio. Advisor: Clarisse Sieckenius de Souza.

Barbosa, S. D. J. & de Souza, C. S. (2000), Extending Software through Metaphors and Metonymies, *in* H. Lieberman (ed.), *Intelligent User Interfaces'2000 (IUI'2000)*, ACM Press, pp.13–20.

Cypher, A. (ed.) (1993), *Watch What I Do: Programming by Demonstration*, MIT Press.

de Souza, C. S. (1993), "The Semiotic Engineering of User Interface Languages", *International Journal of Man–Machine Studies* **39**, 753–73.

de Souza, C. S. (1999), Semiotic Engineering Principles for Evaluating End-user Programming Environments, Monografias da Ciência da Computação PUC-RioInf MCC 10/99, PUC-Rio. Informatics Department. Lucena, C. J. P. (ed.).

de Souza, C. S. & Barbosa, S. D. J. (1996), End-User Programming Environments: The Semiotic Challenges, Monografias da Ciência da Computação PUC-RioInf MCC 16/96, PUC-Rio. Informatics Department. Lucena, C. J. P. (ed.).

DiGiano, C. (1996), "A Vision of Highly-learnable End-user Programming Languages", http://www.idiom.com/~digi/papers/child's-play-96-position/child's-play-96-position.html. Position Paper at Child's Play'96 — Second Workshop on End-user Programming and Education, last visited 2000.06.15.

Dourish, P., Holmes, J., MacLean, A., Marqvardsen, P. & Zbyslaw, A. (1996), Freeflow: Mediating between Representation and Action in Workflow Systems, *in* M. S. Ackerman (ed.), *Proceedings of CSCW'96: ACM Conference on Computer Supported Cooperative Work*, ACM Press, pp.190–8.

Draper, S. W. (1986), Display Managers as the Basis for User–Machine Communication, *in* D. A. Norman & S. W. Draper (eds.), *User Centered System Design: New Perspectives on Human–Computer Interaction*, Lawrence Erlbaum Associates, pp.339–52.

Eco, U. (1976), *A Theory of Semiotics*, Indiana University Press.

Eco, U. (1984), *Semiotics and the Philosophy of Language*, Indiana University Press.

Fischer, G. (1998), Beyond 'Couch Potatoes': From Customers to Designers, *in Proceedings of the 3rd Asia Pacific Computer–Human Interaction Conference*, IEEE Computer Society Press, pp.2–9.

Glance, N. S., Pagani, D. S. & Pareschi, R. (1996), Generalized Process Structure Grammars (GPSG) for Flexible Representations of Work, *in* M. S. Ackerman (ed.), *Proceedings of CSCW'96: ACM Conference on Computer Supported Cooperative Work*, ACM Press, pp.180–9.

Heinl, P., Horn, S., Jablonski, S., Neeb, J., Stein, K. & Teschke, M. (1999), A Comprehensive Approach to Flexibility in Workflow Management Systems, *in International Joint Conference on Work Activities Coordination and Collaboration – WACC'99*, ACM Press, pp.79–88.

Malone, T. W., Lai, K. & Fry, C. (1995), "Experiments with Oval: A Radically Tailorable Tool for Cooperative Work", *ACM Transactions on Office Information Systems* **13**(2), 177–205.

Myers, B. A. (1992), *Languages for Developing User Interfaces*, Jones and Bartlett Publishers, Inc.

Nardi, B. (1993), *A Small Matter of Programming*, MIT Press.

Peirce, C. S. (1931), *Collected Papers*, Harvard University Press.

Prates, R. O. (1998), A Engenharia Semiótica de Linguagens de Interfaces Multi-Usuário, PhD thesis, PUC-Rio. Advisor: Clarisse Sieckenius de Souza.

Prates, R. O., de Souza, C. S. & Barbosa, S. D. J. (2000), "A Method for Evaluating the Communicability of User Interfaces", *Interactions* pp.31–8.

Schwabe, D., Rossi, G. & Barbosa, S. D. J. (1996), Systematic Hypermedia Application Design with OOHDM, *in* C. Marshall, M. Bernstein & S. Poltrock (eds.), *Proceedings of 7th ACM Conference on Hypertext — Hypertext'96*, ACM Press, pp.116–28.

WMC (1999), *Workflow Management Coalition: Terminology and Glossary*. Document Number WFMC-TC-1011, Document Status – Issue 3.0.

Woods, W. A. (1970), "Transition Network Grammars for Natural Language Analysis", *Communications of the ACM* **13**(10), 591–606.

Analysis and Simulation of User Interfaces

Harold Thimbleby

School of Computing Science, Middlesex University,
Bounds Green Road, London N11 2NQ, UK

Tel: *+44 20 8362 6061*
Fax: *+44 20 8362 6411*
EMail: *harold@mdx.ac.uk*
URL: *http://www.cs.mdx.ac.uk/harold*

By taking a mobile phone as a worked example, we show how it and new interfaces can be analysed and simulated. A new interface is shown to reduce the optimal key press costs of accessing the phone's functionality, without losing usability benefits — this is a specific contribution to menu design. However, the approach is not limited to mobile phones, nor just to menus; the techniques are general and can be applied widely. A distinctive feature of the approach is that it is fully inspectable and replicable — this is a contribution to the field of HCI more generally.

Keywords: user interface design, formal methods, menus, mobile phone, new user interfaces.

1   Introduction

The analysis of user interfaces has largely concentrated on issues of human performance, behaviour and cognition. In comparison, device-oriented analyses of user interfaces are rare, which is strange because devices — unlike humans — are precisely known. In the design process, devices themselves are the main areas where usability improvements can be effected. This paper exhibits a range of user interface analyses from a device perspective. An actual device, in commercial production, is used as a case study, and we exhibit a functionally-equivalent user interface that requires under half the key presses to use than the original design on average, and whose worst case cost is just one sixth. The analyses of both the original and alternative user interfaces are described in sufficient detail to be replicated by other usability engineers.

1.1   Contributions to HCI

Often papers in HCI describe ideas that are not replicable; the systems described are incomplete, inaccessible, obsolete or proprietary; the experimental details are not described in sufficient detail; or the methodology used allows vagueness, providing room for mistakes and confusion, which often go unnoticed or may be concealed, accidentally or even deliberately; finally, unspecified craft knowledge is often required to use methods reliably. In contrast the work described in this paper is open, well-defined and fully replicable: all claims and results can easily be reproduced and tested. Indeed, there are several ways to calculate all results claimed, which provides checks and safeguards: if there is anything slightly wrong with our definitions or theories, then the mathematical rigour produces ridiculous conclusions, which we will see and correct. Indeed, automatic and other checks on the mathematics in this paper helped fix typos, most of them of the sort that would easily have been missed in less formal approaches.

A companion paper is available on the World Wide Web, which provides full information behind the results reported here. The method is straight-forwardly mathematical, which means there are many textbooks and other sources of information about it. But, further, the mathematics is 'packaged' as a fully working program, on the Web site, and the benefits claimed can be achieved without delving into the technical details. For example, all the diagrams and results shown in this paper were calculated from a single specification of an interactive device (given as an appendix to this paper). The techniques for analysis used here can be used with other device specifications, merely by changing the appendix, or they can be developed for other purposes.

To show that our approach can handle real designs, we analyse an accurate model of the menu user interface of the Nokia 5110 mobile phone. The general approach to design taken here could be used with any push button device, and would be particularly easy to employ when working within a design process that specifies the feature set of a device. (If we had worked with Nokia, of course we could have avoided reverse-engineering the device's user interface, since the user interface specification should have anyway been directly available.)

1.2   Background

Theoretically the motivation behind this paper is expressed in Thimbleby (1994), and is also illustrated in approaches such as Furnas (1997). Our approach is in contrast to that actually used by Nokia (Kiljander, 1999; Väänänen-Vainio-Mattila & Ruuska, 2000). Kiljander (1999) mentions that Nokia use state transition diagrams informally as story boards; one wonders why they don't use precise specifications of systems, from which informal story boards are derived reliably.

The present paper is a continuation of research going back to Hyperdoc (Thimbleby, 1993), which was a system for simulating and analysing user interfaces to simple push button devices. Hyperdoc was criticised for only handling small devices (Dix et al., 1998); it was also a platform-dependent tool (it ran in HyperCard on the Apple Macintosh) and its inner workings were never published. The present approach is in *Mathematica* (Wolfram, 1996), which is platform-independent, and permits the entire approach, including all its details, to be published. (Actually there is no need to use *Mathematica* — Java, for example, could have been used instead; but *Mathematica* happens to be much better documented than Java.)

We use *Mathematica* for the mathematical calculations — using good tools simplifies presenting results rigorously. *Mathematica* allows user interfaces to be analysed, simulated, checked or have conventional usability experiments run on them; *Mathematica* can also generate specifications of the user interface that can be used by, say, Java or C programs, or even converted to hardware — the Web site associated with this paper has an automatically generated JavaScript simulation for people without access to *Mathematica*. Other advantages of *Mathematica* for HCI work are discussed elsewhere (Thimbleby, 1999), which further suggests how user manuals and other material can also be handled.

Mathematica is a cross between a word processor, graphics program and a symbolic mathematics tool. Like a word processor outliner, sections can be opened or closed to reveal different degrees of detail as needed. What is printed in these proceedings is only part of what the paper actually contains. For example, the *Mathematica* instructions to draw the figures are not needed for most readers of the printed paper, and are therefore concealed; however, the code is still 'inside' the original version of the paper. In the full paper just before each figure there is a piece of *Mathematica* code that generates and either plots or typesets the figure. All versions of the paper were generated automatically from a single master copy (though errors may have crept in during the printing process for the conference proceedings). In short, this paper and its illustrations were not created by a conventional error-prone 'cut and paste' approach.

1.3 The Nokia 5110 User Interface

As a concrete case study, we will be concerned with the Nokia 5110 mobile handset's menu functions, though there are a number of essential functions that are not in the menu (such as quick alert settings and keypad lock). There are 84 features accessible through the menu. A softkey, [−], called 'Navi' by Nokia, selects menu items; keys [∧] and [∨] move up and down within menus. The correction key [C] takes the user up one level of the menu hierarchy, whose structure is illustrated in Figure 1. With reference to Figure 1, the function *Service nos* can be accessed from *Standby* by pressing [−] [the phone now shows *Phone book*], then pressing [−] [shows *Search*], then pressing [∨] [shows *Service nos*] followed by a final press of [−] to access the function itself. All menu items have a numeric code (displayed on the Nokia's LCD panel); for example, *Service nos* can also be accessed by pressing [−][1][2] (no final press of [−] is required).

There are some complications, which we ignore in this paper — they are also ignored in Nokia's User's Guide. For example, inconsistently, the [C] key does not work when shortcuts are being used, so [−][2][C][1] is equivalent to [−][2][1], not to [−][1]. The Nokia 'completes' shortcuts, so that [−][1] in fact selects *Search*, not *Phone book* (see Figure 1). There is no fixed relation between shortcuts and the position of functions in the menu, since some functions may not be supported (e.g. by particular phone operators).

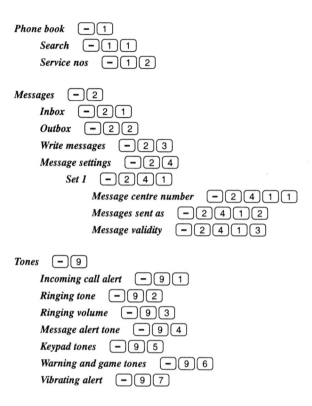

Figure 1: Extracts from the Nokia 5110's menu structure, showing function names and their short cut codes.

There is some ambiguity on what should be taken as a basic function, and what as an option within a function. For example, *Type of view* is treated by the User's Guide as a function, but it has a sub-menu (*Name list, Name number, Large font*). For our definitive list, see the specification of the Nokia in Appendix C.1, which was used to generate all the figures and graphs in this paper. It can easily be edited to do analyses based on any variations.

Figure 2 shows the Nokia's *Standby* function at the top, and each horizontal row downwards is a group of functions that each take an equal minimum number of key presses to access from *Standby* (ignoring the numeric shortcuts). Of the 188 circles, 84 are black: these indicate phone functions of actual use, as opposed to sub-menus that in themselves have no other purpose than structuring the user interface, such as *Options*.

Because of the layout of Figure 2, ⊟ (which selects items from menus, whether sub-menus or functions) moves downwards, and ⓒ (which corrects errors) goes upwards; the ⌃ and ⌄ keys do not move in a systematic direction in this layout. Thus the figure shows the minimum costs of accessing functions, rather than the menu hierarchy (as in Figure 1).

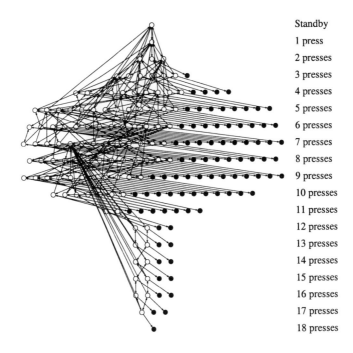

	Standby
	1 press
	2 presses
	3 presses
	4 presses
	5 presses
	6 presses
	7 presses
	8 presses
	9 presses
	10 presses
	11 presses
	12 presses
	13 presses
	14 presses
	15 presses
	16 presses
	17 presses
	18 presses

Figure 2: Visualising the error-free cost of accessing Nokia menu functions. For clarity arrows *from* functions (black dots) are not shown.

Each arrow corresponds to a button press: pressing buttons takes the Nokia from one state to another. Since there are 188 states and four buttons, there are 752 arrows, but for clarity Figure 2 does not show arrows going out of each of the 84 black circles, whether for error-correction (pressing C) or back to *Standby* (pressing −), which not all functions support — otherwise the figure gives an accurate idea of the complexity of the user interface that is the subject of this paper.

2 User Interface Simulation

The specification of the Nokia handset can be used to animate a complete working simulation of the user interface. Interactively, a user can press buttons and the simulated display will show what the Nokia would have shown. Additionally, the simulation can be instrumented so that it collects statistics on user behaviour.

The *Mathematica* code required to run the user interface simulation is simple and brief. After a few lines of support code (see Appendix D), Figure 3 provides the interactive functionality of the user interface: clicking on the buttons makes it work in the full *Mathematica* version of this paper. The complete keypad is about 20 lines

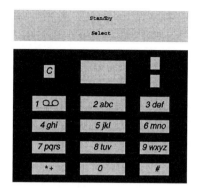

Figure 3: Simulation of the Nokia handset. The picture (which is full size in the *Mathematica* version of this paper) is active code and works when it is clicked.

---

of code, including specifying the key-top fonts and sizes, plus the data structure — also *Mathematica* code — for the graphics symbol on the ⊡ key.

3 User Interface Analysis

A single specification, for the Nokia 5110 menu functions, can be used to support a variety of analyses, as well as provide the basis for generating novel user interfaces that provide the same functionality.

Usability depends on many factors. The analyses, below, while not exhaustive of the sorts of mathematical questions that can be raised, are based on key press costs. A keystroke model could be used to estimate time, but this would take us beyond the space available for this paper; see Silfverberg et al. (2000), whose formula gives 240ms per keystroke, assuming skilled, continuous use of the index finger to press the menu keys. Another measure of usability is the probability that a particular key is used: the Nokia 5110 design appears to have attempted to increase the frequency ⊡ is used — it is a soft key, and reduces the number of other keys required. This creates the visual impression of a simple user interface as well as reducing finger movement. Yet it also means that menu functions (such as the phone's calculator) are inaccessible during phone calls, because in this mode ⊡ ends the phone call. Whether users need, say, a calculator during a phone call and whether this need should override the keypad aesthetics is an empirical question beyond the scope of mathematical analysis. Whatever we choose to analyse mathematically, design trade-offs can be formulated, which then raise interesting insights and questions that suggest further empirical work.

3.1 Goal Weights

From the Nokia specification we can work out the optimal key press sequences to activate any function. The expected optimal number of presses is 8.83 ± 3.29, meaning that if the Nokia is used optimally without error then users will take 8.83 presses on average to activate menu functions with a standard deviation of 3.29. But of course, as well as not always being as efficient, a real user will access some

Function name	Rank	Presses	Probability
Search	1	3	0.0613
Incoming call alert	2	4	0.0306
Inbox	2	4	0.0306
Speed dials	2	4	0.0306
Service nos	2	4	0.0306
...	...	...	...
Português	14	16	0.00438
Svenska	14	16	0.00438
Español	15	17	0.00408
Norsk	15	17	0.00408
Suomi	16	18	0.00383

Figure 4: Summary of functions, ranked by presses and Zipf probabilities.

commands infrequently — especially the ones that Nokia have made less accessible. For example, it takes 11 presses to change the phone's security settings, as against the *Search* function, which only requires 3 presses to access. We would get a more realistic expectation of the number of presses if they were weighted by how likely each function is required by a user.

We could use the simulated handset to obtain weights by getting users to run simulated tasks, but this would take a long time (and many users), as well as begging the question where we could get appropriate distributions of tasks. No doubt Nokia has, over time, collected enough statistics of use to do this accurately. If we had such figures, we could use them. Instead, for the purposes of this paper, it is sufficient to obtain a plausible probability distribution.

We will assume Nokia has arranged things so that more likely, more frequently used, functions take fewer key presses to activate. The Zipf distribution (Zipf, 1949) meets the requirements and is easy to calculate; moreover, the Zipf distribution occurs naturally in many contexts (e.g. it relates the length and frequency of English words) — the frequency of an item is inversely proportional to its cost. Weighting presses by the Zipf probabilities, we obtain an expected number of presses of 7.15 ± 2.95. This number is of course less than the unweighted expectation because we have chosen a probability distribution that makes large numbers less likely.

Figure 4 shows an extract from the phone's functions, ranks, costs and Zipf probabilities, ordered by rank. (With all functions shown the probabilities would sum to 1.)

Given the state probabilities, and other assumptions such as the probability of making errors and of pressing ⒞, we could work out button probabilities. Without known error rates, for this paper we take the probabilities of pressing buttons to be equi-probable (i.e. 0.25) but other values can easily be written into the code in Appendix C.1 if required.

The Nokia allows users to exit some functions returning to the previous position in the menu hierarchy, whereas others enter different modes or return to *Standby*.

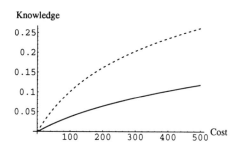

Figure 5: Cost of knowledge graph for the Nokia 5110 function menu. Dashed line is Zipf weights; solid line is uniform weights.

For example, the search function can be used to look up a phone number, which is then dialled. At the end of the phone call, the phone is back in *Standby*, rather than returning to the phone book part of the menu hierarchy. We will assume, for uniformity, that when the user has accessed a function, with probability 1 on the next button press the device is returned to *Standby*.

3.2   Cost of Knowledge Graphs

There are many ways to analyse a user interface from its specification. The *cost of knowledge graph* was introduced and justified for usability analysis by Card et al. (1994) to visualise how easily a user can access the state space of a system. The graph shows the number of goal states a user can access against the number of user actions, that is, the cost of acquiring the knowledge available in each state. The cost of knowledge graph can be constructed from empirical data, from cognitive analysis, or analytically, as we now do. Our approach is probabilistic and does not assume error-free behaviour; the more realistic the probabilities used, the more realistic the evaluations that can be drawn from them. Details of the mathematics are given in Appendix A — for practical purposes (e.g. use by designers, rather than HCI researchers), what is important is the visualisation, rather than the way it is calculated; indeed, for anyone using this paper in its full *Mathematica* form, all that is necessary is to invoke a function that has already been defined, and the graph is drawn automatically.

A cost of knowledge graph for the Nokia menu system is shown in Figure 5. The solid line shows an unweighted cost of knowledge graph, but weighting (by the Zipf probabilities) gives a more realistic measure of knowledge — since the user is less interested in some functions than others, and the Zipf probabilities reflect this well. The dashed line shows the weighted cost of knowledge graph.

The analysis could be refined. For example, we took the probability of pressing Ⓒ as 0.25, which is possibly too high. Nevertheless, the point demonstrated is that with data (whether empirical or estimated) useful insights can be derived. Here we see, for instance, that in "average" use (i.e. as might occur in field studies) to achieve a coverage of 25% takes 455 button presses. (This figure does not translate nicely

Function name	Rank	Presses	Probability
Search	1	3	0.0243
Inbox	1	3	0.0243
Incoming call alert	1	3	0.0243
Speed dials	1	3	0.0243
Service nos	1	3	0.0243
...	...	...	...
Norsk	3	5	0.0081
Español	3	5	0.0081
Suomi	3	5	0.0081

Figure 6: Summary of Huffman costs and probabilities.

into a time, since the cost of knowledge assumes the user acquires knowledge, and thus pauses in each new state.)

Furnas (1997) suggests the pair (maximal outdegree, diameter) is a good indicator of the usability of a device; the original Nokia is (4, 19), compared to the Huffman tree alternative using the same keys discussed below, which is (4, 8). The digit key Huffman tree, also discussed below, is (11, 5) — showing that when more keys are used (here 10 digit keys and one correction key, ⒞) the worst distance between states (the diameter, 5) can be considerably reduced. Many other measures can be obtained from the specification. For example, to test whether every button works correctly in every state takes a *minimum* of 3914 presses, assuming error-free performance. Such a high number suggests that human testing would be inadequate.

4 Alternative User Interfaces

A mobile phone can be controlled with many sorts of user interface. In this paper, following Nokia, we restrict ourselves to tree-structured interfaces. There are other alternatives, which can be much more effective: see Marsden et al. (2000) and Thimbleby (1997) for examples.

The Nokia uses four keys to select from 84 functions. If reducing the number of keystrokes was a design goal, then a Huffman tree (Huffman, 1952) is the most efficient way, in terms of keystrokes, to do this. From the original list of functions, we can construct a Huffman tree using three keys for navigation and one key (retaining ⒞) for correcting errors. Under these assumptions, we achieve an expected optimal number of presses of 4.04 ± 0.53 (or 4.18 ± 0.52 unweighted). See Figure 6 for comparison with the ranking of Nokia functions (Figure 4).

The entries in the Huffman table are in the same overall order as the original Nokia table; this is a consequence of building the Huffman interface on the Zipf probabilities, which were in turn inversely proportional to the ranks of the functions in the original design.

Figure 7 (note the different vertical scales compared to Figure 5) shows that the cost of knowledge graph for the Huffman tree interface is *considerably* better (in terms of speed of access to the device's functions) than the original design; for

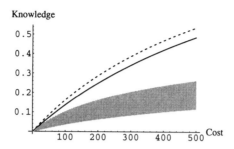

Figure 7: Cost of knowledge graph for the Huffman tree interface (the dashed line is Zipf weights; the solid line is uniform weights). For comparison, the lower grey region represents the range of data from the original Nokia as shown in Figure 5.

example it achieves 25% coverage after 168 presses (compared to 455 presses for the original Nokia). Even so, the model over-estimates the costs because of the assumption of pressing $\boxed{\text{C}}$ with probability 0.25.

A Huffman tree organises functions according to their probability, which would be convenient for a highly skilled user, but might seem arbitrary to a conventional user. There are two obvious improvements: first, the probabilities could be determined from the actual user's operation of the handset — the user interface would then adapt to be optimal for the user's own patterns of behaviour (see Knuth (1985) for an algorithm); secondly, the navigation keys could be left as they are (i.e. with a more-or-less topic-organised structure) and the numeric keys could be used for rapid access, providing shortcut codes.

In fact, the Nokia already uses numeric keys for faster access; some numeric codes are shown in Figure 1. Although the Nokia allocation of numeric codes corresponds to the menu structure, since the menu structure and in particular the order of functions is of little interest to users, the codes are effectively arbitrary — for example, even if a user knows $\boxed{-}\boxed{2}\boxed{4}\boxed{1}$, they are not likely to be able to work out what $\boxed{-}\boxed{2}\boxed{4}\boxed{2}$ is! If we use ten numeric keys and $\boxed{\text{C}}$ instead of just three navigation keys (i.e. creating a Huffman tree with fan-out of 10), we can access functions with 2.98 ± 0.26 (3.01 ± 0.24 unweighted) key presses. Note that using the digit keys means that a menu key is required (otherwise the digits pressed would just dial a phone number), compared to using the dedicated keys where any of them can be pressed immediately without ambiguity. This adds 1 to the costs, which is included in the figures. In comparison the original Nokia shortcuts have higher expected optimum presses of 3.39 ± 0.92 (3.64 ± 0.92 unweighted).

We can use *unallocated* shortcut codes from the Nokia design (for example, $\boxed{-}\boxed{8}\boxed{3}$ is not allocated) and achieve an expected number of presses of 3.09 ± 0.45 (3.29 ± 0.48 unweighted) — which is marginally faster than Nokia's shortcuts. Since these codes are all different from Nokia's, we could have both schemes available at the same time (if we wanted to), so each function would have two codes, Nokia's original and the faster, unallocated codes. Since the codes are different, there is

Design	Min	Max	Weighted	Unweighted
Nokia navigable menu	3	18	7.15 ± 2.95	8.83 ± 3.29
Huffman, 3 keys	3	5	4.04 ± 0.53	4.18 ± 0.52
Nokia digit shortcuts	2	5	3.39 ± 0.92	3.64 ± 0.92
Unallocated codes	2	4	3.09 ± 0.45	3.29 ± 0.48
Huffman, 10 digit keys	2	4	2.98 ± 0.26	3.01 ± 0.24
Shortest codes	2	3	2.69 ± 0.46	2.87 ± 0.34

Figure 8: Summary of expected optimal costs of accessing all goals.

no confusion: either could be used. Since the user presumably doesn't care what the shortcut codes are, they could use Nokia's shortcuts if these are better, or the unallocated codes if these are better. This is having the best of both worlds, and unsurprisingly it works out even faster — at 2.69 ± 0.46 (or 2.87 ± 0.34 unweighted).

All results are summarised in Figure 8. With reference to Figure 8, there appear to be two errors. The Shortest codes have a maximum length shorter than either the Nokia shortcuts or the Unallocated codes, yet it is based on both of them. The explanation is that the Unallocated codes do not take advantage of any of the Nokia's short codes, so some are quite long; the Shortest codes approach makes use of the short Nokia codes, and then has spare short codes of length 3 to replace the longer Nokia codes of length 4 and 5. The second apparent error is that the maximum length of the Shortest codes is 3, but the maximum length of the Huffman codes is 4. Yet Huffman codes are theoretically shortest — so hasn't something gone wrong? The explanation is that Huffman codes are unambiguous (they are prefix-free), but the Nokia as so far described is not.

For example, if a user presses $\boxed{-}\boxed{1}\boxed{7}\boxed{2}$ they get **Memory status**. If they press $\boxed{-}\boxed{1}\boxed{7}$, which is a prefix of that, they first get **Options**, but it auto-completes to **Type of view**, which (also) has shortcut $\boxed{-}\boxed{1}\boxed{7}\boxed{1}$. To avoid the apparent ambiguities, the Nokia effectively has an extra user action, $\boxed{Pause}$, "pressed" when the user delays. Thus **Type of view** has a shortcut $\boxed{-}\boxed{1}\boxed{7}\boxed{Pause}$ — which is not a prefix of $\boxed{-}\boxed{1}\boxed{7}\boxed{2}$. Thus the Shortest codes cost is based on having effectively 12 keys (10 digits and $\boxed{Pause}$ for navigating, plus $\boxed{C}$ for corrections) as compared to the Huffman tree that makes do with 11 keys (10 digits plus $\boxed{C}$). Since the Shortest codes are making use of more "keys," the maximum length of a shortcut can legitimately be less than the maximum length of the Huffman code. It is interesting that by entering the definition of the Nokia straight from the User's Guide, and spotting a potential error in our analysis, we discovered a design feature that was not documented.*

The Shortest codes scheme has advantages — it preserves Nokia's original structure for the menu shortcut codes *and* permits faster access where possible — and it is better than the Huffman code approach, which has no advantages other than reducing key press counts. It is a design worth considering further and evaluating empirically. Figure 9 shows what the new codes look like, compared with the

---

*The 5110 has numerous other timing issues that are not discussed in this paper.

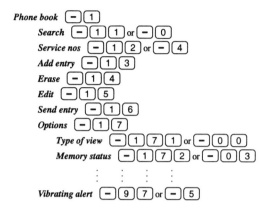

Figure 9: Extract from 'shortest codes' menu. Both shortcuts can be used.

original Nokia codes (compare with Figure 1). For example, to access **Memory status**, the user can press either [–][1][7][2], as specified by Nokia, or they can press [–][0][3], saving a press. (The alternative menu codes in Figure 9 have been allocated so that shorter codes are preferentially allocated to higher Zipf probability functions.)

5 Conclusions

Despite having being around for many years, and having had many opportunities for improvement, consumer electronics, such as mobile phones, video recorders and fax machines, are notorious for having poor user interfaces (Thimbleby, 1992). Certainly it takes skill to perform usability evaluations well, and unfortunately the time pressures of manufacturing often mean usability considerations come too late to have any significant impact. Even if usability studies are done, in the time available, they are unable to cover entire designs — instead, practical evaluation concentrates on usability disasters or marketing features. As ubiquitous bad design proves, conventional usability engineering is relatively ineffective, whether because it is not used, or because it is used but has little impact. The sorts of analyses and simulations presented in this paper can be done automatically, by tools that are in any case required to specify, document and build working products. Ideally, this would help ease technical designers into usability issues. The paper showed that analysis done in this way can raise and help explore interesting design issues.

More generally, this paper showed that a user interface can be specified, simulated and analysed 'on paper'. The work reported here is fully replicable, and can be checked and developed easily. As it happened, the paper exploited *Mathematica*; worthwhile further work would be to embed and cosmetise the appropriate features inside design tools.

Acknowledgements

Ann Blandford and Matt Jones both made very valuable comments. Nokia is a registered trademark of Nokia Corporation, Finland; Navi is a trademark of Nokia Mobile Phones.

Appendix A   The Cost of Knowledge Graph

We are concerned with probability distributions of state occupancy. A vector v represents the probability of the device being in each state; we discussed one such vector above, using Zipf probabilities. With a stochastic transition matrix P, if the distribution is v, one button press later it is vP; two button presses later it is vP^2; three button presses later it is vP^3; ... and so on. (A stochastic transition matrix is a transition matrix, where each transition is a probability. Each row sums to 1; the leading diagonal represents the probability of the device doing nothing in each state.)

If v_0 is the distribution at press zero (typically 1 in standby and zero in all other states) then $v_n = v_0 P^n$ is the distribution at press n. The probability of being in a given state, i, on press n is then $v_n(i)$, which may be written more clearly as $\Pr(\text{in state } i \text{ at press } n)$. The probability the device is not in state i at press n is then $1 - \Pr(\text{in state } i \text{ at press } n)$. Thus the probability it was never in state i over presses 0 to t is the product of these probabilities, with n ranging over 0 to t. The probability it was sometime in state i is therefore 1 minus that:

$$1 - \prod_{n=0}^{t} \left(1 - \Pr(\text{in state } i \text{ at press } n) \right)$$

where $\prod$ is the symbol for a product, just as $\sum$ is the symbol for a sum.

The expected number of states visited to press t is the sum of these probabilities considered over all states. Since we are, more specifically, interested in the proportion of states visited to press t, the following formula is used for plotting the cost of knowledge function:

$$\text{knowledge}(t) = \sum_{i \in \text{States}} w(i) \left(1 - \prod_{n=0}^{t} \left(1 - \Pr(\text{in state } i \text{ at press } n) \right) \right)$$

In this paper we take the state weights $w(i)$ to be the Zipf probabilities, or for 'unweighted' analyses from $\{0, 1/|\text{Goals}|\}$ depending on whether the state is a goal state. Since the weights sum to 1, the measure of knowledge ranges over 0 to 1.

Throughout the paper, costs are given in the form $n \pm \sigma$, meaning n is the expected value and σ the standard deviation. If $c(i)$ is the minimum cost of reaching state i from *Standby* (calculated by a *Mathematica* shortest path function) then the expected cost is $n = w.c$ and the standard deviation is $\sigma = \sqrt{w.(c^2) - (w.c)^2}$.

Appendix B   Utility Functions

This Appendix forms the common *Mathematica* code that creates all the data structures (e.g. the transition matrices) from the basic definitions, which are given in Appendix C. (It has to be placed before the definitions of the various devices.) To save space for the printed paper, this code has been hidden.

Appendix C   Device Specifications

Appendix C.1   Nokia 5110

It is easiest to specify the Nokia 5110 by writing out a definition that is as close a match to the Nokia's User's Guide as possible. We then use a *Mathematica* function to convert this "human readable" specification into a complete device specification.

```
readable[nokia] ^= menu["standby",
    {menu["phone book", {"search", "service nos", "add entry", "erase",
            "edit", "send entry",
            menu["options", {"type of view", "memory status"}],
            "speed dials"}],
      menu["messages", {"inbox", "outbox", "write messages",
            menu["message settings", {menu["set 1",
                    {"message centre number", "messages sent as",
                     "message validity"}],
            menu["common", {"delivery reports", "reply via same centre"}]}],
            "info service", "voice mailbox number"}],
      menu["call register", {"missed calls", "received calls",
            "dialled numbers", "erase recent calls",
            menu["show call duration", {"last call duration",
            "all calls' duration", "received calls' duration",
            "dialled calls' duration", "clear timers"}],
            menu["show call costs", {"last call cost",
            "all calls' cost", "clear counters"}],
            menu["call costs settings", {"call costs' limit",
                    "show costs in"}]}],
      menu["settings", {menu["call settings",
            {"automatic redial", "speed dialling", "call waiting options",
             "own number sending", "automatic answer"}],
      menu["phone settings", {menu["language",
            {"Automatic", "Engish", "Deutsch", "Français", "Nederlands",
             "Italiano", "Dansk", "Svenska", "Norsk", "Suomi", "Español",
             "Português", "<Russian>",† "Eesti", "Latviesu", "Lietuviu",
             "<Arabic>",† "<Hebrew>"†}],
            "cell info display", "welcome note",
            "network selection", "lights"}],
            menu["security settings", {"PIN code request",
                    "fixed dialling", "closed user group",
                    "phone security", "change access codes"}],
            "restore factory settings"}],
      menu["call divert", {"divert all calls without ringing",
            "divert when busy", "divert when not answered",
            "divert when phone off or no coverage", "cancel all diverts"}],
      menu["games", {"memory", "snake", "logic"}], "calculator",
      menu["clock", {"alarm clock", "clock settings"}],
      menu["tones", {"incoming call alert", "ringing tone",
            "ringing volume", "message alert tone", "keypad tones",
            "warning and game tones", "vibrating alert"}]}];
```

This readable tree structure is converted into a list of transitions using the following code. In this example, the button probabilities are set equal at 0.25, but other values can easily be used. The code also gives a name to the specification, as was used, for instance, in Figure 8. (It may seem tedious to provide this code, but it shows *exactly* how the Nokia's keys are assumed to work.)

---

†The Nokia handset displays these items in Arabic, Cyrillic and Hebrew fonts.

```
convert[nokia] := Module[{auxconvert, p = {}, goals = {}, transition},
    transition[from_, button_, prob_, to_] :=
        AppendTo[p, {menuname[from], button, prob, menuname[to]}];
    auxconvert[menu[name_, items_]] :=
        Module[{i}, transition[name, "Navi", 0.25, items[[1]]];
            For[i = 1, i ≤ Length@items, i++,
                transition[items[[i]], "Down", 0.25,
                                items[[If[i == Length@items, 1, i+1]]]];
                transition[items[[i]], "Up", 0.25,
                                items[[If[i == 1, Length@items, i-1]]]];
                transition[items[[i]], "C", 0.25, name];
                If[Head@items[[i]] === menu,
                    auxconvert[items[[i]]],
                    AppendTo[goals, accessed@menuname[items[[i]]]]];
                transition[items[[i]], "Navi", 0.25, Last@goals];
                Map[transition[Last@goals, #, 0.25, "standby"]&,
                        {"C", "Navi", "Up", "Down"}]
            ]
        ]
    ];
    auxconvert[readable[nokia]];
    symbolicGoals[nokia] ^= goals;
    startState[nokia] ^= "standby";
    Map[transition["standby", #, 0.25, "standby"]&, {"C", "Up", "Down"}];
    symbolicTransitions[nokia] ^= p;
    initialise[nokia, "Nokia navigable menu"];
];
convert[nokia];
```

The final line of code (`initialise`) converts the symbolic specification into all the forms required by the body of the paper. It also performs various internal checks (e.g. that probabilities add to 1).

Appendix C.2   Other Device Specifications

The Huffman tree, the Nokia shortcuts and the other device specifications are built automatically from the Nokia specification (as defined in the previous section). The definitions are omitted in the printed version of this paper.

Appendix D   User Interface Code

The user interface code is simple enough to be given in its entirety, even in the printed version of the paper. A function is defined to operate the LCD display panel, which itself is just a *Mathematica* paragraph defined with a grey background and black text, to simulate the Nokia's LCD appearance.

```
lcd[stateno_] := Module[{nb = InputNotebook[]},
    NotebookFind[nb, "LCD", All, CellTags];
    SelectionMove[nb, All, CellContents];
    NotebookWrite[nb, GridBox[{
        {StyleBox[capitalise[FromStateNo[nokia, stateno] /.
            accessed[s_] :> "Do " <> s]]},
        {StyleBox["                    "]},
        {StyleBox[If[stateno == startState[nokia], "Menu", "Select"]]}
    }]]
];
```

There is some special-case code to say when the user activates a function, to capitalise the first letter of state names, and to display the Navi button's prompt as 'Menu' or 'Select' depending on whether the handset is in the start state, *Standby*.

The `press` function, executed when the user presses any button, relies on a function `nextState` that takes the device (whatever it is) from one state to the next, depending on which button is pressed. It would be trivial to modify `press` so that button presses (and timings if required) were recorded for analysis.

```
press[key_] := nextState[stateNumber, key];
```

The rules for the `nextState` function are generated automatically from the device specification:

```
numericTransitions[nokia] /. {from_, button_, prob_, to_}
     :> (nextState[from, button] := lcd[stateNumber = to]);
```

Finally it is necessary to initialise the state to the start state, and display the appropriate text for that state in the LCD panel:

```
lcd[stateNumber = ToStateNo[nokia, startState[nokia]]];
```

After this initialisation, Figure 3 (in the *Mathematica* version of this paper) works and behaves as specified.

References

Card, S. K., Pirolli, P. & Mackinlay, J. D. (1994), The Cost-of-Knowledge Characteristic Function: Display Evaluation for Direct-Walk Dynamic Information Visualizations, *in* B. Adelson, S. Dumais & J. Olson (eds.), *Proceedings of CHI'94: Human Factors in Computing Systems*, ACM Press, pp.238–44.

Dix, A., Finlay, J., Abowd, G. & Beale, R. (1998), *Human–Computer Interaction*, second edition, Prentice–Hall Europe.

Furnas, G. W. (1997), Effective View Navigation, *in* S. Pemberton (ed.), *Proceedings of CHI'97: Human Factors in Computing Systems*, ACM Press, pp.367–74.

Huffman, D. A. (1952), "A Method for the Construction of Minimum-redundancy Codes", *Proceedings of the IRE* **40**(9), 1098–952.

Kiljander, H. (1999), User Interface Prototyping Methods in Designing Mobile Handsets, *in* A. Sasse & C. Johnson (eds.), *Human–Computer Interaction — INTERACT '99: Proceedings of the Seventh IFIP Conference on Human–Computer Interaction*, Vol. 1, IOS Press, pp.118–25.

Knuth, D. E. (1985), "Dynamic Huffman Coding", *Journal of Algorithms* **6**(2), 163–80.

Marsden, G., Thimbleby, H. W., Jones, M. & Gillary, P. (2000), Successful User Interface Design from Efficient Computer Algorithms, *in* G. Szwillus, T. Turner, M. Atwood, B. Bederson, B. Bomsdorf, E. Churchill, G. Cockton, D. Crow, F. Détienne, D. Gilmore, H.-J. Hofman, C. van der Mast, I. McClelland, D. Murray, P. Palanque, M. A. Sasse, J. Scholtz, A. Sutcliffe & W. Visser (eds.), *Companion Proceedings of CHI'2000: Human Factors in Computing Systems (CHI'2000 Conference Companion)*, ACM Press, pp.181–2.

Silfverberg, M., MacKenzie, I. S. & Korhonen, P. (2000), Predicting Text Entry Speed on Mobile Phones, *in* T. Turner, G. Szwillus, M. Czerwinski & F. Paternò (eds.), *Proceedings of CHI'2000: Human Factors in Computing Systems*, ACM Press, pp.9–16.

Thimbleby, H. W. (1992), The Frustrations of a Pushbutton World, *in Encyclopædia Britannica Yearbook of Science and the Future, 1993*, Encyclopædia Britannica Inc., pp.202–219.

Thimbleby, H. W. (1993), Combining Systems and Manuals, *in* J. Alty, D. Diaper & S. Guest (eds.), *People and Computers VIII (Proceedings of HCI'93)*, Cambridge University Press, pp.479–88.

Thimbleby, H. W. (1994), "Formulating Usability", *ACM SIGCHI Bulletin* **26**(2), 59–64.

Thimbleby, H. W. (1997), "Design for a Fax", *Personal Technologies* **1**(2), 101–17.

Thimbleby, H. W. (1999), "Specification-Led Design", *Personal Technologies* **4**(2), 241–54.

Väänänen-Vainio-Mattila, K. & Ruuska, S. (2000), Designing Mobile Phones and Communicators for Consumers' Needs at Nokia, *in* E. Bergman (ed.), *Information Appliances and Beyond: Interaction Design for Consumer Products*, Morgan-Kaufmann, pp.169–204.

Wolfram, S. (1996), *The Mathematica Book*, third edition, Addison–Wesley.

Zipf, G. K. (1949), *Human Behaviour and the Principle of Least Effort*, Addison–Wesley.

Analysing Asynchronous Collaboration

Patrick G T Healey & Nick Bryan-Kinns[†]

Department of Computer Science, Queen Mary and Westfield College, University of London, Mile End, London E1 4NS, UK

EMail: *ph@dcs.qmw.ac.uk*

[†] *School of Computing Science, Middlesex University, Bounds Green Road, London N11 2NQ, UK*

EMail: *N.Bryan-Kinns@mdx.ac.uk*

In this paper we propose a framework for modelling asynchronous collaboration. Drawing on arguments that a task-based approach is inappropriate for the analysis collaborative work, we model collaboration in terms of the artefacts, users, and information flow involved. We illustrate the framework's potential through studies of shared care of diabetic patients, and discuss the implications of this approach for the analysis of collaborative work.

Keywords: evaluation, CSCW, communication, collaboration.

1 Background

Collaboration is an essential part of human activity and the predominant mode of work activity. Computer support for such activity is a relatively recent development in human terms, but a relatively old development in computer science terms. However, the development of effective collaborative systems is frustrated by a paucity of analysis and evaluation techniques that deal effectively with collaborative activity. Although there is now a large body of empirical work on the complex, and often subtle, factors that influence the organisation of collaborative work little progress has been made with techniques or methods that provide for tractable, systematic analyses of a kind that could inform design.

Throughout the literature there are many examples of problems with the use of collaboration support systems. Categories of problems include lack of acceptance; for example Markus's (1990) study of why group work products fail to be accepted by users, poor understanding of the purpose of the such systems by users; for example Orlikowski's (1992) study of people's perceptions of what constitutes a groupware system, and usability problems with particular aspects of systems.

Such problems have led to numerous studies of collaborative systems; for example Rouncefield et al.'s (1994) study of a small office considering the greater introduction of IT, and Grønbæk et al.'s (1992) study of a Danish engineering company, produce similar forms of descriptions by studying work practices. However, as their understanding and descriptions of both the work and the environment are anecdotal and not based on theories or explanations, their findings are difficult to use generally.

Work such as Bowers' (1994) study of the introduction of CSCW tools into an organisation of the UK's central government provide analyses which are inferred from observations of the introduction and use of systems. This analysis highlights the amount of effort that users of groupware systems need to expend to make the systems and their collaborations effective. Bowers' study also uses these explanations to propose design solutions to the problems such as: more sophisticated awareness mechanisms, more sophisticated access mechanisms, and more support for management of the CSCW network.

Conversely, van der Veer et al.'s (1996) Groupware Task Analysis framework (GTA) supports the modelling of people's work in terms of group tasks, the organisational context, and the artefacts involved. Their framework can be used to develop models of group activities, but there is no explicit relationship to models of systems being used. This means that although group work can be described there is no systematic means of identifying problems, nor of explaining why these problems arise, nor designing to support groupwork.

Bannon & Bodker's (1997) discussion of *common information spaces* provides a framework for understanding the properties of information objects that cross between different communities of practice. Such understanding can be used to highlight the amount of effort that is needed to bring information from one community into a shared arena. This effort typically involves packaging and filtering the information to make it comprehensible to the intended audience. Their work is similar to that of Bowers' study discussed previously which considers the amount of effort required to make collaborations effective. However, Bannon et al.'s approach is more powerful as they provide a framework which can be applied to different situations as opposed to Bowers' anecdotal analyses.

An example of work in which theoretically based explanations are produced is Rogers (1992) in which she examines the problems of distributed problem solving. In particular she focused on how problems within troubleshooting arose, and explained these using an ad hoc framework for representing shared understanding between group members. The framework was also used to explain how shared understandings were developed, and how the problems above were addressed. In this way it did not only describe the situations and problems, but also explained how the problems arose, and even provided some insight into how the problems could be resolved.

Inevitably, the investigation of situations in which people collaborate raises the problem of multiple perspectives on the structure and organisation of the joint activity. Participants in a given setting will frequently differ in their view of what actions are involved, how they are integrated and who is responsible for doing what. The management of these differences in perspective are a basic aspect of collaborative activity. For example, Strauss (1985) highlights how cooperative work depends on 'articulation work', a process of negotiating task alignment within a 'working division of labour'. Similarly, Hughes et al. observe that it is a feature of collaborative work that: "the separation, individuation and combination of activities is accomplished in an accountable way through a collectively developed, negotiated and evolving knowledge and practice" (Hughes et al., 1992, p.117). From this viewpoint, the processes of interaction and negotiation which sustain the working division of labour are constitutive of cooperative work.

These phenomena present obvious difficulties for techniques which use task or goal decompositions as the basis of their analyses of collaborative work; cf. Watts & Monk (1998). One of the criticisms most consistently directed at 'conventional' HCI has been that it analyses work in individualistic terms; concentrating on an isolated user engaged in some autonomous task; for example (Schmidt & Bannon, 1992; Heath & Luff, 1992; Jirotka et al., 1992). However, the problem raised above is not with individualistic approaches *per se*, it creates difficulties for any level of analysis (individual, group or higher) at which a privileged decomposition into independent processes, goals or tasks is used. The problem is twofold; not only do different participants in the work take different views on its decomposition, task organisation is continually changing in response to local contingencies and negotiation; for example (Hughes et al., 1992; Bowers et al., 1995; Randall et al., 1995).

In addition to problems with task decomposition, a second, related, consequence of multiple perspectives is that they also engender different views on the significance and meaning of the various artefacts associated with a task. A typical example is provided by Symon et al. (1996) who carried out a detailed analysis of the use of a radiography request form (RF) in a hospital. This work demonstrates, amongst other things, how the different individuals who are involved in processing the RF, including nurses, consultants, house officers, radiographers, clerical staff and secretarial staff all interpret the RF and its function in different, sometimes conflicting, ways. Indeed, Star has suggested that a key factor in the success of a collaborative artefact may be the extent to which its design actually sustains multiple interpretations; for example (Star & Griesemer, 1989).

These difficulties suggest that collaborative activity may require analyses that do not employ notions of task or goal as basic units of analysis and, partly as a result, do not privilege a particular understanding of the objects and artefacts involved. The empirical studies suggest that a promising alternative would be to make communicative processes the central focus of analytic interest. One approach which has developed along these lines is the application of the grounding model for the analysis of interaction with or through computational media (Brennan, 1998; Clark & Brennan, 1991). To date, this model has only been applied to the analysis of local, synchronous interaction. We develop this approach and propose a framework for analysing and comparing the organisation of a broad range of collaborative activities which, we believe, captures those aspects which are most significant for the design of collaborative systems. The rest of this paper is organised as follows. We first outline our approach and follow it with an illustrative example. We then give two further contrastive examples which provide further indications of the framework's use. Implications are then discussed along with the use of the framework to inform design. Finally the paper is summarised.

2 Approach

Our approach takes the artefacts and individuals in a setting as the basic units of analysis. Any object that can be used as a document of collaborative activities is understood as an artefact. This includes familiar examples such as a letter, memo, image, database entry as well as allowing for unconventional cases in which objects such as chairs may be used to assess the current state of the collaborative activity (Anderson, 1996). No attempt is made to determine what a memo or letter specifically means to the various participants in a particular setting, i.e. what it is 'really' a document of. Particular artefacts may be used as documents for a variety of activities, we discriminate artefacts only on formal/physical grounds and they are considered to change only where, for example, they have been annotated, amended or destroyed.

Direct, synchronous interaction is treated in two ways. Firstly, it may itself be documented. For example, a consultation between a GP and a patient will be documented by a number of artefacts. Typically, there will be an appointment in one or more diaries, a list of actions taken on the patient record, a prescription or referral letter and so on. The second feature of synchronous interaction for our purposes is that it provides an opportunity for individuals to align their interpretations of an artefact, whatever those interpretations may be, through grounding. Grounding is the basic process used to update *common ground* in communication and was originally designed to account for how individuals develop a common understanding of utterances or turns during a conversational exchange (Clark & Schaefer, 1989). We extend this approach to cover asynchronous interaction by treating artefacts as, in effect, superordinate 'turns' that are also grounded between individuals.

The principal advantage of thinking in terms of grounding is that it allows us to exploit distinctions in the *state*, or *level of grounding* which one of the partners may be in with respect to the shared artefacts involved. Clark & Brennan (1991) define four states of grounding with respect to conversation, and Brennan (1998) defines eight states with respect to grounding with interactive help systems. We draw on these to define five states of grounding with respect to artefacts:

State 0: Participant (P) is unaware that artefact (A) exists.

State 1: P is aware that A exists.

State 2: P recognises A as being of a particular type.

State 3: P understands the content of A.

State 4: P understands what actions are associated with A.

It should be noted that in the original conversational model, an utterance is understood as successfully grounded at some level only if positive evidence has been obtained, at that level, for the mutual belief that the utterance has been grounded. In the current context this criterion cannot, in general, be satisfied. For collaborations that are distributed widely in space and time there is no reliable means, for analysts or participants, of determining if the right mutual belief has been established. We therefore adopt a weaker criterion and assume that individual beliefs about the level of common ground with respect to an artefact are accurate unless there is evidence to the contrary, i.e. unless we have specific evidence of two or more individuals maintaining discrepant beliefs about each others' common ground with respect to some artefact. We propose initial grounding levels based on observations or records of use. For example, if an individual has seen an artefact we assume they are aware of it (Level 1), if they have filed it without reading we assume they have identified it as being a certain type (Level 2), if they have read it we might assume they have reached some understanding of its content (Level 3) and if they have responded to it in some way we assume they recognise the associated actions (Level 4).

We use this analysis to generate two diagrammatic representations of the informational state of a particular collaborative activity (illustrated in later examples). The first is a Grounding Matrix which summarises the level of grounding for each individual with respect to each relevant artefact. With one exception, this matrix also represents, by default, the mutually assumed level of common ground for a given artefact for each pair of individuals. If the levels of grounding are different for two participants they are assumed to hold the mutual-belief that their common ground is at the lower level. The exception is where, for some individual and some artefact, the level of grounding is zero. In this case, although their collaborators are assumed to know that they are unaware of the artefact, the individual in question has, of course, no beliefs about it or their collaborators' knowledge of it. These defaults are chosen on the assumption that people are normally aware of which artefacts are associated with a particular collaborative activity and are aware of what level of understanding or involvement each of their colleagues have with each artefact. Where there is evidence that the beliefs are in fact discrepant, we take this to be significant and represent it directly within the Matrix. If, for example, participant A believes B's level of grounding with respect to an artefact is higher or lower than it actually is then this is subscripted on A's level of grounding.

To address the specific patterns of information flow a graph representation is used (for example, see Figure 1) which addresses the interactions used to support collaboration, and the different levels of grounding that result from those interactions. Individuals, represented by circles, and artefacts, represented by rectangles, form the nodes of this graph. The arcs between them represent the interactions. Asynchronous interactions are represented as thin lines with filled arrow heads and synchronous interactions as thicker lines with open arrow heads. The artefacts associated with each interaction are linked to that arc by a single line

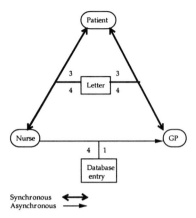

Figure 1: Information flows for patient's eye appointment.

which is labelled to indicate the level of grounding achieved for that artefact through the interaction.

3 Illustrative Example of the Approach

A typical example of problems with support for group work is presented here to illustrate the use of the evaluation framework. This, and later examples, are taken from studies of shared diabetic patient care (Kindberg et al., 1999). Health care for diabetic patients is typically organised in terms of three sectors: primary (GPs, opticians, chiropodists, district nurses), secondary (specialists), and self-help. These sectors relate to different degrees of expertise and specialisation in the treatment they provide. Diabetes is a chronic disease; the aim of the care is to prevent the disease and related problems from worsening. As such the self-help level of care is vital. Patients must ensure that they take, and possibly amend, their treatment every day, that they monitor the levels of sugar in their blood, and that they eat appropriate foods.

The primary sector is the patient's first line of contact. They may visit their GP at regular intervals, and typically visit the optician regularly as diabetes can lead to degeneration of eyesight. If the patient's condition is beyond the treatment of the GP then they are *referred* to a specialist in the secondary sector. The referral acts as a coordinating device; clinicians instigate future activities through referrals and repeat appointments.

One result of the disparate nature of the shared care is that patients are often treated by several clinicians concurrently (in separate sessions). This concurrent working is *loosely-coupled*; the members of the group work semi-autonomously, and over a long period of time towards the group goal of reducing the degeneration of the patient's health. In the example extracts that follow, a nurse arranges an appointment for a patient at an eye clinic just prior to the patient seeing the GP. However, when the patient sees the GP the GP, despite looking through the shared notes and database, is apparently unaware that the appointment has been made until the patient produces the appointment letter. The following extract from the transcript relates to the nurse deciding to refer the patient to the eye clinic.

> Nurse: Have you got another appointment at the L. [eye clinic]?
> Patient: No, I'm under Dr. X. [the GP the patient sees next] and nurses here.
> N: Right … in that case, we need to make an appointment for the next time the camera is available … 6 weeks.
> P: I didn't like the L. — they had wrong address for me and blamed me for not turning up
> P: I was under Dr. whatever-her-name-was in G [a clinic].
> *Nurse looks at paper notes.*
> N: Yes
> *The patient then proceeds to air more grievances about the L. whilst the nurse types at the computer.*
> N: You need to make an appointment.

At this point the nurse has written a letter to arrange an appointment for the patient at the eye clinic and noted the arrangement in the shared database. This letter is printed out at the end of the session and handed to the patient for them to arrange the appointment.

The incident of interest occurs when the patient sees the GP as illustrated in the following transcript extract.

> Patient: I hung on [for an eye examination] because I had it done at the L … I explained to Y. [the nurse] that I can't remember when.
> *The GP (Dr. X.) then looks through both the paper and computer-based patient notes.*
> Dr. X.: Has Y. given you opticians things?
> P: Gave me this letter to tell me to go 'round there.
> *The patient then shows the letter prepared by the nurse to the GP.*
> X: That's fine.
> P: Mr. M [a consultant]. Y said go in a month's time.
> X: He'll send us the result.

Although the nurse has noted that they wrote an appointment letter for the patient and informed them when to visit the eye clinic the GP appears to have missed the information. In fact, the GP spends some time looking through the computer and paper based notes (presumably in an attempt to find out what the nurse has done with respect to arranging for the patient to visit the eye clinic) before asking the patient what the nurse has done Symon et al. (1996) make similar observations in the context of radiography. It is through this interaction that common ground about the appointment with the eye examination is indirectly established for the nurse and the GP.

4 Use of the Framework in Analysing Shared Care

In this example there are two main artefacts of interest: the appointment letter, and the shared database entry. There are three participants: the nurse, the GP, and the patient. From the transcripts, video recordings, and observations carried out at the

	Nurse (N)	Patient (P)	GP (GP)
Appointment letter	4 *GP:1*	3	4
Database entry	4 *GP:4*	0	1

Table 1: Grounding Matrix regarding patient's eye appointment.

time, the Grounding Matrix shown in Table 1 is derived (the numbers refer to levels of grounding as discussed previously).

This illustrates that two artefacts could be used as documents of the patient's eye appointment; the letter and the database entry. Levels of grounding for these artefacts are uneven. The nurse, by virtue of authoring the letter and database entry is assumed to have the highest level of grounding for both. The GP by contrast, has a high level of grounding for the letter but not for the database entry. He reads and confirms the appropriateness of the letter even though it is actually intended for the eye clinic and has only contingently become available to the GP. The organisational expectation is that it is the procedure of making a database entry which should provide the GP with a document of the appointment. We note this by annotating the nurses expectation that the GP will use the database but will only be aware of the letter. However, for whatever reason, the GP has not grounded this information by reading the database and notes. The patient clearly understands the type and meaning of the letter but we assume is not fully aware of the activities it initiates for the various clinicians involved.

The Grounding Matrix highlights one reason why the letter is a more critical artefact in this case than the database entry; it is, on average, more highly grounded for the individuals involved. However, this is also a deviation from the expected pattern of coordination. To account for this we need to consider the interactions involved, illustrated in Figure 1. In this case the nurse and the GP interact asynchronously through the database whereas the patient interacts synchronously with both the nurse and the GP during face to face interactions. Grounding of participants with respect to the artefacts is indicated by the numbers either side of lines connecting interactions to artefacts. For example, the nurse is grounded to Level 4 with the database entry whereas the GP has only reached Level 1.

This captures the fact that, although the database entry provides a direct informational link between the Nurse and GP, it is the indirect channel provided by the letter that underwrites successful coordination in this case. It is effective, we suggest, because there are opportunities for the participants to ground the letter through direct interaction that are not available for the database entry. It may even be that the GP intentionally exploits this fact by preferring to rely on the letter in this case.

5   Further Examples from Studies of Shared Care

Two further illustrative examples are presented here. The first concerns problems with results from visits to other sites, the second illustrates a situation in which support for collaboration is well exploited.

	Nurse	Eye specialist	Patient
Photograph	1	4	2
Results Letter	0	4	0

Table 2: Grounding Matrix regarding patient's eye test.

A typical example of problems concerning coordination between sites occurs when patients attend eye clinics. The purpose of a visit to the eye clinic is for the eye specialist to examine the patient's eyes and determine what treatment is necessary, e.g. cataract removal. The tests performed by the eye specialists inform their diagnoses. However, the results of such tests are also of interest to the referring clinician as indicators of the patient's diabetic condition. Typically such results and information about what the eye specialist intends to do for the patient are not returned to the referring clinician. The following extract of transcript highlights one such situation. First the nurse does not know whether the patient has attended an eye clinic and so has to expend effort extracting this information from the patient (after failing to find any relevant information). Second, at the end of the extract the nurse states that they will have to 'follow that up' which clearly will involve the nurse in extra work. Note that although they are interested in the same artefact (test results), they use them as documents of different things — surgical need or diabetic state.

> Nurse: How are your eyes? Have you had them checked?
> Patient: I didn't 'cos I had them done, but I didn't know when I had them done.
> *At this point the nurse picks up the paper notes — any information from eye clinics will be in the form of a letter.*
> P: Do they photograph them?
> N: Yes.
> P: I had them done at the L.
> N: They never told us.
> *The nurse looks through the notes whilst talking to the patient.*
> N: No correspondence.
> N: At the L.?
> P: Yes.
> N: Need to follow that up.
> *At this point the nurse stops looking through the notes.*
> N: Have you got another appointment?

In this example the Grounding Matrix (Table 2) consists of: the patient, the nurse, the eye specialist; the photograph taken, and the results letter. As before, the eye specialist, as author of the relevant artefacts is assumed to have the highest level of grounding. Note that although we have no evidence to demonstrate that the letter exists, we equally have no reason to believe it doesn't and analyse the example accordingly.

Figure 2 depicts our analysis of the flow of information in this case. The visit to the eye specialist generated two artefacts, a photo of the patient's retina and test results. The expected asynchronous interaction between the nurse and the specialist failed, there is no letter containing test results in the patient record. In response,

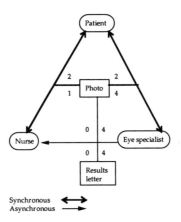

Figure 2: Information flow regarding the patient's eye test.

the nurse uses the synchronous interaction with the patient to establish that a visit to the eye specialist took place. The patient knows that a photograph has been taken (Level 2), but does not necessarily understand the meaning of the photo. The nurse, on the other hand, has only reached the first state of grounding with respect to the photograph; the only evidence they have of its existence is from the patient's report. As the patient does not know about the results letter and the nurse/GP have not received one the nurse has no direct evidence that it exists (Level 0).

The interest of this example lies in the way in which the failure of the asynchronous communication was both detected and dealt with. The nurse uses the interaction with the patient to ground the existence of one artefact, the photo, as a means of determining whether an examination took place and, in turn, to assess whether another artefact, the test results, could be obtained. A variety of factors may be involved in this situation. One possible factor in the failure to feed back the results is that the specialists, who use them for their own purposes, may not appreciate their potential value to the clinicians. Problems of this kind are pervasive in collaboration between individuals with different fields of expertise and are very difficult to address at the level of system design. Also, conflicts of interest and concerns about confidentiality dictate that the simplest solution — making every artefact available to everyone involved in patient care cannot succeed; cf. Symon et al. (1996). What this and the preceding example highlight is how people can cope with these situations through a strategic and indirect use of artefacts and interactions. An effective system or procedure for the support of this coordination would not only attend to the results letter but to understanding which other artefacts could usefully be made available. The analysis framework developed here assists in identifying which artefacts are of greatest relevance to this by attending directly to the levels of grounding and patterns of information flow in each case.

	Nurse (N)	Patient (P)	GP (GP)
Database entry	4	0	4

Table 3: Grounding Matrix for successful information flow.

Of course, communication does not always fail in shared care (if it did it could hardly be referred to as shared care). This final example concerns a situation in which communication is supported by the systems in place. In this example the nurse attempts to find out about the patient's diet; whether it is appropriate for the dietary requirements of attempting to keep diabetes under control. The nurse has a difficult time finding out the relevant information from the patient and so raises concerns with the GP regarding the patient's diet via the shared database using the following comment. From the studies it is clear that such comments serve to both indicate the nurse's opinion about the situation, and as a form of informal request for the GP to pursue the theme with the patient.

> *I found it difficult to ascertain what he was eating etc.*

When the GP sees the patient (shortly after they have seen the nurse) they first read information contained in the shared database. From this they pick up on the nurse's comments regarding diet and start the session with the patient by discussing their diet. The gravity of the GP's concern about the patient's dietary situation is reflected by the amount of time they spend questioning the patient in this initial part of the session, and the fact that they return to the dietary theme two further times in the session.

Essentially the comment helps to establish the GP's understanding of the current state of the shared care; that the patient needs to be further questioned about their diet, and that the patient's diet needs to be carefully monitored in the future (not just by the GP). In terms of the evaluation framework the communication between the Nurse and the GP about the patient's diet is successful; both have grounded to Level 4 as illustrated in Table 3 and Figure 3.

6 Implications

Having illustrated the application of the framework in specific cases we discuss the broader implications of this approach. As the examples show, collaboration of the kind involved in shared diabetic patient care is predominantly asynchronous and typically takes place via artefacts such as letters. Such loosely-coupled work contrasts with the work situations that have most frequently been studied. Schmidt & Bannon note that:

> "... the underlying assumption in most of the CSCW oriented research thus far that the cooperative work arrangement to be supported by a computer artefact is a small, stable, e.g. alitarian, homogeneous and harmonious ensemble of people." (Schmidt & Bannon, 1992, p.15); see also Plowman et al. (1995)

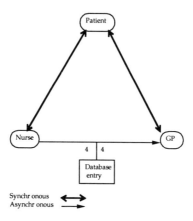

Figure 3: Successful information flow.

In effect, the present framework abstracts over particular episodes of interaction in order to characterise the broader patterns of communication which underwrite coordination. By doing so it has the potential to address a variety of different forms of collaboration, not just tightly-coupled communication. We do not assume that more communication, or higher levels of grounding, are necessarily better or even desirable; cf. Harper & Carter (1994). Rather, this framework offers a means of systematically characterising the pattern and depth of communication in a particular setting and for comparing these patterns between settings. Its potential value consists in the means it offers for assessing the relative importance of various artefacts and individuals to the current work organisation. The key individual(s) in a particular situation can be identified by inspecting the grounding levels across all artefacts for the highest overall score. Similarly, the centrality of particular artefacts can be assessed by looking at the distribution of grounding levels across a group. We believe this framework also clarifies the situations in which workarounds occur and the factors influencing the structure of those workarounds. For example, the preceding analyses highlighted the strategic value to clinicians of exploiting the patient's knowledge of appointment letters or photographs as documents of procedure rather than the artefacts, such as shared databases or results letters that are ostensibly designed for that purpose. This kind of understanding may be of particular value for requirements analysis by facilitating the identification of critical artefacts and interactions. The framework also facilitates higher-level generalisations about patterns of coordination. The Grounding Matrices provide a simple visual representation that indicates the extent to which communication is, for example, fragmented, centralised or diffuse in a given setting. Further, it provides a clear indication of which combinations of participants constitute important coalitions or groups in carrying out the work. We believe it is a strength of this approach that we do not assume, say, an organisational or role-based model of group structure, rather it emerges directly from the pattern of grounding and interaction.

The effectiveness of this framework depends to a significant extent on the ease and accuracy with which the Grounding Matrices and information flow diagrams can be constructed. The kinds of highly detailed analysis which have proved successful for understanding closely-coupled coordination are not practicable for more distributed, largely asynchronous, interaction. An advantage of the current framework is that it is designed to apply to situations in which only partial data is available and does not demand the use of full transcripts or other types of more sophisticated microanalysis. A variety of less intensive techniques, e.g. interview, tracer studies, document audit are available which can establish the critical parameters of the framework; typical patterns of interaction, the set of relevant individuals and artefacts, and the pattern of grounding. A deeper question is whether Grounding Matrices and flow diagrams capture the factors that are of greatest relevance to the conduct of collaborative work. We have argued that task-based analyses are inappropriate in these cases because they impose a particular understanding of the work organisation on a setting. The validity of our alternative approach is currently being assessed in the design and evaluation of system for shared patient care.

7 Design of a Shared Artefact

Using examples like those discussed above we have developed an understanding of the nature and requirements of collaborative work in shared patient care. On the basis of our analysis we have designed a system which aims to engender more effective collaboration through the promotion of higher levels of grounding. This system, referred to as mPathy, is illustrated in a screenshot in Figure 4. See Kindberg et al. (1999) for more detail. For each patient, it provides a shared overview of the history of interactions between the relevant clinicians and other health workers associated with that patient. Each clinician can use the workspace to view who has been active with the patient, and assess the state of the communication between them. The clinicians involved in the patient's care are represented by icons on the left with documents they have added to the workspace arranged from left to right on a time line associated with each clinician. In this example four clinicians are visible: an optician, diabetes sister, GP (C.Day), and specialist (S.Good). The workspace promotes grounding to Level 1 by making all documents in the workspace visible to all the individuals in that workspace. To promote grounding to Level 2 (recognising type), several types of icon are used to distinguish between e.g. letters between clinicians, reviews, or consultation. In the simple case, all documents in the timeline can be read by anyone in the workspace, modified distribution is indicated in two ways. Firstly, a specific intended addressee is indicated by an arrow between participants, for example, on 14 Feb.1997 C.Day sent a letter to the specialist to request a review. Secondly, where, for reasons such as confidentiality, distribution is restricted a padlock appears on the timeline of each individual who is not currently able to read the document. For example, C.Day's consultation and review of the patient's case are not currently available to the optician. Grounding to Level 3 is

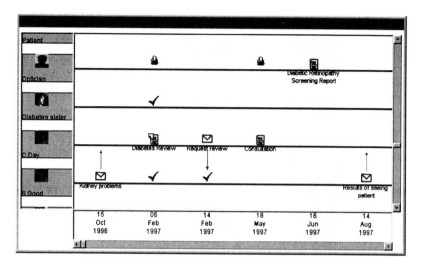

Figure 4: Screenshot of mPathy.

promoted by providing tick marks to indicate when a document has been read by an individual.

The design of the system thus aims to promote both an awareness amongst the clinicians of what patient-related artefacts there are and to underpin their common ground about the current state of patient care.

8 Summary

This paper presented a framework for modelling collaboration in terms of artefacts, information flow, and participants' levels of grounding. This approach contrasts with other work which attempts to model the task and goal structures involved in group work. By concentrating on levels of grounding, our framework abstracts at a level that avoids the problems associated with the fluid nature of tasks and task allocation and which undermine task based approaches. Furthermore, our Grounding Matrices and diagrams of information flow provide simple visual representations which can be employed to highlight and interpret the nature of the collaboration.

Examples of loosely coupled collaboration from studies of clinicians involved in shared care for diabetic patients were used to illustrate the analytic utility of the approach. Similarly, we proposed how such analyses of collaboration could be used to inform design of systems. Our future work involves the further development of the framework for the analysis of other forms of asynchronous collaboration and its use as a basis for making comparative judgements about the adequacy and effectiveness of collaborative systems.

Acknowledgements

The work presented in this paper is part of the Mushroom project funded by UK EPSRC grants GR/L14602 (1996–97) and GR/L64300 (1998–2000). We would like to thank all those involved in the project, especially the clinicians who have given us their valuable time, and the patients who agreed for us to observe them.

References

Anderson, R. (1996), A Security Policy Model for Clinical Information Systems, *in Proceedings of IEEE Symposium on Security and Privacy*, IEEE Computer Society Press, pp.30–45.

Bannon, L. & Bodker, S. (1997), Constructing Common Information Spaces, *in* J. Hughes, W. Prinz, T. Rodden & K. Schmidt (eds.), *Proceedings of ECSCW'97, the 5th European Conference on Computer-Supported Cooperative Work*, Kluwer, pp.81–96.

Bowers, J. (1994), The Work to Make a Network Work: Studying CSCW in Action, *in* R. Furuta & C. Neuwirth (eds.), *Proceedings of CSCW'94: ACM Conference on Computer Supported Cooperative Work*, ACM Press, pp.287–98.

Bowers, J., Button, G. & Sharrock, W. (1995), Workflow from Within and Without: Tehcnology and Cooperative Work on the Print Industry Shopfloor, *in* H. Marmolin, Y. Sundblad & K. Schmidt (eds.), *Proceedings of ECSCW'95, the 4th European Conference on Computer-Supported Cooperative Work*, Kluwer, pp.51–66.

Brennan, S. (1998), The Grounding Problem in Conversations with and Through Computers, *in* S. R. Fussell & R. J. Kreuz (eds.), *Social and Cognitive Approaches to Interpersonal Communication*, Lawrence Erlbaum Associates, pp.201–25.

Clark, H. H. & Brennan, S. E. (1991), Grounding in Communications, *in* L. B. Resnick, J. Levine & S. D. Teasley (eds.), *Perspectives on Socially Shared Cognition*, American Psychology Association, pp.127–49.

Clark, H. H. & Schaefer, E. F. (1989), "Contributing to Discourse", *Cognitive Science* 13(2), 259–94.

Grønbæk, K., Kyng, M. & Mogensen, P. (1992), CSCW Challenges in Large-Scale Technical Projects — A Case Study, *in* J. Turner & R. Kraut (eds.), *Proceedings of CSCW'92: ACM Conference on Computer Supported Cooperative Work*, ACM Press, pp.338–45.

Harper, R. & Carter, K. (1994), "Keeping People Apart: A Research Note", *Computer Supported Cooperative Work* 2(3), 199–207.

Heath, C. & Luff, P. (1992), "Collaboration and Control: Crisis Management and Multimedia Technology in London Underground Control Rooms", *Computer Supported Cooperative Work* 1(1–2), 69–94.

Hughes, J. A., Randall, D. & Shapiro, D. (1992), Faltering from Ethnography to Design, *in* J. Turner & R. Kraut (eds.), *Proceedings of CSCW'92: ACM Conference on Computer Supported Cooperative Work*, ACM Press, pp.115–22.

Jirotka, M., Gilbert, N. & Luff, P. (1992), "On the Social Organsiation of Organisations", *Computer Supported Cooperative Work* 1(1–2), 95–118.

Kindberg, T., Bryan-Kinns, N. & Makwana, R. (1999), Supporting the Shared Care of Diabetic Patients, *in* S. C. Hayne (ed.), *Proceedings of ACM Group'99*, ACM Press, pp.91–100.

Markus, M. L. (1990), Why CSCW Applications Fail: Problems in the Adoption of Interdependent Work Tools, *in* D. G. Tatar (ed.), *Proceedings of CSCW'90: Third Conference on Computer Supported Cooperative Work*, ACM Press, pp.371–80.

Orlikowski, W. J. (1992), Learning from Notes: Organizational Issues in Groupware Implementation, *in* J. Turner & R. Kraut (eds.), *Proceedings of CSCW'92: ACM Conference on Computer Supported Cooperative Work*, ACM Press, pp.362–9.

Plowman, L., Rogers, Y. & Ramage, M. (1995), What are Workplace Studies for?, *in* H. Marmolin, Y. Sundblad & K. Schmidt (eds.), *Proceedings of ECSCW'95, the 4th European Conference on Computer-Supported Cooperative Work*, Kluwer, pp.309–24.

Randall, D., Rouncefield, M. & Hughes, J. A. (1995), Chalk and Cheese: BPR and Ethnomethodologically Informed Ethnography in CSCW, *in* H. Marmolin, Y. Sundblad & K. Schmidt (eds.), *Proceedings of ECSCW'95, the 4th European Conference on Computer-Supported Cooperative Work*, Kluwer, pp.325–40.

Rogers, Y. (1992), Ghosts in the Network: Distributed Troubleshooting in a Shared Working Environment, *in* J. Turner & R. Kraut (eds.), *Proceedings of CSCW'92: ACM Conference on Computer Supported Cooperative Work*, ACM Press, pp.346–55.

Rouncefield, M., Hughes, J. A., Rodden, T. & Viller, S. (1994), "Working with "Constant Interruption": CSCW and the Small Office, *in* R. Furuta & C. Neuwirth (eds.), *Proceedings of CSCW'94: ACM Conference on Computer Supported Cooperative Work*, ACM Press, pp.275–86.

Schmidt, K. & Bannon, L. (1992), "Taking CSCW Seriously: Supporting Articulation Work", *Computer Supported Cooperative Work* **1**(1–2), 7–40.

Star, S. L. & Griesemer, J. R. (1989), "Institutional Ecology, 'Translations' and Boundary Objects: Amateurs and Professionals in Berkeley's Museum of Vertebrate Zoology", *Social Studies of Science* **19**, 387–420.

Strauss, A. (1985), "Work and the Division of Labour", *The Sociological Quarterly* **26**(1), 1–19.

Symon, G., Long, K. & Ellis, J. (1996), "The Coordination of Work Activities: Cooperation and Conflict in a Hospital Context", *Computer Supported Cooperative Work* **5**(1), 1–31.

van der Veer, G. C., Lenting, B. F. & Bergevoet, B. A. J. (1996), "GTA: Groupware Task Analysis — Modeling Complexity", *Acta Psychologica* **91**(3), 297–322.

Watts, L. A. & Monk, A. F. (1998), "Reasoning About Tasks, Activity and Technology to Support Collaboration", *Ergonomics* **41**(11), 1583–606.

Design Innovations

Caring, Sharing Widgets: A Toolkit of Sensitive Widgets

Murray Crease, Stephen Brewster & Philip Gray

Department of Computing Science, University of Glasgow, Glasgow G12 8QQ, UK

Tel: *+44 141 339 8855, +44 141 330 4966*
Fax: *+44 141 330 4913*
EMail: *{murray,stephen,pdg}@dcs.gla.ac.uk*
URL: *http://www.dcs.gla.ac.uk/{˜murray,˜stephen,˜pdg}*

Although most of us communicate using multiple sensory modalities in our lives, and many of our computers are similarly capable of multi-modal interaction, most human–computer interaction is predominantly in the visual mode. This paper describes a toolkit of widgets that are capable of presenting themselves in multiple modalities, but further are capable of adapting their presentation to suit the contexts and environments in which they are used. This is of increasing importance as the use of mobile devices becomes ubiquitous.

Keywords: audio, multi-modal, resource-sensitive, sonically enhanced widgets, toolkit.

1 Introduction

Many modern applications are designed to run on powerful workstations with large monitors and powerful graphical capabilities. Whilst this is often the case, perhaps the user wishes to run the application on a less powerful laptop, or perhaps even on a hand-held device. In these cases, the application will not have access to the same amount of visual output resource available to display its interface. Even if it is the case that the application is running on a powerful workstation with a large monitor, the feedback provided by the graphical interface may be better provided by a different sensory modality or a combination of several modalities.

Or perhaps the application is running on a mobile telephone where graphical feedback is only suitable when the user is not making a call. These examples highlight the need for interface objects, or widgets, which are capable of adapting their presentation according to different requirements: the suitability of different presentation resources, e.g. in a loud environment the use of audio feedback may be unsuitable and the availability of different presentation resources, e.g. the resolution of the screen being used or the number of MIDI channels available. For the widgets to be able to cope with these different demands, they need to be able produce many different forms of output. Whilst it would be possible to build the widgets with built in output in many different output modalities, this would limit the possibilities. It would be better to be able to easily change the widget's output to allow the evaluation and inclusion of new forms. This paper describes a toolkit of such widgets and goes on to discuss some of the issues which arise from the implementation of the toolkit.

2 The Aims of the Toolkit of Resource Sensitive Widgets

The toolkit described in this paper has several aims. Its widgets should be multi-modal, with no one modality assumed to be of any greater importance than any other. We use the phrase modality to refer to a sensory modality so, for example, all auditory output is one sensory modality and all visual output is another modality. The widgets should be sensitive to their environment, adjusting their feedback accordingly. It should be easy for other user interface designers to change the feedback, either personalising the existing feedback or replacing it with a completely new design. Finally, at all times the feedback given to the user should be consistent, regardless of the modality used. That is, regardless of modality, the information given to the user by a widget should be the same.

Most modern human–computer interfaces are based around graphical widgets. This is despite the fact that most of us in our everyday lives use all our different senses to interact with the rest of the world and that many modern computers are capable of generating feedback in modalities other than vision (most notably sound, but in some instances, touch). To rectify this situation, the toolkit's widgets are designed to be multi-modal, with every modality treated equally. Our previous work (Brewster, 1998) has shown that the addition of audio feedback can improve the usability of an interface as has work done by (Gaver, 1989) whilst haptic feedback has also been shown to be effective (Akamatsu & Sato, 1994; Oakley et al., 2000). In these cases, however, the additional feedback was supplemental to the graphical feedback as opposed to being an equal partner. Our toolkit's widgets avoid the assumption that visual feedback is of greater importance than others, allowing for the possibility of widgets which are, for example, audio or haptic only. This is important in situations where the use of visual feedback is limited, e.g. on a mobile device where screen space is limited; impossible, e.g. on a mobile phone when the user has the phone to his/her ear; or unsuitable, e.g. if the user is visually impaired. If the widget is capable of utilising many modalities and makes no assumptions about what modality is best, these situations can be dealt with.

If a widget is capable of utilising multiple modalities equally, it becomes easy to imagine situations where it would be desirable for the widget to switch between modalities. For example, it has been shown that audio feedback can be just as effective as visual feedback in conveying information about the progress of a background task (Crease & Brewster, 1999), and that audio feedback can compensate for a reduction in the size of graphical buttons (Brewster, 1999). This switch may be made by the user to personalise the widget's feedback, or by the system, either to reduce the load on an over-stretched resource or to utilise a more suitable modality for the given context of use. A user may wish to alter the usage of a modality through preference, he/she thinks the sounds are too loud and would like to make them quieter; or through necessity, e.g. an hearing-impaired user has no need for audio feedback. These changes may merely alter the balance of usage for the different modalities, e.g. a little more audio feedback and a little less visual feedback, or may remove a modality all together. The system may change the modalities used by a widget for two reasons. If, for example, there are insufficient resources to meet the demands of a widget in a particular modality the system will reduce the amount of resource required by that modality and may attempt to compensate by increasing the utilisation of a different modality. The other scenario is that the system recognises that the current utilisation of a particular modality is inappropriate in the particular context and will amend the usage appropriately. For example, if the ambient volume in the environment increases, the system may increase the level of the audio feedback given to compensate, or if that is inappropriate, it may switch to a different modality entirely.

When widgets are capable of utilising multiple modalities, the job of designing the widget's feedback becomes harder. Standard graphical widgets are well established and, rightly or wrongly, are almost a de facto standard. Audio feedback, for example, is less well established and there are many conflicting designs for the feedback. For this reason it is important that new designs for the presentation of widgets can be easily included. These designs may replace the existing designs in a particular modality or may supplement the presentation by using other modalities. Modifying or replacing the design of feedback in one modality should not affect the feedback in a different modality if the feedback produced in each modality is independent. For example, if the toolkit currently used audio feedback based around structured, non speech sounds called earcons (Blattner et al., 1989; Brewster et al., 1993) but a designer wished to include an alternative design for audio feedback using everyday sounds representing the events taking place called auditory icons (Gaver, 1986), it should be easy it replace the earcons with auditory icons without affecting the existing visual feedback of the widgets. Additionally, making the introduction of new designs easy, enables designers to incorporate their designs into existing applications decreasing the overhead of evaluating new designs.

Regardless of which modalities are used, it is important that the feedback generated is consistent, both between widgets and within a widget between modalities. If a widget switches between modalities, the overall feedback must give consistent information. If a widget utilises two or more modalities the information given in each must be consistent. For example, if a progress indicator is visible on the screen, but is then covered by a different window, the audio feedback must give information that is consistent with the graphical feedback given previously.

Similarly, different widgets must be presented consistently throughout the system. For example, two different buttons may have different audio styles, e.g. one may use a pop style and one may use a jazz style, but they both must present their information in a way that the user recognises as having the same meaning. To this end, they may use different timbres to achieve their styles, but the same rhythm to maintain consistency. Additionally, clashes between the feedback given by different widgets must be avoided. This issue is usually resolved for graphical feedback by assigning different graphical widgets to different areas in the 2D region which makes up the visual display on a screen. Further, this 2D area simulates a third dimension by allowing the areas occupied by widgets to overlap. For other forms of feedback, the problem is harder to resolve. Two pieces of feedback presented at the same time will attempt to occupy the same 'space' in the output region, potentially causing a clash. It is up to the system to avoid such clashes by limiting the amount of feedback given in such a modality or by somehow modifying the feedback so it no longer clashes, e.g. by ensuring two sounds employ different timbres to aid their distinction, or perhaps using a different modality for one of the pieces of feedback.

2.1   Two Examples

Here are two possible scenarios that illustrate the need for our toolkit:

1. Murray is running an application on a mobile device. He is sitting on a train in a quiet carriage. The application's widgets can only use a limited amount of screen space due to the limited size of the device's screen. To compensate for this, the system utilises audio feedback to supplement the visual feedback. Because the carriage is quiet, the audio feedback is at a low level. At the next station, a family with young children enters the carriage, increasing the ambient volume level. To compensate for this, the system increases the level of the audio feedback. At the next station, Murray gets out and walks along a quiet street in bright sunlight. To compensate for the walking motion, the system increases the level of the audio feedback as it is unable to increase the size of the widgets due to the limited screen size. To compensate for the sun shining on the screen, the system increases the contrast of the screen.

2. When Murray gets home, he switches to using his desktop machine which boasts a large monitor and is attached to an external sound synthesiser. The system is able to utilise a lot of visual feedback because of the large screen, but still uses audio feedback because Murray likes it as a supplement to the visual feedback and the system is capable of producing high quality audio output. The audio feedback is generated using the synthesiser. Murray runs a MIDI sequencer application and starts to compose a tune. When the tune is played, this increases the ambient volume in the room so the system attempts to increase the level of audio feedback to compensate. However, because most of the MIDI channels are used playing the tune, the system is unable to meet this demand. To handle this lack of resource the level of audio feedback generated by the application is decreased and to compensate the graphical feedback is increased.

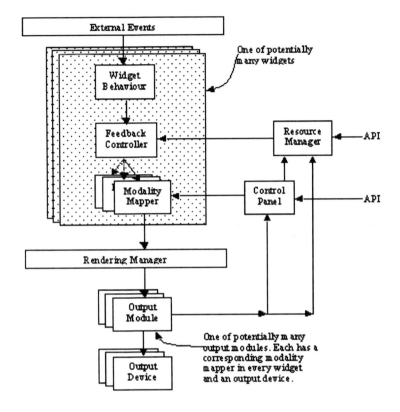

Figure 1: Toolkit architecture.

3 The Toolkit Design

The previous section described the four main requirements to be met by the toolkit. Each widget should be capable of producing feedback in multiple modalities with no preference given to any particular modality. The widgets should be capable of using the modality most suitable or limiting the use of a modality which has limited resources. It should be easy to change the feedback a widget produces in one or more modality with no effect on any other modalities. The feedback given should be consistent, both between widgets and between modalities. This section describes how the design of the toolkit meets these four aims.

3.1 The Toolkit Architecture

Figure 1 shows the architecture of the toolkit. The widget behaviour accepts external events and translates them into requests for feedback. These requests do not specify the modality to be used for the feedback, but rather just the meaning of the feedback, e.g. the mouse is over the widget. By accepting only the events that are relevant to the widget in its current state, the behaviour of the widget is defined.

The requirement that the widgets are multi-modal and treat each modality equally is met by the feedback controller. Because the widget only requests the feedback in terms of semantics, i.e. the mouse is over the widget, the requests can be translated into multiple forms of feedback in different modalities. This is done by the feedback controller which splits the request made by the widget behaviour into suitable requests for feedback in potentially multiple modalities. These requests are given a weight specifying the level or importance for that particular modality. This weight could map to the volume of audio feedback or size in visual feedback, for example. These requests are then passed on to the rest of the toolkit and ultimately result in appropriate feedback being produced.

The requirement that the widgets are sensitive to the available resources and their suitability for the current environment is met by the resource manager. The resource manager receives input from three sources, a control panel, the output modules and from applications that use the toolkit via its API. The control panel allows the users of the system to set the weight for a particular modality. The weight of a modality encompasses two concepts: the level of user preference for a modality, and the level of system resource required to meet requests in a modality. This way, users can set their preference for a particular modality. The output modules can indicate that they have insufficient resource to meet feedback requests to the resource manager, allowing the widgets to be sensitive to the availability of resources. External applications can use the resource manager's API to influence the weight of different modalities. Such applications could monitor the environment allowing the widgets to be sensitive to resource suitability. One such example of this would be an application that monitored the ambient volume level of the environment, changing the weight of the audio feedback so that it can be heard without being too loud.. The resource manager takes the information from these three sources and passes on a weight to the feedback controller for each of the modalities.

The requirement that the widget's feedback is easy to change is met by the output modules and the control panel. Because the widget behaviour does not encapsulate the feedback given by the widget, but merely requests that feedback be given, it is a simple matter to change the feedback of the widgets. To replace one form of auditory feedback with another, for example, it is simply a case of replacing the existing output module with a new one. To supplement the existing feedback with feedback in a different modality, simply add a new output module to the toolkit. The control panel enables the changing of the output of a widget according to user preference. Any options set in the control panel for a widget are added to the request made for feedback in the modality mapper. There is a modality mapper for each output module the widget uses. The parameters that can be set for each output module are supplied by that output module. For example, a visual output module may supply parameters like colour, shape, 3D and an audio module may supply parameters like pitch, jazz, rock, pop.

The requirement that all the feedback for the widgets is consistent both between modalities and between widgets is met by the rendering manager. Again, because the widget's feedback is not encapsulated within the widget, it is possible to alter a widget's feedback so it does not clash with the feedback from other widgets. An example of feedback clashing would be two similar, sounds being played at the same time. The two sounds could interfere with each other, rendering the information they are conveying unintelligible. Because the rendering manager has a global perspective on what feedback is being requested at any given time, it can avoid such clashes by, in this case, perhaps changing the timbres of one of the sounds being played to make them more distinguishable. Another potential inconsistency is the use of two modalities which do not make sense when used together. For example, a button could be presented visually as being wooden, but the audio feedback may present the button in a metallic way. The rendering manager could detect this clash and suggest a change in the feedback. The model of what combinations are acceptable and what are not would have to be built up using information from both the user and the output modules. For example, a user could specify the maximum number of sounds to be played at any one time or an output module could specify preferred output in a different modality.

3.2 An Example

Figure 2 shows a concrete example of how the toolkit works, using a standard button.

4 Related Work

The Seeheim model (Pfaff, 1985) was one of the first user interface models to separate the user interface architecture into monolithic functional blocks. Three functional blocks were defined: the presentation system which handled user input and feedback; the application interface model which defined the application from a users point of view and the dialogue control system which defined the communication between the presentation system and the application interface model. Like Seeheim, our toolkit has a monolithic presentation component (albeit only for output), although the dialogue control system is distributed through out the widgets. The toolkit does not deal with application models because it is solely concerned with the output generated by individual widgets.

MVC (Model, View, Controller) and PAC (Presentation, Abstraction, Control) (Coutaz, 1987) are both agent based models, where an agent is defined to have "state, possess an expertise, and is capable of initiating and reacting to events." (Coutaz et al., 1995). An interface is built using hierarchies of agents. These agents represent an object in the application. In MVC, the model describes the semantics of the object, the view provides the (normally visual) representation of the object and the controllers handles user input. In PAC, the abstraction describes the functional semantics of the object, the presentation handles the users interaction with the object, both input and output and the control handles communication between the presentation and the abstraction as well as between different PAC agents. The toolkit is object-oriented like both MVC and PAC, with each widget (or agent) encapsulated into different objects. The toolkit, however, does not define the whole user interface in terms of a hierarchy of agents, but rather defines the individual widgets without specifying their organisation. Like the MVC model the toolkit separates input and output, although unlike MVC, the toolkit's widgets do not have a controller type object. It would be possible, however, to build an MVC type architecture around the

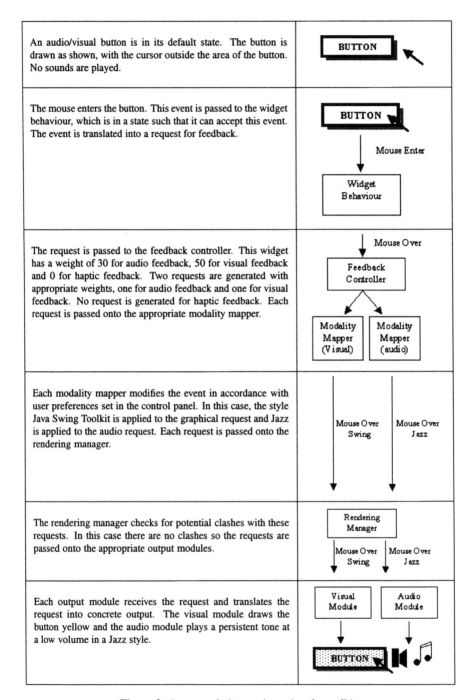

An audio/visual button is in its default state. The button is drawn as shown, with the cursor outside the area of the button. No sounds are played.	
The mouse enters the button. This event is passed to the widget behaviour, which is in a state such that it can accept this event. The event is translated into a request for feedback.	
The request is passed to the feedback controller. This widget has a weight of 30 for audio feedback, 50 for visual feedback and 0 for haptic feedback. Two requests are generated with appropriate weights, one for audio feedback and one for visual feedback. No request is generated for haptic feedback. Each request is passed onto the appropriate modality mapper.	
Each modality mapper modifies the event in accordance with user preferences set in the control panel. In this case, the style Java Swing Toolkit is applied to the graphical request and Jazz is applied to the audio request. Each request is passed onto the rendering manager.	
The rendering manager checks for potential clashes with these requests. In this case there are no clashes so the requests are passed onto the appropriate output modules.	
Each output module receives the request and translates the request into concrete output. The visual module draws the button yellow and the audio module plays a persistent tone at a low volume in a Jazz style.	

Figure 2: An example interaction using the toolkit.

toolkit. The toolkit's architecture has been compared to PAC in the following way: The modality mappers and output modules are abstract and concrete presentation modules, although unlike PAC only handling output. The feedback controller and rendering manager are controllers and the widget behaviour is the abstraction. Unlike PAC, however, the toolkit's abstraction is only aware of the widget's state, but is not aware of the underlying application semantics. This is because the toolkit is designed as an extension of the Java Swing toolkit, allowing it to be easily incorporated into existing Java applications.

The Garnet system (Myers et al., 1990) is a set of tools which allow the creation of highly interactive graphical user interfaces, providing high level tools to generate interfaces using programming by demonstration and a constraints system to maintain consistency. The Garnet toolkit allows the graphical presentation of the toolkit's widgets to be easily modified by changing the prototype upon which the widget is based. Doing this will update all dependent widgets. This is analogous to changing the design of output for a widget in an output module of our toolkit.

The HOMER system (Savidis & Stephanidis, 1995) allowed the development of user interfaces that were accessible to both sighted and non-sighted users concurrently. By employing abstract objects to specify the user interface design independently of any concrete presentation objects, the system was capable of generating two user interfaces which could run concurrently for the same application. This allows sighted and non-sighted users to cooperate using the same application. Unlike our toolkit, the HOMER system developed two interfaces, using two separate modalities rather than have one interface which can switch between multiple modalities as and when required, using several concurrently if appropriate.

Alty & McCartney (1991) created a multimedia process control system that would choose the appropriate modality to present information to a user. This would allow more information to be presented by increasing the bandwidth the interface could use. Additionally, if the preferred modality is unavailable if, for example, it is already being used for output, the system would attempt to present the information using an alternative. It was found, however, to be almost impossible to specify how these switches should be made. To limit the complexity of the system, a user-interface designer would supply it with valid options for output modalities.

The ENO system (Beaudouin-Lafon & Gaver, 1994) is an audio server which allows audio applications to incorporate audio cues. ENO manages a shared resource, audio hardware, handling requests from applications for audio feedback. This shared resource is modelled as a sound space, with requests for sounds made in terms of high level descriptions of the sound. Like ENO, our toolkit manages shared resources, although the toolkit extends the concept by switching between resources according to their suitability and availability. Similarly, the X Windows system (Scheifler & Gettys, 1986) manages a shared resource, this time a graphics server. Again, our toolkit extends this concept by managing resources in multiple modalities and switching between them.

Plasticity (Thevenin & Coutaz, 1999) is the ability of a user interface to be re-used on multiple platforms that have different capabilities. This would minimise the development time of interfaces for different platforms. For example, an interface

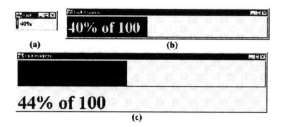

Figure 3: Different visual representations of a progress bar for different visual weights.

could be specified once and then produced for both a workstation with a large screen and a mobile device with limited screen space. This is achieved by specifying the interface using an abstract model, and subsequently building the interface for each platform using that platform's available interactors and resources. Like the toolkit, plasticity allows user interfaces to adapt to available resources, although the toolkit does this at the level of individual widgets whilst plasticity does this at the level of the interface. Additionally, the toolkit attempts to adapt the interface across multiple modalities whereas plasticity is only aimed at visual feedback.

5   Current Implementation

Using Java, the framework of the toolkit has been completely implemented, allowing the widgets to have their presentation changed by both a user and the system. The API to the toolkit is complete, allowing designers to incorporate new forms of feedback into existing widgets, or to add new widgets to the existing set. Currently, the toolkit has been implemented with two widgets, a button and a progress bar; using two modalities, graphics and audio. Graphically, the buttons are Java Swing buttons and the progress bars are drawn from first principles, illustrating the flexibility of the toolkit. Swing buttons were used because this allowed us to take advantage of Swing's built in event handling system. Any changes in the weight of the visual modality are mapped directly to size.

Because the progress bar does not require complex event handling, it could be drawn from first principles. This allowed us to demonstrate the potential for more complex representations for different visual weights. Figure 3 shows the different ways visual weight has been mapped to different graphical representations in this simple example. Figure 3a shows the progress bar at a low visual weight, with the progress bars in Figures 3b & c having successively greater visual weights. Although this increases the work required by the designer of the widget, in this case three visual designs are used rather than one, the work an interface designer is required to do is reduced because it is possible to use the same widget on multiple platforms taking advantage of the multiple designs encapsulated in the output module.

The sounds used to provide the audio feedback for both the button (Brewster, 1998) and the progress bar (Crease & Brewster, 1998) used earcons. Two audio output modules were developed, both of which used similar sounds, but the

```
JButton button = new JButton ("Progress") ;
panel.add(button) ;
```

Figure 4: Adding a standard Swing button to a panel.

```
MButton button = new MButton ("Progress") ;
panel.add(button.getTheWidget()) ;
```

Figure 5: Adding a resource sensitive button to a panel.

mappings for audio weight were different. One simply changed the volume of the sounds in proportion to the audio weight, whilst the other varied the number of sounds played. At low audio weights only the most important sounds were played whilst at higher weights more sounds were played. For example, at a low audio weight only the sound used to indicate a valid selection was played for a button, whilst at higher weights a sound indicating the mouse was over an active button was played and at even higher weights, sounds indicating that the button had been pressed were played. Using the control panel, it is possible to change the output module used dynamically.

To incorporate a resource sensitive widget into a standard Java program requires minimal changes. Figure 4 shows the code necessary to declare a standard Java Swing JButton (here called button) and add it to a JPanel (panel). Figure 5 shows the code necessary to declare a resource sensitive MButton and add it to a JPanel. As can be seen, the only changes to the code required are changing the type of object from JButton to MButton and changing the object passed to the add method of the panel. It is our intention to build a tool which will parse existing code, automatically making these changes, making the transition from standard Swing widgets even easier.

A module was developed for the toolkit which communicated with the resource manager. This module measured the ambient volume of the surrounding environment and adjusted the weight of the audio feedback accordingly. The addition of this module to the toolkit highlights its flexibility and demonstrates how it can be made sensitive to whatever environmental factors are relevant to the user.

6 Discussion

At the moment, the toolkit has a framework to allow widgets to switch between modalities as and when this is suitable. However, further work is required to help understand whether it is possible to define how much feedback in one modality is required to compensate for a reduction in feedback in a different modality. Indeed, it seems unlikely that a generic solution which can automatically handle all possible combinations of modalities and designs could be built. A more realistic target is a semi-automatic system. This would work for specific situations, such as reducing the size of a graphical button to on the display of a mobile computer and compensating by the addition of sound. Brewster (1999) found that using sound in addition to the standard graphical representation of a button on a hand-held device allowed the buttons to be reduced in size. This demonstrates it is possible to set up the toolkit to handle individual scenarios, enabling it to compensate for the reduction in one modality by using another modality.

As can be seen from Figure 1, the toolkit's architecture is heavily biased around output, with no system controls on the input side. The widget's output is configurable, both by users and the system, whereas the input is fixed. To redress this imbalance, the input should be treated in a similar way to the output. This would entail not encapsulating the input behaviour in the widget, but rather separating it out into a different module as has been done with the output. The role of the widget behaviour would no longer include handling input events, but rather to coordinate input and output, providing the base upon the widget is built. In this way, new input mechanisms, for example speech or gesture input, could be designed and added to the widget with the same ease as output mechanisms. As with the output modules, this would reduce the overhead of incorporating and evaluating new input mechanisms into existing widgets.

Another issue which arises from the toolkit design regards the widgets input and output areas, e.g. the screen area used to accept input from a mouse for a widget and to present graphical output for a widget. Because the output, and potentially the input, mechanisms are no longer encapsulated within the widget it is important to avoid inconsistencies. Further, the output area may change over time, compounding the situation. It is therefore important to ensure that the output modules communicate with the input mechanisms to maintain consistency. This dialogue would be controlled by the widget behaviour module described above. Different output modules need to communicate with different input mechanisms. An audio output module has no relevance to a mouse input mechanism. To resolve this, each input mechanism and output module could be associated with an interaction areas. For example, a mouse input mechanism and a graphical output module would be associated with a screen interaction area. A spatialised sound output module and a gesture input mechanism could be associated with a 3D space interaction area in which the output is spatialised and the user then selects a target by gesturing at the area the sound is played in. This is an extension of the concept of a window in X (Scheifler & Gettys, 1986) or a sound space in ENO (Beaudouin-Lafon & Gaver, 1994), where rather than managing a single shared resource, the toolkit manages several, switching between resources when appropriate.

7 Conclusions & Future Work

This paper describes a toolkit of multi-modal, resource sensitive widgets. The toolkit's widgets are capable of presenting themselves in multiple modalities, with no preference for any one modality. If appropriate, the way a widget utilises the different modalities can be varied according to the suitability of the modality for a situation, perhaps substituting a different modality for an unsuitable one. Equally, it is simple to include new designs of feedback in an existing widget without affecting feedback in different modalities allowing the evaluation of new designs without the overhead of building the complete widget and incorporating these new widgets into an application.

Although the mechanism is in place for switching between modalities, more work needs to be done to try and understand the rules, if any, which govern these switches. With the framework it supplies, our toolkit could be useful tool in this research.

Using the toolkit, it is now possible for designers to build interfaces that are suitable for a range of different contexts and environments. This is of increasing importance as the use of mobile devices that can be used in greatly varied environments grows.

Acknowledgements

This work was funded by EPSRC grant GR/L79212.

References

Akamatsu, M. & Sato, S. (1994), "A Multi-modal Mouse with Tactile and Force Feedback", *International Journal of Human–Computer Interaction* **40**(3), 443–53.

Alty, J. & McCartney, C. (1991), Design of a Multi-media Presentation System for a Process Control Environment, *in Eurographics Multimedia Workshop, Session 8: Systems*.

Beaudouin-Lafon, M. & Gaver, W. W. (1994), ENO: Synthesizing Structured Sound Spaces, *in Proceedings of the ACM Symposium on User Interface Software and Technology, UIST'94*, ACM Press, pp.49–57.

Blattner, M. M., Sumikawa, D. A. & Greenberg, R. M. (1989), "Earcons and Icons: Their Structure and Common Design Principles", *Human–Computer Interaction* **4**(1), 11–44.

Brewster, S. (1999), Sound In The Interface To A Mobile Computer, *in* H.-J. Bullinger & J. Zieger (eds.), *Proceedings of the 8th International Conference on Human–Computer Interaction (HCI International '99)*, Lawrence Erlbaum Associates, pp.43–7.

Brewster, S. A. (1998), "The design of sonically-enhanced widgets", *Interacting with Computers* **11**(2), 211–35.

Brewster, S. A., Wright, P. C. & Edwards, A. D. N. (1993), An Evaluation of Earcons for Use in Auditory Human–Computer Interfaces, *in* S. Ashlund, K. Mullet, A. Henderson, E. Hollnagel & T. White (eds.), *Proceedings of INTERCHI'93*, ACM Press/IOS Press, pp.222–7.

Coutaz, J. (1987), "PAC: An Object Oriented Model for Implementing User Interfaces", *ACM SIGCHI Bulletin* **19**(3), 37–41.

Coutaz, J., Nigay, L. & Salber, D. (1995), Agent-based Architecture Modelling for Interactive Systems, *in* P. Palanque & D. Benton (eds.), *Critical Issues In User Interface Engineering*, Springer-Verlag, pp.191–209.

Crease, M. & Brewster, S. (1998), Making Progress With Sounds — The Design And Evaluation Of An Audio Progress Bar, *in* A. Edwards & S. Brewster (eds.), *Proceedings of the International Conference on Auditory Display (ICAD'98)*, BCS.

Crease, M. & Brewster, S. (1999), Scope For Progress: Monitoring Background Tasks With Sound, *in* S. Brewster, A. Cawsey & G. Cockton (eds.), *Human–Computer Interaction — INTERACT '99: Proceedings of the Seventh IFIP Conference on Human–Computer Interaction*, Vol. 2, The Edinburgh Press, pp.19–20.

Gaver, W. W. (1986), "Auditory Icons: Using Sound in Computer Interfaces", *Human–Computer Interaction* **2**(1), 167–77.

Gaver, W. W. (1989), "The SonicFinder: An Interface that Uses Auditory Icon", *Human–Computer Interaction* **4**(1), 67–94.

Myers, B., Giuse, D., Dannenberg, R., Vander Zanden, B., Kosbie, D., Pervin, E., Mickish, A. & Marchal, P. (1990), "Garnet: Comprehensive Support for Graphical, Highly-interactive User Interfaces", *IEEE Computer* **23**(11), 71–85.

Oakley, I., McGee, M., Brewster, S. & Gray, P. (2000), Putting The Feel Into Look And Feel, *in* T. Turner, G. Szwillus, M. Czerwinski & F. Paternò (eds.), *Proceedings of CHI'2000: Human Factors in Computing Systems*, ACM Press, pp.415–22.

Pfaff, G. E. (ed.) (1985), *User Interface Management Systems: Proceedings of the Seeheim Workshop*, Springer-Verlag.

Savidis, A. & Stephanidis, C. (1995), Developing Dual Interfaces for Integrating Blind and Sighted Users: The HOMER UIMS, *in* I. Katz, R. Mack, L. Marks, M. B. Rosson & J. Nielsen (eds.), *Proceedings of CHI'95: Human Factors in Computing Systems*, ACM Press, pp.106–13.

Scheifler, R. W. & Gettys, J. (1986), "The X Window System", *ACM Transactions on Graphics* **5**(2), 79–109.

Thevenin, D. & Coutaz, J. (1999), Plasticity of User Interfaces: Framework and Research Agenda, *in* A. Sasse & C. Johnson (eds.), *Human–Computer Interaction — INTERACT '99: Proceedings of the Seventh IFIP Conference on Human–Computer Interaction*, Vol. 1, IOS Press, pp.110–7.

Extending Eye Tracking to Analyse Interactions with Multimedia Information Presentations

N Hari Narayanan, Dan J Schrimpsher[†]

Intelligent & Interactive Systems Laboratory, Department of Computer Science & Software Engineering, Auburn University, Auburn, AL 36849, USA

EMail: *narayan@eng.auburn.edu*
URL: *http://www.eng.auburn.edu/~narayan*

[†] *Teledyne Brown Engineering, 300 Sparkman Drive, Huntsville, AL 35807, USA*

EMail: *Dan.Schrimpsher@tbe.com*

The explosive growth of the Internet has brought forth Hypermedia Information Presentation Systems into greater prominence. Such systems find use in a variety of domains such as education and advertising. The strongly visual nature of these interactive information delivery tools mandates a new look at techniques for evaluating their usefulness and usability. Tracking the eyes of users as they work with such systems, when combined with traditional evaluation methods from Human–Computer Interaction, can provide a powerful new evaluation approach to the designer. This paper reports on the technical aspects of such an approach that we have developed, and describes a pilot experiment on its application to educational hypermedia.

Keywords: animation, evaluation, eye tracking, interaction analysis, multimedia.

1   Introduction

Ever since the advent of easy-to-use commercial tools like the Apple Hypercard, Hypermedia Information Presentations Systems (HIPS) have found increasing use in a variety of domains. Such a system is designed to convey information to the user, and exploits multimedia representations (e.g. diagrams, pictures, animations, video, text, speech, and sounds) to do so. Furthermore, though such systems may present information in a default sequential structure (such as a series of pages or screens), they also allow non-linear navigation by means of hyperlinks that connect the multiple representations. Education has always been a fertile domain for such systems. The explosive growth of the Internet in recent years has moved HIPS from CD-ROMs to the Web, and tremendously expanded their scope to other domains and users (e.g. commercial Web sites designed both to educate and attract potential customers).

How useful (effective) and usable are such systems? Some of the traditional measures of usability may not be relevant to such systems. For example, learnability of the interface may not be an issue for Web surfers well versed in navigating by pointing and clicking on hyperlinks and graphics. On the other hand, new measures may need to be developed. For instance, a new measure of 'comprehension efficiency' — how much information is comprehended after viewing a HIPS — is quite likely to be useful.

Given the highly graphical nature of HIPS, which typically present multiple visual items on the same screen, another measure relevant to both usability and usefulness is the time users actually spend looking at 'information-carrying' components on the screen (as opposed to looking at merely 'decorative' components or not looking toward the screen at all). Quantitative and qualitative data traditionally used for HIPS evaluation include time on task, keyboard and mouse action logs, pre/post tests, verbal protocols, experimenter observations, structured interviews and systematic questionnaires. However, none of these can reveal information about how users allocate visual attention to and across multiple information carrying components of a HIPS. Therefore, we argue that technology for tracking the eye movements of users as they visually attend to various components of a multimedia information presentation provides a powerful source of data to analyse the *process* of interacting with HIPS, which in turn can throw light on the *outcomes* of such interactions. However, current eye tracking technology suffers from several limitations, not the least of which are high cost and bulkiness of the equipment, and potential for loss of track unless users are physically restrained (or their head motions are tracked, which adds to the cost and bulkiness). Another problem is the lack of general software support for analysing the voluminous data generated (see Section 5 for a discussion in support of this claim).

A research project undertaken in this context is described here. This paper has three aims. The first is to outline an approach to evaluating the usefulness and usability of HIPS (in, but not restricted to, the educational domain). The second is to describe software for aggregating and analysing eye movement data that we have designed and implemented as part of this approach. The third is to discuss the results of applying this approach to an interactive algorithm visualisation designed for computer science undergraduates in a pilot experiment.

2 A Recipe for Evaluation

The primary objective of a HIPS is to effectively convey information to the user. In the educational domain, a useful HIPS is one that is successful in enabling the learner to comprehend complex information on a topic. It is irrelevant whether an ineffective HIPS is usable or not. It does matter if an effective HIPS has poor usability. Therefore, the first question a designer of HIPS needs to ask is whether it produces the desired outcome. In other words, does the system significantly improve the comprehension or knowledge of users? This can be empirically tested by measuring the prior knowledge of a sample of users in a pre-test, having them interact with the HIPS, and then measuring their knowledge improvement in a post-test. But this in itself is not sufficient to justify the time and effort needed to build and deploy a HIPS.

Thus, a second question needs to be asked: does the HIPS provide a significantly better means of conveying information compared to other ways of conveying the same information? This can be empirically tested by a comparative study in which multiple groups of users work with the HIPS as well as other competing techniques of information presentation, in which post-test results are statistically compared to see if the HIPS performs significantly better.

If the HIPS is found to be better, a third question can be asked: why is it better? While the previous two questions dealt with *outcomes* of interacting with a HIPS, the present question has to do with the *process*. As a HIPS can have several components, such as text, diagrams, video clips, animations, and so on, which of these components contribute to its effectiveness is an issue worth pursuing. If a component is found to be ineffective, removing it can benefit both the design (make it more compact) and the user (less interaction objects to deal with). One approach to this is to design and conduct a series of ablation studies in which a complete version of HIPS is compared with versions in which one component (or a group of similar components) has been elided. Then statistical comparisons of post-test results will throw light on the differential contributions of these components. Unfortunately, this is a time and effort intensive approach.

Another way to address this question is to study the micro-structure of interaction by collecting and analysing logs of user interactions with the HIPS. However, since a HIPS screen will typically present multiple information carrying components, collecting only haptic logs (logs of haptic actions such as mouse clicks and key presses) will provide only an incomplete picture. For instance, suppose when the user presses a button labelled 'forward', a page with a chart, some explanatory text and an animation appears. While the haptic log will indicate that the user moved to this page, it will not show whether he or she attended to any of its components. This introduces a need for tracking the visual attention of users. Eye movement data from an eye tracker, when combined with haptic logs, can provide a more complete picture of the interaction process, from which conclusions of the effectiveness or otherwise of specific components can be drawn.

Besides usefulness, eye tracking can also reveal clues about usability (Benel et al., 1991). Unexpected or unusual scanning patterns (such as repeatedly gazing back and forth between two visual components) and fixation patterns (such as staring at a component for a long time) can indicate potential trouble spots in the interface. Information gleaned from an eye tracker can thus complement traditional measures of usability. Such additional information will be quite useful in assessing the usability of the highly visual interfaces of HIPS.

A significant advantage in using eye movements as a source of data is that these are automatic, giving an accurate measure of where one's visual attention is directed. This is information that cannot be accurately obtained by asking a user what he or she is looking at. Interpretation of eye movement data in Human–Computer Interaction (HCI) tasks can be based on the empirically validated eye-mind assumption (Just & Carpenter, 1976) that when a person is performing a cognitive task while looking at a visual display, the location of his or her gaze on the display corresponds to the symbol that he/she is currently processing in working memory. The ability of eye tracking to reveal otherwise unobtainable information about visual interaction has lately generated increasing interest in using this technology for evaluation of computer interfaces (Goldberg & Kotval, 1998).

3   Adding Eye Tracking to the Recipe

Adding eye tracking to the recipe for evaluating HIPS, while clearly beneficial, is also problematic. The technology suffers from several limitations (Jacob, 1991). One difficulty is the sheer volume of eye movement data generated. An eye tracker typically generates 60–250 pairs of screen coordinates per second indicating the locations at which subjects looked. A user who interacts with a HIPS for several minutes can generate enormous amounts of data. Most current eye trackers come with primitive interfaces and rudimentary software for data analysis. As the traditional use of this technology mainly involves static visual stimuli such as text or visual scenes used in psychological research on reading and visual perception (Just & Carpenter, 1976), the available software is tailored to compute and display fixations and scan paths on static stimuli.

We used an ISCAN ETL-400 eye tracker. This system uses an infrared light source that shines an infrared beam on one eye and an infrared camera that processes the resulting corneal and pupil reflections to compute the x and y screen coordinates, at the rate of 60 Hertz, of where the subject is looking. This x–y location is called the subject's point-of-regard (POR). This is the basic eye movement data generated by most eye trackers. The infrared source and the camera are mounted on a pan/tilt assembly and placed at a slightly upward angle on a table below the computer monitor that subjects look at. The system requires a brief calibration step with each user in order for it to be able to compute the POR in screen coordinates. The data output from the ISCAN system consists of a series of quadruples (x, y, p, a) generated 60 times per second. Here x and y provide the POR, p is the pupil dilation (which we ignore at present), and a is an auxiliary byte that contains a code output on the serial line by the stimulus display computer to the eye tracking computer.

The eye tracker tracks two types of eye movements: saccades followed by fixations. Saccades are rapid eye movements that allow the fovea to view a different portion of the display. During a saccade, vision is suppressed and does not become active until its destination has been reached. Often a saccade is followed by one or more fixations when objects in a scene are viewed. During a fixation small eye movements still occur within a general viewing area. There are two general methods used to identify fixations. First, a set area can be identified and any eye movements contained solely within that area for a fixed time period would be termed a fixation. A second method is where the velocities of eye movements are considered. Low velocity eye movements are considered fixations and high velocity eye movements are saccades. The ISCAN system identifies fixations using the first approach. We defined a fixation as the user looking within a 20×20-pixel square for at least 100 milliseconds. After the experimenter defines the parameters of a fixation, the ISCAN software can compute fixations from the POR data.

One aim of our research is to enhance software support for incorporating eye tracking into HCI research, especially for HIPS evaluation. As a first step, we recognised the need for a post-experimental POR data analysis system that computed locations and shifts of a user's visual attention over time across the dynamic elements of a multimedia presentation. To address this need, a software module called GRIP (Gaze Recognising and Information Processing) that incorporates two advances in eye movement data analysis was designed and implemented in C++.

The first advance is that GRIP extends POR data analysis into the realm of dynamic multi-screen and multimedia presentations. GRIP allows the experimenter to interactively indicate spatial regions that contain all components of interest (such as a control panel, a picture, a piece of text, an animation, etc.), identified through a unique integer code, in the HIPS. The HIPS must be instrumented to output the same codes through the serial port to the eye tracking computer whenever the corresponding component comes into the view of the user (for static components) or whenever the user starts/stops a dynamic component such as a video or animation. GRIP combines information about the spatial regions occupied by visual components in various screens, the codes output by the HIPS while the user is interacting with the system, and the raw data from the eye tracker to conduct its analyses.

The second advance is that GRIP aggregates and reduces the voluminous raw data produced by the eye tracker. It first computes *gazes* from the raw POR data. We define a gaze as consecutive fixations within the spatial region of one component. GRIP also computes shifts of visual attention from one component to another as a *jump*. Gazes reveal components that held the user's attention while jumps can reveal interesting patterns in how the user viewed multiple visual components simultaneously present on a screen.

GRIP processes eye movement data in five steps: segment POR data and associate time with data points; aggregate POR data into targets and durations of gazes; aggregate gazes; compute jumps; and aggregate jumps. First, it groups POR data into sections corresponding to the dynamic components visible to the user and computes the time for each POR. Each section is preceded by a list of components visible during that section. Figure 1a shows a sample. This represents the first step in extending eye movement data analysis to dynamic multimedia presentations — associating time stamps and visible dynamic components from the HIPS with POR data. It tells the experimenter which visual elements were present and provides a time-stamped chronological ordering of the POR data that was recorded during that segment of the presentation. However, this is a very large data file, containing 3600 lines per minute of presentation.

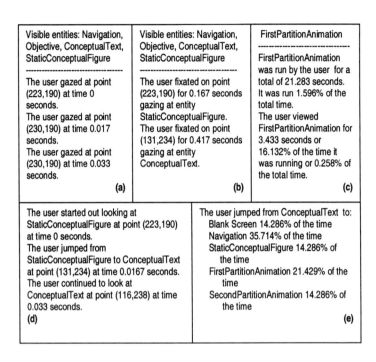

Figure 1: Outputs of GRIP.

The second step is reducing this data by aggregating POR data into fixations. GRIP uses ISCAN software to compute fixations from POR data. It then aggregates consecutive fixations at the same location into gazes and computes timing information. Thus a chronological list of gazes associated with visible components of the multimedia presentation is produced (see Figure 1b for a sample). This, while smaller than the previous file, is still a very large data set.

In the third step, GRIP further aggregates gaze information as shown in Figure 1c. For each component of interest specified by the experimenter, it computes the total time for which the component was visible or active, the percentage of this time with respect to the total time the HIPS was running, total time for which the user gazed at the component, the percentage of this time with respect to the total visible/active time of the component, and the percentage of gaze time with respect to the total running time of the HIPS. These percentages give an indication of interest or indifference by the user and the relative importance (according to the user) of a component in the presentation. This information can be valuable in usefulness (e.g. correlating measured comprehension levels with components that users focused on) and usability (e.g. users staring at a menu for an inordinate amount of time may indicate lack of clarity in labelling) analyses.

The fourth step is to generate a chronological list of gaze switching between different components, called jumps, from the gaze data computed in step two. A sample from this list appears in Figure 1d. In the fifth and final step GRIP computes, for each component of the multimedia presentation, all other visible components to which the user's gaze shifted from that component and the corresponding percentages (with the total number of gaze shifts from the component as a basis). See Figure 1e for an example. This gives the experimenter an idea of conceptual connections between two components. For example, if a subject's gaze jumps from Component 1 to Component 2 95% of the time, it is reasonable to assume that the user is trying to integrate information from the two components in his or her mental model by building representational and referential connections. Narayanan & Hegarty (1998) discuss information integration by making such mental connections in a model of information comprehension from multimedia.

GRIP is designed to be used with multimedia presentations built with any application and running on any computer. There are only two requirements. One is that the experimenter must create a component description file specifying labels and screen coordinates of every visual component of interest in the presentation. This can be done interactively. Second, the stimulus computer running the HIPS should send a code, corresponding to each component when it becomes visible/active, to the eye tracking computer through a serial cable. This code is simply an integer corresponding to the position of the component in the component description file (e.g. the code of the first component is 1). This is easy to do in most multimedia authoring platforms (such as the one we used — Macromedia Director) by adding the corresponding instructions to appropriate event handlers that bring up new screens, start animations, etc. The ISCAN system adds this code to the raw data it generates. Other eye tracking systems can do this as well. More details about the software architecture of GRIP and its source code are available in (Schrimpsher, 1999).

4 A Taste Test

Educating beginning or intermediate computer science students on fundamental computer algorithms is no easy task. Because of the relatively abstract and mathematical nature of algorithms, many students find the subject difficult. Since 1981, researchers have investigated animations of algorithms as potential learning tools for students. However, while several algorithm animations were built as research prototypes and several were deployed in algorithm courses, very few evaluations were done and those that were done indicated no significant learning benefits (Byrne et al., 2000). Motivated by this state of affairs, we have been investigating a novel design approach toward algorithm animations as educational tools since 1997. The key insight to emerge from this research was that for algorithm animations to be effective, they have to be 'chunked' and embedded within a context and knowledge providing HIPS. The resulting system called Hypermedia Algorithm Visualisation (HalVis) proved to be an effective learning tool, with five empirical studies involving over 150 undergraduates showing its superiority to text, lecture and other animations (Hansen et al., 2000).

After answering the first two questions of the HIPS evaluation approach, i.e. showing that HalVis significantly improved the knowledge of students and that it was more beneficial than conventional means, we turned our attention to the third question: why is HalVis better? In developing HalVis, many visual components (e.g. textual descriptions, pseudocode, and three different kinds of animations) that were thought to be useful were included. As a first step toward identifying the components of HalVis that contribute most to learning, we conducted a pilot eye tracking experiment. GRIP, which automates the reduction of eye fixation data into higher level entities called gazes and associates gazes with dynamic interface components of a multimedia presentation, was used to create a readable analysis (excerpts from which appear in Figure 1) of subjects' gaze patterns over the visual elements of HalVis.

This study had the empirical goals of verifying our hypothesis that GRIP provides a useful level of eye movement data analysis, and gaining insights into the relative usefulness of various components of HalVis from gaze patterns.

4.1   The Visual Interface of HalVis

We used a visualisation of the Quicksort algorithm in the experiment. It consists of five different views. The first view, called the Conceptual View, consists of a page that shows a familiar analogy that the student can interact with and animate, with accompanying text (see Figure 2). The analogy shows a line of people arranging themselves in the order of increasing height, using a series of moves illustrated through smooth animation, which capture the essence of the Quicksort algorithm in terms of its fundamental operations. The 'show' buttons provide students with interactive control over this animated analogy.

The second view, called the Detailed View, consists of two pages. The first page provides textual and step-wise (pseudocode) descriptions of the algorithm, with all technical terms in the textual description hyperlinked to another view, called the Fundamental View, which contains basic information about algorithms. The second page of the Detailed View presents a detailed and animated illustration of the Quicksort algorithm in four different panes simultaneously: a smooth graphical animation of the steps of the algorithm (Figure 3, left), pseudocode in which the steps being animated are concurrently highlighted (Figure 3, right), values of important variables used by the algorithm (Figure 3, below the animation pane), and explanatory messages about the events occurring in the animation (Figure 3, below the pseudocode). The algorithm animation in this view provides a micro-level (fine-grained) picture of the algorithm's operation on a small data set.

The next view, called the Populated View, presents a macro-level animated view of the algorithm's behaviour on a large randomly chosen or user input data set (see Figure 4). A novel feature of this module is a facility for the student to make predictions about different parameters of algorithm performance, and then compare those against the actual performance when the animation is running.

The fifth and final view, the Question View, contains a series of questions about the algorithm, which the user may answer and receive feedback. There are two types of questions: one that requires the student to reorder steps of the algorithm correctly, and another with multiple choices. All of these views can be visited in any order

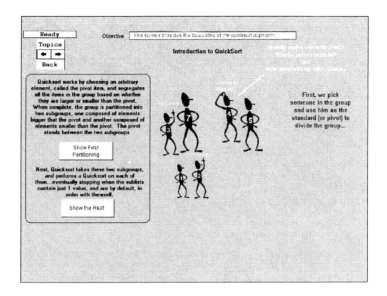

Figure 2: Conceptual View.

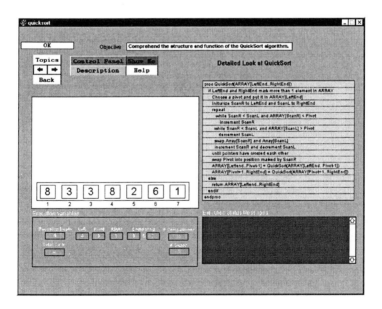

Figure 3: Detailed View — second page.

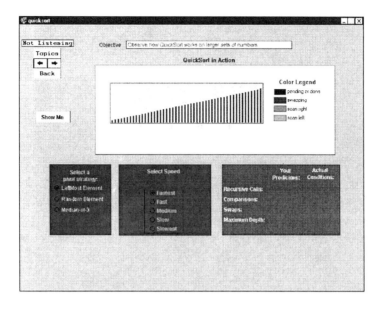

Figure 4: Populated View.

and repeated any number of times. HalVis was originally developed in Asymmetrix Toolbook. The Quicksort visualisation used in our experiment was implemented with Macromedia Director.

4.2   The Experiment

4.2.1   Participants

Seventeen second year computer science students volunteered to participate for extra credit. None of the students had seen the Quicksort algorithm or had any experience with the HalVis system.

4.2.2   Method

Students were first given a pre-test to measure how much they knew about the Quicksort algorithm. They were then given a quick introduction to HalVis' interface. A calibration step required for the eye tracker followed. They were asked to interact with the system until they felt confident they understood the algorithm. Afterwards they were given a post-test. Eye movements were recorded on all subjects and analysed with the GRIP system.

4.2.3   Results

Reliable eye movement data were captured only for nine subjects. Two subjects completed the experiment before a software glitch in HalVis was discovered, three produced eye movements too erratic to extract meaningful data, the eye tracker lost track of two subjects too often due to head movements, and one subject's eyes could not be tracked at all. Analyses described below (a more detailed discussion can be found in Schrimpsher (1999)) are based on data from these nine subjects.

The first analysis was to determine which components were viewed the most as a percentage of the total time spent with HalVis. The top three were the questions (mean(M) = 12.01%, standard deviation (SD) = 9.87), the two algorithm animations in the Detailed and Populated Views (M = 9.15%, SD = 6.97), and the textual description of the algorithm (M = 6.20%, SD = 2.99). It was expected that the animations would hold the students' attention. However, it was surprising to us that students spent quite a bit of time on the questions and the textual description. In order to see if there was a difference in how high performers allocated their visual attention, we did the same analysis on the top five students who showed the most pre- to post-test improvement. They also focused most on the questions (M = 13.51%, SD = 11.84), the two algorithm animations in the Detailed and Populated Views (M = 10.56%, SD = 7.28), and the textual description of the algorithm (M = 5.42%, SD = 2.14).

The second analysis done was based on the percentage of time each component was viewed while it was visible/active within each view, and percentages of gaze shifts across these components. In the Conceptual View, the animations were viewed most (M = 49.41%, SD = 30.71), followed by the textual description of the analogy (M = 18.48%, SD = 9.75). The low standard deviation of text indicates that more students consistently read the text than viewed the animations, suggesting that the importance of text should not be underestimated in HIPS. One-third of all gaze shifts from a graphical component (a static or running animation) in this view were to the textual description. Half of all gaze shifts from the textual description were to a graphical component. This indicates that simultaneous presentation of graphics and explanatory text is important to help learners build an integrated mental model.

In the Detailed View, the animation received the most attention (M = 19.43%, SD = 9.89), followed by the pseudocode highlighted in tandem with the animation (M = 9.81%, SD = 5.87), the explanatory messages (M = 7.05%, SD = 4.04), and the changing values of variables (M = 4.65%, SD = 7.83). The numbers indicate that there is a great deal of variability in how subjects view the components of the Detailed View except the animation. This suggests that the animation is an important component of the Detailed View. Two interesting patterns emerged in gaze shift analysis of this view. One, consistent with the pattern seen in the Conceptual View, is that one-third of gaze shifts from the animation were to the highlighted pseudocode and vice versa. The second was that no gaze shifts occurred from the explanatory messages to the animation. Most gaze shifts from the explanatory messages were to the pseudocode. It appears that, even though the messages were about events happening in the animation when the corresponding steps of the pseudocode were being executed, students used these explanations more as a tool to understand the textual pseudocode rather than the graphical animation.

In the Populated View, as expected, the static and running versions of the animation and its associated control attracted the most attention (M = 52.64%, SD = 37.86). What was surprising was that the facility to make predictions about the algorithm and to compare one's predictions with the actual values while the animation is running did not receive much attention (M = 6.51%, SD = 6.97). This, in the context of the hypothesis that learners making predictions before they watch an algorithm animation are likely to increase their learning (Byrne et al., 2000), indicates that algorithm animation designers need to find a way to encourage students to make and compare their own predictions.

4.2.4 Discussion

This experiment suggests that eye tracking is quite relevant to analysing human interactions with multimedia presentations. It revealed information that could not have been obtained by traditional sources of data such as pre/post tests, questionnaires, experimenter observations, verbal self-reports by subjects and logs of keyboard/mouse actions.

GRIP output revealed that subjects spent the most time viewing questions in HalVis. While a haptic interaction log may have revealed that students spent the most time on the questions page, it could not have confirmed how much of that time was actually spent visually attending to the questions. This becomes an even more salient issue for screens containing multiple visual components. The second item that attracted most attention consisted of two (out of a total of three) kinds of animations HalVis provided. These animations appeared in screens with several other components. Eye tracking helped separate the allocation of visual attention to these components. This is how we were able to detect that the third most 'popular' item was a textual explanation (a step-wise description called pseudocode) of the algorithm that appeared alongside one of the animations. Coarser data such as time spent on the screen containing both this animation and the pseudocode would not have revealed the attention subjects paid to the pseudocode (or the relative lack of attention they paid to the other two significant components on the same screen; see Figure 3).

Analyses of data for each of the three views of HalVis (Conceptual — Figure 2; Detailed — Figure 3; and Populated — Figure 4) by GRIP reinforced the finding that, other than questions, animations capture the most visual attention. The maximum amount of time in each of these views was spent gazing at the animations. The importance of textual descriptions was also reinforced. In the two views that contained text (Conceptual and Detailed), it received the second most attention.

Gaze shift patterns computed by GRIP also painted an interesting picture. The prominence of gaze shifts from an animation to a textual description and vice versa was revealed. Furthermore, in the Detailed View a pattern of gaze shifts among the animation, pseudocode and explanatory messages was also found. None of these fine-grained observations about the *process* of interaction would have been possible without eye tracking.

It must be noted that this was a pilot experiment. While it did achieve the goal of demonstrating the utility of eye tracking and GRIP's eye movement data analyses, the small sample size and other environmental factors caution us from generalising the results. Repeating the experiment with larger sample sizes and conducting statistical analyses on the data obtained are planned for future.

5 Related Work

The use of eye tracking in HCI research has a long, but sporadic, history. Eye tracking has been used both to synthesise (i.e. as an input method; see Salvucci & Anderson

(1999), Sibert & Jacob (2000)) and to analyse interactions. Here we discuss only recent work related to the latter as it is the focus of research reported in this paper.

One HCI task that has been investigated in depth using eye tracking is the visual search of menu items. Aaltonen et al. (1998) report a study in which eye movement data showed that a visual search behaviour called 'sweeps' could possibly account for the systematic and random search strategies previously reported for menu search. Another study employed eye tracking to assess the validity of two cognitive models of menu search (Byrne et al., 1999). Both used data analysis programs tailor-made for the menu search task, which calculated fixations, scan paths, sweeps and selection times from mouse and eye movement data.

Salvucci (1999) describes the use of Hidden Markov Models (HMM) to convert raw eye movement data into a sequence of fixations and to map the fixations into predictions of an HMM-based process model. This results in an interpretation of the eye movements in the context of a specific task like eye-typing. While this provides a powerful method for predicting and interpreting eye movements, it is limited to well-defined tasks for which one can a priori model eye movements.

Faraday & Sutcliffe (1997) report on one of the first studies to track eye movements of subjects viewing a multimedia information presentation. Based on an experiment with six subjects viewing an 18-second presentation, they developed several design guidelines for multimedia. Raw eye movement data was converted to scan paths consisting of saccades and fixations for 5-second intervals, nearby fixations were clustered into an ordered sequence, and overlaid on a frame of the presentation during each interval to produce a visualisation of the data. As data analysis was not the focus of this paper, it is not clear how much of it was done manually. GRIP not only automates this process (except the visualisation), but also takes data analysis to the next level where fixations are aggregated into gazes and gaze shifts automatically. This allows for analysis of complex multimedia presentations over longer periods of time (for example, a session with HalVis typically takes 30–45 minutes).

In summary, a major goal of our research is the development of a general aggregation, analysis and visualisation tool that will integrate and then distill haptic (keyboard/mouse) and visual (eye movement) data to provide designers with useful descriptions and depictions of users' interactions with their systems. The first step towards this goal is reported in this paper. This is in contrast to the data analysis techniques developed and employed in these related works, where either the focus is not on analysis tools or the analyses are highly task-specific.

6 Conclusion

This paper proposed a recipe for evaluating multimedia information presentations, reported on the technical aspects of extending eye tracking for interaction analysis in support of such evaluation, and described a pilot experiment on its application to educational hypermedia. The experiment showed that our system does indeed provide a very useful level of eye movement data analysis. Such a fine-grained analysis of allocation and shifts of visual attention facilitates evaluating and redesigning multimedia information presentations in several ways.

First, it provides data on how users differentially *allocate* visual attention to multiple components that are simultaneously visible on each screen of a dynamic and interactive multimedia information presentation. This can provide unexpected insights on the perceived importance (or unimportance) of these components. For example, while as expected, we found that animations in HalVis attracted a significant amount of visual attention, we were quite surprised at the extent of time spent viewing textual components that appeared alongside the animations. Such information is valuable for redesign. If text is so important in multimedia, extra attention should be paid to making the text comprehensible and relevant. Similarly, in an educational application if a component that the designer feels is important for learning is not being sufficiently attended to, attracting visual attention to that component ought to be a goal for redesign. In an advertising application on the Web, users paying scant attention to a visual component may lead to it being removed instead, as real estate is a scarce resource for Web banners.

Second, it reveals patterns of how users *shift* their visual attention across multiple components that are simultaneously visible on each screen of a dynamic and interactive system. Besides providing insights on the order in which users are visually processing these components, such patterns can also point to potential comprehension problems. When attention shifts occur back and forth between visual components that are different representations of the same object (e.g. multiple perspective views of a three dimensional object, or a description and a diagram of a system), it indicates a comprehension process called 'co-reference resolution' (Narayanan & Hegarty, 1998). Users are trying to build mental connections between these different representations and to integrate information acquired from these representations in their mental models. A high frequency of such back and forth jumps, or a pattern of attention cycling through several visual components, suggests a comprehension bottleneck — a potential target for redesign.

Third, data on attention allocation and shifts can help complete the picture of users' navigation patterns. For the kinds of rich hypermedia information presentations seen on the Web today, containing several visual components on each page, the click-through data that is typically collected on users' movements among pages and through hyperlinks can only paint an incomplete picture of navigation. What is missing is how they visually navigate across components on each page. Automatically synchronising and integrating eye movement data with haptic data to permit navigational analyses is an open problem that we plan to address in future research.

At present we are pursuing further refinements of eye movement data analysis. One refinement is the automatic generation of visualisations of gaze durations and gaze shifts. This will allow the designer to more easily locate interesting patterns of how users allocated their visual attention to and across multiple components of a multimedia presentation, than by reading the textual descriptions that GRIP produces. The second is to provide the designer with interactive control over GRIP's computations, such as grouping and ungrouping visual components for analysis purposes. While eye movement data by itself provides a fine-grained view of users' visual interactions, combining it with logs of keyboard and mouse actions will create a richer and more complete source of data on the interaction process. However, synchronising the visual and haptic logs, aggregating this voluminous data, intelligently analysing it, and presenting the data and analyses in a comprehensible and useful manner to the designer present significant challenges. This is an avenue for our future research on extending eye tracking in support of HCI research.

Acknowledgements

This research was supported by contract N00014-96-11187 and an equipment grant from the Office of Naval Research. The development of HalVis was supported by grants CDA-9616513 and REC-9815016 from the National Science Foundation. Thanks go to Eric Crowe for helping to conduct the experiment.

References

Aaltonen, A., Hyrskykari, A. & Räihä, K.-J. (1998), 101 Spots, or How Do Users Read Menus?, *in* C.-M. Karat, A. Lund, J. Coutaz & J. Karat (eds.), *Proceedings of CHI'98: Human Factors in Computing Systems*, ACM Press, pp.132–9.

Benel, D. C. R., Ottens, D. & Horst, R. (1991), Use of an Eyetracking System in the Usability Laboratory, *in Proceedings of the Human Factors and Ergonomics Society 35th Annual Meeting*, Human Factors and Ergonomics Society, pp.461–5.

Byrne, M. D., Anderson, J. R., Douglas, S. & Matessa, M. (1999), Eye Tracking the Visual Search of Click-down Menus, *in* M. G. Williams, M. W. Altom, K. Ehrlich & W. Newman (eds.), *Proceedings of CHI'99: Human Factors in Computing Systems*, ACM Press, pp.402–9.

Byrne, M. D., Catrambone, R. & Stasko, J. T. (2000), "Evaluating Animations as Student Aids in Learning Computer Algorithms", *Computers and Education* **33**(4), 253–78.

Faraday, P. & Sutcliffe, A. (1997), Multimedia: Design for the Moment, *in* J. D. Hollan & J. D. Foley (eds.), *Proceedings of Multimedia'97*, ACM Press, pp.183–92.

Goldberg, J. H. & Kotval, X. P. (1998), Eye Movement-based Evaluation of the Computer Interface, *in* S. K. Kumar (ed.), *Advances in Occupational Ergonomics and Safety*, IOS Press, pp.529–32.

Hansen, S. R., Narayanan, N. H. & Schrimpsher, D. (2000), "Helping Learners Visualize and Comprehend Algorithms", *Interactive Multimedia Electronic Journal of Computer-enhanced Learning* **2**(1). Electronic journal available at http://imej.wfu.edu/.

Jacob, R. J. K. (1991), "The Use of Eye Movements in Human–Computer Interaction Techniques: What You Look At is What You Get", *ACM Transactions on Office Information Systems* **9**(3), 152–69.

Just, M. A. & Carpenter, P. A. (1976), "Eye Fixations and Cognitive Processes", *Cognitive Psychology* **8**, 441–80.

Narayanan, N. H. & Hegarty, M. (1998), "On Designing Comprehensible Interactive Hypermedia Manuals", *International Journal of Human–Computer Studies* **48**, 267–301.

Salvucci, D. D. (1999), Inferring Intent in Eye-based Interfaces: Tracing Eye Movements with Process Models, *in* M. G. Williams, M. W. Altom, K. Ehrlich & W. Newman (eds.), *Proceedings of CHI'99: Human Factors in Computing Systems*, ACM Press, pp.254–61.

Salvucci, D. D. & Anderson, J. R. (1999), Intelligent Gaze-added Interfaces, *in* M. G. Williams, M. W. Altom, K. Ehrlich & W. Newman (eds.), *Proceedings of CHI'99: Human Factors in Computing Systems*, ACM Press, pp.273–80.

Schrimpsher, D. J. (1999), Where They Look and Why It Matters: Exploiting Gaze Patterns to Analyze Interactions with Algorithm Visualizations, Master's thesis, Computer Science & Software Engineering Department, Auburn University.

Sibert, L. E. & Jacob, R. J. K. (2000), Evaluation of Eye Gaze Interaction, *in* T. Turner, G. Szwillus, M. Czerwinski & F. Paternò (eds.), *Proceedings of CHI'2000: Human Factors in Computing Systems*, ACM Press, pp.282–8.

QTVR Support for Teaching Operative Procedures in Dentistry

Simon A Clark, Betty P Ng[†] & BL William Wong

Multimedia Systems Research Laboratory, Department of Information Science, University of Otago, PO Box 56, Dunedin, New Zealand

Tel: *+64 3 479 8322*
Fax: *+64 3 479 8311*
EMail: *william.wong@stonebow.otago.ac.nz*

[†] *Department of Oral Rehabilitation, School of Dentistry, University of Otago, PO Box 56, Dunedin, New Zealand*

This paper reports on an investigation into the effectiveness of multimedia content in Computer Aided Learning (CAL) tutorials, in particular QuickTime Virtual Reality (QTVR), at teaching operative dentistry. Insights gained from a cognitive task analysis of four dental specialists guided the design of two CAL programs. Both programs made use of a combination of multimedia and QTVR objects of teeth models. The two CAL programs differed only in how the QTVR teeth models were rendered. Forty-nine dental students then participated in an experiment that compared the effectiveness of the CALs at communicating operative dentistry procedures and expertise against traditional-styled dental classroom demonstrations. The results suggest that while the CAL packages can significantly lessen the time required to learn the procedures, the method in which students are taught the procedure had no significant effect upon skill acquisition. Further investigation of this unexpected effect on skill acquisition lead to some implications for the design of future dental-CAL.

Keywords: computer aided learning, operative dentistry, QTVR, CTA, CDM, multimedia.

1   Introduction

The easy access to computing technology and multimedia resources has enabled the development of new teaching and training methods such as self-paced, multimedia-based computer-aided learning (CAL) tutorials. Despite a wide uptake of new training methods there have been few studies in the use of such computing technologies to teach dentistry (Dacanay & Cohen, 1992; Bachman et al., 1998; Matthew et al., 1998). The primary concern with these studies has been the evaluation of the effectiveness of the CAL program as a whole vis-a-vis traditional methods of instruction. Their findings have indicated that there is no difference between the CAL-based and the traditional modes of delivery (Dacanay & Cohen, 1992; Mulligan & Wood, 1993; Plasschaert et al., 1995). These studies, however, have not examined the effectiveness of the manner in which the content information is presented. This paper reports on a study that examined the effectiveness of the way content information, in particular one type of content called QuickTime Virtual Reality (QTVR), is presented rather than the effectiveness of the CAL system as a whole.

2   Background

The objective of this study is to determine if the mode of presenting information affected students' skill acquisition. This was evaluated through a study that evaluated students' performance of an operative dentistry task called a complex amalgam restoration of a lower mandibular molar. This task required the student to fill a cavity in a tooth so as to restore it to its original function and appearance. This study was conducted in three parts:

1. an initial Cognitive Task Analysis (CTA) of four senior dental specialists to identify the expertise, goals and strategies associated with the task;

2. a three-group, between subjects experiment to evaluate the effectiveness of the different CAL designs against traditional classroom delivery; and

3. a post-experiment CTA to help explain the unexpected outcomes from the experiment.

3   Phase I: Initial Cognitive Task Analysis

Cognitive Task Analysis, or CTA, is a method for identifying and describing the cognitive structures, processes that underlie job expertise, and the knowledge and skills required for performing a task (Seamster et al., 1997). Cognitive structures represent the knowledge-base organisation and representational skills required by a person to perform a task. Processes refer to the attention, problem solving, and decision making processes that underlie skillful task performance of that task. CTA differs from traditional Task Analysis (TA) in that the traditional TA largely attempts to identify and study observable behaviours, e.g. a sequence of actions taken to perform a task (Kirwan & Ainsworth, 1992).

Four senior specialists in restorative dentistry at the University of Otago School of Dentistry were interviewed with a CTA technique known as the Critical Decision

Step in Operation	Associated Decision Strategies and Goals
Selection of appropriate matrix band.	Visualisation of size and shape of restoration.
Apply matrix band to prepared tooth.	Visualisation of size and shape of restoration. Prevention of Post-Operative Complications.
Adaptation and stabilisation of matrix band.	Prevention of Post-Operative Complications.
Condensation of amalgam material.	Visualisation of size and shape of restoration.
Remove gross amalgam excess, approximating occlusal surface.	Visualisation of size and shape of restoration.
Remove gross amalgam excess from around matrix band area.	Prevent unnecessary damage to restoration.
Approximate the overlayed and non-overlayed cusps.	Visualisation of size and shape of restoration.
Remove matrix band and wedges.	Prevent unnecessary damage to restoration.
Check for and removal of gingival overhangs.	Prevention of Post-Operative Complications.
Refine approximated tooth to original tooth anatomy.	Visualisation of size and shape of restoration.
Final checking and refining of cusp heights, grooves and fissure detail.	Visualisation of size and shape of restoration.
Check contacts with adjacent teeth.	Prevention of Post-Operative Complications.

Table 1: Steps in operation with associated decision strategies and goals as identified through the CDM analysis.

Method, or CDM (Klein et al., 1989). The CDM is an interview method that employs a retrospective protocol analysis approach to eliciting expert knowledge and decision strategies. Interviewees were asked to recall a particularly memorable incident that they had experienced in the course of their work, and in this case, a particularly memorable amalgam restoration. Cognitive probes, or questions that are designed to probe their memories of the incident, were then used to investigate how those decisions were made, and what factors were considered during the performance of that restoration. The CDM interviews were tape recorded and transcribed for analysis. The interview and data analysis procedures used in this study are from Wong et al. (1997).

Analysis of the CDM interview transcripts revealed twelve steps in the complex amalgam restoration task. The data analysis also revealed a set of implicit expert knowledge underlying the task. Very importantly, the analysis indicated that the experts often would mentally visualise what the original tooth looked like and use this mental image to match and guide their carving of the amalgam restoration. This has been referred to as the visualisation strategy. Table 1 summarises the steps involved in the operation, the associated implicit expertise, and the steps in which this strategy is used.

The expert knowledge, and in particular the visualisation strategy, were then used as the basis for designing the multimedia CAL tutorials and the material for the dental classroom demonstration. This will be discussed next.

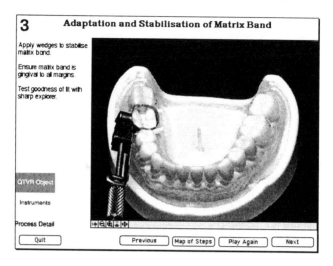

Figure 1: Screen shot of Step 3 showing the matrix band attached in the QTVR mandible.

---

4   Phase II: The Experiment

Two variations of a multimedia CAL tutorial on the complex amalgam restoration were constructed according to the steps and implicit expert knowledge identified in the CTA. Both CAL tutorials were designed around a QuickTime Virtual Reality (QTVR) object representation of the different stages of the amalgam restoration of a molar in the lower mandible or jaw. The photo-realistic QTVR molar and mandible (jaw) can then be rotated and viewed horizontally and vertically. Both CAL tutorials had audio and redundant textual instructions and explanations. From the initial CTAs in Phase I, experts were noted to practise a strategy of visualising the size and shape of the natural tooth. In the first CAL tutorial variation, this visualisation strategy was explicitly supported by embedding a dual-state view of the molar that showed both the stage at which the restoration was at and what the molar should look like as a natural tooth. In the second CAL tutorial, this dual-state view was not provided. A screen shot for Step 3 and the QTVR with the matrix band attached is shown in Figure 1. Figure 2 shows the second view of the dual-state view of the tooth, i.e. what the tooth should look like after the operation. This visualisation view can be presented very quickly by clicking and dragging (in Figure 1) to reveal the second-state view of the QTVR mandible (in Figure 2).

4.1   Running the Experiment

The visualisation and non-visualisation conditions were experimentally compared against the traditional dental classroom demonstration, which is the standard method for teaching an operative dentistry procedure at the School. Forty-nine students attending a course in operative dentistry participated in a three-group, between subjects experiment. The experiment was conducted as part of the students' regular curriculum. Each student was randomly assigned to one of the three conditions. In

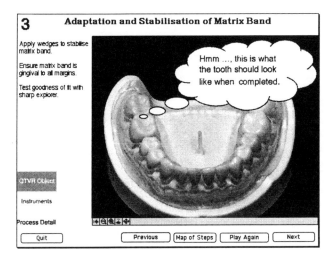

Figure 2: Screen shot of Step 3 showing visualisation state. Thought bubble added.

Figure 3: Dental students participating in the multimedia CAL tutorial conditions.

the control group, students were presented the tutorial using the traditional dental classroom demonstration. The remaining two groups were presented with either the visualisation or non-visualisation variations of the CAL tutorial on the complex amalgam restoration. Figure 3 shows participants in the multimedia CAL tutorial treatments, wearing headphones and each seated in front of a computer performing the amalgam restoration. Each student has his or her own tray of dental instruments located just in front of them.

		Control	Non-Visualisation	Visualisation
Learning	Mean	24.4	*21.2*	*21.1*
Time	Std.Dev.	n/a	*3.32*	*2.58*
(minute)	95% CI	n/a	*19.5–22.9*	*19.7–22.5*
Practical	Mean	35.0	*28.5*	32.0
Time	Std.Dev.	7.29	*6.99*	4.55
(minute)	95% CI	31.88–38.12	*24.9–32.0*	29.5–34.5
Model	Mean	5.6	4.6	5.2
Mark	Std.Dev.	1.29	0.91	1.48
(marks/10)	95% CI	5.1–6.2	4.1–5.1	4.4–6.0

Table 2: Summary results of Learning Time, Practical Time, and Model Mark for each treatment in experiment. Bold italic entries show significant differences against the control based on ANOVA and Bonferroni tests ($p < 0.05$).

Once the students had worked through the tutorials, they were asked to perform the amalgam restoration on teaching models of the lower jaw. The CAL programs were designed to track learning performance by measuring learning time, and time to complete the restorations. The quality of the restorations, another important aspect of learning performance (Bailey, 1996), was graded after the experiment by the teaching staff through a 'blind' assessment of the completed amalgam restoration models. Staff had no knowledge of which experiment group the models they assessed came from. Each model was given a single mark out of 10 (model mark) for the overall quality of the restoration. Seven aspects of an amalgam restoration are considered collectively when deciding on the quality of such a restoration. These aspects are the density and integrity of surface, interproximal contacts, presence or absence of interproximal overhangs, marginal ridge height, cusp height, occlusal morphology, and buccal and lingual contours. Once all the models have been assessed, the marks awarded to each model by the professors are compared and differences are discussed to arrive at an agreeable mark. Although recognising that this not an ideal assessment method, it is still current practice at the School while other research at the School explores alternative assessment techniques (Kirk et al., 1999).

4.2   Results and Analysis

The results from the experiment are summarised in Table 2 and are also charted in Figure 4. The results were analysed in SPSS, a statistical analysis software, to determine if there were a significant difference between groups. The t-tests ($p < 0.05$) and a One-Way Analysis of Variance, ANOVA ($p < 0.05$) showed that:

- Participants who viewed either of the CAL tutorials took three minutes less time to learn the operation than participants who were presented with the traditional dental demonstration. This difference is statistically significant.

- The time taken to perform the operation was significantly faster for participants who viewed the Non-Visualisation treatment than both

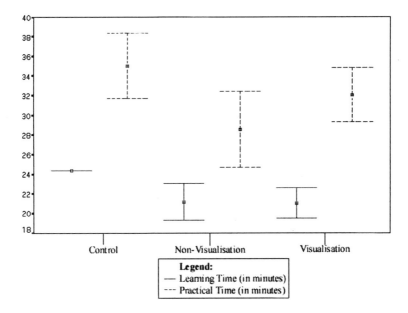

Figure 4: Chart displaying the 95% confidence intervals for Learning Time, and Practical Time.

---

participants who viewed the traditional dental classroom demonstration (control condition) and the Visualisation CAL tutorial.

- There was no significant difference in the marks awarded to the models between the different conditions. This suggests that the skill level attained by the participants is similar for each condition, and that the presentation method had no significant effect on participants' ability to adopt dental expertise.

4.3   Conclusions from the Experiment

Conclusions from this experiment may be summarised as follows:

- As there is no difference in the quality of the restoration, and hence no difference in the level of skill acquired by participants in any of the three conditions, both the CAL tutorial and the traditional classroom demonstration may be said to be equally effective in conveying the required expertise. However, the shorter learning times for participants in the CAL tutorial suggests that the CAL approach is more efficient in conveying this knowledge.

- Providing visualisation support did not seem to help the participant perform the task faster. Instead, participants provided with this additional information appear to take more time to complete their tasks.

- The facility for learner control provided for in both multimedia CAL tutorials allowed participants to learn at a pace that suited them rather than that of the demonstrator as in the traditional classroom method. Students were able to work faster when given the opportunity to do so via an interface that supported learner control. This appeared to help participants learn the operation more quickly than the traditional classroom demonstration method.

These outcomes raised a number of questions, in particular, *why did supporting the visualisation strategy not improve user performance?* This and other questions were further investigated in Phase III of the study. Only the findings that relate to the visualisation question will be discussed next.

5   Phase III: Post-Experiment Cognitive Task Analysis

The purpose of the post-experiment study was to understand how participants used the information available to them when learning and performing the operation, and in this manner, understand why the support for the visualisation strategy appear to be of little benefit. A cognitive task analysis of eight participants from each group of the experiment, was conducted using the same Critical Decision Method technique employed in Phase I.

5.1   *The Critical Decision Method Interview*

To set the scene, each student was first asked to reflect on his or her participation in the earlier experiment. They were asked to describe the learning and practical sessions as they had experienced them. Each event and associated decision points were identified and organised on a timeline.

Each participant was probed to explore the rationale behind each decision point, to identify the cues they had attended to, the knowledge they needed or learned in order to perform the operation, the experience and previous training they had drawn on to carry on with the operation, and the helpfulness of the aids they were presented with. The eight interviews were transcribed and analysed. Data from the interviews were compared between the CAL-based tutorials and the traditional classroom tutorial.

5.2   *Results from the Interviews*

The analysis identified several issues that provide clues to answer the question, *Why did supporting the visualisation strategy not improve user performance?* These are summarised below.

5.2.1   *Visualisation Support Used, But Not During Practical*

Participants found being able to see the desired surface of the tooth helpful during the learning stage. It made them aware of how the restoration should be carved. However, the participants interviewed reported that they did not use this information while performing the task. Time constraints caused by the fast hardening amalgam forced them to concentrate on completing the job.

5.2.2   *Effects of Time Constraint on Practical Phase of Experiment*

Due to the time-constrained nature of the operation, particularly in the carving stages, as the amalgam sets within a minute or two, many participants did not feel they had the time to view the CAL during the practical phase of the experiment. Instead, participants tended to replay the voice instructions to 'jog their memory' while they concentrated on carving the amalgam.

5.2.3   Pressure of Assessed Nature of Task

Participants were often spending an excessive amount of time performing the practical task. This was because they knew their carvings were to be assessed and therefore wished to make the molar look as best they could. This is despite the fact that the amalgam would have set, and made the task difficult to complete.

5.2.4   Want for Better Visual Quality

Participants have in the past been exposed to high quality images in their regular demonstrations, such as video broadcast of operating procedures, and high quality photographs in textbooks. Such expectations led the participants to believe that what they would see in the CAL tutorials would be at least of the same visual quality. Despite steps taken to ensure that the QTVR objects and animations were of high visual quality (e.g. a professional quality Nikon SLR camera with a 1280x1024 CCD was used to photograph the models), constraints on the available computer memory and display resolution meant the desired visual quality was simply not obtainable. However, participants were still able to use the visual detail presented to them in the QTVR models. Together with the positions of the opposite and adjacent teeth on their models, and their prior knowledge of tooth morphology (the structure of teeth) enabled them to carve the finer anatomical details of the mandibular molar. Thus despite the lower than expected visual quality, the interviewees still considered the CAL better than traditional demonstrations.

5.2.5   Desire Full Motion Animation/ Video of Operating Procedures

Another common theme uncovered was a desire for animation and video clips of the procedures in the operation. The existing animations were sufficient for the participants to understand what they had to do, but they thought that the CAL would be improved by being able to show the 'actual strokes' of the procedures.

5.2.6   Learner Control — Increased Motivation, but No Replacement for a Demonstrator

Participants indicated that the self-paced and interactive nature of the CAL tutorial was advantageous. They were able to learn at their own pace and to repeat aspects of the operation that they were uncertain about. But many participants still felt that they needed assistance from demonstrators during the actual performance of the task.

5.2.7   CALs More Suitable as a Pre-demonstration Learning Tool

Participants found that the explicit presentation of detail given in the multimedia CAL tutorials were very useful as a pre-demonstration learning tool, i.e. *before* the tutorial begins, rather than for concurrent support of task performance. The explicit detail included the ability to see what the restoration should look like at the end of each step, and when specific instruments should be used. Although it would be mentioned in traditional dental classroom demonstrations, it is often not made explicit details such as what specific instruments should be used and when. Participants also revealed that although they could learn how to perform the operation from the CAL, some would still prefer a demonstrator to be with them *during the practical phase* of the operation, to correct potential mistakes.

5.3   Discussion

This section will discuss the results in terms of the question, *why did supporting the visualisation strategy not improve user performance?* The CTA results suggest that the facility for visualisation was used and found to be helpful by the students, but due to the time pressure they experienced coupled with the fact that the restored models were to be assessed, its use did not feature significantly during the practical phase of the experiment. The students chose to concentrate on the carving task and on occasions would play the voice-over instructions to jog their memory about the steps in the procedure rather than spend time interacting with the QTVR model.

The second factor that could account for the apparent ineffectiveness of the visualisation support is that students wanted better visual quality in the QTVR models to enable them to see fine detail such as fissures and tooth contours which are essential for restoring the tooth to their original form. This need for high quality imagery was also identified in other studies; for example Sellen & Telford (1998). As the fine detail could not be seen easily, students simply relied on their memory of what they had examined during the learning phase.

Thirdly, learning how to carve an amalgam restoration is a highly procedural and practical skill. Videos or animations showing the carving procedure in relation to the specific tooth would have provided the time and motion based dimension necessary to teach procedural knowledge. Other research also supports the notion that video is preferred to text when supporting procedural task performance (Norris & Wong, 1997). The absence of video or animation within the QTVR model to support a time and motion based task provides further explanation for the QTVR model not playing a significant role during the practical phase.

Finally, the interviewees indicated that it was important to have feedback on whether the procedure they were performing is correct. The QTVR model was not designed to inform the student when he or she performs the procedure incorrectly. At the moment, the student may choose to check his or her work against the QTVR model, which shows what the carved restoration should look like at each stage. Currently, a tutor walking around the class to check their work is providing this feedback. Ideally, force-feedback devices such as the haptic PHANToM hand-piece reported in (Oakely et al., 1999) would be useful in providing visual, interactive, and, eventually expert and intelligent feedback.

In summary, it appears that while the facility to support visualisation was used during the learning phase, the time constraints coupled with the limitations in terms of the need for better visual quality, support for the demonstration of movement and animation, and the provision of real-time feedback during practice, it was not referred to during the practical phase to make a significant impact to student practical outcomes. These shortcomings implied that there would be no significant advantage between the CAL program that did and the one that did not support the visualisation strategy. Also, study also suggests that in its current form, the QTVR-based multimedia CALs are more suitable for use as a pre-demonstration learning tool.

6 Conclusion

This study investigated whether the provision of explicit support for identified cognitive strategies can improve student performance in learning an operative dentistry task such as the complex amalgam restoration. Through a CTA with senior dental experts, 12 steps in the restoration operation, two task goals, and a visualisation strategy were identified. This visualisation strategy then guided the development of two QTVR-based multimedia CAL programs. The programs were then experimentally evaluated against the traditional classroom demonstration method. The results indicated that the presence of support for the visualisation strategy did not lead to significantly better student outcomes. Further investigation of this unexpected outcome indicated that although support for the visualisation strategy was important, it was just as important that students could easily see the fine details of the tooth morphology, and that there should be animation or movies embedded in the QTVR model or within the CAL program to demonstrate how the operative procedures are performed. Finally, it is important that real-time feedback on the correctness of the students' work during the carving session be provided. These conclusions suggest the need for a form of CAL different from the usual electronic textbook, hypermedia, or problem-based learning implementations, to teach operative dental procedures. Further research is being planned to investigate the possible use of virtual reality, haptic technologies, and alternative modalities of interaction, for an operative dental simulator.

References

Bachman, M. W., Lua, M. J., Clay, D. J. & Rudney, J. D. (1998), "Comparing Traditional Lecture vs. Computer-based Instruction for Oral Anatomy", *Journal of Dental Education* **62**(8), 587–91.

Bailey, R. W. (1996), *Human Performance Engineering*, Prentice–Hall.

Dacanay, L. S. & Cohen, P. A. (1992), "A Meta-analysis of Individualized Instruction in Dental Education", *Journal of Dental Education* **56**(3), 183–9.

Kirk, E. E. J., Monteith, D. B., Lewis, G. R. & Purton, D. G. (1999), "Variability in Teacher-assessment and Student Self-evaluation of Performance", *Journal of Dental Research* **78**(Special Issue), 408.

Kirwan, B. & Ainsworth, L. K. (1992), *A Guide to Task Analysis*, Taylor & Francis.

Klein, G. A., Calderwood, R. & Macgregor, D. (1989), "Critical Decision Method for Eliciting Knowledge", *IEEE Transactions in Systems, Man and Cybernetics* **19**(3), 462–72.

Matthew, I. R., Pollard, D. J. & Frame, J. W. (1998), "Development and Evaluation of a Computer-aided Learning Package for Minor Oral Surgery Teaching", *Medical Education* **32**(1), 89–94.

Mulligan, R. & Wood, G. J. (1993), "A Controlled Evaluation of Computer-assisted Training Simulations in Geriatric Dentistry", *Journal of Dental Education* **57**(1), 16–24.

Norris, B. E. & Wong, W. B. L. (1997), Supporting Task Performance: Is Text or Video Better, *in* M. J. Smith, G. Salvendy & R. J. Koubek (eds.), *Proceedings of the 7th International Conference on Human–Computer Interaction (HCI International '97)*, Vol. 2, Elsevier Science, pp.24–9.

Oakely, I., Brewster, S., Glendye, A. & Masters, M. M. (1999), Haptic Visualisation, *in* S. Brewster, A. Cawsey & G. Cockton (eds.), *Human–Computer Interaction — INTERACT '99: Proceedings of the Seventh IFIP Conference on Human–Computer Interaction*, Vol. 2, The Edinburgh Press, pp.97–8.

Plasschaert, A. J. M., Wilson, N. H. F., Cailleteau, J. G. & Verdonschot, E. H. (1995), "Opinions and Experiences of Dental Students and Faculty Concerning Computer-Assisted Learning", *Journal of Dental Education* **59**(11), 1034–40.

Seamster, T. L., Redding, R. E. & Kaempf, G. L. (1997), *Applied Cognitive Task Analysis in Aviation*, Avebury Publishing Ltd.

Sellen, P. & Telford, A. (1998), "The Impact of Computers in Dental Education", *Primary Dental Care* **5**(2), 73–6.

Wong, W. B. L., Sallis, P. J. & O'Hare, D. (1997), Eliciting Information Portrayal Requirements: Experiences with the Critical Decision Method, *in* H. Thimbleby, B. O'Conaill & P. Thomas (eds.), *People and Computers XII (Proceedings of HCI'97)*, Springer-Verlag, pp.397–415.

Solutions for Elderly Visually Impaired People Using the Internet

Mary Zajicek & Sue Hall[†]

School of Computing and Mathematical Sciences, Oxford Brookes University, Oxford OX3 OBP, UK

EMail: *mzajicek@brookes.ac.uk*

[†] *Department of Family and Lifespan Studies, School of Health Care, Oxford Brookes University, Oxford OX3 OBP, UK*

EMail: *shall@brookes.ac.uk*

This paper is concerned with problems that elderly visually impaired users encounter when using the World Wide Web for the first time. It reports the results of an evaluation, conducted with BrookesTalk (a Web browser for blind and visually impaired people), with special reference to the problems experienced by elderly visually impaired users. The authors seek to identify the source of their problems and describe a software solution that offers support for those with fluid memory loss, and low levels of confidence.

Keywords: elderly users, visual impairment, memory loss, World Wide Web, interface, speech.

1 Introduction

This paper addresses problems encountered by elderly visually impaired people using the Internet. It is based on interdisciplinary work carried out in the School of Computing and Mathematical Sciences, where a Web browser specially for the elderly visually impaired has been built, and on research based in the Department of Family and Lifespan Studies in the School of Health Care.

The studies described below show that elderly visually impaired users experience great difficulty in getting going on the Internet when they have no previous experience in computing. Studies of Age Associated Memory Impairment (AAMI) show how disadvantaged elderly people are when using computer applications. This coupled with their visual impairment demands a new interface modality to support elderly visually impaired people learning to use computer applications.

This paper describes preliminary studies carried out with a specially modified Web browser for the blind, which speaks out instructions to the user as they use the application. The idea is to reduce reliance on 'fluid' memory, the most significant age associated memory loss and to support the users' development of strategies and processes until they become resident in the 'crystalline' memory. Instructions can be switched off as processes become understood and of course, if necessary, all instructions can be switched on again. The authors also looked at the effect of personal support in getting elderly visually impaired users up and running with the World Wide Web.

2 Difficulties Experienced by Elderly First Time Users on the Internet

The difficulties experienced by elderly visually impaired users were demonstrated during trials using a function key driven, Web browser for the blind and visually impaired, developed within our research group. The system called BrookesTalk was distributed free to over 200 blind and visually impaired users and an evaluation of how users were interacting with the browser was performed using an online questionnaire and follow-up telephone interview (Zajicek & Arnold, 1999).

Browser uptake by elderly visually impaired first time users was very disappointing, 82% of this group were unable get up and running. Analysis of their interaction showed that they were unable to build useful conceptual models of the functionality of BrookesTalk or of the workings of the Web. Their confidence in making the decisions needed for the construction of conceptual models was low and they became confused and frustrated. For example some subject users were unsure as to the functionality of a link. Sighted users are able to see the link, how it is placed in the page, and how it relates to other text on the page. They could also follow the link to reinforce their concepts and easily return to their original position. It is not as easy for visually impaired users to try out a link, see what happens, and learn from the experience. In addition, elderly users find difficulty in remembering sequences of actions they have previously performed.

These users also found difficulty in understanding the way a computer application works. Some 'borrowed' the model of a video recorder and expected one press of a button to make everything 'happen'. They were afraid that they would 'break' the software if they did something wrong. The concept of dialogue and learning to use a language at the interface through trial-and-error was very new to them. Other problems stemmed from a lack of understanding of the relationship between the function keys and functions they represent and the concept of mapping the task in hand onto the appropriate sequence of functions to achieve a goal.

Elderly visually impaired users interviewed on the telephone appeared not have the skill or confidence to try out functions to see how they work in order to build up a conceptual model of the system. Impaired memory as described below seriously interferes with exploratory activity that involves remembering many combinations of actions and outcomes.

Poorly developed conceptual models of the Web, as distinct from the browser, also form a major impediment to successful Web use, for blind and visually impaired users. Sighted users rely on complex and contextual, conceptual models and many visual clues to help them find information on the Web (Zajicek et al., 1998a).

Four important inter-relating conceptual models were identified for Web search:

- The model of the workings of the search engine.

- The model of the results page of a given search engine.

- The model of the Web site being visited.

- The model of the page.

Elderly visually impaired users find difficulty in constructing any of these models for the reasons established above.

3 Difficulties Faced by the Elderly

3.1 Memory Loss

Age related memory changes and their effects on learning are no doubt at the heart of the difficulties which older people have in accessing the Internet. It is generally agreed that old age is associated with a decline in intellectual skills which affects the absorption of new information. (Stuart-Hamilton, 1999). This is not a global decline; some skills are not affected by ageing and research has shown that certain types of memory are unaffected by ageing (Marighetto et al., 1999; Park, 1998). Others have shown that Age Associated Memory Impairment (AAMI) is associated with damage to different areas of the brain such as the hippocampus (Marighetto et al., 1999) or the frontal lobe (Rabbitt, 1997). These changes take place at a sub-clinical level in 'normal' elderly subjects as part of the general ageing process.

The importance of these changes for the older would-be Internet user is that while the 'crystalline' memory — i.e. fixed, pre-learned and unchanging knowledge and skills — is relatively unaffected, the 'fluid' memory is more likely to be subject to AAMI. Fluid memory is described by Stuart-Hamilton (1995) as "the ability to solve problems for which there are no solutions derivable from formal training or cultural practices". This definition fits precisely the 'suck-it-and-see' type of learning required for Internet use, described elsewhere in this paper and it can therefore be hypothesised that the request for a button to press for the right answer represents not only a need for familiar technology but for a learning method which makes the user feels more confident in their own ability to learn. Other research shows that older people are less able to retrace and navigate a route than younger people (Wilkniss et al., 1997). This can be seen as analogous to using the Internet which features a navigational system for information organisation.

Stuart-Hamilton also found that older people develop a range of strategies to compensate for AAMI, acquired through years of experience. This is illustrated in the BrookesTalk study described in Section 2, by the efforts of the older to identify a similar type of technology which they can relate to, i.e. the reliance on the VCR as the nearest model to a computer application.

It is generally agreed that older people are still able to learn but knowledge of the effects of AAMI indicates the need for a different type of interaction, which uses aspects of cognition that are less likely to be impaired.

3.2   Perceptions of the Internet

Given that the older person is capable of learning to use the Internet, what are the barriers which cause resistance, and sometimes fear of learning to use it? Although there is at present little hard research into the impact of the explosion of new technology into the lives of older people, much can be deduced from the way in which the Internet is marketed and reported in more traditional media. (Some of the following material is taken from an interview with an older non-user who was responding to the question "Why don't you use the Internet?"

To begin with, older people do not, generally see the Internet as being for, or relevant to them. Conceptually and technologically, the information super-highway has not been explained in terms which they are familiar with and one has only to look at the range of literature and magazines available on the topic to realise that they are unlikely to appeal to the older reader. Television and newspaper advertising features children and younger adults. Instead, they are likely to see newspaper stories featuring Internet stalking, fraud and crime, bringing the threat of events which they already fear into their own homes. Even non-computer owners express fears of having their personal details made available on the Web.

McMellon et al. (1997) coined the term 'Cyberseniors' and describe two groups of Internet users — the technology lovers, indulging a lifelong fascination with technology and the technology users who are pragmatic and see computers as another tool to achieve what they require. However this ignores the far greater group who are either technophobes who fear the power of the Internet, or who cannot see any gain to be made from using it rather than their traditional modes of communication.

Proponents of the Internet tend to emphasise its convenience and find it hard to understand why older people do not embrace the opportunities to reduce travelling and use of the telephone. However this shows a lack of understanding of how much an older person's world may be reduced already. Physical, psychological and social factors combine to shrink the available options. Retirement, loss of income, disability and sensory impairment, decrease independence and control over one's environment. As our informant pointed out, the contact with the bank clerk, post office worker or doctor's receptionist may be the only human contact of that day, and the trip to the shop or the bank may be the only physical exercise that the older person gets. 'Convenient' technology therefore becomes counter-productive. Gardner & Helmes (1999) report a study in Australia which illustrates the complexity of the relationship between physical and mental well being and the willingness of the ability to learn. Internal locus of control — the individual's sense of control of their own life and environment has, for a long time, been seen as an indicator of well-being, but the authors comment that self-directed learning readiness was a better predictor of well-being than locus of control.

3.3 Technology Acceptance

Technology Acceptance Models (TAMS) have been developed for looking at the factors that affect the uptake of technology (Zajicek & Arnold, 1999). The perception of the usefulness of the technology weighed against the time taken to learn it is a major factor.

Allied to this is the fear of failure. Learning to use the Internet represents a considerable investment of time and energy. According to our informant there is a fear that the failure to learn sufficient skills to be able to use the Net efficiently is a waste of a limited amount of time and energy. Is it worth the expenditure? The amount to be learned is also an important factor. Many learners would have to master keyboard skills before attempting to master the Internet. The 'qwerty' keyboard appears illogical and difficult to follow, and for many older people typing is not an essential tool; it may be seen rather as a dauntingly skilled occupation.

4 A Partial Solution

We see that several factors affect the take up of the Internet by elderly visually impaired people. The authors decided to concentrate on compensating for memory loss and visual impairment in the partial solution provided. Users' confidence in their own abilities was also studied, by offering individual help to half the subject users in the study described below.

Users' perception of the Internet and their levels of confidence and technology acceptance are important factors, but not easy to control at the interaction level. It was assumed that the subject users have a reasonably high level of technology acceptance as they, or their family, had originally requested a trial copy of BrookesTalk.

At the interaction level difficulties can be attributed to two interrelated factors which interfere with conceptual model development, age associated memory impairment and visual impairment both of which reduce the user's ability to benefit from visual clues and contexts. To accommodate of memory loss and visual impairment, a speaking front end was built onto BrookesTalk. The idea is to support the user in their construction of conceptual models by 'talking' them through their interaction. For each possible state of BrookesTalk an optional spoken output is provided. The user is informed as to where they are in the interaction and which actions are possible at this point. Optional further details are also available to describe the consequences of each action. After listening to the message the user chooses an option, presses the appropriate function key and then receives another message describing the new state of the system.

The spoken output for those who have just started up BrookesTalk would be:

Welcome to BrookesTalk your speaking Web browser. There is currently no page loaded. Would you like to:

Enter the URL of a page, press F1.
Start an Internet search, press F2.
Change the settings of the browser, press F7.
Hear more details about options available to you, press F3.
Repeat the options, press return.

With these messages reinforcing the users' knowledge of the state of the system and explaining to them what they can do next, it is hoped that the development of conceptual models will be supported through repetition and that the user will no longer need to rely on memory. The user can function initially with virtually no conceptual models at all, by using the system in a similar way to a telephone answering system and simply responding to questions.

The aim of the speaking front end was to familiarise the user with the steps needed to achieve Web interaction goals so that eventually the spoken instructions would be superfluous and the user would 'know' which function key to press for the required result.

5   A Pilot Study to Evaluate the Solution

The aim of the study was:

- To determine whether the presence of personal support plays a significant role in the uptake of the Internet.

- To determine whether it is possible to increase uptake of the Internet by elderly visually impaired users by offering the computer based support described above.

- To determine, if users can use the Web with the support provided, whether they are able to wean themselves off the support and use the browser unaided.

To carry out the first aim of the study, the enhanced version of BrookesTalk was piloted with two groups of four elderly visually impaired users. All the subjects were drawn from the group who had been unable to get going with the non-enhanced BrookesTalk in the previous large-scale study.

Group A was given written instructions for using the enhanced version of BrookesTalk and were observed as they carried out a set of Internet search tasks prepared for them.

Group B attended a demonstration of the use of the enhanced version of BrookesTalk and then were observed as they carried out the same set of Internet search tasks as Group A, with a helper in attendance for each person.

The helper provided support by answering 'yes' or 'no' to users' questions. In this way users could confirm decisions they were making at the interface and talk through strategies as they developed. This was assumed to increase confidence in the development of conceptual models. Further support than yes or no answers, was considered too difficult to monitor for consistency.

The set of tasks was performed in three one-hour sessions, completed within a week. Every effort was made to match individuals in the two different groups for intellectual ability, memory, level of family support and level of visual impairment.

	With personal support	Without personal support
Subject 1	3	
Subject 2	1	
Subject 3	3	
Subject 4	4	
Subject 5		2
Subject 6		1
Subject 7		2
Subject 8		1

Table 1: Ratings for subjects using enhanced and non-enhanced BrookesTalk.

At the end of the period of observation, users were rated on their level of use of BrookesTalk and hence their level of use the Web, as follows:

1. Not able to use the enhanced BrookesTalk unaided at all.

2. Able to use the enhanced BrookesTalk unaided.

3. Able to use non-enhanced BrookesTalk adequately.

4. Able to use non-enhanced BrookesTalk successfully.

The authors fully acknowledged that a user's rating gives a very crude measurement of the richness of interaction that was observed as they struggled to use the Web. However, the purpose of the study was to indicate whether personal support, or the speaking front end enhancement, appeared to be able to increase uptake of the World Wide Web for users who had previously been unable to use it. Users' ratings are shown in Table 1.

5.1 The Effect of Personal Support

Average ratings for those who received personal support were 2.75 compared to 1.5 for those who worked unaided. These figures indicate that individual support can make the difference for some users between getting up and running on the Web or not. These findings are in line with other work (Zajicek & Arnold, 1999; Zajicek et al., 1998b) which discovered other user groups who are unable to use computers unaided and for whom offline support was essential.

It is unclear at this point which aspects of the personal support offered were most valuable, the software demonstration or the confidence afforded by the availability of individual help. The nature of the support and how it should be incorporated into user requirements is a complex issue but must be addressed if this type of user is to participate in information technology.

5.2   The Effect of the Speaking Front End Enhancement

The rating of 2 for Subject 5 and Subject 7 in Group B, those who did not receive individual support, represent an improvement in their ability to use the Web due to the enhancement. They had been unable to use the non-enhanced BrookesTalk previously. These results indicate that the 'talking the user through' approach has something to offer and enables users to achieve interaction where it had previously been impossible. The authors plan to experiment to find optimum sentences, and voices, for talk through which may improve ratings still further.

5.3   The Ability to Move to Non-enhanced BrookesTalk

The rating of subjects 1, 3 and 4, who received individual support indicates that the enhanced BrookesTalk does go some way to enabling users to build 'crystalline' conceptual models i.e. models that work without re-evaluation.

However we see that users who did not receive individual help were unable to progress on to non-enhanced BrookesTalk. These results need further investigation. Possibly the time spent practising with set tasks was too short for this group.

6   Conclusion

The results of the pilot study indicate that personal support is very important for elderly visual impaired users using a computer application for the first time. They also indicate that application 'talk through' has a part to play where memory impairment precludes the building of strategies and experimental learning at the interface. The combined effect of these two factors appears to be significant although the level of their individual effects is unclear at the moment.

References

Gardner, D. K. & Helmes, E. (1999), "Locus of Control and Self-directed Learning as Predictors of Well Being in the Elderly", *Australian Psychologist* **34**(2), 99–103.

Marighetto, A., Etchamendy, N., Touzani, K., Torrea, C. C., Yee, B. K., Rawlins, J. N. P. & Jaffard, R. (1999), "Knowing which and knowing what: A Potential Mouse Model for Age-related Human Declarative Memory Decline", *European Journal of Neuroscience* **11**(9), 3312–22.

McMellon, C. A., Schiffman, L. G. & Sherman, E. (1997), "Consuming Cyberseniors: Some Personal and Situational Circumstances that Influence their Online Behaviour", *Advances in Consumer Research* **24**, 517–21.

Park, D. C. (1998), "Ageing and Memory: Mechanisms Underlying Age Differences in Performance", *Australian Journal on Ageing* **17**(1), 69–72.

Rabbitt, P. (1997), "The Alan Welford Memorial Lecture — Ageing and Human Skill: A 40th Anniversary", *Ergonomics* **40**(10), 962–81.

Stuart-Hamilton, I. (1995), *Dictionary of Psychological Testing, Assessment and Treatment*, Jessica Kingsley.

Stuart-Hamilton, I. (1999), Intellectual Changes in Late Life, *in* E. Woods (ed.), *Psychological Problems of Ageing Chichester*, John Wiley & Sons, pp.27–44.

Wilkniss, S. M., Jones, M. G., Korol, D. L., Gold, P. E. & Manning, C. A. (1997), "Age-related Differences in an Ecologically Based Study of Route Learning", *Psychology and Ageing* **12**(2), 372–5.

Zajicek, M. & Arnold, A. (1999), The 'Technology Push' and The User Tailored Information Environment, *in* A. Kobsa & C. Stephanidis (eds.), *Proceedings of 5th European Research Consortium for Informatics and Mathematics Workshop on 'User Interfaces for All'*, GMD Forschungszentrum Informationstechnik GmbH, pp.5–11.

Zajicek, M., Powell, C. & Reeves, C. (1998a), A Web Navigation Tool for the Blind, *in* A. Karshmer & M. Blattner (eds.), *Proceedings of the 3rd ACM/SIGRAPH on Assistive Technologies*, ACM Press, pp.204–06.

Zajicek, M., Wheatley, B. & Winstone-Partridge, C. (1998b), Improving the Performance of the Tourism and Hospitality Industry in the Thames Valley, Technical Report CMS-TR-99-04, Oxford Brookes University.

Usability and System Evaluation

Using Incident Reporting to Combat Human Error

Chris Johnson

Department of Computing Science, University of Glasgow,
Glasgow G12 8QQ, UK

Tel: *+44 141 330 6053*
Fax: *+44 141 330 4913*
EMail: *johnson@dcs.gla.ac.uk*
URL: *http://www.dcs.gla.ac.uk/~johnson*

Incident reporting schemes enable users to provide direct feedback about the safety of the systems that they operate. Many schemes now also include questions that are specifically designed to elicit information about the usability of computer-based applications. They, therefore, provide a good source of information about the contextual factors that frustrate the operation of many interactive applications in complex working environments. This paper argues that such schemes can yield valuable insights about the nature of Human–Computer Interaction (HCI). Conversely, there is also a need to apply HCI research to improve incident reporting systems. Many of the online forms and Web-based interfaces that are being used in industry are poorly designed.

Keywords: incident reporting, human error, managerial failure.

1   Introduction

Accident reports, typically, record the events leading to fatalities, injuries, environmental damage or other significant losses. Recent work has argued that such major accidents are rare and atypical events (Reason, 1998). They are often the result of complex chains of human 'error' and system 'failure' that are unlikely to be replicated during subsequent interaction. As a result, many organisations have turned their attention towards incident reporting as a means of improving safety (van der Schaaf, 1996; van Vuuren, 1998). These schemes are increasingly capturing incidents that stem from problems in the interaction between people and computer-based systems (Busse & Johnson, 1999). This paper, therefore, argues that incident reporting systems can yield valuable insights that can be used to guide the subsequent development of human–computer interfaces.

Conversely, HCI has much to contribute to the design and operation of incident reporting systems (Johnson, 1999a). The most obvious example of this potential contribution is in the application of basic interface design principles to the growing number of incident reporting systems that are being developed on the Web (Staender et al., 1999). Many of these sites ignore basic guidelines about the selection of appropriate fonts, the choice of appropriate language and the layout of the fields that are used to request information about an incident. There are other areas in which HCI might contribute to incident reporting. In particular, previous insights into the causes and consequences of human error have not universally informed the analysis and interpretation of those incidents that are identified by existing systems (Busse, 2000). Later sections will also argue that observation techniques and workplace analysis can also be recruited to support the interpretation of the snap-shots that are provided by individual reports about human 'error' and systems 'failure'.

1.1   Why Bother?

Many different authors have identified the benefits of incident reporting (van der Schaaf, 1996; Reason, 1998; Busse & Johnson, 1999). The following list summarises the arguments in favour of incident reporting systems:

1. *Incident reports help to find out why accidents DON'T occur.* Many incident reporting forms identify the barriers that prevent adverse situations from developing into a major accident. These help analysts to identify where additional support is required in order to guarantee the future benefits of those safeguards.

2. *The higher frequency of incidents permits quantitative analysis.* Many accidents stem from atypical situations. They, therefore, provide relatively little information about the nature of future failures. In contrast, the higher frequency of incidents provides greater insights into the relative proportions of particular classes of human 'error' and systems 'failure'.

3. *They provide a reminder of hazards.* Incident reports provide a means of monitoring potential problems as they recur during the lifetime of an application. The documentation of these problems increases the likelihood that recurrent failures will be noticed and acted upon (Johnson, 1999a).

4. *Feedback keeps staff 'in the loop'.* Incident reporting schemes provide a means of encouraging staff participation in safety improvement. In a well-run system, they can see that their concerns are treated seriously and are acted upon by the organisation. This again illustrates the common concerns that motivate incident reporting schemes and user centred design.

5. *Data (and lessons) can be shared.* Incident reporting systems provide the raw data for comparisons both within and between industries. If common causes of incidents can be observed then, it is argued, common solutions can be found. However, in practice, the lack of national and international standards for incident reporting prevents designers and managers from gaining a clear view of the relative priorities of such safety improvements.

6. *Incident reporting schemes are cheaper than an accident.* These is an argument that the relatively low costs of managing an incident reporting scheme should be offset against the costs of failing to prevent an accident. This is a persuasive argument. However, there is also a concern that punitive damages may be levied if an organisation fails to act upon the causes of an incident that subsequently contribute towards an accident.

7. *May be required to do it.* The final argument in favour of incident reporting is that these schemes are increasingly being required by regulatory agencies as evidence of an appropriate safety culture. An important motivation behind this paper is that argument that HCI practitioners now have an opportunity to influence national and international policy in this area. In particular, it is important to ensure that proposed schemes explicitly consider usability issues as important precursors to incidents and accidents.

2 An Example Incident Report

Figure 1 presents part of an incident report from the Federal Aviation Authorities' (FAA) Aviation Safety Reporting Systems (ASRS). This system is frequently used as a model for other incident reporting systems (Johnson, 1999a). The forms are available online via a site that is maintained by NASA Ames. They receive the reports that initially are not anonymous. Providing that there are no grounds for criminal prosecution, Ames personnel extract any details that might be used to identify the people involved. The report is then analysed for subsequent statistical analysis, see below. Figure 1 describes an Air Traffic Control incident in which the controller reports a collision between two aircraft that he directed to runway 19. He gave the initial instructions while he was simultaneously interacting with a computerised information system. As can be seen, this transcript represents the output from an initial analysis process. Informal free text descriptions of the incident, the NARRATIVE, are supported by more strongly typed information about the systems that were involved, FACILITY IDENTIFIER, about the nature of the incident, ANOMALY DESCRIPTIONS. It also provides information about the people or systems that identified the problem, ANOMALY DETECTOR, and how they helped to mitigate its effects, ANOMALY RESOLUTION. This report is one of almost half a million in the ASRS database that describe similar interaction problems. It is important, however, to raise a note of caution. Later sections will describe the reporting biases that prevent at least some of this data from being accepted at face value.

ACCESSION NO.:	425641	DATE:	9901
REPORTED BY:	CTLR;;;	FLIGHT CONDITIONS:	VMC
PERSONS FUNC.:	TWR, GC. FDMAN. CD; FLC, PLT; FLC, PLT;		
FACILITY ID:	TEB FACILITY	STATE:	NJ
FACILITY TYPE:	TWR; ARPT;	FACILITY ID.:	TEB; TEB;
AIRCRAFT TYPE:	SMA; SMT;	ANOMALY DETECTOR:	CKPIT/FLC;
ANOMALY DESC.:	CONFLICT/GROUND CRITICAL;		
ANOMALY RESOL.:	NOT RESOLVED/UNABLE;		
ANOMALY CONSEQUENCES:	NONE;		

NARRATIVE: ON OR ABOUT XA50Z CESSNA ACFT X REQUESTED TAXI AND BEACON CODE FOR VFR FLT TO BED. WHILE I WAS TYPING INFO IN THE ARTS KEY PACK, ACFT Y CALLED FOR AN IFR CLRNC TO IAG. AFTER GETTING THE BEACON CODE FOR ACFT X, I READ IT TO HIM AND GAVE HIM TAXI FROM FBO-X TO RWY 19 AND HE ACKNOWLEDGED. I THEN READ ACFT Y HIS CLRNC TO IAG AND TOLD HIM TO ADVISE WHEN HE WAS READY TO TAXI. HE SAID HE WAS READY AND I ASKED IF HE COULD ACCEPT THE RWY 19 DALTON DEP, TO WHICH HE ANSWERED IN THE AFFIRMATIVE. I AMENDED HIS CLRNC TO THE RWY 19 DALTON DEP AND INSTRUCTED HIM TO TAXI TO RWY 19. AT XB55Z ACFT X RPTED A COLLISION WITH ACFT Y ON TXWY P. ACFT Y APPARENTLY WAS UNAWARE OF THE INCIDENT.

SYNOPSIS: ATCT CTLR AT TEB CLRS A C172 AND A C402 TO RWY 19 AND WHILE TAXIING, THE C172 PLT RPTS COLLIDING WITH THE C402.

REFERENCE FACILITY ID:	TEB	FACILITY STATE:	NJ
DIST. & BEARING FROM REF:	0		
AGL ALTITUDE:	0,0		

Figure 1: Excerpt from the ASRS Air Traffic Control Collection (Aug. 1999).

---

3 The Incident Reporting Process

In order to obtain reports about human 'error' and systems 'failure', users must be convinced that they will contribute to the overall success and safety of application processes. This depends upon feedback mechanisms that show users how their contributions have affected working practices. Figure 2 illustrates this feedback loop (Busse & Johnson, 1999). Incident reports are firstly analysed to identify common factors and to identify priorities for actions. These priorities are then acted upon and any changes are communicated back to the users who generated the initial reports.

4 The Elicitation of Incident Reports

The first stage in any reporting process is to design the forms that are to be submitted. Traditionally, text-based forms have been used to collect information about incidents from members of staff. However, this can create considerable problems for the installation and maintenance of reporting schemes across departments, institutions and national organisations. The logistics of providing every nurse in the UK with access to a paper-based incident reporting form are potentially prohibitive (Johnson, 2000). Many reporting schemes are now following the route taken by NASA and the FAA. In particular, they are distributing report forms over the Internet. Most simply provide Word or PDF templates that can be completed and then mailed

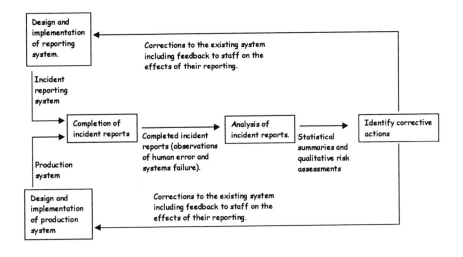

Figure 2: Anatomy of an Incident Reporting System.

back to the reporting agency. Other systems have been developed to exploit the online submission of incident reports. This creates considerable opportunities for investigation agencies to respond immediately in the aftermath of an incident. It also creates considerable ethical and security problems if agencies are to ensure that any reports, which are submitted over the Internet, come from a 'genuine' source. Figure 3 illustrates one of these Web-based reporting forms. Staender et al. (1999) have pioneered this approach to support incident reporting within Swiss Anaesthesia Departments. Web-based submission provides a cost-effective way of ensuring widespread coverage. However, it is important to emphasise the importance of HCI techniques in the development of incident reporting systems. If users perceive the difficult of completing the form to outweigh any perceived benefits then they are unlikely to complete their report. If any of the fields are unclear then users may find difficulty in accurately categorising the incident. If particular incident classifications are continually presented before certain others, for example operator thoughtlessness before poor display layout, then this can bias users towards the earlier cause. Each of these interface design issues has a profound impact on the way in which the form is completed. This has a knock-on effect on any analysis and hence ultimately affects remedial actions. Unless these issues are considered then there is a danger that ad hoc interfaces will bias the ways in which organisations respond to incidents involving safety-critical systems.

   The elicitation of incident reports raises a number of further issues. A practical concern is what to do if no incidents are reported? In most instances it is naïve to assume that the interface is, therefore, absolutely safe (Perrow, 1984). Instead,

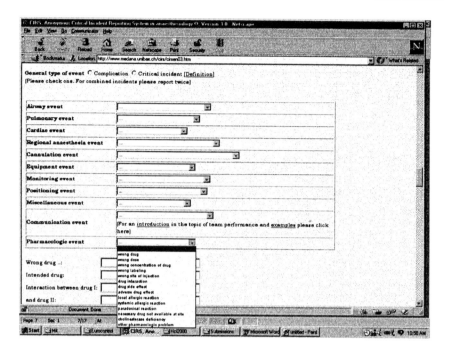

Figure 3: Swiss Critical Incident in Anaesthesia Reporting System (CIRS).

it may be important to focus incident reporting around a particular topic or task that is known to be problematic and then broaden the scheme out once initial participation is established. Alternatively, some organisations force their staff to complete a form at the end of each procedure even if only to explicitly indicate that no incident has arisen. This mirrors Norman's (1990) argument that it is often critical to understand not simply 'critical incidents' but also the prerequisites for successful task completion in HCI more generally.

5 The Analysis of Incident Reports

There are further ways in which incident reporting systems might directly benefit from recent work in human–computer interaction. For example, there is a growing body of work devoted to the causes of operator error during interaction with complex, technological systems (Reason, 1998). However, the incidents that are reported through these schemes are seldom in a form where they fit neatly into the categories that have been proposed by previous research (Johnson, 1999b). Incidents often involve complex dependent failures where many different systems and operators interact to attack the defences that ultimately safeguard the system. Each individual report may only contain observations about this complex web of causes from a particular user's viewpoint. For example, the nurse's view can often be very different from a clinician's observations of an incident (Busse & Johnson, 1999).

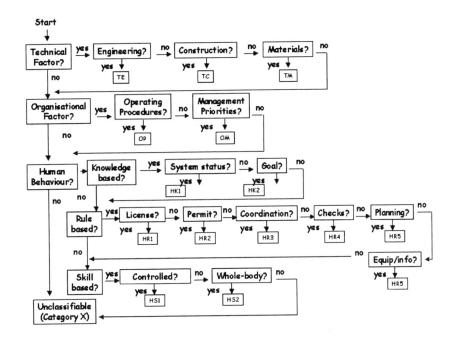

Figure 4: Classification Scheme for Chemical Industry (van der Schaaf, 1996).

In anonymous reporting systems, these problems are exacerbated by the problems of correlation independent reports about the same event.

HCI has much to contribute to the field of incident reporting in the categorisation and analysis of human error. There is a broad and diverse literature about operator failure within the field of HCI. This work provides cognitive frameworks and taxonomies that can be used to represent and reason about the causes of slips, lapses and mistakes. It is difficult to under-emphasise the importance of this work in shaping the analytical procedures that have been adopted within incident reporting. In particular, Reason's (1990) Generic Error Modelling approach has provided the backbone for many existing systems. However, there are some important limitations. As its name suggests GEMS is a generic system. Recent work in the field of incident reporting continues to emphasise the importance of domain dependent analytical frameworks (van Vuuren, 1998). For example, Figures 4 & 5 illustrate two different analytical tools that can be used to classify the causal factors that lie behind the observation information in an incident report. Both were based on the managerial factors identified in Reasons later work and alsoRasmussen's (1983) earlier SKR approach to human cognition and error. However, Figure 4 illustrates the scheme that was developed for incident reporting in the Chemical industry while Figure 5

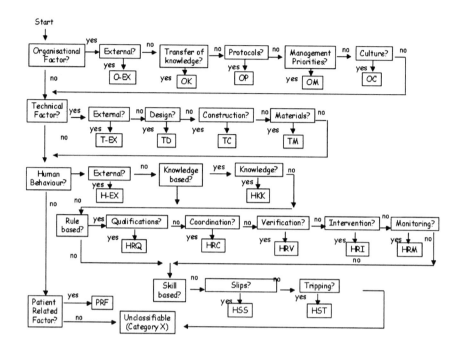

Figure 5: Classification Scheme for Clinical Environments (van Vuuren, 1998).

---

illustrates the analytical framework that was developed to support incident reporting within a number of UK NHS trusts.

There are a number of differences between these two different schemes. For example, patient related factors are clearly not an issue within the chemical industry. Conversely, the issuing of a licence or permit to perform an action is an important feature of Chemical incidents but plays little or no part in the medical classification scheme. It is important to emphasise that Figures 4 & 5 are supported by considerable fieldwork in the application of these schemes by domain specialists. This work in incident reporting, therefore, provides valuable insights into those contextual factors that complicate the task of applying generic error models, such as Reason's GEMS, from HCI research to support error analysis in complex, real-world environments.

The previous figures illustrate how incident reporting schemes have blended generic insights about the causes of user 'error' with the pragmatics that arise during the close observation of error in particular industries. Incident reporting schemes are also being used to validate theories about more detailed aspects of human–computer interaction. For example, Figure 6 provides the results of a study that was conducted into Endsley's three level model of situation awareness (Jones & Endsley, 1996). The

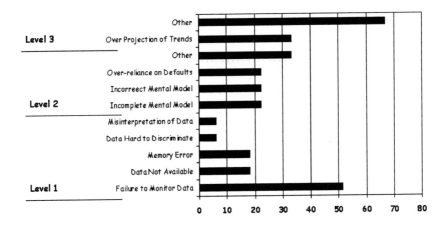

Figure 6: Use of incident data to validate models of situation awareness.

causal factors behind thirty-three air traffic control incidents in the ASRS database were analysed to determine whether or not any loss of situation awareness could be explained in terms of Endsley's abstract model. This work is signification not only because it provides insights into situation awareness in safety-critical aspects of HCI. Endsley's research on situation awareness has increasing relevance for more 'mainstream' applications. For example, it has been used to model the problems that users experience when they must coordinate many different concurrent, distributed tasks. The data provided by incident reporting systems has, therefore, been used to inform much recent research into safety-critical HCI. These insights have, in turn, helped to inform observations about more general forms of human–computer interaction.

Analytical methods that have been pioneered in HCI can also be used to significantly improve existing practices within incident reporting. In particular, they can be used to probe beyond the observation information that is provided by individual reports to gain a greater understanding of the organisational and cultural precursors to each incident. Each incident report only provides a snapshot of events. In order to understand the causal factors behind these events, analysts must have a deep understanding of the context in which an incident occurs. This creates a 'Catch-22' problem. Considerable domain expertise is required to identify the salient features of an incident in domains as complex as neonatal intensive care or en-route air traffic control. However, there are very few domain experts who have the human factors and HCI training required to go beyond the surface causes of an incident to diagnose any systemic factors. One means of addressing this problem is to exploit observational techniques that have been developed within HCI. This enables HCI practitioners and human factors experts to observe the working context in which incidents occur. It also better equips these analysts to participate in the incident analysis sessions that are critical in identifying the causes that lie behind each report. We are currently extending observation HCI techniques in this way (Busse & Johnson, 1999). We have introduced an incident reporting system into a Neonatal Intensive Care Unit in a Glasgow hospital. An innovative feature of this work has been the introduction of an HCI/human factors analyst into the Unit both to promote the system and to observe working practices within the Unit. This is a long-term research initiative and so it is premature to comment in detail on the results. However, we hope that it will yield a number of insights. Not only can it help to interpret the reports that are submitted to the system but it may also help us to understand the reporting biases that we have observed in our previous reporting schemes. Not all of the staff will contribute to the system and even within particular staff groupings there are noticeable patterns of contributory behaviour. Such patterns can only be explained by detailed and situated observations of the interactions between and within the groups involved in different work activities.

6   The Application of Incident Reports

There are further ways in which incident reporting schemes can be improved by a greater application of techniques that were originally pioneered within the field of human–computer interaction. For instance, it is possible to recruit ideas from design rationale to justify the corrective actions that must be taken in the aftermath of an incident. This is critically important. Unless analysts identify a clear justification for corrective actions, in terms of the incidents that are reported, then there is a danger that any incident reporting scheme will make only a minimal contribution to the safety of an interactive system. Design rationale notations provide a graphical overview of the arguments that support development decisions (Buckingham Shum, 1996). For example Figure 7 illustrates some of the design options that were considered following an incident involving two ships on the Heath Reef in Australia (Johnson, 1999a). In particular, it considers the arguments for and against computer-based and manual systems to improve situation awareness amongst crew members. The first option is to force all ships to notify their position to an existing automated monitoring system. This is supported by the criteria that it would provide an external means of ensuring that crews comply with regulations. The Reefrep system could monitor and log the reporting behaviour of each vessel. The development of such a system is not supported by the affect that it would have upon crew workload because they would have to ensure that they explicitly reported their position and requested details of any other vessels in the area. The second design option is to use crew training procedures as a means of ensuring adequate levels of situation awareness. This is not supported by the possibility of performing external checks.

A major limitation with the previous figure is that it provides little or no indication of the status or source of the criteria that are represented. In other words, we have no means of assessing the evidence that external checks are, indeed, difficult to perform on crew training practices. Such problems can be avoided by integrating design rationale techniques, such as the QOC notation shown in Figure 7, with previous findings about human 'error' and system 'failure' from incident reporting systems. Figure 8 illustrates a notation that was developed to provide a graphical

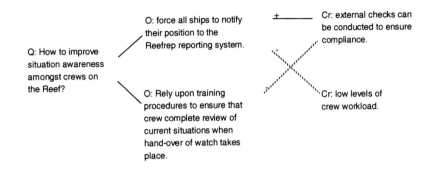

Figure 7: QOC diagram showing options for improved situation awareness.

overview of the findings in incident and accident reports. Conclusions, Analysis, Evidence (CAE) diagrams connect the conclusions of an incident panel to the lines of argument that explain those conclusions and finally to the available evidence that supports or weakens a line of argument. In Figure 7, the Australian Marine Incident Investigation Unit concluded that the Fremantle's crew made several human 'errors'. These mistakes included their failure to complete adequate contingency and passage planning. This analysis is supported by evidence that the crew failed to identify the waters off Heath Reef as being restricted for deep draught vessels. This is documented on page 29 of the report. The human errors also included a lack of awareness about the other traffic on the reef. This is supported by evidence that both the Fourth Officer and the Commander assumed that the River Embley was some 2.5 miles away when they were, in fact, much closer. This evidence is cited on page 18 of the report. The Fremantle's crew also lacked experience of encounters within the Great Barrier Reef. This analysis depends upon two related pieces of evidence. Firstly, that the Fourth office was on the bridge in the lead up to the collision *and* secondly that this officer was undergoing training in watch keeping. Finally, human factors problems led to the collisions because the decision to apply 20 degrees of starboard helm was based upon incomplete and scanty information. The Commander's surprise at the consequences of his decision, cited on page 18 of the report, provide evidence for this assertion.

Figure 8 explicitly illustrates the way in which pieces of evidence contribute to an analyst's findings about the precursors to human 'error' and systems 'failure'. The intention is to provide a road map for the analysis that is conducted after an incident report has been submitted. Figure 9 goes on to show how this graphical approach to incident reporting can be linked to the design rationale notations that were originally developed within the field of Human–Computer Interaction. The Australian Marine Incident Investigation Unit found that the crew was unaware of other ships in their

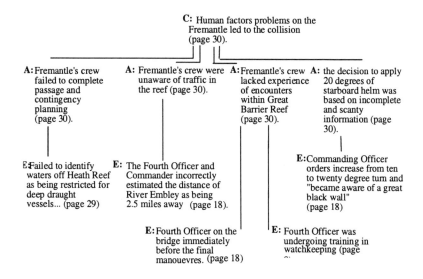

Figure 8: Conclusion, Analysis, Evidence Diagram for the Fremantle Collision.

vicinity. A link is then drawn to the QOC diagram to show that this finding justifies designers in considering how to improve situation awareness amongst the crews in the Reef area. It is important not to underestimate the benefits that such links provide. For instance, it is relatively easy to provide well considered solutions to the problems that are addressed in safety cases. It is less easy to know what problems should be anticipated during the development of safety-critical interfaces (Reason, 1990). By linking development documents directly to the products of accident investigations, it is possible to ensure that designers base their subsequent development decisions at least partly upon those problems that have arisen with previous applications. Figure 9 epitomises the main argument in this paper. It combines QOC diagrams from HCI and CAE diagrams that have been used in incident and accident reporting. The QOC diagram provides a graphical overview of the reasons for and against particular design options. The CAE diagram provides an overview of why those options were ever considered in the first place. It, therefore, captures the way in which incident reporting systems can be used to direct and focus the future development of interactive systems.

7 Conclusions

This paper has argued that there are considerable mutual benefits to be obtained if there was a greater exchange of ideas between people working in the areas of incident reporting and human–computer interaction. For the HCI community, incident reporting schemes provide:

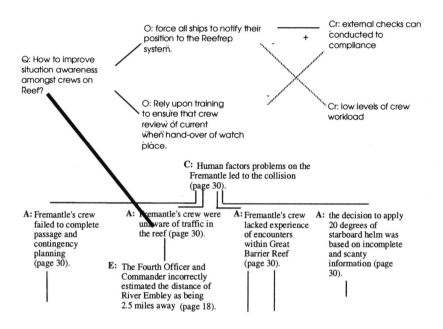

Figure 9: Using previous incidents to justify questions in QOC diagrams.

- Insights into the organisational and domain dependent precursors to human error.

- Means of validating models of human error, such as Endersley's work on situation awareness, that have a wider applicability within HCI.

- Means of identifying the weaknesses that lead to problems in human–computer interaction.

- Means of identifying the human, organisational and technological defences that prevent incidents from developing into major accidents.

For incident reporting, findings in the field of human–computer interaction can provide:

- A range of observational and workplace analysis techniques that can be used to validate findings about the precursors to particular incidents.

- A range of basic interface design expertise that is essential as incident reporting systems are being implemented over the World Wide Web.

- A number of human error models, and models of human–computer interaction in general, that can be used to improve our understanding of the precursors of particular incidents.

- Greater guidance about the techniques and approaches that can be used to prevent future instances of operator 'error' and to mitigate those incidents that cannot be prevented.

These lists are incomplete. They are the result of an initial involvement by a number of HCI practitioners in the setting up and maintenance of incident reporting schemes in aviation and medicine. More work is needed to identify future areas of mutual benefit. There is, however, a very real danger that if this collaboration does not take place then incident reporting schemes will continue to rely on poorly designed forms that prevent, rather than promote, the reporting of potential accidents. Existing incident reporting schemes may also continue to depend on classification schemes that reveal little understanding of the cognitive, organisational and technological causes of human 'error'. Conversely, there is a danger that HCI researchers may neglect an essential source of information about the mechanisms that jeopardise and preserve the safety of interactive systems in many working domains.

Acknowledgements

Thanks are due to the members of the Glasgow Accident Analysis Group and the Glasgow Interactive Systems group.

References

Buckingham Shum, S. (1996), Analyzing the Usability of a Design Rationale Notation, *in* T. P. Moran & J. M. Carroll (eds.), *Design Rationale: Concepts, Techniques and Use*, Lawrence Erlbaum Associates, pp.185–215.

Busse, D. (2000), Integrating Cognitive Modelling and Workplace Studies to Support Incident Analysis in Intensive Care Units, PhD thesis, Department of Computing Science, University of Glasgow.

Busse, D. & Johnson, C. W. (1999), Human Error in an Intensive Care Unit: A Cognitive Analysis of Critical Incidents, *in* J. Dixon (ed.), *17th International Systems Safety Conference*, The Systems Safety Society, pp.138–47.

Johnson, C. W. (1999a), A First Step Toward the Integration of Accident Reports and Constructive Design Documents, *in* M. Felici, K. Kanoun & A. Pasquini (eds.), *Proceedings of 18th International Conference SAFECOMP'99*, Springer-Verlag, pp.286–96.

Johnson, C. W. (1999b), "Why Human Error Analysis Fails to Support Systems Development", *Interacting with Computers* **11**(5), 517–24.

Johnson, C. W. (2000), "Guest Editorial, Combating the Challenges of Human 'Error' in Clinical Systems", *Topics in Healthcare Information Management* **4**(20), v–vii.

Jones, D. G. & Endsley, M. R. (1996), "Sources of Situation Awareness Errors in Aviation", *Aviation, Space and Environmental Medicine* **67**(6), 507–12.

Norman, D. (1990), The 'Problem' With Automation: Inappropriate Feedback and Interaction not 'Over-Automation', *in* D. E. Broadbent, J. Reason & A. Baddeley (eds.), *Human Factors in Hazardous Situations*, Clarendon Press, pp.137–45.

Perrow, C. (1984), *Normal Accidents: Living With High-risk Technologies*, Basic Books.

Rasmussen, J. (1983), "Skill, Rules, Knowledge: Signals, Signs and Symbols and Other Distinctions in Human Performance Models", *IEEE Transactions in Systems, Man and Cybernetics* **13**(3), 257–66.

Reason, J. (1990), *Human Error*, Cambridge University Press.

Reason, J. (1998), *Managing the Risks of Organisational Accidents*, Ashgate.

Staender, S., Kaufman, M. & Scheidegger, D. (1999), Critical Incident Reporting in Anaesthesiology in Switzerland Using Standard Internet Technology, *in* C. W. Johnson (ed.), *Proceedings of the 1st Workshop on Human Error and Clinical Systems*, Glasgow University, pp.10–13. Published as a Glasgow Interactive Systems Group technical report GIST-99-1, available at http://www.dcs.gla.ac.uk/ˉjohnson/papers/HECS_99/, last accessed 2000.06.25.

van der Schaaf, T. (1996), PRISMA: A Risk Management Tool Based on Incident Analysis, *in Proceedings of the International Workshop on Process Safety Management and Inherently Safer Processes*, pp.242–51.

van Vuuren, W. (1998), Organisational Failure, PhD thesis, Technical University of Eindhoven, Netherlands.

Do Users Always Know What's Good For Them? Utilising Physiological Responses to Assess Media Quality

Gillian M Wilson & M Angela Sasse

Department of Computer Science, University College London, Gower Street, London WC1E 6BT, UK

Tel: *+44 20 7679 3462*

Fax: *+44 20 7387 1397*

EMail: *{g.wilson,a.sasse}@cs.ucl.ac.uk*

URL: *http://www.cs.ucl.ac.uk/Staff/G.Wilson/*

Subjective methods are widely used to determine whether audio and video quality in networked multimedia applications is sufficient. Recent findings suggest that, due to contextual factors, users often accept levels of media quality known to be below the threshold required for such tasks. Therefore, we propose the use of physiological methods to assess the *user cost* of different levels of media quality. Physiological responses (HR, GSR and BVP) to two levels of video quality (5 vs. 25 frames per second — fps) were measured in a study with 24 users. Results showed that there was a statistically significant effect of frame rate, in the direction that 5fps caused responses to indicate stress. However, only 16% of the users noticed the difference subjectively. We propose a 3-tier assessment method that combines task performance, user satisfaction and user cost to obtain a meaningful indication of the media quality required by users.

Keywords: evaluation methods, empirical evaluation, subjective assessment, user cost, audio, video, videoconferencing, physiological measurements.

1 Introduction

Multimedia conferencing (MMC) allows users to communicate using audio, video and shared-workspace tools in real time. In recent years, MMC has become more widely used, including in areas such as healthcare and distance education. Computer workstations and high-bandwidth networks can deliver high-quality audio and video, but higher quality is usually more expensive. Since most users — individual or corporate — do not want to pay more than necessary for their communications, it is important to determine the level of media quality that supports effective and comfortable interaction between users collaborating on a specific task. The point at which increased quality has no further benefit to the user should also be considered, since this allows efficient use of bandwidth.

Establishing such quality thresholds is essential for network providers and multimedia application developers. Currently, subjective methods are widely used to assess audio and video quality. However, there are problems associated with the use of those methods and when used as the single means of assessing whether quality is adequate, the results obtained may give a misleading impression about the impact on the user (see Section 2). This paper presents a new method for assessing media quality in the context of networked applications: physiological responses to media quality are being taken as an objective measure of user cost. Such methods should be part of a traditional HCI evaluation approach that considers task performance, user satisfaction and user cost, to obtain a reliable indication of how quality affects users.

Section 2 presents a critical review of existing methods for assessing media quality, and the rationale for the new assessment method. Section 3 describes an experimental study whose results demonstrate the validity of this method. The implications of the results are discussed in Section 4; conclusions and future work follow in Section 5.

2 Evaluating Multimedia Quality

In media quality assessment to date, audio and video quality have been treated as uni-dimensional phenomena, which can be described using a one-dimensional rating scale such as those recommended by the International Telecommunications Union (ITU) (see Section 2.1). However, this approach is unsuitable in the assessment of media quality in a complex environment, such as videoconferencing, since many factors contribute to users' perception (Watson & Sasse, 1998): loudness, intelligibility, naturalness, pleasantness of tone and listening effort required are known to contribute to audio quality (Kitawaki & Nagabuchi, 1998). With video quality, variables such as brightness, background stability, speed in image reassembling, outline definition, 'dirty window' and the mosaic/blocking effect all contribute to its perceived quality (Gili Manzanaro et al., 1991).

2.1 Current Assessment Methods

At present, the most widely used assessment method for audio and video quality is the subjective rating scales recommended by the ITU, which is an international organisation in which governments and the private sector coordinate global telecommunication networks and services. It is the leading publisher of telecommunications regulatory and standards information.

The assessment scales recommended by the ITU fall into three categories: those for speech transmission over telephone networks, image quality over television systems, and multimedia systems. Generally, a short section of material is played, after which the viewer/listener rates their opinion on a 5-point quality or impairment scale, usually labelled with the terms 'Excellent', 'Good', 'Fair', 'Poor', 'Bad'. A Mean Opinion Score (MOS) (ITU, 2000) is computed by way of an average score. However, recent research at UCL has illustrated the unsuitability of these scales when applied to network audio and video (Watson & Sasse, 1998).

2.2 Problems with ITU Scales

The MOS scales were originally designed to assess high-quality television pictures and toll-quality audio. They are primarily concerned with establishing if viewers/listeners can detect a particular degradation in quality, and this assessment is usually carried out without any reference to task. However, when it comes to determining the media quality required in networked applications, the question asked by network providers, application developers and users is: *What level of quality is good enough?*

Audio and video delivered over digital networks is subject to unique impairments, such as packet loss, so the quality can vary during a session. However, the short duration of the test material used by the scales discussed above is not long enough to allow users to form an opinion on whether the quality is good enough in the context of longer interactive use, such as videoconferencing. In order to account for the fact that network conditions can be variable, a dynamic measuring scale is now recommended by the ITU for video assessment — ITU BT.500–8.

The final problem regards assessment via the 5-point scale. Firstly, the 5-point scale does not reflect the multi-dimensional nature of audio and video quality and the potential interaction between different types of impairment (see Section 2 introduction). Secondly, the labels on the scale do not represent equal intervals (Jones & McManus, 1986; Teunissen, 1996), so caution must be exercised when interpreting data gathered using such scales (Watson & Sasse, 1998).

Attempts to improve the scales have been made by our research group at UCL. Watson & Sasse (1997) developed an unlabelled scale and showed that users were consistent in their quality ratings of audio segments when using it. A dynamic version of this unlabelled scale, the QUality ASsessment Slider, QUASS (Bouch et al., 1998), allows users to continuously rate the quality of audio and video in a meaningful context. A drawback of this method is that continuous rating interferes with user's primary task; e.g. participating in a tutorial via videoconferencing.

2.3 Problems with Subjective Assessment

Subjective assessment is cognitively mediated. One example of this process is the finding that users accepted significantly lower media quality when a notion of financial cost was attached to the level of quality (Bouch & Sasse, 1999). The quality that users rated as acceptable in this study has been demonstrated to be insufficient in a number of experimental and field studies. Another example is Wilson & Descamps's (1996) finding that the same video quality receives lower ratings when the task being performed is difficult. This evidence indicates that contextual variables can influence users' subjective assessment of quality.

Knoche et al. (1999) argue that, because it is not possible for users to register what they do not consciously perceive, subjective measurements are fundamentally flawed. As a more effective method, they recommend *task performance*. As HCI researchers, we agree that task performance is an essential element of usability, yet cannot be used as its only measure.

Subjective assessment methods capture the degree of *user satisfaction* with quality, which is important but not necessarily a reliable indicator of the impact that quality has on the user. We argue that both task performance and user satisfaction need to be used in conjunction with a measure of *user cost*, as part of a 3-tier approach. User cost is an explicit — if often disregarded — element of the traditional HCI evaluation framework.

2.4 Objective Measurements of User Cost

There are subjective approaches to determining user cost — rather than user satisfaction — via rating scales, yet like all subjective rating methods they are cognitively mediated. We thus decided to investigate the use of objective methods of assessing the impact of media quality on the user. One way to determine this, is to monitor physiological responses that are indicative of stress and discomfort. When a user is presented with insufficient audio and video quality in a task context — e.g. when making a business decision in a videoconference meeting — he or she must expend extra effort on decoding information at the perceptual level. If the user is struggling to decode the information, this should induce a response of discomfort or stress, even if the user is still capable of performing his/her main task — e.g. participating in the business decision. Autonomous physiological responses are not subject to cognitive mediation (see Section 2.5) and collecting such measurements need not interfere with task completion.

2.5 Physiological Measurements

Psychophysiology explores the relationship between the mind and body and the interactive influence they have upon each other. The nervous system of humans is separated into the central nervous system (CNS) and the peripheral nervous system (PNS) (see Figure 1). The PNS comprises the somatic nervous system (SNS) and the autonomic nervous system (ANS). The ANS is divided into sympathetic and parasympathetic divisions.

The sympathetic division mobilises the body's energetic responses. Thus, when faced with a stressful situation, the sympathetic division prepares the body for the 'fight or flight' response by, e.g. releasing glucose into the bloodstream for energy, and dilating the walls of the blood vessels to speed up blood flow to the limbs. When the stressful situation has passed, the parasympathetic division takes over to return the body to equilibrium.

We decided to concentrate on the following responses as indicators of stress: Heart Rate (HR), Blood Volume Pulse (BVP) and Galvanic Skin Resistance (GSR). They were adopted as they are non-invasive, i.e. they do not require samples of body fluids to be taken. In addition, they are relatively easy to measure with standard monitoring equipment.

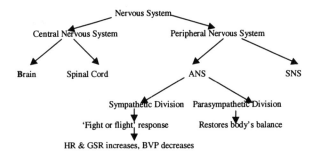

Figure 1: Diagram illustrating the nervous system of humans.

Heart rate is considered to be a valuable indicator of overall activity level, with a high heart rate being associated with an anxious state and vice versa (Frijda, 1986). Seyle (1956) has linked GSR to stress and ANS arousal. GSR is also known to be the fastest and most robust measure of stress (Cacioppo & Louis, 1990), with an increase in the resistance of the skin being associated with stress. BVP is an indicator of blood flow: the BVP waveform exhibits the characteristic periodicity of the heart beating: each beat of the heart forces blood through the vessels. The overall envelope of the waveform pinches when a person is startled, fearful or anxious, thus a decrease in BVP amplitude is indicative of a person under stress.

HR rises under stress in order to increase blood flow to the working muscles, thus preparing the body for the 'fight or flight' response. The function of a decreased BVP under stress is to divert blood to the working muscles in order to prepare them for action. This means that blood flow is reduced to the extremities, like a finger. The precise reason for GSR increasing under stress is not known. One theory is that it occurs in order to toughen the skin, thus protecting it against mechanical injury, (Wilcott, 1967) as it has been observed that skin is difficult to cut under profuse sweating (Edelberg & Wright, 1962). A second theory is that GSR increases to cool the body in preparation for the projected activity of 'fight or flight'.

The equipment used to measure the physiological responses in this experiment and throughout this research is the ProComp, manufactured by Thought Technology Ltd (see http://www.thoughttechnology.com/). This equipment is lightweight and the sensors are small. At present they are placed on three fingers, however we are looking at the possibility of placing sensors on the feet, e.g. Healey et al. (1999), to allow ease of typing.

To measure GSR, two electrodes are placed on adjacent fingers and a small voltage is applied. The skin's capacity to conduct the current is measured. Photoplethysmography is used to measure HR and BVP: a sensor is attached to a finger — this applies a light source and the light reflected by the skin is measured. At each contraction of the heart, blood is forced through the peripheral vessels, which produces an engorgement of the vessel under the light source. Thus, the volume and the rate at which blood is pumped through the body are detected.

2.5.1   Problems with Measuring Physiological Responses

Measuring physiological signals in response to multimedia quality can be problematic. One of the main issues is how to separate stress and other emotions, such as excitement about the situation or task, in an experiment. This is a problem as the physiological patterns accompanying each emotion are not clearly understood (Cacioppo & Louis, 1990), however recent research at the Massachusetts Institute of Technology (MIT) Media Laboratory (Vyzas & Picard, 1999) has shown that eight emotions can be distinguished between with eighty-percent accuracy, which is an encouraging result. We are using the following methods to address this problem in our experiments, by ensuring that there is no stress placed on participants by factors other than the quality:

- In our lab-based trials, we hold the environment as constant and minimally stressful as possible. An example of this is that we make sure that stressful environmental events, like the phone ringing, do not occur: we need to determine the effects the quality has in isolation before we can account for environmental events in the field.

- We measure the baseline responses of participants for fifteen minutes, prior to any experimentation occurring. This allows participants, and the sensors, time to settle down and allows us to have a set of baseline physiological readings with which to compare responses in an experiment.

- We discard the first five minutes of physiological responses in experiments to ensure that the change from baseline measurements being taken to the experiment commencing is not affecting results.

- We administer subjective assessments of user cost, i.e. scales of discomfort, to allow people to comment on how they feel during the experiment. Physiological measurements identify problems but do not aid problem resolution: subjective assessment is still needed for this purpose.

- Finally, we carefully design the tasks used in our experiments to ensure that they are engaging, yet minimally stressful (see Section 3.1 for an example). The tasks used in our experiments are taken from the taxonomy of tasks performed in networked multimedia environments developed by the ETNA project (see Section 5.2)*.

3   Experimental Study

Results of investigations have generally found that the addition of video to an audio stream does not improve task performance in the context of MMC. The exceptions to this are where conflict resolution or negotiations are required (Short et al., 1976) or when communication is particularly difficult. This could be when participants in the conference do not share the same first language (Veinott et al., 1997).

---

*The ETNA Project — http://www-mice.cs.ucl.ac.uk/multimedia/projects/etna/, last accessed 2000.06.10.

Other research claims that addition of a video channel benefits the process of communication rather than its result. This could be by making the conversation more fluent between people (Daly-Jones et al., 1998). It has often been found that users consider the video to be of subjective benefit: people said they preferred the video to be there, e.g. Tang & Isaacs (1993). Therefore, it can be presumed that video is not a prerequisite for a user to perform a task, yet without the video channel greater effort must be expended (Monk et al., 1996).

Synchronisation between audio and video ('lip synch') is perceived at around 16 frames per second (fps), and full motion video is defined at 25fps — television quality. High frame rates require a lot of bandwidth, which is not available or affordable for many users. Studies looking at the outcome of a task (as opposed to how communication was conducted, e.g. the number of turns taken) found no impairment in task performance from using low video frame rates, e.g. Kies et al. (1996). It must be noted here that the task being performed is a major factor in the requirements for frame rate. For example, a task that uses 'video-as-data', e.g. a neurosurgeon performing an operation where detailed and rapidly changing information is relayed to help critical surgical decisions (Nardi et al., 1997), requires a high frame rate.

Recent research using subjective assessment and measures of task performance found that users do not notice the difference between 12fps and 25fps when involved in an engaging task (Anderson et al., 2000). In addition, there is no significant difference in task performance at these two frame rates. However the difference between the same two frame rates is noticed when the data are short video clips in isolation (O'Malley et al., in press).

If users do not subjectively notice such differences in frame rate when engaged in a task, does this imply that it has no effect on them physiologically? It needs to be determined if high frame rates are necessary for the user to be satisfied with the quality and to allow them to complete their task without significant user cost. If it is discovered that frame rate does not have a significant impact upon the user, then bandwidth could be conserved and resources would be better allocated elsewhere.

3.1 Method

To investigate the subjective and physiological effects of video frame rate, a full experiment investigating the effects of 5fps and 25fps was devised. We created these 'very low' and 'very high' quality conditions, as we wanted to determine if the difference in frame rate was still not noticed when it became more extreme than used by Anderson et al. (2000).

Twenty-four volunteer participants watched two recorded interviews, which were acted between a university admissions tutor and two school pupils applying to University College London. The tutor and students played themselves in scripted interviews, which had been designed with the help of an admissions tutor to mimic typical interactions in such interviews and to ensure that the content of the interviews was not unduly stressful.

The interviews were conducted using IP (Internet Protocol) videoconferencing tools on a high-quality computer screen. Audio quality was good and did not vary during the sessions. The interviews began at 16fps for five minutes: these results

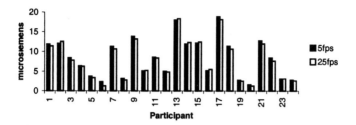

Figure 2: Mean GSR for each participant at 5fps and 25fps.

were disregarded in order to account for any change in physiological measurements due to the experiment beginning (see Section 2.5.1). The interviews lasted fifteen minutes each. Participants saw two interviews at 5–25–5fps or 25–5–25fps: each frame rate was held for a period of five minutes (the frame rate changed twice in order to counteract any expectancy effect). The task was to make a judgement on the suitability of the candidates. The following hypotheses were posited:

- There will be different physiological responses to the two frame rates: 5fps will cause more stress.

- Participants will not subjectively register the frame rate change.

Participants rated the audio/video quality throughout the interviews using the QUASS tool (Bouch et al., 1998). After they had watched both interviews, a questionnaire was administered. This addressed how participants felt during the experiment and asked their opinions on the audio and video quality. Physiological measurements were taken throughout the experiment, and baseline responses were gathered for fifteen minutes before the experiment began.

3.2   Results

The mean GSR, HR and BVP responses at both frame rates are shown in Figure 2, 3 and 4 respectively.

A Multivariate Analysis of Variance (MANOVA) was performed on the data with the independent variables frame rate and order of presentation. There was no significant effect of order of presentation on any of the signals: GSR ($F(1,22) = 0.383, p = 0.542$); HR ($F(1,22) = 1.139, p = 0.297$); BVP ($F(1,22) = 0.680, p = 0.418$). There was a significant effect of frame rate on each of the signals: GSR ($F(1,22) = 9.925, p = 0.005$); HR ($F(1,22) = 9.415, p = 0.006$); BVP ($F(1,22) = 5.074, p = 0.035$). Examination of the direction of the means showed that GSR and HR significantly increased at 5fps whereas BVP significantly decreased at 5fps: these results are indicative of stress.

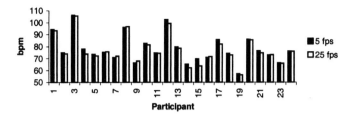

Figure 3: Mean HR for each participant at 5fps and 25fps.

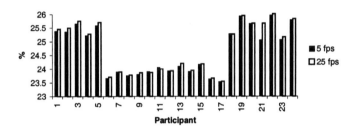

Figure 4: Mean BVP for each participant at 5fps and 25fps

4 Discussion of Results

The results from this experiment show that there was a statistically significant effect of frame rate on participants' physiological responses in the direction predicted: 5fps caused responses indicative of stress. Thus, Hypothesis 1 is supported. The questionnaire results showed that 84% of participants did not notice the frame rate change subjectively, thus Hypothesis 2 is supported. In addition, there was no significant correlation between subjective and physiological results, which indicates that physiological measurements are tapping into a mechanism that subjective, cognitively mediated, responses do not register.

These results are important as they indicate that, when users are engaged in a task, they do not subjectively notice the difference between two extreme frame rates during or after the task, however the difference is registered physiologically. Thus, the difference in quality does have a physiological impact upon the user. The direct implication of these results is that at very low frame rates, as used in this experiment, users have to work harder at the same task. Application designers and network providers should consider this information.

The findings from this experiment imply that acceptable quality levels required for a task and those that result in unacceptable user cost should not be determined by subjective assessment alone, as they may not pick up important but subconscious effects.

5   Discussion

5.1   Conclusions

Three main conclusions can be made from this research. Firstly, different levels of media quality cause different physiological responses in users and can be detected through common physiological measurement techniques.   Secondly, subjective assessment and measures of task performance do not pick up all the effects of poor quality in the short-term, e.g. in an hour-long experimental study. It is possible that the negative effects of poor quality would emerge in these assessment methods in longer-term studies, yet for laboratory-based experiments physiological responses give a more instant account of how the quality affects the user.   We therefore argue that the 3-tier approach to multimedia quality assessment, as described in Section 2.3, needs to be utilised to determine if a certain level of media quality is usable. Furthermore, we suggest that the largely neglected question of user cost should be given due attention in usability evaluation of any technology, and that objective measures — such as physiological responses — may be more reliable measures of user cost than subjective methods, which are cognitively mediated.

Critics of this approach may argue that it is not proven that stress responses are a reliable indicator that a factor — e.g. a level of media quality — is actually bad for the user. In our view, it is reasonable to assume that a significant deviation from baseline responses in the direction of stress indicates that the user has to work harder, and that this might manifest itself in a usability problem with prolonged use. At a time where the negative effects of stress in the workplace are debated, indications that a particular aspect of technology — such as the level of video quality — may be inducing stress deserves further investigation.

5.2   Contributions

Our continuing work in this area aims to produce two substantive contributions. Firstly, the minimum levels of multimedia quality for certain tasks at which users can successfully perform, without significant user cost, will be determined. The impact of problems caused by the network will be investigated, such as audio packet loss, delay and lip synchronisation. However, quality is not uni-dimensional and encompasses more than variables affected by the network. Thus, the effects of other contributing factors must be examined, e.g. volume differences between speakers and image size. This will allow network providers to allocate resources with the users requirements clearly specified, thus improving applications for the end user.

These findings will be incorporated into the ETNA Project, which aims to produce a taxonomy of real-time multimedia tasks and applications, and to determine the maximum and minimum audio/video quality thresholds for a number of these tasks. This will greatly assist network providers and application designers, as they will have guidelines on the quality they need to deliver for specific tasks.

Secondly, this research aims to build a utility curve. Utility curves provide a mechanism by which the network state can be related to the end user. Such curves are usually formulated by the results of subjective assessment, however by using physiological measurements an adaptive application could be built. This would enable the application to receive continuous feedback on the state of the user. In the future a user 'wearing' a discrete computer, like those being developed at MIT Media Lab, could have their physiological responses fed into a videoconferencing application. If the computer detected that the user was under stress, it would automatically adjust the variable of the videoconference causing stress to reduce user cost and increase user satisfaction. If network congestion was occurring, the computer would then refer to the utility curve to deliver the next best quality possible.

Finally, a methodological contribution will be made: guidelines stating the best physiological measurements to indicate a specific impairment in quality will be produced. This will pave the way for much needed further research in this area.

5.3 Future Applications

We are currently in discussions with BT about the possibility of using physiological measurements as a method of stress detection to evaluate a new interface that has been developed. The MUI (Motivational User Interface) was developed by Bournemouth University and BT's Bournemouth '150' call centre (Millard et al., 1999). It aims to motivate and provide feedback to call centre operators, thus reflecting their positive attitude back to the customer. BT wants to determine if operators are put under more or less stress when using the MUI, as opposed to the traditional interface. In addition there is interest in developing an adaptive application, whereby the application would modify itself if the operator became stressed.

This example of industrial interest illustrates that the ability to detect discomfort and stress unconsciously has wide-ranging implications in product assessment. It can also be used in areas like teaching, stress control and providing 'emotionally sympathetic' user interfaces.

Acknowledgements

Gillian Wilson is funded through an EPSRC CASE studentship award with BT Labs. Many thanks to Dr Janet McDonnell of the Computer Science department at UCL, for her help in creating the interview task.

References

Anderson, A., Smallwood, L., MacDonald, R., Mullin, J., Fleming, A. & O'Malley, O. (2000), "Video Data and Video Links in Mediated Communication: What Do Users Value", *International Journal of Human–Computer Studies* **52**(1), 165–87.

Bouch, A. & Sasse, M. A. (1999), Network Quality of Service: What do Users Need, *in Proceedings of the 4th International Distributed Conference*.

Bouch, A., Watson, A. & Sasse, M. A. (1998), QUASS — A Tool for Measuring the Subjective Quality of Real-time Multimedia Audio and Video, *in* J. May, J. Siddiqi & J. Wilkinson (eds.), *Adjunct Proceedings of HCI'98*, pp.94–5.

Cacioppo, J. T. & Louis, G. T. (1990), "Inferring Psychological Significance from Physiological Signals", *American Psychologist* **45**(1), 16–28.

Daly-Jones, O., Monk, A. & Watts, L. (1998), "Some Advantages of Videoconferencing Over High-quality Audio Conferencing: Fluency and Awareness of Attentional Focus", *International Journal of Human–Computer Studies* **45**, 21–58.

Edelberg, R. & Wright, D. J. (1962), "Two GSR Effector Organs and their Stimulus Specificity". Paper Read at the Society for Psychophysiological Research.

Frijda, N. H. (1986), The Emotions, Chapter Physiology of Emotion, *in Studies in Emotion and Social Interaction*, Cambridge University Press, pp.124–75.

Gili Manzanaro, J., Janez Escalada, L., Hernandez Lioreda, M. & Szymanski, M. (1991), Subjective Image Quality Assessment and Prediction in Digital Videocommunications, Technical Report COST 212 HUFIS Report.

Healey, J., Seger, J. & Picard, R. W. (1999), Quantifying Driver Stress: Developing a System for Collecting and Processing Biometric Signals in Natural Situations, Technical Report TR-483, Affective Computing Group, MIT. http://vismod.www.media.mit.edu/tech-reports/TR-483/index.html.

ITU (2000), "ITU-R BT.500-8 Methodology for the Subjective Assessment of the Quality of Television Pictures", http://www.itu.int/publications/itu-t/iturec.htm. Last accessed 2000.06.11.

Jones, B. L. & McManus, P. R. (1986), "Graphic Scaling of Qualitative Terms", *SMPTE Journal* pp.1166–71.

Kies, J. K., Williges, R. C. & Rosson, M. B. (1996), Controlled Laboratory Experimentation and Field Study Evaluation of Videoconferencing for Distance Learning Applications, Technical Report, Virginia Tech. http://www.hci.ise.vt.edu/ hcil/.

Kitawaki, N. & Nagabuchi, H. (1998), "Quality Assessment of Speech Coding and Speech Synthesis Systems", *IEEE Communications Magazine* pp.36–44.

Knoche, H., De Meer, H. G. & Kirsh, D. (1999), Utility Curves: Mean Opinion Scores Considered Biased, *in* S. Crowcroft, S. Bhatti & C. Diot (eds.), *Proceedings of 7th International Workshop on Quality of Service*, IEEE/IFIP, pp.12–4.

Millard, N., Coe, T., Gardner, M., Gower, A., Hole, L. & Crowle, S. (1999), "The Future of Customer Contact", *BT Technical Journal* . http://www.bt.co.uk/bttj/vol18no1/today.htm.

Monk, A., McCarthy, J., Watts, L. & Daly-Jones, O. (1996), Measures of Process, *in* M. MacLeod & D. Murray (eds.), *Evaluation for CSCW*, Springer-Verlag, pp.125–40.

Nardi, B., Kuchinsky, A., Whittaker, S., Leichner, R. & Schwarz, H. (1997), Video-as-data: Technical and Social Aspects of a Collaborative Multimedia Application, *in* K. Finn, A. Sellen & S. Wilbur (eds.), *Video-mediated Communication*, Lawrence Erlbaum Associates, pp.487–518.

O'Malley, C., Anderson, A. H., Mullin, J., Fleming, A., Smallwood, L. & MacDonald, R. (in press), "Factors Affecting Perceived Quality of Digitised Video: Tradeoffs between Frame Rate, Resolution and Encoding Format", *Applied Cognitive Psychology* .

Seyle, H. (1956), *The Stress of Life*, McGraw-Hill.

Short, J., Williams, E. & Christie, B. (1976), *The Social Psychology of Telecommunications*, John Wiley & Sons.

Tang, J. C. & Isaacs, E. A. (1993), "Why Do Users Like Video: Study of Multimedia Supported Collaboration", *Computer Supported Cooperative Work* **1**, 163–96.

Teunissen, K. (1996), "The Validity of CCIR Quality Indicators Along a Graphical Scale", *SMPTE Journal* pp.144–9.

Veinott, E. S., Olson, J. S., Olson, G. M. & Fu, X. (1997), Video matters! When Communication Ability is Stressed, Video Helps, *in* S. Pemberton (ed.), *Proceedings of CHI'97: Human Factors in Computing Systems*, ACM Press, pp.315–6.

Vyzas, E. & Picard, R. W. (1999), Offline and Online Recognition of Emotion Expression from Physiological Data, Technical Report TR-488, Affective Computing Group, MIT. ftp://whitechapel.media.mit.edu/pub/tech-reports/TR-488/abstract.html.

Watson, A. & Sasse, M. A. (1997), Multimedia Conferencing via Multicast: Determining the Quality of Service required by the End User, *in* M. Gambari & I. Richardson (eds.), *Proceedings of AVSPN '97 — International Workshop on Audio-visual Services over Packet Networks*, pp.189–94.

Watson, A. & Sasse, M. A. (1998), Measuring Perceived Quality of Speech and Video in Multimedia Conferencing Applications, *in* H. J. Zhang & L. Carr (eds.), *Proceedings of Multimedia'98*, ACM Press, pp.55–60.

Wilcott, R. C. (1967), "Arousal Sweating and Electrodermal Phenomena", *Psychological Bulletin* **67**, 58–72.

Wilson, F. & Descamps, P. T. (1996), "Should We Accept Anything Less than TV Quality: Visual Communication". Paper presented at International Broadcasting Convention, 12th-16th September 1996.

Embodiment and Interface Metaphors: Comparing Computer Filing Systems

Mark Treglown

School of Computer Science and Information Technology, University of Nottingham, Jubilee Campus, Wollaton Road, Nottingham NG8 1BB, UK

Tel: *+44 115 951 4793*

Fax: *+44 115 951 4254*

EMail: *M.Treglown@cs.nott.ac.uk*

Designing graphical user interfaces according to a metaphor, where the appearance and behaviour of on-screen objects can be accounted for, in part, in terms of users' existing knowledge structures, remains controversial. A number of influential and best-selling texts have promoted the use of metaphor as an approach to interface design, and many influential systems have employed this design approach, while other authors discourage the use of metaphor for its preventing an accurate account and mental model of the interface being developed. The understanding of metaphor as previously employed in HCI is undergoing reconsideration, and experientialist, non-objectivist, approaches such as that devised by George Lakoff and his colleagues are now starting to be promoted. We test a claim that experientialist approaches to metaphor can be used to compare competing interface designs by contrasting a number of metaphors for electronic filing systems. From this, we suggest that even a recent radical interface design has failings and relies on similar conceptual structures for its understanding as designs it seeks to overthrow.

Keywords: embodiment, experientialism, metaphor, data filing systems.

1   Introduction

It has been suggested that HCI researchers and interface designers are forced to work in a *theory gap*, as it not clear what sort of practice user interface design is to know whether the designer should act as craftsman, scientist, or engineer (Long & Dowell, 1989). In addition, because none of the disciplines that contribute to an understanding of HCI can yet contribute a sufficient body of knowledge, interface design is not a well-defined procedure. A consequence of this is that the interface designer must choose from among many tens of task and user knowledge elicitation methods; requirements elicitation methods; development lifecycle models; user interface toolkits; implementation languages; and usability inspection and analysis methods, all of which may be combined in yet more tens of ways during a design task. Interface design must therefore include as a large sub-task the constraint of the available choices to a manageable set of approaches, strategies, tools, and methods. One method of constraining the design task, while addressing the need to provide user interfaces that are successful and which can be learned and employed with a minimum of effort, is to design a user interface metaphor for the task domain to be, perhaps partly, implemented in software. The metaphor constrains the appearance and behaviour of on-screen objects, or the commands that alter the system's state, so that users' existing knowledge structures can be employed to understand the unfamiliar electronic system, and to suggest tasks that the system supports. The use of metaphors in the user interface is an approach that has been advocated by many best-selling HCI texts, for example Hix & Hartson (1993), Nielsen (1993).

By contrast, the use of analogy and metaphor in user interface designs has also been criticised by many authors, including Halasz & Moran (1982), Kay (1990) and Norman (1998), for not providing the user with a complete and useful mental model of an application. The notion of user interface metaphor that these authors, among others, criticise is that described by Erickson (1990), Madsen (1994) and Marcus (1994), where familiar real-world objects are recruited and evaluated as candidate representations for functionality provided by a computing system. The difficulties of such a notion in practice are well-known, the scope of a metaphorical source domain (or vehicle) is necessarily limited and there will often be aspects of the target domain (or topic) of the computer-based application that the metaphor cannot account for. Alternatively, aspects of the source domain may have no counterparts in the electronic domain, resulting in performance of tasks that the system cannot reliably respond to. Such failures prompt discussion of 'literal' interface features, magical features, and interface behaviour that is neither (Smith, 1987), discussion of to what extent magical features should replace literal features in actual designs (Nelson, 1990), and proposals for visual representations that should replace the use of metaphors (Nardi & Zarmer, 1993).

2   An Embodied Theory of Metaphor

The assumptions underlying the arguments of both those who promote and criticise metaphor-based in user interface designs are similar, however, and these assumptions tend to not fully take into account current accounts of what metaphors are, and how they are understood. Many authors now are beginning to appreciate that metaphor

John went out of the room.
Pump out the air.
Let out your anger.
Pick out the best theory.
Drown out the music.
Harry weaselled out of the contract.

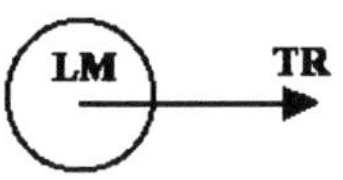

Figure 1: OUT$_1$ (Johnson, 1987, reproduced with permission).

pervades understanding and description of the world (Lakoff & Johnson, 1980). Disciplines other than HCI, however, show a greater appreciation of detecting and generating similarities between domains and understanding metaphors being central to our cognitive facilities (Clancey, 1997; Clark, 1989), and of our experience and consciousness being structured by our embodied interaction with the world (Varela et al., 1991).

A recent theory of metaphor that does take these aspects of embodied cognition into account is that proposed by George Lakoff and his colleagues (Lakoff, 1987; Johnson, 1987; Lakoff, 1993; Lakoff & Johnson, 1999). This theory has been found able to help the designer reason about users' understanding of metaphor-based graphical user interfaces and is starting to be promoted as a tool and representation system for this purpose (Rohrer, 1995; Benyon & Imaz, 1999; Treglown, 1999). In this section we introduce the Lakoff/Johnson theory in order to employ it below to analyse and compare a number of user interface designs that support tasks performed in the same task domain. These are uses to which Benyon & Imaz (1999) claim the theory can be put, but which have not been previously attempted.

2.1 Image Schemata

The Lakoff/Johnson theory of metaphor rejects many of the assumptions of the theories of metaphor that have been applied previously in HCI. Concepts, in particular, are not thought to obtain their semantics from being mirrors of external reality, as in the objectivist tradition assumed by some theories of cognition, and by many theories of metaphor. Instead, concepts obtain meaning by being grounded in representations of regularities in patterns of interaction with the physical world, these representations are termed *image schemata* (Johnson, 1987). Figures 1–3 show depictions of three OUT schemata underlying a number of situations and utterances. It should be noted that the depictions of image schema shown are only *depictions*, but they serve to illustrate the bodily experiences captured in, and described by, the schemata. In the schemata shown, LM is the 'landmark' in relation to which TR, the 'trajector', moves. Considering the schema OUT$_1$ and the sentence "John went out of the room", the circle (LM) represents the room as a container, and John moves along the arrow (as TR) out of the room. The diagram does not represent much information, such as the actual shape of the room, or the vector along which John moves, but instead "gives only one idealised image of the actual schema ... It is, rather, a continuous, active, dynamic recurring structure of experiences of similar spatial movements of a certain kind." (Johnson, 1987, p.36).

Pour out the beans.
Roll out the red carpet.
Send out the troops.
Hand out the information.
Write out your ideas.

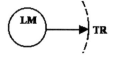

Figure 2: OUT$_2$ (Johnson, 1987, reproduced with permission).

The train started out for Chicago.

Figure 3: OUT$_3$ (Johnson, 1987, reproduced with permission).

Clearly OUT schemata are not sufficient to capture all patterns of interaction with the physical world. A number of schemata that are said by Johnson (1987) to be pervasive in human understanding are listed in Table 1. A number of authors contribute to the notion that image schemata can ground understanding of user interfaces. For example, Jackendoff (1983) and Fauconnier (1985) discuss correspondence mappings between photographs, and images in other media, and the mental representations from which language descriptions and motor actions to manipulate them can be derived. For Fauconnier, among others, although not for Jackendoff, these mental representations take the form of image schemata. Regier (1996) demonstrates how a number of image schemata can be represented and learned from labelled demonstrations in the form of computer animations. His work also shows that interface animation should demonstrate clear, prototypical, examples of concepts to be understood, and from which metaphorical mappings must be made, if the interface is to be fully understood. Bailey et al. (1997) report on the beginnings of work showing how image schemata-like representations can be used to guide execution by the sensorimotor system of the physical action that the representation captures.

2.2 Understanding Metaphor

In the Lakoff/Johnson theory of metaphor, metaphors are as previously understood — asymmetric and partial mappings between conceptual domains. These mappings project the image schema structure of the source domain onto the target domain in a way that is consistent with the Invariance Principle, which is defined and employed below. A conceptual system possessed by the user is said to contain thousands of metaphorical mappings which are highly structured, these mappings vary in universality, some, according to Lakoff & Johnson's findings, seem to be universal to all people, others seem specific to certain cultures. Thus we may later find that, beyond issues of software internationalisation, the conceptual system assumed by some interface designs differs radically from that possessed by the user.

Container	Balance	Compulsion
Blockage	Counterforce	Restraint Removal
Enablement	Attraction	Mass-count
Path	Link	Centre–Periphery
Cycle	Near–Far	Scale
Part–Whole	Merging	Splitting
Full–Empty	Matching	Superimposition
Iteration	Contact	Process
Surface	Object	Collection

Table 1: Examples of pervasive image schemata.

3 Comparing Filing Systems

Even with the increasing adoption of personal digital assistants and mobile networked information appliances, users must still perform information storage and retrieval tasks, especially when the devices are used to create new data files, rather than just to explore an existing information space. A number of alternative metaphors and representations for filing systems, the one application that all users of a system will interact with at some time, have been proposed, all of which have claimed advantages over competing designs. Benyon & Imaz (1999) suggest that an experientialist approach to cognition, where concepts are given form by direct and indirect experience of the world, such as the Lakoff/Johnson theory of metaphor, allows us to model concepts and representations and to discuss alternative metaphors and their relative strengths and weaknesses. In this section we compare a number of computer-based filing systems to examine Benyon & Imaz's (1999) suggestion. Previous applications of the Lakoff/Johnson theory of metaphor (Rohrer, 1995; Treglown, 1999) have only examined very different types of system in an effort to test in general the applicability of the experientialist approach to reasoning about user interface designs.

3.1 Data Mountain

Data Mountain (Robertson et al., 1998) provides an interface for storing and retrieving Web documents. The Data Mountain is a texture-mapped rectangular plane segment angled at 60° to a horizontal plane extending away from the viewer into the screen. The Data Mountain is intended to replace the 'favourites' or 'bookmarks' mechanism of World Wide Web browsers as a means of noting and returning later to Web pages of interest to the user. Thumbnail icons, reductions of a Web page to icon size, may be placed on the mountain in locations meaningful to the user and icons may occlude others. If icons are placed at the top of the mountain they will appear smaller than icons placed at the foot of the mountain due to being rendered in perspective.

Data Mountain permits casual arrangement of icons, collecting them together in space to allow ad hoc categorisation, and allowing spatial memory to aid in locating the bookmark sought. Landau & Jackendoff (1993) argue that different mental systems are responsible for representing 'what' an object is, and 'where' an object is. Data Mountain, it should be noted, is, like Bolt and Negroponte's Spatial Data Management System, and the Perspective Wall (Mackinlay et al., 1991), an example of the use of a *spatial* metaphor (Jones & Dumais, 1986) in user interface design, in being concerned with *where* the bookmark sought is. The difference between 'what' and 'where', and users' abilities to remember spatial location is apparent in the Data Mountain system, with users proving able to find the bookmark sought even when the thumbnail images are removed leaving only blank icons (Czerwinski et al., 1999). Memory for spatial location can, though, be further refined into *coordinate spatial relationships* and *categorical spatial relationships* (Kosslyn, 1994), there being evidence that different mental systems and hemispheres of the brain are involved in storing these different relationships. Coordinate spatial relationships encode distance between objects, and their relative position. It is likely that Data Mountain and other spatial metaphors employ these mental representations for performing the actions involved in selecting the bookmarks sought.

Spatial metaphors can be contrasted with *spatialisation* metaphors (Demasco et al., 1994; Regier, 1996) that are grounded in spatial distinctions such as in/out, above/below, and front/back, that are captured in image schema and which make up categorical spatial relationships. The use of these sorts of distinctions is, however, at best limited in interaction with the Data Mountain. The use of the description 'mountain' to describe the depiction of the information space can evoke the MOUNTAIN IS BODY metaphor, in which locations on a mountain are mapped to parts of the body and their relative location. Lakoff & Johnson (1980), unfortunately, suggest that the mountain is a poor concept to ground in the body, only making reference to 'the foot of the mountain', as we did above, is meaningful. This leads others (Bederson et al., 1996) to claim that the MOUNTAIN IS BODY metaphor is a dead metaphor, incapable of providing useful insight. The systems discussed below rely on greater use of spatialisation metaphors in descriptions of interaction with them.

3.2   File and Folder Hierarchies

The desktop metaphor, the user interface metaphor with which most users will be familiar, adopts a data filing system based on files and folders which denote data files and (typically acyclic) graph structures of directories in the file space. Malone's (1983) oft-cited study of the ways in which people organise and move papers and collections of documents in their offices differentiated between 'neat' and 'tidy' offices. The demands of neat offices better suit the data file and hierarchical folder representation, but both types of data organisation in offices can be accounted for in the same way. Rather than employ existing suggested methods for metaphor-based design, and collect nouns and verbs from protocols to determine the objects and actions that the implemented interface should support, like Madsen (1994), we seek the *structure* of the metaphor used to understand the existing process or domain. Analysing the verbal protocols provided by Malone (1983), we see that data file organisation is often structured in terms of a CONTAINER schema. Johnson (1987) observes that human beings constantly experience their bodies as containers and also as things in containers (for example, inside rooms). The notion of containment,

Figure 4: The containment schema.

captured in an image schema, is depicted in Figure 4.

The containment schema has the structural elements of an interior, a boundary, and an exterior. Like many image schemata its internal structure is said to yield a basic 'logic'. This logic is described by Lakoff (1987, p.272) as follows:

"Everything is either inside a container or out of it — P or not P. If container A is in container B and X is in A, then X is in B — which is the basis for modus ponens: If all A's are B's and X is an A, then X is a B."

Johnson (1987, p.22) identifies a number of consequences, or entailments, of the structure of in-out schemata of the sort that will ground understanding of actions that bring about or change instances of containment, these consequences being:

i. The experience of containment typically involves protection from, or resistance to, external forces ...

ii. Containment also limits and restricts forces within the container ...

iii. Because of this restraint of forces, the constrained object gets a relative fixity of location ...

iv. This relative fixing of location within the container means that the contained object becomes either accessible or inaccessible to the view of some observer. It is either held so that it can be observed, or else the container itself blocks or hides the object from view.

v. Finally, we experience transitivity of containment. If B is *in* A, then whatever is *in* B is also *in* A."

In Treglown (1999) it is suggested that the complexity and directness of user interfaces are a function of the structure of the image schema that grounds the metaphors, and whether or not a design breaks the Invariance Principle. This being the requirement that:

"Metaphorical mappings preserve the cognitive topology (that is, the image-schema structure) of the source domain, in a way consistent with the inherent structure of the target domain." (Lakoff, 1993, p.215).

The image schema that grounds a metaphor will also suggest tasks and actions that the user interface must implement, as can be seen by comparing the logic of containment with the window manipulation and file movement features in file management systems such as Microsoft Windows and the Apple Macintosh Finder. For example, scrollbars are needed on a directory window to bring hidden data files icons into view (Consequence *iv*). Data files within a folder that is moved to another part of the file space remain within their immediate sub-hierarchy (Consequence *iii*). Also, in Unix, a non-empty sub-directory of a directory to be deleted requires an additional or modified use of the 'rm' command (Consequence *i*). The file and folder metaphor for data file organisation differs from Data Mountain in relying more on categorical spatial relationships than on coordinate spatial relationships, but the latter representation is likely to be used to locate the file of interest once the file is visible within an open folder window.

3.3   Piles

The folder is only one form of data file organisation possible. Despite argument to the contrary (Fertig et al., 1996), the conclusion reached by Barreau & Nardi (1995) and Nardi & Barreau (1997) is that users prefer location-based search of files, and that the locations of files serve as reminders of tasks to be performed. They also state that most users archive relatively little information and avoid elaborate filing schemes. Their proposed requirements for data filing systems and filing tasks are thus not satisfied, and indeed are made more difficult, by the desktop metaphor.

Malone's (1983) study of how documents and information resources are arranged in the physical office differentiates between files and piles. In Malone's terminology *files* are comprised of elements (such as individual data files or folders) that are explicitly titled and arranged in order (typically alphabetical or chronological). Groups, such as drawers in filing cabinets, may also be explicitly titled and systematically arranged, but they need not be. In *piles*, though, the individual elements (papers, folders, and so on) are not necessarily titled, and they are not generally ordered in a particular way.

In a computer-based file organisation system based on a pile metaphor (Mander et al., 1992), the folder metaphor is not adopted in any form. Instead, individual data files are arranged in pile structures which can be casually arranged on the root window. The pile metaphor, like other metaphors, has difficulties that arise from the limits of its scope to account for all of an electronic pile's behaviour. Some behaviour is magical and improves usability, for example, a pile never topples over as a result of being stacked too high.

For our current analysis, however, it is also possible to claim from an examination of Malone's (1983) protocols, in terms of the Lakoff/Johnson theory of metaphor, that the pile metaphor is grounded in the same logic of containment as the folder metaphor for data file organisation. This should be clear from considering attributes of a physical pile, documents are *in* a pile, all but the document upper-most on the pile are hidden from view, and the spatial extent and boundary of the pile are clearly defined. As with the folder metaphor, the image schema that grounds understanding of the pile suggests tasks and actions that the electronic domain should support. These include tasks to locate and remove files in the pile, and to construct new piles from existing piles according to new, more immediately relevant, criteria. Most of the design effort and user testing reported by Mander et al. (1992) has concerned the details of possible interface solutions to the tasks that a pile must support, including methods for locating a data file wanted and removing it from the pile. Considering again the distinction between coordinate and categorical spatial representations, it is likely that coordinate spatial representations are used to locate a pile on the root window, but deciding whether the data file sought is a in a candidate pile relies on a categorical spatial relationship decision.

3.4   Lifestreams

Lifestreams is a recent, radical, interface design prompted by a number of objections to other filing system interfaces, particularly to the suggested need to support location-based search mechanisms. Fertig et al. (1996) note that Barreau & Nardi's (1995) studies of users of the Apple Macintosh and a number of PC-based operating systems show the following similarities between users:

1. A preference for location-based search for finding files (in contrast to logical, text-based search).

2. The use of file placement as a critical reminding function.

3. The use of three types of information: ephemeral, working and archived.

4. The 'lack of importance' of archiving files.

Fertig et al. claim that similarities 1, 2, and 4 are artefacts of the computing systems studied rather than statements of the way users actually acquire, organise, and maintain information. Fertig et al.'s Lifestreams system proposes a new metaphor that replaces traditional files and directories. Lifestreams is claimed to be based upon the metaphor of a time-ordered stream of documents, every document created by the user or sent to the user via electronic mail is stored in the lifestream. The tail of the stream contains old documents and denotes the past. In the present, in the head of the stream, items such as work in progress and recently arrived electronic mail are shown. The claims made for Lifestreams include that the system supports reminding and archiving inherently in the model, and also that it aids in locating information by ephemeral and working information typically being in the 'present' part of the stream.

As can be seen in the stream segment shown in Figure 5, the lifestream forms a diagonal line of documents across the display. Documents in the present are shown in the bottom right-hand corner of the screen, younger documents occlude older documents so that the rear-most document in the top left-hand corner of the display is the oldest one rendered. After a period of time, documents 'fall off' the edge of the screen and are automatically archived, but may easily be retrieved. A scrollbar allows the span of time parameter to be altered changing the set of documents that are shown in the display. In order to move into the future, however, so that reminders may be introduced, the Lifestreams system 'clock' must be altered by a function reached from a menu option. Lifestreams is proposed as an alternative to the desktop metaphor, in having the 'organisational metaphor' of a time-ordered

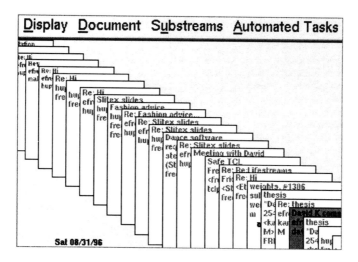

Figure 5: A portion of a lifestream ©, 1996 Eric Freeman.

The Location of the Observer	→	The Present
The Space in Front of the Observer	→	The Future
The Space Behind the Observer	→	The Past

Table 2: Mappings for the TIME ORIENTATION metaphor.

stream of documents. It is possible, however, to employ the Lakoff/Johnson theory to also critique Lifestreams. The frequent use of the word 'stream' to describe the Lifestreams interface is to employ an appealing metaphor evoking the 'flow' of time, but, in terms of the metaphors that describe our understanding of time, Lifestreams has faults, and may not differ considerably from the systems it seeks to replace.

Physics cannot yet provide a full account of the nature of time (Davies, 1995), and so we can only refer to time, and to the flow of time, metaphorically. While Lifestreams adopts a metaphor in which the passage of time maps onto the position and motion of objects, Lifestreams does not adopt the common MOVING TIME metaphor, which is based on the following schema:

> "There is a lone, stationary observer facing in a fixed direction. There is an indefinitely long sequence of objects moving past the observer from front to back. The moving objects are conceptualised as having fronts in their direction of motion." (Lakoff & Johnson, 1999, p.141)

This schema combines with a TIME ORIENTATION metaphor, the mappings of which are shown in Table 2, to produce a set of composite mappings shown in Table 3.

Comparing the composite metaphor for the flow of time with the Lifestreams system, one should not conclude that the Lifestreams interface metaphor is not

The Location of the Observer	→	The Present
The Space in Front of the Observer	→	The Future
The Space Behind the Observer	→	The Past
Objects	→	Times
The Motion of Objects Past the Observer	→	The 'Passage' of Time

Table 3: A Composite metaphor for the passage of time.

grounded in a pattern of interaction that people can understand easily, only that the schema that grounds the Lifestreams concept is one unfamiliar to many people. For Chilean speakers of the Aymara language (Lakoff & Johnson, 1999, p.141) the metaphor 'The Past is in Front' is familiar and is grounded by the notion of being able to see the results of what you have just done in front of you. Thus while Lifestreams may prove to have an acceptable level of usability, its design appears to conflict with the culture and everyday experience of embodied interaction with the world of most of its intended user population.

One can also question whether Lifestreams is as radical an alternative to electronic support for the notions of piles and folders as it is claimed to be. The analysis of piles and folders above shows that both these forms of file organisation can be understood in terms of the same grounding image schemata and in terms of metaphors with similar mappings. Similar claims can be made for how Lifestreams is understood. While the MOVING TIME metaphor underlies Lifestreams (albeit combined with a time orientation metaphor unfamiliar to many potential users), the MOVING TIME metaphor and the MOVING OBSERVER metaphor (the other mutually exclusive metaphor used to describe temporal events in language) are both extensions of an EVENT FOR TIME metonymy, in which:

"Times are then conceptualised as locations or bounded regions in space or as objects or substances that move. Events are then located with respect to those locations in space or objects that move." (Lakoff & Johnson, 1999, p.155)

Thus, in Lifestreams newly edited or created documents and reminders are located with respect to locations or bounded regions in the part of the display denoting the stream. We could therefore undertake an analysis similar to that for folders and piles of how present, ephemeral, and sub-streamed documents are referred to and find that manipulation of items within the categories formed in these regions of time is reasoned about in the same way as a pile or folder. It could be proposed that time-based search (when did I create that file?) is as prone to the same difficulties and advantages as location-based search (where did I leave that file?), especially in terms of the consequences of conceptualisations of file spaces arising from the EVENT FOR TIME metonymy and the use of areas in the visual field to denote temporal events.

4   Conclusions

A number of authors confronted by the theory gap in HCI adopt the view that development of theory should be, if not abandoned entirely, downplayed in favour of acquiring design experience and design principles that provide immediate input into design tasks. Accounts of spatial cognition, reflected in user interface designs, show that spatial metaphor-based designs, and also many of the detailed design choices that need to be made with systems based upon spatialisation metaphors, benefit from immediate evaluation and comparison of alternative designs. Spatialisation metaphors, where understanding comes from more structured and complex representations of patterns of physical experience, do, though, rely on theory, not only for suggesting interface designs, but also for being able to compare designs, as we hope to have demonstrated above. Further work applying the experientialist approach, and the Lakoff/Johnson theory of metaphor in particular, will address whether the structure of image schemata can suggest more detailed user interface designs rather than just be a tool of analysis. There is no reason as yet to expect that this might be the case, for the reason that most existing input technologies do not permit the user's existing motor representations and task-oriented action sequences (Jeannerod, 1997) to be applied directly to alter the state of on-screen objects. A larger scale project is to further explore issues of culture and software internationalisation by cataloguing and developing structures of the schemata relied on to understand interface components, to identify the designs that are likely to fail in a particular culture. The experientialist approach we have adopted, echoing Benyon & Imaz's (1999) promotion and prior (Treglown, 1999) application of it, is proving to be a useful and successful method for these tasks.

Acknowledgements

I would like to thank Tim O'Shea, Debbie Stone and Vanessa Evers for their helpful comments on the doctoral thesis from which some sections of this article are taken. Figures 1–3 are © The University of Chicago, 1987, and are reproduced with permission. Figure 5 is © Eric Freeman, 1996, and reproduced with his kind permission.

References

Bailey, D., Feldman, J., Narayanan, S. & Lakoff, G. (1997), Modeling Embodied Lexical Development, *in* M. G. Shafto & P. Langley (eds.), *Proceedings of the 19th Annual Conference of the Cognitive Science Society*, Lawrence Erlbaum Associates, pp.19–24.

Barreau, D. & Nardi, B. A. (1995), "Finding and Reminding: File Organisation from the Desktop", *ACM SIGCHI Bulletin* 27(3), 39–43.

Bederson, B. B., Hollan, J. D., Perlin, K., Meyer, J., Bacon, D. & Furnas, G. (1996), "Pad++: A Zoomable Graphical Sketchpad for Exploring Alternate Interface Physics", *Journal of Visual Languages and Computing* 7, 3–31.

Benyon, D. & Imaz, M. (1999), "Metaphors and Models: Conceptual Foundations of Representations in Interactive Systems Development", *Human–Computer Interaction* 14, 159–89. Special issue on Representations in Interactive System Development.

Clancey, W. J. (1997), *Situated Cognition*, Cambridge University Press.

Clark, A. (1989), *Microcognition*, MIT Press.

Czerwinski, M. P., van Dantzich, M., Robertson, G. & Hoffman, H. (1999), The Contribution of Thumbnail Image Mouse-over Text and Spatial Location Memory to Web Page Retrieval in 3D, *in* A. Sasse & C. Johnson (eds.), *Human–Computer Interaction — INTERACT '99: Proceedings of the Seventh IFIP Conference on Human–Computer Interaction*, Vol. 1, IOS Press, pp.163–70.

Davies, P. C. W. (1995), *About Time*, Viking.

Demasco, P., Newell, A. F. & Arnott, J. L. (1994), The Application of Spatialization and Spatial Metaphor to Augmentive and Alternative Communication, *in* E. P. Glinert (ed.), *ASSETS'94: Proceedings of The First Annual International ACM/SIGCAPH Conference on Assistive Technologies*, ACM Press, pp.31–8.

Erickson, T. D. (1990), Working with Interface Metaphors, *in* B. Laurel (ed.), *The Art of Human–Computer Interface Design*, Addison–Wesley, pp.65–73.

Fauconnier, G. (1985), *Mental Spaces*, MIT Press.

Fertig, S., Freeman, E. & Gelernter, D. (1996), "Finding and Reminding Reconsidered", *ACM SIGCHI Bulletin* **28**(1), 66–9.

Halasz, F. & Moran, T. P. (1982), Analogy Considered Harmful, *in Proceedings of CHI'82: Human Factors in Computing Systems*, ACM Press, pp.383–6.

Hix, D. & Hartson, H. R. (1993), *Developing User Interfaces: Ensuring Usability through Product and Process*, John Wiley & Sons.

Jackendoff, R. (1983), *Semantics and Cognition*, MIT Press.

Jeannerod, M. (1997), *The Cognitive Neuroscience of Action*, Blackwell.

Johnson, M. (1987), *The Body in the Mind: The Bodily Basis of Reason and Imagination*, University of Chicago Press.

Jones, W. & Dumais, S. (1986), "The Spatial Metaphor for User Interfaces: Experimental Tests of Reference by Location versus Name", *ACM Transactions on Office Information Systems* **4**(1), 42–63.

Kay, A. (1990), User Interface: A Personal View, *in* B. Laurel (ed.), *The Art of Human–Computer Interface Design*, Addison–Wesley, pp.191–207.

Kosslyn, S. M. (1994), *Image and Brain*, MIT Press.

Lakoff, G. (1987), *Women, Fire and Dangerous Things: What Categories Reveal About the Mind*, University of Chicago Press.

Lakoff, G. (1993), The Contemporary Theory of Metaphor, *in* A. Ortony (ed.), *Metaphor and Thought 2nd edition*, Cambridge University Press, pp.202–51.

Lakoff, G. & Johnson, M. (1980), *Metaphors We Live By*, University of Chicago Press.

Lakoff, G. & Johnson, M. (1999), *Philosophy in the Flesh*, Basic Books.

Landau, B. & Jackendoff, R. (1993), "'What' and 'Where' in Spatial Language and Spatial Cognitions", *Behavioural and Brain Sciences* **16**, 217–65.

Long, J. & Dowell, J. (1989), Conceptions of the Discipline of HCI: Craft, Applied Science and Engineering, *in* A. Sutcliffe & L. Macaulay (eds.), *People and Computers V (Proceedings of HCI'89)*, Cambridge University Press, pp.9–34.

Mackinlay, J. D., Robertson, G. G. & Card, S. K. (1991), The Perspective Wall: Details and Context Smoothly Integrated, *in* S. P. Robertson, G. M. Olson & J. S. Olson (eds.), *Proceedings of CHI'91: Human Factors in Computing Systems (Reaching through Technology)*, ACM Press, pp.173–9.

Madsen, K. H. (1994), "A Guide to Metaphorical Design", *Communications of the ACM* **37**, 57–62.

Malone, T. (1983), "How Do People Organize Their Desks? Implications for the Design of Office Information Systems", *ACM Transactions on Office Information Systems* **1**(1), 99–112.

Mander, R., Salomon, G. & Wong, Y. Y. (1992), A 'Pile' Metaphor for Supporting Casual Organization of Information, *in* P. Bauersfeld, J. Bennett & G. Lynch (eds.), *Proceedings of CHI'92: Human Factors in Computing Systems*, ACM Press, pp.627–634.

Marcus, A. (1994), "Metaphor Mayhem: Mismanaging Expectation and Surprise Interactions", *Interactions* **1**(1), 41–3.

Nardi, B. A. & Barreau, D. (1997), "Finding and Reminding Revisited: Appropriate Metaphors for File Organization at the Desktop", *ACM SIGCHI Bulletin* **29**(1), 76–8.

Nardi, B. A. & Zarmer, C. L. (1993), "Beyond Models and Metaphors: Visual Formalisms in User Interface Design", *Journal of Visual Languages and Computing* **4**, 5–33.

Nelson, T. H. (1990), The Right Way to Think about Software Design, *in* B. Laurel (ed.), *The Art of Human–Computer Interface Design*, Addison–Wesley, pp.235–43.

Nielsen, J. (1993), *Usability Engineering*, Academic Press.

Norman, D. A. (1998), *The Invisable Computer*, MIT Press.

Regier, T. (1996), *The Human Semantic Potential*, MIT Press.

Robertson, G., Czerwinski, M., Larson, K., Robbins, D., Thiel, D. & van Dantzich, M. (1998), Data Mountain: Using Spatial Memory for Document Management, *in* B. Schilit (ed.), *Proceedings of the ACM Symposium on User Interface Software and Technology, UIST'98*, ACM Press, pp.153–62.

Rohrer, T. (1995), Feeling Stuck in a GUI Web: Metaphors, Image-schemas, and Designing the Human–Computer Interface, Technical Report, University of Oregon. http://darkwing.uoregon.edu/ rohrer/gui4web.htm.

Smith, R. B. (1987), Experiences with the Alternate Reality Kit: An Example of the Tension Between Literalism and Magic, *in* J. M. Carroll & P. P. Tanner (eds.), *Proceedings of CHI+GI 1987: Human Factors in Computing Systems and Graphics Interface*, ACM Press, pp.61–7.

Treglown, M. (1999), Is the Trashcan Being Ironic? Evaluating Direct Manipulation Interfaces using a Contemporary Theory of Metaphor, *in* R. Paton & I. Neilson (eds.), *Visual Representations and Interpretations*, Springer-Verlag, pp.173–80.

Varela, F. J., Thompson, E. & Rosch, E. (1991), *The Embodied Mind*, MIT Press.

A Comprehension-based Model of Web Navigation and Its Application to Web Usability Analysis

Muneo Kitajima, Marilyn H Blackmon[†] & Peter G Polson[†]

National Institute of Bioscience and Human-Technology, 1–1 Higashi, Tsukuba, Ibaraki 305–8566, Japan

Tel: *+81 298 61 6731*
Fax: *+81 298 61 6732*
EMail: *kitajima@nibh.go.jp*

[†] *Institute of Cognitive Science, University of Colorado at Boulder, Boulder, CO 80309–0344, USA*

Tel: *+1 303 492 5622*
EMail: *{ppolson,blackmon}@psych.colorado.edu*

CoLiDeS, a comprehension-based cognitive model of Web navigation, offers a theoretical explanation of the impasses users often encounter during information search and retrieval from the WWW, and also identifies the determinants of success cases. In this model, acting on a single Web page screen object is regarded as the outcome of a multi-step process:

- **parsing the current display containing up to about 200 screen objects into five to ten top-level schematic objects;**

- **focusing on one of these top-level schematic objects;**

- **comprehending and elaborating the screen objects within the focused-on area; and then**

- **selecting one of the actual screen objects as the target for the next action, the object whose representation bears the highest degree of semantic similarity to the user's goal.**

Keywords: Web navigation, usability, comprehension-based cognitive model, information retrieval, semantic similarity, scent, hierarchical site structure, attention management, action planning, forward search, impasse.

1 Introduction

According to published findings, users find typical Web navigation tasks to be very difficult and have low success rates, even when they are first taken to a particular Web site containing the information sought (Spool et al., 1999). The pragmatic goal of our research program is to improve users' success rates in finding information on typical Web sites. To accomplish that goal we are currently engaged in a three-prong research program:

- developing a theoretical model;

- conducting extensive empirical testing of the model, combining controlled laboratory research and usability testing of real-world Web sites; and

- building tools and tutorials for Web site developers.

Due to space limitations, this paper will focus on describing the theoretical model, a comprehension-based, simulation model of Web site navigation derived from earlier models of Kitajima & Polson (1995; 1997). Our strategy in this paper is to highlight the ingredients of success, providing integrated, detailed explanations of what is known about the attributes of Web pages that support successful navigation.

We plan to ultimately build a theoretically based design methodology practical enough for Web site developers to put to wide use (Wharton et al., 1994), but even now developers will find valuable uses for our model. Empirical results (Larson & Czerwinski, 1998) and guidelines summarising successful design practice and usability research findings (see http://www.useit.com/alertbox/ — last accessed 2000.06.10) typically focus on one attribute of a site design at a time and may be contradictory when applied to particular site designs. A theoretical model can be a powerful tool for mediating such tradeoffs by showing how two or more attributes interact to determine usability of a Web page, collection of pages, or Web site. A model can also be a powerful tool for reasoning about design decisions for which there are no relevant empirical data or guidelines.

The key claim of the model presented in this paper is that comprehension of texts and images is the core process underlying Web navigation. Comprehension processes build and compare the mental representations of screen objects on a Web page in preparation for selecting and clicking one particular hyperlink or image. The primary assumption of the model is that users act on the hyperlink, image, or other screen object they perceive as being most similar to the representation of their current goal. By similarity we mean semantic similarity — similarity of meaning.

2 The CoLiDeS Model

The model we have developed to understand cognitive processes of users navigating the Web is called CoLiDeS, an acronym for *Co*mprehension-based *Li*nked model of *De*liberate *S*earch. CoLiDeS extends a series of earlier models developed by Kitajima & Polson (1995; 1997) and the entire series of models is based on Kintsch's construction-integration theory of text comprehension (Kintsch, 1998). Previous models in the series simulated both performing/learning by exploration (Kitajima & Polson, 1997) and skilled use in complex applications hosted on systems with graphical user interfaces (Kitajima & Polson, 1995). CoLiDeS shares with its predecessors assumptions about the underlying cognitive architecture, comprehension processes, and action planning processes.

All models in the series, CoLiDeS included, are based on the claim that both exploration and skilled use involve serious problems of attention management. In contrast to previous models in the series, CoLiDeS incorporates more complete and realistic attention management mechanisms. These attention management mechanisms provide a principled explanation of how the user focuses on a subset of the screen objects and selects one screen object (e.g. a pull-down menu or hypertext link) on a Web page.

The four cognitive processes most central to the CoLiDeS model are *parsing, focusing on, comprehension*, and *selection*. Section 2.1 explains how *parsing* builds mental representations of Web pages. Section 2.2 portrays how *selecting* the next action depends upon *comprehension* of a set of screen objects. As Section 2.3 shows, *focusing on* a subset of the screen objects on a Web page guides both the comprehension and action selection processes. Section 2.4 examines patterns in the entire sequence of actions — the entire click stream — selected by a particular user to accomplish her goal.

2.1 Representation of the Screen Objects on Web Pages

CoLiDeS assumes that each object on the screen — action graphic, iconic link, hypertext link, navigation bar item, or paragraph, for example — is represented as a screen object if it is a meaningful unit and/or a target for action. A Web page can contain from 100 to 200 screen objects competing for a user's attention. Users manage this complexity by scanning and constructing a schematic representation of a page that contains from 5 to 10 top-level schematic objects — referred to here as 'parsing the page'.* Parsing the page into top-level schematic objects is critical to avoiding getting lost in the complexity of a Web page.

A mixture of bottom-up and top-down processes determines the collection of schematic objects defined by a page. Bottom-up processes utilise low-level perceptual features that guide how the user parses the Web page into visually related regions. Top-down processes are controlled by a user's knowledge of the conventional elements of a typical page for a given Web site or type of Web site

---

*Tullis (1998) used nine standard elements that appeared on each page when he worked on redesigning the Internet at Fidelity Investments. The number we describe in the paper is an approximate value that we derived from his experience and from the similarity of his nine standard elements to the conventional page elements defined by best-practice guides to Web site design. The number is also in accord with the number of items that can be held in working memory, classically estimated at seven plus or minus two.

Figure 1: An example of standard elements for online bookstores.

and by the user's knowledge of print conventions that enable the user to scan the configuration of heading texts to identify meaning-related units. Consistent or enforced interface conventions enable users to quickly grasp an accurate schematic representation for individual pages in a Web site (Tullis, 1998). Frequent Web users can assume the existence of many top-level schematic objects, such as site and sub-site navigation bars, browser application menus and window controls, site search engine, and advertising banners and promotions.

Each top-level schematic object encompasses a cluster of screen objects. The top-level parsing always employs schematic objects for its representation. Each schematic object can be regarded as a conceptual label that distinguishes it from the remaining regions on the page. Each top-level schematic object, in turn, contains a collection of lower-level schematic objects and/or actual objects. Examples of actual objects include text links, navigation buttons and other image links, text discourse communicating content, brief texts used for banners, and images, such as a site logo or images of products for sale.

Figure 1 shows how a frequent user of a particular online bookstore might parse its home page by applying both knowledge-driven top-down processes and perception-driven bottom-up processes. The user would be apt to identify such schematic objects as window controls and the browser menu, because such features are consistently present in any Web browser application familiar to the user. Another easily identifiable area is the interactive window for the site search engine. Experienced users will probably define a browse area containing a list of related links, for example, the area labelled 'Browse Books' in Figure 1.

Such site-specific areas as site navigation buttons and a site navigation tab consistently appear at the same position on every page of this particular Web site, as shown in Figure 1. The site navigation tab conjointly displays both an upper menu of sub-sites and a lower menu with crucial navigation options for one particular sub-site or for the site home page. Users familiar with e-commerce sites will also tend to distinguish a promotion area encompassing an assortment of featured products the business hopes the customer will buy. In Figure 1, the site navigation tab area, a schematic object, contains only actual screen objects, text links with the labels WELCOME, BOOKS, etc. In contrast, the promotion area contains both another level of schematic objects — more specific promotion areas — and an assortment of actual objects — text links.

2.2 Action Planning Processes Guided by User's Goal

This section describes the comprehension process and the selection process applied to a given set of alternative objects. This set of objects can be a set of schematic objects, as illustrated by the superimposed labels of Figure 1, or they can be a set of actual screen objects, as shown by the hyperlinks nested under 'Browse Books' in Figure 1. Kitajima & Polson (1995; 1997) have defined the comprehension and selection processes. Elaboration plays a central role in the comprehension process by extracting information from the user's long-term memory store of knowledge to augment the representations of the goal and the set of objects. The user then selects the next action on the basis of the elaborated representations.

2.2.1 Elaboration of Goal, Schematic Objects, and Actual Objects

To plan the next action the user must comprehend and compare what the probable consequences would be for selecting various screen objects as candidates for action. To decide how selecting any given screen object might contribute to accomplishing the user's current goal, the user elaborates candidate objects. The user interprets the intended meaning of screen objects and their associated texts by relying on the extensive amount of knowledge in long-term memory (LTM), which stores both domain knowledge and knowledge of interface conventions.

The elaboration process can be applied to the current goal as well as to schematic/actual screen objects, as the following examples clarify:

Elaborate goal: The concise goal representation, *browse books on chaos theory*, might be elaborated with a subgoal in a richer representation, such as *browse books on chaos theory by [the subgoal of] selecting a link that matches chaos theory, which is a mathematical formalism for describing complex indeterminate physical systems.*

Elaborate schematic object: Similarly, the schematic object 'Button Bar' in the Browser Application Menu might be represented after elaboration as a series of buttons for controlling various display properties, such as fonts, size, and style. The ability to elaborate this schematic object comes from knowledge acquired from experience with typical button bars in browser applications and/or other computer applications.

Elaborate actual object: In the same vein, the user could elaborate the actual object represented by the image **A** with the word 'Larger' printed beneath it, constructing the elaborated representation "a button which can be clicked to enlarge the size of the font displayed in the browser window by one unit". The elaboration of the intended meaning comes from knowledge associated with the interface convention combined with the semantic meaning of the image A^* joined with the word 'Larger' printed under the image.

2.2.2 Selection by Constraint Satisfaction

Each of the elaborated schematic/actual objects is related to some degree with the elaborated goal. Furnas (1997) and Pirolli & Card (1999) use the term *scent* to describe the degree of relatedness. This metaphor evokes the image of a user searching for information by following a trail, repeatedly pursuing whatever object currently provides the highest degree of scent. In the CoLiDeS model three independent factors interplay conjunctively to define the degree of relatedness:

- The degree of similarity between the elaborated object's representation and the elaborated goal.

- The frequency with which the user has encountered a particular object on a particular navigation path.

- Whether the representation of the unelaborated current goal has a literal matching with the actual object.

CoLiDeS assumes that the competition among the objects based on these three factors be resolved by the constraint satisfaction process incorporated into Kintsch's (1998) construction-integration architecture. Each schematic/actual object is related to the current goal in degree of similarity, frequency, and literal matching. Each screen object is also related to each of the other screen objects in degree of similarity, frequency, and literal matching. Thus, when the selection is performed there exists a very complicated network of relationships with multiple measures of relatedness. The constraint satisfaction process deals with the competition among the various degrees of relatedness, enabling the user to single out the objects closest to the user's current goal.

Similarity: The model assumes that the degree of similarity between schematic or actual objects and the current goal is defined by their distance in a semantic space. We use Latent Semantic Analysis (LSA) to compute the degree of similarity within a particular semantic space. As Landauer & Dumais (1997) explain, LSA is a data analysis technique that generates a high dimensional space, typically a space with about 300 dimensions. LSA applies singular value decomposition, a mathematical procedure similar to factor analysis, to a huge terms-by-documents co-occurrence matrix. Each word can be represented as a vector in the 300-dimensional space.

The vector of each word varies according to the knowledge of the user, and the LSA Web site, http://lsa.colorado.edu/, currently offers a variety of LSA semantic spaces, most importantly an encyclopaedia space and five spaces representing the general reading knowledge typical of users in grades 3,

6, 9, 12 or first-year college. These grade-defined spaces are constructed by incorporating the appropriate texts from the Touchstone Applied Science Associates, Inc. (TASA) corpus, which provides a variety of texts, novels, newspaper articles, and other information that has typically been read by students who have attained these age-grade levels.

In LSA analyses any cluster of terms is represented as a linear combination of the constituent vectors. The degree of semantic relatedness between two terms or documents is measured by the cosine value between the corresponding two vectors. Cosines are analogous to correlations. Each cosine value lies somewhere between +1 (identical) and -1 (opposite), and near-zero values are unrelated. By using LSA, it is possible to measure the relationship between the representation of a user's goal and the representation of each screen object.

Frequency: The model assumes that the screen elements on frequently navigated paths are more likely to be selected. For example, a frequent user of Web sites with site navigation tab menus would have a propensity to navigate a Web site using the site tab menu. Analogously, a person who had often used site search engines would be more apt to focus on the search window than someone who had previously located information primarily by browsing.

Literal Matching: When the representation of the current goal literally matches the representation of the schematic or actual object, partially or completely, the number of matches is counted when selecting an object from the screen.

2.3   *Attention Management Mechanisms*

CoLiDeS assumes that attention management mechanisms are crucial for guiding the user toward acting on a particular screen object. Immediately after being transported to a new Web page, the user parses the page, generates a schematic representation of the display — illustrated by the collection of top-level schematic objects in Figure 1. A particular schematic object rapidly grabs the user's attention. If there are lower-level schematic objects nested under the *focussed-on* top-level schematic object, then the user parses the top-level schematic area as a representation of lower-level schematic objects. Then one of these lower-level schematic objects grabs the user's attention, making available the information in that area. By this point, if not before, the user is *focusing on* an area that contains actual objects, meaning screen objects on which the user can act. The user then comprehends and compares these actual objects in relation to the current goal and selects one object as a target for the next action.

   If, for example, a user wants to enlarge the font size for the page, her attention must be successively drawn to a series of particular schematic/actual screen objects as follows:

- *Parse* the home page, representing it as 5–10 top-level schematic objects, and *focus on* the Browser Application Menu to make available the information contained in the area.

- *Parse* the Browser Application Menu area, consisting of multiple schematic objects — Tab Menu (vertical at left edge), Button Bar, Address Bar accompanied by a Go To Button, Status Bar, and Featured Sites Bar — and *focus on* Button Bar, a particular lower-level schematic object, to make available actual objects to act upon.

- *Comprehend* the set of button objects and *select/click* the button object with the image **A** (intended to mean 'increase font size') with the clarifying text label 'Larger' printed beneath the image.

As shown in this simple example, the interplay of *focus on* with the other three processes is crucial to determining which screen object is acted upon. If the user first focuses on the Browser Application Menu and then on the Button Bar, the user is apt to accurately comprehend the consequences of clicking the '**A**/Larger' button and select that action. At present CoLiDeS models both the *focus on* and *select* processes using constraint satisfaction to resolve competition among objects related by varying degrees of similarity (LSA cosines), frequency, and literal matching. The difference between the two processes is that *select* results after comprehending actual screen objects that are competing potential targets for action and *focus on* results after scanning and representing top-level schematic objects that compete for the user's attention.

2.4   Outcomes of Action Sequences

So far the discussion has been limited to analysing a single action at a time, a single click in the user's click stream. This section enlarges the perspective to the full sequence of actions, analysing patterns in the entire click stream required to accomplish the user's goal. Two prototype patterns can be distinguished. The first pattern is forward search, in which the user moves smoothly forward step by step towards the goal. The second pattern is an erratic navigation path, exhibiting backtracking to previously visited pages and/or detours resulting from confrontations with one or more impasses.

Forward search: This is an action sequence that avoids impasses. Obviously this is the ideal pattern Web site designers should aim to support, and CoLiDeS offers insights into how to increase the percentage of typical users who can accomplish their goals with forward search.

Impasses: Forward search can fail when no screen object is similar to the user's goal — no target of action is available that can satisfy the similarity, frequency, or literal matching measures. This situation presents an impasse that results in the user backtracking, taking detours, and becoming lost in the site. To resume forward search and move towards accomplishing her goal, the user must first find a way to solve the impasse.

An example of pure forward search is shown in Figure 2 and discussed in detail in Section 3.1. Causes of impasses and methods of solution are described in detail in Section 3.2.

3   Simulation of Web Navigation: Browse Books at Online Stores

In order to demonstrate how the CoLiDeS processes are performed, this section describes simulations of Web navigation by CoLiDeS. The task we consider is a task commonly performed by both frequent and novice Web users: browsing for a narrow class of items at an online shopping site. More specifically, the simulated task was locating and browsing books on chaos theory at online bookstores. The success case described in Section 3.1 was accomplished with flawless forward search. In contrast, Section 3.2 analyses impasses frequently confronted by users attempting the same or similar tasks at various e-commerce sites. The success case illustrates how CoLiDeS simulations can help designers gather evidence that a particular site design enables pure forward search for a sample of prototypical user goals. The analysis of impasses shows how useful CoLiDeS simulations can be for identifying usability problems on a particular Web site.

3.1   Success Case: Pure Forward Search

Figure 2 displays a CoLiDeS simulation that exemplifies pure forward search. For this simulation the user was assumed to be familiar with site navigation tabs and to have general reading knowledge equivalent to the average college freshman. In addition, the user is assumed to have previously acquired sufficient knowledge of chaos theory to construct the following well-elaborated subgoal for the goal of browsing books on chaos theory:

> I am searching for a link for chaos theory. Chaos theory is the hottest scientific theory since relativity, a new paradigm in the realm of mathematics, mathematicians' and scientists' breakthrough discovery of order in chaos, and a mathematical formalism for describing complex, indeterminate physical systems in complicated equations. Chaos theory overturns deterministic theories of classical physics, showing that systems obeying precise laws can behave in a random fashion, and showing the emergence of order from disorder and the generation of random patterns from chaos and uncertainty.

This goal was entered into the LSA analysis to compute the cosines displayed in steps 2.6 and 2.8 of Figure 2. These cosines measure the degree of similarity between the user's goal and the relevant text labels that appear on Web pages the user visited to complete the task.

Figure 2 outlines a ten-step trace (see steps 2.1 to 2.10 in Figure 2) of the simulation of the success case. The same two-part cycle is repeated five times during the simulation. Each cycle begins when a new Web page appears in the browser, and CoLiDeS parses the page into top-level schematic objects and focuses on one of the top-level schematic objects (odd-numbered steps). To complete the cycle CoLiDeS comprehends the set of actual screen objects nested within the top-level schematic object and selects the object that is semantically most similar or identical with the user goal (even-numbered steps). The action of selecting a link transports CoLiDeS to a new Web page and the start of a new cycle. For each step, the highlighted object is the one CoLiDeS has focused on or selected.

Window Controls	Browser Application Menu	Site Navigation Buttons	**Site Navigation Tab**	Home Page Tab Menu	Site Search Engine	Browse	Promotions

2.1: Parse the home page as the above 8 schematic objects and *focus on area* Site Navigation Tab

WELCOME	**BOOKS**	MUSIC	VIDEO	TOYS & GAMES	ELECTRONICS, E-CARDS	AUCTIONS

2.2: Comprehend above set of 7 subsite tabs in the area Site Navigation Tab, noting links most similar/identical to the user's goal, and *select/click tab* BOOKS

2.3: Parse BOOKS subsite main page as 8 areas shown in Figure 1 and *focus on area* Subsite Tab Menu

BOOK SEARCH	**BROWSE SUBJECTS**	BESTSELLERS	FEATURED IN THE MEDIA
AWARD WINNERS	COMPUTERS & INTERNET	KIDS	BUSINESS & INVESTING

2.4: Comprehend the above set of 8 menu options, noting links most similar/identical to the user's goal, and *select/click tab* BROWSE SUBJECTS

Window Controls	Browser Application Menu	Site Navigation Buttons	Site Navigation Tab	Subsite Tab Menu	**Browse Subjects**	Promotions

2.5: Parse the BROWSE SUBJECTS page and *focus on central area with header* Browse Subjects

Science & Nature 0.41	Science Fiction 0.35	Home & Garden 0.08	23 other book-subject links, all with LSA cosine values ranging from +0.07 to –0.07

2.6: Comprehend the list of 26 alphabetically-arranged links to subjects in the area Browse Subjects, noting links most similar/identical to the user's goal, shown above, and *select/click link* Science & Nature

Window Controls	Browser Application Menu	Site Navigation Buttons	Site Navigation Tab	Subsite Tab Menu
Site Search Engine	Browse Window	**Browse Science & Nature**	Great Gifts in Science & Nature	Promotions

2.7: Parse Science & Nature web page and *focus on boxed area with header* Browse Science & Nature

Physics 0.57	Biological Sciences 0.39	Mathematics 0.37	Behavioural Sciences 0.37	Evolution 0.35	Chemistry 0.29
16 other book-subject links, all with LSA cosine values ranging from +0.27 to –0.01					

2.8: Comprehend the list of 22 alphabetically-arranged links to subjects within the category Science & Nature, noting links most similar/identical to the user's goal, shown above, and *select/click link* Physics

Window Controls	Browser Application Menu	Site Navigation Buttons	Site Navigation Tab	Subsite Tab Menu
Site Search Engine	Browse Window	**Browse Physics**	Promotions	

2.9: Parse Physics web page and *focus on boxed area with header* Browse Physics

General	Acoustics & Sound	Astrophysics	Biophysics	**Chaos & Systems**	21 other book-subject links

2.10: Comprehend the list of 26 alphabetically-arranged links to subjects within the category Physics, noting links most similar/identical to the user's goal and *select/click link* Chaos & Systems

Figure 2: Simulation of 'Browse books on chaos' at Amazon.com.

3.2   When Forward Search Fails: Impasses and Their Solution

Impasses are commonly encountered while searching for information or products on the Web, and the difficulty of solving an impasse frequently results in the user abandoning the site without completing the task, yielding no sales for e-commerce sites and frustration for the user. This section will first describe how users try to cope with impasses and then analyse two distinct types of impasses. One type of impasse is due to inadequate scent for the target item on Web pages visited along the trail (Larson & Czerwinski, 1998; Pirolli & Card, 1999). Another type of impasse can be traced to flaws in the hierarchical structure of a particular Web site (Dumais & Landauer, 1984; Phillips et al., 1985; Landauer, 1995).

3.2.1   How Users Respond to Impasses

Forward search breaks down if a user cannot find any link that is sufficiently similar to the user's goal, leaving the constraint satisfaction process with no target of action that satisfies the similarity, frequency, or literal matching measures. Under such conditions the user's goal often offers little, if any, guidance.

There are several possible actions in this case:

- The user can shift attention and focus on another schematic object on the page, attempting to find an acceptable forward move. For example, scanning the headings may have attracted the user to focus on the actual objects in one area of the page, but the heading may have been misleading or misinterpreted or there may have been two or more objects with a similar degree of scent. The user may then search for an acceptable link under a different heading printed on the same page.

- The user can backtrack to a previously visited Web page, most commonly by clicking the browser application back button one or more times. For example, if the user was surprised by the new Web page that appeared as a result of her last click, backtracking can erase the effects of her mistaken prediction.

- A more complex alternative is to focus on a subset of the navigation links on the page and try to elaborate the links using information from other sources, such as the site architecture and/or general search strategies for the Web. For example, if the user has been browsing for information in a hierarchically structured site and has reached a dead end, the user may abandon browsing and try the site search engine. Alternatively, the user may revise her model of the site architecture and conclude she has previously been searching for the information in the wrong place, deciding to browse for the desired information in a different part of the hierarchical structure instead.

Successful solutions for impasses can thus require extensive knowledge of the Web site architecture (something only frequent users of the particular site have) and/or well developed search strategies for the Web (something only expert Web users have).

3.2.2   Causes of Impasses: Inadequate Scent

As the success case in Figure 2 shows, CoLiDeS estimates information scent by measuring the LSA cosine value of the correct link(s) in relation to the cosine values for competing links that could potentially lead the user astray. LSA cosines increase with richness of meaning, clarity, specificity, and lack of ambiguity — generally correlated with increased text length — for either the user goal or the text labels attached to the hyperlinks the user is considering. We have done cognitive walkthroughs (Wharton et al., 1994) of many Web sites using representations of user goals that are realistic for these Web sites and measuring the LSA cosines between each of these goals and the texts for each of the link labels available on the page. Several distinct sources of inadequate scent have emerged.

- Users encounter inadequate scent — and, therefore, more impasses — on Web pages that use short and/or ambiguous link labels. Various alternative link label texts — with or without link titles — can be objectively evaluated by comparing their LSA cosines in relation to the spectrum of typical user goals for a particular Web site.

- If all the link labels on a Web page are highly general, none of the LSA cosines for link labels may exceed 0.20 and five or six low-scent link labels (ranging from 0.10 to 0.20) may compete for the user's attention. In such a case the user experiences difficulty finding any link worth clicking on the page. When link labels are very general, they are slightly similar to just about everything but not very similar to anything in particular. The antidote is greater specificity that makes individual links distinct from each other.

- Sometimes a link for a featured item has high specificity but lacks adequate scent nevertheless, because the link label text uses a technical term or brand name with little or no meaning for most users. CoLiDeS or potential customers can select the correct link by literal matching, but only if they happen to know the precise technical term or brand name. To repair the inadequate scent the Web site designer can add link label and/or link title text describing the featured item in terms common within the LSA semantic space for general reading knowledge of typical users.

- When the highest cosines on the Web page deceptively lure the user to follow unproductive search paths, it generates an unusually difficult kind of impasse to solve. For example, we tested several medical/health Web sites using the query of a real user seeking information about diabetes. On one home page LSA cosines indicated that the user's attention would be pulled strongly towards a set of disease conditions. Five of the ten links nested within that area had cosines ranging from 0.33 to 0.46, but none provided more than an indirect path to some cross-referenced information on diabetes. The best link to diabetes information, unfortunately, was 'Library' with a cosine of only 0.03.

- Although some users arrive at a Web site with well-formulated goals and abundant relevant knowledge, others do not. Opportunely, LSA can accommodate any and all varieties of user goals, even rambling, ill-informed user goals that reduce scent and presumably raise the frequency of impasses. For example, we repeated the simulation of browsing for books on chaos theory with less elaborated and minimally elaborated goal representations, showing that each reduction in elaboration produced substantially lower LSA cosines. LSA could enable simulations to explore how to design a Web site that interacted with users to gradually expand the user's goal elaboration and goal-related knowledge, thereby potentially improving the success rate for users who arrive at a Web site with poorly elaborated goals.

3.2.3 Causes of Impasses: Flaws in Hierarchical Structure

Online bookstores — like most complex Web sites — have a hierarchical site structure several layers deep. To find books on a particular subject the user must drill down to a terminal node by selecting link labels for increasingly narrower categories. The browsing path down through any hierarchical structure is liable to present several types of hazards:

- The top-level categories may be so general that none are more than weakly similar to a particular subject, reducing the probability that the user will select the correct link, i.e. the link that leads to the correct terminal node. This situation of inadequate scent has already been covered in Section 3.2.2.

- The Web site designers may have misclassified either the terminal node or some middle level of the hierarchy, so that picking links closest to the user's goal may not lead to the correct terminal node.

- Even if an information architect says the terminal node is optimally categorised, the real issue is whether there is enough information scent at each click along the trail to ensure that the user can get to the correct terminal node. According to amazon.com, the primary classification for 'Chaos & Systems' is under 'Mathematics', but there would be no success case in Figure 2 if Amazon.com had not also decided to nest 'Chaos & Systems' under 'Physics'. The LSA cosines suggest that many users would click 'Evolution' to get to 'Chaos & Systems', so cross-classifying 'Chaos & Systems' under 'Evolution' and perhaps additional subjects would be effective for further reduction of the incidence of user impasses.

- The terminal nodes in the hierarchy may not be sufficiently specific, so that the terminal node retrieves an unreasonably large number of books. This happened when the simulation was run on a competing online bookstore site, where 'Physics' turned out to be a terminal node, presenting the user with the task of browsing 6519 books.

- There may not be a terminal node that closely matches the user's goal. For the case at hand, there may be no terminal node for books on chaos theory, not because the terminal nodes are not sufficiently specific but because that particular terminal node was not used.

To the naïve Web user, search engines may seem to present a superior alternative to browsing through hierarchically organised Web sites, but key word searching has its own set of hazards. If the user enters key words describing the particular subject — such as 'chaos' and 'theory' — into the site search engine, the search engine may or may not return results similar to those the user finds by browsing.

4 Useful Applications of CoLiDeS

4.1 *Theoretical Understanding of Key Usability Guidelines*

The CoLiDeS model offers a theoretical explanation of existing, agreed-upon usability guidelines that have been developed independently. Three well-known, agreed-upon usability guidelines are briefly considered in this section as examples of guidelines that can be explained by CoLiDeS.

4.1.1 *User Navigation Is Goal Driven, Dominated by Local Decisions*

Usability experts have noted that users' behaviour on Web sites is very goal driven and that users focus immediately on scanning the content area of the Web page, ignoring navigation aids and resisting constructing a representation of the site structure unless required to solve impasses. CoLiDeS claims that the major determinate of successful navigation is the quality of the descriptions of the consequences of clicking on a link. The most promising measure of users' accuracy in predicting the consequences of clicking on a link appears to be the LSA cosines between link label texts and a spectrum of representative user goals. To enable users to navigate by forward search, the Web site designer must ensure that clicking the link with the highest LSA cosine consistently carries the user closer to meeting her goal.

4.1.2 *Link Labels Must Be Clear, Not Ambiguous, to Users*

Unambiguous link labels facilitate smooth forward search, enabling users to accurately predict where they will end up if they click on a link. Adding clear verbal labels to an icon reduces the ambiguity inherent in icons without verbal labels (Nielsen & Sano, 1995; Rogers, 1986; Vaughan, 1998). Higher success rates in finding information are correlated with longer link labels (7–12 words), because long link labels generally carry more information and are less ambiguous than the short labels more typically found on Web pages (Spool et al., 1999). An alternative to long link labels is to retain short link labels and add link titles containing important supplementary information (a maximum of 60–80 characters) that becomes visible to the user when the cursor lands on the link label (Nielsen, 2000). CoLiDeS uses LSA to assess which links are highly similar to any given user goal, and ideally just one link label will be similar to the goal. In a case where multiple links on a Web page are similar to the user's goal, the Web site designer should ensure that selecting any of the competing links — not just one 'correct' link — will carry the user towards accomplishing the goal.

4.1.3 *Lower Success Rate for Web Sites Organised in a Deep Hierarchy*

The impasses outlined in Section 3.2 illustrate many reasons why searches through hierarchical spaces so often fail. Descriptions of top-level objects in deep hierarchies are very general and unlikely to provide much scent (Larson & Czerwinski, 1998) for any user's goal, especially an unelaborated one. In contrast, in a broad, shallow structure, a larger number of more specific headings appear on a Web page, raising the probability of a close semantic match to a user's goal. In a well-designed site scent increases as the user moves deeper into the hierarchy and closer to accomplishing her goal. For the elaborated goal in Section 3.1, for example, 'Science & Nature' (third level down) has a cosine of 0.41, 'Physics' (fourth level down) has a cosine of 0.57, and 'Chaos and Systems Theory' (fifth level down) has a cosine of 0.76.

A modest change in the probability of selecting the correct link at each level has a major impact on the overall success rate. A separate advantage of breadth is reducing the number of levels the user must drill through. If the user has an 90% probability of picking the correct link at each level then drilling down through two levels results in an 81% (0.9^2) overall chance of success, but drilling down through six levels reduces the overall probability of success to 53% (0.9^6). Just as important, a user trying to solve an impasse is less likely to get lost when backing up through two levels than when backing up through six levels.

4.2 Way to Resolve Tradeoffs Among Guidelines

Individual guidelines for Web site design have an inherent limitation: there are always contradictions and tradeoffs among guidelines, and also among the empirical results of usability studies. A unique contribution of a model like CoLiDeS is to provide guidance in balancing the tradeoffs and resolving the contradictions. For example, the guideline that stipulates long labels (Spool et al., 1999) can contradict the guideline recommending designing text to be concise and highly scannable (Nielsen, 2000). CoLiDeS offers a resolution of the contradiction. CoLiDeS emphasises scannability for the text the user relies upon to parse a Web page, but unambiguous, high-scent, long text labels when the user is comprehending a set of actual objects and selecting one for the next action.

4.3 Insight into Forward Search Success Cases

CoLiDeS provides a well-integrated, intuitive theoretical foundation for explaining the determinants of successful navigation by pure forward search. The best defence against usability problems is a good offence: CoLiDeS can help designers test a particular site design to determine whether user goals can be accomplished with pure forward search — the ideal scenario that would increase success rates for information searches on the Web.

4.4 Key Design Goal: Higher Information Retrieval Success Rates

Empirical usability studies have reported dismal success rates for information search and retrieval on the Web (Nielsen, 2000; Spool et al., 1999). Problems with inadequate scent and flaws in hierarchical site structures present serious usability problems for information search and retrieval, and this paper has demonstrated how CoLiDeS can explain these problems and suggest solutions. In addition, CoLiDeS can simulate solutions to impasses, although that complex topic is beyond the scope of this paper. If we can increase our understanding of the ways users wiggle out of impasses, it may be possible for designers to create second-chance search paths when minimum-path forward search is out of reach.

References

Dumais, S. T. & Landauer, T. K. (1984), "Describing Categories of Objects for Menu Retrieval Systems", *Behavior Research Methods, Instruments and Computers* **16**(2), 242–8.

Furnas, G. W. (1997), Effective View Navigation, *in* S. Pemberton (ed.), *Proceedings of CHI'97: Human Factors in Computing Systems*, ACM Press, pp.367–74.

Kintsch, W. (1998), *Comprehension: A Paradigm for cognition*, Cambridge University Press.

Kitajima, M. & Polson, P. G. (1995), "A Comprehension-Based Model of Correct Performance and Errors in Skilled Display-based Human–Computer Interaction", *International Journal of Human–Computer Interaction* **43**(1), 65–99.

Kitajima, M. & Polson, P. G. (1997), "A Comprehension-based Model of Exploration", *Human–Computer Interaction* **12**(4), 345–89.

Landauer, T. K. (1995), *The Trouble with Computers: Usefulness, Usability and Productivity*, MIT Press.

Landauer, T. K. & Dumais, S. T. (1997), "A Solution to Plato's Problem: The Latent Semantic Analysis Theory of Acquisition, Induction, and Representation of Knowledge", *Psychological Review* **104**(2), 211–40.

Larson, K. & Czerwinski, M. (1998), Web Page Design: Implications of Memory, Structure and Scent for Information Retrieval, *in* C.-M. Karat, A. Lund, J. Coutaz & J. Karat (eds.), *Proceedings of CHI'98: Human Factors in Computing Systems*, ACM Press, pp.25–32.

Nielsen, J. (2000), *Designing Web Usability*, New Riders Publishing.

Nielsen, J. & Sano, D. (1995), "SunWeb: User Interface Design for Sun Microsystem's Internal Web", *Computer Networks and ISDN Systems* **28**(1/2), 179–88.

Phillips, D. A., Hearty, P. J., Latremouille, S., Treurniet, W. C. & Whalen, T. E. (1985), "Behavioural Research in Telematics", *Canadian Psychology/Psychologie Canadienne* **26**(3), 219–30.

Pirolli, P. & Card, S. (1999), "Information Foraging", *Psychological Review* **106**(4), 643–75.

Rogers, Y. (1986), Evaluating the Meaningfulness of Icon Sets to Represent Command Operations, *in* M. D. Harrison & A. Monk (eds.), *People and Computers: Designing for Usability (Proceedings of HCI'86)*, Cambridge University Press, pp.586–603.

Spool, J. M., Scanlon, T., Schroeder, W., Snyder, C. & DeAngelo, T. (1999), *Web Site Usability: A Designer's Guide*, Morgan-Kaufmann.

Tullis, T. S. (1998), A Method for Evaluating Web Page Design Concepts, *in* C.-M. Karat, A. Lund, J. Coutaz & J. Karat (eds.), *Proceedings of CHI'98: Human Factors in Computing Systems*, ACM Press, pp.323–4.

Vaughan, M. (1998), "Testing the Boundaries of Two User-centred Design Principles: Metaphors and Memory Load", *International Journal of Human–Computer Interaction* **10**(3), 265–82.

Wharton, C., Rieman, J., Lewis, C. & Polson, P. (1994), The Cognitive Walkthrough Method: A Practitioners Guide, *in* J. Nielsen & R. L. Mack (eds.), *Usability Inspection Methods*, John Wiley & Sons, pp.105–140.

Multimedia and Learning: Patterns of Interaction

Sandra Cairncross & Mike Mannion[†]

HCI Research Group, School of Computing, Napier University, 219 Colinton Road, Edinburgh EH14 1DJ, UK

EMail: *s.cairncross@napier.ac.uk*

[†] *Computing Department, Glasgow Caledonian University, Cowcaddens Road, Glasgow G4 0BA, UK*

EMail: *M.A.G.Mannion@gcal.ac.uk*

Many people argue that interactive multimedia has the potential to create high quality learning environments which actively engage the learner, thereby promoting deep learning. However there is little reported empirical evidence to support this claim. This paper explains some interactive techniques commonly used for educational applications and describes the results of experimental trials into learner learning using these techniques. Our results show that whilst there is some evidence that the use of interactive multimedia can aid learner learning, its effect and benefits are not as clear cut as its proponents suggest.

Keywords: interactivity, multimedia, learning, engagement.

1   Introduction

Most universities and further education colleges are now using interactive multimedia and associated learning technologies to deliver part of their curricula to learners. This trend is set to continue. There is a growing need to offer greater flexibility in product delivery to learners because of changing patterns of learner availability, resulting in increased numbers of learners studying off-campus or on a part-time basis. These patterns are emerging from changes to learner funding and strong encouragement from the government, industry and higher and further education or continued professional development and life-long learning.

There is also a renewed emphasis on promoting more effective or deep learning. The MacFarlane report (CSUP, 1992) noted that learners must not only acquire extensive knowledge or facts about their subject area but that they should also exhibit critical and independent thinking. Increasingly learners are expected to interact vigorously and critically with content rather than just reproduce parts of it. Entwistle et al. (1992) have characterised this approach as deep learning or learning by transforming knowledge as opposed to surface learning or learning by reproducing knowledge.

Multimedia has much to offer within this context; having the potential to create high quality learning environments. In particular the key elements of multiple media, learner control over the delivery of information and interactivity can be used to enhance the learning process (Cairncross & Mannion, 1999). Mayes (1995) argues learning can only occur as a by-product of understanding and this is best achieved through performing tasks. In the context of multimedia assisted learning this implies interactivity.

However is interactive multimedia fulfilling its promise and leading to better understanding? Rogers & Scaife (1997) point out that many multimedia applications fail to live up their claims of providing enhanced learning environments. Learners often focus on the dynamic elements, for example surfing through video clips, rather than engaging with the material. They argue that greater attention must be paid to designing interactions which are effective in supporting learning i.e. which promote internal cognitive activities, such as reflection. There are few reports explaining how learners actually interact with applications and the resultant learning that can provide a deeper insight into what circumstances learners learn best.

There is a growing emphasis on learner centred approaches to education, through, for example, providing environments in which learners are encouraged to take responsibility for their own learning within a supportive framework (Grabinger & Dunlap, 1995). In creating such environments the interactive multimedia designer has to select from a range of techniques to create an application in which a user is given freedom to explore whilst having guidance where necessary. Whilst some studies have found that such an approach can lead to improvements in learning (Pang & Edmonds, 1999), the efficacy of interactive multimedia applications in promoting deep and meaningful learning needs further investigation. This work will inform the definition of guidelines for the design and integration of such applications based on sound pedagogical principles.

This paper explains some interactive multimedia techniques commonly used for educational applications and describes the results of experiments into learner performance using these techniques. In a first experiment we compared learner performance using three different versions of an interactive multimedia application in which each version contained different levels of interactivity. We called these levels: dynamic exposition, suggested discovery and discovery only. In a second experiment we examined in more detail the effect of contextual factors on the suggested discovery version. Our results show that whilst there is some evidence that the use of interactive multimedia can aid learner learning, its effect and benefits are not as clear cut as its proponents suggest. In particular learners do not always make full use of the available interactive features and contextual factors have a significant impact on performance.

The rest of this paper is organised as follows. Section 2 describes interactive multimedia and learning. Section 3 describes the first experiment, which compared performance using different versions of an application. Section 4 and 5 describe the second experiment, in which the application was redesigned and performance under different learning conditions compared. The results of usability evaluations from both experiments are discussed in Section 6 and the impact of contextual factors explored in Section 7. Conclusions and suggestions for further research are given in Section 8.

2   Interactive Multimedia and Learning

Academic learning is often perceived as an activity in which learners are passive recipients of de-contextualised abstract concepts. However Laurillard (1993) argues in favour of an approach whereby learning is placed in the context of concrete experiences and activities. Interactive multimedia can facilitate this, by providing an integrated environment incorporating exposition, examples, tutorials and simulations.

Interactivity in multimedia assisted learning applications can and should go further than simply allowing a learner to choose their own path through an application by pointing and clicking at various menus items and buttons. If deep learning is to be promoted then an application should actively engage a learner in carrying out tasks which allow them to apply the new knowledge being presented as well as encouraging reflection on that experience. Learners can interact with multimedia packages in many ways, including:

- Selecting or manipulating virtual objects on screen to reveal the outcome of some action.

- Running simulations of experiments and industrial processes.

- Participating in games and role-playing.

- Completing online assessments.

Interactivity allows learning by discovery to take place. It actively engages a learner and allows them to put the new knowledge being presented into practice. For example using a simulation a learner can be supported in viewing the consequences of taking alternative courses of action which lead to both positive and negative outcomes. In virtual experiments, learners can manipulate objects on screen, allowing them to experiment safely, to examine the consequences of taking alternative approaches and to come to a deeper understanding of the subject.. Assessment procedures can then be incorporated into an application and learners can be given instant feedback on their progress to date, strengthening the learning process. The results of online assessments can be stored to file and be accessed at a later date by staff and learners, allowing progress to be monitored.

Many applications (Boyle, 1997; Phillips, 1998) have already been developed which embody interactivity and engage a learner in active learning. The children's edutainment producer, Dorling Kindersley, has produced a number of interactive educational applications for children. In *Castle Explorer* a user can undertake a spying mission in which they have to uncover certain key pieces of information. Such an approach is likely to encourage purposeful navigation in pursuit of facts rather than random browsing. In *I Love Maths* and *I Love Spelling* a user has to compete video-game style against a virtual adversary in order to save the world from destruction. Rogers & Scaife (1997) report on a virtual ecosystem, *PondWorld*, which can be used by children to find out about food chains.

However whilst these packages are successful in engaging the learner in activity and are enjoyable to use, there is little empirical data about how effective the learning is and there are few guidelines for the design of learning activities based on sound pedagogical principles. Aldrich et al. (1998) explore the notion of interactivity further and outline the need to identify in a systematic manner those interactivities which support effective learning and those which are largely gratuitous.

3 Experiment 1: Learning With Different Interactive Multimedia Approaches

In earlier work (Cairncross & Smith, 1999) we found that the inclusion of interactive features does not always lead to deeper learning. A primary aim of this study was to produce guidelines for embedding virtual experiments into a supportive learning framework where guidance, background theory and exercises can be included.

Three versions of an application to teach learners about analogue to digital conversion process were developed. The application was designed to replace a two-hour lecture. One version (dynamic exposition) took an explanation based approach. Animations were used to illustrate the conversion process in order to promote better recall (Faraday & Sutcliffe, 1997). Interactivity was limited to menu selection, and navigation and control over the playback of animations. In many respects this version can be thought of as a dynamic electronic textbook.

The remaining two versions provided the learners with a similar process overview and animations. However one section, concerning digital output quality, was replaced with a virtual converter for the learners to experiment with in order to discover relationships for themselves rather than being presented with a summary of the effects. Active experimentation (Kolb, 1984) is an essential part of the learning process but that experimentation must be purposeful if it is to be successful. As Laurillard (1993) points out discovery learning implies that the learner has some skills as a researcher, and is able to make appropriate mental connections. However some learners may require assistance during their exploration. To address this issue, one version of the virtual converter gave suggestions for areas to explore (suggested discovery), whereas the other did not (discovery only).

A user-centred approach was taken to their development with the design being informed by consideration of general psychological considerations when interacting

Post-test 1 (carried out immediately afterwards)			
Condition	Numbers of Learners	Mean Test Score	Standard Deviation
1 Dynamic Exposition	20	52%	22
2 Suggested Discovery	20	47%	23
3 Discovery Only	25	46%	21
All		48 %	22
Post-test 2 (carried out following week)			
Condition	Numbers of Learners	Mean Test Score	Standard Deviation
1 Dynamic Exposition	9	41%	19
2 Suggested Discovery	9	37%	17
3 Discovery Only	9	45%	24
All		41 %	20

Table 1: Learner results of analogue to digital conversion assessment.

with computers as well as the learning process itself. Usability testing was carried out by contextual observation, getting feedback from learners and heuristic evaluation by practitioners. This ensured that each version was of a comparable standard without any major design flaws which could impact on understanding.

Learners who were taking a Level 2 undergraduate module in Industrial Systems were divided into three groups on a matched basis and each group was assigned to one of the three versions on a random basis. The learners then worked through the application in a tutorial session. On completion a post-test about analogue to digital conversion was administered to measure immediate learning. A second post-test was carried out the following week in order to measure retention.

On analysing the test results (Table 1), no significant differences in performance between the three groups emerged. Learners using the dynamic exposition version actually did best in Post-test 1. In all cases performance deteriorated between the two tests, reflecting normal patterns of forgetfulness. Students using the discovery only version appear to have retained more than the other groups but they started with a lower score in Post-test 1. It would be wrong to conclude from the results that interactivity does not lead to better learning performance, only that it does not always automatically do so.

Most learners spent between 30 and 60 minutes using the application. It can be argued deep learning cannot take place in a tutorial session by itself and would have to be complemented by further study and opportunities to apply the knowledge gained and reflect on that experience. External or environmental factors can also influence the outcome.

On completing the application learners were asked to fill in a usability questionnaire using a five point Likert scale (Table 3). In general the feedback was positive in that the overwhelming majority of learners (93%) either agreed or strongly agreed that they found the application easy to use. 58% of learners enjoyed using the application.

60% of learners across all three versions agreed or strongly agreed that they now had a good understanding of the topic with 9% disagreeing and the remainder remaining neutral. 87% of learners felt that the animation illustrating key stages of the conversion process helped their understanding. However as the mean test score was below 50% these results must be treated with some caution and are perhaps more suggestive that the learners were not good judges of their own ability. This may be a general trait or it may have been that the application lulled them into a false sense of security.

Moreover even though the majority (72%) of learners using the two versions with the virtual experiment felt that the ability to experiment helped their understanding, there is no evidence that this is indeed the case. It is possible that any interaction was at a physical level of changing the setting and passively watching the results rather than actively engaging with the content and using the experiment in a systematic manner.

A majority of learners (68%) agreed that they would like to use more interactive multimedia learning application although only 58% said that they would definitely use this application when revising. Selected interviews revealed that learners value personal contact with tutors and other learners, and would prefer to use such applications in a computer based tutorial rather than in isolation at home, a finding which is in keeping with other studies (Davidson & Goldfinch, 1998).

4   Experiment 2: Learning Performance and Context of Use

In a second experiment we examined the contribution of the context of use on successful learning. Draper et al. (1995) highlighted the need to take an integrative approach when investigating the efficacy of learning technologies stressing that learning in higher education depends on the whole teaching and learning environment not just the material itself. The situation of use can impact on performance. Integration into the curriculum needs to be considered as well as the design of the application itself (Milne & Heath, 1997). One of the benefits of interactive multimedia learning applications is that it can allow the learner to study at a time and place convenient to them, thereby reducing class contact. However, as discussed previously, many learners prefer to use learning applications in a classroom setting. It is not clear however whether meeting this preference leads to better performance. It was decided to focus on a single version of the application and to compare the performance of learners who had been introduced the application in class time compared to those who had not. To maintain consistency with the previous experiment the application was used to replace a lecture.

We chose to modify the suggested discovery version of the analogue to digital conversion application. This approach was chosen, as, despite our earlier findings, it is believed to be potentially the most beneficial to learners. For example Grabinger & Dunlap (1995) describe the benefits that active discovery approaches can bring. Other studies that have found improved learning performance with learners using a guided discovery approach (Pang & Edmonds, 1999). We revised the application, by extending its scope and adding extra features:

- Online assessment.

- Section on practical examples.

- Second virtual experiment.

- Improved graphics.

- Pause and Reflect questions.

The section on online assessment was added in response to feedback from focus groups. It offers the learner an opportunity to test and receive feedback on their understanding. The section on practical examples of analogue to digital converters was also added in order to make the theory less abstract by relating it to practice. The second virtual experiment was added to allow learners to observe the effect of changing the sampling rate in the frequency domain in order to assist learners in visualising the effects of aliasing, a concept which many learners find difficult.

A number of learners who had used the previous version had commented that whilst they found the interface easy to use, aesthetically they found it uninspiring. The graphical layout was also improved with better quality graphics, customised buttons and an improved colour scheme. Some of these graphical layout modifications were prototyped before the experiment, shown to learners and modified as a result of feedback.

Attention was also directed at incorporating features, including pause and reflect questions, that would encourage learners to cognitively engage with the material being presented. Vygotsky (1962; 1978) argued individuals absorb new knowledge from the outside world through internalisation. New information is often best made sense of and absorbed through considering it from different angles, through thinking it over, either through internal dialogue or discussion with others. Reflection is crucial for internalisation to occur. To this end a series of 'pause and reflect' interactions were incorporated into the application. Clicking on these revealed a question which was intended to encourage the learner to reflect on what they had just been learning, Having done so they could then reveal the answer. An attempt was also made to promote discussion on the content. For example in the section on online assessment learners were asked to discuss their answers to questions fellow classmates or to seek advice from a class tutor where they had got the answer wrong and where unsure as to why.

The revised learning application was then used by a new group of undergraduate learners taking the Level 2 module on Industrial Systems. This time the class was divided on a matched basis into two groups, with group A being asked to come along to their normal timetabled tutorial to use the application followed by self-study and group B being asked to use the application on a self-study basis only. The application was made available from both internal university networks and the World Wide Web.

Selected learners from group A were observed when using the application to understand how they made use of interactive features and whether they were truly

	Numbers of Learners	Mean Test Score	Standard Deviation
Industrial Systems: Post-test 1			
	25	43%	21
Industrial Systems: Post-test 2			
Condition			
Group A: Tutorial and Self Study	11	34%	15
Group B: Self Study Only	7	30%	12
Multimedia Technology: Post-test 2			
	45	45%	14

Table 2: Learner results of analogue to digital conversion assessment using enhanced suggested discovery multimedia application.

engaging with the content or not. Such an insight can assist in designing scenarios to support active learning. All learners in that group were given a post test immediately afterwards (the same test that learners in the first experiment were given). Learners from group A were also asked to complete a usability questionnaire. We compared performance and attitude of learners using the enriched version of the application with that of those using the original version.

Two weeks after the start of the trial all learners sat the second post-test to compare performance between the two conditions. Although this was the same second post-test as used in the previous experiment care was taken in comparing performance with the learners in the first cohort as both the application used and the experimental conditions were different.

A parallel study was also conducted with another group of learners taking a module on Multimedia Technology, comprised of mainly post-graduate learners on a conversion masters programme with a small number of direct entrants into the third year of undergraduate programmes. These learners essentially did the same as Group A above except that they did not sit the first post-test, due to time constraints.

Over 80 learners are registered on the Industrial Systems module. 28 learners from Group A took part in the laboratory based sessions with 11 of those doing the second post-test. 3 learners declined to do the first post-test. Only 7 learners from Group B sat the second post-test. 45 out of the 100 plus learners registered on the Multimedia Technology module sat the test. Results relating to performance are given in Table 2.

5 Exploring Interactivity

Learners in Group A spent on average 45 to 90 minutes using the application in the tutorial sessions, compared with 30 to 60 minutes for those using the original version. However this did not result in improved performance. Learners using the revised version scored an average of 43% in Post-test 1 afterwards compared to a combined average of 48% in the previous cohort.

This may be because the increased time was not necessarily spent in interactivity or cognitive activity. The majority of learners did not have enough time in the laboratory session to work through the online assessment, analysis of tracking data reveals that learners on average spent a quarter of their time when using the application in the section on practical examples, a section with supplementary material that was not tested and which involved no interactivity, save advancing through the content and reading it.

Learners using the revised application were found to make more use of the virtual experiments. Tracking data reveals that on average learners reset the time based simulation 11.5 times and the frequency simulation 3.5 times, compared to an average of 8.6 times for the previous version. These observations suggested that initially learners were exploring the interface to discover how the virtual experiment worked rather than systematically exploring and comparing different settings. Analysis of individual questions revealed learners using the revised application did considerably better in questions relating to aliasing, scoring an average of 44% compared to 33% with the previous version. The interactive graphical representation afforded by the virtual frequency domain experiment appears to have improved understanding of this particular aspect.

Whilst the majority of learners selected the 'pause and reflect' option, none of them actually paused to reflect — they all read the question and then immediately selected the button to reveal the answer. One can lead a learner to cognitive activities but this in itself does not guarantee that they will think. One option would be to include a delay effect so that the answer cannot be revealed until a certain amount of time has passed. However this takes control away from the learner and could prove irritating and counterproductive. Moreover there is no guarantee that the time would be spent on reflection.

Learners worked through the application in a linear fashion, starting with the introduction and working through each section in turn, completing one section before commencing the next. This approach may not necessarily be the most efficient or effective. As discussed previously learners in the second study spent much of their initial time in the laboratory on a supplementary section, which was not being assessed at that stage. It would appear that learners require guidance in making most effective use of their time, particularly when that time is limited.

The focus groups from experiment one revealed that learners preferred to use such applications in a classroom setting rather than on their own. Learners particularly valued the opportunity to seek advice when unsure about something. However the observations in the laboratory revealed that by and large the learners worked through the application on their own, and only a minority sought advice from the tutors present or fellow class mates. Whilst the presence of the observers may have prevented this it would appear that a valuable opportunity for discussion is being lost and perhaps performance would be improved if learners were asked to work through the application together. One pair of learners were asked to do this and whilst they spent less time using the application they did discuss the 'pause and reflect' questions before revealing the answer.

	1998 Study (65 learners)			1999 Study (28 learners)		
Question	A/SA	N	D/DS	A/SA	N	D/DS
I found this application easy to use	93	8	0	86	7	7
I enjoyed using application	58	33	9	57	18	25
I now have a good understanding of analogue to digital conversion	60	31	9	29	46	25
I found the extra features (help, glossary, study guide,) helpful.	88	5	8	64	11	25
The animations helped me understand the subject better	87	8	6	74	19	7
I felt in control of my learning at all times	72	20	8	50	36	14
I would like to use more interactive multimedia learning applications	68	23	10	46	25	29
I will use this application when revising	57	27	16	71	14	14
I found Virtual Analogue to Digital Converter easy to use	78	22	0	59	26	15
I feel that the ability to experiment has helped me understand this subject better	72	25	3	52	33	15
I found the online assessment section helpful				56	30	15
I found that the online questions helped me test my understanding				74	7	19

A = agree, SA = strongly agree, N = neither agree or disagree, D = disagree, SD = strongly disagree, all figures are percentages not all rows add up to 100 due to rounding.

Table 3: Summary of usability evaluations.

6   Usability Evaluation

In addition to assessing educational performance feedback, learners' attitudes to using both version of the application was also sought. The results are summarised in Table 3.

The redesigned application with its higher production values did not lead to increased levels of enjoyment and indeed 25% of the learners using the new version disagreed with the statement "I enjoyed using the application" compared to only 9% of those using the original version. This may be linked to ease of use in that no learners from the first study disagreed with the statement "I found this application easy to use" whereas a small minority from the second study did so. Similar attitudes were also found with regard to using the virtual converters.

The second group may also have felt more challenged by the version they used; it was wider in scope and more complex. As Gilmore (1995) point out maximising ease of use for educational applications may be counterproductive and learners can actually perform better when faced with more challenging interfaces. Moreover, whilst the second group of learners expressed less satisfaction with using the application the majority did realise that further work was required: 29% agreed with the statement "I now have a good understanding of Analogue to Digital Conversion" and 25% disagreeing, compared to 60% and 9% respectively for the previous version. Given the relatively poor performance of both groups in the post-tests this at least is a more realistic assessment of their learning.

Usability in this context is complex. It is not enough for learning applications to be easy to learn to use; they must also be easy to learn from. Davies & Brailsford (1994) term the latter educatability, which is measures a product's educational effectiveness, as distinct from learnability, which measures the ease with which the product functions are learned and remembered. Others (Draper et al., 1994; Milne & Heath, 1997) also recognise the need to evaluate both the human–computer interface and educational effectiveness.

Deep learning requires effort on that the part of the learner. Moreover this is unlikely to occur in a single session. Bahrich & Phelps (1987) found that spacing this effort over a period of time (distributed practice), leads to better subsequent recall than achieved with massed practice, that is when sessions are crammed all together at once. Whilst an application may not be universally liked or immediately understood it can be more effective if learners realise that they have not covered the material in a single session and recognise that further study is required.

However it is not enough for learners to realise that further study is required, the must also carry out that further study. This does not always happen and so the context of use must also be considered.

7 Contextual Factors

As can be seen from Table 2, the performance of learners on the Industrial Systems module in the second post-test was considerably worse than that of learners on the Multimedia Technology module. This can be attributed to differences in the learner populations taking the two modules and to differences in the timing of the trials.

The application was used with learners on the Multimedia Technology module in Weeks 3 and 4 of the semester, prior to many courseworks being handed out, whereas it was used in Weeks 8 to 10 with learners on the Industrial Systems module, when a number of courseworks were due to be handed in. It is likely therefore that the learners in the former group had the time to follow up their initial session in the tutorial with self-study whereas learners in the later group concentrated on more pressing concerns.

A survey of learners at the last Industrial Systems lecture at the end of term bears this out. Attendance was much lower than average at 19 and of those only 6 (32%) had used the application for self-study. Of the remainder, the majority cited lack of time as the main reason why they had not yet used the application. One learner commented that the reason they had not used it was "because I have not yet started revision", which suggests a strategic approach to learning. Only 2 of the 13 learners who had not used the application gave dislike of interactive learning applications as their reason for not using it.

It appears that learners on the Industrial Systems module performed poorly not because of deficiencies in the application itself but because they were not sufficiently motivated to use it, primarily due to other demands on their time. Interviews with learners also revealed that some learners prefer the discipline of coming to classes and they find this easier than managing their own time.

Learners from the second group, not only had fewer demands on their time, but also were primarily enrolled on multimedia programmes as opposed to more general computing programmes. This perhaps gave then an added impetus for using the application: to examine and explore an interactive learning application, as well as learning about the topic. Even so with an average of 45% it hardly be argued that they all came to a deep understanding of the application.

A key challenge facing designers of interactive learning applications is how best to motivate learners so that deep learning is encouraged. The design and delivery of instructional material can impact on this. In particular Entwistle et al. (1992) found that overloading a course with content tends to induce surface approaches to learning whereas courses where learners experience freedom in learning and which introduce learners to the broader aspects of their discipline appear to encourage a deep approach. Moreover resistance to new ways of studying and learning may be greater when learners are feeling overloaded.

If interactive multimedia is going to be used to its full potential then its integration into the curriculum must carefully be considered. Failure to do so may result in it not being used regardless of well it is designed.

8 Conclusions

Multimedia offers many benefits, in particular multiple media, delivery control and interactivity, and has the potential to provide high quality learning environments. Whilst it is important that the design of interactive learning applications should be informed by HCI theory and learning considerations this in itself is not enough to guarantee its effectiveness from an educational point of view. Our findings indicate that it is not enough to provide interactive features, such as virtual experiments or reflective questions, as many learners do not make full use of them, requiring support to do so. Whilst learners are interacting with the learning applications our studies indicate that they are not always actively engaging with the material. Further work is required to determine why this is the case and how best to promote their use. Options which we plan to explore involve setting learners a task or problem to solve and providing the learning application as a resource to assist them in doing so and encouraging learners to work collaboratively when using the application.

We have also found that motivation impacts on learning and it may be that some learning applications are failing learners not because the applications themselves are deficient but because the learners lack the motivation to use them due to competing demands on their time. It is also possible that learners require additional support in learning how to learn from interactive learning applications.

Further research is needed, both into the efficacy of interactive learning applications and also into how learners are actually engaging with and learning from the material. We need to consistently design applications which truly engage the learner, so that they are interacting with the content as well as the application and integrate them into the curriculum so that they are used to the full by learners.

Acknowledgements

The authors would like to thank Sun-Hea Choi for her work in redeveloping the application and all the learners who took part in the studies.

References

Aldrich, F., Rogers, Y. & Scaife, M. (1998), "Getting to Grips with Interactivity: Helping Teachers Assess the Educational Value of CD-Roms", *British Journal of Educational Technology* **29**(4), 321–32.

Bahrich, H. P. & Phelps, E. (1987), "Retention of Spanish Vocabulary Over Eight Years", *Journal of Experimental Psychology: Learning, Memory and Cognition* **13**, 344–9.

Boyle, T. (1997), *Design for Multimedia Learning*, Prentice–Hall.

Cairncross, S. & Mannion, M. (1999), "How Multimedia Functions in Engineering", *Engineering Science & Education Journal* **8**(3), 100–7.

Cairncross, S. & Smith, S. (1999), Integrating Interactive Multimedia Into The Curriculum, *in Proceedings of 16th International Conference on Technology and Education.*

CSUP (1992), Teaching and Learning in an Expanding Higher Education System: A Report of a Working Party of the Committee of Scottish University Principals, Technical Report, SCFC Edinburgh.

Davidson, K. & Goldfinch, J. (1998), How to Add VALUE in Evaluation Studies, Learning Technology Dissemination Initiative, Technical Report, Heriot-Watt University Edinburgh.

Davies, P. & Brailsford, T. (1994), Guidelines for Multimedia Courseware Developers in Higher Education Volume 1: Delivery, Production and Provision, Technical Report, UCoSDA, University of Nottingham.

Draper, S. W., Brown, M. I., Edgerton, E., Henderson, F. P., McAteer, E., Smith, E. D. & Watt, H. D. (1994), Observing and Measuring the Performance of Educational Technology, TLTP Report, Technical Report, University of Glasgow.

Draper, S. W., Henderson, F. P., Brown, M. I. & McAteer, E. (1995), "Integrative Evaluation: An Emerging Role for Classroom Studies of CAL", *Journal of Computers and Education* **26**(1–3), 17–32.

Entwistle, N., Thomson, S. & Tait, H. (1992), Guidelines for Promoting Effective Learning in Higher Education, Technical Report, Centre for Research on Learning and Instruction, University of Edinburgh.

Faraday, P. & Sutcliffe, A. (1997), Multimedia: Design for the Moment, *in* J. D. Hollan & J. D. Foley (eds.), *Proceedings of Multimedia'97*, ACM Press, pp.183–92.

Gilmore, D. (1995), Interface Design: Have We Got it Wrong?, *in* K. Nordby, P. H. Helmersen, D. J. Gilmore & S. A. Arnessen (eds.), *Human–Computer Interaction — INTERACT '95: Proceedings of the Fifth IFIP Conference on Human–Computer Interaction*, Chapman & Hall.

Grabinger, S. & Dunlap, J. (1995), "Rich Environments for Active Learning: A Definition", *Association for Learning Technology Journal* **3**(2), 5–34.

Kolb, D. (1984), *Experiential Learning: Experiences as the Source of Learning and Development*, Prentice–Hall.

Laurillard, D. (1993), *Rethinking University Teaching: A Framework for the Effective Use of Educational Technology*, Routledge.

Mayes, J. T. (1995), Learning Technolgy and Groundhog Day, *in* W. Strang, V. Simpson & D. Slater (eds.), *Hypermedia at Work: Practice and Theory in Education*, University of Kent Press, pp.21–37.

Milne, J. & Heath, S. (1997), Evaluation Handbook For Successful CAL Courseware Development, Technical Report, University of Aberdeen.

Pang, K. W. & Edmonds, E. A. (1999), Modelling the Learner in a World Wide Web Guided Discovery Hypertext Learning Environment in Human–Computer Interaction, *in* A. Sasse & C. Johnson (eds.), *Human–Computer Interaction — INTERACT '99: Proceedings of the Seventh IFIP Conference on Human–Computer Interaction*, Vol. 1, IOS Press, pp.597–604.

Phillips, R. (1998), *The Developers Handbook to Interactive Multimedia: A Practical Guide for Educational Applications*, Kogan Page.

Rogers, Y. & Scaife, M. (1997), How Can Interactive Multimedia Facilitate Learning, *in* J. Lee (ed.), *Proceedings of First International Workshop on Intelligence and Multimodalities in Multimedia*, The Live Oak Press, pp.123–42.

Vygotsky, L. S. (1962), *Thought and Language*, MIT Press.

Vygotsky, L. S. (1978), *Mind In Society. The Development of Higher Psychological Processes*, Harvard University Press.

Low Cost Remote Evaluation for Interface Prototyping

Lynne Dunckley, Dean Taylor, Malcolm Storey & Andy Smith[†]

The Open University, Walton Hall, Milton Keynes MK7 6AA, UK

Tel: *+44 1908 652 349*
EMail: *L.Dunckley@open.ac.uk*

[†] *University of Luton, Park Square, Luton, Bedfordshire LU1 3JU, UK*

The increasing incidence of distributed information systems has led to the requirement for remote usability evaluations. The development of network systems and the Internet has created both the necessity and the opportunity to involve remote users much earlier in the development cycle. This paper describes the application of remote evaluation methods to the rapid prototyping development of a software product. The methods used include critical incident reporting, electronic questionnaires and written current protocols for asynchronous remote evaluation used in a context centred manner.

Keywords: remote usability evaluation, rapid prototyping, Internet, written current protocols.

1 Introduction

Information systems are being developed to support increasingly complex and unstructured tasks. Many of these systems are distributed, involving geographically remote users. The growth of network and particularly Web technology means users are communicating with central systems using a wide range of machines and operating systems. Developers of these systems often have limited access to representative users for usability testing in laboratories and the cost of transporting users and evaluators to remote locations can be prohibitive. The network itself and the remote work setting are also intrinsic parts of the system which produce usage patterns that are difficult to reproduce in a laboratory setting.

This paper describes a method for low cost remote evaluation (LCR) in the context of incremental design and its application to the development of a real-world software product. The LCR method attempts to capture the users' response to prototype interfaces in a contextual manner and provides a framework to simulate a remote conversation between the developer and the user. The next sections describe previous research that strongly influenced the development.

1.1   Remote Evaluation Approaches

Networks such as the Internet and the Web make it possible to distribute prototypes rapidly at low cost to large numbers of users, linked to groupware technologies such as news groups and e-mail lists. Several researchers (Hartson et al., 1996) have already noted these opportunities to create remote evaluation systems. In general two types of data collection have been used. Firstly the *subjective approach* can range from user reports, user-identified 'critical incidents' to questionnaires, interviews and ethnographic techniques. Secondly the *objective approach* involves automatically collecting data (for example counts, sequence, timing of actions) through audio and video recording, conferencing; automatic software and psychological event monitoring.

It is possible to collect such large amounts of feedback that this causes a problem in terms of time and resources needed to sift through to extract key parts. Although objective methods capture detailed feedback information that is difficult to collect by subjective methods, many methods need one-to-one observer-user resources which makes them resource intensive. Another problem is the context, which is vital to interpret the meaning of the users' actions, is missing.

A key benefit of the subjective approach is the ability to capture aspects of the users' needs, thought processes and subjective experiences which are difficult to collect using the objective approach. Subjective data needs expert interpretation. Users, it has been suggested, speculate on problems that may be encountered by others and anticipate problems even when these are unfounded and not supported by the evidence. Although there are problems with this approach, particularly if the intention is to collect usability issues and not merely list software bugs we concluded that a subjective remote evaluation approach should be investigated which would:

- Capture the user's experience in a real world context.

- Collect users' subjective experience as they actually used the interface.

- Prompt the user remotely and asynchronously.

- Constrain the user's reports to actually experience and not speculation.

1.2   Critical Incident Reports

The application of critical incident reports to remote evaluation has been described by Hartson and co-workers. Castillo et al. (1998) introduced the concept of user-reported critical incident gathering as a method based on previous work about critical incident reports (Hartson et al., 1996) where each contextualised report was sent asynchronously to a network queue for evaluators. The results showed users were capable of self-reporting high, medium and low severity critical incidents encountered during task performance. With minimum training users could recognise and report critical incidents effectively and rank their severity reasonably well. Self-reporting does not interfere with users getting real work done, according to Hartson et al. (1996), who concluded that the identification of critical incidents is the single most important information associated with task performance in a usability-oriented context. This information is lost in the objective approach because it is not captured immediately as it arises. The objective approach, it is argued, consists of applying complex pattern recognition to regain a small portion of the lost information. Hartson et al. (1996) reasoned that processing this data in search of usability problems is like looking for a needle in a haystack. Critical incidents are an attempt to get the users to deliver the needles directly.

Hartson et al. (1996) found that when experts analysed the user feedback without knowing what the user was trying to do, the experts had difficulty guessing what was happening and identifying associated usability problems. Comparing remote and laboratory based evaluation, the principal problem exposed in their study was the need to prompt the users continually for the verbal protocol that is so essential for establishing task context and to know what the user was trying to do and why the users were having trouble. When asked for a running commentary the users did not speak much without prompting. This problem is exacerbated by remote evaluation since the experimenters were not present and they concluded there was a clear need for user prompting.

This paper describes the evaluation of a prototype using the LCR as part of an incremental design involving remote users. The evaluation combined a novel subjective method with critical incident reports. The results of the evaluation and factors which might influence the effectiveness of the method are discussed.

1.3   Basis of the Method

There are two key activities involved in this approach which was based on a method reported by Smith et al. (1999) for the evaluation of high fidelity prototypes linked to the subsequent redesign process. Firstly 'developer-user contextual inquiry' (DUCE) sessions involve users interacting with working or semi-working prototypes in real-life scenarios while verbalising their experience. Following the DUCE sessions experts extract significant user comments relevant to usability issues from the transcripts of the audio video records of the DUCE sessions. Secondly within 'team evidence analysis' (TEA) sessions the evidence extracted is discussed and refined by a team of developers into design factors for the next prototype.

There are a number of methods that are variously known by the terms think-aloud, verbal protocol and cooperative evaluation. Many experts recommend thinking-aloud for most ordinary applications. Cooperative evaluation is a variation of thinking-aloud in which the user is encouraged to see himself as a collaborator in the evaluation rather than just a subject. This is claimed to be less constrained and the user is encouraged to actively criticise the system by the evaluator who is not necessarily the designer. An experimental study was reported by Wright & Monk

For each task/goal
  Ask the user to explain what he / she is attempting
  For each sub task
    Ask the user to explain what he / she is attempting
    For each stage in Norman's model of interaction
    Consider asking a question from the check list
    Next stage
  Next sub task
Next task

Figure 1: Eliciting user comments in a DUCE Session.

(1991) in which the conversational approach was contrasted with the pure think-aloud procedure in terms of the number of usability problems identified. However a significant factor in the maintenance of human-human dialogue appears to be the expertise of the participants. Falzon (1990) describes dialogues between experts and non-experts (e.g. patient–doctor) which are analogous to developer-user situations where the expert speaker soon assumes control of the conversation and the remaining exchange of information follows a sequence of 'yes/no' questions and answers. This is in contrast with the situation where the expert perceives the other speaker as expert in the domain. Another problem is highlighted by Goguen (1996) who criticises such 'think-aloud' methods as 'unnatural' for the reason that language is intrinsically social; it is created for a conversational partner. As a result a person imagines a partner with certain desires and tries to address these desires, at the expense of accuracy and reliability.

The DUCE approach is based on integrating contextual inquiry approaches (Holtzblatt & Jones, 1993; Beyer & Holtzblatt, 1998) with think-aloud methods with the particular aim of promoting developer-user conversations which the developer does not dominate. A key part of the method is the establishment of a conversation between the user and the developer supported by a series of questions structured within Norman's seven stages of action. The overall process is as shown in Figure 1. Video and audio recordings of the DUCE sessions are made, and these provide the evidence on which the key design factors are derived. Investigations of variations of this basic method had led to conclusions that DUCE sessions provide rich sources of user evidence for prototype enhancement and that TEA sessions were more effective than individual developer introspection.

We adapted this method for low cost remote evaluation to test the method with a real-world case study. This would involve changing the nature of the DUCE sessions to collect data of the same richness remotely. For reasons that will become clear the new method can be called the 'write-along DUCE' approach.

2 Electronic Assessment Case Study

The Open University is the major provider of distance-learning education at university level in the UK and Europe. A continuous assessment system is a major vehicle in delivering the distance learning. Students complete between 3 and 7 tutor marked assessments (TMAs) for each course. These are marked by associate lecturers usually located in the same geographic area as their students; the results are returned to the Open University and extensive feedback is returned to each student with the script. The feedback takes the form of annotations (ticks, comments and marks e.g. 5/12) and an overall comment is also attached to each script identifying strengths, weaknesses and future action. The provision of feedback is much more crucial for distance learners since this replaces face-to-face tutorials.

Over the last few years the Open University has been moving to delivering course and assessment material to students via the Internet and e-mail systems. An e-TMA system was developed to handle script submission and return, and additional 'marking tool' software has been developed to assist the on-screen marking of scripts. As part of the on-going development of this system its functionality and usability is being reviewed. The e-TMA system can be viewed as a decision support system that is designed to support markers in their tasks of evaluating students' work and providing feedback.

The case study describes the use of remote evaluation within an incremental design to produce a new marking tool. The software development was subject to considerable organisational pressure as the new marking tool was required for the next course presentations. The evaluation provided a number of challenges. The lecturers operate on a part-time basis, often work in evenings and weekends, usually from their home. The Open University recommends a Windows 95 platform, but in practice users may be connected by machines running any of the Windows operating systems, and some may be using Windows emulators on other operating systems.

3 Design of the Remote Evaluation Package

The new Marking Tool system would be a separate tool which would work with Microsoft Word or in stand-alone mode to capture scores and feedback for non-text e-TMAs such as HTML and graphical files. After considering the options that were feasible in the time scale and with the equipment available, it was decided that the incremental development should be divided into two phases. The first phase would focus on an initial prototype which would not be fully functional but would have sufficient functionality and interface structure (menus, icons, buttons) to test the concept in some detail, focusing on usability, spatial layout and navigation. This prototype would be evaluated using the modification of the DUCE session and the design refined through TEA sessions. The second phase would evaluate a fully functional prototype which would incorporate the changes made in the light of the previous evaluation. The evaluation of the second prototype would be mainly based on the use of a usability questionnaire. In addition it was decided to incorporate ideas presented by Hartson et al. (1996) on critical incident reports.

Both prototypes would be e-mailed to the users as installation files, together with sample unmarked e-TMAs and the remote evaluation package. A range of different typical e-TMAs was provided. The initial prototype did not include the functionality to up-load and down-load e-TMAs to the central system via the auto-zipping functions. The evaluation and the rebuild were scheduled five weeks apart to meet organisational requirements.

3.1   Design of Remote Data Collection

There were a number of constraints on the nature of data collection which influenced the adaptation of the DUCE sessions. These included practical difficulties in using verbal protocols remotely with this kind of user. Previous remote evaluation experiments tend to have taken place in organisational settings, with a single group of remote users in their normal work environment which could to some extent be controlled, and where audio and video equipment could be set up. In contrast the e-TMA Marking Tool involved individual users who where geographically widely distributed. Their social context is usually the home, with background family noise. Video recording and video conferencing were not feasible options as most of the users would not have equipment, and previous experiments with low cost video conferencing using *Netmeeting* had highlighted problems particularly with audio quality. Problems with low cost software utilities have also been reported by Shah et al. (1998) when they investigated practical use of multimedia tools available for communication and collaboration on the Internet between remote users. They found problems linking audio tools (e.g. Freetel and PowWow) with other applications since speed of processing of the tools were greatly reduced.

The possibility of using verbal protocols through telephone links was also considered but there were problems both because this would have disrupted the users' work, and made communication with the evaluator, who could not see the interface, difficult. Asynchronous evaluation would also be an advantage because of the time distribution of the users' work patterns. In view of this, it was decided to simulate the 'think-aloud DUCE' method by converting the DUCE session to an electronic form in which the users would write their responses while interacting with the prototype. However there was concern that the actual process would cause the users to proceed differently so that the usability problems encountered would not be genuine. The remote evaluation package comprised three sections:

- Detailed evaluation form.

- Critical incident report form.

- Summary form of nine open-ended evaluation questions.

The questions used in the framework were modified from those prepared by Carroll & Rosson (1991) for scenario based design and are structured under Norman's seven stages of action model. This cognitive model was chosen because it includes goal — action — feedback, which was considered to be particularly suited to interface evaluation in the context of design decisions. The overall process remained as presented in Figure 1. For each window the questions were tailored to link the window to its intended task. The task scenario consisted of four tasks:

- Selecting courses and scripts to mark.

- Setting part marks for the standard mark scheme.

- Marking sample scripts.

Norman's Stage	Remote Evaluation Questions
Form a goal	How does the screen help you select a way of achieving your task?
Form an intention	What is the most important information visible when you start to allocate the score and make comments?
Specify the action sequence	How does the Score Allocation window make it obvious how to allocate scores and make comments?
Execute the action	
Perceive the resultant system state	How has the Score Allocation window changed in order to show what you have achieved?
Interpret the resultant state	How do you know what you have done is correct
Evaluate the outcome.	How would you recognise any mistakes? What action would you take to correct any mistakes?

Figure 2: Remote evaluation framework — sample questions.

- Saving completed marked scripts.

The task scenarios used were not action specific so facilitating user flexibility in goal selection. With each task a number of questions were provided which the users were asked to answer while carrying out the tasks, not retrospectively and were given the option of completing these online in Word or printing the forms and completing them manually. Sample questions adapted to the write-along method are shown in Figure 2.

3.2   First Prototype Design

The design of the Marking Tool prototype had been subject to some conflicting objectives. The software would need to be operated with the minimum of support and technical backup by the remote users. The usage pattern would be one of fairly long gaps followed by intensive use for short periods. Visibility and affordance of design were therefore crucial issues. The Marking Tool consisted of four different windows which worked in conjunction with a Word document window displaying the e-TMA. The most complex tasks were associated with the Score Allocation window (shown in Figure 3). The user is required to enter the score and can then attach a comment to each score. (The score and the comment are automatically embedded in the Word document at the position of the cursor.) When marking manually this order is not crucial and could even interleave but in the interface the score had to be entered first, followed by the comment. This was a sound design rationale because the score is essential and the comment optional and the user could forget to add the score. However the importance of this action sequence needed to be conveyed to the user. Another problem was associated with the visibility of the comments. With the previous version it had been discovered that extensive comments could disrupt the format and display of the e-TMA returned to the student. In an attempt to address this, comments could be embedded so that they could be glimpsed when the cursor passed over the score in the Word document.

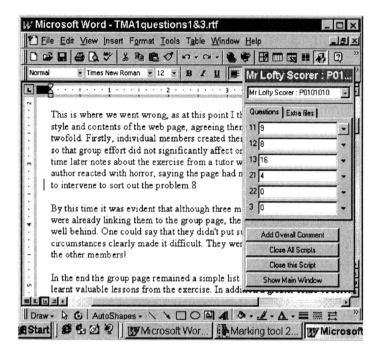

Figure 3: Word and score allocation window.

It was decided that the users would not be issued with a user guide because we wanted the investigation to focus on the affordance and visibility of the interface and not be influenced by the quality of a user guide. This was a difficult decision since the remote evaluation would not provide the guidance usually available from an evaluator to a participant in cooperative evaluation. The users were asked to complete the tasks but deliberately not told how to use the Marking Tool to accomplish the tasks. The users would have to rely on past experience, the task context and the information provided by the interface itself, although a help-line was available. The remote evaluation package was piloted within the development team before it was used and it was decided that the prototype was sufficiently robust for the exercise to be feasible. The package also included a critical incident report form and a brief outline of what a critical incident was and how to rate it. The report asked the users which windows were open at the time the incident took place but there was no screen or video capture. Fourteen volunteers completed the evaluation.

4 Results of Remote Evaluation

The remote evaluation and subsequent TEA session identified a significant number of usability problems leading to the identification of a large number of design changes. After these were implemented a second prototype was evaluated remotely using an electronic usability questionnaire. The second evaluation showed that

Window	Design/usability issues	Critical incidents	Design changes
1 Select Assignment	4		5
2 Marking Tool	10	1	9
3 Main Window	7		6
4 Score Allocation	17	1 med; 2 high	17
Total	38	4	37

Table 1: Summary of usability problems identified.

the improvement to the design had been significant and that the second prototype was much easier to use and achieved much higher levels of user satisfaction. The refined product is now in use. Having established the overall success of the remote evaluation method it was decided to look at the method itself in more detail, particularly the users' responses to establish factors which could influence its effectiveness and user acceptance.

4.1 Detailed Analysis of Users' Responses

Based on data extracted from the analysis of user comments, Table 1 summarises the number of separate design issues/usability problems identified by the design team during the TEA session. The same issues were identifiable from many comments. Table 1 shows the number of critical incidents reported, and the design changes, grouped by each window. The contribution of the critical incident reports is discussed later.

Most usability problems identified were derived from the remote DUCE responses; 81 design issues in total, 38 separate usability problems. The majority of users' comments read convincingly as though written while looking and exploring the screen. They had a 'stream-of-consciousness' quality. It was interesting that these users were not inhibited in expressing themselves in writing (Table 2) and were not paying attention to grammatical expression or spelling. This lack of inhibition is a well-known phenomenon in email when communication is similarly spontaneous.

4.2 Review of Effectiveness of Remote Evaluation

In order to consider the effectiveness of the adaptation of the DUCE sessions to what became an asynchronous write-along style, the evaluation framework and results were reviewed. We were concerned that interactive communication studies reported that pairs of subjects who solved problems through communication by sound only, exchanged ten times the number of messages compared with those who communicated in writing — reflecting the inconvenience of writing and the consequent need for economy of expression (Chapanis et al., 1972). Therefore, we used the word count of the users' responses as an indication of the richness of evidence and their ability to express what they thought about using the interface in writing. The word count could be compared with the usefulness of the responses in terms of the ease with which design/usability problems could be identified in the TEA session, giving an indication of its efficiency. The word count of every user for

Q1	*How does the score allocation window help you select a way of achieving your task.*
User 1	It gives you a box for each question.
User 2	It provides spaces for the marks to be written in and it specifies what part/question the marks are for. I was confused by the option 'Go to Question' as I thought it would reposition the cursor against the appropriate question number that was selected.
Q2	*How does the Score Allocation window make it obvious how to allocate scores and make comments?*
User 1	I am not sure it does. Zero in box made me experiment with putting score in and I discovered that if you clicked on arrow that this helped you position score in script.
User 2	There is a question tab at the top of the list of numbers for that question. The window shows a list of marks against a list of text fields. It seemed obvious to insert marks in the text fields and against each of the marks listed. To add a comment the arrow is raised and the text box is displayed whenever you scroll over it.
User 3	Well, no I'm not sure. Your marking tool is confused. Blast. I pressed Yes for 'I am sure' and now it has put the mark in a silly place in the script.
Q3	*What is the most important information visible when you start to allocate the score and make comments?*
User 1	Put cursor where you want score to go, score shown in document.
User 2	The most visible information on the window was the marks alongside each of the text fields and the labelled buttons at the bottom of the window. It seemed fairly obvious what to do with these elements within the window.
User 3	The student's work of course. What else would I be reading.
Q4	*How has the Score Allocation window changed in order to show what you have achieved?*
User 1	It records score on script in blue.
User 2	It clearly shows the score, but the comments can only be viewed if you scroll over the mark with the mouse and wait for a rectangular box to appear. This is followed by a pop up text box that displays the message.
User 3	It hasn't. It is wrong at the moment I have deleted the score but the window shows a mark.
Q5	*How does the Marking Tool let you know you are making progress with the whole task?*
User 1	Status box changes part marked etc.
User 2	In the main screen the status moves to Fully Marked if all the marks have been entered and the action called mark changes to remark.
User 3	I don't know I'm stuck.

Table 2: Samples of users' write-along responses.

Gender	Task	Mean Word Count	Users	Average Usability Issues	Total Usability Issues
Male	1	45.7	8	1.2	9
	2	156.0	8	1.2	9
	3	238.2	8	4.8	38
	Overall	146.7	24	2.4	56
Female	1	189.4	5	0.8	4
	2	186.8	5	1.2	5
	3	294.8	5	3.0	16
	Overall	223.7	15	1.7	25
All	1	101.0	13	1.1	13
	2	167.8	13	1.2	14
	3	260.0	13	4.1	54
	Overall	176.3	39	2.1	81

Table 3: Mean word count and problems identified from user responses grouped by gender and task.

Task 1	Task 2	Task 3
0.67	0.74	0.95

Table 4: Correlation coefficients — word count vs. problems identified for each task.

every question was measured. Table 3 groups this data by task and by gender and relates it to the usability problems the design team was able to identify.

Each task was associated with a different subset of windows from the Marking Tool. However the results for task 4 were not included in the detailed study as few usability problems had been reported for this task. One user's results were also excluded from the detailed study since a critical incident prevented him completing tasks 3 and 4. It can be seen that as the task complexity increased (from task 1 to task 3) the mean word count and usability issues identified also increased. The results presented in Table 3 suggest that the average number of words used by users increased as the tasks and the interfaces became more complex. The relationship between word count and number of usability issues identified was investigated by calculating the correlation coefficients for the different tasks. These results (Table 4) show increased correlation suggesting the user's response became more focused as the task complexity increased and that the method is more effective for more complex tasks.

However this could also reflect a learning effect in relation to the evaluation method although the suggestion that for simple tasks the users may provide rambling descriptions but as task complexity increases their descriptions become more focused and concise, was supported by inspection of the users' forms.

Factor	Sum of squares	df	Mean squares	F	Eta²
Combined	220443	3	73481.1	2.8	
Gender	54729.2	1	54729.2	2.1	0.05
Task	165714	2	82857.1	3.2	0.15
Residual	855542	33	25925.5		

Table 5: ANOVA word count.

Factor	Sum of squares	df	Mean squares	F	Eta²
Combined	80.68	3	26.89	9.49	
Gender	4.63	1	4.63	0.21	0.026
Task	76.05	2	38.03	13.42	0.42
Residual	93.47	33	2.83		

Table 6: ANOVA usability issues.

4.3 Effect of Gender and Task Complexity

The results from Table 3 suggested that male users might be more taciturn than female users and this hypothesis was investigated by two-way ANOVA and MANOVA by gender and task and the results summarised in Tables 5 & 6. As can be seen the results for word count (Table 5) lead us to accept the null hypothesis for gender and the combined factors (no effect) but reject the null hypothesis for the task factor (some effect).

When the gender and task factors are investigated in terms of the number of usability issues identified, the nature of the tasks is highly significant, while gender has no effect (see Table 6). This is supported by the observation that task 3, involving the addition of marks and comments, was much more difficult to complete than the others.

4.4 Remote Evaluation Compared with Heuristic Evaluation

The application of this remote evaluation method has not directly compared the effectiveness of the 'write-along DUCE' method with the original 'think-aloud' mode. Since this was a real application with very tight time constraints, it would not have been possible to carry out such an experiment. However it was possible to gauge the effectiveness of the write-along DUCE method by comparison with heuristic evaluation of the prototype interface. Therefore an HCI expert was asked to carry out an heuristic evaluation using the same task framework but not the questions. The expert evaluation identified a total of 14 usability problems (0 for task 1; 5 for task 2; 9 for task 3, 0 for task 4;) a larger number than any single user. The problems he missed were generally associated with users' responses based on their domain knowledge and expectations of task completion. He identified one problem concerning metaphor that had not been identified by the remote evaluation exercise.

4.5 Users' Views of Remote Evaluation

Post evaluation interviewing of users showed that users completed the evaluation package online by opening another independent copy of Word, although some of them had also printed out a copy. Some users confessed to 'being unable to resist exploring the prototype and finding they got ahead of the question'. Users felt the evaluation did not seriously interrupt them in completing the tasks although not being totally natural. Expressing themselves in writing seems quite natural and did not inhibit them. Some found it difficult to understand what the questions were asking but, since these were repeated in slightly different variants for all the tasks, they felt they understood by the end of the exercise and could express themselves fully. This learning effect could have made some contribution to the correlation changes shown in Table 4.

4.6 Critical Incident Reports

When critical incident reports were used in the remote evaluation of the first prototype, few users reported critical incidents. Those reported tended to be software bugs associated with instability of the prototype. Despite the low response for the first evaluation it was decided to include a critical incident report section again in the evaluation of the second prototype. The tasks set were less specific but included extracting and loading e-TMAs to the central system. The users were also encouraged to explore the system and try the available options. This resulted in the return of 12 critical incidents reports. Of these 11 were concerned with bugs, some involving the operating system, and 2 were usability problems. Several users captured the screen when the incident occurred and returned these with the reports even though they had not been asked to do so. It was concluded that these reports are very useful for identifying software bugs remotely, particularly those which can result from the interaction of different systems and applications. In addition screen capture was useful in identifying the cause, although this needs careful interpretation with stacked-window applications.

The remote evaluation of the second prototype used an electronic questionnaire consisting of 33 statements linked to a five point Likert scale (strongly agree to strongly disagree) which were focused on the screen layout, icons, error messages and navigation.

5 Conclusions and Future Work

Contextual inquiry attempts to gain meaningful information about users' work by helping users articulate their current work procedures. The remote evaluation method, based upon a 'write-along DUCE' technique, applied the same concepts to enable users to articulate the way in which they would use a prototype interface to complete their normal tasks. Users may not recall problems with the interface outside the context of actually doing work. Unless the evaluation focuses on specific tasks and context, users tend to evaluate prototypes in abstract terms referring to their general view of the interface and about whether they like the font, colours etc. and such information had been collected through open-ended questions for the first evaluation. Although the remote evaluation method uses a question and answer framework it has done so in a style to empower the user by simulating direct conversation with the remote developer on equal terms. Holtzblatt & Jones (1993) describe active engagement as having the sense of a stream of consciousness discussion and this feeling was recognisable in many of the users' responses.

The one element that was a problem in the write-along DUCE method which cannot arise in think-aloud protocols is that users get tempted to explore and interact before they have completed the written answer. An actual observer can prevent this in a way which is difficult to simulate in remote evaluation. One possible extension is to combine the write-along method with audio prompts and reminders, although these could add to task disruption. The benefits of this method in comparison the cooperative evaluation techniques are the ease of administration and low resource costs which combined should allow the method to be used with much larger numbers of users. Another advantage in terms of cost and time is that the evaluation sessions do not have to be transcribed although experts still need to sift the written material to provide evidence for the TEA sessions. For geographically and temporally distributed applications the asynchronous nature of the evaluation is a considerable advantage over cooperative evaluation techniques. To summarise the results:

- The remote evaluation based on the DUCE session was effective in providing information from which the developer team could identify usability problems that lead to design changes.

- The evaluation framework (Figure 2) provides a generic framework for remote evaluation.

- Users were able to articulate their experience of using the interface, regardless of their gender and task complexity.

- Users need to get used to the conversational style of the DUCE framework, repetition of the style of questions for each task assists this.

- Since there is some evidence of a learning effect in terms of the questions being asked, the evaluation design should ensure less complex tasks are encountered first.

- The problem of users getting ahead in the evaluation needs to be addressed.

- Users were able to understand the concepts of critical incidents and report these effectively. Screen dumps are helpful in interpreting the incident reports.

The method used was highly efficient in terms of the resources needed to extract the usability problems from the users' responses — the method has a high signal to noise ratio. Subsequent experiments are needed to compare the effectiveness of the LCR method with cooperative evaluation techniques and to investigate the effects of using audio prompts or active agent technology to enforce the conversational nature of the evaluation. Another interesting issue is whether this method is suitable for other cultures in view of Evers (2000) report of difficulties using think-aloud protocols with some cultures. Future work needs to be carried out to compare the two modes write-along vs. think-aloud with remote users. Another question arises in relation to the kind of user. The users for this application were articulate and confident in expressing their views in writing. The method needs to be tested with users with disabilities such as dyslexia and with users from different cultural backgrounds. In addition the effects of supplementing the method with the collection of objective data needs to be investigated.

References

Beyer, H. & Holtzblatt, K. (1998), *Contextual Design: Defining Customer-centered Systems*, Morgan-Kaufmann.

Carroll, J. M. & Rosson, M. B. (1991), "Deliberated evolution: Stalking the View Matcher in Design Space", *Human–Computer Interaction* **6**(3-4), 281–318.

Castillo, J. C., Hartson, H. R. & Hix, D. (1998), Remote Usability Evaluation: Can Users Report their own Critical Incidents, *in* C.-M. Karat, A. Lund, J. Coutaz & J. Karat (eds.), *Proceedings of CHI'98: Human Factors in Computing Systems*, ACM Press, pp.253–4.

Chapanis, A., Ochsman, R., Parrish, R. & Weeks, G. (1972), "Studies in Interactive Communication: The Effects of Four Communication Modes on the Behaviour of Teams During Cooperative Problem Solving", *Human Factors* **14**(6), 487–509.

Evers, V. (2000), Cross-cultural Understanding of Interface Design, PhD thesis, Institute of Educational Technology, Open University.

Falzon, P. (1990), Human–Computer Interaction: Lessons from Human–Human Communication, *in* P. Falzon (ed.), *Cognitive Ergonomics*, Academic Press, pp.51–68.

Goguen, J. (1996), Formality and Informality in Requirements Engineering, *in Proceedings of Fourth International Conference on Requirements Engineering*, IEEE Computer Society Press, pp.102–8.

Hartson, R., Castillo, J., Kelso, J., Kamler, J. & Neale, W. (1996), Remote Evaluation: The Network as an Extension of the Usability Laboratory, *in* G. van der Veer & B. Nardi (eds.), *Proceedings of CHI'96: Human Factors in Computing Systems*, ACM Press, pp.228–35.

Holtzblatt, K. & Jones, S. (1993), Contextual Inquiry: A Participatory Technique for System Design, *in* D. Schuler & A. Namioka (eds.), *Participatory Design: Principles and Practices*, Lawrence Erlbaum Associates, pp.177–210.

Shah, D., Candy, L. & Edwards, E. (1998), "An Investigation into Supporting Collaboration over the Internet", *Computer Communications* **20**(16), 1458–66.

Smith, A., Dunckley, L. & Smith, L. (1999), Importance of Collaborative Design in Computer Interface Design, *in* M. A. Hanson, E. J. Lovesey & S. A. Robertson (eds.), *Proceedings of Contemporary Ergonomics '99*, Taylor & Francis, pp.494–8.

Wright, P. C. & Monk, A. F. (1991), "A Cost-effective Evaluation Method for Use by Designers", *International Journal of Man–Machine Studies* **35**(6), 891–912.

Are Passfaces†More Usable Than Passwords? A Field Trial Investigation

Sacha Brostoff & M Angela Sasse

Department of Computer Science, University College London, Gower Street, London WC1E 6BT, UK

Tel: *+44 20 7679 3039*

Fax: *+44 20 7387 1397*

EMail: {*s.brostoff,a.sasse*} *@cs.ucl.ac.uk*

The proliferation of technology requiring user authentication has increased the number of passwords which users have to remember, creating a significant usability problem. This paper reports a usability comparison between a new mechanism for user authentication — Passfaces — and passwords, with 34 student participants in a 3-month field trial. Fewer login errors were made with Passfaces, even when periods between logins were long. On the computer facilities regularly chosen by participants to log in, Passfaces took a long time to execute. Participants consequently started their work later when using Passfaces than when using passwords, and logged into the system less often. The results emphasise the importance of evaluating the usability of security mechanisms in field trials.

Keywords: task performance, evaluation, passwords, security, human memory.

1 Introduction

Most computers contain and process data which needs to be protected, and many other technologies — such as mobile phones — require some sort of access control. On most computer systems, this is done through a process of user identification and authentication (Garfinkel & Spafford, 1996). Through *identification*, the user's

---

†Passfaces™ have been used by kind permission of the patent and trademark holding company, Id-Arts (http://www.id-arts.com/).

right to access a system is established. Once a user's identity is established, the *authentication* mechanism verifies that the user is who he says he is.

There are three types of user authentication: examining what the user *knows, possesses* or *is* (Menkus, 1988). *Knowledge-based authentication* uses a secret word or phrase shared between the user and the computer system, with the user revealing the secret to the computer to prove their authenticity. *Token-based authentication* uses a physical token that is difficult to obtain or forge. *Biometric authentication* relies on the uniqueness of details in a person's anatomy or behaviour — a user whose characteristics match the electronic equivalent of those characteristics recorded in the computer is accepted as valid. Examples of such characteristics used currently include fingerprints (Roddy & Stosz, 1997), retinal patterns (Arthur, 1997), signatures, keystroke dynamics in typing (Obaidat & Sadoun, 1997), and voice properties (Kim, 1995).

Today, knowledge-based authentication is the most widely used mechanism, in the form of the *password*. Many companies require multiple computer systems throughout their businesses. Business is using an ever increasing number of computer systems, and so more users are acquiring more passwords. However, there is plenty of evidence that passwords are neither usable nor secure. Many users forget their passwords (Zviran & Haga, 1993), and with the number of passwords per user increasing, the rate of forgetting increases further (Adams et al., 1997). A visible consequence is that password users require extensive support (Murrer, 1999). Support takes the form of a password reset, estimated at up to £40 a reset (Charles Brennan, personal communication, 2000). With a typical support requirement of 1 password reset per 4–5 users per month, this represents a considerable cost: a company with 100 to 120 thousand employees would have 25,000 password resets a month.

Despite the large amount of money invested in it, password mechanisms often are not as secure as expected. The passwords chosen by most users are relatively easy to crack (Davis & Ganesan, 1993; Adams & Sasse, 1999). The continuing increase of networked systems introduces an additional risk, since passwords sent across networks in plain text can be intercepted through mechanisms such as packet sniffing (Garfinkel & Spafford, 1996).

Given the number and quality of problems associated with passwords, why are they still so widely used? In our experience, staff responsible for computer security — system administrators and IT managers — are generally reluctant to change existing security mechanisms. Despite mounting evidence of password problems, they feel that sticking with "the devil you know" is safer than experimenting with new mechanisms. A closer examination of the alternatives explains that reluctance — other mechanisms have their own problems.

1.1 Token-based Authentication

Token-based authentication requires token construction and distribution, which is far from trivial and has led to documented financial loss (Anderson, 1994). The token must be physically presented to the computer system, which requires additional hardware for reading the token. Both token and token reader cost money, and a reader must be available at every point a user might be authenticated. As costs of tokens and readers fall, this will be less of an issue. However, presentation of a valid token does not prove ownership — the token may have been stolen. And although a token may be hard to forge, it does not mean it is impossible or uneconomic to do so (Svigals, 1994). For these reasons, tokens are mostly used for identification only as part of a two-factor procedure (see below); the user still needs to authenticate him/herself through some other means, usually a password.

1.2 Biometric Authentication

Biometric authentication raises issues of trust among many users, who fear it could be used to track them constantly, as in the Big Brother scenario. But there are problems beyond potential mis-use by an unaccountable entity. Since users' biometric characteristics (such as the shape of face or fingerprints) cannot be easily changed, it is paramount that the security of the characteristic is protected. There are, however, many points at which a description characteristic may be illicitly gained without maiming the actual owner: digital representations of the characteristic must be stored somewhere to compare against the user being authenticated. If somebody else obtains the digital representation of the characteristic, the user can be impersonated with impunity (Kim, 1995). The digital representation may have to be transmitted across a computer network during authentication, and so could be intercepted (using mechanisms such as packet sniffing — see above). Finally, analogue copies of a biometric characteristic may be left behind by the user from which the digital representation can be replicated, such as fingerprints on a beer glass, speech on an answering machine, or a signature on a form. Unlike the President of the USA, most users are not trailed by secret service agents who systematically break their beer glasses for them; thus, the chore of safeguarding of these characteristics falls on the user.

As with token-based authentication, structural or physiological biometrics require special hardware, which is expensive. Behavioural biometrics — such as keystroke dynamics — do not necessarily require costly hardware, but are not popular with users since they can be used to monitor productivity as well (Deane et al., 1995).

To make tokens or biometrics sufficiently secure, they have to be combined with another mechanism into a two-step procedure, using a second mechanism to shore up the weaknesses of the first. A combination of two mechanisms requiring special hardware would double the already high cost associated with these methods. Therefore, a combination of tokens or biometrics with a knowledge-based mechanism is likely to remain the most common form of access control — such as the cash card and Personal Identification Number (PIN). Using tokens or biometrics for user identification reduces the cognitive load of traditional computer login procedures, since the user no longer has to recall the specific user-id or account name for a particular system. Adams (1996) found that for users with many different systems and varying account names, recalling the user id presents a significant load in itself. But overall, the introduction of tokens and biometrics will lead to a further increase in the total number of knowledge-based items users have to recall for access procedures.

1.3   Improving Knowledge-based Mechanisms

The majority of users in Adams & Sasse's (1999) study reported they could not cope with the number of passwords they had; consequently, they wrote passwords down and/or disclosed them to others, breaking the most elementary rule of knowledge-based authentication. Many security professionals would regard this 'remedy' as unacceptable. However, the cost of resetting forgotten passwords has reached such proportions in some organisations that their security staff regard "writing passwords down and storing them in a safe place" as the lesser evil. Given that the number of applications requiring user authentication in some form is increasing rapidly — consider mobile phones, Personal Digital Assistants (PDAs), remote access to services and encryption — many individual and corporate users will face serious security problems unless usability of knowledge-based mechanisms is improved.

What are the options for improving the usability of knowledge-based authentication mechanisms? The biggest problem with passwords is that users forget them easily (Zviran & Haga, 1990; 1993). Recall is one of many routes to remembering which have been assessed in psychological experiments (Baddeley, 1997). To be secure, i.e. not be guessable, a password must be a random combination of numbers, symbols and letters (Garfinkel & Spafford, 1996). Unfortunately, these types of passwords are more difficult for people to recall than meaningful — guessable — ones, such as names. It has also been established that *cued recall* leads to better remembering than recall alone, and *recognition* has better accuracy than cued recall (Parkin, 1993; Baddeley, 1997). As well as using more powerful modes of remembering, it is possible to use authentication items (in place of passwords) that are more memorable, without being guessable. These include pass-sentences, (Spector & Ginzberg, 1994) longer strings of meaningful words; associative passwords, (Zviran & Haga, 1993) a form of cued recall; and Passfaces, which utilise recognition of images rather than recall of words.

1.4   Passfaces

The enrolment procedure allows users to first select whether their Passface set is male or female. They then select 4 faces, and are directed to consider the characteristics of their selections, and why they selected them. The users are then twice taken through the Passfaces login procedure, with their Passfaces indicated to them. They complete enrolment by correctly identifying their 4 Passfaces twice in a row with no prompting, then (in this field trial only) entering an enrolment password.

To log in, users select their Passfaces from a grid of faces displayed on the screen. This study uses the standard implementation of the Passfaces demonstration toolkit, requiring participants to memorise 4 faces, and correctly select all 4: one in each of 4 grids of nine faces (see Figure 1 for an example grid). The grids are presented one at a time on the screen, and the order of presentation remains constant, as do the faces contained in each grid. However, no grid contains faces found in the other grids, and the order of faces within each grid is randomised. These features help secure a user's Passface combination against detection through shoulder-surfing and packet-sniffing.

Figure 1: Example Passfaces grid.

Passfaces were shown to be memorable in a study involving 77 staff and students of Goldsmiths College (Valentine, 1998). All participants went through the Passfaces enrolment procedure, and 3 conditions were tested. The first condition had 29 participants logging in every working day for 2 weeks. Participants correctly recalled their Passfaces in 99.98% of logins. The second condition had 29 participants log in approximately 7 days after enrolment. On their first attempt, 83% logged in successfully. Everyone in this condition logged in by his or her 3rd attempt. The third condition had 19 participants login only once approximately 30 days after enrolment, with 84% of participants remembering their Passfaces at the first attempt, and the remainder remembering their Passfaces by the third attempt.

Passfaces have also proved to be memorable over long periods without use*. The participants were contacted and asked to log in again on average 5.4 months after they had last used their Passfaces. 56 participants completed the follow up study. Overall, 72% of participants remembered their Passfaces on the first attempt, and 84% had remembered their Passfaces by the third attempt. Participants who had originally been in the everyday use condition remembered their Passfaces the best, with 87% remembering them at the first attempt and 100% by the third attempt (Valentine, 1999). There have been similar studies of password memorability. In most cases the password is selected by the participant, who is then asked to recall it after an interval that varies between studies. The intervals and the resulting memorability are shown in Table 1.

A comparison of the results (Table 1) suggests that Passfaces are more memorable than traditional passwords, and hence a solution to the usability problem described above. However, there has been no direct comparison of Passfaces and passwords. The participants were different and the intervals over which the words

---

*Password resets are most often required after holidays. Internal helpdesks and those of Internet Service Providers experience a surge of calls after the Christmas break and the end of the holidays. In one case, more than 60% of calls to the help desk were due to forgotten passwords.

Interval	Passwords (% remembered)	Passfaces (% remembered)	Study
1 day	—	99.98 (1st attempt)	(Valentine, 1998)
1 week	—	100 (by 3rd attempt)	(Valentine, 1998)
2 weeks	77 (1st attempt)	—	(Bunnell et al., 1997)
1 month	—	100 (by 3rd attempt)	(Valentine, 1998)
3 months	35 (1st attempt)	—	(Zviran & Haga, 1990)
3 months	27.2 (1st attempt)	—	(Zviran & Haga, 1993)
5 months	—	72 (by 3rd attempt)	(Valentine, 1998)

Table 1: Memorability of passwords and Passfaces over different intervals.

and faces were recalled were of different lengths. A final concern is that the situation under which the mechanisms were tested was somewhat artificial — users were prompted by experimenters to log in, rather than observed using the mechanism to access the systems in the context of their normal activities.

The goal of the study reported in this paper is to compare passwords and Passfaces with the same participants in a field trial, with participants using authentication mechanisms to gain access to a real system as part of a real task.

2 The Field Trial

2.1 Participants

Thirty-six first year undergraduate students in Information Management taking a one-term course in Systems Analysis participated in the trial. Thirty-four students logged in frequently enough to be included in the study.

2.2 Trial Context

As part of the course, the students had to complete 6 assignments online on the Web over a period of 10 weeks; the coursework was authored and managed through the TACO system (Sasse et al., 1998). To interact with TACO, students used computers at the University (mostly PCs running Windows 3.1 with 486 processors, and some Macs running MacOs 8.1 with 601 processors) or from home. Students can practise each question set as often as they like before submitting an assessed version; since they receive scores and feedback, frequent practice tends to result in better grades. Users of TACO are required to go through authentication before being allowed to interact with courseworks. Logging in usually consists of being identified by entering a username, and then authenticated by entering a system-generated password (both of which had been previously supplied to the user through a secure channel). A facility allowing participants to change passwords and a facility to select and use Passfaces were added to TACO. Each of these facilities required participants to supply the system-generated password before they could select their user-generated password or Passfaces set. In addition, the modified authentication system allowed logging of interactions taking place during the login (i.e. keystrokes), thus making it possible to count successful and failed logins, and reconstruct what participants typed.

2.3 The System

The password mechanism of TACO is executed at the server side, and appears instantaneous to users. However, the Passfaces mechanism is executed at the user's computer. There are two versions, one using *Active X* and the other using *Java* technologies. Both require users initially to download the Passfaces mechanism and the Passfaces themselves. *Active X* allows these to be stored on the user's computer, such that subsequent uses of Passfaces appear instantaneous, but is not supported by the versions of the Web browsers (Netscape 3 and 4.03) available on the computers commonly used by this cohort of students. Since the *Java* version does not support local storage, the Passfaces set and mechanism must be downloaded for each log in. The user must wait for this download across busy university networks. In addition, for each initial use of the Passfaces system in a session, the user must wait for a software package to load that converts the *Java* to a working Passfaces mechanism. On the slowest computers available to participants, a Passface login took up to 3 minutes, while a password login was completed in seconds[†].

Passface enrolment has been described in Section 1.4. In contrast to Passfaces, the password enrolment procedure is relatively brief. Guidance about the selection of cryptographically strong password content is displayed on screen, and users are required to submit a password of their choosing twice, and their enrolment password. If the enrolment password is correct, and both submissions of the chosen password match, then enrolment is complete.

TACO was further changed to offer participants reminders of their passwords/Passfaces. On their request, participants were emailed a copy of their password, or sent the address of a Web page where they could view their Passface. TACO log files were enhanced so that the failure or success of login attempts could be determined, and all requests for reminders were recorded.

2.4 Procedure

A repeated-measures design was used, with each student using both passwords and Passfaces. The design was counterbalanced to take account of order effects, with half the participants using the mechanisms in order PW–PF (passwords then Passfaces) and the other half in order PF–PW (Passfaces then passwords). This maximised power for the test of difference between Passfaces and passwords (a simple between-groups design would have insufficient power to detect differences between Passface and passwords given the relatively small sample size).

Participants were pseudo-randomly assigned to PW–PF or PF–PW with the aid of a random number table. Participants were given enrolment passwords (on paper slips) at the start of term, to authenticate them for their subsequent selection of passwords or Passfaces. Participants used the Web-based coursework system as normal to complete course-works.

Halfway through the term (marked by the lecture-free Reading Week) the authentication mechanisms used by students were changed over (those using

---

[†]Participants were pointed towards more powerful computers on which the Passfaces login was much faster, but the majority of students continued accessing the system from the old machines. The specification of machine used not only affected the speed of the login, but also the time it took to complete the coursework exercises.

passwords were now using Passfaces, and vice versa). Participants were required to re-enrol, and *new* enrolment passwords were distributed by email to all participants and on paper slip by request.

3 Results

Logins and login problem rates were analysed, followed by reminders, time taken before first use of the system, and number of logins. This paper will describe each variable's effect using the effect size indicator *d*, which is the distance in standard deviations between the means of two groups. The following sections may describe differences between groups that are small in absolute terms, counter-intuitively, as being due to large effects. In the context of effect sizes, *large*, *medium* and *small* have technical definitions; see Rosenthal & Rosnow (1991) or Clark-Carter (1997), for further information about effect size and statistical power.

3.1 Problem Rates

Task performance is an important part of usability, and is often measured by time and errors. In the context of passwords, an easy type of error to record is a failed login attempt. Failed login attempts are user costs, and so should be minimised where possible. If two people have the same number of failed logins but different numbers of successful logins then counting the absolute number of failed login attempts is misleading. We will therefore use login failure *rate* as one of our measures of usability.

The numbers of successful and unsuccessful logins were used to calculate each participant's failure rate for logging in (problems÷(problems+successes)) for both passwords and Passfaces. Table 2 shows descriptive statistics for login failure rate, with authentication mechanism and order of presentation of authentication mechanism as the independent variables.

Passwords had a login failure rate of 15.1%, while Passfaces for the same participants produced a login failure rate of 4.9%. Thus, the number of login problems occurring with Passfaces was approximately a third that of passwords.

A mixed ANOVA was performed on the data, testing authentication mechanism (repeated measure) and order of presentation (between groups measure) as the main effects and the interaction between them (Table 3). The test of authentication mechanism achieved a power of 0.924 (better than the recommended level), and showed that the difference between Passfaces' and passwords' error rate was highly significant ($F(1,31) = 12.31, p = 0.001$), and that authentication mechanism had a large effect on login problem rate ($d = 1.26$).

The ANOVA achieved a power of 0.861 in testing order of presentation, slightly bettering the recommended value. Order effects were not predicted but there was a highly significant difference ($F(1,31) = 9.92, p = 0.004$) between the login problem rates of those who were presented with passwords first (PW–PF) and those who were presented with them last (PF–PW). Order of presentation had a large effect ($d = 1.13$).

The ANOVA, operating at 0.704 — slightly less than recommended power, also showed that the effect of order of use was different for each authentication mechanism ($F(1,31) = 6.68, p = 0.015$). This difference was large ($d = 0.93$). The PF–PW group had a login error rate of 5.5% with Passfaces, whilst the PW–PF group

Group	Mean	N	95% CI for Mean	Std.Err.	Std.Dev.	Min.	Max.
Mechanism							
Passwords	0.15	33	0.09/0.21	0.03	0.16	0	0.57
Passfaces	0.05	34	0.02/0.08	0.02	0.09	0	0.38
Order							
PW–PF	0.06	34	0.03/0.08	0.01	0.07	0	0.29
PF–PW	0.14	33	0.08/0.20	0.03	0.17	0	0.57
Order × Mechanism							
PW–PF							
Passwords	0.07	17	0.03/0.11	0.02	0.08	0	0.29
Passfaces	0.04	17	0.01/0.08	0.02	0.07	0	0.20
PF–PW							
Passwords	0.24	16	0.12/0.33	0.05	0.18	0	0.57
Passfaces	0.05	17	0.00/0.11	0.01	0.11	0	0.38

Table 2: Descriptive statistics of login error rates. Mechanism, Order, and Order × Mechanism are significantly different.

Source of Variation	SS	DF	MS	F	Sig. of F
(Between groups measure)					
Within + Residual	0.44	31	0.01		
Mechanism	0.17	1	0.17	12.31	0.001
Order × Mechanism	0.09	1	0.09	6.68	0.015
(Repeated measure)					
Within + Residual	0.42	31	0.01		
Order	0.13	1	0.13	9.92	0.004

Table 3: ANOVA table for login error rates.

had an error rate of 4.3%. Thus, PF–PW had an error rate more than 25% higher than PW–PF.

The difference was in the other direction for passwords. The PW–PF group had a password login error rate of 7.1%; while PF–PW had an error rate of 23.6%. The error rate for PW–PF was less than a third of that of PF–PW. Using PF–PW had a detrimental effect on both their password and Passfaces login failure rate, but much more so for passwords.

As explained in Section 2.2, the experimental apparatus captured failed password login attempts. By comparing the failed attempt with the participant's correct password, problem types could be inferred. This helps to diagnose the causes of password login problems, and to prioritise them. Table 4 shows the relative frequencies of password problems encountered during the experiment. The most frequent problem was entering a previous TACO password in place of the current one. The next most frequent problem was substituting a password-like sequence for the correct password.

Problem type	Proportion
Previous (TACO) password used	37%
Other password used	15%
'ENTER' only	9%
Character missing	6%
Additional character	5%
Part of password only	5%
Admin. problem	4%
System problem	3%
Wrong character	2%
2 passwords mixed	1%
Capitals not used correctly	1%
User ID entered instead of password	1%

Table 4: Password problems encountered by participants.

Separate analyses of login error rates for each error type would be preferable to the lumped together measure employed here, as would analysis of Passface error types. Such analysis would suffer from the small data set available to this study, and technical issues prevented the recording of Passface login errors. These analyses will, however, become feasible when data sets from studies in progress are added to the data presented here.

3.2 Reminders

The previous section measured the numbers and types of errors made in task completion — logging in. This section looks at the prevalence of not being able to do the task — giving up on logging in and calling in the helpdesk. This is an important measure of authentication mechanism usability, because it is such a large cost to industry (see Section 1).

Participants in this experiment were offered a facility to have a reminder of their password or Passfaces sent to them by e-mail. Automatic reminders are now widely employed in many e-commerce systems as a means of reducing the number of password-related calls to helpdesks, even though sending passwords in unencrypted email is not secure.

Descriptive statistics of password/Passface reminders are shown in Table 5. A mixed ANOVA was performed on the data, with dependent variable being the number of reminders per participant, and the independent variables authentication mechanism (repeated measure) and order in which the mechanisms were used (between groups measure). The results are shown in Table 6.

When using passwords, users requested 0.15 reminders on average, approximately two thirds more than when using Passfaces (mean of 0.09). However, the difference is not significant ($F(1,32) = 0.27, p = 0.605$). Power analysis showed that the ANOVA only achieved a power of 0.055 in testing the effect of mechanism, and therefore had only a 5.5% chance of detecting a real effect. Further analysis showed that mechanism had a small effect on number of reminders ($d = 0.18$).

Group	Mean	N	95% CI for Mean	Std.Err.	Std.Dev.	Min.	Max.
Mechanism							
Passwords	0.15	34	-0.05/0.34	0.10	0.56	0	3
Passfaces	0.09	34	-0.01/0.19	0.05	0.29	0	1
Order							
PW–PF	0.00	34	0.00/0.00	0.00	0.00	0	0
PF–PW	0.24	34	0.02/0.45	0.10	0.61	0	3
Order × Mechanism							
PW–PF							
Passwords	0.00	17	0.00/0.00	0.00	0.00	0	0
Passfaces	0.00	17	0.00/0.00	0.00	0.00	0	0
PF–PW							
Passwords	0.29	17	-0.10/0.69	0.20	0.77	0	3
Passfaces	0.18	17	-0.03/0.38	0.10	0.39	0	1

Table 5: Descriptive statistics of password/Passfaces reminders. Order is significantly different.

Source of Variation	SS	DF	MS	F	Sig. of F
(Within groups effects)					
Within + Residual	6.88	32	0.22		
Mechanism	0.06	1	0.06	0.27	0.605
Order × Mechanism	0.06	1	0.06	0.27	0.605
(Between groups effects)					
Within + Residual	5.12	32	0.16		
Order	0.94	1	0.94	5.89	0.021

Table 6: ANOVA table for password/Passfaces reminders.

Rosenthal & Rosnow (1991) show that 400 participants would be required for a test to achieve significance at the 0.05 level (2 tailed) for an effect of this size. If this small effect were real, then multiplied by the large scale of corporate computer use, Passfaces could make an appreciable difference in helpdesk costs.

Order of use of the authentication mechanisms had a large effect on participants' mean number of reminders ($d = 0.85$). The PF–PW group had a mean number of 0.24 reminders, whereas PW–PF required none. The ANOVA reached a power of 0.65 in testing order of use. This difference between the groups was unexpected.

Whereas login error rates showed an interaction between the effects of order of use and authentication mechanism, reminders did not ($F(1,32) = 0.27, p = 0.605$). As with the effect of method on participants' mean number of reminders, the test for order x mechanism achieved a power of only 0.05, having a small effect ($d = 0.18$) that if real would have required 400 participants to detect.

Group	Mean	N	95% CI for Mean	Std.Err.	Std.Dev.	Min.	Max.
Mechanism							
Passwords	16.36	33	13.98/18.75	1.17	6.72	5	36
Passfaces	20.00	34	17.84/22.16	1.06	6.20	11	35
Order							
PW–PF	17.38	34	14.94/19.83	1.20	7.00	5	32
PF–PW	19.06	33	16.83/21.29	1.10	6.30	11	36
Order × Mechanism							
PW–PF							
Passwords	11.18	17	9.47/12.88	0.81	3.32	5	15
Passfaces	23.59	17	22.11/25.07	0.70	2.87	17	32
PF–PW							
Passwords	21.88	16	19.40/24.35	1.16	4.65	15	36
Passfaces	16.41	17	13.01/19.81	1.60	6.61	1	35

Table 7: Descriptive statistics for day of first use of target application. Mechanism and Order × Mechanism are significantly different.

3.3 Time Before First Use

The popularity of a system may be measured by the speed with which users adopt it. In a work-related piece of software such as a login mechanism, usability is a good starting point for popularity. The speed with which people took up each authentication mechanism could be viewed as an indicator of usability. This is particularly the case in a domain where time is limited — students have coursework deadlines which must be met.

Participants' coursework consisted of multiple-choice and free-response questions that were distributed, responded to by participants, marked and corrections displayed all via Web pages. Practice questions were made available (practice coursework), which participants could use whenever and as often as they wished and for which marks were not formally recorded. We observed that Passface users were waiting longer before submitting practice or assessed coursework than password users. Data regarding the date of first use of the system were collected from system logs, and descriptive statistics for these are shown in Table 7. These same data were added to a mixed ANOVA, the results of which are shown in Table 8.

As in previous sections, the independent variables were authentication mechanism (repeated measure) and order of use of authentication mechanisms (between groups measure). As authentication mechanism is a repeated measure, each participant experiences first use of a system twice, once for passwords and once for Passfaces.

Passfaces were first used on average 4 days later than passwords. The ANOVA achieved better than recommended power (0.859) and showed that this difference was highly statistically significant ($F(1,63) = 9.55, p = 0.003$), and was equivalent to a medium sized effect ($d = 0.78$). This finding shows a usability advantage for

Source of Variation	SS	DF	MS	F	Sig. of F
Within + Residual	1332.46	63	21.15		
Order	51.91	1	51.91	2.45	0.122
Mechanism	202.04	1	202.04	9.55	0.003
Order × Mechanism	1337.05	1	1337.05	63.22	0.000
(Model)	1602.62	3	534.21	25.26	0.000
(Total)	2935.07	66	44.47		

Table 8: ANOVA table for day of first use of target application.

Group	Mean	N	95% CI for Mean	Std.Err.	Std.Dev.	Min.	Max.
Passwords	33.91	34	27.00/40.83	3.40	19.81	0.00	92.00
Passfaces	12.32	34	9.92/14.73	1.18	6.88	2.00	29.00

Table 9: Descriptive statistics for number of login attempts.

passwords, where previous sections gave the advantage to Passfaces. A synthesis of these apparently contradictory results can be achieved by examining evidence from the number of logins made (Section 3.4 below) and from participants' anecdotes.

The ANOVA did not detect a significant difference in first use dates due to order of use ($F(1,63) = 2.45, p = 0.112$). However, the observed effect size was small ($d = 0.39$). Due to the limited number of participants available, the test achieved a power of only 0.338 (a one in three chance of detecting a real effect) for the order of use effect. Assuming this small effect does exist, it would require 400 participants to detect; cf. (Rosenthal & Rosnow, 1991).

Because each participant contributed data for 2 first courseworks (one for each authentication method) and the two deadlines were on different days (days 15 and 24) we would predict a strong interaction effect between authentication mechanism and order of mechanism use. This is in fact the case. As this is merely an artefact of the experimental design, it will not be further reported.

3.4 Number of Login Attempts

To help interpret the results of the time before first use analysis, descriptive (Table 9) and inferential statistics (Table 10) were calculated for the number of login attempts for each participant. The experimental apparatus counted a login attempt as a successful or unsuccessful submission of passwords/Passfaces. It could not record logins interrupted before a password or Passface was entered. For example, a login attempt was not recorded if cancelled by a participant while Passfaces were downloading.

Overall, the authentication mechanism had a large effect ($d = 2.6$) on the number of logins attempted. Participants attempted to use the coursework system with Passfaces approximately a third of the amount they attempted to use it with passwords ($F(1,32) = 53.92, p = 0.000$, highly significant; observed *power* = 1.0).

Source of Variation	SS	DF	MS	F	Sig. of F
(Within groups effects)					
Within + Residual	4702.18	32	146.94		
Mechanism	7922.88	1	7922.88	53.92	0.000
Order × Mechanism	52.94	1	52.94	0.36	0.553
(Between groups effects)					
Within + Residual	9691.00	32	302.84		
Order	72.06	1	72.06	0.24	0.629

Table 10: ANOVA table for number of attempted logins recorded.

There were no significant order effects ($F(1,32) = 0.24, p = 0.63$, not sig.; observed *power* = 0.06), or interaction effects between order and authentication mechanism ($F(1,32) = 0.36, p = 0.55$, not sig.; observed *power* = 0.36). Should these small effects ($d = 0.17$ and 0.21 respectively) exist, 800 participants would be required for a similar ANOVA to class them as statistically significant.

Not only was there a delay before Passfaces were used, they were used less frequently. The *time* part of our analysis suggests a usability problem for Passfaces in this field trial, but the *errors* analysis shows them to have a usability advantage. Passfaces could be said to trade some login speed for greater memorability. It is argued below that several factors greatly exaggerated this trade off, causing one usability problem whilst solving another.

4 Discussion

4.1 *Performance of the Authentication Mechanisms*

There was no significant difference between the number of reminders asked for by participants when using passwords or Passfaces. This measure of usability is relevant to helpdesks — where forgotten passwords would need to be reset. From this perspective the mechanisms appear to be equal (for users similar to those in the study). From the participants' point of view however, they are not equal.

Passfaces had a login problem rate of less than a third of the login problem rate of passwords in this study. In particular, the PF–PW group of participants experienced nearly a 1 in 4 password login failure rate, 3 times higher than PW–PF's. This finding is unexpected — how might it be explained?

Participants were randomly assigned to PW–PF or PF–PW groups, so the differences should not be due to participant differences between groups. Since every participant used both passwords and Passfaces, every participant also necessarily underwent a transition from using one mechanism to the other. It is likely that something related to this transition is responsible.

The protocol used to move participants from the mechanism they first used to the second was different to the protocol used to start them on the first mechanism at the beginning of the experiment. During induction, participants were informed of enrolment details via paper slips handed out in the first few lectures. During changeover, participants received emails with their changeover information, in addition to verbal and hard copy notification. It seems, however, unlikely this difference in procedure could have caused such severe problems for password users.

We know that the largest problem encountered by password users was attempting login with defunct passwords (Table 4). Why should participants in the PF–PW group be more susceptible to password confusion than participants in the PW–PF group?

It is a counter-intuitive finding. A simple hypothesis would be that people have problems changing passwords, because they confuse the password they *previously* used for the one they should now be using. However, this would not explain the large difference between the groups, who both had opportunities to make the slip.

Using this hypothesis we may even predict a difference in the *opposite* direction to the one found. Assuming a schema model of human performance such as Reason's (1990) (and that passwords are schemata), participants who changed from passwords to Passfaces (PW–PF group) would have had their self-selected passwords at high levels of activation due to frequency and recency of use and links to related schemata, and so these passwords should offer high levels of interference to recall and use of the current password (but do not). In contrast, the (PF–PW) group which suffered extreme interference in password recall and use suffered it at the expense of an enrolment password that had been used once more than a month previously, and which being a non-word would have little relation to other contents of participants' memories.

A second possible explanation of the finding is that password and Passfaces use are competing skills, and that Passface use de-skills the participant in password use. This would effect all passwords systems participants may use. To test this hypothesis, each group should undergo the suspect transition and contribute data from more than one password protected system. To assess the de-skilling effect's duration might require repetitions of the suspect transition, and observation over longer periods.

A similar but alternate interpretation is that Passface use inhibits password use on the system in which Passfaces were previously used. For example, assuming Passfaces are easier to remember than passwords, participants may use the same effort in processing passwords that they used for the Passfaces — leading to an insufficiently deep level of password processing, and so poorer memory for the password. We feel that this explanation is unlikely, as participants were often alarmed at the prospect of having to remember the faces — and so would be likely to process the Passfaces to a deep level.

Another explanation of the finding is possible: that Passfaces are simply more resistant to confusion at changeover time than passwords. The Passfaces patent holding company intends to control their distribution to minimise possible confusion between different sets of Passfaces (Paul Barratt, personal communication, 1999). However, to properly support this explanation of the results would require a new experiment in which both authentication mechanisms are equivalently used; with system chosen Passfaces protecting participants' Passface selection (as passwords protect password selection). This would allow comparisons of mistaken use of defunct secrets in the two systems. In the wider context, this would assess the untested claim that Passfaces are resistant to confusion with previous/other Passfaces.

Overall, login failures are user-costs, and so should be minimised. There were no restrictions on login attempts in this field trail. In industrial contexts the consequences may be more severe — authentication systems may enforce delays between login attempts, or *"3 strikes"* policies to reduce the password guessing opportunities of hackers. The present findings have a more detrimental effect in such settings.

4.2 Login Frequency

The strengths of the present study have been to provide detailed observations of both authentication mechanisms in longer-term use with real users and real tasks in a real system environment. However, the reality of the study environment (many of the machines available to the participants were old and underpowered) led to significantly longer login times with Passfaces. When using Passfaces, participants attempted to login with a third of the frequency with which they did using passwords. They also started their attempts a mean of four days later than when using passwords. When using Passfaces participants, therefore, had less practice for coursework and had less opportunity for practice. This did not reduce their final mark (when using Passfaces participants scored 6% higher though the difference was not significant, $F(1,202) = 3.71, p = 0.56, d = 0.27$ small effect, *power* $= 0.48$). Whilst the detailed impact of this usage bias needs to be explored in a future study, its existence also demonstrates the importance of evaluating the usability of security mechanisms in context.

Combining our knowledge of the study environment with anecdotal evidence (several participants commented unfavourably to their course lecturer on the time taken to login with Passfaces) suggests an explanation for the delayed and reduced Passface use. On finding Passface use to be slow on college facilities (anecdotal evidence), participants abandoned their attempts to use them (reduced use, see Section 3.4) until close to the deadline for submitting the coursework (delayed used, see Section 3.3).

Anecdotal evidence suggests that the use of more up-to-date computing facilities can lead to dramatic gains in user acceptance: a participant who had strenuously objected to using Passfaces because of slow and erratic system response during enrolment attempted it with faster equipment (PII 300/Win95) after a discussion with the experimenter. The participant withdrew all objections.

4.3 Psychology of Authentication Mechanisms

The primary component of any knowledge-based authentication system is human memory. Psychology has much substantive knowledge that can be used to explain password problems, and in intervention. Being a real world activity, password use involves a complicated knit of contextual factors as well as the laboratory capabilities and mechanisms of human memory. Understanding the current field trial would involve partitioning the effects of at least: levels of processing (Craik & Lockhart, 1972), pro-active (Baddeley, 1997), retro-active (Tulving & Psotka,

1971) and within-list interference (Wickens, 1992), free and cued recall (Parkin, 1981) and recognition (Parkin, 1993), whether the item being remembered is a word, picture (Nelson et al., 1977) or face (Bahrick et al., 1975), group working practices and perceptions of threat (Adams & Sasse, 1999), the use of prompts (Cohen, 1996), and individual differences such as absent-mindedness (Reason, 1990). A thorough understanding of the psychology underlying the remembering of secrets in knowledge-based authentication will require a research program spanning these and more topics.

5 Conclusions and Further Work

5.1 Passfaces

Passfaces showed a third the login failure rate of passwords, despite having users with a third the frequency of use (less frequent means the memory task was more difficult). This performance difference was partly due to the password confusions of participants who had recently changed from Passfaces to passwords. While Passfaces' low error rate may be due to their superiority over passwords, there are other explanations that need to be ruled out.

Passfaces have been shown to be very memorable over long intervals in previous studies (Valentine, 1998; 1999). Implemented appropriately (with more powerful computers and in *ActiveX* rather than *Java*), we predict that Passfaces would offer better performance than passwords for users who log in infrequently (less than once every two weeks).

Passfaces are a security mechanism designed with many theoretical advantages over passwords. They have been tested in previous studies under laboratory conditions and shown to perform well. This study tested Passfaces and passwords in a group of real users' work contexts, and with a number of unpredicted results. Consideration of task and environmental context in which a system is used is a fundamental part of human–computer interaction methods. However, security research and implementation do not often concern themselves with user costs, nor consider the context of system use as their source (Adams & Sasse, 1999). Developers ignore contextual factors at their peril; this study reminds us that evaluators do also. Security mechanisms designed and *tested* outside users' work contexts may shine on paper and in laboratory settings, yet may behave unexpectedly in practice.

5.2 Passwords

In this study, password users experienced substantial login failure rates (in one condition as high as 1 in 4 attempts failing). Passwords can therefore have user costs beyond the resets observed by computer helpdesks. Whilst user report data has identified similar problems to the present study (Adams & Sasse, 1999), the extent of failure had not been quantified in the security or HCI literature to date. This study therefore represents a step forward in the evaluation of user-authentication mechanisms, and computer security mechanisms more widely.

Research of this kind, however, is likely to remain rare. Security personnel and systems administrators are duty bound to prevent dissemination of data that might aid attackers. This makes even the collection of security system usability data, such as the capturing of failed login attempts, possible only in unusual circumstances.

5.3 *Further Work*

Passfaces implementation with older computing services may have led to reduced and delayed system use. The increasing power of computing infrastructure is inevitable. As the increase occurs, the resources that Passfaces require will become ubiquitous. Passfaces should therefore be tested with up to date hardware and software facilities — recent CPUs and Web browser *Active X* support. If these facilities are not available, speed of the authentication mechanisms' responses to user input should be measured and included in analyses, and response times made similar by retarding the password mechanism.

This experiment raised the possibility that Passface use interfered with password use. To assess this possibility an experiment is needed that authenticates Passface selection with Passfaces, and which repeats the transition from Passfaces to passwords.

The study raised the issue of confusing previous authentication secrets with new, when this was found to be participants' largest source of password error. Although Passfaces have been designed to reduce similar confusions, their ability to do this has not been tested. Studies are required of the relative effects of transition from previous to new secrets in both passwords and Passfaces. More widely, studies should be made of the contributions of different psychological phenomena to authentication mechanism usability.

Every user has at least one password story, and user reports are easy to gather. Future studies should augment user reports with objective data, even though it is hard to obtain.

Acknowledgements

Sacha Brostoff's PhD research is funded by a grant from BT. The authors would like to thank Charles Brennan for his contribution to the research project of which this is a small part. We would also like to thank Id-Arts Ltd. for permitting us to use Passfaces, and for their support in adapting and integrating the Passfaces demonstration toolkit into the experimental apparatus.

References

Adams, A. (1996), Reviewing Human Factors in Password Security Systems, Master's thesis, University College London, London.

Adams, A. & Sasse, M. A. (1999), "Users Are Not the Enemy: Why Users Compromise Security Mechanisms and How to Take Remedial Measures", *Communications of the ACM* **42**(12), 40–6.

Adams, A., Sasse, M. A. & Lunt, P. (1997), Making Passwords Secure and Usable, *in* H. Thimbleby, B. O'Conaill & P. Thomas (eds.), *People and Computers XII (Proceedings of HCI'97)*, Springer-Verlag, pp.1–19.

Anderson, R. J. (1994), "Why Cryptosystems Fail", *Communications of the ACM* **37**(11), 32–40.

Arthur, C. (1997), "Your Eye. The Ultimate Id Card", The Independent. Tuesday 2nd December.

Baddeley, A. (1997), *Human Memory: Theory and Practice*, revised edition, Psychology Press.

Bahrick, H. P., Bahrick, P. O. & Wittlinger, R. P. (1975), "Fifty Years of Memory for Names and Faces: A Cross-sectional Approach", *Journal of Experimental Social Psychology* **104**(1), 54–75.

Bunnell, J., Podd, J., Henderson, R., Napier, R. & Kennedy-Moffat, J. (1997), "Cognitive, Associative and Conventional Passwords: Recall and Guessing Rates", *Computers and Security* **16**(7), 629–41.

Clark-Carter, D. (1997), "The Account Taken of Statistical Power in Research Published in the British Journal of Psychology", *British Journal of Psychology* **88**(1), 71–83.

Cohen, G. (1996), *Memory in the Real World*, second edition, Psychology Press.

Craik, F. I. M. & Lockhart, R. S. (1972), "Levels of Processing: A Framework for Memory Research", *Journal of Verbal Learning and Verbal Behavior* **11**(6), 671–84.

Davis, C. & Ganesan, R. (1993), BApassword: A New Proactive Password Checker, in L. Reiner & D. Gilbert (eds.), *Proceedings of the National Computer Security Conference '93, the 16th NIST/NSA Conference*, USA Government, pp.1–15.

Deane, F., Barrelle, K., Henderson, R. & Mahar, D. (1995), "Perceived Acceptability of Biometric Security Systems", *Computers and Security* **14**(3), 225–31.

Garfinkel, S. & Spafford, G. (1996), *Practical Unix and Internet Security*, second edition, O'Reilly.

Kim, H.-J. (1995), "Biometrics, Is It a Viable Proposition for Identity Authentication and Access Control?", *Computers and Security* **14**(3), 205–14.

Menkus, B. (1988), "Understanding the Use of Passwords", *Computers and Security* **7**(2), 132–6.

Murrer, E. (1999), "Fingerprint Authentication", *Secure Computing* **10**(3), 26–30.

Nelson, D. L., Reed, U. S. & Walling, J. R. (1977), "Picture Superiority Effect", *Journal of Experimental Psychology: Learning, Memory and Cognition* **2**(5), 523–8.

Obaidat, M. & Sadoun, B. (1997), "Verification of Computer Users Using Keystroke Dynamics", *IEEE Transactions in Systems, Man and Cybernetics* **27**(2), 261–9.

Parkin, A. J. (1981), "Determinants of Cued Recall", *Psychological Research* **1**(4), 291–300.

Parkin, A. J. (1993), *Memory: Phenomena, Experiment and Theory*, Blackwell.

Reason, J. (1990), *Human Error*, Cambridge University Press.

Roddy, A. R. & Stosz, J. D. (1997), "Fingerprint Features - Statistical Analysis and System Performance Estimates", *Proceedings of the IEEE* **85**(9), 1390–421.

Rosenthal, R. & Rosnow, R. (1991), *The Essentials of Behavioural Research*, second edition, McGraw-Hill.

Sasse, M. A., Harris, C., Ismail, I. & Monthienvichienchai, P. (1998), Support for Authoring and Managing Web-based Coursework: The TACO Project, *in* R. Hazemi, S. Hailes & S. Wilbur (eds.), *The Digital University: Reinventing the Academy*, Springer-Verlag, pp.155–75.

Spector, Y. & Ginzberg, J. (1994), "Pass Sentence — A New Approach to Computer Code", *Computers and Security* **13**(2), 145–60.

Svigals, J. (1994), "Smartcards — A Security Assessment", *Computers and Security* **13**(2), 107–14.

Tulving, E. & Psotka, A. (1971), "Retroactive Inhibition in Free Recall: Inaccessibility of Information in the Memory Store", *Journal of Educational Psychology* **87**(1), 1–8.

Valentine, T. (1998), An Evaluation of the Passface™ Personal Authentication System, Technical Report, Goldmsiths College, University of London.

Valentine, T. (1999), Memory for Passfaces™ After a Long Delay, Technical Report, Goldsmiths College, University of London.

Wickens, C. D. (1992), *Engineering Psychology and Human Performance*, Harper Collins.

Zviran, M. & Haga, W. J. (1990), "Cognitive Passwords: The Key to Easy Access Control", *Computers and Security* **9**(8), 723–36.

Zviran, M. & Haga, W. J. (1993), "A Comparison of Password Techniques for Multilevel Authentication Mechanisms", *The Computer Journal* **36**(3), 227–37.

An Evaluation of Cone Trees

Andy Cockburn & Bruce McKenzie

Department of Computer Science, University of Canterbury,
Christchurch, New Zealand

Tel: *+64 3 364 2987 x7768*
Fax: *+64 3 364 2569*
EMail: *{andy, bruce}@cosc.canterbury.ac.nz*
URL: *http://www.cosc.canterbury.ac.nz/~andy*

Cone Trees are an appealing interactive 3D visualisation technique for hierarchical data structures. They were originally intended to maximise effective use of available screen space and to better exploit the abilities of the human perceptual system. Prior work has focused on the fidelity of the visualisation rather than providing empirical user studies. This paper describes the design, implementation and evaluation of a low-fidelity animated and rapidly interactive 3D cone tree system. Results of the evaluation show that our subjects were slower at locating data using cone trees than when using a 'normal' tree browser, and that their performance deteriorated rapidly as the branching factor of the data-structure increased. Qualitative results, however, indicate that the subjects were enthusiastic about the cone tree visualisation and that they felt it provided a better 'feel' for the structure of the information space.

Keywords: Cone Trees, visualisation, evaluation, navigation, structural views.

1 Introduction

Interactive visualisations of complex information spaces are designed to improve the ability of users to work with, and navigate through, rich data spaces. Examples include the three-dimensional data displays provided by cone trees (Robertson et al., 1991), the Data Mountain (Robertson et al., 1998), the Perspective Wall (Mackinlay et al., 1991), and the rich 2D displays of the Information Mural (Jerding & Stasko, 1998). While the sophistication of visualisations is dramatically increasing, there has been a surprising lack of empirical evaluation to provide evidence of improvements in efficiency and usability.

This paper focuses on cone trees, which were proposed as a visualisation technique that would "shift some of the user's cognitive load to the human perceptual system" while maximising the effective use of the available screen space (Robertson et al., 1991). They provide an animated 3D visualisation of hierarchical data structures. When a level in the hierarchy is expanded, its contents are arranged around the bottom of an inverted cone. The user's perspective is normally slightly above or below the display, allowing them to 'reach through' the hierarchy to select items. Cones can be rotated to bring data items to the foreground of the display.

Although cone trees have been used in several research systems, for example Cat-a-Cone (Hearst & Karadi, 1997) and LyberWorld (Hemmje et al., 1994), a fundamental limitation of the work on cone trees is the lack of empirical investigation into their usability and effectiveness. As Robertson et al. (1991) state, "Formal user studies are needed". With the exception of a small study by Carriere & Kazman (1995) which compared a cone tree system with a command-line interface, we are unaware of any prior attempt to quantitatively evaluate cone trees.

In this paper we describe the quantitative and qualitative evaluation of a small cone tree system. Although the interface fidelity of our implementation is low when compared to that of prior work, our focus is on creating a rapidly interactive interface that contains the full set of 3D functionality of previous systems. Our research objective is to produce reliable and repeatable results of usability.

The structure of the paper is as follow. First, we describe the interface and functionality of our cone tree implementation. Next, the evaluation method and results are described, followed by implications for further and related work. Conclusions are then presented.

2 A Minimal Cone Tree Implementation

Our cone tree system is designed to support users navigating through hierarchical file systems[*]. Figure 1(a) shows a single cone displaying the contents of the directory "/users/andy/places/vMed". Directories are distinguished from files by text colour; directories are red, files are blue. Directory contents are arranged around the cone in alphabetical order in an anti-clockwise direction from the front[†]. To explore the contents of any directory (or to hide its contents) the user clicks on the directory name with the middle mouse-button, as shown in Figure 1(b). To help the user identify the text-tags associated with expanded directories in cluttered displays, their background is coloured yellow ("/users/andy/places/vMed" and "Australia" in Figure 1(b)). When a parent cone is contracted and re-expanded, its previous display state is immediately restored, including the rotation and expansion state of all child cones in the hierarchy.

User controlled cone rotation is a fundamental requirement in supporting exploration of the data contained in the visualisation. It is essential that rotation

---

[*] It would be trivial to modify the system to work with almost any hierarchical data.

[†] This order is the default produced by the UNIX command `ls` which is used as our control in the evaluation.

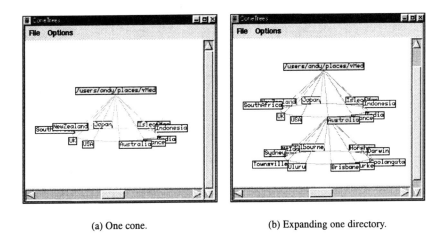

(a) One cone.   (b) Expanding one directory.

Figure 1: Basic cone tree interface.

is both rapid and animated. Rapidity is necessary to ensure that users see rotation as a 'lightweight' operation that does not disrupt their interaction with the system. Animation is needed to help the user maintain their sense of orientation within the data-space by easing the mapping between the pre- and post-rotation states. To rotate a cone, the user clicks on a text item with the left mouse button. The clicked item immediately turns green (to highlight the target), and the cone is smoothly rotated in the direction yielding the smallest angle change until the target is at the front of the cone. A configuration option allows users to choose whether child cones are dynamically rotated with the parent (providing a smooth animated display of the rotation of the entire hierarchy) or are redisplayed only when the animation of the parent cone is complete. This is a user-controlled trade-off between the fidelity of the visualisation and the speed of interaction. In our evaluations, all rotations took less than half a second, and the dynamic rotation option was disabled.

The presentation, placement and management of text identification tags in cone trees raises several complex interface design trade-offs. Our system uses a variety of techniques to ease the conflict between display-space clutter and support for item identification. By default, every item in every cone has a non-transparent text label that is implicitly raised above all other labels when the mouse cursor enters it. Non-transparent labels have the disadvantage that they can occlude other items, but our experiments with opaque and translucent labels showed that they greatly aid text legibility. In dense cones, many text labels can be displayed in close proximity, particularly at a cone's left and right extremities. This makes the implicit item raising feature difficult to use. In such circumstances the user can 'shuffle' the stacking order of text labels by right-clicking an item with the mouse.

A variety of configuration options allow the user to tailor the cone visualisation, including the following:

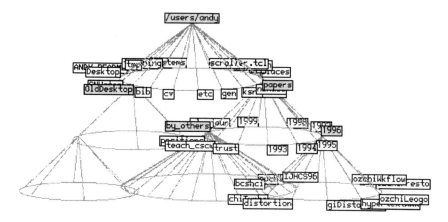

Figure 2: A hierarchy viewed with the "One named cone per level" option.

Constant/Variable cone radius: The variable cone radius option makes each cone's radius dependent on the number of items contained in the cone. This reduces the occurrence of occluded text items within each cone, but increases the occurrence of overlapping cones when several dense cones are displayed at the same level in the hierarchy.

One named cone per level: When the user displays more than one cone at any level in the hierarchy, portions of the cones are likely to collide. Although layout algorithms can reduce collisions between cone text labels, see (Carriere & Kazman, 1995), collisions cannot be completely avoided because of the effects of cone rotation. For instance, child cones that are displayed with maximum separation (the left and right extremities of the cone) will collide and occlude each other at the front and back positions if the parent is rotated through 90 degrees.

To ease this problem, the user can select a "One named cone per level" option which removes the text labels from all but the most recently expanded cone at each level. To maintain the user's sense of structure in the data space, the construction lines of all cones are displayed as normal (Figure 2).

User's perspective angle: To enhance the 3D interaction capabilities of the system, the user can shift their vertical angle of perspective. This is controlled by a slider widget that ranges from a side-on view (Figure 3(a)), through tilted views (Figure 3(b)), to a vertically downward view (Figure 3(c)).

Cone height: The final configuration option allows users to control the height of each cone.

Our cone tree interface also allows the user to view and manipulate the hierarchy using a normal holophrasting (Smith et al., 1984) tree browser similar to those

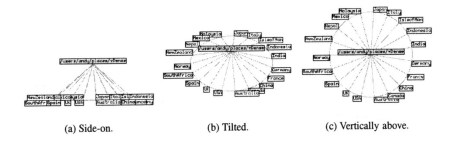

   (a) Side-on.   (b) Tilted.   (c) Vertically above.

Figure 3: Changing the user's perspective.

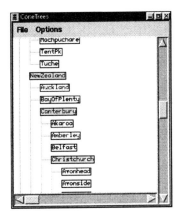

Figure 4: The 'tree browser' control interface.

used for file management in Windows Explorer and MacOS (see Figure 4). All interface controls and representation schemes are the same in both interfaces: the middle mouse button expands and contracts directories, text labels for directories are coloured red while those for files are coloured blue, and the background of the text labels of expanded directories are coloured yellow. This interface is used in the control for the experiment described in the following section.

3 Evaluation

The aim of the evaluation is to compare the efficiency of the cone tree interface for simple hierarchical navigation tasks with that of 'normal' tree interfaces, and to detect qualitative usability issues. We are also interested in the support provided by cone trees for navigating through hierarchies of different depths (number of levels in the hierarchy) and densities (number of items in each cone).

The experiment is a three-way factorial design with the following independent variables: depth, density, and interface type. The depth variable has two levels:

'shallow' for search paths of length two (for example, "Find California in the USA"), and 'deep' for search length four (for example, "Find Newport in Los Angeles in California in the USA"). The density variable has three levels: 'sparse', 'medium' and 'dense' for fan-out values of 6, 10 and 20 files or directories contained within each directory. Robertson et al. (1991) stated that cone trees become cluttered and ineffective at a branching factor of 30, so our choice of 20 as a maximum branching factor is fairly conservative. The two levels in the interface type variable are 'cone tree' and 'normal tree'.

Each subject completed seven paired tasks, with the pairing repeating the same task for the cone and normal tree interfaces. Experimental conditions for each task are summarised in Table 1. The first six task pairs covered all combinations of the independent variables, and they tested the subjects' ability to navigate through a stated series of directories to locate a named file. Tasks 1 to 6 all start from a fully contracted state with only the top-level directory name showing. Task 7 interleaved the subjects' completion of Task 6 (the deep and dense condition). In contrast to Tasks 1 to 6, Task 7 starts from an expanded system state, testing the subjects' ability to return to a previously visited file (the one visited in Task 1). The interleaved order between Tasks 6 and 7, then, was 6.1, 7.1, 6.2, 7.2, and the system state is only reset to a fully contracted state prior to Tasks 6.1 and 6.2.

The interface order used for each task (cone, then normal, or vice-versa) was varied between each task and between each subject to control any learning effect. In addition, we tested the response times to ensure that order had no significant effect on task completion times (as summarised in the results).

In selecting the navigational paths for each task, three sample paths were generated for each depth (see right hand column of Table 1). These tasks were then rotated round the three levels of the density independent variable for each of the subjects. We could not use random selection of navigational paths because of the difficulty of providing a familiar hierarchy with fan-out of 20 to four levels of depth (requiring 160,000 meaningful place names).

Task completion times were measured by the software which recorded all user actions and their timing.

3.1 Subject Details and Treatment

Twelve volunteer subjects, all Computer Science professionals or graduate students, took part in the evaluation. Each subject participated in a single half-hour session.

The first ten minutes of each session was spent introducing the subject to the two interfaces. Most of the subjects were familiar with the normal tree style of interface, but they were given several sample tasks to ensure they were familiar with the mouse bindings used to display and hide directory contents. The subjects were also given sample tasks in the cone tree interface, and they were encouraged to experiment with the interface mechanisms for rotating, expanding and contracting cones, as well as the techniques for shuffling text-labels and scrolling round the display. The various configuration options, such as the ability to change the user's angle of perspective, were neither described nor used in the evaluation. The introductory session continued until the subjects reported that they felt comfortable with both interfaces.

Task	Depth	Density	Paths (rotated between Tasks 1–3 and 4–6)
1	Shallow	Sparse (6)	France to Buoux
2		Medium (10)	Australia to Sydney
3		Dense (20)	Isle of Man to Chasms
4	Deep	Sparse (6)	UK to Yorkshire to York to Shambles
5		Medium (10)	USA to California to Los Angeles to Newport
6		Dense (20)	New Zealand to Canterbury to Christchurch to Sumner
7†	Shallow	Dense (20)	Return to the Task 1 file

† Note: Task 7 is interleaved with Task 6

Table 1: Conditions for the seven pairs of tasks.

The subjects were informed that they would carry out fourteen tasks involving following, as quickly as possible, a specified series of directories to reach a particular file. They were told that the file structure was a geographical hierarchy of countries, regions, cities and places.

Each task was introduced to the subject via a graphical user interface that controlled the experimental condition (the selection of the navigational path and the order of the interfaces). It displayed the path that the subject had to navigate through in large red text, and the subjects were asked to read the path out loud prior to being told to start.

After each task the subjects recorded their level of agreement with two statements: "It was easy to see the data needed", and "Overall the normal/cone tree interface was effective for the task." Responses were recorded using a five-point Likert scale. Once all of the tasks were completed, the subjects were asked for comments about the interfaces.

4 Results

This section reports the quantitative results of the experiment. Qualitative results are reported in the following section.

All of the subjects were able to complete the tasks fairly rapidly. The mean time for task completion across all conditions was 8.3 seconds, and the minimum and maximum times across all tasks were 1.9 seconds (using the normal tree in Task 1) and 29.2 seconds (using the cone tree in Task 6). Figure 5(a) shows the means and standard deviations for the two interfaces in each of the tasks.

Three-way analysis of variance (ANOVA) with repeated measures reveals that the main effects for each of the independent variables are significant. The mean task times for the normal tree and cone tree interfaces were 6.7 and 9.9 seconds, providing a reliable difference ($F(1,11) = 71.98, p < 0.001$). The means for the shallow and

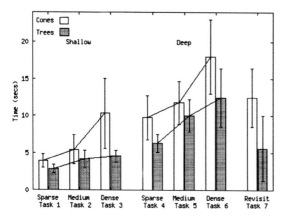

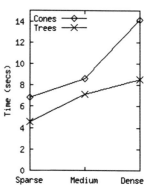

(a) Mean task completion times and standard deviations in seconds for the cone tree and normal tree interfaces across density and depth independent variables.

(b) The interaction between factors interface type and density.

Figure 5: Results.

deep conditions were 5.2 and 11.4 seconds ($F(1,11) = 133.9, p < 0.001$). Finally, the means for the three levels of the density factor were also significantly different at 5.7, 7.9 and 11.3 seconds for the levels sparse, medium and dense ($F(2,22) = 64.1, p < 0.001$). Summarising the main effects: the subjects followed the paths more quickly using the normal-tree interface than when using the cone tree interface; unsurprisingly, they took more time to follow deep navigational paths than shallow paths; finally, the subjects took longer to follow paths in densely populated data sets.

There is a significant interaction between the density and type independent variables ($F(2,22) = 12.8, p < 0.001$). The effect of the interaction is clear in Figure 5(b): using the cone interface, the time taken for the dense condition increases dramatically from that for the medium and sparse conditions, while using the normal tree interface, there is a more gradual increase between the sparse, medium and dense conditions. A Tukey honest significant difference for this interaction is 7.2 (maintaining α at the 0.05 level), revealing that only the mean for the 'dense' and 'cone' condition yields significant differences from any other condition.

There is no interaction between the depth and type factors ($F(1,11) = 0.77, p = 0.4$). This shows that while the subjects took longer to complete deep tasks than shallow ones, there were no significant differences in the rate of degradation in their performance between the two interfaces.

The main effects and interactions detailed above describe the subjects' behaviour in Tasks 1 to 6, which involved following a single path starting with a single unexpanded directory in an otherwise clear display. In contrast, Task 7 investigates the differences in the support for following paths when starting from a partially explored representation of the data-structure.

	Task 1	Task 2	Task 3	Task 4	Task 5	Task 6	Task 7
	"It was easy to see the data needed"						
Cone: Mean(Std.Dev.)	3.92(0.9)	3.42(0.79)	2.42(1.0)	3.75(0.97)	3.08(0.9)	2.67(1.5)	3.17(1.47)
Tree: Mean(Std.Dev.)	4.58(0.51)	4.5(0.52)	4.08(0.9)	4.5(0.52)	3.92(0.67)	3.83(0.84)	4.33(0.49)
Paired T(11)	-2.35	-4.17	-4.43	-2.69	-3.08	-2.55	-2.76
p	0.039	0.002	0.001	0.021	0.01	0.03	0.019
	"Overall the interface was effective for the task"						
Cone: Mean(Std.Dev.)	4.17(0.72)	3.67(0.78)	2.83(0.94)	3.67(0.98)	3.33(0.78)	3.0(1.54)	3.17(1.34)
Tree: Mean(Std.Dev.)	4.75(0.45)	4.67(0.49)	4.17(0.83)	4.58(0.52)	3.83(0.72)	3.75(0.45)	4.25(0.45)
Paired T(11)	-2.55	-3.63	-4.0	-2.93	-2.17	-1.83	-2.6
p	0.027	0.004	0.002	0.014	0.053*	0.095*	0.025

Table 2: Responses to the Likert questions (1 = strongly disagree, 5 = strongly agree). * marks differences that are *not* significant at the 0.05 level.

The mean time for completing Task 7 with the cone interface (12.5 seconds, s.d. 3.9) was more than twice that using the normal tree interface (5.6 seconds, s.d. 4.4), providing a significant difference (paired t-test, $t(11) = 4.4, p < 0.01$).

Our experimental design assumed that the interface order used for each task would not significantly influence the subjects' task completion time. Our control for order involved varying the interface that each subject used first, both between tasks and between subjects. To confirm that order was not a confounding factor in our experiment, we calculated a per-subject difference between task completion time using the cone and normal tree interfaces for each task. We then compared these values between the subjects that used the cone interface first, and those that used the normal tree interface first. None of these differences were significant at the 0.05 level (unpaired t-tests, p values 0.06, 0.73, 0.13, 0.36, 0.57, 0.95, 0.36 for Tasks 1 to 7).

The subjects' responses to the questionnaire also yielded significant results. The mean responses to the question "It was easy to see the data needed" were significantly different between interfaces for all tasks (see Table 2). Similarly, in all but Tasks 5 and 6 there were significant differences in the responses about the overall effectiveness of the interfaces. Figure 6 shows that the subjects rated both interfaces more poorly as the data density increased; however, the ratings decreased more rapidly for the cone interface. Note that subjects rated the overall effectiveness of the cone tree interface higher than their assessment of the ease of seeing the data.

5 Discussion

The quantitative results show that the subjects took longer to complete their tasks when using the cone interface, and that they rated the cone interface more poorly than the normal one for seeing and interacting with the data structure. There were, however, many positive comments about the cone interface, and half of the subjects performed at least one of the tasks more rapidly using cones.

The most common positive comment about the cone interface was that it made it easier to see the structure and population of the explored data-space (reported by five of the subjects). Four of the subjects felt that their lack of familiarity with the

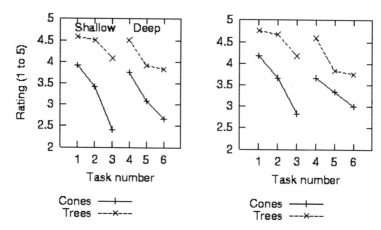

Figure 6: Likert responses by task for the two interfaces: "It was easy to see the data needed" (left); "Overall the interface was effective for the task" (right).

cone interface was a major factor in their task completion times, and they believed they would be able to become much more efficient with more experience. The most common negative comment concerned the difficulty of finding the desired text label amongst the clutter of overlapping labels in dense tasks.

The ability to rotate cones received both positive and negative comments. Three participants commented that rotation was a good alternative to scrolling, with one adding that he disliked scrolling. In contrast, one subject stated that he found rotation disorienting, stating that that it was "easy to lose landmarks".

Despite the fact that our results show that cone trees were not as effective for the tasks in our study, the subjects' comments indicate that several factors could have contributed towards an overly negative set of results. These factors are as follows:

Experimental tasks and conditions: The tasks in our study are characterised by 'text-based search and locate'. These tasks were selected because of the predominantly text-based nature of most file-organisation schemes. However, it seems likely that the 3D organisation of cone trees is inherently poor at representing text labels. Our subjects' comments indicated that cone trees may be more effective in providing users with a sense of structure and population. Therefore, there is reason to suspect that cone trees may perform relatively better in tasks such as "find the most densely populated directory" or "find the deepest directory".

The constant screen real-estate used in both interface conditions is also likely to have detrimentally affected the subjects' performance with the cone interface. The need for vertical scrolling could have been removed in the cone tree interface if we had allowed the subjects to maximise the window. However, if we had allowed this for the cone interface, we would also have had to allow it for the normal tree interface, with a consequent reduction in the amount of scrolling required in both conditions.

Familiarity: As mentioned above, with more training, it is likely that the subjects would have improved their task completion times using the cone tree interface.

Interface fidelity: Previous work with cone trees has focused primarily on the fidelity of the 3D cone representation. Our interface is crude by comparison, but this compromise allowed us to achieve rapid animated interaction, even for large data-structures. Two of the subjects (who had prior experience with VRML representations of cone trees) commented on the relatively poor rendering of cones, but no subjects stated that their performance was detrimentally affected by this. Enhanced cone representation, such as shading and shadowing, might improve subject performance, and future evaluations should determine if this is the case.

6 Conclusions

Cone tree visualisations of hierarchical data structures were first described by Robertson et al. (1991). Since then, there have been numerous refinements on the concept, but there has been a notable absence of empirical studies to demonstrate their effectiveness. This paper provides an empirical foundation for future work on the usability of cone tree interfaces. Results show that our subjects were significantly slower at locating named files in a hierarchical data structure when using our cone tree interface than when using a 'normal' tree interface. Subject performance also deteriorated rapidly with cone trees as the density (branching factor) of the data structure increased.

Despite relatively poor task performance times, many subjects were enthusiastic about the cone tree interface. In particular, several subjects stated that cone trees provided a better feel for the structure of the data-space. In our further work we will investigate the effectiveness of using cone trees in different types of navigation tasks, and we will explore the effects of enhancing the interface's 3D visual cues.

Availability

The cone tree interface is written in Tcl/Tk and is available on request from the first author.

References

Carriere, J. & Kazman, R. (1995), Visualizing Huge Hierarchies: Beyond Cone Trees, *in Proceedings of the 1995 IEEE Symposium on Information Visualization, October 1995, Atlanta, Georgia*, IEEE Computer Society Press, pp.74–81.

Hearst, M. A. & Karadi, C. (1997), Cat-a-Cone: An Interactive Interface for Specifying Searches and Viewing Retrieval Results using a Large Category Hierarchy, *in* N. Belkin, A. Narasimhalu & P. Willett (eds.), *SIGIR'97 Proceedings of the Twentieth Annual International ACM SIGIR Conference on Research and Development in Information Retrieval*, ACM Press, pp.246–55.

Hemmje, M., Kunkel, C. & Willet, A. (1994), LyberWorld — A Visualization User Interface Supporting Fulltext Retrieval, *in* W. Croft & C. van Rijsbergen (eds.), *SIGIR'94*

Proceedings of the Seventeenth Annual International ACM SIGIR Conference on Research and Development in Information Retrieval, ACM Press, pp.249–59.

Jerding, D. F. & Stasko, J. T. (1998), "The Information Mural: A Technique for Displaying and Navigating Large Information Spaces", *IEEE Transactions on Visualization and Computer Graphics* 4(3), 257–71.

Mackinlay, J. D., Robertson, G. G. & Card, S. K. (1991), The Perspective Wall: Details and Context Smoothly Integrated, *in* S. P. Robertson, G. M. Olson & J. S. Olson (eds.), *Proceedings of CHI'91: Human Factors in Computing Systems (Reaching through Technology)*, ACM Press, pp.173–9.

Robertson, G., Czerwinski, M., Larson, K., Robbins, D., Thiel, D. & van Dantzich, M. (1998), Data Mountain: Using Spatial Memory for Document Management, *in* B. Schilit (ed.), *Proceedings of the ACM Symposium on User Interface Software and Technology, UIST'98*, ACM Press, pp.153–62.

Robertson, G. G., Mackinlay, J. D. & Card, S. K. (1991), Cone Trees: Animated 3D Visualizations of Hierarchical Information, *in* S. P. Robertson, G. M. Olson & J. S. Olson (eds.), *Proceedings of CHI'91: Human Factors in Computing Systems (Reaching through Technology)*, ACM Press, pp.189–94.

Smith, S. R., Barnard, D. T. & Macleod, I. A. (1984), "Holophrasted Displays in an Interactive Environment", *International Journal of Man–Machine Studies* 20(4), 343–55.

The Evaluation of Desperado — A Computerised Tool to Aid Design Reuse

Nicola J Lambell, Linden J Ball[†] & Thomas C Ormerod[‡]

Department of Psychology, University of Plymouth, Drake Circus, Plymouth PL4 8AA, UK

Tel: *+44 1752 233 147*
Fax: *+44 1752 233 176*
EMail: *n.lambell@plymouth.ac.uk*
URL: *psy.plym.ac.uk/staff/nlhp.html*

[†] *Institute of Behavioural Sciences, University of Derby, Mickleover, Derby DE3 5GX, UK*

[‡] *Department of Psychology, Lancaster University, Fylde College, Lancaster LA1 4YF, UK*

The reuse of previous design knowledge when tackling a current problem is a potentially important way to improve design efficiency. However, unguided reuse is fraught with problems. Our current goal is to try and limit the problems associated with reuse in engineering contexts by means of a computer-based support tool which guides the effective encoding of information for subsequent reuse. This paper presents an evaluation of such a tool that we have developed, which is known as Desperado. The evaluation involved observing academic designers working on a short design brief, either with or without Desperado. Our observational data are reported in conjunction with designers' subjective experiences of using Desperado. It was found that whilst the introduction of the system changed the nature of the users' design work, these changes were primarily associated with a better exploration and evaluation of possible design options.

Keywords: design representation, design reuse, design rationale, design support, minimal representation, information retrieval, information indexing, usability issues.

1   Introduction

The reuse of previous design ideas is an attractive proposition. It could reduce development costs, maintain quality, improve productivity, avoid repetition of design effort and maintain upward product compatibility and consistency with company standards. The reuse of software code and specifications has been shown to benefit software engineers (Sutcliffe & Maiden, 1990) and work has been undertaken to produce appropriate tools to support this process; see Tracz (1988) for an overview of past research, and Pena-Mora & Vadhavkar (1997) as an example of more recent research. Supporting reuse should not, however, be limited to software designing. Reuse is applicable in all areas of design and with the appropriate tools could actively enhance innovation in these areas. The notion of *innovative* design-reuse sounds at first like an oxymoron. However, providing access to previous design options enables the maintenance of innovation over time. When designers know that ideas, if not implemented immediately, may be useful for future projects, they may explore them more creatively.

1.1   Issues in Design Reuse

In spite of the potential benefits associated with reuse, unguided reuse is fraught with problems that tend to reduce designers' willingness to reuse and the effectiveness of their actual reuse activity. Ball et al. (in press) present an in-depth discussion of such problems that we summarise here. First, designers appear to demonstrate difficulties in recognising potentially reusable information in previous designs (Woodfield et al., 1987), a problem which is exacerbated the further into the past the previous design recedes (Busby, 1998). Sutcliffe & Maiden (1990) similarly found that inexperienced designers tended to reuse specifications based on surface features rather than deep-level analogies. This resulted in the erroneous transfer of domain knowledge.

Second, designers are inclined to underestimate the amount of modification required on those occasions when they do recognise relevant candidate designs (Busby, 1998). In addition, when modifying designs, because designers tend to rely heavily on their memory of previous information they are also likely to replicate the faults of the original design (Ball et al., 1998; Busby, 1997; Busby, 1998). This problem is especially problematic given the absence of efficient indexing of previous design information.

Third, the invocation of previous design ideas may restrict the range of options that are explored by designers (Ormerod et al., 1999). Even expert designers engage in minimal solution-search behaviours and reveal severe *satisficing* tendencies — often becoming fixated upon single solutions rather than exploring alternatives in order to improve choices; see Ball et al. (1998) for a review of evidence and explanations of such tendencies in the reuse of design solutions.

Finally, as Banker et al. (1993) have noted, at an organisational level design companies may provide little incentive for reusing previous designs, whilst at an individual level designers may be reluctant due to problems of quality assurance (Busby, 1998). However, our own experience (Ormerod et al., 1999) suggests that many design companies and individual designers are currently becoming more proactive in their attempt to capitalise upon the potential benefits of design reuse.

Despite the problems that confront designers reusing past solutions, we believe that there is considerable potential for cost-effective design reuse in innovative design practice if such limiting factors can be eliminated or ameliorated. The task remains to develop a support system that addresses these problems.

1.2 Using Design Rationale to Support Design Reuse

Our research on supporting design reuse is focussed within the context of engineering design. The approach we adopt has been guided by the notion of 'design rationale' (DR). DR involves the documenting of the underlying reasoning behind the design of an artifact and describes the actual design process which culminated in a set of particular design features (Moran & Carroll, 1996). The documenting of DR itself can lead to a better understanding of the issues involved, aid maintenance and redesign, improve critical reflection and reasoning, and enable more efficient communication between designers. Of primary importance to our aims is the notion that documenting of DR can aid reuse and limit some of the problems discussed previously.

Lee (1997) suggests that DR can serve as an index of past knowledge, thereby improving the ability of designers to spot relevant designs. Pena-Mora & Vadhavkar (1997) used DR to help index software code to promote reuse. DR itself is also potentially reusable. It would additionally improve the understanding of previous designs as it provides a common language of understanding, enabling designers to assess the implications of attempting to modify a previous design (McKerlie & MacLean, 1994) and providing a means of checking the integrity of previous designs to overcome quality assurance problems. Thus the current problems of reuse to do with understanding, adaptation, indexing and relevance could all be reduced by reusing DR and by using DR to index previous solutions. However, the benefits of DR for reuse depend heavily on the technique used to capture and represent DR.

Shipman & McCall (1997) distinguish between three different perspectives on DR: argumentation, documentation and communication. The Argumentation approach focuses on capturing the thinking itself in an orderly way. Documentation focuses on recording decisions and the actual thinking is fairly implicit. Communication captures information in the form of communications such as emails, faxes and design-meeting notes and much of the DR is implicit within these communications. Shipman & McCall argue that the communication approach is the most effective method of capturing all of the DR involved in a design but it is difficult to index and therefore retrieve relevant DR. The argumentation approach, on the other hand, has more problems associated with effective capture of DR but is very useful for retrieval of relevant DR. Thus the argumentation approach would seem to be the most suitable for supporting reuse.

There are several different argumentation techniques, the two most widely considered being the Issue Based Information Systems (IBIS) approach developed by Rittel & Weber (1973; Rittel, 1984) and the Questions, Options and Criteria, or QOC approach pioneered by MacLean et al. (1991). Both of these representations provide structural components to enable the development of a graphical network of nodes and links which captures the design rationale.

Proponents of the issue-based approach tend to consider DR to be a record or a history of design deliberations. IBIS seeks to capture the key design issues that are articulated in the course of the conversation between stakeholders, along with the various positions that are raised in response to these issues and the pros and cons of these various positions. In contrast, MacLean et al. do not see DR as being a record but a co-product of design which is constructed in addition to the artifact itself. QOC seeks to represent and explain the relationship between an artifact and its alternative design possibilities (Options) using Questions and Criteria, to guide the construction and evaluation of these design alternatives. Whilst both approaches would be suitable candidates for our computer support tool, the QOC approach was chosen for several reasons.

First, the QOC notation is more consistent with recent empirical observations that design activity, in both individual and cooperative contexts, seems to be naturally segmented in terms of Questions and their associated Options and Criteria (Ball & Ormerod, 2000). The IBIS approach, on the other hand, appears to suffer from the lack of an explicit criterion space (Lee & Lai, 1996), and thus seems less reflective of natural design activity than the QOC formalism (MacLean et al., 1991). Second, the evaluation of Options in relation to plausible alternatives is fundamental to QOC, and is especially useful for reuse as it specifies not only the reasoning behind an artifact but also offers a host of plausible alternatives which can be reused, thereby challenging satisficing behaviours, design fixation and confirmation biases (McKerlie & MacLean, 1994). Third, the assessment of Options against Criteria is useful for design modifications since the Criteria emphasise what was considered important when Questions and Options were first examined. As such, the negative implications of a change in the design are readily apparent since certain Criteria will no longer be satisfied. Questions also help to shape ideas better thus making it much easier to detect relevant rationales. Finally, it is noteworthy that proponents of the QOC approach emphasise its value for design reuse (McKerlie & MacLean, 1994), whereas advocates of IBIS-based models explicitly state that reusability is a secondary concern (Conklin & Burgess-Yakemovic, 1996).

Our approach to encoding DR is based on the notion of Questions, Options and Criteria but does not fully implement the complete philosophy associated with this approach. For example it does not support a hierarchical representation. The next section describes the system and the encoding of Questions, Options and Criteria to aid effective reuse of design ideas.

2 System Description

2.1 Overview of the System

The development of Desperado involved phases of needs analysis, requirements specification, conceptual and detailed design, and implementation. The development was also informed by frequent discussions with end user companies and from ethnographic data collected at the beginning of this project (Ball & Ormerod, 2000). Desperado is now in its second phase of development; see Ball et al. (in press) for a detailed discussion of the implementation of Desperado I and subsequent development of Desperado II. The current version of Desperado has a Web-browser oriented front-end written in HTML and JavaScript connecting to a relational database using Filemaker Pro.

Desperado is based around the notion of a 'design episode'. This is the unit of encoding which is the basis of the indexing of reusable information. An episode is focussed around the notion of Questions, Options and Criteria. It begins with the pursuit of a Question and the subsequent encoding of relevant indices (such as user and client information) pertaining to that Question. It then enables the exploration of Options and Criteria pertaining to that Question and the storage of other relevant documents. Distinctions between the end of one episode and the beginning of a subsequent episode are determined by shifts from one Question to another. Thus Desperado supports structured, goal-oriented shifts in activity which are thought to be the hallmark of design expertise (Ball & Ormerod, 1995; Ball et al., 1997) as well as allowing for more opportunistic shifts to emergent design issues (Sen, 1997) to facilitate crucial aspects of design flexibility.

Desperado was designed to provide an environment for the simultaneous encoding and reuse of design information during ongoing design work. Relevant episodes from the database are made available for retrieval during encoding. The system additionally provides pop-up menus with information from previous design episodes. These menus promote reuse of key terminology whilst also ensuring naming consistency and reducing the need for manual data entry.

The prompting of relevant previous episodes and prioritisation of information in the pop-up menus are performed by an interpreter. This interpreter uses prioritisation data to rank order previous episodes and labels. There are five sources of prioritisation data: time of episode, user selected defaults, key word matching, frequency of retrieval, and weighting derived during the process of rating Options against Criteria and weightings based on whether an Option was adopted or not. The interpreter contains an algorithm which evaluates the value of the data from each design episode and then it presents the most appropriate episodes and labels at the top of the retrieval menu and pop-up menus.

2.2   Guided Encoding and Retrieval

The system provides a sequenced procedural dialogue that elicits information from users. This method of information elicitation makes the process of encoding, reusing and designing interactive. The four phases are:

Phase 1: Data-oriented encoding. The first phase in the encoding of an episode involves specifying the design Question to be pursued and the encoding of episode indices. These indices consist of information pertaining to: the user, the component function, the stage of design (e.g. requirements vs. conceptual vs. detailed design), the scope of the design activity (e.g. project-specific, organisational) and episode type (e.g. notes, meeting). During encoding the system provides pop-up menus containing previous episode labels and relevant episodes for reuse.

Phase 2: QOC encoding. This involves the elicitation of the Options and Criteria that relate to the Question specified in Phase 1, and the subsequent cross-rating of Options and Criteria together with associated decision-making. Again, relevant episodes are made available in the retrieval window. Additionally, users can access previous Option and Criteria names directly via the pop-up menus.

Phase 3: Indexing of supplementary documentation. This involves the indexing of relevant design documents such as CAD files and requirements specifications.

Phase 4: Specification of 'consequents'. This involves the specification of Questions that emerge as a result of the current episode. The notion of consequents resembles the construct of dependencies (McCall, 1991) where answering a design Question may depend upon how other Questions are answered.

The are also five modes of system use and a user can only be in one mode at a time. A user can:

- browse sequentially though all of the episodes in the database;

- search for specific episodes in the database using keywords;

- explore system-prompted episodes that appear as suggestions in a retrieval menu;

- create a new episode and then submit it for storage in the database; and

- edit an existing episode.

These distinctions between modes of system use are aimed at preventing the erroneous loss of information from the database (i.e. you cannot edit an episode unless you are specifically in edit mode) and enabling user-initiated reuse (via searching and retrieving of existing information) as well as system-initiated prompts.

3   The Evaluation Study

3.1   Aims

The purpose of this study was to evaluate the usability and effectiveness of the Desperado system (at an interface level and at the more fundamental level of encoding QOCs during ongoing design). Direct observations of participants using Desperado whilst designing were complemented by data from a post experimental questionnaire. These evaluation techniques enabled objective and subjective insights into participants' use of Desperado, including its direct affect upon their design behaviour.

3.2 Design

For this study we developed three design briefs in consultation with managers at end-user companies. The first brief related to the design of an automated car-rental facility, the second to the design of an automated cloakroom, and the third to the design of an automated short-loan library facility. All three briefs shared analogous deep- and surface-level features. For example, they all involved automation of non-automatic facilities, they all focussed on product conceptualisation, and all involved inputs and outputs to the system. The briefs were designed to be non-routine since Buckingham Shum et al. (1997) found that participants had some difficulties implementing QOC analysis on routine design tasks. The briefs were, therefore, based on design concepts that participants would not be familiar with, but for which they would possess the necessary skills in their repertoire to tackle them effectively.

The experiment involved three sessions and each session was uniquely associated with one of the three design briefs. This arrangement enabled control of the information available to the designers for reuse during each session. In Session 1, all participants worked on the car-rental brief, using pen and paper only. In Session 2 (the cloakroom brief) the Control group used pen and paper only while the Desperado group used Desperado with encoding mode (i.e. without retrieval). In Session 3 (the short-loan library brief) the Control group used pen and paper only while the Desperado group used Desperado with encoding and retrieval. At this stage Desperado was seeded with design work from the previous session which was available for retrieval.

This experimental design allowed the effects of encoding to be partialled out from those of retrieval. It also allowed comparisons to be made within-participant (Session 1 vs. 2 vs. 3) and within design brief (Control vs. Desperado Sessions 1, 2 and 3). The inclusion of a control group also allowed us to consider the natural occurrence of reuse.

Eighteen MSc students from Lancaster University were paid £15 per session and 15 participants completed all three sessions (seven Control and eight Desperado). These students were all trained in mechanical and/or electronic engineering and had an average of six years of academic and company-based experience. All participants had attended an introductory course on the concepts of documentation and DR. After Session 1, participants were matched according to their verbalisation ability and the clarity of their transcripts. One person from the pair was then randomly assigned to the Desperado condition and the other remained a Control.

Design sessions were separated by intervals of about two months. During each session each participant spent approximately one hour developing a conceptual design to meet the brief. Participants made notes and sketches, and, where appropriate, encoded and retrieved design episodes using Desperado. All participants were instructed to produce concurrent think-aloud verbalisations during the experiment and were told that we were interested in capturing the initial hour of their normal design process.

All of the participants in the Desperado condition received an overview and training exercise in their first encounter with Desperado and a top-up training exercise in their second encounter. The training and exercises were based on a design brief about the development of a sealing system for milk cartons. Participants were familiar with this design problem from their Master's studies. The training was deliberately brief to allow a conservative evaluation of Desperado.

The data were analysed to examine the nature of reuse and the usability of the Desperado system. Additionally, participants' transcripts were coded in terms of Questions, Options and Criteria. This allowed comparisons to be made concerning the nature of design activity for participants working with and without Desperado.

3.3 Design of Usability Questionnaire

Henderson et al. (1995) found that direct observation tended to fail to produce any useful insights into how to improve computer programs whereas questionnaire data lacked the ability to pinpoint directly the nature and location of possible problems with a system. Thus it was decided to combine the two techniques in order to maximise the informativeness of our usability data. This two-pronged approach to usability analysis was considered to be the most suitable for enabling a comparison of participants' behaviour and their subjective experience of the system and for providing clear insight into possible areas of improvement. Subjective experience was considered to be important because it was felt that demonstrating the system's usefulness was not sufficient in itself to ensure that people would use the system in the future. It was hypothesised that people would not use the system unless they explicitly felt that they would gain something from it.

The first two sections of the questionnaire required participants to rate statements about the Desperado system and their use of QOC analysis on a five-point Likert scale. Half of the statements were phrased positively and half were phrased negatively. Additional space was provided below each statement to enable justifications of their ratings and a number of open-ended questions. The design was informed by Henderson et al.'s research that established that feedback would enable greater insight into participants' perceptions than just simple ratings. The statements employed and the questions asked were also informed by their questionnaire. Our statements and questions are discussed individually in the results section. The questionnaire was given to participants at the end of Session 3.

4 Results

4.1 Observational Data

Full analysis of our extensive data-set is ongoing and the present analysis is therefore based on a subset of data (four participants from each condition). Initial analysis of the transcripts was centred on identifying specific episodes that were present (for the Desperado groups, these episodes were in the main directly retrieved from the databases for each participant). Episodes were then coded according to elements comprising the episode-specific Question, Options and Criteria (in many instances, the Questions in the Control group transcripts were inferred from the presence of Option/Criteria clusters). A key aim of our QOC-based analysis was to enable comparison of design activity between Desperado and Control conditions (e.g. in terms of the mean number of Options that were generated per Question, and the mean number of Criteria per Question).

In addition, a composite hierarchy of QOC elements was produced for each transcript in order to examine further aspects of the nature and quality of design work within the Desperado and Control conditions. First, the hierarchy permitted an examination of the quantity of 'basic design functions' (i.e. key, high-level aspects of the artifact) that each designer developed in their design session — thus providing an index of the *breadth* of design work undertaken. Second, the hierarchy allowed for an assessment of the number of 'design levels traversed' during a session — thus providing a measure of the maximum *depth* to which each designer explored the problem. Third, the hierarchy facilitated the identification of the 'design view' of each Question and Option element — which allowed us to examine the impact of Desperado on the *type* of work that the designers were engaging in. The design view was coded according to whether the designer was exploring the Question or Option from a functional-, structural-, procedural- or optimisation-oriented perspective. For example, Questions such as "How does the machine collect keys on return?" were coded as being functionally-oriented whereas Questions such as "When should the keys be dispensed?" were considered to be procedurally-oriented. The design-view coding scheme was developed in the light of insights deriving from MacLean et al. (1991) work as well as initial, informal analysis of our protocols.

Table 1 presents the results of the episode and QOC analyses, and Table 2 presents a summary of the design-view characteristics. While caution should be exercised in the interpretation of the data in Table 1 and 2, owing to the relatively small number of designers being considered, it seems clear that Desperado is having an impact upon design activity. The effects can be interpreted both as negative and positive.

Table 1 shows that the Control group are generating a broadly equivalent number of total and unique design Questions across all design sessions, whereas the Desperado group demonstrate a marked decline in Question generation after the introduction of the system (i.e. at Sessions 2 and 3). The Control group are also developing the design hierarchy in apparently greater depth and breadth than the Desperado group. This is indicated by the marked decline in the number of Design Levels Traversed and Basic Design Functions addressed in Sessions 2 and 3. These findings may suggest that the Desperado group achieved less coverage of the design brief. However, this is only to be expected. Not only do the people in the Desperado group carry the burden of interacting with a relatively unfamiliar system, but they are also required to undertake the additional requirement of documenting their design rationale (in the form of Option and Criterion encoding and rating). The latter point is particularly important, since over two thirds of interactions that participants made with Desperado were to rate Options under Criteria. In contrast, there was scant evidence in the protocols of the Control group for participants undertaking the systematic evaluation of Options under all the Criteria that they generated. It is also worth noting a decrease in the time taken per Question between Sessions 2 and 3 for the Desperado group, which suggests a strong system-learning effect.

Positive evidence for Desperado comes from inspection of the mean number of Options and Criteria considered per Question. The Desperado group considered up to three times as many Options per Question as the Control group, and up to six

Session Characteristics	Control			Desperado		
	Session 1	Session 2	Session 3	Session 1	Session 2	Session 3
Design Levels Traversed	6.8 (0.96)	7.3 (0.58)	7 (1)	6.3 (0.58)	4.3 (0.58)	4.3 (0.58)
Basic Design Functions	11 (1.63)	9 (1)	10.7 (0.58)	10.7 (1.15)	3 (2)	4.7 (1.15)
Minutes Taken per Question	1.12	1.3	0.88	0.76	13.86	6.67
Total Questions	53 (9.1)	51 (11.6)	70 (19.1)	88 (18.5)	4 (1.2)	9 (1.7)
Unique Questions	33 (2.1)	30 (5.5)	40 (14.9)	55 (9.2)	4 (1.2)	9 (1.7)
Total Options per Question	1.1	1.5	1.1	1.2	3.8	2.6
Unique Options per Question	0.9	1.2	0.9	1.1	3.0	2.0
Total Criteria per Question	0.6	0.8	0.5	0.6	3.5	3.2
Unique Criteria per Question	0.5	0.6	0.4	0.5	2.8	1.4

Note: Standard deviations are presented in parenthesis. Design Levels Traversed provides a measure of the depth to which design work was carried out, while Basic Design Function provides a measure of the breadth of key design aspects developed in each session. The term 'Total' refers to all Q, O or C elements coded within a session (and includes repeat mentions of such elements during a designer's attempt at the task). The term 'Unique' reflects a count of the unique occurrences of a Q, O or C element within a session (e.g. if a designer mentioned the Criterion of 'cost' several times during their design activity, then this would only be scored once in the Unique category).

Table 1: Mean design-activity scores across sessions of the Control and Desperado conditions.

times as many Criteria. This is important, since the pursuit of multiple Options is precisely the kind of innovative design behaviour that Desperado was intended to encourage as a way of overcoming satisficing in design. We are also encouraged by the increased number of Criteria considered for each Question, since this suggests that Desperado is encouraging reflective design.

There are clearly some problems with Desperado II, that require attention in future versions. For example, it is apparent from Table 2 that whilst a small but significant proportion of the Control group's time was spent engaging in procedurally-oriented design work, there was a complete absence of any procedure-orientated work after the introduction of the system in the Desperado condition. This suggests that the system is inhibiting one kind of view that designers naturally adopt. We remain encouraged, however, by the finding that the use of Desperado continues to support structure-, function- and optimisation-oriented design work.

Session Characteristics	Control			Desperado		
	Session 1	Session 2	Session 3	Session 1	Session 2	Session 3
% Function-oriented	35.8 (13.6)	31.9 (8.9)	41.0 (7.1)	36.4 (3.4)	29.6 (10.8)	41.0 (10.8)
% Structure-oriented	49.1 (16.3)	56.9 (4.2)	35.9 (12)	46.8 (10.6)	69.2 (10.4)	57.4 (9.3)
% Procedure-oriented	12.7 (10.9)	7.1 (7.4)	22.9 (13.9)	16.1 (9.8)	0	0
% Optimisation-oriented	2.4 (3.24)	3.7 (5.0)	0.2 (0.3)	0.7 (1.1)	1.2 (2.1)	1.6 (2.7)

Note: Standard deviations are presented in parenthesis. The design-view characteristic scores refer to the percentage of episode elements in each stage for which participants held each design view.

Table 2: Design-view characteristics.

Our examination of the design protocols obtained in this study allow a number of observations to be made about the nature of reuse activity in design. There was some evidence that the designers in the Control condition were forming spontaneous analogies to previously encountered design concepts (e.g. some designers drew links between their current designs and known aspects of ATM/cash-point machines). Designers in the Control condition also showed evidence for the recognition of similarities across the design briefs, but demonstrated little explicit evidence for the reuse of their previously generated design Options and Criteria. In contrast, designers in Session 3 of the Desperado condition engaged in the frequent reuse of Options and Criteria generated in Session 2. Such reuse, however, was primarily restricted to QOC elements that were available in the prioritised pop-up menus rather than from the designer actively retrieving and browsing previous episodes prompted by the prioritisation interpreter. Protocol analysis suggests two reasons for this. First, the relatively short time (six weeks, on average) between Sessions 2 and 3 meant that participants could remember their own episodes. Secondly, the pop-up menus allowed them to access relevant information without the need to retrieve whole episodes.

In one sense these latter findings are disappointing, since by not retrieving whole episodes, participants were not accessing the detailed design rationale information (e.g. the Option/Criterion ratings). However, we are encouraged by evidence that there are reusable elements beyond solution options. We suspect that the failure to browse previous episodes may be an artifact of the small scale of the study. With a larger database, longer time intervals between sessions, and episodes from multiple users, we believe that prompted episode retrieval will play a greater role.

4.2 Questionnaire Data

Our descriptive analysis of the questionnaire data was based on the full data-set. Participants' responses were assigned numerical values, whereby 1 = strongly disagree and 5 = strongly agree. All questions were converted to produce positive scores. The key outcomes from these analyses are presented below.

4.2.1 Section 1 of Questionnaire — Ratings and Comments About QOC

1. *QOC was easy to understand* (M = 4.13, SD = 0.35). On the whole participants thought that QOC was very easy to understand and made little comment to support this rating.

2. *QOC was expressive enough* (M = 3.25, SD = 0.89). QOC was not quite expressive enough, some felt thinking in QOC terms interrupted their thought processes and forced oversimplification. However, others felt that the ability to add notes overcame this as it allowed them to expand on the QOC representation.

3. *QOC helped understanding of design deliberations* (M = 3.75, SD = 0.71). Generally QOC helped participants to make sense of their design deliberations. It helped them to clarify individual points and was flexible enough for them to adapt it to what they wanted. One person felt that it would be more useful to implement on a larger scale project.

4. *QOC aided design work* (M = 2.75, SD = 1.16). Participants were generally undecided as to whether QOC aided their design work, perhaps because some felt that it slowed them down so much. However, many of the participants felt that to some extent QOC provided them with a convenient break in which to think.

5. *Would use QOC when designing in the future* (M = 3.88, SD = 0.35). Participants felt that they would probably use QOC again or a similar design rationale approach. A few mentioned that they would use QOC again but possibly in their heads or on paper.

4.2.2 Section 2 of Questionnaire — Ratings and Comments About the Desperado System in General

1. *Desperado aided their design work* (M = 3.25, SD = 0.89). They were undecided as to whether the system as a whole aided their design work. Some commented on the fact that it slowed them down so that they produced less. Others felt that it regulated their work and allowed them to keep track of their choices.

2. *Making previous design work accessible aided their design work* (M = 4, SD = 0.58). Participants felt that making their previous design work accessible did aid their designing. They felt that it jogged their memory and prompted alternative solutions. One person, however, felt that it stopped them thinking.

3. *Easy to navigate through the system* (M = 2.5, SD = 1.31). Participants did not think it was particularly easy to navigate through the system. They found that it was difficult to establish which mode they were working in.

4. *Would use Desperado in the future* (M = 3.56, SD = 0.53). Participants tended to suggest that they would use Desperado again in the future. It was considered to have potential and be particularly useful when working as part of a team to provide structure and traceability. One participant felt that they would use Desperado after they had sketched their ideas out on paper as a means of documentation.

5. *The retrieval part of the system aided their design work* (M = 4, SD = 0.58). Participants thought that the ability to retrieve previous designs was advantageous. They felt it was useful to check similar previous design work and to browse through to recap on previous ideas. One participant felt the choice to browse or ignore it was worth commenting on, however, one participant voiced concern as to scaling up issues when there are lots of episodes in the database.

6. *The system was easy to use* (M = 3.56, SD = 0.5). Participants though it was fairly easy to use but voiced concerns over the awkwardness of the interface and how it improved once you got used to it. This is reflected in Question 7 below.

7. *The system was easier to use the second time* (M = 4.6, SD = 0.52). Participants felt that the system was much easier to use once they became more familiar with it.

4.2.3 Section 3 of the Questionnaire — Open Question Section on the System as a Whole

1. *What do you understand to be the purpose of the Desperado system?* References were made to aiding design, recording the design process, tracking current design, structuring design and supporting the derivation of Criteria and functionality.

2. *What do you most like about the system?* References were made to the ability to reselect Criteria and identify possibly missed Options, being able to use ideas from previous projects, referencing similar past designs. One participant commented on the ability to format everything the same to allow comparison of ideas.

3. *What do you most dislike about the system?* References were made to the slowness of the system, refilling of boxes from pop-up menus was thought to be tedious, the fact that the boxes provided required everything to be so brief, in particular the difficulty in expanding on Criteria. One participant suggested that it did not allow functional decomposition.

4. *How could Desperado be improved?* The most common response was the introduction of a hierarchical facility which enabled participants to view the history of the project and to provide an overview of the Questions considered throughout the whole project.

5. *Participants were asked whether they thought that their design work differed when Desperado was introduced and if yes, to explain how if they could.* Four participants thought that the system changed the nature of their designing: some positively and some negatively. Some participants made reference to it slowing the whole process down whilst others commented on their work being more structured. One participant felt that he concentrated more on deciding between safe Options than innovative solutions thus encouraging him to produce a safe design.

6. *Participants were asked to define what they thought was meant by the terms, Questions, Options, and Criteria.* All participants' responses were rated by an independent rater who was not involved in the experiment proper. It was found that 96% of all responses were rated as being within the definitions of the terms as defined by MacLean et al. Thus participants demonstrated a clear and common understanding of the QOC terminology.

7. *Any other comments.* One participant expressed the opinion that using the system was good fun, another added that he thought his usual design approach was quite random and Desperado helped to organise his work. One participant requested the inclusion of more examples during the learning phase of the experiment.

5   Conclusion

The observational data were encouraging. Despite showing less coverage of the design brief than Control participants, participants using Desperado demonstrated a more comprehensive evaluation of Criteria against Options and a greater production of Options per Question. Spontaneous reuse of analogous designs was observed but there was little evidence that explicitly retrieving prompted episodes aided design. Instead, participants tended to reuse Criteria and Option names through the pop-up menus. The absence of explicit reuse of complete episodes is partially a product of seeding the database with each participant's own design work. To address this issue we have constructed a version of Desperado which is seeded with 50 design episodes that were collected at our end-user companies and we are currently testing this system on a group of professional designers who are unfamiliar with these specific episodes.

The usability data suggested that people could readily think in QOC terms and provided a useful structure for their design deliberations. The difficulty seemed to be that the QOC formalism was not expressive enough to capture all aspects of our participants' design work; see (Buckingham Shum, 1996) for similar arguments. This is supported by the complete absence of any coding of procedural information in the database. The Desperado system as a whole was also viewed fairly favourably and despite a lack of participants using explicitly retrieved design information, participants felt that this information provided a useful memory aid. They also reported that reusing Criteria and Options from the pop-up menus was useful during ongoing design.

The major concerns voiced were interface difficulties — especially issues of navigation and limitations of the current pop-up menus. Perhaps a more fundamental problem was the inability to provide participants with a hierarchical overview of their design deliberations. This hierarchical overview is associated with the traditional approach to QOC analysis and is an important omission in our system. These problems are currently being addressed.

It appears that using Desperado did change the nature of participants' designing, and this was explicitly reported in the questionnaire. On the whole these changes were fairly positive, suggesting that Desperado improved participants' reasoning about Options and Criteria. However, one major concern is the finding that using Desperado precluded a complete coverage of the design brief. We suggest that a number of factors must be borne in mind in assessing the negative impact of Desperado use. The first is that participants received minimal training in the use of Desperado. It can take many sessions for designers to gain sufficient familiarity with any system so that it does not impact upon their design productivity, and this is undoubtedly the case with Desperado. For example, we suspect that there is a natural level of encoding detail that participants will adopt when using the system, such that they become selective in the kinds of design episode that they encode. The evaluation study may have created a demand characteristic among participants to encode episodes continuously rather than selectively as one might expect in natural design environments. Second, there is clearly a trade-off between designing in breadth, as seen with Control participants, and designing that focuses on multiple design Options and Criteria, as seen with Desperado users. Clearly in a realistic context, there are situations where a rapid and superficial exploration of a design problem is valuable. However, reflective and evaluative design practice as seen with the Desperado group is also clearly advantageous. In the short term, the Control group may have made more progress, but it may be ephemeral. Over continued use of the Desperado system we might start to see the benefits to designers of having a detailed record of previous work to draw upon during a project. Exploring this issue represents an avenue for future research.

Acknowledgements

This research was supported by an ESRC Cognitive Engineering Programme grant (L127251027). We are grateful to the managers and designers in our end user companies for their extensive assistance. We also thank Simon Slavin and Simon Lock for their assistance with the programming and Andy Morley for help with the formatting.

References

Ball, L. J. & Ormerod, T. C. (1995), "Structured and Opportunistic Processing in Design: A Critical Discussion", *International Journal of Human–Computer Studies* **43**, 131–51.

Ball, L. J. & Ormerod, T. C. (2000), "Applying Ethnography in the Analysis and Support of Expertise in Engineering Design", *Design Studies* **21**(4), 403–21.

Ball, L. J., Evans, J. S. B. T., Dennis, I. & Ormerod, T. C. (1997), "Problem Solving Strategies and Expertise in Engineering Design", *Thinking and Reasoning* **3**(4), 247–70.

Ball, L. J., Lambell, N. J., Ormerod, T. C., Slavin, S. & Mariani, J. (in press), "Representing Design Rationale to Support Innovative Design Reuse: A Minimalist Approach", *Automation in Construction* .

Ball, L. J., Maskill, L. & Ormerod, T. C. (1998), "Satisficing in Engineering Design: Causes, Consequences and Implications for Design Support", *Automation in Construction* **7**(2–3), 213–27.

Banker, R. D., Kauffman, R. J. & Zweig, D. (1993), "Repository Evaluation of Software Reuse", *IEEE Transactions on Software Engineering* **19**(4), 379–89.

Buckingham Shum, S. (1996), Analyzing the Usability of a Design Rationale Notation, *in* Moran & Carroll (1996), pp.185–215.

Buckingham Shum, S. J. B., MacLean, A., Bellotti, V. M. E. & Hammond, N. V. (1997), "Graphical Argumentation and Design Cognition", *Human–Computer Interaction* **12**(3), 267–300.

Busby, J. S. (1997), Why Engineering Designers Don't Learn From Feedback, *in Proceedings of the International Conference on Engineering Design (ICED'97)*, Vol. 2, pp.105–10.

Busby, J. S. (1998), Causal Explanations of the Absence of Reuse in Engineering Design Organisations, *in Proceedings of the Engineering Design Conference (EDC'98)*, pp.475–82.

Conklin, E. J. & Burgess-Yakemovic, K. C. (1996), A Process-oriented Approach to Design Rationale, *in* Moran & Carroll (1996), pp.357–91.

Henderson, R. R., Smight, M. C., Podd, J. & Varela-Alvarez, H. (1995), "A Comparison of the Four Prominent User-based Methods for Evaluating the Usability of Computer Software", *Ergonomics* **38**(10), 2030–44.

Lee, J. & Lai, K.-Y. (1996), What's in Design Rationale, *in* Moran & Carroll (1996), pp.251–80.

Lee, J. T. (1997), "Design Rationale Systems: Understanding the Issues", *IEEE Expert Intelligent Systems and Their Applications* **12**(3), 78–85.

MacLean, A., Young, R. M., Bellotti, V. M. E. & Moran, T. P. (1991), "Questions, Options and Criteria: Elements of Design Space Analysis", *Human–Computer Interaction* **6**(3-4), 201–50. Reprinted as MacLean et al. (1996).

MacLean, A., Young, R. M., Bellotti, V. M. E. & Moran, T. P. (1996), Questions, Options and Criteria: Elements of Design Space Analysis, *in* Moran & Carroll (1996), pp.53–105. Reprint of MacLean et al. (1991).

McCall, R. (1991), "PHI: A Conceptual Foundation for Design Hypermedia", *Design Studies* **12**(1), 30–41.

McKerlie, D. & MacLean, A. (1994), "Reasoning with Design Rationale: Practical Experience with Design Space Analysis", *Design Studies* **15**, 214–26.

Moran, T. P. & Carroll, J. M. (eds.) (1996), *Design Rationale: Concepts, Techniques and Use*, Lawrence Erlbaum Associates.

Ormerod, T. C., Mariani, J. A., Ball, L. J. & Lambell, N. J. (1999), Desperado: Three-in-one Indexing for Innovative Design, *in* A. Sasse & C. Johnson (eds.), *Human–Computer Interaction — INTERACT '99: Proceedings of the Seventh IFIP Conference on Human–Computer Interaction*, Vol. 1, IOS Press, pp.336–43.

Pena-Mora, F. & Vadhavkar, S. (1997), "Augmenting Design Patterns with Design Rationale", *AI-EDAM — Artificial Intelligence for Engineering Design Analysis and Manufacturing* **11**(2), 93–108.

Rittel, H. W. J. (1984), Second Generation Design Methods, *in* N. Cross (ed.), *Developments in Design Methodology*, John Wiley & Sons, pp.317–27.

Rittel, H. W. J. & Weber, M. M. (1973), "Dilemmas in a General Theory of Planning", *Policy Sciences* **4**, 155–69. Reprinted as Rittel & Weber (1984).

Rittel, H. W. J. & Weber, M. M. (1984), Dilemmas in a General Theory of Planning, *in* N. Cross (ed.), *Developments in Design Methodology*, John Wiley & Sons, pp.135–44. Reprint of Rittel & Weber (1973).

Sen, A. (1997), "The Role of Opportunism in the Software Design Reuse Process", *IEEE Transactions on Software Engineering* **23**(7), 418–36.

Shipman, F. M. & McCall, R. J. (1997), "Integrating Different Perspectives on Design Rationale: Supporting the Emergence of Design Rationale from Design Communication", *AI-EDAM — Artificial Intelligence for Engineering Design Analysis and Manufacturing* **11**(2), 141–54.

Sutcliffe, A. G. & Maiden, N. A. M. (1990), Software Reusability; Delivery Productivity Gains or Short Cuts, *in* D. Diaper, D. Gilmore, G. Cockton & B. Shackel (eds.), *Proceedings of INTERACT '90 — Third IFIP Conference on Human–Computer Interaction*, Elsevier Science, pp.895–901.

Tracz, W. (1988), *Software Reuse: Emerging Technology*, IEEE Publications.

Woodfield, S. N., Embley, D. W. & Scott, D. T. (1987), "Can Programmers Reuse Software", *IEEE Software* **4**(4), 52–60.

Author Index

Keyword Index